W9-BEF-434

SOCIOLOGICAL THEORY

ORIGIN 1897

FOUNDERS Émile Durkheim, Robert Ezra Park, Ernest Burgess, Clifford Shaw, Walter Reckless, Frederic Thrasher

MOST IMPORTANT WORKS Durkheim, *The Division of Labor in Society* (1893), and *Suicide: A Study in Sociology* (1897); Park, Burgess, and John McKenzie, *The City* (1925); Thrasher, *The Gang* (1926); Shaw et al., *Delinquency Areas* (1925); Edwin Sutherland, *Criminology* (1924)

CORE IDEAS A person's place in the social structure determines his or her behavior. Disorganized urban areas are the breeding ground of crime. A lack of legitimate opportunities produces criminal subcultures. Socialization within the family, the school, and the peer group controls behavior.

MODERN OUTGROWTHS Strain Theory, Cultural Deviance Theory, Social Learning Theory, Social Control Theory, Social Reaction Theory, Labeling

Émile Durkheim

Corbis/Bettmann

MULTIFACTOR/INTEGRATED THEORY

ORIGIN About 1930

FOUNDERS Sheldon and Eleanor Glueck

MOST IMPORTANT WORKS Sheldon and Eleanor Glueck: *Five Hundred Delinquent Women* (1934); *Later Criminal Careers* (1937); *Criminal Careers in Retrospect* (1943); *Juvenile Delinquents Grown Up* (1940); *Unraveling Juvenile Delinquency* (1950)

CORE IDEAS Crime is a function of environmental, socialization, physical, and psychological factors. Each makes an independent contribution to shaping and directing behavior patterns. Deficits in these areas of human development increase the risk of crime. People at risk for crime can resist antisocial behaviors if these traits and conditions can be strengthened.

MODERN OUTGROWTHS Developmental Theory, Life Course Theory, Latent Trait Theory

Harvard Law School Library

Sheldon and Eleanor Glueck

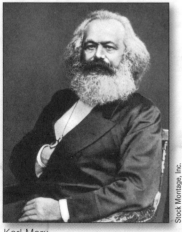

Stock Montage, Inc.

Karl Marx

Thomson™ NOW!

ThomsonNOW™ for Siegel's *Criminology*, 10th Edition

Just what you need to know and do NOW!

ThomsonNOW for *Criminology* is an easy-to-use online resource that helps you study in less time to get the grade you want—NOW. Students like you who use **ThomsonNOW** find they are studying more *efficiently* because they spend their time on what they still need to master rather than on information they already have learned.

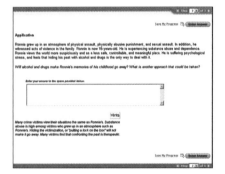

How does it work?

If your text came packaged with an access code, you can immediately start using **ThomsonNOW**. Take the diagnostic *Pre-test* to assess your current understanding. Based on your score, **ThomsonNOW** will build your unique and complete *Personalized Study* plan, directing you to specific text sections, *Narrative Figures* from the text, and *Topic Review* activities to help you master and retain the material in this book.

Log on today and use ThomsonNOW to . . .

▶ **Manage** your time
▶ **Prepare** for class
▶ **Practice** key concepts learned in class
▶ **Study** for exams more effectively
▶ **Get the grade** you want!

If you did not receive an access code with your text, you may purchase one a **www.ichapters.com**.

CRIMINOLOGY

TENTH EDITION

CRIMINOLOGY

Larry J. Siegel
University of Massachusetts, Lowell

THOMSON

WADSWORTH

Australia • Brazil • Canada • Mexico • Singapore
Spain • United Kingdom • United States

THOMSON

WADSWORTH

Criminology, **Tenth Edition**

Larry J. Siegel

Senior Acquisitions Editor, Criminal Justice: Carolyn Henderson Meier

Development Editor: Shelley Murphy

Assistant Editor: Meaghan Banks

Editorial Assistant: Jill Nowlin

Technology Project Manager: Lauren Keyes

Marketing Manager: Terra Schultz

Marketing Assistant: Ileana Shevlin

Marketing Communications Manager: Tami Strang

Project Manager, Editorial Production: Jennie Redwitz

Creative Director: Rob Hugel

Art Director: Vernon Boes

Print Buyer: Judy Inouye

Permissions Editor: Mardell Glinski-Schultz

Production Service: Linda Jupiter, Jupiter Productions

Text Designer: Tani Hasegawa

Photo Editor/Researcher: Linda L Rill

Illustrators: John and Judy Waller

Copy Editor: Lunaea Weatherstone

Proofreader: Mary Kanable

Indexer: Linda Webster

Cover Designer: Yvo, Yvo Riezebos Design

Cover Image: Naoki Okamoto/SuperStock

Compositor: Pre-Press PMG

© 2009, 2006 Thomson Wadsworth, a part of The Thomson Corporation. Thomson, the Star logo, and Wadsworth are trademarks used herein under license.

ALL RIGHTS RESERVED. No part of this work covered by the copyright hereon may be reproduced or used in any form or by any means—graphic, electronic, or mechanical, including photocopying, recording, taping, Web distribution, information storage and retrieval systems, or in any other manner—without the written permission of the publisher.

Printed in Canada

1 2 3 4 5 6 7 12 11 10 09 08

ExamView® and *ExamView Pro*® are registered trademarks of FSCreations, Inc. Windows is a registered trademark of the Microsoft Corporation used herein under license. Macintosh and Power Macintosh are registered trademarks of Apple Computer, Inc. Used herein under license.

© 2009 Thomson Learning, Inc. All Rights Reserved. Thomson Learning WebTutor™ is a trademark of Thomson Learning, Inc.

Library of Congress Control Number: 2007928663

Student Edition:
ISBN-13: 978-0-495-39102-9
ISBN-10: 0-495-39102-6

Loose-leaf Edition:
ISBN-13: 978-0-495-50755-0
ISBN-10: 0-495-50755-5

Thomson Higher Education
10 Davis Drive
Belmont, CA 94002-3098
USA

For more information about our products, contact us at:
Thomson Learning Academic Resource Center
1-800-423-0563

For permission to use material from this text or product, submit a request online at **http://www.thomsonrights.com.** Any additional questions about permissions can be submitted by e-mail to **thomsonrights@thomson.com.**

This book is dedicated to my kids, Eric, Andrew, Julie, and Rachel, and to my grandkids, Jack, Kayla, and Brooke. It is also dedicated to Jason Macy (thanks for marrying Rachel) and Therese J. Libby (thanks for marrying me).

ABOUT THE AUTHOR

Larry J. Siegel was born in the Bronx in 1947. While living on Jerome Avenue and attending City College of New York in the 1960s, he was swept up in the social and political currents of the time. He became intrigued with the influence contemporary culture had on individual behavior: Did people shape society or did society shape people? He applied his interest in social forces and human behavior to the study of crime and justice. After graduating from CCNY, he attended the newly opened program in criminal justice at the State University of New York at Albany, earning both his M.A. and Ph.D. degrees there. After completing his graduate work, Dr. Siegel began his teaching career at Northeastern University, where he was a faculty member for nine years. After leaving Northeastern, he held teaching positions at the University of Nebraska–Omaha and Saint Anselm College in New Hampshire. He is currently a professor at the University of Massachusetts–Lowell. Dr. Siegel has written extensively in the area of crime and justice, including books on juvenile law, delinquency, criminology, criminal justice, and criminal procedure. He is a court certified expert on police conduct and has testified in numerous legal cases. The father of four and grandfather of three, Larry Siegel and his wife, Terry, now reside in Bedford, New Hampshire, with their two dogs, Watson and Cody.

BRIEF CONTENTS

PART ONE

CONCEPTS OF CRIME, LAW, AND CRIMINOLOGY

CHAPTER 1
Crime and Criminology 2

CHAPTER 2
The Nature and Extent of Crime 28

CHAPTER 3
Victims and Victimization 64

PART TWO

THEORIES OF CRIME CAUSATION

CHAPTER 4
Rational Choice Theory 90

CHAPTER 5
Trait Theories 120

CHAPTER 6
Social Structure Theories 160

CHAPTER 7
Social Process Theories 196

CHAPTER 8
Social Conflict, Critical Criminology, and Restorative Justice 228

CHAPTER 9
Developmental Theories: Life Course and Latent Trait 254

PART THREE

CRIME TYPOLOGIES

CHAPTER 10
Interpersonal Violence 284

CHAPTER 11
Political Crime and Terrorism 318

CHAPTER 12
Property Crime 344

CHAPTER 13
Enterprise Crime: White-Collar and Organized Crime 370

CHAPTER 14
Public Order Crime 400

CHAPTER 15
Cyber Crime and Technology 438

PART FOUR

THE CRIMINAL JUSTICE SYSTEM

CHAPTER 16
Criminal Justice: Process and Perspectives 464

CHAPTER 17
Police and the Courts: Investigation, Arrest, and Adjudication 484

CHAPTER 18
Punishment and Correction 524

CONTENTS

Preface xix

████████ **PART ONE**

CONCEPTS OF CRIME, LAW, AND CRIMINOLOGY 1

CHAPTER 1

Crime and Criminology 2

What Is Criminology? 4
Criminology and Criminal Justice 4
Criminology and Deviance 4
A Brief History of Criminology 5
Classical Criminology 5
Nineteenth-Century Positivism 6
The Chicago School and Beyond 8
Social-Psychological Views 9
Conflict and Crime 9
Integrating Diverse Prospectives: Developmental
    Criminology 10
Contemporary Criminology 10
**What Criminologists Do: The Criminological
Enterprise** 11
Criminal Statistics and Research Methodology 11

▮ *Comparative Criminology:
    International Crime Trends* 12

Law and Society: The Sociology of Law 14
Theory Construction and Testing 14
Criminal Behavior Systems and Crime Typologies 14
Penology and Social Control 15
Victimology: Victims and Victimization 15
How Criminologists View Crime 16
The Consensus View of Crime 16
The Conflict View of Crime 17
The Interactionist View of Crime 17
Defining Crime 18

Crime and the Criminal Law 18
Common Law 19
Contemporary Criminal Law 19

▮ *PROFILES IN CRIME:
    The Mother of All Snakeheads* 21

The Evolution of Criminal Law 21

▮ *The Criminological Enterprise:
    The Elements of Criminal Law* 22

Ethical Issues in Criminology 23
What to Study? 24
Whom to Study? 24
How to Study? 24

CHAPTER 2

The Nature and Extent of Crime 28

Primary Sources of Crime Data 30
The Uniform Crime Report (UCR) 30

▮ *PROFILES IN CRIME: A Pain in the Glass* 31

Self-Report Surveys 34
The National Crime Victimization Survey (NCVS) 36
Evaluating the
    Primary
    Sources
    of Crime
    Data 36
**Secondary
Sources of Crime
Data** 37
Cohort Data:
    Longitudinal
    and Retrospective 37
Experimental Data 37
Observational and Interview Data 38
Meta-Analysis and Systematic Review 38
Data Mining 39
Crime Mapping 39

Crime Trends 39
Trends in Violent Crime 39

▍ *The Criminological Enterprise:*
Explaining Crime Trends 40

Trends in Property Crime 42
Trends in Victimization Data (NCVS Findings) 43
Trends in Self-Reporting 43
What the Future Holds 44
Crime Patterns 45
The Ecology of Crime 45
Use of Firearms 46
Social Class, Socioeconomic Conditions, and Crime 46

▍ *Policy and Practice in Criminology:*
Should Guns Be Controlled? 48

Age and Crime 51
Gender and Crime 52
Race and Crime 54
Chronic Offenders/Criminal Careers 56

CHAPTER 3
Victims and Victimization 64

Problems of Crime Victims 66
Economic Loss 66
System
Abuse 66
Long-Term
Stress 67
Fear 67
Antisocial
Behavior 68
**The Nature of
Victimization** 68
The Social
Ecology of

Victimization 69
The Victim's Household 69
Victim Characteristics 69
Victims and Their Criminals 72
Theories of Victimization 73
Victim Precipitation Theory 73
Lifestyle Theory 73
Deviant Place Theory 74
Routine Activities Theory 74

▍ *The Criminological Enterprise:*
Crime and Everyday Life 76

Caring for the Victim 77
The Government's Response to Victimization 78
Victims and Self-Protection 80
Victims' Rights 81

▍ *PROFILES IN CRIME: Jesse Timmendequas*
and Megan's Law 82

PART TWO
THEORIES OF CRIME CAUSATION 89

CHAPTER 4
Rational Choice Theory 90

The Development of Rational Choice Theory 92
The Classical Theory of Crime 92
Contemporary Choice Theory Emerges 93
The Concepts of Rational Choice 94
Offense- and Offender-Specific Crimes 94
Structuring Criminality 94

▍ *PROFILES IN CRIME:*
Looting the Public Treasury 95

Structuring Crime 97
Is Crime Rational? 98
Is Theft Rational? 98
Is Drug Use Rational? 98
Is Violence Rational? 98
Eliminating Crime 100
Situational Crime Prevention 100

▍ *Comparative Criminology: CCTV or Not CCTV?*
Comparing Situational Crime Prevention Efforts
in Great Britain and the United States 103

General Deterrence 104

▍ *The Criminological Enterprise: Does Capital*
Punishment Deter Murder? 108

Specific Deterrence 108
Incapacitation 110
Public Policy Implications of Choice Theory 111
Just Desert 112

CHAPTER 5
Trait Theories 120

Foundations of Trait Theory 122
Sociobiology 123
Modern Trait Theories 123
Biosocial Trait Theories 124
Biochemical Conditions and Crime 124

▍ *Comparative Criminology: Diet and Crime:*
An International Perspective 126

Neurophysiological Conditions and Crime 129
Arousal Theory 132
Genetics and Crime 132

Evolutionary Theory 135
Evaluation of the Biosocial Branch of Trait Theory 136
Psychological Trait Theories 136
Psychodynamic Theory 137

▮ *PROFILES IN CRIME: Andrea Yates* 140

Behavioral Theory 141

▮ *The Criminological Enterprise:*
The Media and Violence 142

Cognitive Theory 144
Psychological Traits and Characteristics 146
Personality and Crime 146
Intelligence and Crime 147

▮ *The Criminological Enterprise:*
The Antisocial Personality 148

Public Policy Implications of Trait Theory 149

CHAPTER 6
Social Structure Theories 160

Socioeconomic Structure and Crime 162
The Underclass 163
Child Poverty 163
Minority Group Poverty 164

▮ *Race, Culture, Gender, and Criminology:*
There Goes the Neighborhood 165

Social Structure Theories 166
Social Disorganization Theory 167
The Social Ecology School 170
Collective Efficacy 170
Strain Theories 174
The Concept of Anomie 175
Merton's Theory of Anomie 176
Macro-Level Theory: Institutional Anomie
Theory 177
Micro-Level Theory: General Strain
Theory 178
Sources of Strain 179
Coping with Strain 180
Evaluating GST 181
Cultural Deviance Theories 181
Conduct Norms 182
Focal Concerns 182
Theory of Delinquent Subcultures 182

▮ *PROFILES IN CRIME: A Life in the Drug*
Trade 184

▮ *Race, Culture, Gender, and Criminology:*
The Code of the Streets 185

Theory of Differential Opportunity 186
Evaluating Social Structure Theories 187
Public Policy Implications of Social
Structure Theory 188

CHAPTER 7
Social Process Theories 196

Socialization and Crime 198
Family Relations 198
Educational Experience 200
Peer Relations 201
Institutional Involvement and Belief 201
The Effects of Socialization on Crime 202
Social Learning Theory 203
Differential Association
Theory 203
Differential
Reinforcement
Theory 206
Neutralization
Theory 207
Are Learning Theories
Valid? 208

▮ *The Criminological*
Enterprise:
When Being Good Is Bad 209

Social Control Theory 210
Self-Concept and Crime 210
Hirschi's Social Bond Theory 211

▮ *PROFILES IN CRIME: Alpha Dog* 213

Social Reaction Theory 214
Interpreting Crime 215
Differential Enforcement 215
Consequences of Labeling 216
Primary and Secondary Deviance 217
Research on Social Reaction Theory 217
Is Labeling Theory Valid? 218
Evaluating Social Process Theories 218
Public Policy Implications of Social Process Theory 219

▮ *The Criminological Enterprise: Storylines* 220

CHAPTER 8
Social Conflict, Critical Criminology,
and Restorative Justice 228

Marxist Thought 230
Productive Forces and Productive Relations 230
A Marxist Vision of Crime 232
Creating a Critical Criminology 232
Contemporary Critical Criminology 234
How Critical Criminologists Define Crime 234
How Critical Criminologists View the Cause
of Crime 235
Globalization 236
Instrumental vs. Structural Theory 236
Instrumental Theory 237
Structural Theory 237

Research on Critical Criminology   237

▌ *PROFILES IN CRIME: Mumia Abu-Jamal*   238

Critique of Critical Criminology   239
Emerging Forms of Critical Criminology   239
Left Realism   239
Critical Feminist Theory   240
Power–Control Theory   241
Peacemaking Criminology   242
Critical Theory and Public Policy   243
The Concept of Restorative Justice   243
Reintegrative Shaming   244
The Process of Restoration   245
The Challenge of Restorative Justice   246

▌ *Comparative Criminology: Restoration in the International Community*   248

CHAPTER 9
Developmental Theories: Life Course and Latent Trait   254

Foundations of Developmental Theory   256
Life Course Fundamentals   257
Disruption Promotes Criminality   257
Changing Life Influences   257
Life Course Concepts   258
Problem Behavior Syndrome   258
Pathways to Crime   258
Age of Onset/Continuity of Crime   259
Adolescent-Limiteds and Life Course Persisters   261
Theories of the Criminal Life Course   261
Sampson and Laub: Age-Graded Theory   262

▌ *The Criminological Enterprise: Shared Beginnings, Divergent Lives*   266

Latent Trait Theories   267
Crime and Human Nature   269
General Theory of Crime   269

▌ *PROFILES IN CRIME: James Paul Lewis, Jr.: "Crimes Against Humanity"*   272

Evaluating Developmental Theories   275
Public Policy Implications of Developmental Theory   276

▬▬▬ PART THREE
CRIME TYPOLOGIES   283

CHAPTER 10
Interpersonal Violence   284

The Causes of Violence   286
Psychological/Biological Abnormality   286
Evolutionary Factors/Human Instinct   286
Substance Abuse   287
Socialization and Upbringing   287
Exposure to Violence   288
Cultural Values/Subculture of Violence   289

▌ *Comparative Criminology: The Honor Killing of Women and Girls*   290

Forcible Rape   290
History of Rape   291
Rape and the Military   291
Incidence of Rape   292
Types of Rape and Rapists   292
The Causes of Rape   293
Rape and the Law   294
Murder and Homicide   296
Degrees of Murder   296
The Nature and Extent of Murder   297
Murderous Relations   297
Serial Murder   299
Mass Murderers   300
Assault and Battery   301
Nature and Extent of Assault   301
Assault in the Home   302
Robbery   304
Acquaintance Robbery   305
Rational Robbery   306
Emerging Forms of Interpersonal Violence   306
Hate Crimes   306
Workplace Violence   308
Stalking   309

CHAPTER 11
Political Crime and Terrorism   318

Political Crime   320
The Nature of Political Crimes   320
The Goals of Political Crime   320
Becoming a Political Criminal   321
Types of Political Crimes   321
Election Fraud   321
Treason   322
Espionage   323
State Political Crime   324

▌ *PROFILES IN CRIME: Aldrich Hazen Ames*   325

Terrorism   326

▌ *The Criminological Enterprise: Want to Torture? Get a Warrant*   327

Terrorist and Guerilla   328
Terrorist and Insurgent   328
Terrorist and Revolutionary   329
A Brief History of Terrorism   329
Religious Roots   329
Political Roots   330

Contemporary Forms of Terrorism 330
  Revolutionary Terrorists 331
  Political Terrorists 331
  Nationalist Terrorism 332
  Retributive Terrorism 333
  State-Sponsored Terrorism 334
  Cult Terrorism 334
  Criminal Terrorism 335
How Are Terror Groups Organized? 335
What Motivates the Terrorist? 336
  Psychological View 336
  Socialization View 336
  Ideological View 336
  Alienation View 336
  Explaining State Terrorism 336
Response to Terrorism 337
  Fighting Terrorism with Law Enforcement 337
  Confronting Terrorism with the Law 339

CHAPTER 12

Property Crime 344

A Brief History of Theft 346
Theft in the Nineteenth Century: Train Robbery and Safecracking 347
Contemporary Theft 348
  Occasional Thieves 348
  Professional Thieves 348
  Sutherland's Professional Criminal 349
  The Professional Fence 349

▌ *The Criminological Enterprise:*
  Confessions of a Dying Thief 350

The Occasional Fence 351
Larceny/Theft 352
  Larceny Today 352

▌ *PROFILES IN CRIME:*
  Invasion of the Body Snatchers 353

Shoplifting 353
Bad Checks 355
Credit Card Theft 355

▌ *PROFILES IN CRIME: Credit Card Con* 356

Auto Theft 356
False Pretenses or Fraud 358
Confidence Games 359
Embezzlement 359
Burglary 360
  The Nature and
    Extent of
    Burglary 360
  Planning to
    Burgle 361
  Commercial
    Burglary 361

▌ *Race, Culture, Gender, and Criminology: Are There Gender Differences in Burglary?* 362

  Careers in Burglary 363
Arson 364
  The Juvenile Fire Starter 365
  Professional Arson 365

CHAPTER 13

Enterprise Crime: White-Collar and Organized Crime 370

Enterprise
Crime 372
  Crimes of
    Business
    Enterprise 372
White-Collar Crime 372
  Redefining White-Collar Crime 372
  Extent of White-Collar Crime 373
Components of White-Collar Crime 374
  Stings and Swindles 374
  Chiseling 375
  Individual Exploitation of Institutional Position 376
  Influence Peddling and Bribery 376

▌ *The Criminological Enterprise: Tyco,*
  Enron, and WorldCom: Enterprise
  Crime at the Highest Levels 378

Embezzlement and Employee Fraud 380
Client Fraud 380

▌ *PROFILES IN CRIME: When the Flu Bug Bites* 381

Corporate Crime 382
The Causes of White-Collar Crime 385
  Rational Choice: Greed 385
  Rational Choice: Need 386
  Rationalization/Neutralization View 386
  Cultural View 387
  Self-Control View 387
White-Collar Law Enforcement Systems 387
  Controlling White-Collar Crime 388
  Is the Tide Turning? 389
Organized Crime 390
  Characteristics of Organized Crime 390
  Activities of Organized Crime 390
  The Concept of Organized Crime 391
  The Mob: Cosa Nostra 391
  Contemporary Organized Crime Groups 391
  Controlling Organized Crime 392

■ *Comparative Criminology:*
   Russian Organized Crime 393

   The Future of Organized Crime 394

CHAPTER 14
Public Order Crime 400

Law and Morality 402
   Debating Morality 402
   Social Harm 403
   Moral Crusades and Crusaders 404
   Moral Crusades Today 404
Sexually Related Offenses 405
Paraphilias 405
Prostitution 406

   ■ *PROFILES IN CRIME: John Evander Couey*
      and the Jessica Lunsford Murder Case 407

   Incidents of Prostitution 407
   International Sex Trade 408
   Types of Prostitutes 408

   ■ *Comparative Criminology: International*
      Trafficking in Prostitution 410

   Becoming a Prostitute 410
   Controlling Prostitution 412
   Legalize Prostitution? 412
Pornography 413
   Child Pornography 413
   Does Pornography Cause Violence? 414
   Pornography and the Law 415
   Controlling Pornography 415
Substance Abuse 416
   When Did Drug Use Begin? 416
   Alcohol and Its Prohibition 418
   The Extent of Substance Abuse 418
   AIDS and Drug Use 420
   What Causes Substance Abuse? 420
   Is There a Drug Gateway? 421
   Types of Drug Users 421
   Drugs and Crime 423
   Drugs and the Law 424
   Drug Control Strategies 425

   ■ *Policy and Practice in Criminology:*
      Drug Abuse Resistance Education 428

   Drug Legalization 429

CHAPTER 15
Cyber Crime and Technology 438

Cyber Theft: Cyber Crimes for Profit 440
   Computer Fraud 441
   Distributing Illegal Sexual Material 441

   Denial-of-Service Attack 442
   Illegal Copyright Infringement 442
   Internet Securities Fraud 443
   Identity Theft 443
   Etailing Fraud 445

   ■ *PROFILES IN CRIME: Cyber Vandalizing NASA* 446

Cyber Vandalism: Cyber Crime
with Malicious Intent 446
   Worms, Viruses, Trojan Horses, Logic Bombs,
      and Spam 446
   Website Defacement 447
   Cyber Stalking 448
   Cyber Bullying 448
   Cyber Spying 449
Cyber Terrorism: Cyber Crime
with Political Motives 449
   Why Terrorism in Cyberspace? 450
   Cyber Attacks 450
   Funding Terrorist Activities 451
The Extent and Costs of Cyber Crime 451
Controlling Cyber Crime 452
   International Treaties 453
   Cyber Crime Enforcement Agencies 454
   Local Enforcement Efforts 454
Information Technology in Criminal Justice 455
IT, Crime, and Civil Liberties 455

   ■ *Policy and Practice in Criminology: Biometric*
      Technology 456

PART FOUR
THE CRIMINAL JUSTICE SYSTEM 463

CHAPTER 16
Criminal Justice: Process and Perspectives 464

Origins of the American Criminal
Justice System 466
What Is the
Criminal Justice
System? 467
The Process of
Justice 469

   ■ *Policy and*
      Practice in
      Criminology:
      The Juvenile
      Justice System in the New Millennium 472

   Going through the Justice Process 474

Criminal Justice and the Rule of Law   474
Concepts of Justice   476
  Crime Control Model   476

  ▌ *PROFILES IN CRIME: Two Wrongs Don't*
  Make a Right   477

  Justice Model   478
  Due Process Model   478
  Rehabilitation Model   478
  Nonintervention Model   479
  Restorative Justice Model   480
Visions of Justice Today   480

CHAPTER 17

Police and the Courts: Investigation, Arrest, and Adjudication   484

The Police and Society   486
Law Enforcement Agencies Today   486
  Federal Law Enforcement   486
  County Law Enforcement   487
  State Police   487
  Metropolitan Police   487
Preventing and Deterring Crime   489
  Proactive Patrol   489
  Targeting Crimes   489
  Making Arrests   490
  Adding Patrol Officers   490
  Using Technology   490
Investigating Crime   491
  Are Investigations Effective?   491

  ▌ *PROFILES IN CRIME: James Ford Seale:*
  Mississippi Burning   492

  The Arrest Process   492
  Legal Controls over Police Investigation   493
  Custodial Interrogation   494
  Search and Seizure   495

  ▌ *The Criminological Enterprise: Police Violence*   496

Changing the Police Role   497
  Community-Oriented Policing (COP)   498
  Problem-Oriented Policing   499
  Technology and the Future of Policing   499
The Adjudication Process   500
Court Structure   500
  State Courts   500
  Federal Courts   500
  Court Case Flow   500
Actors in the Judicatory Process   501
  Prosecutor   502

  Defense Attorney   504
  Judge   505
Pretrial Procedures   507
  Bail   507
  Plea Bargaining   511
The Criminal Trial   513
  Jury Selection   513
  The Trial Process   514
  Trials and the Rule of Law   516
  What the Future Holds   518

CHAPTER 18

Punishment and Correction   524

A Brief History of Punishment   526
  Reforming Correctional Punishment   527
  The Rise of the Prison   527
  Competing Correctional Models   527
The Goals of Criminal Punishment   528
  Imposing Punishment   528
  Sentencing Structures   528

  ▌ *Race, Culture, Gender, and Criminology:*
  Does Race Matter?   534

The Death Penalty   534
  The Death Penalty Debate   534

  ▌ *Comparative Criminology: International*
  Use of the Death Penalty   538

  Legal Issues   539
Correcting Criminal Offenders   539
  Contemporary Corrections   539
Probation   540
  Probation Services   540
  Probation Rules and Revocation   541
  Success of Probation   541
Intermediate Sanctions   542
  Fines   542
  Forfeiture   543
  Restitution   543
  Split Sentencing and Shock Probation   543
  Intensive Probation Supervision   544
  Home Confinement/Electronic
    Monitoring   544
  Residential Community Corrections   544
  Boot Camps/Shock Incarceration   545
  Can Alternatives Work?   545
Jails   545
  Jail Populations   545
Prisons   546
  Types of Prisons   546
  Prison Inmates: Male   548
  Living in Prison   549

Prison Inmates: Female   550
Correctional Treatment   551
Prison Violence   552
Corrections and the Rule of Law   553
Cruel and Unusual Punishment   553

▌ *The Criminological Enterprise:*
The Problems of Reentry   554

Parole   554
The Parolee in the Community   556
How Effective Is Parole?   556

Glossary   565

Case Index   583

Name Index   585

Subject Index   607

Photo Credits   633

PREFACE

During the summer of 2007, my family and I, along with the rest of the nation, debated the behavior of Michael Vick. On August 27, 2007, the star quarterback pleaded guilty to charges of criminal conspiracy stemming from his involvement in a dog-fighting ring. Vick had been accused of torturing and executing dogs who lost their matches. My family, dog lovers all, were shocked and dismayed by the accusations. As we debated the case over dinner, my wife and some of my kids glanced over at our two beloved cockapoos, Watson and Cody, and demanded that Vick receive the harshest punishment possible. My son Andrew sagely observed that we were eating cheeseburgers at the time. "Isn't it a bit hypocritical to consume the flesh of dead animals, killed for our pleasure, and condemn the behavior of someone accused of killing animals?" And, he went on to note, some of our friends in New Hampshire were hunters who routinely shot and killed moose and deer. "Why is it legal to hunt and kill defenseless animals if we are so concerned about animal welfare?" My wife Terry was swayed by the argument and announced that she was becoming a vegan. The conversation turned to fishing, fox hunting, raising chinchillas for fur coats, bull fighting, and boiling lobsters alive (the latter activity a staple of New England culture). Why were these practices, which involved the killing of innocent creatures, legal while dog fighting was condemned and its practitioners imprisoned? While some argue that it is the method of killing that counts, I am not sure that the victims would agree.

The Vick case raises many important issues. As our dinnertime debate suggests, there are still many questions on the definition of what is legal versus criminal, moral versus immoral. Who defines morality? Where do you draw the line between legal and criminal activity, and who gets to draw it?

In addition, the Vick case raises questions about the motivation and cause of crime: Why would a talented football star such as Michael Vick, who had recently signed a contract for more than $100 million, risk everything in an illegal and depraved dog-fighting scheme? Was it a product of a troubled childhood? Improper and damaged socialization? An impulsive personality? Or had he simply chosen to engage in risky and reckless behavior because he thought he was above the law? And finally, what punishment should Michael Vick receive? Would a prison sentence serve the public interest?

Should he eventually be allowed to return to the NFL? Can someone like Vick be restored to society, and if so, does he deserve restoration?

The general public is greatly concerned by cases such as the Michael Vick incident. I too share this concern. For the past 37 years I have been able to channel my personal interest into a career as a teacher of criminology. My goal in writing this text is to help students generate the same curiosity about issues of crime and justice. What could be more important or fascinating than a field of study that deals with such wide-ranging topics as the motivation for mass murder, the effects of violent media on young people, drug abuse, and organized crime? Criminology is a dynamic field, changing constantly with the release of major research studies, Supreme Court rulings, and governmental policy. Its dynamism and diversity make it an important and engrossing area of study.

Because interest in crime and justice is so great and so timely, this text is designed to review these ongoing issues and cover the field of criminology in an organized and comprehensive manner. It is meant as a broad overview of the field, designed to whet the reader's appetite and encourage further and more in-depth exploration. Several major themes recur throughout the book.

▍ **Competing Viewpoints:** In every chapter an effort is made to introduce students to the diversity of thought that characterizes the discipline. One reason that the study of criminology is so important is that debates

continue over the nature and extent of crime and the causes and prevention of criminality. Some experts view criminal offenders as society's victims, unfortunate people who are forced to violate the law because they lack hope of legitimate opportunity. Others view aggressive, antisocial behavior as a product of mental and physical abnormalities, present at birth or soon after, which are stable over the life course. Still another view is that crime is a function of the rational choice of greedy, selfish people who can only be deterred through the threat of harsh punishments. All chapters explore how different theoretical frameworks cover different aspects of criminology. Students are helped in this regard by Concept Summary boxes that compare different viewpoints, showing each view's main points and strengths.

▍ **Critical Thinking:** It is important for students to think critically about law and justice and to develop a critical perspective toward the social and legal institutions entrusted with crime control. Throughout the book, students are asked to critique research highlighted in boxed material and to think outside the box. To aid in this task, each chapter ends with a Thinking Like a Criminologist feature that presents a scenario that can be analyzed with the help of material found in the chapter.

▍ **Diversity:** Diversity is a key issue in criminology, and the text attempts to integrate issues of racial, ethnic, gender, and cultural diversity throughout. The book includes material on international issues such as the use of the death penalty abroad, as well as gender issues such as the rising rate of female criminality. To help with the coverage of diversity issues, Race, Culture, Gender, and Criminology boxes cover diversity issues. In Chapter 18, for example, there is an in-depth discussion on how race influences sentencing in criminal courts. There are also Comparative Criminology boxes, which focus on criminological issues abroad or compare the justice process in the United States with other nations.

▍ **Currency and Immediacy:** Throughout the book, every attempt is made to use the most current research and to cover the most immediate topics. The idea is to show students the major trends in criminological research and justice policy. Most people who use the book have told me that this is one of its strongest features. I have attempted to present current research in a balanced fashion, though this sometimes can be frustrating to students. For example, while some experts find that a defendant's race negatively affects sentencing in the criminal courts, other criminologists conclude that race has little influence. Which position is correct? While it is comforting to reach an unequivocal conclusion about an important topic, sometimes that is simply not possible. In an effort to be objective and fair, each side of important criminological debates is presented in full. Throughout the text, Criminological Enterprise boxes review important research in criminology. For example, in Chapter 2 the feature "Explaining Crime Trends" discusses research

that helps explain why crime rates continue to rise and fall.

▍ **Social Policy:** There is a focus on social policy throughout the book so that students can see how criminological theory has been translated into crime prevention programs. Because of this theme, Policy and Practice in Criminology boxes are included throughout the text. These show how criminological ideas and research can be put into action. For example, in Chapter 18, there is a Policy and Practice in Criminology box called "The Problems of Reentry." This box discusses the long-term effects of an increasing prison population. It presents the provocative view that rather than deterring or preventing crime, imprisoning large numbers of offenders has had an opposite effect: It causes the crime rate to increase. What is the cause of this unexpected phenomenon?

In sum, the primary goals in writing this text are:

1. To provide students with a thorough knowledge of criminology and show its diversity and intellectual content.

2. To be as thorough and up-to-date as possible.

3. To be objective and unbiased.

4. To describe current theories, crime types, and methods of social control, and analyze their strengths and weaknesses.

5. To show how criminological thought has influenced social policy.

TOPIC AREAS

The tenth edition has been revised more extensively than previous editions. Two new chapters are included, one covering political crime and terrorism and the other cyber crime. The section on criminal justice has been streamlined and contains three rather than four chapters. The text is now divided into four main sections or topic areas.

Part One provides a framework for studying criminology. The first chapter defines the field and discusses its most basic concepts: the definition of crime, the component areas of criminology, the history of criminology, the concept of criminal law, and the ethical issues that confront the field. Chapter 2 covers criminological research methods, and the nature, extent, and patterns of crime. Chapter 3 is devoted to the concept of victimization, including the nature of victims, theories of victimization, and programs designed to help crime victims.

Part Two contains six chapters that cover criminological theory: Why do people behave the way they do? Why do they commit crimes? These views focus on choice (Chapter 4), biological and psychological traits (Chapter 5), social structure and culture (Chapter 6), social process and socialization (Chapter 7), social conflict (Chapter 8), and human development (Chapter 9).

Part Three is devoted to the major forms of criminal behavior. The chapters in this section cover interpersonal violence (Chapter 10), political crime and terrorism (Chapter 11), common theft offenses (Chapter 12), white-collar and organized crimes (Chapter 13), public order crimes, including sex offenses and substance abuse (Chapter 14), and cyber crime (Chapter 15).

Part Four contains three chapters that cover the criminal justice system. Chapter 16 provides an overview of the entire justice system, including the process of justice, the major organizations that make up the justice system, and concepts and perspectives of justice. Chapter 17 focuses on the arrest and adjudication process. And Chapter 18 delves into the topics of punishment and correction.

GOALS AND OBJECTIVES

The tenth edition has been carefully structured to cover relevant material in a comprehensive, balanced, and objective fashion. Every attempt has been made to make the presentation of material interesting and contemporary. No single political or theoretical position dominates the text; instead, the many diverse views that are contained within criminology and characterize its interdisciplinary nature are presented. While the text includes analysis of the most important scholarly works and scientific research reports, it also includes a great deal of topical information on recent cases and events, including some recent cyber scams, the Virginia Tech shooting, and the effects of excessive CEO pay.

NEW IN THE TENTH EDITION

▪ **Chapter 1, "Crime and Criminology,"** now begins with the story of Douglas Richard Stevens, who used the Internet to arrange sexual meetings with underage minors. The chapter contains new developments in law and theory, including research on the falsely convicted. There is a new Profiles in Crime box entitled "The Mother of All Snakeheads," which talks about the activities of Cheng Chui Ping, one of the most powerful underworld figures in New York.

▪ **Chapter 2, "The Nature and Extent of Crime"** A Profiles in Crime box details the fraud schemes of Ronald and Mary Evano, who turned dining in restaurants into a profitable, albeit illegal, scam. UCR, NCVS, and self-report data are all updated and recent trends in crime explored.

▪ **Chapter 3, "Victims and Victimization,"** now begins with the tragic story of Imette St. Guillen, a young graduate student who was killed after stopping in for a late-night drink in The Falls bar, a popular New York City night spot. The chapter contains new information on the

suffering experienced by rape survivors and the long-term stress experienced by crime victims. Chapter 3 also now covers the Justice for All Act of 2004 and "stand your ground" laws, as well as presenting a new Profiles in Crime box on Jesse Timmendequas and Megan's Law.

▪ **Chapter 4, "Rational Choice Theory,"** begins with the story of Johnny Ray Gasca, an infamous "movie pirate" who made a fortune illegally copying and selling feature films. The new Profiles in Crime box "Looting the Public Treasury" tells the story of Albert Robles: mayor, councilman, and deputy city manager of South Gate, California, who used his position for personal gain. There is new material on situational crime prevention efforts, including how efforts to ban alcohol influence DWI arrests. Research looks at how perception of punishment shapes criminal choices and the effect of deterrence strategies on crime rates.

▪ **Chapter 5, "Trait Theories,"** begins with the story of Seung-hui Cho and the Virginia Tech massacre. A Profiles in Crime box looks at the case of Andrea Yates, a young mother who killed her children in a fit of depression. We include new information on international studies measuring the effects of diet on crime and recent research on the effects of maternal smoking and alcohol on children's development. New research on the effects of environmental pollution on behavior is presented. And new studies on the effects of depression and mental illness on crime are discussed.

▪ **Chapter 6, "Social Structure Theories,"** begins with a new vignette on gangs in Los Angeles. There is a Profiles in Crime box on life in the drug trade, information on the neighborhood context of policing, as well as the association of neighborhood structure and parenting processes. There are new data on the evolving wealth structure of society and the issue of race and poverty. Recent research on the effects of exposure to community violence and neighborhood disadvantage is reported. And the chapter covers the latest research on topics such as fear of crime, and collective and street efficacy.

▪ **Chapter 7, "Social Process Theories,"** now opens with a compelling vignette on the case of Genarlow Wilson, a young man imprisoned for what he believed was consensual sex. There is a new Profiles in Crime box on Jesse James Hollywood, whose story was made into the motion picture *Alpha Dog*. Two new Criminological Enterprise features are presented: "When Being Good Is Bad," an expansion of neutralization theory, and "Storylines," which looks at the stories criminals tell to understand their motivations. Also included is new research on childhood predictors of criminality, the effects of bad parenting, parent–adolescent processes and reduced risk for delinquency, and the influence of fathers on male delinquency.

▪ **Chapter 8, "Social Conflict, Critical Criminology, and Restorative Justice,"** now begins with a vignette on executive pay trends. There is a Profiles in Crime box on Mumia Abu-Jamal, an activist accused of a murder many supporters believe he did not commit; a new Comparative Criminology feature on restoration programs around the world; and new research on genocide, feminist criminology, and race and crime.

■ **Chapter 9, "Developmental Theories: Life Course and Latent Trait,"** now opens with a vignette focusing on Troy Victorino, the notorious Xbox killer. New research covers such issues as the effects of family instability, self-control and victimization, cultural invariance, and the development of self-control.

■ **Chapter 10, "Interpersonal Violence,"** has expanded coverage of the causes of violence. It begins with a new vignette on the Duke University lacrosse team scandal, in which three young men were charged with a rape they did not actually commit but which still made national headlines. There is a new Comparative Criminology feature on honor killing of women and girls. Chapter 10 includes new research on violence and residential choice, the violent brain, and men who sexually abuse their own partners. A new analysis of the roots of serial murder and stalking is provided, as are new sections on psychological and social learning views of rape causation. The section on rape law changes has been updated with a new discussion on consent.

■ **Chapter 11, "Political Crime and Terrorism,"** is a new chapter for the tenth edition, and it begins with a vignette on the 9/11 attacks. There is a new Profiles in Crime box on master spy Aldrich Ames. Topics covered include political crimes such as voter fraud, espionage, and treason. The coverage on the nature and cause of terrorism is expansive, and the chapter delves into material on the history of terrorism, comparing terrorists to guerillas and insurgents, and what is being done to thwart terror attacks. A Criminological Enterprise feature on the use of torture is included.

■ **Chapter 12, "Property Crime,"** begins with the story of a thief who specialized in the theft of rare maps. Two new Profiles in Crime boxes have been added, one called "Invasion of the Body Snatchers," about people who stole dead body parts for resale, and another on credit card cons. Also added is a new Criminological Enterprise feature on the confessions of a dying thief. The chapter contains new material on street life and auto theft and on embezzlement. And a new section called "Planning to Burgle" shows how burglars decide to commit their crimes.

■ **Chapter 13** has expanded coverage and more focus on white-collar crime than in the previous edition, so it has been retitled **"Enterprise Crime: White-Collar and Organized Crime."** We begin the chapter with a new vignette on Medicare fraud, and there is a new Profiles in Crime box called "When the Flu Bug Bites," about a scam to sell fake flu shots. We discuss the federal government's Operation Bullpen, aimed at stopping chiseling in the sports memorabilia industry (including photos with fake autographs!), and also discuss international bribery used to secure business contracts. There is new material on influence peddling in government and an update on the Tyco and Enron cases. Lastly, a new section covers health care fraud and the rationalization/neutralization theory of white-collar crime.

■ **Chapter 14, "Public Order Crime,"** now begins with a vignette on a political candidate who had worked as a male prostitute and how that revelation ruined his career. There is more information on the international trade in prostitution and the coercion of women from the former Soviet Union into prostitution. A new Profiles in Crime box covers John Evander Couey and the Jessica Lunsford murder case. And the data on drug use and abuse and drug control strategies have all been updated.

■ **Chapter 15, "Cyber Crime and Technology,"** is new to this edition. It begins with a vignette that tells of an international Internet fraud scheme. There is coverage of computer fraud, distributing illegal sexual material, denial-of-service attacks, illegal copyright infringement, identity theft, e-tailing fraud, website defacement, cyber stalking, cyber bullying, and cyber spying, and a Policy and Practice box on biometric identification. Also included is a section on cyber terrorism and efforts to control it and other forms of cyber crime.

■ **Chapter 16, "Criminal Justice: Process and Perspectives,"** includes the latest material on important criminal justice issues concerning the police, courts, and corrections. There are updated data on the number of people behind bars and trends in the correctional population, and an interesting new Profiles in Crime box entitled "Two Wrongs Don't Make a Right" about a theft scheme at the Miami Airport gone very wrong.

■ **Chapter 17, "Police and the Courts: Investigation, Arrest, and Adjudication,"** is a new chapter that looks at the process of arrest and adjudication, as well as information on how police conduct investigations. We begin with the story of Booker T. Hudson, Jr., whose arrest led to a Supreme Court case that redefined the "no knock entry" rule. The chapter also includes a new Profiles in Crime box that discusses James Ford Seale, whose arrest for a civil rights era killing illustrates that some investigations take many years. The use of technology in court administration and its future direction is described in some detail as well.

■ **Chapter 18, "Punishment and Correction,"** is also new in the tenth edition. It describes how punishment is applied and how those convicted of criminal acts are treated or corrected. It begins with a vignette on Rachel Holt, a sixth-grade teacher found guilty of having sex with a student, and raises the question of whether her punishment fits the crime. The material on sentencing guidelines has been updated in light of Supreme Court decisions shaping and restricting their use. There is new material on the international use of the death penalty and on the problems of prisoner reentry.

FEATURES

This text contains many kinds of pedagogy that help students analyze material in greater depth and also link it to other material in the book.

▌ **Profiles in Crime** are new to the tenth edition and are designed to present students with case studies of actual criminals and crimes to help illustrate the position or views within the chapter.

▌ **The Criminological Enterprise** boxed inserts review important issues in criminology and reflect the major subareas of the field: measuring crime, creating theory, crime typologies, legal theory, and penology. For example, in Chapter 2, "Explaining Crime Trends" discusses the social and political factors that cause crime rates to rise and fall.

▌ **Policy and Practice in Criminology** boxes show how criminological ideas and research can be put into action. A Policy and Practice in Criminology box in Chapter 2, "Should Guns Be Controlled?" examines the pros and cons of the gun control debate, an issue that is being reexamined in the aftermath of the Virginia Tech killings.

▌ **Race, Culture, Gender, and Criminology** boxes cover issues of racial, sexual, and cultural diversity. For example, in Chapter 6, a Race, Culture, Gender, and Criminology box entitled "There Goes the Neighborhood" discusses the work and thoughts of William Julius Wilson, one of the nation's leading sociologists.

▌ **Comparative Criminology** boxes compare criminological policies, trends, and practices in the United States with those abroad. For example, in Chapter 13 a Comparative Criminology box looks at organized crime in Russia.

▌ **Connections** are short inserts that link the material to other areas covered in the book. For example, a Connections box in Chapter 14 links the question of pornography causing violence to the Chapter 5 discussion of whether watching media causes violence.

▌ **Chapter Outlines** provide a roadmap to coverage and serve as a useful review tool.

▌ **Learning Objectives** are presented at the beginning of each chapter to help students get the most out of the chapter coverage.

▌ **Thinking Like a Criminologist** sections near the end of each chapter present challenging questions or issues that students must use their criminological knowledge to answer or confront. Applying the information learned in the text will help students begin to "think like criminologists."

▌ **Doing Research on the Web** accompanies every Thinking Like a Criminologist feature and guides students to websites that will help them answer the criminological questions posed.

▌ **Critical Thinking Questions** accompany each of the boxed features above, and more are presented at the end of each chapter to help students develop their analytical abilities.

▌ Each chapter ends with a **Chapter Summary** and a list of **Key Terms**.

ANCILLARIES

A number of supplements are provided by Wadsworth to help instructors use *Criminology,* Tenth Edition in their courses and to aid students in preparing for exams. Supplements are available to qualified adopters. Please consult your local sales representative for details.

For the Instructor

▌ **Instructor's Resource Manual** Fully updated and revised by Joanne Ziembo-Vogl, the *Instructor's Resource Manual* for this edition includes learning objectives, detailed chapter outlines, key terms and figures, class discussion exercises, worksheets, lecture suggestions, and a complete test bank. Each chapter's test bank contains approximately 80 multiple-choice, true-false, fill-in-the-blank, and essay questions, which are coded according to difficulty level and Bloom's taxonomy. The Test Bank also includes a full answer key. Also presented is a Resource Integration Guide, which will help you make maximum use of the rich supplement package available for this text by integrating media, Internet, video, and other resources into each chapter.

▌ **ExamView® Computerized Testing** The comprehensive *Instructor's Resource Manual* described above is backed up by ExamView, a computerized test bank available for PC and Macintosh computers. With ExamView, an easy-to-use assessment and tutorial system, you can create, deliver, and customize tests and study guides (both print and online) in minutes. You can easily edit and import your own questions and graphics, change test layouts, and reorganize questions. And using ExamView's complete word processing capabilities, you can enter an unlimited number of new questions or edit existing questions.

▌ **JoinIn™ on TurningPoint®** Spark discussion and assess your students' comprehension of chapter concepts with interactive classroom quizzes and background polls developed specifically for use with this edition of *Criminology.* Also available are polling/quiz questions that enable you to maximize the educational benefits of the ABC® News video clips we custom select to accompany this textbook. Wadsworth's exclusive agreement with TurningPoint lets you run our tailor-made Microsoft® PowerPoint® slides in conjunction with the "clicker" hardware of your choice. Enhance how your students interact with you, your lecture, and each other. *For college and university adopters only. Contact your local Wadsworth representative to learn more.*

■ **PowerLecture CD** This instructor resource includes Microsoft® PowerPoint® lecture slides with graphics from the text, making it easy for you to assemble, edit, publish, and present custom lectures for your course. The PowerLecture CD also includes video-based polling and quiz questions that can be used with the JoinIn on TurningPoint personal response system, and integrates ExamView testing software for customizing tests of up to 250 items, which can be delivered in print or online. Finally, all of your media teaching resources in one place!

■ **WebTutor™ ToolBox on Blackboard® and WebCT®** A powerful combination: easy-to-use course management tools for whichever program you use combined with content from this text's rich companion website, all in one place. You can use ToolBox as is, from the moment you log on, or if you prefer, you can customize the program with web links, images, and other resources.

■ **The Wadsworth Criminal Justice Video Library** So many exciting new videos—so many great ways to enrich your lectures and spark discussion of the material in this text! A list of our unique and expansive video programs follows. Or visit **www.thomsonedu.com/criminaljustice/media_center/** for a complete, up-to-the-minute list of all of Wadsworth's video offerings—available in VHS and DVD format—as well as clip lists and running times. The library includes these selections and many others:

- *ABC Videos:* Featuring short, high-interest clips from current news events and specially developed for courses including Introduction to Criminal Justice, Criminology, Corrections, Terrorism, and White-Collar Crime, these videos are perfect for use as discussion starters or lecture launchers to spark student interest. The brief video clips provide students with a new lens through which to view the past and present, one that will greatly enhance their knowledge and understanding of significant events and open up to them new dimensions in learning. Clips are drawn from such programs as *World News Tonight, Good Morning America, This Week, Prime-Time Live, 20/20,* and *Nightline,* as well as numerous ABC News specials and material from the Associated Press Television News and British Movietone News collections.

- *The Wadsworth Custom Videos for Criminal Justice:* Produced by Wadsworth and Films for the Humanities, these videos include short (5- to 10-minute) segments that encourage classroom discussion. Topics include white-collar crime, domestic violence, forensics, suicide and the police officer, the court process, the history of corrections, prison society, and juvenile justice.

- *Court TV Videos:* One-hour videos presenting seminal and high-profile cases, such as the interrogation of Michael Crowe and serial killer Ted Bundy, as well as crucial and current issues such as cyber crime, double

jeopardy, and the management of the prison on Riker's Island.

- *A&E American Justice:* Forty videos to choose from, on topics such as deadly force, women on death row, juvenile justice, strange defenses, and Alcatraz.

- *Films for the Humanities:* Nearly 200 videos to choose from on a variety of topics such as elder abuse, supermax prisons, suicide and the police officer, the making of an FBI agent, domestic violence, and more.

- *Oral History Project:* Developed in association with the American Society of Criminology, the Academy of Criminal Justice Society, and the National Institute of Justice, these videos will help you introduce your students to the scholars who have developed the criminal justice discipline. Compiled over the last several years, each video features a set of Guest Lecturers—scholars whose thinking has helped to build the foundation of present ideas in the discipline.

■ **Classroom Activities for Criminal Justice** This valuable booklet, available to adopters of any Wadsworth criminal justice text, offers instructors the best of the best in criminal justice classroom activities. Containing both tried-and-true favorites and exciting new projects, its activities are drawn from across the spectrum of criminal justice subjects, including introduction to criminal justice, criminology, corrections, criminal law, policing, and juvenile justice, and can be customized to fit any course. Novice and seasoned instructors alike will find it a powerful tool to stimulate classroom engagement.

■ **Internet Activities for Criminal Justice** In addition to providing a wide range of activities for any criminal justice class, this useful booklet helps familiarize students with Internet resources they will use both as students of criminal justice and in their criminal justice careers. *Internet Activities for Criminal Justice* allows instructors to integrate Internet resources and addresses on important topics such as criminal and police law, policing organizations, policing challenges, corrections systems, juvenile justice, criminal trials, and current issues in criminal justice. Available to adopters of any Wadsworth criminal justice text, and prepared by Christina DeJong of Michigan State University, this booklet will bring current tools and resources to the criminal justice classroom.

■ **The Wadsworth Criminal Justice Resource Center: www.thomsonedu.com/criminaljustice** Designed with the instructor in mind, this website features information about Wadsworth's technology and teaching solutions, as well as several features created specifically for today's criminal justice student. Supreme Court updates, timelines, and hot-topic polling can all be used to supplement in-class assignments and discussions. You'll also find a wealth of links to careers and news in criminal justice, book-specific sites, and much more.

For the Student

■ **ThomsonNOW™** This unique, interactive online resource is the most exciting assessment-centered student learning tool ever offered for this course. ThomsonNOW determines each student's unique study needs by having him take a chapter pre-test and then offers him a personalized study plan that focuses his study time on the concepts he needs to master. Personalized study includes ABC News clips with questions, career profile videos, concept learning modules with assessments, integrated simulations, interactive diagrams, animations, Microsoft® PowerPoint® lectures, topic reviews, an e-book, and more. Once the student has completed his personalized study plan, a post-test evaluates his improved comprehension of chapter content. At any time the student can view his pre-/post-test scores, and all scores and gradable assignments flow directly into the instructor's grade book.

■ **Study Guide** An extensive student guide has been developed and updated for this edition by Joanne Ziembo-Vogl. Because students learn in different ways, the guide includes a variety of pedagogical aids. Each chapter is outlined and summarized, major terms and figures are defined, and worksheets and self-tests are provided.

■ **Mobile Content Study Guide** Students can finally study anytime and anywhere they want using Wadsworth's EAudio for *Criminology*. Our exclusive EAudio content, which can be downloaded to any MP3 player, includes a review of all key terms and concepts, as well as a summary of the chapter. With this unique supplement, students can quiz themselves on each chapter's vocabulary and key concepts as they go or review important material before tests—even if they don't have their textbook on hand or aren't at their desk.

■ **Careers in Criminal Justice Website: www.thomsonedu.com/login** This unique website gives students information on a wide variety of career paths, including requirements, salaries, training, contact information for key agencies, and employment outlooks. Several important tools help students investigate the criminal justice career choices that are right for them.

- *Career Profiles:* Video testimonials from a variety of practicing professionals in the field as well as information on many criminal justice careers, including job descriptions, requirements, training, salary and benefits, and the application process.
- *Interest Assessment:* Self-assessment tool to help students decide which careers suit their personalities and interests.
- *Career Planner:* Résumé writing tips and worksheets, interviewing techniques, and successful job search strategies.
- *Links for Reference:* Direct links to federal, state, and local agencies where students can get contact information and learn more about current job opportunities.

■ **Handbook of Selected Supreme Court Cases, Third Edition** This supplementary handbook covers almost 40 landmark cases, each of which includes a full case citation, an introduction, a summary from WestLaw, excerpts from the case, and the decision. The updated edition includes *Hamdi v. Rumsfeld, Roper v. Simmons, Ring v. Arizona, Atkins v. Virginia, Illinois v. Caballes,* and much more.

■ **Current Perspectives: Readings from InfoTrac® College Edition** These readers, designed to give students a deeper taste of special topics in criminal justice, include free access to InfoTrac College Edition. The timely articles are selected by experts in each topic from within InfoTrac College Edition. They are available for free when bundled with the text.

- *Terrorism and Homeland Security*
- *Cyber Crime*
- *Juvenile Justice*
- *Public Policy and Criminal Justice*
- *Crisis Management and National Emergency Response*
- *Racial Profiling*
- *New Technologies and Criminal Justice*
- *White-Collar Crime*

■ **Terrorism: An Interdisciplinary Perspective** Available for bundling with each new copy of *Criminology*, Tenth Edition, this 80-page booklet discusses terrorism in general and the issues surrounding the events of September 11, 2001. This information-packed booklet examines the origins of terrorism in the Middle East, focusing on Osama bin Laden in particular, as well as issues involving bioterrorism, the specific role played by religion in Middle Eastern terrorism, globalization as it relates to terrorism, and the reactions to and repercussions of terrorist attacks.

■ **Crime Scenes 2.0: An Interactive Criminal Justice CD-ROM** Recipient of several *New Media Magazine Invision Awards*, this interactive CD-ROM allows your students to take on the roles of investigating officer, lawyer, parole officer, and judge in excitingly realistic scenarios. Available free when bundled with every new copy of Criminology, Tenth Edition. An online instructor's manual for the CD-ROM is also available.

■ **Mind of a Killer CD-ROM (bundle version)** Voted one of the top 100 CD-ROMs by an annual *PC Magazine survey, Mind of a Killer* gives students a chilling glimpse into the realm of serial killers, with over 80 minutes of video and 3D simulations, an extensive mapping system, a library, and much more.

■ **Internet Guide for Criminal Justice, Second Edition** Intended for the novice user, this guide provides students with the background and vocabulary necessary to navigate and understand the Web, then provides them with a wealth of criminal justice websites and Internet project ideas.

ACKNOWLEDGMENTS

The preparation of this text would not have been possible without the aid of my colleagues who helped by reviewing the previous editions and giving me important suggestions for improvement. Reviewers for the tenth edition are:

Christopher Bader, *Baylor University*
David Bogumil, *California Polytechnic State University–Pomona*
Peggy Bowen, *Alvernia College*
Pearl Jacobs, *Sacred Heart University*
H. W. Mannle, *Tennessee Tech*
Anna-Maria Marshall, *University of Illinois at Urbana–Champaign*
Jennifer Schulenberg, *Sam Houston State University*

Reviewers of the previous editions include: M. H. Alsikafi, Alexander Alvarez, Thomas Arvanites, Patricia Atchison, Timothy Austin, Agnes Baro, Bonnie Berry, James Black, Joseph Blake, David Bordua, Stephen Brodt, Michael Brown, Thomas Calhoun, Mike Carlie, Mae Conley, Thomas Courtless, Mary Dietz, Carol DiMambro, Edna Erez, Stephen Gibbons, Dorothy Goldsborough, Edward Green, Julia Glover Hall, Marie Henry, Denny Hill, Alfred Himelson, Dennis Hoffman, Gerrold Hotaling, Joseph Jacoby, Sterling Jenkins, Casey Jordan, John Martin, Pamela Mayhall, James McKenna, Steven Messner, Ellyn K. Ness, Linda O'Daniel, Hugh O'Rourke, Nikos Passos, Gary Perlstein, William Pridemore, Jim Ruiz, Louis San Marco, Kip Schelgel, Theodore Skotnick, Mark Stetler, Kathleen Sweet, Gregory Talley, Kevin Thompson, Charles Tittle, Paul Tracy, Ruth Triplett, Charles Vedder, Joseph Vielbig, Ed Wells, Angela West, Michael Witkowski, Cecil Willis, Janet Wilson, and Joanne Ziembo-Vogl.

My colleagues at Wadsworth did their typically outstanding job of aiding me in the preparation of the text and gave me counseling and support. My editor Carolyn Henderson Meier is a real pro and gave me a lot of TLC, while I only give her GRIEF. The fantastic Shelley Murphy is a terrifically superb development editor who is always there for me. I really could not do another edition without her. My photo editor and friend Linda Rill did a thorough, professional job in photo research as usual. I have worked with Linda Jupiter, the book's production editor, many times and she is always great and also a close friend and confidant. Many thanks to Lunaea Weatherstone for her special and professional attention to the copyediting process. The fabulous Jennie Redwitz somehow pulls everything together as production manager and Terra Schultz is the quintessential marketing manager. All in all a terrific team!

Larry Siegel
Bedford, New Hampshire

PART ONE

CONCEPTS OF CRIME, LAW, AND CRIMINOLOGY

CHAPTER 1
Crime and Criminology

CHAPTER 2
The Nature and Extent of Crime

CHAPTER 3
Victims and Victimization

How is crime defined? How much crime is there, and what are the trends and patterns in the crime rate? How many people fall victim to crime, and who is likely to become a crime victim? How did our system of criminal law develop, and what are the basic elements of crimes? What is the science of criminology all about?

These are some of the core issues that will be addressed in the first three chapters of this text. Chapter 1 introduces students to the field of criminology: its nature, area of study, methodologies, and historical development. Concern about crime and justice has been an important part of the human condition for more than 5,000 years, since the first criminal codes were set down in the Middle East. Although criminology—the scientific study of crime—is considered a modern science, it has existed for more than 200 years. Chapter 1 introduces students to one of the key components of criminology—the development of criminal law. It also discusses the social history of law, the purpose of law, and how law defines crime. Chapter 2 focuses on the acquisition of crime data, crime rate trends, and observable patterns within the crime rate. Chapter 3 is devoted to victims and victimization. Topics include the affects of victimization, the cause of victimization, and efforts to help crime victims.

Crime and Criminology

CHAPTER OUTLINE

What Is Criminology?
Criminology and Criminal Justice
Criminology and Deviance

A Brief History of Criminology
Classical Criminology
Nineteenth-Century Positivism
The Chicago School and Beyond
Social-Psychological Views
Conflict and Crime
Integrating Diverse Perspectives: Developmental
Criminology
Contemporary Criminology

What Criminologists Do: The Criminological Enterprise
Criminal Statistics and Research Methodology
Comparative Criminology: International Crime Trends
Law and Society: The Sociology of Law
Theory Construction and Testing
Criminal Behavior Systems and Crime Typologies
Penology and Social Control
Victimology: Victims and Victimization

How Criminologists View Crime
The Consensus View of Crime
The Conflict View of Crime
The Interactionist View of Crime
Defining Crime

Crime and the Criminal Law
Common Law
Contemporary Criminal Law
PROFILES IN CRIME: The Mother of All Snakeheads
The Evolution of Criminal Law
The Criminological Enterprise: The Elements of Criminal Law

Ethical Issues in Criminology
What to Study?
Whom to Study?
How to Study?

CHAPTER OBJECTIVES

Pg:4 1. Understand what is meant by the field of criminology

2. Know the historical context of criminology

3. Recognize the differences among the various schools of criminological thought

4. Be familiar with the various elements of the criminological enterprise

5. Be able to discuss how criminologists define crime

6. Recognize the concepts of criminal law

7. Know the difference between evil acts and evil intent

8. Describe the various defenses to crime

9. Show how criminal law is undergoing change

10. Be able to discuss ethical issues in criminology

© Guergui Pinkhassov/Magnum Photos

On December 7, 2005, Douglas Richard Stevens, 53, of Ontario, Canada, began communicating online with "Jane," whom he believed had a ten-year-old daughter named Mary. Using the screen name "ontm4momanddaughter," Stevens told "Jane" that he wanted to engage in sexual acts with "Mary" and bragged about previous conquests of girls he met online. He arranged to meet "Jane" and "Mary" in Atlanta so that he could sexually molest "Mary." When he arrived, federal law enforcement agents arrested Stevens in a restaurant parking lot. "Jane" and "Mary" never existed and were in fact identities created and used by an undercover FBI agent working as part of the FBI's Safe Child Task Force, designed to lure predators such as Stevens. He was indicted by a federal grand jury in January 2006 on charges that included using a computer to entice a minor to engage in sexual activity and traveling across state lines to engage in sexual acts with the minor. Stevens pleaded guilty to both counts and on June 9, 2006, he was sentenced to 12 years in prison.[1]

The Stevens case illustrates the evolution of criminal behavior in contemporary society. The computer and Internet have enabled people to engage in criminal activities unknown a decade ago. Besides crimes like the one Stevens committed, these range from identity theft to online securities fraud.

The reach of crime has become truly international, creating new challenges for law enforcement authorities. The questions about crime and its control raised by the Stevens case and others have spurred interest in criminology, an academic discipline that uses the scientific method to study the nature, extent, cause, and control of criminal behavior. Unlike political figures and media commentators—whose opinions about crime may be colored by personal experiences, biases, and election concerns—criminologists remain objective as they study crime and its consequences.[2]

Criminology is a multidisciplinary science. Criminologists hold degrees in a variety of diverse fields, most commonly sociology, but also criminal justice, political science, psychology, public policy, economics, and the natural sciences.

For most of the twentieth century, criminology's primary orientation was sociological, but today it can be viewed as an integrated approach to the study of criminal behavior. How this field developed, its major components, and its relationship to crime law and deviance are some of the topics discussed in this chapter.

This text analyzes criminology and its major subareas of inquiry. It focuses on the nature and extent of crime, the causes of crime, and patterns of criminal behavior. This chapter introduces and defines criminology: What are its goals? What is its history? How do criminologists define crime? How do they conduct research? What ethical issues face those wishing to conduct criminological research?

WHAT IS CRIMINOLOGY?

Criminology is the scientific approach to studying criminal behavior. In their classic definition, preeminent criminologists Edwin Sutherland and Donald Cressey state:

> Criminology is the body of knowledge regarding crime as a social phenomenon. It includes within its scope the processes of making laws, of breaking laws, and of reacting toward the breaking of laws. . . . The objective of criminology is the development of a body of general and verified principles and of other types of knowledge regarding this process of law, crime, and treatment.[3]

Sutherland and Cressey's definition includes some of the most important areas of interest to criminologists:

▮ *Crime as a social phenomenon.* Although some criminologists believe that individual traits and characteristics may play some role in the cause of criminals' antisocial behavior, most believe that social factors are at the root cause of crime. Even the most disturbed people are influenced by their environment and their social interactions and personal relationships.

▮ *The processes of making laws.* Sutherland and Cressey's definition recognizes the association between crime and the criminal law and shows how the law defines crime. Nonetheless, how and why laws are created and why some are strengthened and others eliminated is of great interest to criminologists.

▮ *Of breaking laws and reacting toward the breaking of laws.* At its core, the purpose of criminology is to understand both the onset of crime and the most effective methods for its elimination. Why do people commit illegal acts, and what can be done to convince them—and others who are contemplating crime—that it is in their best interests to turn their back on criminality? These concepts are naturally bound together: it is impossible to effectively control crime unless we understand its cause.

▮ *Development of a body of general and verified principles.* Sutherland and Cressey recognize that criminology is a social science and criminologists must use the scientific method when conducting research. Criminologists are required to employ valid and reliable experimental designs and sophisticated data analysis techniques or else lose standing in the academic community.

Criminology and Criminal Justice

Although the terms *criminology* and *criminal justice* may seem similar, and people often confuse the two or lump them together, there are major differences between these fields of study. Criminology explains the etiology (origin), extent, and nature of crime in society, whereas criminal justice refers to the study of the agencies of social control—police, courts, and corrections. While criminologists are mainly concerned with identifying the suspected cause of *crime*, criminal justice scholars spend their time identifying effective methods of *crime control*.

Since both fields are crime-related, they do overlap. Some criminologists devote their research to justice and social control and are concerned with how the agencies of justice operate, how they influence crime and criminals, and how justice policies shape crime rates and trends. Conversely, criminal justice experts often want to design effective programs of crime prevention or rehabilitation and to do so must develop an understanding of the nature of crime and its causation. It is common, therefore, for criminal justice programs to feature courses on criminology and for criminology courses to evaluate the agencies of justice.

Criminology and Deviance

Criminology is also related to the study of deviant behaviors—those actions that depart from social norms, values, and beliefs. Included within the broad spectrum of deviant acts are behaviors ranging from violent crimes to joining a nudist colony. However, significant distinctions can be made between these two areas of study because many crimes are not unusual or deviant, and many deviant acts are neither illegal nor criminal.

Take, for instance, substance abuse. Selling and/or possessing recreational drugs, such as marijuana, may be illegal, but can it actually be considered deviant? A significant percentage of the population have used or are using drugs; more than half of all high school students have tried drugs before they graduate.[4] Therefore, it is erroneous to argue that all crimes are deviant behaviors that depart from the norms of society.

CONCEPT SUMMARY 1.1

CRIMINOLOGY: CRIMINAL JUSTICE AND DEVIANCE

CRIMINOLOGY

Criminology explores the etiology (origin), extent, and nature of crime in society. Criminologists are concerned with identifying the nature, extent, and cause of crime.

Criminal Justice

Criminal justice refers to the agencies of social control that handle criminal offenders. Criminal justice scholars engage in describing, analyzing, and explaining operations of the agencies of justice, specifically the police departments, courts, and correctional facilities. They seek more effective methods of crime control and offender rehabilitation.

Overlapping Areas of Concern

Criminal justice experts cannot begin to design effective programs of crime prevention or rehabilitation without understanding the nature and cause of crime. They require accurate criminal statistics and data to test the effectiveness of crime control and prevention programs.

Deviance

Deviance refers to the study of behavior that departs from social norms. Included within the broad spectrum of deviant acts are behaviors ranging from violent crimes to joining a nudist colony. Not all crimes are deviant or unusual acts, and not all deviant acts are illegal.

Overlapping Areas of Concern

Under what circumstances do deviant behaviors become crimes? When does sexually oriented material cross the line from merely suggestive to obscene and therefore illegal? If an illegal act becomes a norm, should society reevaluate its criminal status? There is still debate over the legalization and/or decriminalization of abortion, recreational drug use, possession of handguns, and assisted suicide.

Similarly, many deviant acts are not criminal even though they may be both disturbing and shocking to the conscience. Suppose a passerby witnesses someone floundering in the ocean and makes no rescue attempt. Most people would condemn the onlooker's coldhearted behavior as callous, immoral, and deviant. However, no legal action could be taken since a private citizen is not required by law to risk his or her own life to save another's. There is no legal requirement that a person rush into a burning building, brave a flood, or jump into the ocean to save someone from harm. They may be deviant and not share commonly held values, but according to the law, they are not criminals.

In sum, criminologists are concerned with the concept of deviance and its relationship to criminality, whereas those sociologists who study deviant behaviors often want to understand and/or identify the line that separates criminal from merely unusual behaviors. The shifting definition of deviant behavior is closely associated with our concepts of crime. The relationships among criminology, criminal justice, and deviance are illustrated in Concept Summary 1.1.

🖱 **www** The principal purpose of the **Office on National Drug Control Policy (ONDCP)** is to establish policies, priorities, and objectives for the nation's drug control program, the goals of which are to reduce illicit drug use, manufacturing, and trafficking; reduce drug-related crime and violence; and reduce drug-related health consequences. To read more about their efforts, access their website via www.thomsonedu.com/criminaljustice/siegel.

A BRIEF HISTORY OF CRIMINOLOGY

How did the study of criminology develop? It is actually a relatively new field of study. Although written criminal codes have existed for thousands of years, these were restricted to defining crime and setting punishments. What motivated people to violate the law remained a matter for conjecture.

During the early Middle Ages (1200–1400), superstition and fear of satanic possession dominated thinking. People who violated social norms or religious practices were believed to be witches or possessed by demons. The prescribed method for dealing with the possessed was burning at the stake, a practice that survived into the seventeenth century. Beginning in the mid-thirteenth century, the jurisdiction of central governments reached a significantly broader range of social behaviors. Human problems and conflicts began to be dealt with in a formalized and legal manner.[5] Nonetheless, superstition and harsh punishments did not end quickly. The authorities were on guard against Satan's offspring, who engaged in acts ranging from witchcraft to robbery. Between 1581 and 1590, Nicholas Remy, head of the Inquisition in the French province of Lorraine, ordered 900 sorcerers and witches burned to death; likewise, Peter Binsfield, the bishop of the German city of Trier, ordered the death of 6,500 people. An estimated 100,000 people were prosecuted throughout Europe for witchcraft during the sixteenth and seventeenth centuries. It was also commonly believed that some families produced offspring who were unsound or unstable and that social misfits were inherently damaged by reason of their "inferior blood."[6] It was common practice to use cruel tortures to extract confessions, and those convicted of violent or theft crimes suffered extremely harsh penalties, including whipping, branding, maiming, and execution. Almost all felons were punished with death; the law made little distinction between thieves and murderers.

Classical Criminology

During the eighteenth century, social philosophers such as Jeremy Bentham began to embrace the view that human behavior was a result of rational thought processes. According to Bentham's utilitarianism, people choose to act when, after weighing costs and benefits, they believe that their actions will bring them an increase in pleasure and a reduction of pain. It stands to reason that criminal behavior could be eliminated or controlled if would-be law violators could be convinced that the pain of punishment exceeds the benefits of crime. Cesare Beccaria (1738–1794) applied these principles to criminal behavior in his famous treatise, "On Crimes and Punishment." He agreed that people want to achieve pleasure and avoid pain. He suggested that harsh punishments and routine use of torture were inappropriate and excessive. If every felon were punished with death, he reasoned, there would be little incentive for criminals not to escalate the severity of their crimes. To deter crime, the pain of punishment must be administered in a fair, balanced, and proportionate amount, just enough to counterbalance the pleasure obtained from crime. Beccaria stated his famous theorem like this:

> In order for punishment not to be in every instance, an act of violence of one or many against a private citizen, it must be essentially public, prompt, necessary, the least possible in the given circumstances, proportionate to the crimes, and dictated by the laws.[7]

The writings of Beccaria and his followers form the core of what today is referred to as classical criminology. As originally conceived in the eighteenth century, classical criminology theory had several basic elements:

▌ In every society people have free will to choose criminal or lawful solutions to meet their needs or settle their problems.

▌ Criminal solutions can be very attractive because for little effort they hold the promise of a huge payoff.

▌ A person will choose not to commit crime only if they believe that the pain of expected punishment is greater than the promise of reward. This is the principle of deterrence.

▌ In order to be an effective crime deterrent, punishment must be severe, certain, and swift enough to convince potential criminals that "crime does not pay."

This classical perspective influenced penal practices for more than 200 years. The law was made proportionate to crime so that the most serious offenses earned the harshest punishments. Executions were still widely used but slowly began to be employed for only the most serious crimes. The catchphrase was "let the punishment fit the crime."

As the nineteenth century was coming to a close, a new vision of the world challenged the validity of classical theory and presented an innovative way of looking at the causes of crime.

Nineteenth-Century Positivism

During the late nineteenth century, the scientific method was beginning to take hold in Europe. Rather than rely on pure thought and reason, contemporary scientists began to use careful observation and analysis of natural phenomena in their experiments. This movement inspired new discoveries in biology, astronomy, and chemistry. Charles Darwin's (1809–1882) discoveries on the evolution of man encouraged a nineteenth-century "cult of science." Darwin's discoveries encouraged other scholars to be certain that all human activity could be verified by scientific principles. If the scientific method could be applied to the study of the natural world, then why not use it to study human behavior?

Auguste Comte (1798–1857), considered the founder of sociology, applied scientific methods to the study of society. According to Comte, societies pass through stages that can be grouped on the basis of how people try to understand the world in which they live. People in primitive societies consider inanimate objects as having life (for example, the sun is a god); in later social stages, people embrace a rational, scientific view of the world. Comte called this final stage the positive stage, and those who followed his writings became known as positivists.

As we understand it today, positivism has two main elements:

▌All true knowledge is acquired through direct observation and not through conjecture or belief. Statements that cannot be backed up by direct observation—for instance, "all babies are born innocent"—are invalid and worthless.

▌The scientific method must be used if research findings are to be considered valid. This involves such steps as identifying problems, collecting data, forming hypotheses, conducting experiments, and interpreting results (see Exhibit 1.1).

According to the positivist tradition, social processes are a product of the measurable interaction between relationships and

The Trial of George Jacobs, August 5, 1692 by T. H. Matteson (1855). Oil on canvas 39×53 inches. #1.246 Peabody Essex Museum, Salem, MA

▌ During the Middle Ages, superstition and fear of satanic possession dominated thinking. People who violated social norms or religious practices were believed to be witches or possessed by demons. The prescribed method for dealing with the possessed was burning at the stake, a practice that survived into the seventeenth century. This painting, *The Trial of George Jacobs, August 5, 1692* by T. H. Matteson (1855), depicts the ordeal of Jacobs, a patriarch of Salem, Massachusetts. During the witch craze, he had ridiculed the trials, only to find himself accused, tried, and executed.

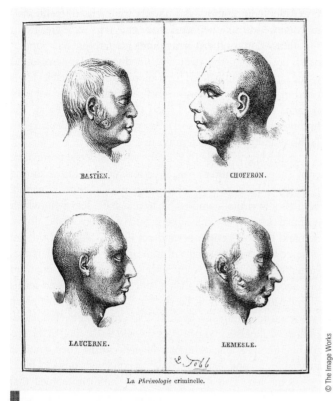

BASTIEN.   CHOFFRON.

LAUCERNE.   LEMESLE.

La *Phrénologie* criminelle.

© The Image Works

Early positivists believed the shape of the skull was a key determinant of behavior. These drawings from the nineteenth century illustrate "typical" criminally shaped heads.

EXHIBIT 1.1

Elements of the Scientific Method

Observation
Identify problem and collect data and facts

Hypothesis
Develop a reasonable explanation to account for or predict the data observed and the facts collected

Test Hypothesis
Test hypothesis using control groups and experimental methods

Interpretation
Analyze data using accepted statistical techniques

Conclusion
Interpret data and verify or disprove accuracy of hypothesis

events. Human behavior therefore is a function of a variety of forces. Some are social, such as the effect of wealth and class; others are political and historical, such as war and famine. Other forces are more personal and psychological, such as an individual's brain structure and his or her biological makeup or mental ability. Each of these influences and shapes human behavior. People are neither born "good" nor "bad," and are neither "saints" nor "sinners." They are a product of their social and psychological traits, influenced by their upbringing and environment.

Biological Positivism The earliest "scientific" studies applying the positivist model to criminology were conducted by **physiognomists**, such as J. K. Lavater (1741–1801), who studied the facial features of criminals to determine whether the shape of ears, nose, and eyes and the distance between them were associated with antisocial behavior. **Phrenologists**, such as Franz Joseph Gall (1758–1828) and Johann K. Spurzheim (1776–1832), studied the shape of the skull and bumps on the head to determine whether these physical attributes were linked to criminal behavior. Phrenologists believed that external cranial characteristics dictate which areas of the brain control physical activity. The brain, they suggested, has 30 different areas or faculties that control behavior. The size of a brain could be determined by inspecting the contours of the skull—the larger the organ, the more active it was. The relative size of brain organs could be increased or decreased through exercise and self-discipline.[8] Though phrenology techniques and methods

are no longer practiced or taken seriously, these efforts were an early attempt to use a "scientific" method to study crime.

By the early nineteenth century, abnormality in the human mind was being linked to criminal behavior patterns.[9] Philippe Pinel (1745–1826), one of the founders of French psychiatry, claimed that some people behave abnormally even without being mentally ill. He coined the phrase *manie sans delire* to denote what today is referred to as a **psychopathic personality**. In 1812, an American, Benjamin Rush (1745–1813), described patients with an "innate preternatural moral depravity."[10] Another early criminological pioneer, English physician Henry Maudsley (1835–1918), believed that insanity and criminal behavior were strongly linked. He stated: "Crime is a sort of outlet in which their unsound tendencies are discharged; they would go mad if they were not criminals, and they do not go mad because they are criminals."[11] These early research efforts shifted attention to brain functioning and personality as the keys to criminal behavior. When Sigmund Freud's (1856–1939) work on the unconscious gained worldwide notoriety, the psychological basis of behavior was forever established.

In Italy, Cesare Lombroso (1835–1909), a physician who served much of his career in the Italian army, was studying the cadavers of executed criminals in an effort to scientifically determine whether law violators were physically different from people of conventional values and behavior.[12] Lombroso believed that serious offenders—those who engaged in repeated assault- or theft-related activities—were "born criminals" who had inherited a set of primitive physical traits that he referred to as **atavistic anomalies**. Physically, born criminals were throwbacks to more primitive savage people. Among the crime-producing traits Lombroso identified were enormous jaws and strong canine teeth common to carnivores and savages who devour raw flesh. These criminogenic traits can be acquired through *indirect heredity*, from a degenerate family whose members suffered from such ills as insanity, syphilis, and alcoholism, or *direct heredity*—being the offspring of criminal parents.

Lombroso's version of criminal anthropology was brought to the United States via articles and textbooks that adopted his ideas. He attracted a circle of followers who expanded on his vision of **biological determinism**. His scholarship helped stimulate interest in a **criminal anthropology**.[13] Ironically, his work was actually more popular in the United States than it was in Europe, and by the turn of the century, American social thinkers were discussing "the science of penology" and "the science of criminology."[14]

Lombroso's version of strict biological determinism is no longer taken seriously (later in his career even he recognized that not all criminals were biological throwbacks). Today, those criminologists who suggest that crime has some biological basis also believe that environmental conditions influence human behavior. Hence, the term **biosocial theory** has been coined to reflect the assumed link between physical and mental traits, the social environment, and behavior.

Social Positivism At the same time that biological positivists were conducting their experiments, other positivists were using social data to scientifically study the major changes that were taking place in nineteenth-century society and in so doing helping to create the field of sociology.

Sociology seemed an ideal perspective from which to study society. After thousands of years of stability, the world was undergoing a population explosion. The population estimated at 600 million in 1700 had risen to 900 million by 1800. People were flocking to cities in ever-increasing numbers. Manchester, England, had 12,000 inhabitants in 1760 and 400,000 in 1850; during the same period, the population of Glasgow, Scotland, rose from 30,000 to 300,000.

The development of machinery such as power looms had doomed cottage industries and given rise to a factory system in which large numbers of people toiled for extremely low wages. The spread of agricultural machines increased the food supply while reducing the need for a large rural workforce; these excess laborers further swelled city populations. At the same time, political, religious, and social traditions continued to be challenged by the scientific method.

Quetelet and Durkheim The application of sociological concepts to criminology can be traced to the works of pioneering sociologists L. A. J. (Adolphe) Quetelet (1796–1874) and (David) Émile Durkheim (1858–1917). Quetelet instigated the use of data and statistics in performing criminological research. Durkheim, considered one of the founders of sociology, defined crime as a normal and necessary social event.[15] These two perspectives have been extremely influential on modern criminology. L. A. J. (Adolphe) Quetelet was a Belgian mathematician who began (along with a Frenchman, Andre-Michel Guerry) what is known as the **cartographic school of criminology**.[16] This approach made use of social statistics that were being developed in Europe in the early nineteenth century. Statistical data provided important demographic information on the population, including density, gender, religious affiliations, and wealth.

Quetelet studied data gathered in France (called the *Comptes generaux de l'administration de la justice*) to investigate the influence of social factors on the propensity to commit crime. In addition to finding a strong influence of age and sex on crime, Quetelet also uncovered evidence that season, climate, population composition, and poverty were related to criminality. More specifically, he found that crime rates were greatest in the summer, in southern areas, among heterogeneous populations, and among the poor and uneducated. He also found crime rates to be influenced by drinking habits.[17] Quetelet identified many of the relationships between crime and social phenomena that still serve as a basis for criminology today. His findings that crime had a social basis were a direct challenge to Lombrosian biological determinism.

According to Émile Durkheim's vision of social positivism, crime is part of human nature because it has existed during periods of both poverty and prosperity.[18] Crime is *normal* because it is virtually impossible to imagine a society in which criminal behavior is totally absent. Such a society would almost demand that all people be and act exactly alike. Durkheim believed that the inevitability of crime is linked to the differences (heterogeneity) within society. Since people are so different from one another and employ such a variety of methods and forms of behavior to meet their needs, it is not surprising that some will resort to criminality. Even if "real" crimes were eliminated, human weaknesses and petty vices would be elevated to the status of crimes. As long as human differences exist, then, crime is inevitable and one of the fundamental conditions of social life.

Some may find it surprising, but Durkheim argued that crime can even be useful and, on occasion, healthy for society. He held that the existence of crime paves the way for social change and indicates that the social structure is not rigid or inflexible. Put another way, if such differences did not exist, it would mean that everyone behaved the same way and agreed on what is right and wrong. Such universal conformity would stifle creativity and independent thinking. To illustrate this concept, Durkheim offered the example of the Greek philosopher Socrates, who was considered a criminal and put to death for corrupting the morals of youth simply because he expressed ideas that were different from what people believed at that time.

Durkheim reasoned that another benefit of crime is that it calls attention to social ills. A rising crime rate can signal the need for social change and promote a variety of programs designed to relieve the human suffering that may have caused crime in the first place. In his influential book, *The Division of Labor in Society*, Durkheim described the consequences of the shift from a small, rural society, which he labeled "mechanical," to the more modern "organic" society with a large urban population, division of labor, and personal isolation.[19] From this shift flowed **anomie**, or norm and role confusion, a powerful sociological concept that helps describe the chaos and disarray accompanying the loss of traditional values in modern society. Durkheim's research on suicide indicated that anomic societies maintain high suicide rates; by implication, anomie might cause other forms of deviance as well.

The Chicago School and Beyond

The primacy of sociological positivism as the intellectual basis of criminology was secured by research begun in the early twentieth century by Albion W. Small (1854–1926), who organized the famed sociology department at the University of Chicago.

Referred to as the Chicago School, urban sociologists such as W. I. Thomas (1863–1947), Robert Ezra Park (1864–1944), Ernest W. Burgess (1886–1966), and Louis Wirth (1897–1952) pioneered research on the social ecology of the city. In 1915, Robert Ezra Park called for anthropological methods of description and observation to be applied to urban life.[20] He was concerned about how neighborhood structure developed, how isolated pockets of poverty formed, and what social policies could be used to alleviate urban problems. In response, Chicago School sociologists carried out an ambitious program of research and scholarship on urban topics, including criminal behavior patterns. Harvey Zorbaugh's *The Gold Coast and the Slum*,[21] Frederick Thrasher's *The Gang*,[22] and Louis Wirth's *The Ghetto*[23] are classic examples of objective, highly descriptive accounts of urban life. Park, with Ernest Burgess, studied the social ecology of the city and found that some neighborhoods formed so-called natural areas of wealth and affluence, while others suffered poverty and disintegration.[24] Regardless of their race, religion, or ethnicity, the everyday behavior of people living in these areas was controlled by the social and ecological climate.

This body of research inspired a generation of scholars to conclude that social forces operating in urban areas create "natural areas" for crime.[25] These urban neighborhoods maintain such a high level of poverty that critical institutions of socialization and control, such as the school and the family, begin to break down. While normally these social institutions can apply the social control necessary to restrain deviant behaviors, because they are weak, people are free to engage in exciting and enticing law-violating behaviors. As crime rate soars and residents are afraid to leave their homes at night, the neighborhood becomes *socially disorganized*—unable to apply social control. It can no longer muster the cohesion needed to protect its residents from crime, drug abuse, and violence. Criminal behavior is not then a function of personal traits or characteristics but is linked to environmental conditions that fail to provide residents with proper human relations and development.

The Chicago School sociologists initiated the view that crime and social ecological conditions were linked. Neighborhood conditions, and not individual pathologies, influence and shape the direction of crime rates.

Social-Psychological Views

During the 1930s and 1940s, another group of sociologists began to link social-psychological interactions to criminological behavior. Sociological social psychology (also known as psychological sociology) is the study of human interactions and relationships, and emphasizes such issues as group dynamics and socialization.

According to this school of thought, an individual's relationship to important social processes, such as education, family life, and peer relations, is the key to understanding human behavior. Poverty and social disorganization alone are not sufficient to cause criminal activity because, after all, many people living in the most deteriorated areas never commit criminal offenses. Something else was needed. Research seemed to show that children who grow up in homes wracked

by conflict, attend inadequate schools, and/or associate with deviant peers become exposed to pro-crime forces.

In this view, socialization, rather than social structure, is key to understanding crime. But what element of socialization had the greatest effect? To Edwin Sutherland, the preeminent American criminologist, it was the learning of criminal attitudes from older, more experienced law violators. Crime was a learned behavior similar to any other, such as driving and playing sports. Another view, developed by Chicago-trained sociologist Walter Reckless, was that crime occurs when children develop an inadequate self-image, rendering them incapable of controlling their own misbehavior. Criminologists seized upon this concept of control and suggested that it was a key element in a criminal career: people became crime prone when social forces proved inadequate to control their behavior.

Both of these views—learning and control—link criminality to the failure of socialization, the interactions people have with the various individuals, organizations, institutions, and processes of society that help them mature and develop.

By mid-century, most criminologists had embraced either the structural/ecological view or the socialization view of crime. However, these were not the only positions on how social institutions influence human behavior. In Europe, the writings of another social thinker, Karl Marx (1818–1883), had pushed the understanding of social interaction in another direction and sowed the seeds for a new approach in criminology.[26]

Conflict and Crime

In his *Communist Manifesto* and other writings, Marx described the oppressive labor conditions prevalent during the rise of industrial capitalism. His observations of the economic structure convinced Marx that the character of every civilization is determined by its mode of production—the way its people develop and produce material goods (materialism). The most important relationship in industrial culture is between the owners of the means of production—the capitalist bourgeoisie—and the people who do the actual labor, the proletariat. The economic system controls all facets of human life; consequently, people's lives revolve around the means of production. The exploitation of the working class, he believed, would eventually lead to class conflict and the end of the capitalist system.

Though these writings laid the foundation for a Marxist-based criminology, decades passed before the impact of Marxist theory was realized. In the United States during the 1960s, social and political upheaval was fueled by the Vietnam War, the development of an antiestablishment counterculture movement, the civil rights movement, and the women's movement. Contemporary sociologists interested in applying Marx's principles to the study of crime began to analyze the socioeconomic conditions in the United States that promoted class conflict and crime. What emerged from this intellectual ferment was a Marxist-based critical criminology that indicted the capitalist economic system as producing the conditions that support a high crime rate. The critical view of crime developed in the 1960s has played a significant role in criminology ever since.

Integrating Diverse Perspectives: Developmental Criminology

During the twentieth century some criminologists began to integrate sociological, psychological, and economic elements into more complex developmental views of crime causation. Hans Eysenck published *Crime and Personality* in 1964 and proclaimed that antisocial behavior was linked to psychological conditions that were a product of heredity.[27] His controversial theory integrated social, biological, and psychological factors, a vision that upset the sociologists who controlled the field at that time.[28]

However, it is Sheldon (1896–1980) and Eleanor (1898–1972) Glueck who are today considered founders of the developmental branch of criminological theory. While at Harvard University in the 1930s, they conducted research on the careers of known criminals to determine the factors that predicted persistent offending, making extensive use of interviews and records in their elaborate comparisons of criminals and noncriminals.

connections

Because Eysenck's theory is essentially psychological, there will be more on his views in our Chapter 5 discussion of individual traits that produce crime. The Gluecks are revisited in Chapter 9, Developmental Theories, because they are more closely associated with that area of scholarship.

The Gluecks' research focused on early onset of delinquency as a harbinger of a criminal career: "[T]he deeper the roots of childhood maladjustment, the smaller the chance of adult adjustment."[29] They also noted the stability of offending careers: children who are antisocial early in life are the most likely to continue their offending careers into adulthood.

The Gluecks identified a number of personal and social factors related to persistent offending, the most important of which was family relations. This factor was considered in terms of quality of discipline and emotional ties with parents. The adolescent raised in a large, single-parent family of limited economic means and educational achievement was the most vulnerable to delinquency. Not restricting their analysis to social variables, the Gluecks measured such biological and psychological traits as body type, intelligence, and personality, and found that physical and mental factors also played a role in determining behavior. Children with low intelligence, who had a background of mental disease, and who had a powerful ("mesomorph") physique were the most likely to become persistent offenders.

Integrating biological, social, and psychological elements, the Gluecks' research suggested that the initiation and continuity of a criminal career was a developmental process influenced by both internal and external situations, conditions, and circumstances. While impressive, their research was heavily criticized by sociologists such as Edwin Sutherland who wanted to keep criminology within the field of sociology and feared or disparaged efforts to integrate biological or psychological concepts into the field.[30] Following Sutherland's critique, the Gluecks' work was ignored for quite some time until criminologists began to revisit their data and use contemporary methods to reanalyze their results. Today, upon reflection, it is now considered one of the foundations for the developmental theory model that is influential in the field today. Developmental models track the natural history of a criminal career. Rather than limiting their purpose to finding the root cause of crime, developmental criminologists examine the life course of a criminal career and ponder such issues as why people begin to commit crime, why they escalate their criminal activities, why they stop committing crime, and if they do stop, why some begin again. Contemporary developmental theories will be discussed in Chapter 9.

Contemporary Criminology

The various schools of criminology developed over the past 200 years. Though they have evolved, each continues to have an impact on the field. For example, classical theory has evolved into rational choice and deterrence theories. Rational choice theorists today argue that criminals are rational and use available information to decide if crime is a worthwhile undertaking. A sub-branch of rational choice theory, deterrence theory, holds that this choice is structured by the fear of punishment. Biological positivism has undergone similar transformation. Although criminologists no longer believe that an inherited characteristic can by itself determine the course of behavior, some are convinced that behavior is altered when an individual's biological and psychological traits interact with environmental influences. Biological and psychological criminologists study the association between criminal behavior and such traits as diet, hormonal makeup, personality, and intelligence.

The sociological tradition, linked back to Quetelet and Durkheim, maintains that individuals' lifestyles and living conditions directly control their criminal behavior. Contemporary structural and social ecological theory holds that (a) a person's place in the social structure controls his or her behavioral choices, and (b) due to the ecological conditions faced by those at the bottom of the social structure, they cannot achieve success and thus experience anomie, strain, failure, and frustration.

Sociological social psychology theories remain influential with contemporary criminologists. In their modern incarnation, they suggest that individuals' learning experiences and socialization directly control their behavior. In some cases, children learn to commit crime by interacting with and modeling their behavior after others they admire, whereas other criminal offenders are people whose life experiences have shattered their social bonds to society. These current social process theories will be discussed in Chapter 7.

The writings of Marx and his followers also continue to be influential. Many criminologists still view social and political conflict as the root cause of crime. The inherently unfair economic structure of the United States and other advanced capitalist countries is the engine that drives the high crime rate. Critical criminology, the contemporary form of Marxist/conflict theory, will be discussed further in Chapter 8. The developmental, multifaceted views of the Gluecks have morphed into a developmental criminology that has received a great deal of attention from contemporary criminologists; these views of crime are

CONCEPT SUMMARY 1.2

CRIMINOLOGICAL PERSPECTIVES

The major perspectives of criminology focus on individual (biological, psychological, and choice theories), social (structural and process theories), political and economic (conflict theory), and multiple (developmental theory) factors.

Classical/Choice Perspective

Situational forces. Crime is a function of free will and personal choice. Punishment is a deterrent to crime.

Biological/Psychological Perspective

Internal forces. Crime is a function of chemical, neurological, genetic, personality, intelligence, or mental traits.

Structural Perspective

Ecological forces. Crime rates are a function of neighborhood conditions, cultural forces, and norm conflict.

Process Perspective

Socialization forces. Crime is a function of upbringing, learning, and control. Peers, parents, and teachers influence behavior.

Conflict Perspective

Economic and political forces. Crime is a function of competition for limited resources and power. Class conflict produces crime.

Developmental Perspective

Multiple forces. Biological, social-psychological, economic, and political forces may combine to produce crime.

analyzed in Chapter 9. Each of the major perspectives is summarized in Concept Summary 1.2.

WHAT CRIMINOLOGISTS DO: THE CRIMINOLOGICAL ENTERPRISE

Regardless of their theoretical orientation, criminologists are devoted to the study of crime and criminal behavior. As two noted criminologists, Marvin Wolfgang and Franco Ferracuti, put it: "A criminologist is one whose professional training, occupational role, and pecuniary reward are primarily concentrated on a scientific approach to, and study and analysis of, the phenomenon of crime and criminal behavior."[31]

Because criminologists have been trained in diverse fields, including sociology, criminal justice, political science, psychology, economics, and the natural sciences, criminology is today an interdisciplinary science. As a result, several subareas, reflecting different orientations and perspectives, are now contained within the broader arena of criminology. Taken together, these subareas make up the criminological enterprise. Criminologists may specialize in a subarea in the same way that psychologists might specialize in a subfield of psychology, such as cognition, development, perception, personality, psychopathology, or sexuality. Some of the more important criminological specialties are described next and summarized in Concept Summary 1.3.

Criminal Statistics and Research Methodology

Those criminologists who devote themselves to criminal statistics and research methodology engage in a number of different tasks, including:

▮ Devising accurate methods of collecting crime data

▮ Using these tested methods to measure the amount and trends of criminal activity

▮ Using valid crime data to determine who commits crime and where it occurs

▮ Measuring the effect of social policy and social trends on crime rate changes

▮ Using crime data to design crime prevention programs and then measuring their effectiveness

The media loves to sensationalize crime and report on lurid cases of murder and rape. The general public is influenced by these stories, becoming fearful and altering their behavior to avoid victimization.[32] These news accounts, proclaiming crime waves, are often driven by the need to sell newspapers and/or increase TV viewership. Media accounts can be biased and inaccurate, and it is up to criminologists to set the record straight. Criminologists therefore try to create valid and reliable measurements of criminal behavior. They create techniques to access the records of police and court agencies and use sophisticated statistical methods to understand underlying patterns and trends. They develop survey instruments and then use them with large samples to determine the actual number of crimes being committed and the number of victims who suffer criminal violations: How many people are victims of crime, and what percentage reports the crime to police?

Criminologists are also interested in helping agents of the criminal justice system develop effective crime control policies that rely on accurate measurement of crime rates. A recent (2007) analysis by Jacqueline Cohen and her associates used advanced statistical techniques to predict where crime will take place, based on past criminal activities. Police departments can allocate patrol officers based on these predictions.[33]

The development of valid methods to measure crime and the accuracy of crime data are crucial aspects of the criminological enterprise. Without valid and reliable crime data sources, efforts to conduct research on crime and create criminological theories would be futile. It is also important to determine why crime rates vary across and within regions in order to gauge the association between social and economic forces and criminal activity. Criminal statistics may be used to make international comparisons in order to understand why some countries are crime free while others are beset by antisocial activities. This is the topic of the Comparative Criminology box "International Crime Trends" on the next page.

INTERNATIONAL CRIME TRENDS

In 1981, there were 88 residential burglaries per 1,000 households in the United States, compared with 41 per 1,000 households in England (including Wales). Ten years later, the U.S. rate had decreased to 54 per 1,000 households, but the English rate had increased to 68 per 1,000 households.

The English experience is not unique. Crime rates appear to be increasing around the world even as they decline in the United States. Asian countries now report an upswing in serious criminal activities. Cambodian officials are concerned with drug production/trafficking and human trafficking. Drugs produced in neighboring countries are being trafficked into Cambodia for local consumption, and drug traffickers routinely use Cambodia as a transit country for distributing narcotics around the world. The trafficking of Cambodian women into Thailand for sexual activities and the presence of a large number of Vietnamese women in Cambodia who are engaged in prostitution are also major concerns. Even Japan, a nation renowned for its low crime rate, has experienced an upsurge in crime linked to its economy. Japan's economic bubble burst in 1990 and more than 15 years of economic stagnation has resulted in climbing numbers of reported crime.

Similarly, China, another relatively safe nation, has experienced an upswing in violent crime. Chinese police handled almost 5 million criminal cases in 2005, and though this number was down slightly from the previous year, the decline comes after years of steady increases. And though crime declined in general, theft and robbery remain a serious problem, especially in public places such as railway stations, long-distance bus stations, and passenger docks. The Chinese Ministry of Public Security reports these trends:

- Criminals are targeting richer people and/or entities.
- Car theft is on the rise.
- Criminal cases happen more often in public spaces—meaning that the streets are becoming less safe than they used to be.
- The average age of criminals is lowering—more kids are involved in illegal activities.
- New types of criminal activities are emerging: blackmailing, cons, and prostitution via the Web.

Though these trends are alarming, making international comparisons is often difficult because the legal definitions of crime vary from country to country. There are also differences in the way crime is measured. For example, in the United States, crime may be measured by counting criminal acts reported to the police or by using victim surveys, whereas in many European countries crime is measured by the number of cases solved by the police. Despite these problems, valid comparisons can still be made about crime across different countries using a number of reliable data sources. The United Nations Survey of Crime Trends and Operations of Criminal Justice Systems (UNCJS) is the most well known source of information on cross-national data. The International Crime Victims Survey (ICVS) is conducted in 60 countries and managed by the Ministry of Justice of the Netherlands, the Home Office of the United Kingdom, and the United Nations Interregional Crime and Justice Research Institute. INTERPOL, the international police agency, collects data from police agencies in 179 countries. The World Health Organization (WHO) has conducted surveys on global violence. The *European Sourcebook of Crime and Criminal Justice Statistics* provides data from police agencies in 36 European nations.

International Crime Rates

What do these various sources tell us about international crime rates?

Homicide

Many nations, especially those experiencing social or economic upheaval, have murder rates much higher than the United States. Colombia has about 63 homicides per 100,000 people and South Africa has 51, compared to fewer than 6 in the United States. During the 1990s there were more homicides in Brazil than in the United States, Canada, Italy, Japan, Australia, Portugal, Britain, Austria, and Germany taken together. Why are murder rates so high in nations like Brazil? Law enforcement officials link the upsurge in violence to drug trafficking, gang feuds, vigilantism, and disputes over trivial matters in which young, unmarried, uneducated males are involved. Others find that local custom and practice underpin the homicide rate. India has experienced a shocking form of violence against women known as bride burning. A woman may be burned to death if her family fails to provide the expected dowry to the groom's family or if she is suspected of premarital infidelity. Many Indian women commit suicide to escape the brutality of their situation.

Rape

Until 1990, U.S. rape rates were higher than those of any Western nation, but by 2000, Canada took the lead. Violence against women is related to economic hardship and the social status of women. Rates are high in poor nations in which women are oppressed. Where women are more emancipated, the rates of violence against women are lower.

For many women, sexual violence starts in childhood and adolescence and may occur in the home, school, and community. Studies conducted in a wide variety of nations ranging from the Cameroon to New Zealand found high rates of reported forced sexual initiation. In some nations, as many as 46 percent of adolescent women and 20 percent of adolescent men report sexual coercion at the hands of family members, teachers, boyfriends, or strangers.

Sexual violence has significant health consequences, including suicide, stress, mental illnesses, unwanted pregnancy, sexually transmitted diseases, HIV/AIDS, self-inflicted injuries, and, in the case of child sexual abuse, adoption of high-risk behaviors such as multiple sexual partners and drug use.

Robbery
Countries with more reported robberies than the United States include England and Wales, Portugal, and Spain. Countries with fewer reported robberies include Germany, Italy, and France, as well as Middle Eastern and Asian nations.

Burglary
The United States has lower burglary rates than Australia, Denmark, Finland, England and Wales, and Canada. It has higher reported burglary rates than Spain, Korea, and Saudi Arabia.

Vehicle Theft
Australia, England and Wales, Denmark, Norway, Canada, France, and Italy now have higher rates of vehicle theft than the United States.

Child Abuse
A World Health Organization report found that child physical and sexual abuse takes a significant toll around the world. In a single year, about 57,000 children under 15 years are murdered. The homicide rates for children aged 0 to 4 years are over twice as high as rates among children aged 5 to 14 years. Many more children are subjected to nonfatal abuse and neglect; 8 percent of male and 25 percent of female children up to age 18 experience sexual abuse of some kind.

Why the Change?
Why are crime rates increasing around the world while leveling off in the United States? Some conservative commentators reason that the get-tough crime control policies instituted in the United States have resulted in increases in conviction and punishment rates—an outcome that may help lower crime rates. In 1981 it was estimated that 15 in every 1,000 U.S. burglary offenders were convicted, compared with 28 in every 1,000 English burglary offenders. Ten years later, the U.S. conviction rate had increased to 19 per 1,000 offenders, while the English rate had decreased to 10 per 1,000 offenders. In addition, the death penalty is commonly employed in the United States, whereas it has been abolished in many European nations.

Crime rates may be spiraling upward abroad because nations are undergoing rapid changes in their social and economic makeup. In eastern Europe, the fall of Communism has brought about a transformation of the family, religion, education, and economy. These changes increase social pressures and result in crime rate increases. Some Asian societies, such as China, are undergoing rapid industrialization, urbanization, and social change. The shift from agricultural to industrial and service economies has produced political turmoil and a surge in their crime rates. For example, the island of Hong Kong, long a British possession but now part of the People's Republic of China, is experiencing an upsurge in club drugs. Tied to the local dance scene, ecstasy and ketamine use has skyrocketed, in synch with the traditional drug of choice, heroin. In sum, the crime problems we experience at home are not unique to the United States.

CRITICAL THINKING

1. While risk factors at all levels of social and personal life contribute to violence, people in all nations who experience change in societal-level factors—such as economic inequalities, rapid social change, and the availability of firearms, alcohol, and drugs—seem the most likely to get involved in violence. Can anything be done to help alleviate these social problems?

2. The United States is notorious for employing much tougher penal measures than Europe. Do you believe our tougher measures explain why crime is declining in the United States while increasing abroad?

Sources: James Finckenauer and Ko-lin Chin, *Asian Transnational Organized Crime and Its Impact on the United States* (Washington, DC: National Institute of Justice, 2007); Zhu Zhe, "Nationwide Crime Rate Shows Drop," *China Daily News*, 20 January 2006, www.chinadaily.com.cn/english/doc/2006–01/20/content_513862.htm (accessed March 14, 2007); Mauro Marescialli, "Crime in China: Some Statistics," Danwei Organization, www.danwei.org/ip_and_law/crime_in_china_some_statistics.php (accessed March 14, 2007); Dag Leonardsen, "Crime in Japan: Paradise Lost?" *Journal of Scandinavian Studies in Criminology and Crime Prevention* 7 (2006): 185–210; Karen Joe Laidler, "The Rise of Club Drugs in a Heroin Society: The Case of Hong Kong," *Substance Use and Misuse* 40 (2005): 1,257–1,279; Virendra Kumar and Sarita Kanth, "Bride Burning," *Lancet* 364 (2004): 18–19; Etienne Krug, Linda Dahlberg, James Mercy, Anthony Zwi, and Rafael Lozano, *World Report on Violence and Health* (Geneva: World Health Organization, 2002); Gene Stephens, "Global Trends in Crime: Crime Varies Greatly Around the World, Statistics Show, but New Tactics Have Proved Effective in the United States. To Keep Crime in Check in the Twenty-First Century, We'll All Need to Get Smarter, Not Just Tougher," *The Futurist* 37 (2003): 40–47; David P. Farrington, Patrick A. Langan, and Michael Tonry, *Cross-National Studies in Crime and Justice* (Washington, DC: Bureau of Justice Statistics, 2004); Pedro Scuro, *World Factbook of Criminal Justice Systems: Brazil* (Washington, DC: Bureau of Justice Statistics, 2003).

Law and Society: The Sociology of Law

The sociology of law, also referred to as the study of law and society, is a subarea of criminology concerned with the role social forces play in shaping criminal law and, concomitantly, the role of criminal law in shaping society. Criminologists interested in studying the social aspects of law focus on such topics as:

▪ The history of legal thought

▪ How social forces shape the definition and content of the law

▪ The impact of legal change on society

▪ The relationship between law and social control

▪ The effect of criminalization/legalization on behaviors

Some criminologists who study law and society consider the role of law in the context of criminological theory. They try to understand how legal decision making influences individuals, groups, and the criminal justice system. Others try to identify alternatives to traditional legal process—for example, by designing nonpunitive methods of dispute resolution. Some seek to describe the legal system and identify and explain patterns of behavior that guide its operation. Others use the operations of law as a perspective for understanding culture and social life.[34]

Because the law is constantly evolving, criminologists are often asked to determine whether legal change is required and what shape it should take. Computer fraud, airplane hijacking, ATM theft, and cyber stalking did not exist when the nation was founded. Consequently, the law must be revised to reflect cultural, societal, and technological changes. In fact, the Supreme Court has often considered empirical research supplied by criminologists on such topics as racial discrimination in the death penalty before it renders an opinion.[35] The research conducted by criminologists then helps shape the direction of their legal decision making.

Theory Construction and Testing

Social theory can be defined as a systematic set of interrelated statements or principles that explain some aspect of social life. At their core, theories should serve as models or frameworks for understanding human behavior and the forces that shape its content and direction.

Because, ideally, theories are based on verified *social facts*—readily observed phenomenon that can be consistently quantified and measured—criminological theorists use the scientific method to test their theories. They gather data, derive *hypotheses*—testable expectations of behavior that can be derived from the theory—and then test them using valid empirical research methods. For example, general deterrence theory (see Chapter 4) states that the more people fear punishment the less willing they are to commit crime. If this statement is accurate, then logically there should be a significant association between police levels and crime. To test this theory, a number of hypotheses can be derived:

H1: The greater the number of police on the street, the lower the crime rate.

H2: Cities with the most police officers per capita will also have the lowest crime rates.

H3: Adding more police officers to the local force will cause the crime rate to decline.

H4: Cities that reduce the size of their police forces will experience an upsurge in criminal activity.

The validity of the theory would be damaged if research data showed that cities with large police forces had crime rates similar to those with smaller per capita forces, or that cities that have added police officers experience little decline in their crime rate. In contrast, if research shows that adding police reduces crime and this effect could be observed at different times in a number of different locales, then the theory might eventually become an accepted element of social thought.

Sometimes criminologists use innovative methods to test theory. When Dennis Wilson sought to determine whether adding police would deter crime, he used data from the National Hockey League to test the hypothesis that adding an enforcement agent (i.e., an additional referee) would deter law violations (i.e., penalties). His analysis of game data supported the theory that adding police would bring the crime rate down: as the number of refs increase, serious penalties that are potentially harmful decline![36]

Criminal Behavior Systems and Crime Typologies

Criminologists who study criminal behavior systems and crime typologies focus their research on specific criminal types and patterns: violent crime, theft crime, public order crime, and organized crime. Numerous attempts have been made to describe and understand particular crime types. Marvin Wolfgang's famous 1958 study, *Patterns in Criminal Homicide*—considered a landmark analysis of the nature of homicide and the relationship between victim and offender—found that victims often precipitate the incident that results in their death.[37] Edwin Sutherland's analysis of business-related offenses helped coin a new phrase—white-collar crime—to describe economic crime activities.

Criminologists also conduct research on the links between different types of crime and criminals. This is known as a **crime typology**. Some typologies focus on the criminal, suggesting the existence of offender groups, such as professional criminals, psychotic criminals, amateur criminals, and so on. Others focus on the crimes, clustering them into categories such as property crimes, sex crimes, and so on.

Research on criminal behavior systems and crime types is important because it enables criminologists to understand why people commit specific sorts of crime, and using this information, gives them the tools to devise crime reduction strategies. In one recent study, Arielle Baskin-Sommers and Ira Sommers analyzed the relationship between methamphetamine use and violence among young adults. To understand the association, Sommers and Sommers conducted in-depth life history interviews with

New York City Police Department Sergeant Rafi Ovanessian checks the contents of a commuter's backpack as he goes into the subway at 96th Street. New York ramped up security on its subway system after receiving a specific threat of a terrorist attack. Some criminologists focus their attention on a specific crime problem such as terrorism in order to understand its nature and extent and to help plan programs that can control or eliminate its occurrence.

more than 100 individuals who used methamphetamine for a minimum of three months. They found that about one-third committed violent acts while under the influence of methamphetamine. Incidents included domestic, drug, and gang related violence. Although the association between drug use and violence is strong, about two-thirds of the meth users remained nonviolent. Consequently, Sommers and Sommers conclude that while methamphetamine use is a *risk factor*, violence is not an inevitable outcome of even chronic methamphetamine use.[38] These results show that violence reduction policies should not be limited to reducing drug abuse since most abusers are nonviolent.

Penology and Social Control

The study of penology involves the correction and control of known criminal offenders; it is the segment of criminology that overlaps criminal justice. Criminologists conduct research that is designed to evaluate justice initiatives in order to determine their efficiency, effectiveness, and impact. For example, should capital punishment continue to be employed or is its use simply too risky? To explore this issue, Samuel Gross and his colleagues looked at death row inmates who were later found to be innocent. His sample of 340 death row inmates (327 men and

13 women), exonerated after having served years in prison, indicated that about half (144 people) were cleared by DNA evidence. Collectively, they had spent more than 3,400 years in prison for crimes they did not commit—an average of more than ten years each. Gross and his colleagues found that exonerations from death row are more than 25 times more frequent than exonerations for other prisoners convicted of murder, and more than 100 times more frequent than for all imprisoned felons.[39] How many wrongful convictions might be uncovered if all criminal convictions were given the same degree of scrutiny as death penalty cases? The Gross research illustrates how important it is to evaluate penal measures in order to determine their effectiveness and reliability.

Victimology: Victims and Victimization

In two classic criminological studies, one by Hans von Hentig and the other by Stephen Schafer, the critical role of the victim in the criminal process was first identified. These authors were the first to suggest that victim behavior is often a key determinant of crime and that victims' actions may actually precipitate crime. Both men believe that the study of crime is not complete unless the victim's role is considered.[40] For those studying the role of the victim in crime, these areas are of particular interest:

▌ Using victim surveys to measure the nature and extent of criminal behavior not reported to the police

▌ Calculating the actual costs of crime to victims

▌ Measuring the factors that increase the likelihood of becoming a crime victim

▌ Studying the role of the victim in causing or precipitating crime

▌ Designing services for the victims of crime, such as counseling and compensation programs

The study of victims and victimization has uncovered some startling results. For one thing, criminals have been found to be at greater risk for victimization than noncriminals.[41] Rather than being the passive receptors of criminal acts who are in the "wrong place at the wrong time," crime victims may engage in high risk lifestyles that increase their own chance of victimization and make them highly vulnerable to crime. The various elements of the criminological enterprise are summarized in Concept Summary 1.3.

connections

In recent years, criminologists have devoted ever-increasing attention to the victim's role in the criminal process. It has been suggested that a person's lifestyle and behavior may actually increase the risk that he or she will become a crime victim. Some have suggested that living in a high-crime neighborhood increases risk; others point at the problems caused by associating with dangerous peers and companions. For a discussion of victimization risk, see Chapter 3.

CONCEPT SUMMARY 1.3

THE CRIMINOLOGICAL ENTERPRISE

These subareas constitute the discipline of criminology.

Criminal Statistics and Research Methodology

Gathering valid crime data. Devising new research methods; measuring crime patterns and trends.

The Sociology of Law/Law and Society

Determining the origin of law. Measuring the forces that can change laws and society.

Theory Construction and Testing

Predicting individual behavior. Understanding the cause of crime rates and trends.

Criminal Behavior Systems and Crime Typologies

Determining the nature and cause of specific crime patterns. Studying violence, theft, organized, white-collar, and public order crimes.

Penology and Social Control

Studying the correction and control of criminal behavior. Using scientific methods to assess the effectiveness of crime control and offender treatment programs.

Victimology/Victims and Victimization

Studying the nature and cause of victimization. Aiding crime victims; understanding the nature and extent of victimization; developing theories of victimization risk.

HOW CRIMINOLOGISTS VIEW CRIME

Professional criminologists usually align themselves with one of several schools of thought or perspectives in their field. Each perspective maintains its own view of what constitutes criminal behavior and what causes people to engage in criminality. This diversity of thought is not unique to criminology; biologists, psychologists, sociologists, historians, economists, and natural scientists disagree among themselves about critical issues in their fields. Considering the multidisciplinary nature of the field of criminology, fundamental issues such as the nature and definition of crime itself is cause for disagreement among criminologists.

A criminologist's choice of orientation or perspective depends, in part, on his or her definition of crime. This section discusses the three most common concepts of crime used by criminologists.

The Consensus View of Crime

According to the **consensus view**, crimes are behaviors believed to be repugnant to all elements of society. The

substantive criminal law, which is the written code that defines crimes and their punishments, reflects the values, beliefs, and opinions of society's mainstream. The term "consensus" is used because it implies that there is general agreement among a majority of citizens on what behaviors should be outlawed by the criminal law and henceforth viewed as crimes. As the eminent criminologists Edwin Sutherland and Donald Cressey put it:

> Criminal behavior is behavior in violation of the criminal law. . . . [I]t is not a crime unless it is prohibited by the criminal law [which] is defined conventionally as a body of specific rules regarding human conduct which have been promulgated by political authority, which apply uniformly to all members of the classes to which the rules refer, and which are enforced by punishment administered by the state.[42]

This approach to crime implies that it is a function of the beliefs, morality, and rules established by the existing legal power structure. According to Sutherland and Cressey's statement, criminal law is applied "uniformly to all members of the classes to which the rules refer." This statement reveals the authors' faith in the concept of an "ideal legal system" that deals adequately with all classes and types of people. Laws prohibiting theft and violence may be directed at the neediest members of society, whereas laws that sanction economic acts such as insider trading, embezzlement, and corporate price-fixing are aimed at controlling the wealthiest. The reach of the criminal law is not restricted to any single element of society.

Social Harm The consensus view of crime links illegal behavior to the concept of **social harm**. Though people generally enjoy a great deal of latitude in their behavior, it is agreed that behaviors that are harmful to other people and society in general must be controlled. Social harm is what sets strange, unusual, or **deviant behavior**—or any other action that departs from social norms—apart from criminal behaviors.[43]

connections

The associations among crime, social harm, and morality are best illustrated in efforts to criminalize acts considered dangerous to the public welfare because they involve behaviors that offend existing social values. These so-called public order crimes include pornography, prostitution and drug use. Though "victims" are often willing participants, some people believe it is society's duty to save them from themselves. To read more about crime, morality, and social harm, see Chapter 14.

This position is not without controversy. Although it is clear that rape, robbery, and murder are inherently harmful and their control justified, behaviors such as drug use and prostitution are more problematic because the harm they inflict is only on those who are willing participants. According to the consensus view, society is justified in controlling these so-called victimless crimes because public opinion holds that they undermine the social fabric and threaten the general well-being of society. Society has a duty to protect all its members—even those who choose to engage in high-risk behaviors.

According to the consensus view, crimes are behaviors believed to be repugnant to all elements of society. Do you agree with the artist's implied sentiment that spraying graffiti on a wall is not really a crime? Why do you think this remains an outlawed behavior?

- Price-fixing
- Police brutality
- Assassinations and war-making
- Violations of human dignity
- Denial of physical needs and necessities, and impediments to self-determination
- Deprivation of adequate food
- Blocked opportunities to participate in political decision making[45]

The Conflict View of Crime

The conflict view depicts society as a collection of diverse groups—owners, workers, professionals, students—who are in constant and continuing conflict. Groups able to assert their political power use the law and the criminal justice system to advance their economic and social position. Criminal laws, therefore, are viewed as acts created to protect the haves from the have-nots. Critical criminologists often compare and contrast the harsh penalties exacted on the poor for their "street crimes" (burglary, robbery, and larceny) with the minor penalties the wealthy receive for their white-collar crimes (securities violations and other illegal business practices), though the latter may cause considerably more social harm. While the poor go to prison for minor law violations, the wealthy are given lenient sentences for even the most serious breaches of law. Rather than being class neutral, criminal law reflects and protects established economic, racial, gendered, and political power and privilege.[44]

Crime, according to this definition, is a political concept designed to protect the power and position of the upper classes at the expense of the poor. Even crimes prohibiting violent acts, such as armed robbery, rape, and murder, may have political undertones. Banning violent acts ensures domestic tranquility and guarantees that the anger of the poor and disenfranchised classes will not be directed at their wealthy capitalist exploiters. According to this conflict view of crime, "real" crimes would include the following acts:

- Violations of human rights due to racism, sexism, and imperialism
- Unsafe working conditions
- Inadequate child care
- Inadequate opportunities for employment and education
- Substandard housing and medical care
- Crimes of economic and political domination
- Pollution of the environment

The Interactionist View of Crime

The interactionist view of crime traces its antecedents to the symbolic interaction school of sociology, first popularized by pioneering sociologists George Herbert Mead, Charles Horton Cooley, and W. I. Thomas.[46] This position holds that (a) people act according to their own interpretations of reality, through which they assign meaning to things; (b) they observe the way others react, either positively or negatively; and (c) they reevaluate and interpret their own behavior according to the meaning and symbols they have learned from others.

According to this perspective, there is no objective reality. People, institutions, and events are viewed subjectively and labeled either good or evil according to the interpretation of the evaluator. Some people might consider the hit film *Borat: Cultural Learnings of America for Make Benefit Glorious Nation of Kazakhstan* as obscene, degrading, and offensive, while others view the same film as a laugh riot. The same interactions help define crime:

- The content of the criminal law and consequently the definition of crime often depend on human interaction and perceptions. Alcohol is legal, marijuana is not. It could easily be the other way around. Gay marriage is legal in some jurisdictions, illegal in others.

- Deciding whether an individual act is considered a crime is also a function of interaction and labeling. When an argument results in the death of one of the participants, a jury may be asked to decide whether it was murder, self-defense, or merely an accidental fatality. Each person on the jury may have their own interpretation of what took place, and whether the act is labeled a crime depends on their interpretation of events.

- The process in which people are defined or labeled as criminal is also subjective. One person is viewed as an unrepentant hard-core offender and sent to a maximum security prison. Another, who has committed essentially the same crime, is considered remorseful and repentant and given probation in the community. Though their acts are similar the treatment they receive is quite different.

According to the interactionist view, the definition of crime reflects the preferences and opinions of people who hold social

CONCEPT SUMMARY 1.4

THE DEFINITION OF CRIME

The definition of crime affects how criminologists view the cause and control of illegal behavior and shapes their research orientation.

Conflict View

▌ The law is a tool of the ruling class.

▌ Crime is a politically defined concept.

▌ "Real crimes" are not outlawed.

▌ The law is used to control the underclass.

Consensus View

▌ The law defines crime.

▌ The law reflects public opinion.

▌ Agreement exists on outlawed behavior.

▌ Laws apply to all citizens equally.

Interactionist View

▌ Moral entrepreneurs define crime.

▌ Crimes are illegal because society defines them that way.

▌ The definition of crime evolves according to the moral standards of those in power.

power in a particular legal jurisdiction. These people use their influence to impose their definition of right and wrong on the rest of the population. Conversely, criminals are individuals people choose to label or **stigmatize** as outcasts or deviants because they have violated social rules. In a classic statement, sociologist Howard Becker argued, "The deviant is one to whom that label has successfully been applied; deviant behavior is behavior people so label."[47] Crimes are outlawed behaviors because society defines them that way, not because they are inherently evil or immoral acts.

The interactionist view of crime is similar to the conflict perspective; both suggest that behavior is outlawed and considered criminal when it offends people who hold social, economic, and political power. However, unlike the conflict view, the interactionist perspective does not attribute capitalist economic and political motives to the process of defining crime. Instead, interactionists see the criminal law as conforming to the beliefs of "moral crusaders" or **moral entrepreneurs**, who use their influence to shape the legal process in the way they see fit.[48] Laws against pornography, prostitution, and drugs are believed to be motivated more by moral crusades than by economic values.

The three main views of crime are summarized in Concept Summary 1.4.

Defining Crime

It is possible to take elements from each school of thought to formulate an integrated definition of crime, such as this one:

> *Crime is a violation of societal rules of behavior as interpreted and expressed by a criminal legal code created by people holding social and political power. Individuals who violate these rules are subject to sanctions by state authority, social stigma, and loss of status.*

This definition combines the consensus position that the criminal law defines crimes with the conflict perspective's emphasis on political power and control and the interactionist concept of labeling and stigma. Thus crime, as defined here, is a political, social, and economic function of modern life.

CRIME AND THE CRIMINAL LAW

No matter which definition of crime we embrace, criminal behavior is tied to the criminal law. It is therefore important for all criminologists to have some understanding of the development of criminal law, its objectives, its elements, and how it evolves.

The concept of criminal law has been recognized for more than 3,000 years. Hammurabi (1792–1750 BCE), the sixth king of Babylon, created the most famous set of written laws of the ancient world, known today as the Code of Hammurabi. Preserved on basalt rock columns, the code established a system of crime and punishment based on physical retaliation ("an eye for an eye"). The severity of punishment depended on class standing: if convicted of an unprovoked assault, a slave would be killed, whereas a freeman might lose a limb.

More familiar is the Mosaic Code of the Israelites (1200 BCE). According to tradition, God entered into a covenant or contract with the tribes of Israel in which they agreed to obey his law (the 613 laws of the Old Testament, including the Ten Commandments), as presented to them by Moses, in return for God's special care and protection. The Mosaic Code is not only the foundation of Judeo-Christian moral teachings but also a basis for the U.S. legal system. Prohibitions against murder, theft, and perjury, preceded, by several thousand years, the same laws found in the modern United States.

Though ancient formal legal codes were lost during the Dark Ages, early German and Anglo-Saxon societies developed legal systems featuring monetary compensation for criminal violations. Guilt was determined by two methods. One was compurgation, in which the accused person swore an oath of innocence with the backing of 12 to 25 oath helpers, who would attest to his or her character and claims of innocence. The second was trial by ordeal, which was based on the principle that divine forces would not allow an innocent person to be harmed. It involved such measures as having the accused place his or her hand in boiling water or hold a hot iron. If the wound healed, the person was found innocent; if the wound did not heal, the accused was deemed guilty. Another version, trial by combat, allowed the accused to challenge his accuser to a duel, with the outcome determining the legitimacy of the accusation. Punishments included public flogging, branding, beheading, and burning.

Common Law

After the Norman conquest of England in 1066, royal judges began to travel throughout the land, holding court in each shire several times a year. When court was in session, the royal administrator, or judge, would summon a number of citizens who would, on their oath, tell of the crimes and serious breaches of the peace that had occurred since the judge's last visit. The royal judge would then decide what to do in each case, using local custom and rules of conduct as his guide. Courts were bound to follow the law established in previous cases unless a higher authority, such as the king or the pope, overruled the law.

The present English system of law came into existence during the reign of Henry II (1154–1189), when royal judges began to publish their decisions in local cases. Judges began to use these written decisions as a basis for their decision making, and eventually a fixed body of legal rules and principles was established. If a new rule was successfully applied in a number of different cases, it would become a precedent. These precedents would then be commonly applied in all similar cases—hence the term common law. Crimes such as murder, burglary, arson, and rape are common-law crimes whose elements were initially defined by judges. They are referred to as *mala in se,* or inherently evil and depraved. When the situation required, the English parliament enacted legislation to supplement the judge-made common law. Crimes defined by Parliament, which reflected existing social conditions, were referred to as *mala prohibitum*, or statutory crimes.

Before the American Revolution, the colonies, then under British rule, were subject to the common law. After the colonies acquired their independence, state legislatures standardized common-law crimes such as murder, burglary, arson, and rape by putting them into statutory form in criminal codes. As in England, whenever common law proved inadequate to deal with changing social and moral issues, the states and Congress supplemented it with legislative statutes, creating new elements in the various state and federal legal codes. Table 1.1 lists a number of crimes that were first defined in common law.

Contemporary Criminal Law

Criminal laws are now divided into felonies and misdemeanors. The distinction is based on seriousness: a felony is a serious offense; a misdemeanor is a minor or petty crime. Crimes such as murder, rape, and burglary are felonies; they are punished with long prison sentences or even death. Crimes such as unarmed assault and battery, petty larceny, and disturbing the peace are misdemeanors; they are punished with a fine or a period of incarceration in a county jail.

Regardless of their classification, acts prohibited by the criminal law constitute behaviors considered unacceptable and impermissible by those in power. People who engage in these acts are eligible for severe sanctions. By outlawing these behaviors, the government expects to achieve a number of social goals:

▮ *Enforcing social control.* Those who hold political power rely on criminal law to formally prohibit behaviors believed to threaten societal well-being or to challenge their authority. For example, U.S. criminal law incorporates centuries-old prohibitions against the following behaviors harmful to others: taking another person's possessions, physically harming another person, damaging another person's property, and cheating another person out of his or her possessions. Similarly, the law prevents actions that challenge the legitimacy of the government, such as planning its overthrow, collaborating with its enemies, and so on.

▮ *Discouraging revenge.* By punishing people who infringe on the rights, property, and freedom of others, the law shifts the burden of revenge from the individual to the state. As Oliver Wendell Holmes stated, this prevents "the greater evil of private retribution."[49] Although state retaliation may offend the sensibilities of many citizens, it is greatly preferable to a system in which people would have to seek justice for themselves.

▮ *Expressing public opinion and morality.* Criminal law reflects constantly changing public opinions and moral values. *Mala in se* crimes, such as murder and forcible rape, are almost universally prohibited; however, the prohibition of legislatively created *mala prohibitum* crimes, such as traffic offenses and gambling violations, changes according to social conditions and attitudes. Criminal law is used to codify these changes.

▮ *Deterring criminal behavior.* Criminal law has a social control function. It can control, restrain, and direct human behavior through its sanctioning power. The threat of punishment associated with violating the law is designed to prevent crimes before they occur. During the Middle Ages, public executions drove this point home. Today criminal law's impact is felt through news accounts of long prison sentences and an occasional execution.

▮ *Punishing wrongdoing.* The deterrent power of criminal law is tied to the authority it gives the state to sanction or punish offenders. Those who violate criminal law are subject to physical coercion and punishment.

▮ *Maintaining social order.* All legal systems are designed to support and maintain the boundaries of the social system they serve. In medieval England, the law protected the feudal system by defining an orderly system of property transfer and ownership. Laws in some socialist nations protect the primacy of the state by strictly curtailing profiteering and individual enterprise. Our own capitalist system is also supported and sustained by criminal law. In a sense, the content of criminal law is more a reflection of the needs of those who control the existing economic and political system than a representation of some idealized moral code.

Some of the elements of the contemporary criminal law are discussed in The Criminological Enterprise feature "The Elements of Criminal Law."

Table 1.1 Common-Law Crimes

Crime	Description	Example
Crimes Against the Person		
First-Degree Murder	Unlawful killing of another human being with malice aforethought and with premeditation and deliberation.	A woman buys poison and pours it into a cup of coffee her husband is drinking, intending to kill him for the insurance benefits.
Voluntary Manslaughter	Intentional killing committed under extenuating circumstances that mitigate the killing, such as killing in the heat of passion after being provoked.	A husband coming home early from work finds his wife in bed with another man. The husband goes into a rage and shoots and kills both lovers with a gun he keeps by his bedside.
Battery	Unlawful touching of another with intent to cause injury.	A man seeing a stranger sitting in his favorite seat in a cafeteria goes up to that person and pushes him out of the seat.
Assault	Intentional placing of another in fear of receiving an immediate battery.	A student aims an unloaded gun at her professor and threatens to shoot. He believes the gun is loaded.
Rape	Unlawful sexual intercourse with a female without her consent.	After a party, a man offers to drive a young female acquaintance home. He takes her to a wooded area and, despite her protests, forces her to have sexual relations with him.
Robbery	Wrongful taking and carrying away of personal property from a person by violence or intimidation.	A man armed with a loaded gun approaches another man on a deserted street and demands his wallet.
Inchoate (Incomplete) Offenses		
Attempt	An intentional act for the purpose of committing a crime that is more than mere preparation or planning of the crime. The crime is not completed, however.	A person places a bomb in the intended victim's car so that it will detonate when the ignition key is used. The bomb is discovered before the car is started. Attempted murder has been committed.
Conspiracy	Voluntary agreement between two or more persons to achieve an unlawful object or to achieve a lawful object using means forbidden by law.	A doctor conspires with a con man to fake accidents and then bring the false "victims" to his office so he can collect medical fees from an insurance company.
Solicitation	With the intent that another person engage in conduct constituting a felony, a person solicits, requests, commands, or otherwise attempts to cause that person to engage in such conduct.	A terrorist approaches a person he believes is sympathetic to his cause and asks him to join in a plot to blow up a government building.
Crimes Against Property		
Burglary	Breaking and entering of a dwelling house of another in the nighttime with the intent to commit a felony.	Intending to steal some jewelry and silver, a young man breaks a window and enters another's house at 10 P.M.
Arson	Intentional burning of a dwelling house of another.	A worker, angry that her boss did not give her a raise, goes to her boss's house and sets it on fire.
Larceny	Taking and carrying away the personal property of another with the intent to keep and possess the property.	While shopping, a woman sees a diamond ring displayed at the jewelry counter. When no one is looking, the woman takes the ring, places it in her pocket, and walks out of the store without paying.

Source: Developed by Therese J. Libby, J.D.

THE MOTHER OF ALL SNAKEHEADS

© AP Images/Jane Rosenberg

Cheng Chui Ping was one of the most powerful underworld figures in New York. Known as "the Mother of all Snakeheads"—meaning she was top dog in the human smuggling trade—to her friends in Chinatown she was "Sister Ping."

Cheng was an illegal immigrant herself. Born in 1949 in the poor farming village of Shengmei in Fujian province, she left her husband and family behind and set out for the West, traveling via Hong Kong and Canada before ending up in New York in 1981.

She opened a grocery store and started other ventures that became fronts for her people trafficking business. For more than a decade, Cheng smuggled as many as 3,000 illegal immigrants from her native China into the United States—charging upwards of $40,000 per person. To ensure her clients paid their smuggling fees, Sister Ping hired members of the Fuk Ching, Chinatown's most feared gang, to transport and guard them in the United States.

In addition to running her own operation, Sister Ping helped other smugglers by financing large vessels designed for human cargo. She also ran a money transmitting business out of her Chinatown variety store. She used this business to collect smuggling fees from family members of her own "customers," and also collected ransom money on behalf of other alien smugglers.

Conditions aboard the smuggling vessels were often inhumane. The voyages were dangerous, and on at least one occasion a boat capsized while offloading people to a larger vessel and fourteen of her "customers" drowned. The *Golden Venture*, a smuggling ship Sister Ping helped finance for others, was intentionally grounded off the coast of Rockaway, Queens, in early June 1993 when the offloading vessel failed to meet it in the open sea. Many of the passengers could not swim and ten drowned.

Cheng Chui Ping was indicted in 1994 when members of the Fuk Ching gang cooperated with federal agents. After her indictment, Cheng fled to China, where she continued to run a smuggling operation. In April 2000, Hong Kong police arrested her at the airport. Cheng fought extradition but was eventually delivered to the United States in July 2003. She was convicted in New York less than two years later on multiple counts, including money laundering, conspiracy to commit alien smuggling, and other smuggling-related offenses, and was sentenced to 35 years in prison.

The activities of Sister Ping illustrate how the law must evolve to confront newly emerging social problems such as illegal immigration. Other areas include cyber crime, drug importation, and terrorism. Unfortunately, the law is sometimes slow to change, and change comes only after conditions have reached a crisis. How might laws be changed to reduce illegal immigration? Should people caught entering the country illegally be charged with a felony and imprisoned?

Sources: FBI News release, "Sister Ping Sentenced to 35 Years in Prison for Alien Smuggling, Hostage Taking, Money Laundering and Ransom Proceeds Conspiracy," 16 March 2006, http://newyork.fbi.gov//dojpressrel/pressrel06/sispter_ping031606.htm (accessed March 14, 2007); BBC news, "Cheng Chui Ping: 'Mother of snakeheads,'" http://news.bbc.co.uk/2/hi/americas/4816354.stm (accessed March 14, 2007).

The Evolution of Criminal Law

The criminal law is constantly evolving in an effort to reflect social and economic conditions. Sometimes legal changes are prompted by highly publicized cases that generate fear and concern. A number of highly publicized cases of celebrity stalking, including Robert John Bardo's fatal shooting of actress Rebecca Schaeffer on July 18, 1989, prompted more than 25 states to enact stalking statutes that prohibit "the willful, malicious, and repeated following and harassing of another person."[50] Similarly, after 7-year-old Megan Kanka of Hamilton Township, New Jersey, was killed in 1994 by a repeat sexual offender who had moved into her neighborhood, the federal government passed legislation requiring that the general public be notified of local pedophiles (sexual offenders who target children).[51] California's sexual predator law, which took effect on January 1, 1996, allows people convicted of sexually violent crimes against two or more victims to be committed to a mental institution after their prison terms have been served.[52]

The criminal law may also change because of shifts in culture and social conventions, reflecting a newfound tolerance of behavior condemned only a few years before. In an important 2003 case, *Lawrence v. Texas*, the Supreme Court declared that laws banning sodomy were unconstitutional because they

THE ELEMENTS OF CRIMINAL LAW

Although each state and the federal government have unique methods of defining crime, there are significant uniformities and similarities that shape the essence of almost all criminal law codes. Although the laws of California, Texas, and Maine may all be somewhat different, the underlying concepts that guide and shape their legal systems are universal. The question remains: regardless of jurisdictional boundaries, what is the legal definition of a crime—and how does the criminal law deal with it?

Legal Definition of a Crime

Today, in all jurisdictions, the legal definition of a crime involves the elements of the criminal acts that must be proven in a court of law if the defendant is to be found guilty. For the most part, common criminal acts have both mental and physical elements, both of which must be present if the act is to be considered a legal crime. In order for a crime to occur, the state must show that the accused committed the guilty act, or *actus reus*, and had the *mens rea*, or criminal intent, to commit the act. The *actus reus* may be an aggressive act, such as taking someone's money, burning a building, or shooting someone; or it may be a failure to act when there is a legal duty to do so, such as a parent's neglecting to seek medical attention for a sick child. The

mens rea (guilty mind) refers to an individual's state of mind at the time of the act or, more specifically, the person's intent to commit the crime.

Actus Reus

To satisfy the requirements of *actus reus*, guilty actions must be voluntary. Even though an act may cause harm or damage, it is not considered a crime if it was done by accident or was an involuntary act. For example, it would not be a crime if a motorist obeying all the traffic laws hit a child who ran into the street. If the same motorist were drinking or speeding, then his action would be considered a vehicular crime because it was a product of negligence. Similarly, it would not be considered a crime if a babysitter accidentally dropped a child and the child died. However, it would be considered manslaughter if the sitter threw the child down in anger or frustration and the blow caused the child's death. In some circumstances of *actus reus*, the use of words is considered criminal. In the crime of sedition, the words of disloyalty constitute the *actus reus*. If a person falsely yells "fire" in a crowded theater and people are injured in the rush to exit, that person is held responsible for the injuries, because the use of the word in that situation constitutes an illegal act.

Typically, the law does not require people to aid others in distress, such as entering a burning building to rescue people trapped by a fire. However,

failure to act is considered a crime in certain instances:

- *Relationship of the parties based on status.* Some people are bound by relationship to give aid. These relationships include parent/child and husband/wife. If a husband finds his wife unconscious because she took an overdose of sleeping pills, he is obligated to save her life by seeking medical aid. If he fails to do so and she dies, he can be held responsible for her death.

- *Imposition by statute.* Some states have passed laws requiring people to give aid. For example, a person who observes a broken-down automobile in the desert but fails to stop and help the other parties involved may be committing a crime.

- *Contractual relationships.* These relationships include lifeguard and swimmer, doctor and patient, and babysitter or au pair and child. Because lifeguards have been hired to ensure the safety of swimmers, they have a legal duty to come to the aid of drowning persons. If a lifeguard knows a swimmer is in danger and does nothing about it and the swimmer drowns, the lifeguard is legally responsible for the swimmer's death.

Mens Rea

In most situations, for an act to constitute a crime, it must be done with criminal

violated the due process rights of citizens because of their sexual orientation. In its decision, the Court said:

> *Although the laws involved . . . here . . . do not more than prohibit a particular sexual act, their penalties and purposes have more far-reaching consequences, touching upon the most private human conduct, sexual behavior, and in the most private of places, the home. They seek to control a personal relationship that, whether or not entitled to formal recognition in the law, is within the liberty of persons to choose without being punished as criminals. The liberty protected by the Constitution allows homosexual persons the right to choose to enter upon relationships in the confines of their homes and their own private lives and still retain their dignity as free persons.*

As a result of the decision, all sodomy laws in the United States are now unconstitutional and therefore unenforceable.[53]

The future direction of U.S. criminal law remains unclear. Certain actions, such as crimes by corporations and political corruption, will be labeled as criminal and given more attention. Other offenses, such as recreational drug use, may be reduced in importance or removed entirely from the criminal law system. In addition, changing technology and its ever-increasing global and local roles in our lives will require modifications in criminal law. Such technologies as automatic teller machines and cellular phones have already spawned a new generation of criminal acts such as identity theft and software piracy. The globalization of crime will present even more

intent, or *mens rea*. Intent, in the legal sense, can mean carrying out an act intentionally, knowingly, and willingly. However, the definition also encompasses situations in which recklessness or negligence establishes the required criminal intent.

Criminal intent also exists if the results of an action, although originally unintended, are certain to occur. When Timothy McVeigh planted a bomb in front of the Murrah Federal Building in Oklahoma City, he did not intend to kill any particular person in the building. Yet the law would hold that McVeigh or any other person would be substantially certain that people in the building would be killed in the blast, and McVeigh therefore had the criminal intent to commit murder.

Strict Liability

Though common-law crimes require that both the *actus reus* and the *mens rea* must be present before a person can be convicted of a crime, several crimes defined by statute do not require *mens rea*. In these cases, the person accused is guilty simply by doing what the statute prohibits; intent does not enter the picture. These strict liability crimes, or public welfare offenses, include violations of health and safety regulations, traffic laws, and narcotic control laws. For example, a person stopped for speeding is guilty of breaking the traffic laws regardless of whether he or she intended to go over the speed limit or did it by accident.

The underlying purpose of these laws is to protect the public; therefore, intent is not required.

Criminal Defenses

When people defend themselves against criminal charges, they must refute one or more of the elements of the crime of which they have been accused. A number of different approaches can be taken to create this defense.

First, defendants may deny the *actus reus* by arguing that they were falsely accused and that the real culprit has yet to be identified. Second, defendants may claim that although they engaged in the criminal act of which they are accused, they lacked the *mens rea* (intent) needed to be found guilty of the crime.

If a person whose mental state is impaired commits a criminal act, it is possible for the person to excuse his or her criminal actions by claiming that he or she lacked the capacity to form sufficient intent to be held criminally responsible. Insanity, intoxication, and ignorance are types of excuse defenses. A defendant might argue that because he suffered from a mental impairment that prevented him from understanding the harmfulness of his acts, he lacked sufficient *mens rea* to be found guilty as charged.

Another type of defense is justification. Here the individual usually admits committing the criminal act but maintains that he or she should not be held

criminally liable because the act was justified. Among the justification defenses are necessity, duress, self-defense, and entrapment. A battered wife who kills her mate might argue that she acted out of duress; her crime was committed to save her own life.

Persons standing trial for criminal offenses may thus defend themselves by claiming that they did not commit the act in question, that their actions were justified under the circumstances, or that their behavior can be excused by their lack of *mens rea*. If either the physical or mental elements of a crime cannot be proven, then the defendant cannot be convicted.

CRITICAL THINKING

1. Should the concept of the "guilty mind" be eliminated from the criminal law and replaced with a strict liability standard? (If you do the crime, you do the time.)

2. Some critics believe that current criminal defenses, such as the battered wife defense or the insanity defense, allow people to go free even though they committed serious criminal acts and are actually guilty as charged. Do you agree?

Sources: Joshua Dressler, *Cases and Materials on Criminal Law* (American Casebook Series) (Eagan, MN: West Publishing, 2003); Joel Samaha, *Criminal Law* (Belmont, CA: Wadsworth Publishing, 2001).

challenges, as the Profiles in Crime feature "The Mother of All Snakeheads" illustrates on page 21.

ETHICAL ISSUES IN CRIMINOLOGY

A critical issue facing students of criminology involves recognizing the field's political and social consequences. All too often, criminologists forget the social responsibility they bear as experts in the area of crime and justice. When government

agencies request their views of issues, their pronouncements and opinions become the basis for sweeping social policy. The lives of millions of people can be influenced by criminological research data.

Debates over gun control, capital punishment, and mandatory sentences are ongoing and contentious. Some criminologists have successfully argued for social service, treatment, and rehabilitation programs to reduce the crime rate, but others consider them a waste of time, suggesting instead that a massive prison construction program coupled with tough criminal sentences can bring the crime rate down. By accepting their roles as experts on law-violating behavior, criminologists place themselves in a position of power; the potential consequences of their actions are enormous. Therefore, they must be aware of the ethics of their profession and be prepared to defend their work in the light of public scrutiny. Major ethical issues include these:

▌ What to study?

▌ Whom to study?

▌ How to study?

What to Study?

Under ideal circumstances, when criminologists choose a subject for study, they are guided by their own scholarly interests, pressing social needs, the availability of accurate data, and other similar concerns. Nonetheless, in recent years, a great influx of government and institutional funding has influenced the direction of criminological inquiry. Major sources of monetary support include the Justice Department's National Institute of Justice, the National Science Foundation, and the National Institute of Mental Health. Private foundations, such as the Edna McConnell Clark Foundation, have also played an important role in supporting criminological research.

Though the availability of research money has spurred criminological inquiry, it has also influenced the direction research has taken. State and federal governments provide a significant percentage of available research funds, and they may also dictate the areas that can be studied. In recent years, for example, the federal government has spent millions of dollars funding long-term cohort studies of criminal careers. Consequently, academic research has recently focused on criminal careers. Other areas of inquiry may be ignored because there is simply not enough funding to pay for or sponsor the research.

A potential conflict of interest may arise when the institution funding research is itself one of the principal subjects of the research project. Governments may be reluctant to fund research on fraud and abuse of power by government officials. They may also exert a not-so-subtle influence on the criminologists seeking research funding: if criminologists are too critical of the government's efforts to reduce or counteract crime, perhaps they will be barred from receiving further financial help. This situation is even more acute when we consider that criminologists typically work for universities or public agencies and are under pressure to bring in a steady flow of research funds or to maintain the continued viability of their agency. Even when criminologists maintain discretion of choice, the direction of their efforts may not be truly objective. The objectivity of research may be questioned if studies are funded by organizations that have a vested interest in the outcome of the research. For example, a study on the effectiveness of the defensive use of handguns to stop crime may be tainted if the funding for the project comes from a gun manufacturer whose sales may be affected by the research findings. Efforts to show that private prisons are more effective than state correctional facilities might be tainted if the researchers received a research grant from a corporation that maintains private prisons.

Whom to Study?

A second major ethical issue in criminology concerns who will be the subject of inquiries and study. Too often, criminologists focus their attention on the poor and minorities while ignoring the middle-class criminal who may be committing white-collar crime, organized crime, or government crime. Critics have charged that by "unmasking" the poor and desperate, criminologists have justified any harsh measures taken against them. For example, a few social scientists have suggested that criminals have lower intelligence quotients than the average citizen, and that because minority group members have lower than average IQ scores, their crime rates are high.[54] This was the conclusion reached in *The Bell Curve*, a popular though highly controversial book written by Richard Herrnstein and Charles Murray.[55] Although such research is often methodologically unsound, it brings to light the tendency of criminologists to focus on one element of the community while ignoring others. The question that remains is whether it is ethical for criminologists to publish biased or subjective research findings, paving the way for injustice.

How to Study?

Ethics are once again questioned in cases where subjects are misled about the purpose of the research. When white and African American individuals are asked to participate in a survey of their behavior or an IQ test, they are rarely told in advance that the data they provide may later be used to prove the existence of significant racial differences in their self-reported crime rates. Should subjects be told about the true purpose of a survey? Would such disclosures make meaningful research impossible? How far should criminologists go when collecting data? Is it ever permissible to deceive subjects to collect data? Criminologists must take extreme care when they select subjects for their research studies to ensure that they are selected in an unbiased and random manner.[56]

When criminological research efforts involve experimentation and treatment, care must be taken to protect those subjects who have been chosen for experimental and control groups. For example, it may be unethical to provide a special treatment program for one group while depriving others of the same opportunity. Conversely, criminologists must be careful to protect subjects from experiments that may actually cause them harm. An examination of the highly publicized Scared Straight program, which brought youngsters into contact with hard-core prison inmates who gave them graphic insights into prison life (to scare them out of a life of crime), discovered that the young subjects may have been harmed by their experience. Rather than being frightened into conformity, subjects actually increased their criminal behavior.[57]

THINKING LIKE A CRIMINOLOGIST

You have been experimenting with various techniques to identify a sure-fire method to predict violence-prone behavior in delinquents. Your procedure involves brain scans, DNA testing, and blood analysis. When used with samples from incarcerated adolescents, your procedure has been able to distinguish with 80 percent accuracy between youths with a history of violence and those who are exclusively property offenders.

Your research indicates that if any youth were tested with your techniques, potentially violence-prone career criminals easily could be identified for special treatment. For example, children in the local school system could be tested, and those who are identified as violence prone carefully monitored by teachers. Those at risk for future violence could be put into special programs as a precaution.

Some of your colleagues argue that this type of testing is unconstitutional because it violates the subjects' Fifth Amendment right against self-incrimination. There is also the problem of error: Some kids may be falsely labeled as violence prone.

Writing Exercise Write a brief paper (two double-spaced pages) explaining how you would answer your critics. Is it fair and/or ethical to label people as "potentially" criminal and violent even though they have not yet exhibited any antisocial behaviors? Do the risks of such a procedure outweigh its benefits?

Doing Research on the Web To help answer your critics, review these Web-based resources:

- Read about the "DNA Testing of Criminals" prepared by Angela Blann.
- Learn more about "Arresting Developments in DNA" Typing by Phillip B. C. Jones.
- Read Nicole Rafter's take on biological theories of crime to learn more about the biological testing of criminals.
- Learn more about the effects of stigma as it pertains to mental health.

These websites can be accessed via **www.thomsonedu.com/criminaljustice/siegel.**

SUMMARY

- Criminology is the scientific approach to the study of criminal behavior and society's reaction to law violations and violators. It is essentially an interdisciplinary field; many of its practitioners were originally trained as sociologists, psychologists, economists, political scientists, historians, and natural scientists.

- Criminology has a rich history, with roots in the utilitarian philosophy of Beccaria, the biological positivism of Lombroso, the social theory of Durkheim, and the political philosophy of Marx.

- The criminological enterprise includes subareas such as criminal statistics, the sociology of law, theory construction, criminal behavior systems, penology, and victimology.

- When they define crime, criminologists typically hold one of three perspectives: the consensus view, the conflict view, or the interactionist view.

- The consensus view holds that criminal behavior is defined by laws that reflect the values and morals of a majority of citizens.

- The conflict view states that criminal behavior is defined in such a way that economically powerful groups can retain their control over society.

- The interactionist view portrays criminal behavior as a relativistic, constantly changing concept that reflects society's current moral values. According to the interactionist view, behavior is labeled as criminal by those in power; criminals are people society chooses to label as outsiders or deviants.

- The criminal law is a set of rules that specify the behaviors society has outlawed.

- The criminal law serves several important purposes. It represents public opinion and moral values; it enforces social controls; it deters criminal behavior and wrongdoing; it punishes transgressors; and it banishes private retribution.

- The criminal law used in U.S. jurisdictions traces its origin to the English common law. In the U.S. legal system, lawmakers have codified common-law crimes into state and federal penal codes.

- Every crime has specific elements. In most instances, these elements include both the *actus reus* (guilty act) and the *mens rea* (guilty mind)—the person's state of mind or criminal intent.

- At trial, a defendant may claim to have lacked *mens rea* and, therefore, to not be responsible for a criminal action. One type of defense is excuse for mental reasons, such as insanity, intoxication, necessity, or duress. Another type of defense is justification by reason of self-defense or entrapment.

- The criminal law is undergoing constant reform. Some acts are being decriminalized—their penalties are being reduced—while penalties for others are becoming more severe.

- Ethical issues arise when information-gathering methods appear biased or exclusionary. These issues may cause serious consequences because research findings can significantly impact individuals and groups.

- **Thomson**NOW™ Maximize your study time by using ThomsonNOW's diagnostic study plan to help you review this chapter. The Personalized Study plan will help you identify areas on which you should concentrate; provide interactive exercises to help you master the chapter concepts; and provide a post-test to confirm you are ready to move on to the next chapter.

KEY TERMS

criminology (4)
criminologists (4)
criminal justice (4)
scientific method (4)
justice (4)
utilitarianism (5)
classical criminology (6)
positivism (6)
physiognomist (7)
phrenologist (7)
psychopathic personality (7)
atavistic anomalies (7)
biological determinism (8)
criminal anthropology (8)

biosocial theory (8)
cartographic school of criminology (8)
anomie (8)
Chicago School (9)
social ecology (9)
social psychology (9)
socialization (9)
ecological view (9)
socialization view (9)
bourgeoisie (9)
proletariat (9)
rational choice (10)
criminological enterprise (11)
crime typology (14)

consensus view (16)
substantive criminal law (16)
social harm (16)
deviant behavior (16)
conflict view (17)
interactionist view (17)
stigmatize (18)
moral entrepreneurs (18)
common law (19)
mala in se (19)
mala prohibitum (19)
statutory crimes (19)
stalking statutes (22)

CRITICAL THINKING QUESTIONS

1. Beccaria argued that the threat of punishment controls crime. Are there other forms of social control? Aside from the threat of legal punishments, what else controls your own behavior?

2. What research method would you employ if you wanted to study drug and alcohol abuse at your own school?

3. Would it be ethical for a criminologist to observe a teenage gang by "hanging" with them, drinking, and watching as they steal cars? Should he report that behavior to the police?

4. Can you identify behaviors that are deviant but not criminal? What about crimes that are illegal but not deviant?

5. Do you agree with conflict theorists that some of the most damaging acts in society are not punished as crimes? If so, what are they?

6. If you could change the criminal law, what behaviors would you legalize? What would you criminalize? What might be the consequences of your actions—in other words, are there any hidden drawbacks?

NOTES

1. FBI, news release, "Canadian Man Pleads Guilty to Traveling to Georgia to Engage in Sexual Activity with a 10-Year-Old Girl," March 15, 2006, Department of Justice News Release, "Canadian Man Sentenced for Traveling to Georgia to Engage in Sexual Activity with a 10-Year-Old Girl," www.usdoj.gov/usao/gan/press/2006/03-15-06.pdf (accessed May 11, 2007).

2. John Hagan and Alberto Palloni, "Sociological Criminology and the Mythology of Hispanic Immigration and Crime," *Social Problems* 46 (1999): 617–632.

3. Edwin Sutherland and Donald Cressey, *Principles of Criminology*, 6th ed. (Philadelphia: J. B. Lippincott, 1960), p. 3.

4. Monitoring the Future, "Teen Drug Use Continues Down in 2006, Particularly among Older Teens; but Use of Prescription-Type Drugs Remains High," December 21, 2006, www.monitoringthefuture.org/pressreleases/06drugpr.pdf.

5. Alan Harding, Medieval Law and the Foundations of the State (New York: Oxford University Press, 2002).

6. Eugen Weber, *A Modern History of Europe* (New York: W. W. Norton, 1971), p. 398.

7. Marvin Wolfgang, *Patterns in Criminal Homicide* (Philadelphia: University of Pennsylvania Press, 1958).

8. Nicole Rafter, "The Murderous Dutch Giddler: Criminology, History and the Problem of Phrenology," *Theoretical Criminology* 9 (2005): 65–97.

9. Nicole Rafter, "The Unrepentant Horse-Slasher: Moral Insanity and the Origins of Criminological Thought," *Criminology* 42 (2004): 979–1,008.

10. Described in David Lykken, "Psychopathy, Sociopathy, and Crime," *Society* 34 (1996): 29–38.

11. See Peter Scott, "Henry Maudsley," in *Pioneers in Criminology*, ed. Hermann Mannheim (Montclair, NJ: Prentice Hall, 1981).

12. To read about Lombroso, go to http://jahsonic.com/Lombroso.html (accessed May 11, 2007).

13. Nicole Hahn Rafter, "Criminal Anthropology in the United States," *Criminology* 30 (1992): 525–547.

14. Ibid., p. 535.

15. See, generally, Robert Nisbet, *The Sociology of Émile Durkheim* (New York: Oxford University Press, 1974).

16. L. A. J. Quetelet, *A Treatise on Man and the Development of His Faculties* (Gainesville, FL: Scholars' Facsimiles and Reprints, 1969), pp. 82–96.

17. Ibid., p. 85.

18. Émile Durkheim, *Rules of the Sociological Method,* reprint ed., trans. W. D. Halls (New York: Free Press, 1982).

19. Émile Durkheim, *The Division of Labor in Society,* reprint ed. (New York: Free Press, 1997).

20. Robert E. Park, "The City: Suggestions for the Investigation of Behavior in the City Environment," *American Journal of Sociology* 20 (1915): 579–583.

21. Harvey Zorbaugh, *The Gold Coast and the Slum* (Chicago: University of Chicago Press, 1929).

22. Frederick Thrasher, *The Gang* (Chicago: University of Chicago Press, 1927).

23. Louis Wirth, *The Ghetto* (Chicago: University of Chicago Press, 1928).

24. Robert Park, Ernest Burgess, and Roderic McKenzie, *The City* (Chicago: University of Chicago Press, 1925).

25. Ibid.

26. Karl Marx and Friedrich Engels, *Capital: A Critique of Political Economy,* trans. E. Aveling (Chicago: Charles Kern, 1906); Karl Marx, *Selected Writings in Sociology and Social Philosophy,* trans. P. B. Bottomore (New York: McGraw-Hill, 1956). For a general discussion of Marxist thought, see Michael Lynch and W. Byron Groves, *A Primer in Radical Criminology* (New York: Harrow and Heston, 1986), pp. 6–26.

27. Hans Eysenck, *Crime and Personality* (London: Methuen, 1964).

28. Nicole Hahn Rafter, "H. J. Eysenck in Fagin's Kitchen: The Return to Biological Theory in 20th-Century Criminology," *History of the Human Sciences* 19 (2006): 37–56.

29. Sheldon Glueck and Eleanor Glueck, *Unraveling Juvenile Delinquency* (Cambridge: Harvard University Press, 1950), p. 48.

30. John Laub and Robert Sampson, "The Sutherland-Glueck Debate: On the Sociology of Criminological Knowledge," *The American Journal of Sociology* 96 (1991): 1,402–1,440.

31. Marvin Wolfgang and Franco Ferracuti, *The Subculture of Violence* (London: Social Science Paperbacks, 1967), p. 20.

32. Mirka Smolej and Janne Kivivuori, "The Relation between Crime News and Fear of Violence," *Journal of Scandinavian Studies in Criminology and Crime Prevention* 7 (2006): 211–227.

33. Jacqueline Cohen, Wilpen Gorr, and Andreas Olligschlaeger, "Leading Indicators and Spatial Interactions: A Crime-Forecasting Model for Proactive Police Deployment," *Geographical Analysis* 39 (2007): 105–127.

34. The Sociology of Law Section of the American Sociological Association, www.departments.bucknell.edu/soc_anthro/soclaw/textfiles/Purpose_soclaw.txt (accessed March 21, 2007).

35. Rosemary Erickson and Rita Simon, *The Use of Social Science Data in Supreme Court Decisions* (Champaign, IL : University of Illinois Press, 1998).

36. Dennis Wilson, "Additional Law Enforcement as a Deterrent to Criminal Behavior: Empirical Evidence from the National Hockey League," *Journal of Socio-Economics* 34 (2005): 319–330.

37. Wolfgang, *Patterns in Criminal Homicide*.

38. Arielle Baskin-Sommers and Ira Sommers, "Methamphetamine Use and Violence among Young Adults," *Journal of Criminal Justice* 34 (2006): 661–674.

39. Samuel Gross, Kristen Jacoby, Daniel Matheson, Nicholas Montgomery, and Sujata Patil, "Exonerations in the United States, 1989 through 2003," *Journal of Criminal Law and Criminology* 95 (2005): 523–559.

40. Hans von Hentig, *The Criminal and His Victim* (New Haven: Yale University Press, 1948); Stephen Schafer, *The Victim and His Criminal* (New York: Random House, 1968).

41. Linda Teplin, Gary McClelland, Karen Abram, and Darinka Mileusnic, "Early Violent Death among Delinquent Youth: A Prospective Longitudinal Study," *Pediatrics* 115 (2005): 1,586–1,593.

42. Edwin Sutherland and Donald Cressey, *Criminology,* 8th ed. (Philadelphia: J. B. Lippincott, 1960), p. 8.

43. Charles McCaghy, *Deviant Behavior* (New York: MacMillan, 1976), pp. 2–3.

44. Michael Lynch, Raymond Michalowski, and W. Byron Groves, *The New Primer in Radical Criminology: Critical Perspectives on Crime, Power and Identity,* 3rd ed. (Monsey, NY: Criminal Justice Press, 2000), p. 59.

45. Michael Lynch and W. Byron Groves, *A Primer in Radical Criminology* (Albany, NY: Harrow and Heston, 1989).

46. See Herbert Blumer, *Symbolic Interactionism* (Englewood Cliffs, NJ: Prentice Hall, 1969).

47. Howard Becker, *Outsiders: Studies in the Sociology of Deviance* (New York: Free Press, 1963), p. 9.

48. Ibid.

49. Oliver Wendell Holmes, *The Common Law,* ed. Mark De Wolf (Boston: Little, Brown, 1881), p. 36.

50. National Institute of Justice, *Project to Develop a Model Anti-stalking Statute* (Washington, DC: National Institute of Justice, 1994).

51. "Clinton Signs Tougher 'Megan's Law,'" *CNN News Service,* 17 May 1996.

52. Associated Press, "Judge Upholds State's Sexual Predator Law," *Bakersfield Californian,* 2 October 1996.

53. *Lawrence et al. v. Texas,* No. 02-102. June 26, 2003.

54. See, for example, Michael Hindelang and Travis Hirschi, "Intelligence and Delinquency: A Revisionist Review," *American Sociological Review* 42 (1977): 471–486.

55. Richard Herrnstein and Charles Murray, *The Bell Curve* (New York: Free Press, 1994).

56. Victor Boruch, Timothy Victor, and Joe Cecil, "Resolving Ethical and Legal Problems in Randomized Experiments," *Crime and Delinquency* 46 (2000): 330–353.

57. Anthony Petrosino, Carolyn Turpin-Petrosino, and James Finckenauer, "Well-Meaning Programs Can Have Harmful Effects! Lessons from Experiments of Programs Such as Scared Straight," *Crime and Delinquency* 46 (2000): 354–379.

The Nature and Extent of Crime

CHAPTER OUTLINE

Primary Sources of Crime Data
The Uniform Crime Report (UCR)
PROFILES IN CRIME: A Pain in the Glass

Self-Report Surveys
The National Crime Victimization Survey (NCVS)
Evaluating the Primary Sources of Crime Data

Secondary Sources of Crime Data
Cohort Data: Longitudinal and Retrospective
Experimental Data
Observational and Interview Data
Meta-Analysis and Systematic Review
Data Mining
Crime Mapping

Crime Trends
Trends in Violent Crime

The Criminological Enterprise: Explaining Crime Trends

Trends in Property Crime
Trends in Victimization Data (NCVS Findings)
Trends in Self-Reporting
What the Future Holds

Crime Patterns
The Ecology of Crime
Use of Firearms
Social Class, Socioeconomic Conditions, and Crime
Policy and Practice in Criminology:
Should Guns Be Controlled?

Age and Crime
Gender and Crime
Race and Crime
Chronic Offenders/Criminal Careers

CHAPTER OBJECTIVES

Pg. 30 & 58

1. Be familiar with the various forms of crime data
2. Know the problems associated with collecting data
3. Be able to discuss the recent trends in the crime rate
4. Be familiar with the factors that influence crime rates
5. Be able to discuss the patterns in the crime rate
6. Be able to discuss the association between social class and crime   *Pg 51*
7. Recognize that there are stable age, gender, and racial patterns in crime
8. Describe the pros and cons of gun control   *48, 49*
9. Be familiar with Wolfgang's pioneering research on chronic offending   *36*
10. Be able to discuss the discovery of the chronic offender and the effect it has had on criminology   *58*

On May 31, 2003, Eric Rudolph was arrested behind a grocery store in rural western North Carolina after five years on the run. Rudolph had detonated a bomb that exploded outside a Birmingham abortion clinic on January 29, 1998, killing a police officer and critically injuring a clinic nurse. He also set off a bomb that killed one person and injured 150 others in a park in downtown Atlanta during the 1996 Olympics and was involved in the 1997 bombings of a gay nightclub and a building that housed an abortion clinic. Rudolph's crime spree is believed to have been motivated by his extreme political beliefs. He was a member of a white supremacist group called the Army of God and an ardent anti-Semite who claimed that the Holocaust never happened and that the Jews now control the media and the government. Ironically, soon after he was arrested, the court appointed Richard S. Jaffe, a practicing Jew, to lead Rudolph's defense team.[1] On April 8, 2005, Rudolph agreed to plead guilty to all the attacks of which he was accused in order to avoid the death penalty; he was sentenced to four consecutive life terms.[2]

© Erik S. Lesser/Getty Images

Stories such as Rudolph's help convince most Americans that we live in a violent society. When people read headlines about a violent crime spree such as Rudolph's, they begin to fear crime and take steps to protect themselves, perhaps avoiding public places and staying at home in the evening.[3] Are Americans justified in their fear of violent crime? Should they barricade themselves behind armed guards? Are crime rates actually rising or falling? Where do most crimes occur, and who commits them?

To answer these and similar questions, criminologists have devised elaborate methods of crime data collection and analysis. Without accurate data on the nature and extent of crime, it would not be possible to formulate theories that explain the onset of crime or to devise social policies that facilitate its control or elimination. For example, some political figures want to reduce or eliminate immigration because they believe that immigrants commit a lot of crime and are actively engaged in drug dealing. Unless criminologists can produce accurate measures of immigrant crime rates, such hearsay and speculation could be used to shape critically important national policies. (To find out how immigration actually influences crime rates, read the The Criminological Enterprise feature "Explaining Crime Trends" later in this chapter.)

Accurate data collection is also critical in order to assess the nature and extent of crime, track changes in the crime rate, and measure the individual and social factors that may influence criminality.

In this chapter, we review how crime data are collected on criminal offenders and offenses and what this information tells us about crime patterns and trends. We also examine the concept of criminal careers and discover what available crime data can tell us about the onset, continuation, and termination of criminality. We begin with a discussion of the most important sources of crime data.

PRIMARY SOURCES OF CRIME DATA

The primary sources of crime data routinely used by criminologists around the globe are surveys and official records collected, compiled, and analyzed by government agencies such as the federal government's Bureau of Justice Statistics or the Federal Bureau of Investigation (FBI). Criminologists use these techniques to measure the nature and extent of criminal behavior and the personality, attitudes, and background of criminal offenders. It is important to understand how these data are collected to gain insight into how professional criminologists approach various problems and questions in their field. What are these primary sources, how are they collected, and how valid are their findings?

EXHIBIT 2.1

Part I Crime Offenses

Criminal Homicide

Murder and Nonnegligent Manslaughter The willful (nonnegligent) killing of one human being by another. Deaths caused by negligence, attempts to kill, assaults to kill, suicides, accidental deaths, and justifiable homicides are excluded. Justifiable homicides are limited to (a) the killing of a felon by a law enforcement officer in the line of duty and (b) the killing of a felon, during the commission of a felony, by a private citizen.

Manslaughter by Negligence The killing of another person through gross negligence. Traffic fatalities are excluded. Although manslaughter by negligence is a Part I crime, it is not included in the crime index.

Forcible Rape

The carnal knowledge of a female forcibly and against her will. Included are rapes by force and attempts or assaults to rape. Statutory offenses (no force used—victim under age of consent) are excluded.

Robbery

The taking or attempting to take anything of value from the care, custody, or control of a person or persons by force or threat of force or violence and/or by putting the victim in fear.

Aggravated Assault

An unlawful attack by one person upon another for the purpose of inflicting severe or aggravated bodily injury. This type of assault usually is accompanied by the use of a weapon or by means likely to produce death or great bodily harm. Simple assaults are excluded.

Burglary/Breaking or Entering

The unlawful entry of a structure to commit a felony or a theft. Attempted forcible entry is included.

Larceny/Theft (except motor vehicle theft)

The unlawful taking, carrying, leading, or riding away of property from the possession or constructive possession of another. Examples are thefts of bicycles or automobile accessories, shoplifting, pocket picking, or the stealing of any property or article that is not taken by force and violence or by fraud. Attempted larcenies are included. Embezzlement, con games, forgery, worthless checks, and so on are excluded.

Motor Vehicle Theft

The theft or attempted theft of a motor vehicle. A motor vehicle is self-propelled and runs on the surface and not on rails. Specifically excluded from this category are motorboats, construction equipment, airplanes, and farming equipment.

Arson

Any willful or malicious burning or attempt to burn, with or without intent to defraud, a dwelling house, public building, motor vehicle, or aircraft, personal property of another, or the like.

Source: FBI, *Uniform Crime Report*, 2006.

The Uniform Crime Report (UCR)

The most important source of crime data is probably the Uniform Crime Report (UCR), collected from local law enforcement agencies by the Federal Bureau of Investigation

A PAIN IN THE GLASS

From 1997 to 2005, Ronald and Mary Evano turned dining in restaurants into a profitable albeit illegal scam. They used the "waiter, there is glass in my food" ruse in restaurants and supermarkets stretching from Boston to Washington, D.C. Though crude, their efforts paid big dividends. They allegedly swindled insurance companies out of $200,000 and conned a generous helping of food establishments and hospitals along the way. To top it off, in order to look authentic, the Evanos actually did eat glass.

How did the Evanos pull off their scam? After ordering or buying food at restaurants, hotel bars, or supermarkets, either Ronald or Mary would "discover" glass in his or her food. They would then complain of the incident to management and fill out a report.

After leaving the food establishment, the Evanos would check into the emergency room at the local hospital complaining of severe stomach pain. After presenting fake IDs and Social Security cards to hospital staff, they would allow doctors to examine them. In some cases, x-rays would show actual pieces of glass in their stomachs (but none of it came from the food they purchased). Once released from the hospital, the couple would continue getting medical treatment for stomach pain. After racking up several thousand dollars in bills, they would file an insurance claim for their extensive "pain and suffering."

The scheme unraveled when the Insurance Fraud Bureau of Massachusetts noticed a pattern of glass-eating claims in the state. The private industry organization eventually realized that most claims were being filed by the same couple and contacted federal authorities who then traced the couple's trail of insurance fraud across three states and the District of Columbia.

On March 16, 2006, the Evanos were indicted on mail fraud, identity theft, Social Security fraud, and making false statements on health care matters. Ronald was arrested less than a month later, but Mary—his partner in crime—is still on the lam.

Sources: Department of Justice Press Release, "Man Arrested in Glass-Eating Fraud Scheme," April 14, 2006, http://boston.fbi.gov/dojpressrel/pressrel06/evanoranald_indict.htm (accessed March 14, 2007); Federal Bureau of Investigation, "Bizarre Meal Ticket: The Couple Who Ate Glass," November 8, 2006, www.fbi.gov/page2/nov06/glass110806.htm (accessed March 14, 2007); Insurance Journal, "Mass. Couple Charged in Glass-Eating Insurance Fraud," April 16, 2006, www.insurancejournal.com/news/east/2006/04/17/67327.htm (accessed March 14, 2007).

and published yearly. The UCR includes both crimes reported to local law enforcement departments and the number of arrests made by police agencies. It is the best known and most widely cited source of official criminal statistics.[4] The FBI receives and compiles records from more than 17,000 police departments serving a majority of the U.S. population. Its major unit of analysis involves Part I crimes: murder and nonnegligent manslaughter, forcible rape, robbery, aggravated assault, burglary, larceny, arson, and motor vehicle theft. Exhibit 2.1 defines these crimes. All other crimes are referred to as Part II crimes.

The FBI tallies and annually publishes the number of reported Part I offenses by city, county, standard metropolitan statistical area, and geographical divisions of the United States. In addition to these statistics, the UCR shows the number and characteristics (age, race, and gender) of individuals who have been arrested for both Part I and Part II crimes, except traffic violations.

Compiling the Uniform Crime Report The methods used to compile the UCR are quite complex. Each month law enforcement agencies report the number of Part I crimes known to them. These data are collected from records of all crime complaints that victims, officers who discovered the infractions, or other sources reported to these agencies.

Whenever criminal complaints are found through investigation to be unfounded or false, they are eliminated from the actual count. However, the number of actual offenses known is reported to the FBI whether or not anyone is arrested for the crime, the stolen property is recovered, or prosecution ensues.

In addition, each month law enforcement agencies also report how many crimes were cleared. Crimes are cleared in two ways: (1) when at least one person is arrested, charged, and turned over to the court for prosecution, or (2) by exceptional means, when some element beyond police control precludes the physical arrest of an offender (for instance, the offender leaves the country). Data on the number of clearances involving the arrest of only juvenile offenders, data on the value of property stolen and recovered in connection with Part I offenses, and detailed information pertaining to criminal homicide are also reported. Traditionally, slightly more than 20 percent of all reported Part I crimes are cleared by arrest each year (Figure 2.1). The Profiles in Crime feature "A Pain in the Glass" shows how one atypical crime was solved.

Violent crimes are more likely to be solved than property crimes because police devote more resources to these more serious acts. For these types of crime, witnesses (including the victim) are frequently available to identify offenders, and in many instances the victim and offender were previously acquainted.

Figure 2.1 Crime Cleared by Arrest

More serious crimes such as murder and rape are cleared at much higher rates than less serious crimes such as larceny. Factors may include the fact that police spend more resources solving serious crimes and that there is more likely to be an association between victim and offender in serious crimes. Arson is not included in most calculations because it is not reported by all police departments.

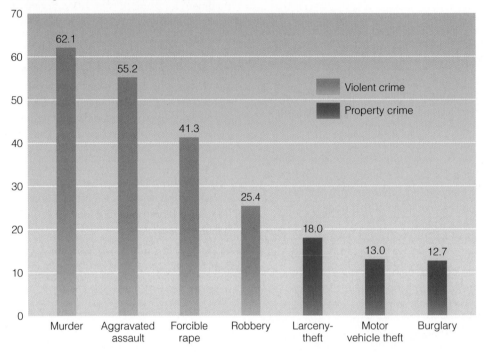

Percentage of Part I crimes cleared by arrest

Source: FBI, *Crime in the United States*, 2005.

The UCR uses three methods to express crime data. First, the number of crimes reported to the police and arrests made are expressed as raw figures (e.g., 16,692 murders occurred in 2005). Second, crime rates per 100,000 people are computed. That is, when the UCR indicates that the murder rate was 5.7 in 2005, it means that almost 6 people in every 100,000 were murdered between January 1 and December 31 of 2005. This is the equation used:

$$\frac{\text{Number of Reported Crimes}}{\text{Total U.S. Population}} \times 100{,}000 = \text{Rate per } 100{,}000$$

Third, the FBI computes changes in the number and rate of crimes over time. The murder rate increased from 5.5 to 5.9 and the number of murders increased 3.4 percent between 2004 and 2005.

Validity of the Uniform Crime Report Despite criminologists' continued reliance on the UCR, its accuracy has been suspect. The three main areas of concern are reporting practices, law enforcement practices, and methodological problems.

1. *Reporting practices.* Some criminologists claim that victims of many serious crimes do not report these inci-

dents to police; therefore, these crimes do not become part of the UCR. The reasons for not reporting vary. Some victims do not trust the police or have confidence in their ability to solve crimes. Others do not have property insurance and therefore believe it is useless to report theft. In other cases, victims fear reprisals from an offender's friends or family or, in the case of family violence, from their spouse, boyfriend, and/or girlfriend.[5]

According to surveys of crime victims, less than 40 percent of all criminal incidents are reported to the police. Some of these victims justify not reporting by stating that the incident was "a private matter," that "nothing could be done," or that the victimization was "not important enough."[6] These findings indicate that the UCR data may significantly underrepresent the total number of annual criminal events.

2. *Law enforcement practices.* The way police departments record and report criminal and delinquent activity also affects the validity of UCR statistics. Some police departments define crimes loosely—reporting a trespass as a burglary or an assault on a woman as an attempted rape—whereas others pay strict attention to FBI guidelines. These reporting practices may help explain

CONCEPT SUMMARY 2.1

DATA COLLECTION METHODS

Uniform Crime Report

▌ Data is collected from records of police departments across the nation. It includes crime reported to police and arrests.

▌ Strengths of the UCR are that the data is collected in a consistent and stable fashion.

▌ Weaknesses of the UCR are that it omits crimes not reported to police, omits most drug usage, and may contain reporting errors.

National Crime Victimization Survey

▌ Data is collected from a large national survey that includes crime victims.

▌ Strengths of the NCVS are that it includes crimes not reported to the police, uses careful sampling techniques, and is a yearly survey.

▌ Weaknesses of the NCVS are that it relies on victims' memory and honesty, and it omits substance abuse.

Self-Report Surveys

▌ Data is collected from anonymous respondents.

▌ Strengths of self-report surveys are that they include unreported crimes, substance abuse, and offenders' personal information.

▌ Weaknesses of self-report surveys are that they rely on the honesty of offenders and that they omit offenders who refuse to participate and/or are otherwise unavailable and who may be the most deviant.

SECONDARY SOURCES OF CRIME DATA

In addition to these main sources of crime data, a number of other techniques are used by criminologists to gather data on specific crime problems and trends, to examine the lives of criminal offenders, and to assess the effectiveness of crime control efforts:

Cohort Data: Longitudinal and Retrospective

Collecting cohort data involves observing a group of people who share a like characteristic over time. For example, researchers might select all girls born in Albany, New York, in 1970 and then follow their behavior patterns for 20 years. The research data might include their school experiences, arrests, hospitalizations, and information about their family life (divorces, parental relations). The subjects might be given repeated intelligence and physical exams; their diets might be monitored.

Data could be collected directly from the subjects during interviews and meetings with family members. Criminologists might also examine records of social organizations, such as hospitals, schools, welfare departments, courts, police departments, and prisons. School records contain data on students' academic performance, attendance, intelligence, disciplinary problems, and teacher ratings. Hospitals record incidents of drug use and suspicious wounds, which may be indicative of child abuse. Police files contain reports of criminal activity, arrest data, personal information on suspects, victim reports, and actions taken by police officers. Court records enable researchers to compare the personal characteristics of offenders with the outcomes of their court appearances, conviction rates, and types of sentence. Prison records contain information on inmates' personal characteristics, adjustment problems, disciplinary records, rehabilitation efforts, and length of sentence served. If the cohort is carefully drawn, it may be possible to determine which life experiences produce criminal careers.

Because it is extremely difficult, expensive, and time-consuming to follow a cohort over time, another approach is to take an intact cohort from the past and collect data from their educational, family, police, and hospital records. This format is known as a retrospective cohort study.[36] For example, a cohort of girls who were in grade school in 1980 could be selected from school attendance records. A criminologist might then acquire their police and court records over the proceeding two decades to determine (a) which ones developed a criminal record and (b) whether school achievement predicts adult criminality.

Experimental Data

Sometimes criminologists are able to conduct controlled experiments to collect data on the cause of crime. They may want to directly test whether (a) watching a violent TV show will (b) cause viewers to act aggressively. This test requires experimental research. To conduct experimental research, criminologists manipulate or intervene in the lives of their subjects to see the outcome or the effect of the intervention. True experiments usually have three elements: (1) random selection of subjects, (2) a control or comparison group, and (3) an experimental condition. Using this approach to find out the effects of viewing violent media content, a criminologist might have one group of randomly chosen subjects watch an extremely violent and gory film (such as *Hostel* or *Saw*) while another randomly selected group views something more mellow (such as *The Princess Diaries* or *Happy Feet*). If the subjects who watched the violent film were significantly more aggressive than those who watched the nonviolent film, an association between media content and behavior would be supported. The fact that both groups were randomly selected would prevent some preexisting condition from invalidating the results of the experiment.

Because it is sometimes impossible to randomly select subjects or manipulate conditions, criminologists may be forced to rely on what is known as a *quasi-experimental design*. A criminologist may want to measure whether kids who were abused as children are more likely to become violent as teens. Of course,

Criminologists observe people in their home setting and interview them in order to gain insight into their behavior, attitudes, and values. Some specialize in gang research. Here, members of the Pico Norte 19th Street Gang pose flashing their hand signs in El Paso, Texas. The gang, an offshoot of the Los Juaritos gang from Ciudad Juarez, Mexico, has become the most notorious gang in the city with some 60 active members. The gang is known also for being a "clean gang"—not involved in drug trafficking or part of older gangs that have become involved in large organized crime schemes. Some 650 known gang members, the majority of Hispanic origin, operate in El Paso. When interviewed, members say they joined the gang to gain respect among their peers and to protect themselves against other gangs; they consider the group a part of their family. Interviews can provide information unavailable with other research methods.

it is impossible to randomly select youth, assign them to two independent groups, and then purposely abuse members of one group in order to gauge their reactions. To get around this dilemma, a criminologist may follow a group of kids who were abused and compare them with a matched group who, though similar in every other respect, were never abused in order to discover if the battered kids were more likely to become violent teens. Because the subjects were not randomly assigned, it is impossible to know whether there was something in the abused group that made them more crime prone than the kids who were not abused.

True criminological experiments are relatively rare because they are difficult and expensive to conduct; they involve manipulating subjects' lives, which can cause ethical and legal roadblocks; and they require long follow-up periods to verify results. Nonetheless, they have been an important source of criminological data.

Observational and Interview Data

Sometimes criminologists focus their research on relatively few subjects, interviewing them in depth or observing them as they go about their activities. This research often results in the kind of in-depth data absent in large-scale surveys. In one such effort Claire Sterk-Elifson focused on the lives of middle-class female

drug abusers.[37] The 34 interviews she conducted provide insight into a group whose behavior might not be captured in a large-scale survey. Sterk-Elifson found that these women were introduced to cocaine at first "just for fun": "I do drugs," one 34-year-old lawyer told her, "because I like the feeling. I would never let drugs take over my life."[38] Unfortunately, many of these subjects succumbed to the power of drugs and suffered both emotional and financial stress.

Another common criminological method is to observe criminals firsthand to gain insight into their motives and activities. This may involve going into the field and participating in group activities, as was done in sociologist William Whyte's famous study of a Boston gang, *Street Corner Society*.[39] Other observers conduct field studies but remain in the background, observing but not being part of the ongoing activity.[40]

Meta-Analysis and Systematic Review

Meta-analysis involves gathering data from a number of previous studies. Compatible information and data are extracted and pooled together. When analyzed, the grouped data from several different studies provide a more powerful and valid indicator of relationships than the results provided from a single study. A systematic review is another widely accepted means of evaluating the effectiveness of public policy interventions. It involves collecting the findings from previously conducted scientific studies that address a particular problem, appraising and synthesizing the evidence, and using the collective data to address a particular scientific question.

Through these well-proven techniques, criminologists can identify what is known and what is not known about a particular problem and use the findings as a first step for carrying out new research. Criminologists David Farrington and Brandon Welsh used a systematic review and a meta-analysis in order to study the effects of street lighting on crime.[41] After identifying and analyzing 13 relevant studies, Farrington and Welsh found evidence showing that neighborhoods that improve their street lighting do in fact experience a reduction in crime rates. Their findings should come as no great surprise. It seems logical that well-lit streets would have fewer robberies and thefts because (a) criminals could not conceal their efforts under the cover of darkness, and (b) potential victims could take evasive action if they saw a suspicious-looking person lurking about. However, their analysis produced an unusual finding: improving lighting caused the crime rate to go down during the day just as much as it did during the night! Obviously, the crime-reducing

a small argument to end in a duel or, at least, a brawl if a person's personal or family honor was impugned or questioned. Today, honor-based killings can still be found, such as in areas of Turkey, where any critical remark about a person's reputation is dealt with by aggression against the source of "rumors." In contemporary society, cultural change, such as a reduction in the number of single-parent families, high school dropout rates, racial conflict, and teen pregnancies, can influence crime rates.

Crime rates may drop when economic conditions change or when an alternative criminal opportunity develops. The decline in the burglary rate over the past decade may be explained in part by the abundance and subsequent decline in price of commonly stolen merchandise such as VCRs, DVDs, cell phones, TVs, and digital cameras. Improving home and commercial security devices may also discourage would-be burglars, convincing them to turn to other forms of crime such as theft from motor vehicles. On the other hand, new targets may increase crime rates: subway crime increased in New York when thieves began targeting people carrying iPods and expensive cell phones.

CRITICAL THINKING

While crime rates have been declining in the United States, they have been increasing in Europe. Is it possible that factors that correlate with crime rate changes in the United States have little utility in predicting changes in other cultures? What other factors may increase or reduce crime rates?

Sources: Robert J. Sampson and Lydia Bean, "Cultural Mechanisms and Killing Fields: A Revised Theory of Community-Level Racial Inequality," in *The Many Colors of Crime: Inequalities of Race, Ethnicity, and Crime in America,* ed. Ruth D. Peterson, Lauren Krivo, and John Hagan (New York: New York University Press, 2006): 8–36; Ramiro Martinez, Jr., Matthew Lee, and Amie Nielsen, "Local Context and Determinants of Drug Violence in Miami and San Diego: Does Ethnicity and Immigration Matter?" *International Migration Review* 38 (2004): 131–157; Martin Killias, "The Opening and Closing of Breaches: A Theory on Crime Waves, Law Creation and Crime Prevention," *European Journal of Criminology* 3 (2006): 11–31; Matthew Miller, David Hemenway, and Deborah Azrael, "State-level Homicide Victimization Rates in the U.S. in Relation to Survey Measures of Household Firearm Ownership, 2001–2003," *Social Science and Medicine* 64 (2007): 656–664; Alfred Blumstein, "The Crime Drop in America: An Exploration of Some Recent Crime Trends," *Journal of Scandinavian Studies in Criminology and Crime Prevention* 7 (2006): 17–35; Thomas Arvanites and Robert Defina, "Business Cycles and Street Crime," *Criminology* 44 (2006): 139–164; David Fergusson, L. John Horwood, and Elizabeth Ridder, "Show Me the Child at Seven: The Consequences of Conduct Problems in Childhood for Psychosocial Functioning in Adulthood," *Journal of Child Psychology and Psychiatry and Allied Disciplines* 46 (2005): 837–849; Fahui Wang, "Job Access and Homicide Patterns in Chicago: An Analysis at Multiple Geographic Levels Based on Scale-Space Theory," *Journal of Quantitative Criminology* 21 (2005): 195–217; Gary Kleck and Ted Chiricos, "Unemployment and Property Crime: A Target-Specific Assessment of Opportunity and Motivation as Mediating Factors," *Criminology* 40 (2002): 649–680; Michael Brick, "An iPod Crime Wave? How Terrible. On Second Thought," *New York Times,* 2 May 2005; Steven Levitt, "Understanding Why Crime Fell in the 1990s: Four Factors that Explain the Decline and Six that Do Not," *Journal of Economic Perspectives* 18 (2004): 163–190; Michael White, James Fyfe, Suzanne Campbell, and John Goldkamp, "The Police Role in Preventing Homicide: Considering the Impact of Problem-Oriented Policing on the Prevalence of Murder," *Journal of Research in Crime and Delinquency* 40 (2003): 194–226; Jeffrey Johnson, Patricia Cohen, Elizabeth Smailes, Stephanie Kasen, and Judith Brook, "Television Viewing and Aggressive Behavior During Adolescence and Adulthood," *Science* 295 (2002): 2,468–2,471; Brad Bushman and Craig Anderson, "Media Violence and the American Public," *American Psychologist* 56 (2001): 477–489; Anthony Harris, Stephen Thomas, Gene Fisher, and David Hirsch, "Murder and Medicine: The Lethality of Criminal Assault 1960–1999," *Homicide Studies* 6 (2002): 128–167; Steven Messner, Lawrence Raffalovich, and Richard McMillan, "Economic Deprivation and Changes in Homicide Arrest Rates for White and Black Youths, 1967–1998: A National Time-Series Analysis," *Criminology* 39 (2001): 591–614; John Laub, "Review of the Crime Drop in America," *American Journal of Sociology* 106 (2001): 1,820–1,822; John J. Donohue and Steven D. Levitt, "The Impact of Legalized Abortion on Crime," *The Quarterly Journal of Economics* 116 (2001): 379–420.

about 18 percent, and the property crime rate declined more than 25 percent. And because there are so many more property crimes than violent crimes, the decline in theft-related offenses means that the overall crime rate is still falling.

Trends in Victimization Data (NCVS Findings)

According to the latest NCVS survey, at last count (2005) U.S. residents age 12 or older experienced about 23 million violent and property victimizations. In 2005 about 16 million households experienced one or more property crimes or had a member age 12 or older who experienced one or more violent crimes.[47]

Reported victimizations have declined significantly during the past 30 years; in 1973 an estimated 44 million victimizations were recorded. Between 1993 and 2005 the violent crime rate decreased 58 percent, from 50 to 21 victimizations per 1,000 persons age 12 or older, and the property crime rate declined at about the same rate (from 319 to 154 crimes per 1,000 households). Figure 2.5 shows the recent trends in violent crime victimization, and Figure 2.6 shows trends in property victimization. In the figures, each line plot shows the range within which the true victimization rate was likely to fall.

Trends in Self-Reporting

Self-report results appear to be more stable than the UCR. When the results of recent self-report surveys are compared with various studies conducted over a 20-year period, a uniform pattern emerges. The use of drugs and alcohol increased markedly in the 1970s, leveled off in the 1980s, and then began to increase in the mid-1990s until 1997, when the use

Figure 2.4 Homicide Rate Trends

Rate per 100,000 population

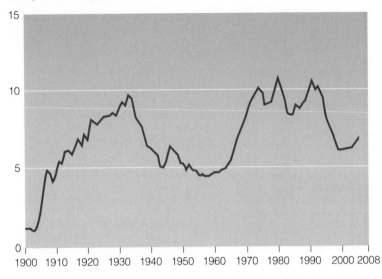

Source: Bureau of Justice Statistics, *Violent Crime in the United States* (Washington, DC, 1992). Updated with data from FBI, *Crime in the United States*, 2005.

of most drugs began to decline. Theft, violence, and damage-related crimes seem more stable. Although a self-reported crime wave has not occurred, neither has there been any visible reduction in self-reported criminality. Table 2.1 contains data from the most recent (2006) Monitoring the Future (MTF) survey. A surprising number of these *typical* teenagers reported involvement in serious criminal behavior: about 13 percent reported hurting someone badly enough that the victim needed medical care (7 percent said they did it more than once); about 27 percent reported stealing something worth less than $50, and another 9 percent stole something worth more than $50; 28 percent reported shoplifting; 13 percent damaged school property.

If the MTF data are accurate, the crime problem is much greater than FBI data would lead us to believe. There are approximately 40 million youths between the ages of 10 and 18. Extrapolating from the MTF findings, this group accounts for more than 100 percent of all theft offenses reported in the UCR. More than 3 percent of the students said they used a knife or a gun in a robbery. At this rate, high school students commit 1.2 million armed robberies per year. In comparison, the UCR tallied about 230,000 armed robberies for all age groups. Over the past decade, the MTF surveys indicate that, with a few exceptions, self-reported participation in theft, violence, and damage-related crimes seems to be more stable than the trends reported in the UCR arrest data.

What the Future Holds

It is risky to speculate about the future of crime trends because current conditions can change rapidly, but some criminologists believe that crime rates may eventually rise as the number of teens in the population increases.

Not all criminologists believe we are in for an age-driven crime wave. Some, such as Steven Levitt, dispute the fact that the population's age makeup contributes as much to the crime rate as suggested by Fox and others.[48] Even if teens commit more crime in the future, he finds that their contribution may be offset by the aging of the population, which will produce a large number of senior citizens, a group with a relatively low crime rate.

Criminologists Darrell Steffensmeier and Miles Harer predict a much more moderate increase in crime than previously believed possible.[49] Steffensmeier and Harer agree that the age structure of society is one of the most important determinants of crime rates, but they believe the economy, technological change, and social factors help moderate the crime rate.[50] They

Figure 2.5 Trends in Violent Crime Victimizations

Violent victimizations per
1,000 population age 12 or over

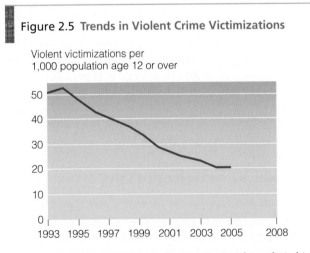

Source: National Crime Victimization Survey, www.ojp.usdoj.gov/bjs/pub/pdf/cv05.pdf.

Figure 2.6 Trends in Property Crime Victimizations

Property victimizations per
1,000 households

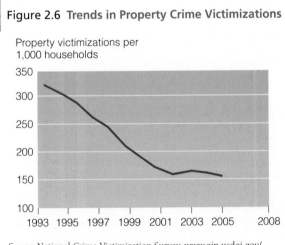

Source: National Crime Victimization Survey, www.ojp.usdoj.gov/bjs/pub/pdf/cv05.pdf.

Table 2.1 Survey of Criminal Activity of High School Seniors, 2006

Crime	Percentage Engaging in Offenses	
	Committed at Least Once	Committed More Than Once
Set fire on purpose	2	2
Damaged school property	6	5
Damaged work property	3	3
Auto theft	3	2
Auto part theft	2	2
Break and enter	12	13
Theft, less than $50	12	15
Theft, more than $50	5	5
Shoplift	11	14
Gang fight	9	8
Hurt someone badly enough to require medical care	6	5
Used force or a weapon to steal	2	2
Hit teacher or supervisor	1	2
Participated in serious fight	7	5

Source: Monitoring the Future, 2006 (Ann Arbor, MI: Institute for Social Research, 2006).

note that American culture is being transformed because baby boomers, now in their late 50s and 60s, are exerting a significant influence on the nation's values and morals. As a result, the narcissistic youth culture that stresses materialism is being replaced by more moralistic cultural values.[51] Positive social values have a "contagion effect"; those held by the baby boomers will have an important influence on the behavior of all citizens, even crime-prone teens. The result may be a moderation in the potential growth of the crime rate.

Such prognostication is reassuring, but there is, of course, no telling what changes are in store that may influence crime rates either up or down. Technological developments such as e-commerce on the Internet have created new classes of crime. Concern about the environment in rural areas may produce a rapid upswing in environmental crimes ranging from vandalism to violence.[52] Although crime rates have trended downward, it is too early to predict that this trend will continue into the foreseeable future. The recent uptick in murder may foretell an overall increase in the general crime rate.

CRIME PATTERNS

Criminologists look for stable crime rate patterns to gain insight into the nature of crime. The cause of crime may be better understood by examining the rate. If criminal statistics consistently show that crime rates are higher in poor neighborhoods in large urban areas, then the cause of crime may be related to poverty and neighborhood decline. If, in contrast, crime rates are spread evenly across society, and rates were equal in poor and affluent neighborhoods, this would

provide little evidence that crime has an economic basis. Instead, crime might be linked to socialization, personality, intelligence, or some other trait unrelated to class position or income. In this section we examine traits and patterns that may influence the crime rate.

The Ecology of Crime

Patterns in the crime rate seem to be linked to temporal and ecological factors. Some of the most important of these are discussed here.

Day, Season, and Climate Most reported crimes occur during the warm summer months of July and August. During the summer, teenagers, who usually have the highest crime levels, are out of school and have greater opportunity to commit crime. People spend more time outdoors during warm weather, making themselves easier targets. Similarly, homes are left vacant more often during the summer, making them more vulnerable to property crimes. Two exceptions to this trend are murders and robberies, which occur frequently in December and January (although rates are also high during the summer).

Crime rates also may be higher on the first day of the month than at any other time. Government welfare and Social Security checks arrive at this time, and with them come increases in such activities as breaking into mailboxes and accosting recipients on the streets. Also, people may have more disposable income at this time, and the availability of extra money may relate to behaviors associated with crime such as drinking, partying, gambling, and so on.[53]

Temperature Weather effects (such as temperature swings) may have an impact on violent crime rates. Traditionally, the association between temperature and crime was thought to resembles an inverted U-shaped curve: crime rates increase with rising temperatures and then begin to decline at some point (85 degrees) when it may be too hot for any physical exertion[54] (see Figure 2.7). However, criminologists continue to debate this issue:

- Some believe that crime rates rise with temperature (i.e., the hotter the day, the higher the crime rate).[55]

- Others have found evidence that the curvilinear model is correct.[56]

- Some research shows that a rising temperature will cause some crimes to continually increase (such as domestic assault), whereas others (such as rape) will decline after temperatures rise to an extremely high level.[57]

Crime rates peak during the summer months in most areas and then decline in the fall and winter. A surveillance camera tape shows David Willingham (right) and Megan Franklin as they rob a convenience store in Tucson, Arizona, in August 2005. The couple, who robbed the store while wearing clown suits, was sentenced to three years in prison each. What does this seasonal effect tell us about the cause of crime?

If in fact there is an association between temperature and crime, how can it be explained? The relationship may be due to the stress and tension caused by extreme temperature. The human body generates stress hormones (adrenaline and testosterone) in response to excessive heat; hormonal activity has been linked to aggression.[58]

One way to combat the temperature–crime association: turn off your air conditioner! James Rotton and Ellen Cohn found that assaults in air-conditioned settings increase as the temperature rose; assaults in non–air-conditioned settings decline after peaking at moderately high temperatures.[59]

Figure 2.7 Relationship between Temperature and Crime

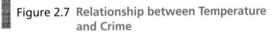

Crime rate

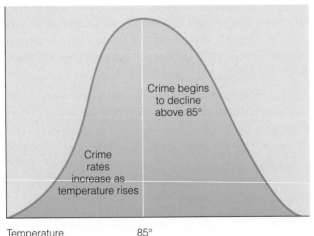

Crime begins to decline above 85°

Crime rates increase as temperature rises

Temperature   85°

Regional Differences Large urban areas have by far the highest violence rates; rural areas have the lowest per capita crime rates. Exceptions to this trend are low population resort areas with large transient or seasonal populations—such as Atlantic City, New Jersey. Typically, the western and southern states have had consistently higher crime rates than the Midwest and Northeast (see Figure 2.8) This pattern has convinced some criminologists that regional cultural values influence crime rates; others believe that regional differences be explained by economic differences.

Use of Firearms

Firearms play a dominant role in criminal activity. According to the NCVS, firearms are typically involved in about 20 percent of robberies, 10 percent of assaults, and more than 5 percent of rapes. According to the UCR, about two-thirds of all murders involved firearms; most of these weapons were handguns.

Because of these findings, there is an ongoing debate over gun control. International criminologists Franklin Zimring and Gordon Hawkins believe the proliferation of handguns and the high rate of lethal violence they cause is the single most significant factor separating the crime problem in the United States from the rest of the developed world.[60] Differences between the United States and Europe in nonlethal crimes are only modest at best—and getting smaller over time.[61]

In contrast, some criminologists believe that personal gun use can actually be a deterrent to crime. Gary Kleck and Marc Gertz have found that as many as 400,000 people per year use guns in situations in which they later claim that the guns "almost certainly" saved lives. Even if these estimates are off by a factor of 10, it means that armed citizens may save 40,000 lives annually. Although Kleck and Gertz recognize that guns are involved in murders, suicides, and accidents, which claim more than 30,000 lives per year, they believe their benefit as a crime prevention device should not be overlooked.[62] Because this is so important, the Policy and Practice in Criminology feature "Should Guns Be Controlled?" discusses this issue in some detail.

Social Class, Socioeconomic Conditions, and Crime

It makes logical sense that crime is a lower-class phenomenon. After all, people at the lowest rungs of the social structure have the greatest incentive to commit crimes. Those unable to obtain desired goods and services through conventional means

Figure 2.8 Regional Crime Rates for Violent and Property Crimes

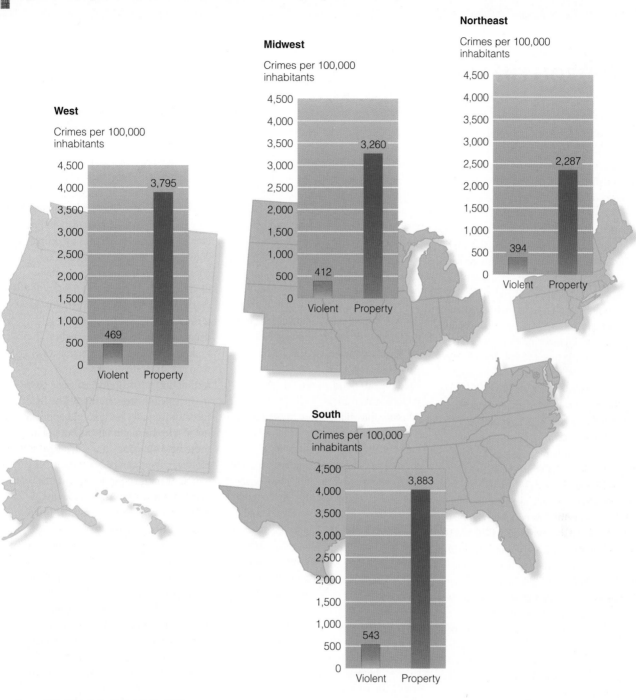

West

Crimes per 100,000 inhabitants

469 (Violent)
3,795 (Property)

Midwest

Crimes per 100,000 inhabitants

412 (Violent)
3,260 (Property)

Northeast

Crimes per 100,000 inhabitants

394 (Violent)
2,287 (Property)

South

Crimes per 100,000 inhabitants

543 (Violent)
3,883 (Property)

Source: FBI, *Crime in the United States*, 2005.

may consequently resort to theft and other illegal activities—such as selling narcotics—to obtain them. These activities are referred to as **instrumental crimes**. Those living in poverty are also believed to engage in disproportionate amounts of **expressive crimes**, such as rape and assault, as a result of their rage, frustration, and anger against society. Alcohol and drug abuse, common in impoverished areas, help fuel violent episodes.[63]

When measured with UCR data, official statistics indicate that crime rates in inner-city, high-poverty areas are generally higher than those in suburban or wealthier areas.[64] Surveys of prison inmates consistently show that prisoners were members of the lower class and unemployed or underemployed in the years before their incarceration.

An alternative explanation for these findings is that the relationship between official crime and social class is a function

SHOULD GUNS BE CONTROLLED?

To millions of Americans, the massacre of more than 30 people at Virginia Tech on April 16, 2007, was a graphic reminder of the association between guns and crime. How could an obviously mentally unbalanced person such as Seung-Hui Cho be able to purchase a deadly automatic weapon? Under Virginia's existing gun laws, Cho was legally entitled to purchase the Glock 19 9mm semiautomatic from a gun dealer and leave with it on the same day. Though he was a disturbed loner, the Commonwealth has no waiting period to buy a gun and his status as a permanent resident alien made no difference. If he had taken the time to apply for a permit to carry a concealed weapon, he would have received it without a fuss—in Virginia, law enforcement authorities must issue a permit to anyone who requests one if the applicant doesn't fit into a narrow range of disqualifying categories, one of which is having a criminal record, which Cho did not.

Could Cho's rampage been avoided if the sale of handguns could be eliminated or strictly controlled? The association between guns and crime has spurred many Americans to advocate controlling the sale of handguns and banning the cheap mass-produced handguns known as Saturday night specials. In contrast, gun advocates view control as a threat to personal liberty and call for severe punishment of criminals rather than control of handguns. They argue that the Second Amendment to the U.S. Constitution protects the right to bear arms.

The Miller Case

Seventy years ago, in *United States v. Miller*, 307 U.S. 174 (1939), the Supreme Court ruled that the Second Amendment must be interpreted as intending to guarantee the states' rights to maintain and train a militia and not a personal right to bear arms. Jack Miller had wanted to avoid registering a sawed-off shotgun, which he possessed for personal use. The Court ruled, "In the absence of any evidence tending to show that possession or use of a shotgun having a barrel of less than 18 inches in length at this time has some reasonable relationship to the preservation or efficiency of a well-regulated militia, we cannot say that the Second Amendment guarantees the right to keep and bear such an instrument." Because Miller's shotgun was not for a militia-type purpose, it was not protected by the Second Amendment. The purpose of the Second Amendment was to support the national defense. Therefore, the only purpose for which owning and carrying a gun is protected under the Second Amendment is as part of "a well regulated militia," acting on behalf of the national government.

Since the Miller case, efforts to control handguns have come from many different sources. States and many local jurisdictions have laws banning or restricting sales or possession of guns; some regulate dealers who sell guns. The Federal Gun Control Act of 1968, which is still in effect, requires that all dealers be licensed, fill out forms detailing each trade, and avoid selling to people prohibited from owning guns, such as minors, ex-felons, and drug users. Dealers must record the source and properties of all guns they sell and carefully account for their purchase. Gun buyers must provide identification and sign waivers attesting to their ability to possess guns. Unfortunately, the resources available to enforce this law are meager.

On November 30, 1993, the Brady Handgun Violence Prevention Act was enacted, amending the Gun Control Act of 1968. The bill was named after former Press Secretary James Brady, who was severely wounded in the attempted assassination of President Ronald Reagan by John Hinckley in 1981. The Brady Law imposes a waiting period of five days before a licensed importer, manufacturer, or dealer may sell, deliver, or transfer a handgun to an unlicensed individual. The waiting period applies only in states without an acceptable alternate system of conducting background checks on handgun purchasers. Beginning November 30, 1998, the Brady Law changed, providing an instant check on whether a prospective buyer is prohibited from purchasing a weapon. Federal law bans gun purchases by people convicted of or under indictment for felony charges, fugitives, the mentally ill, those with dishonorable military discharges, those who have renounced U.S. citizenship, illegal aliens, illegal drug users, and those convicted of domestic violence misdemeanors or who are under domestic violence restraining orders (individual state laws may create other restrictions). The Brady Law now requires background approval not just for handgun buyers but also for those who buy long guns and shotguns. However, there can be gaps in the system. One of these prevented Virginia from reporting Cho's legal status to the federal National Instant Criminal Background Check System. In the aftermath of the shooting, Virginia's Governor Timothy Kaine addressed this problem by issuing an executive order closing this gap in the law. In addition, the Federal Violent Crime Control and Law Enforcement Act of 1994 banned a group of military-style semiautomatic firearms (that is, assault weapons). However, this ban on assault weapons was allowed to lapse in 2004.

Although gun control advocates see this legislation as a good first step, some question whether such measures will ultimately curb gun violence. When Jens Ludwig and Philip Cook compared two sets of states—thirty-two that installed the Brady Law in 1994 and eighteen states plus the District of Columbia that already had similar types of laws prior to

1994—they found that there was no evidence that implementing the Brady Law contributed to a reduction in homicide. However, there is evidence that legislation targeting specific crimes can bring positive results. A number of states have instituted laws restricting access to firearms by individuals who are subject to a restraining order or have been convicted of a domestic violence misdemeanor, or allowing law enforcement officers to confiscate firearms at a domestic violence scene. Research indicates that taking guns out of the hands of domestic abusers can lower rates of intimate partner homicides.

Another approach is to severely punish people caught with unregistered handguns. The most famous attempt to regulate handguns using this method is the Massachusetts Bartley-Fox Law, which provides a mandatory one-year prison term for possessing a handgun (outside the home) without a permit. A detailed analysis of violent crime in Boston after the law's passage found that the use of handguns in robberies and murders did decline substantially (in robberies by 35 percent and in murders by 55 percent in a two-year period). However, these optimistic results must be tempered by two facts: rates for similar crimes dropped significantly in comparable cities that did not have gun control laws, and the use of other weapons, such as knives, increased in Boston.

Can Guns Be Outlawed?

Even if outlawed or severely restricted, the government's ability to control guns is problematic. If legitimate gun stores were strictly regulated, private citizens could still sell, barter, or trade handguns. Unregulated gun fairs and auctions are common throughout the United States; many gun deals are made at gun shows with few questions asked. People obtain firearms illegally through a multitude of unauthorized sources, including unlicensed dealers, corrupt licensed dealers, and "straw" purchasers (people who buy guns for those who cannot purchase them legally).

If handguns were banned or outlawed, they would become more valuable; illegal importation of guns might increase as it has for other controlled substances (for instance, narcotics). Increasing penalties for gun-related crimes has also met with limited success because judges may be reluctant to alter their sentencing policies to accommodate legislators. Regulating dealers is difficult, and tighter controls on them would only encourage private sales and bartering. Relatively few guns are stolen in burglaries, but many are sold to licensed gun dealers who circumvent the law by ignoring state registration requirements or making unrecorded or misrecorded sales to individuals and unlicensed dealers. Even a few corrupt dealers can supply tens of thousands of illegal handguns.

Is There a Benefit to Having Guns?

Not all experts are convinced that strict gun control is a good thing. Some, such as Gary Kleck, a leading advocate of gun ownership, argues that guns may actually inhibit violence. He finds that Americans use guns for defensive purposes more than 2 million times a year. Although this figure seems huge, it must be viewed in the context of total gun ownership: almost 50 million households own a gun; more than 90 million, or 49 percent of the adult U.S. population, live in households with guns; and about 59 million adults personally own guns. Considering these numbers it is not implausible that 3 percent of the people (2.5 million) with access to guns could have used one defensively in a given year.

Guns have other uses. In many assaults, Kleck reasons, the aggressor does not wish to kill but only scare the victim. Possessing a gun gives aggressors enough killing power so that they may actually be inhibited from attacking. Guns may also enable victims to escape serious injury. Victims may be inhibited from fighting back without losing face; it is socially acceptable to back down from a challenge if the opponent is armed with a gun. Guns then can deescalate a potentially violent situation. The benefits of gun ownership, he concludes, outweigh the costs.

Does Defensive Gun Use Really Work?

While this research is persuasive, many criminologists are still skeptical about the benefits of carrying a handgun. Tomislav Kovandzic and his colleagues used data for all large U.S. cities (population over 100,000) to examine the impact of right-to-carry concealed handgun laws on violent crime rates from 1980 to 2000 and found that carry laws have little effect on local crime rates. And though Kleck's research shows that carrying a gun can thwart crimes, other research shows that defensive gun use may be more limited than he believes: people who carry guns may be at greater risk of victimization than those who do not. Even people with a history of violence and mental disease are less likely to kill when they use a knife or other weapon than when they employ a gun. Do guns kill people or do people kill people? Research indicates that even the most dangerous people are less likely to resort to lethal violence if the gun is taken out of their hands.

CRITICAL THINKING

1. Should the sale and possession of handguns be banned?

2. Which of the gun control methods discussed do you feel would be most effective in deterring crime?

Sources: E. R Vigdor and J.A. Mercy, "Do Laws Restricting Access to Firearms by Domestic Violence Offenders Prevent Intimate Partner Homicide?" *Evaluation Review* 30 (2006): 313–346; Gary Kleck and Jongyeon Tark, "Resisting Crime: The Effects of Victim Action on the Outcomes of Crimes." *Criminology* 42 (2005): 861–909; Robert Martin

(continued)

(continued)

and Richard Legault, "Systematic Measurement Error with State-Level Crime Data: Evidence from the 'More Guns, Less Crime' Debate," *Journal of Research in Crime and Delinquency* 42 (2005): 187–210; Tomislav Kovandzic, Thomas Marvell, and Lynne Vieraitis, "The Impact of 'Shall-Issue' Concealed Handgun Laws on Violent Crime Rates: Evidence From Panel Data for Large Urban Cities," *Homicide Studies* 9 (2005): 292–323; Tomislav Kovandzic and Thomas Marvell, "Right-to-Carry Concealed Handguns and Violent Crime: Crime

Control through Gun Control?" *Criminology and Public Policy* 2 (2003): 363–396; Lisa Hepburn and David Hemenway, "Firearm Availability and Homicide: A Review of the Literature," *Aggression and Violent Behavior* 9 (2004): 417–440; Matthew Miller, Deborah Azrael, and David Hemenway, "Rates of Household Firearm Ownership and Homicide across U.S. Regions and States, 1988–1997," *American Journal of Public Health* 92 (2002): 1,988–1,993; John Lott, Jr., "More Guns, Less Crime: Understanding Crime and Gun-Control Laws," *Studies in Law and Economics,* 2nd ed. (Chicago: University of Chicago Press, 2001); John Lott, Jr., and David

Mustard, "Crime, Deterrence, and Right-to-Carry Concealed Handguns," *Journal of Legal Studies* 26 (1997): 1–68; Anthony A. Braga and David M. Kennedy, "The Illicit Acquisition of Firearms by Youth and Juveniles," *Journal of Criminal Justice* 29 (2001): 379–388; Gary Kleck and Marc Gertz, "Armed Resistance to Crime: The Prevalence and Nature of Self-Defense with a Gun," *Journal of Criminal Law and Criminology* 86 (1995): 150–187; Jens Ludwig and Philip Cook, "Homicide and Suicide Rates Associated with the Implementation of the Brady Violence Prevention Act," *Journal of the American Medical Association* 284 (2000): 585–591.

of law enforcement practices, not actual criminal behavior patterns. Police may devote more resources to poor areas, and consequently apprehension rates may be higher there. Similarly, police may be more likely to formally arrest and prosecute lower-class citizens than those in the middle and upper classes, which may account for the lower class's overrepresentation in official statistics and the prison population.

Class and Self-Reports Self-report data have been used extensively to test the class–crime relationship. If people in all social classes self-report similar crime patterns, but only those in the lower class are formally arrested, that would explain higher crime rates in lower-class neighborhoods. However, if lower-class people report greater criminal activity than their middle- and upper-class peers, it would indicate that official statistics accurately represent the crime problem.

Surprisingly, early self-report studies conducted in the 1950s, specifically those conducted by James Short and F. Ivan Nye, did not find a direct relationship between social class and youth crime.[65] They found that socioeconomic class was related to official processing by police, courts, and correctional agencies but not to the actual commission of crimes. In other words, although lower- and middle-class youth self-reported equal amounts of crime, the lower-class youths had a greater chance of being arrested, convicted, and incarcerated and becoming official delinquents. In addition, factors generally associated with lower-class membership, such as broken homes, were found to be related to institutionalization but not to admissions of delinquency. Other studies of this period reached similar conclusions.[66]

For more than 20 years after the use of self-reports became widespread, a majority of self-report studies concluded that a class–crime relationship did not exist: if the poor possessed more extensive criminal records than the wealthy, this difference was attributable to differential law enforcement and not to class-based behavior differences. That is, police may be more likely to arrest lower-class offenders and treat the affluent more leniently.

Almost 30 years ago, Charles Tittle, Wayne Villemez, and Douglas Smith published what is still considered the definitive review of the relationship between class and crime.[67] They concluded that little if any support exists for the contention that crime is primarily a lower-class phenomenon. Consequently, Tittle and his associates argued that official statistics probably reflect class bias in processing lower-class offenders. In a subsequent article written with Robert Meier, Tittle once again reviewed existing data on the class–crime relationship and found little evidence of a consistent association between class and crime.[68] More recent self-report studies generally support Tittle's conclusions: there is no direct relationship between social class and crime.[69]

Tittle's findings have sparked significant debate in the criminological community. Many self-report instruments include trivial offenses such as using a false ID or drinking alcohol, which may invalidate findings. It is possible that affluent youths frequently engage in trivial offenses such as petty larceny, using drugs, and simple assault but rarely escalate their criminal involvement. Those who support a class–crime relationship suggest that if only serious felony offenses are considered, a significant association can be observed.[70] Some studies find that when only serious crimes, such as burglary and assault, are considered, lower-class youths are significantly more delinquent than their more affluent peers.[71]

The Class–Crime Controversy The relationship between class and crime is an important one for criminological theory. If crime is related to social class, it follows that economic and social factors, such as poverty and neighborhood disorganization, cause criminal behavior. If class and economic conditions are not related to crime rates, the cause of crime may be found at an individual level, related more to a person's psychological and biological makeup than their economic predicament.

One reason that a true measure of the class–crime relationship has so far eluded criminologists is that the methods now

The poor may have an economic incentive to commit crime, but so do the more affluent members of society. Here, former Hewlett-Packard company chairwoman Patricia Dunn pleads not guilty during her arraignment in a Santa Clara County Superior Court in San Jose, California, November 15, 2006. She was charged with four counts of felony identity theft and fraud for allegedly instigating the company's ill-fated spying probe into boardroom leaks. The association between class and crime is clouded by the fact that members of all economic strata engage in illegal activities.

the social structure.[76] Income inequality, poverty, and resource deprivation are all associated with the most serious violent crimes, including homicide and assault.[77] Members of the lower class are more likely to suffer psychological abnormality, including high rates of anxiety and conduct disorders, conditions that may promote criminality.[78]

Communities that lack economic and social opportunities also produce high levels of frustration; their residents believe they are relatively more deprived than residents in more affluent areas and may then turn to criminal behavior to relieve their frustration.[79] Family life is disrupted, and law-violating youth groups thrive in a climate that undermines adult supervision.[80] Conversely, when the poor are provided with economic opportunities via welfare and public assistance, crime rates drop.[81] The debate is far from over. Although crime rates may be higher in lower-class areas, poverty alone cannot explain why a particular individual becomes a chronic violent criminal; if it could, the crime problem would be much worse than it is now.[82]

employed to measure social class vary widely. Some widely used measures of social class, such as father's occupation and education, are only weakly related to self-reported crime, but others, such as unemployment or receiving welfare, are more significant predictors of criminality.[72]

It is also possible that the association between class and crime is difficult to calculate because it is quite complex and cannot be explained with a simple linear relationship (that is, the poorer you are, the more crime you commit).[73] Class and economic conditions may affect some crimes and some people differently than they affect others. Some subgroups in the population (e.g., women, African Americans) seem more deeply influenced by economic factors than others (e.g., males, European Americans).[74] Job loss seems to affect young adults more than it does teens. Younger adults are affected not only when they experience job loss but when only low-wage jobs are available.[75]

These findings show why the true relationship between class and crime is difficult to determine. The effect may be obscured because its impact varies within and between groups.

Does Class Matter? Like so many other criminological controversies, the debate over the true relationship between class and crime will most likely persist. The weight of recent evidence seems to suggest that serious, official crime is more prevalent among the lower classes, whereas less serious and self-reported crime is spread more evenly throughout

connections

If class and crime are unrelated, then the causes of crime must be found in factors experienced by members of all social classes—psychological impairment, family conflict, peer pressure, school failure, and so on. Theories that view crime as a function of problems experienced by members of all social classes are reviewed in Chapter 7.

Age and Crime

There is general agreement that age is inversely related to criminality. Criminologists Travis Hirschi and Michael Gottfredson state: "Age is everywhere correlated with crime. Its effects on crime do not depend on other demographic correlates of crime."[83]

Regardless of economic status, marital status, race, sex, and so on, younger people commit crime more often than their older peers; research indicates this relationship has been stable across time periods ranging from 1935 to the present.[84] Official statistics tell us that young people are arrested at a disproportionate rate to their numbers in the population; victim surveys generate similar findings for crimes in which assailant age can be determined. Whereas youths under 18 collectively make up about 6 percent of the total U.S. population, they account for about 25 percent of serious crime arrests and 17 percent of arrests for all crimes. As a general rule, the peak age for property

Figure 2.9 **Relationship between Age and Serious Crime Arrests**

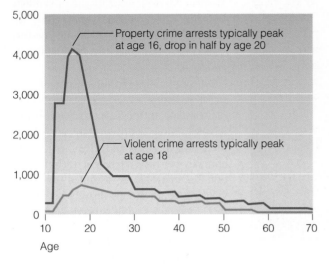

Arrest rate per 100,000 persons

Property crime arrests typically peak at age 16, drop in half by age 20

Violent crime arrests typically peak at age 18

Source: FBI, *Uniform Crime Report*, 2005.

Table 2.2 **Percentage of High School Seniors Admitting to at Least One Offense during the Past 12 Months, by Gender**

Delinquent Acts	Males	Females
Serious fight	14	9
Gang fight	21	16
Hurt someone badly	17	5
Used a weapon to steal	5	2
Stole less than $50	30	25
Stole more than $50	13	7
Shoplift	25	25
Breaking and entering	27	22
Arson	4	2
Damaged school property	17	6

Source: Monitoring the Future, 2006 (Ann Arbor, MI: Institute for Social Research, 2007).

crime is believed to be 16, and for violence 18 (Figure 2.9). In contrast, adults 45 and over, who make up about a third of the population, account for only 7 percent of serious crime arrests. The elderly are particularly resistant to the temptations of crime; they make up more than 14 percent of the population and less than 1 percent of arrests. Elderly males 65 and over are predominantly arrested for alcohol-related matters (such as public drunkenness and drunk driving) and elderly females for larceny (such as shoplifting). The elderly crime rate has remained stable for the past twenty years.[85]

Aging Out of Crime Most criminologists agree that people commit less crime as they age.[86] Crime peaks in adolescence and then declines rapidly thereafter. According to criminologist Robert Agnew, this peak in criminal activity can be linked to essential features of adolescence in modern, industrial societies. Because adolescents are given most of the privileges and responsibilities of adults in these cultures, they also experience:

- A reduction in supervision
- An increase in social and academic demands
- Participation in a larger, more diverse, peer-oriented social world
- An increased desire for adult privileges
- A reduced ability to cope in a legitimate manner and increased incentive to solve problems in a criminal manner[87]

Adding to these incentives is the fact that young people, especially the indigent and antisocial, tend to discount the future.[88] They are impatient, and because their future is uncertain, they are unwilling or unable to delay gratification. As they mature, troubled youths are able to develop a long-term life view and resist the need for immediate gratification.[89]

Aging out of crime may be a function of the natural history of the human life cycle.[90] Deviance in adolescence is fueled by the need for money and sex and reinforced by close relationships with peers who defy conventional morality. At the same time, teenagers are becoming independent from parents and other adults who enforce conventional standards of morality and behavior. They have a new sense of energy and strength and are involved with peers who are similarly vigorous and frustrated. Adults, on the other hand, develop the ability to delay gratification and forgo the immediate gains that law violations bring. They also start wanting to take responsibility for their behavior and to adhere to conventional mores, such as establishing long-term relationships and starting a family.[91] Research does show that people who maintain successful marriages are more likely to desist from antisocial behaviors than those whose marriages fail.[92]

Gender and Crime

Male crime rates are much higher than those of females. Victims report that their assailant was male in more than 80 percent of all violent personal crimes. The most recent Uniform Crime Report arrest statistics (2005) indicate that males account for more than 80 percent of all arrests for serious violent crimes and 68 percent of the arrests for serious property crimes; murder arrests are 8 males to 1 female. MTF data also show that males commit more serious crimes, such as robbery, assault, and burglary, than females. However, although the patterns in self-reports parallel official data, the ratios are smaller. In other words, males self-report more criminal behavior than females, but not to the degree suggested by official data (Table 2.2). How can these differences be explained?

Explaining Gender Differences in the Crime Rate Early criminologists pointed to emotional, physical, and psychological differences between males and females to explain the differences in crime rates. Cesare Lombroso's 1895 book, *The Female Offender*, argued that a small group of female criminals lacked "typical" female traits of "piety, maternity, undeveloped intelligence, and weakness."[93] In physical appearance as well as in their emotional makeup, delinquent females appeared closer to men than to other women. Lombroso's theory became known as the masculinity hypothesis; in essence, a few "masculine" females were responsible for the handful of crimes women commit.

Another early view of female crime focused on the supposed dynamics of sexual relationships. Female criminals were viewed as either sexually controlling or sexually naive, either manipulating men for profit or being manipulated by them. The female's criminality was often masked because criminal justice authorities were reluctant to take action against a woman.[94] This perspective is known as the chivalry hypothesis, which holds that much female criminality is hidden because of the culture's generally protective and benevolent attitude toward women.[95] In other words, police are less likely to arrest, juries are less likely to convict, and judges are less likely to incarcerate female offenders.

Although these early writings are no longer taken seriously, some criminologists still believe that gender-based traits are a key determinant of crime rate differences. Among the suspected differences include physical strength and hormonal influences. According to this view, male sex hormones (androgens) account for more aggressive male behavior, and gender-related hormonal differences explain the gender gap in the crime rate.[96]

Socialization and Development Although there are few gender-based differences in aggression during the first few years of life, girls are socialized to be less aggressive than boys and are supervised more closely by parents.[97] Differences in aggression become noticeable between ages 3 and 6 when children are first socialized into organized peer groups such as the day care center or school. Males are more likely then to display physical aggression whereas girls display relational aggression—excluding disliked peers from play groups, gossiping, and interfering with social relationships.

Males are taught to be more aggressive and assertive and less likely to form attachments to others. They often view their aggression as a gender-appropriate means to gain status and power, either by joining deviant groups and gangs or engaging in sports. Even in middle-class suburbs, they may seek approval by knocking down or running through peers on the playing field, while females literally cheer them on. The male search for social approval through aggressive behavior may make them more susceptible to criminality, especially when the chosen form of aggression is antisocial or illegal. Recent research by Jean Bottcher found that young boys perceive their roles as being more dominant than young girls.[98] Male perceptions of power, their ability to have freedom and hang with their friends, helped explain the gender differences in crime and delinquency.

In contrast, girls are encouraged to care about other people and avoid harming them; their need for sensitivity and understanding may help counterbalance the effects of poverty and family problems. And because they are more verbally proficient, many females may develop social skills that help them deal with conflict without resorting to violence. Females are taught to be less aggressive and to view belligerence as a lack of self-control—a conclusion that is unlikely to be reached by a male.

Girls are usually taught—directly or indirectly—to respond to provocation by feeling anxious and depressed, whereas boys are encouraged to retaliate. Overall, when they are provoked, females are much more likely to feel distressed than males, experiencing sadness, anxiety, and uneasiness. Although females may get angry as often as males, many have been taught to blame themselves for harboring such negative feelings. Females are therefore much more likely than males to respond to anger with feelings of depression, anxiety, fear, and shame. Although females are socialized to fear that their anger will harm valued relationships, males react with "moral outrage," looking to blame others for their discomfort.[99]

Cognitive Differences Psychologists note significant cognitive differences between boys and girls that may impact on their antisocial behaviors. Girls have been found to be superior to boys in verbal ability, whereas boys test higher in visual-spatial performance. Girls acquire language faster, learning to speak earlier and faster with better pronunciation. Girls are far less likely to have reading problems than boys, whereas boys do much better on standardized math tests (this difference is attributed by some experts to boys receiving more attention from math teachers.) In most cases these cognitive differences are small, narrowing, and usually attributed to cultural expectations. When given training, girls demonstrate an ability to increase their visual-spatial skills to the point that their abilities become indistinguishable from the ability of boys.

Cognitive differences may contribute to behavioral variations. Even at an early age, girls are found to be more empathic than boys—that is, more capable of understanding and relating to the feelings of others.[100] Empathy for others may help shield girls from antisocial acts because they are more likely to understand a victim's suffering. Girls are more concerned with relationship and feeling issues, and they are less interested than boys are in competing for material success. Boys who are not tough and aggressive are labeled sissies and cry babies. In contrast, girls are expected to form closer bonds with their friends and share feelings. When faced with conflict, women might be more likely to attempt to negotiate, rather than to either respond passively or to physically resist, especially when they perceive increased threat of harm or death.[101]

Feminist Views In the 1970s liberal feminist theory focused attention on the social and economic roles of women in society and their relationship to female crime rates.[102] This view suggested that the traditionally lower crime rate for women could be explained by their "second-class" economic and social position. As women's social roles changed and their lifestyles became more like men's, it was believed that their crime rates would converge. Criminologists, responding to this research, began to refer to the "new female criminal." The rapid increase in the female crime rate, especially in what had traditionally been male-oriented crimes (such as burglary and larceny), supports the feminist view. In addition, self-report studies seem to indicate that (a) the pattern of female criminality, if not its frequency, is quite similar to that of male criminality, and (b) the factors that predispose male criminals to crime have an equal impact on female criminals.[103]

Is Convergence Likely? Although male arrest rates are still considerably higher than female rates, female arrest rates seem to be increasing at a faster pace; it is possible that they may eventually converge. Women are committing more crime and young girls are joining gangs in record numbers.[104]

Although these trends indicate that gender differences in the crime rate may be eroding, some criminologists remain skeptical about the data. They find that gender-based crime rate differences are still significant; the "emancipation of women" may have had relatively little influence on female crime rates.[105] For one thing, many female criminals come from the socioeconomic class least affected by the women's movement; their crimes seem more a function of economic inequality than women's rights. For another, the offense patterns of women are still quite different from those of men. Though males still commit a disproportionate share of serious crimes such as robbery, burglary, murder, and assault, most female criminals are still engaging in petty property crimes such as welfare and credit card fraud, and public order crimes such as prostitution.[106] How then can increases in female arrest rates be explained? According to Darrell Steffensmeier and his associates, these arrest trends may be explained more by changes in police activity than in criminal activity: police today may be more willing to arrest girls for minor crimes; police are making more arrests for crimes that occur at school and in the home; police are responding more vigorously to public demands for action and therefore are less likely to use their discretion to help females.[107] Police may also be abandoning their traditional deference toward women in an effort to be "gender neutral." In addition, changing laws such as dual arrest laws in domestic cases, which mandate both parties be taken into custody, result in more women suffering arrest in domestic incidents.[108]

Race and Crime

Official crime data indicate that minority group members are involved in a disproportionate share of criminal activity. African Americans make up about 12 percent of the general population, yet they account for about 40 percent of Part I violent crime arrests and 30 percent of property crime arrests. They also are responsible for a disproportionate number of Part II arrests (except for alcohol-related arrests, which detain primarily white offenders).

It is possible that these data reflect true racial differences in the crime rate, but it is also likely that they reflect bias in the justice process. We can evaluate this issue by comparing racial differences in self-report data with those found in official delinquency records. Charges of racial discrimination in the justice process would be substantiated if whites and blacks self-reported equal numbers of crimes, but minorities were arrested and prosecuted far more often.

Early efforts by noted criminologists Leroy Gould in Seattle, Harwin Voss in Honolulu, and Ronald Akers in seven

© AP Images/Steve Yeater

Empirical evidence shows that, in at least some jurisdictions, young African American males are treated more harshly by the criminal and juvenile justice systems than are members of any other group. Elements of institutional racism have become so endemic that terms such as "DWB" (Driving While Black) are now part of the vernacular, used to signify the fact that young African American motorists are routinely stopped by police.

midwestern states found virtually no relationship between race and self-reported delinquency.[109] These research efforts supported a case for police bias in the arrest decision. Other, more recent self-report studies that use large national samples of youths have also found little evidence of racial disparity in crimes committed.[110] Monitoring the Future data indicate that, if anything, black youths self-report less delinquent behavior and substance abuse than whites.[111] These and other self-report studies seem to indicate that the delinquent behavior rates of black and white teenagers are generally similar and that differences in arrest statistics may indicate a differential selection policy by police.[112] Suspects who are poor, minority, and male are more likely to be formally arrested than suspects who are white, affluent, and female.[113]

Racial differences in the crime rate remain an extremely sensitive issue. Although official arrest records indicate that African Americans are arrested at a higher rate than members of other racial groups, self-report data, which indicates greater equality between the races, suggest arrest rate differences are an artifact of justice system bias.[114] Some critics charge that police

54   PART ONE   CONCEPTS OF CRIME, LAW, AND CRIMINOLOGY

officers routinely use "racial profiling" to stop African Americans and search their cars without probable cause or reasonable suspicion. Police officers, they glibly suggest, have created a new form of traffic offense called DWB, "driving while black."[115] National surveys of driving practices show that young black and Latino males are more likely to be stopped by police and suffer citations, searches, and arrests, as well as be the target of force even though they are no more likely to be in the possession of illegal contraband than white drivers.[116]

Although the official statistics (such as UCR arrest data) may reflect discriminatory justice system practices, African Americans are arrested for a disproportionate amount of serious violent crime, such as robbery and murder, and it is improbable that police discretion and/or bias *alone* could account for these proportions. It is doubtful that police routinely release white killers, robbers, and rapists while arresting violent black offenders who commit the same offenses.[117] How can these racial differences in serious crimes be explained?

Racism and Discrimination To explain racial and ethnic differences in the violent crime rate, criminologists focus on the impact of economic deprivation and the legacy of racism discrimination on personality and behavior.[118] The fact that U.S. culture influences African American crime rates is underscored by the fact that black violence rates are much lower in other nations—both those that are predominantly white, such as Canada, and those that are predominantly black, such as Nigeria.[119]

Some criminologists view black crime as a function of socialization in a society where the black family was torn apart and black culture destroyed in such a way that recovery has proven impossible. Early experiences, beginning with slavery, have left a wound that has been deepened by racism and lack of opportunity.[120] Children of the slave society were thrust into a system of forced dependency and ambivalence and antagonism toward one's self and group.

In an important work, *All God's Children: The Bosket Family and the American Tradition of Violence*, crime reporter Fox Butterfield chronicles the history of the Boskets, a black family, through five generations.[121] He focuses on Willie Bosket, who is charming, captivating, and brilliant. He is also one of the worst criminals in the New York State penal system. By the time he was in his teens, he had committed more than 200 armed robberies and 25 stabbings. Butterfield shows how early struggles in the South, with its violent slave culture, led directly to Willie Bosket's rage and violence on the streets of New York City. Beginning in South Carolina in the 1700s, the southern slave society was a place where white notions of honor demanded immediate retaliation for the smallest slight. According to Butterfield, contemporary black violence is a tradition inherited from white southern violence. The need for respect has turned into a cultural mandate that can provoke retaliation at the slightest hint of insult.

Institutional Racism Racism is still an element of daily life in the African American community, a factor that undermines faith in social and political institutions and weakens confidence in the justice system. According to the racial threat theory, as the percentage of African Americans in the population increases so too does the amount of social control that police direct at blacks.[122]

While the racial threat theory has received only mixed support, there is a significant body of research showing that the justice system may be racially biased.[123] Research shows that black and Latino adults are less likely to receive bail in violent crime cases than whites, and that minority juveniles are more likely to be kept in detention pending trial in juvenile court.[124] There is also evidence that African Americans, especially those who are indigent or unemployed, receive longer prison sentences than whites with the same employment status. It is possible that judges impose harsher punishments on unemployed African Americans because they view them as "social dynamite," considering them more dangerous and more likely to recidivate than white offenders.[125] Yet when African Americans are victims of crime, their predicaments receive less public concern and media attention than that afforded white victims.[126] Murders involving whites (and females) are much more likely to be punished with death than those whose victims are black males, a fact not lost on the minority population.[127]

In his book *Search and Destroy*, correctional reformer Jerome Miller spells out how millions of young African Americans acquire a criminal record each year because police officers abuse their authority. Conservative politicians complain about providing welfare because they believe government should stay out of people's lives, but they do not mind the traumatic intrusion to the black community being made by agents of the criminal justice system who seem bent on "identifying and managing unruly groups."[128] Differential enforcement practices take their toll on the black community. A national survey found that more that 13 percent of all African American males have lost the right to vote, that in seven states 25 percent have been disenfranchised, and in two states, Florida and Alabama, 33 percent of black males have lost their voting privileges.[129] It is not surprising that African Americans of all social classes hold negative attitudes toward the justice system and view it as an arbitrary and unfair institution.[130]

Economic and Social Disparity Racial and ethnic differentials in crime rates may also be tied to economic and social disparity. Racial and ethnic minorities are often forced to live in high crime areas where the risk of victimization is significant. People who witness violent crime and are victimized may themselves engage in violence.[131]

Racial and ethnic minorities face a greater degree of social isolation and economic deprivation than the white majority, a condition that has been linked by empirical research to high violence rates.[132] Not helping the situation is the fact that during tough economic times, blacks and whites may find themselves competing for shrinking job opportunities. As economic competition between the races grows, interracial homicides do likewise; economic and political rivalries lead to greater levels of interracial violence.[133]

Even during times of economic growth, lower-class African Americans are left out of the economic mainstream, a fact that meets with a growing sense of frustration and failure.[134] As a result of being shut out of educational and economic opportunities enjoyed by the rest of society, this population may be prone to the lure of illegitimate gain and criminality. African Americans living in lower-class inner-city areas may be disproportionately violent because they are exposed to more violence in their daily lives than other racial and economic groups.[135] Many black youths are forced to attend essentially segregated schools that are underfunded and deteriorated, a condition that elevates the likelihood of their being incarcerated in adulthood.[136]

Family Dissolution Family dissolution in the minority community may be tied to low employment rates among African American males, which places a strain on marriages. The relatively large number of single, female-headed households in these communities may be tied to the high mortality rate among African American males due in part to their increased risk of early death by disease and violence.[137] When families are weakened or disrupted, their social control is compromised. It is not surprising that divorce and separation rates are significantly associated with homicide rates in the African American community.[138]

connections

According to some criminologists, racism has created isolated subcultures that espouse violence as a way of coping with conflict situations. Exasperation and frustration among minority group members who feel powerless to fit into middle-class society are manifested in aggression. This view is discussed further in Chapter 10, which reviews the subculture of violence theory.

Is Convergence Possible? Considering these overwhelming social problems, is it possible that racial crime rates will soon converge? One argument is that if economic conditions improve in the minority community, differences in crime rates will eventually disappear.[139] A trend toward residential integration, underway since 1980, may also help reduce crime rate differentials.[140] Convergence in crime rates will occur if economic and social obstacles can be removed.

In sum, the weight of the evidence shows that although there is little difference in the self-reported crime rates of racial groups, Hispanics and African Americans are more likely to be arrested for serious violent crimes. The causes of minority crime have been linked to poverty, racism, hopelessness, lack of opportunity, and urban problems experienced by all too many African American citizens.

Chronic Offenders/Criminal Careers

Crime data show that most offenders commit a single criminal act and upon arrest discontinue their antisocial activity. Others commit a few less serious crimes. A small group of criminal offenders, however, account for a majority of all criminal offenses. These persistent offenders are referred to as **career criminals** or **chronic offenders**. The concept of the chronic or career offender is most closely associated with the research efforts of Marvin Wolfgang, Robert Figlio, and Thorsten Sellin.[141] In their landmark 1972 study, *Delinquency in a Birth Cohort*, they used official records to follow the criminal careers of a cohort of 9,945 boys born in Philadelphia in 1945 from the time of their birth until they reached 18 years of age in 1963. Official police records were used to identify delinquents. About one-third of the boys (3,475) had some police contact. The remaining two-thirds (6,470) had none. Each delinquent was given a seriousness weight score for every delinquent act.[142] The weighting of delinquent acts allowed the researchers to differentiate between a simple assault requiring no medical attention for the victim and serious battery in which the victim needed hospitalization. The best-known discovery of Wolfgang and his associates was that of the so-called chronic offender. The cohort data indicated that 54 percent (1,862) of the sample's delinquent youths were repeat offenders, whereas the remaining 46 percent (1,613) were one-time offenders. The repeaters could be further categorized as nonchronic recidivists and chronic recidivists. The former consisted of 1,235 youths who had been arrested more than once but fewer than five times and who made up 35.6 percent of all delinquents. The latter were a group of 627 boys arrested five times or more, who accounted for 18 percent of the delinquents and 6 percent of the total sample of 9,945 (Figure 2.10).

The chronic offenders (known today as "the chronic 6 percent") were involved in the most dramatic amounts of delinquent behavior: They were responsible for 5,305 offenses, or 51.9 percent of all the offenses committed by the cohort. Even more striking was the involvement of chronic offenders in serious criminal acts. Of the entire sample, the chronic 6 percent committed 71 percent of the homicides, 73 percent of the rapes, 82 percent of the robberies, and 69 percent of the aggravated assaults.

Wolfgang and his associates found that arrests and court experience did little to deter the chronic offender. In fact, punishment was inversely related to chronic offending: the more stringent the sanction chronic offenders received, the more likely they would be to engage in repeated criminal behavior.

In a second cohort study, Wolfgang and his associates selected a new, larger birth cohort, born in Philadelphia in 1958, which contained both male and female subjects.[143] Although the proportion of delinquent youths was about the same as that in the 1945 cohort, they again found a similar pattern of chronic offending. Chronic female delinquency was relatively rare— only 1 percent of the females in the survey were chronic offenders. Wolfgang's pioneering effort to identify the chronic career offender has been replicated by a number of other researchers in a variety of locations in the United States.[144] The chronic offender has also been found abroad.[145]

What Causes Chronicity? As might be expected, kids who have been exposed to a variety of personal and social problems at an early age are the most at risk to repeat offending; a concept referred to as **early onset**. One important study

Figure 2.10 Distribution of Offenses in the Philadelphia Cohort

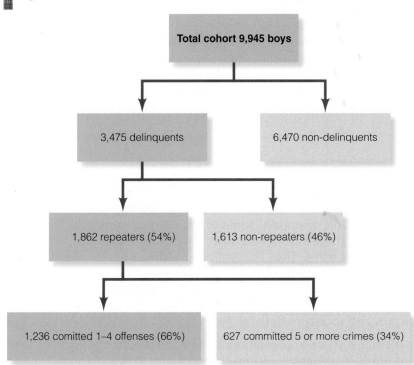

Total cohort 9,945 boys

3,475 delinquents — 6,470 non-delinquents

1,862 repeaters (54%) — 1,613 non-repeaters (46%)

1,236 comitted 1–4 offenses (66%) — 627 committed 5 or more crimes (34%)

Source: Marvin Wolfgang, Robert Figlio, and Thorsten Sellin, *Delinquency in a Birth Cohort* (Chicago: University of Chicago Press, 1972). Reprinted with permission of University of Chicago Press.

of delinquent offenders in Orange County, California, conducted by Michael Schumacher and Gwen Kurz, found several factors (see Exhibit 2.2) that characterized the chronic offender, including problems in the home and at school.[146] Other research studies have found that involvement in criminal activity (such as getting arrested before age 15), relatively low intellectual development, and parental drug involvement, were key predictive factors for chronicity.[147] Offenders who accumulate large debts, use drugs, and resort to violence are more likely to persist.[148] In contrast, those who spend time in a juvenile facility and later in an adult prison are more likely to desist.[149]

Persistence: The Continuity of Crime One of the most important findings from the cohort studies is that persistent juvenile offenders are the ones most likely to continue their criminal careers into adulthood.[150] Paul Tracy and Kimberly Kempf-Leonard followed up all subjects in the second 1958 cohort and found that two-thirds of delinquent offenders desisted from crime, but those who started their delinquent careers early and who committed serious violent crimes throughout adolescence were the most likely to persist as adults.[151] This phenomenon is referred to as persistence or the continuity of crime.[152]

Children who are found to be disruptive and antisocial as early as age 5 or 6 are the most likely to exhibit stable, long-term patterns of disruptive behavior throughout adolescence.[153] They have measurable behavior problems in areas such as learning and motor skills, cognitive abilities, family relations, and other areas of social, psychological, and physical functioning.[154]

Youthful offenders who persist are more likely to abuse alcohol, get into trouble while in military service, become economically dependent, have lower aspirations, get divorced or separated, and have a weak employment record.[155] They do not specialize in one type of crime; rather, they engage in a variety of criminal acts, including theft, use of drugs, and violent offenses.

Implications of the Chronic Offender Concept The findings of the cohort studies and the discovery of the chronic offender have revitalized criminological theory. If relatively few offenders become chronic, persistent criminals, then perhaps they possess some individual trait that is responsible for their behavior. Most people exposed to troublesome social conditions, such as poverty, do not become chronic offenders, so it is unlikely that social conditions alone can cause chronic offending. Traditional theories of criminal behavior have failed to distinguish between chronic and occasional offenders. They concentrate more on explaining why people begin to commit crime and pay scant attention to why people stop offending. The discovery of the chronic offender 30 years ago forced criminologists to consider such issues as persistence and desistance in

EXHIBIT 2.2

Characteristics That Predict Chronic Offending

School Behavior/Performance Factor

- Attendance problems (truancy or a pattern of skipping school)
- Behavior problems (recent suspensions or expulsion)
- Poor grades (failing two or more classes)

Family Problem Factor

- Poor parental supervision and control
- Significant family problems (illness, substance abuse, discord)
- Criminal family members
- Documented child abuse, neglect, or family violence

Substance Abuse Factor

- Alcohol or drug use (by minors in any way but experimentation)

Delinquency Factor

- Stealing pattern of behavior
- Runaway pattern of behavior
- Gang member or associate

Source: Michael Schumacher and Gwen Kurz, *The 8% Solution: Preventing Serious Repeat Juvenile Crime* (Thousand Oaks, CA: Sage, 1999).

their explanations of crime; more recent theories account for not only the onset of criminality but also its termination.

The chronic offender has become a central focus of crime control policy. Apprehension and punishment seem to have little effect on the offending behavior of chronic offenders, and most repeat their criminal acts after their correctional release.[156] Because chronic offenders rarely learn from their mistakes, sentencing policies designed to incapacitate chronic offenders for long periods of time without hope of probation or parole have been established. Incapacitation rather than rehabilitation is the goal. Among the policies spurred by the chronic offender concept are mandatory sentences for violent or drug-related crimes, "**three strikes**" policies, which require people convicted of a third felony offense to serve a mandatory life sentence, and "truth in sentencing" policies, which require that convicted felons spend a significant portion of their sentence behind bars. Whether such policies can reduce crime rates or are merely "get tough" measures designed to placate conservative voters remains to be seen.

THINKING LIKE A CRIMINOLOGIST

The planning director for the State Department of Juvenile Justice has asked for your advice on how to reduce the threat of chronic offenders. Some of the more conservative members of her staff seem to believe that these kids need a strict dose of rough justice if they are to be turned away from a life of crime. They believe juvenile delinquents who are punished harshly are less likely to recidivate than youths who receive lesser punishments such as community corrections or probation. In addition, they believe that hard-core, violent offenders deserve to be punished; excessive concern for offenders and not their acts ignores the rights of victims and society in general.

The planning director is unsure whether such an approach can reduce the threat of chronic offending. Can tough punishment produce deviant identities that lock kids into a criminal way of life? She is concerned that a strategy stressing punishment will have relatively little impact on chronic offenders and, if anything, may cause escalation in serious criminal behaviors. She has asked you for your professional advice.

Writing Exercise Write a letter to the planning director outlining your recommendations for dealing with chronic offenders in the state juvenile justice system. On the one hand, the system must be sensitive to the adverse effects of stigma and labeling. On the other hand, the need for control and deterrence must not be ignored. Is it possible to reconcile these two opposing views?

Doing Research on the Web To help formulate your recommendations, review these Web-based resources:

▪ Eric B. Schnurer and Charles R. Lyons, "Turning Chronic Juvenile Offenders into Productive Citizens: Comprehensive Model Emerging."

▪ For an international view, see "Juvenile Offending: Predicting Persistence and Determining the Cost-Effectiveness of Intervention."

These websites can be accessed via **www.thomsonedu.com/criminaljustice/siegel.**

SUMMARY

▪ Criminologists use various research methods to gather information that will shed light on criminal behavior. These include surveys, cohort studies, official record studies, experiments, observations, meta-analysis, and systematic reviews.

▪ The FBI's Uniform Crime Report is an annual tally of crime reported to local police departments. It is the nation's official crime database.

▪ The National Crime Victimization Survey (NCVS) employs large national samples in order to estimate the total number of criminal incidents, including those not reported to police.

- Self-report surveys ask respondents about their own criminal activity. They are useful in measuring crimes rarely reported to police, such as drug usage.

- Each data source has its strengths and weaknesses, and although different from one another, they actually agree on the nature of criminal behavior.

- Crime rates peaked in the early 1990s and have been in sharp decline ever since. The murder rate has undergone a particularly steep decline.

- A number of factors are believed to influence the crime rate, including the economy, drug use, gun availability, and crime control policies such as adding police and putting more criminals in prison.

- It is difficult to gauge future trends. Some experts forecast an increase in crime, while others foresee a long-term decline in the crime rate.

- The data sources show stable patterns in the crime rate.

- Ecological patterns show that some areas of the country are more crime prone than others, that there are seasons and times for crime, and that these patterns are quite stable.

- There is also evidence of gender and age gaps in the crime rate: men commit more crime than women, and young people commit more crime than the elderly. Crime data show that people commit less crime as they age, but the significance and cause of this pattern is not completely understood.

- Similarly, racial and class patterns appear in the crime rate. However, it is unclear whether these are true differences or a function of discriminatory law enforcement. Some criminologists suggest that institutional racism, such as police profiling, accounts for the racial differences in the crime rate. Others believe that high African American crime rates are a function of living in a racially segregated society.

- One of the most important findings in the crime statistics is the existence of the chronic offender, a repeat criminal responsible for a significant amount of all law violations. Chronic offenders begin their careers early in life and, rather than aging out of crime, persistently offend into adulthood. The discovery of the chronic offender has led to the study of developmental criminology—why people persist, desist, terminate, or escalate their deviant behavior.

- **ThomsonNOW** Maximize your study time by using ThomsonNOW's diagnostic study plan to help you review this chapter. The Personalized Study plan will help you identify areas on which you should concentrate; provide interactive exercises to help you master the chapter concepts; and provide a post-test to confirm you are ready to move on to the next chapter.

KEY TERMS

Uniform Crime Report (UCR) (30)
Part I crimes (31)
Part II crimes (31)
cleared crimes (31)
National Incident-Based Reporting System (NIBRS) (33)
self-report survey (34)
sampling (34)
population (34)
cross-sectional survey (34)

National Crime Victimization Survey (NCVS) (36)
cohort (37)
retrospective cohort study (37)
meta-analysis (38)
systematic review (38)
instrumental crimes (47)
expressive crimes (47)
aging out (52)
masculinity hypothesis (53)

chivalry hypothesis (53)
liberal feminist theory (53)
career criminal (56)
chronic offender (56)
early onset (56)
persistence (57)
continuity of crime (57)
three strikes (58)

CRITICAL THINKING QUESTIONS

1. Would you answer honestly if a national crime survey asked you about your criminal behavior, including drinking and drug use? If not, why not? If you would not answer honestly, do you question the accuracy of self-report surveys?

2. How would you explain gender differences in the crime rate? Why

do you think males are more violent than females?

3. Assuming that males are more violent than females, does that mean crime has a biological rather than a social basis (because males and females share a similar environment)?

4. The UCR reports that crime rates are higher in large cities than in small

towns. What does that tell us about the effects of TV, films, and music on teenage behavior?

5. What social and environmental factors do you believe influence the crime rate? Do you think a national emergency would increase or decrease crime rates?

NOTES

1. Information on the Rudolph case can be obtained at www.cnn.com/2003/US/05/31/rudolph.arrest/ (accessed June 13, 2007).

2. Cited on http://en.wikipedia.org/wiki/Eric_Rudolph (accessed June 13, 2007).

3. Mirka Smolej and Janne Kivivuori, "The Relation Between Crime News and Fear of Violence," *Journal of Scandinavian Studies in Criminology and Crime Prevention* 7 (2006): 211–227.

4. FBI, *Crime in the United States, 2005* (Washington, DC: U.S. Government Printing Office, 2006). Herein cited in notes as FBI, Uniform Crime Report, and referred to in text as Uniform Crime Report or UCR. When possible, data has been updated with preliminary 2006 results.

5. Richard Felson, Steven Messner, Anthony Hoskin, and Glenn Deane, "Reasons for Reporting and Not Reporting Domestic Violence to the Police," *Criminology* 40 (2002): 617–648.

6. Shannan Catalano, *Criminal Victimization 2005* (Washington, DC: Bureau of Justice Statistics, 2006). Herein cited as NCVS, 2005.

7. Duncan Chappell, Gilbert Geis, Stephen Schafer, and Larry Siegel, "Forcible Rape: A Comparative Study of Offenses Known to the Police in Boston and Los Angeles," in *Studies in the Sociology of Sex*, ed. James Henslin (New York: Appleton Century Crofts, 1971), pp. 169–193.

8. Patrick Jackson, "Assessing the Validity of Official Data on Arson," *Criminology* 26 (1988): 181–195.

9. Lawrence Sherman and Barry Glick, "The Quality of Arrest Statistics," *Police Foundation Reports* 2 (1984): 1–8.

10. David Seidman and Michael Couzens, "Getting the Crime Rate Down: Political Pressure and Crime Reporting," *Law and Society Review* 8 (1974): 457.

11. Ariel Hart, "Report Finds Atlanta Police Cut Figures on Crimes," *New York Times*, 21 February 2004, p. A3.

12. Robert Davis and Bruce Taylor, "A Proactive Response to Family Violence: The Results of a Randomized Experiment," *Criminology* 35 (1997): 307–333.

13. Robert O'Brien, "Police Productivity and Crime Rates: 1973–1992," *Criminology* 34 (1996): 183–207.

14. Leonard Savitz, "Official Statistics," in *Contemporary Criminology*, eds. Leonard Savitz and Norman Johnston (New York: Wiley, 1982), pp. 3–15.

15. FBI, *UCR Handbook* (Washington, DC: U.S. Government Printing Office, 1998), p. 33.

16. Lynn Addington, "The Effect of NIBRS Reporting on Item Missing Data in Murder Cases," *Homicide Studies* 8 (2004): 193–213.

17. Michael Gottfredson and Travis Hirschi, "The Methodological Adequacy of Longitudinal Research on Crime," *Criminology* 25 (1987): 581–614.

18. A pioneering effort in self-report research is A. L. Porterfield, *Youth in Trouble* (Fort Worth, TX: Leo Potishman Foundation, 1946); for a review, see Robert Hardt and George Bodine, *Development of Self-Report Instruments in Delinquency Research: A Conference Report* (Syracuse, NY: Syracuse University Youth Development Center, 1965). See also Fred Murphy, Mary Shirley, and Helen Witner, "The Incidence of Hidden Delinquency," *American Journal of Orthopsychology* 16 (1946): 686–696.

19. See John Paul Wright and Francis Cullen, "Juvenile Involvement in Occupational Delinquency," *Criminology* 38 (2000): 863–896.

20. Christiane Brems, Mark Johnson, David Neal, and Melinda Freemon, "Childhood Abuse History and Substance Use Among Men and Women Receiving Detoxification Services," *American Journal of Drug and Alcohol Abuse* 30 (2004): 799–821.

21. Lloyd Johnston, Patrick O'Malley, and Jerald Bachman, *Monitoring the Future, 2006* (Ann Arbor, MI: Institute for Social Research, 2006).

22. D. Wayne Osgood, Lloyd Johnston, Patrick O'Malley, and Jerald Bachman, "The Generality of Deviance in Late Adolescence and Early Adulthood," *American Sociological Review* 53 (1988): 81–93.

23. Leonore Simon, "Validity and Reliability of Violent Juveniles: A Comparison of Juvenile Self-Reports with Adult Self-Reports Incarcerated in Adult Prisons," paper presented at the annual meeting of the American Society of Criminology, Boston, November 1995, p. 26.

24. Stephen Cernkovich, Peggy Giordano, and Meredith Pugh, "Chronic Offenders: The Missing Cases in Self-Report Delinquency Research," *Journal of Criminal Law and Criminology* 76 (1985): 705–732.

25. Terence Thornberry, Beth Bjerregaard, and William Miles, "The Consequences of Respondent Attrition in Panel Studies: A Simulation Based on the Rochester Youth Development Study," *Journal of Quantitative Criminology* 9 (1993): 127–158.

26. Julia Yun Soo Kim, Michael Fendrich, and Joseph S. Wislar, "The Validity of Juvenile Arrestees' Drug Use Reporting: A Gender Comparison," *Journal of Research in Crime and Delinquency* 37 (2000): 419–432.

27. Donald Tomaskovic-Devey, Cynthia Pfaff Wright, Ronald Czaja, and Kirk Miller, "Self-reports of Police Speeding Stops by Race: Results from the North Carolina Reverse Record Check Survey," *Journal of Quantitative Criminology* 22 (2006): 279–297.

28. See Spencer Rathus and Larry Siegel, "Crime and Personality Revisited: Effects of MMPI Sets on Self-Report Studies," *Criminology* 18 (1980): 245–251; John Clark and Larry Tifft, "Polygraph and Interview Validation of Self-Reported Deviant Behavior," *American Sociological Review* 31 (1966): 516–523.

29. Mallie Paschall, Miriam Ornstein, and Robert Flewelling, "African-American Male Adolescents' Involvement in the Criminal Justice System: The Criterion Validity of Self-Report Measures in Prospective Study," *Journal of Research in Crime and Delinquency* 38 (2001): 174–187.

30. Jennifer Roberts, Edward Mulvey, Julie Horney, John Lewis, and Michael Arter, "A Test of Two Methods of Recall for Violent Events," *Journal of Quantitative Criminology* 21 (2005): 175–193.

31. Lila Kazemian and David Farrington, "Comparing the Validity of Prospective, Retrospective, and Official Onset for Different Offending Categories," *Journal of Quantitative Criminology* 21 (2005): 127–147.

32. Catalano, NCVS, 2005

33. L. Edward Wells and Joseph Rankin, "Juvenile Victimization: Convergent Validation of Alternative Measurements," *Journal of Research in Crime and Delinquency* 32 (1995): 287–307.

34. Barbara Warner and Brandi Wilson Coomer, "Neighborhood Drug Arrest Rates: Are They a Meaningful Indicator of Drug Activity? A Research Note," *Journal of Research in Crime and Delinquency* 40 (2003): 123–139.

35. Alfred Blumstein, Jacqueline Cohen, and Richard Rosenfeld, "Trend and Deviation in Crime Rates: A Comparison of UCR and NCVS Data for Burglary and Robbery," *Criminology* 29 (1991): 237–248. See also Michael Hindelang, Travis Hirschi, and Joseph Weis, *Measuring Delinquency* (Beverly Hills: Sage, 1981).

36. David Farrington, Lloyd Ohlin, and James Q. Wilson, *Understanding and Controlling Crime* (New York: Springer-Verlag, 1986), pp. 11–18.

37. Claire Sterk-Elifson, "Just for Fun? Cocaine Use among Middle-Class Women," *Journal of Drug Issues* 26 (1996): 63–76.

38. Ibid., p. 63.

39. William F. Whyte, *Street Corner Society* (Chicago: University of Chicago Press, 1955).

40. Herman Schwendinger and Julia Schwendinger, *Adolescent Subcultures and Delinquency* (New York: Praeger, 1985).

41. David Farrington and Brandon Welsh, "Improved Street Lighting and Crime Prevention," *Justice Quarterly* 19 (2002): 313–343.

42. Colleen McCue, Emily Stone, and Teresa Gooch, "Data Mining and Value-Added Analysis," *FBI Law Enforcement Bulletin* 72 (2003): 1–6.

43. Jerry Ratcliffe, "Aoristic Signatures and the Spatio-Temporal Analysis of High Volume Crime Patterns," *Journal of Quantitative Criminology* 18 (2002): 23–43.

44. Clarence Schrag, *Crime and Justice: American Style* (Washington, DC: U.S. Government Printing Office, 1971), p. 17.

45. Thomas Bernard, "Juvenile Crime and the Transformation of Juvenile Justice: Is There a Juvenile Crime Wave?" *Justice Quarterly* 16 (1999): 336–356.

46. FBI, *Crime in the United States, 2006*, Preliminary data, www.fbi.gov/ucr/06prelim/index.html (accessed June 5, 2007).

47. Catalano, NCVS, 2005.

48. Steven Levitt, "The Limited Role of Changing Age Structure in Explaining Aggregate Crime Rates," *Criminology* 37 (1999): 581–599.

49. Darrell Steffensmeier and Miles Harer, "Did Crime Rise or Fall During the Reagan Presidency? The Effects of an 'Aging' U.S. Population on the Nation's Crime Rate," *Journal of Research in Crime and Delinquency* 28 (1991): 330–339.

50. Darrell Steffensmeier and Miles Harer, "Making Sense of Recent U.S. Crime Trends, 1980 to 1996/1998: Age Composition Effects and Other Explanations," *Journal of Research in Crime and Delinquency* 36 (1999): 235–274.

51. Ibid., p. 265.

52. Ralph Weisheit and L. Edward Wells, "The Future of Crime in Rural America," *Journal of Crime and Justice* 22 (1999): 1–22.

53. Ellen Cohn, "The Effect of Weather and Temporal Variations on Calls for Police Service," *American Journal of Police* 15 (1996): 23–43.

54. R. A. Baron, "Aggression as a Function of Ambient Temperature and Prior Anger Arousal," *Journal of Personality and Social Psychology* 21 (1972): 183–189.

55. Brad Bushman, Morgan Wang, and Craig Anderson, "Is the Curve Relating Temperature to Aggression Linear or Curvilinear? Assaults and Temperature in Minneapolis Reexamined," *Journal of Personality and Social Psychology* 89 (2005): 62–66.

56. Paul Bell, "Reanalysis and Perspective in the Heat-Aggression Debate," *Journal of Personality and Social Psychology* 89 (2005): 71–73.

57. Ellen Cohn, "The Prediction of Police Calls for Service: The Influence of Weather and Temporal Variables on Rape and Domestic Violence," *Journal of Environmental Psychology* 13 (1993): 71–83.

58. John Simister and Cary Cooper, "Thermal Stress in the U.S.A.: Effects on Violence and on Employee Behaviour," *Stress and Health* 21 (2005): 3–15.

59. James Rotton and Ellen Cohn, "Outdoor Temperature, Climate Control, and Criminal Assault," *Environment and Behavior* 36 (2004): 276–306.

60. See generally Franklin Zimring and Gordon Hawkins, *Crime Is Not the Problem: Lethal Violence in America* (New York Oxford University Press, 1997).

61. Ibid., p. 36.

62. Gary Kleck and Marc Gertz, "Armed Resistance to Crime: The Prevalence and Nature of Self-Defense with a Gun," *Journal of Criminal Law and Criminology* 86 (1995): 219–249.

63. Robert Nash Parker, "Bringing 'Booze' Back In: The Relationship between Alcohol and Homicide," *Journal of Research in Crime and Delinquency* 32 (1995): 3–38.

64. Victoria Brewer and M. Dwayne Smith, "Gender Inequality and Rates of Female Homicide Victimization across U.S. Cities," *Journal of Research in Crime and Delinquency* 32 (1995): 175–190.

65. James Short and F. Ivan Nye, "Extent of Unrecorded Juvenile Delinquency, Tentative Conclusions," *Journal of Criminal Law, Criminology, and Police Science* 49 (1958): 296–302.

66. Ivan Nye, James Short, and Virgil Olsen, "Socio-Economic Status and Delinquent Behavior," *American Journal of Sociology* 63 (1958): 381–389; Robert Dentler and Lawrence Monroe, "Social Correlates of Early Adolescent Theft," *American Sociological Review* 63 (1961): 733–743. See also Terence Thornberry and Margaret Farnworth, "Social Correlates of Criminal Involvement: Further Evidence of the Relationship between Social Status and Criminal Behavior," *American Sociological Review* 47 (1982): 505–518.

67. Charles Tittle, Wayne Villemez, and Douglas Smith, "The Myth of Social Class and Criminality: An Empirical Assessment of the Empirical Evidence," *American Sociological Review* 43 (1978): 643–656.

68. Charles Tittle and Robert Meier, "Specifying the SES/Delinquency Relationship," *Criminology* 28 (1990): 271–301.

69. R. Gregory Dunaway, Francis Cullen, Velmer Burton, and T. David Evans, "The Myth of Social Class and Crime Revisited: An Examination of Class and Adult Criminality," *Criminology* 38 (2000): 589–632.

70. Delbert Elliott and Suzanne Ageton, "Reconciling Race and Class Differences in Self-Reported and Official Estimates of Delinquency," *American Sociological Review* 45 (1980): 95–110.

71. See also Delbert Elliott and David Huizinga, "Social Class and Delinquent Behavior in a National Youth Panel: 1976–1980," *Criminology* 21 (1983): 149–177. For a similar view, see John Braithwaite, "The Myth of Social Class and Criminality Reconsidered," *American Sociological Review* 46 (1981): 35–58; Hindelang, Hirschi, and Weis, *Measuring Delinquency*, p. 196.

72. David Brownfield, "Social Class and Violent Behavior," *Criminology* 24 (1986): 421–439.

73. Douglas Smith and Laura Davidson, "Interfacing Indicators and Constructs in Criminological Research: A Note on the Comparability of Self-Report Violence Data for Race and Sex Groups," *Criminology* 24 (1986): 473–488.

74. Dunaway, Cullen, Burton, and Evans, "The Myth of Social Class and Crime Revisited."

75. Lauren Krivo and Ruth D. Peterson, "Labor Market Conditions and Violent Crime among Youth and Adults," *Sociological Perspectives* 47 (2004): 485–505.

76. Judith Blau and Peter Blau, "The Cost of Inequality: Metropolitan Structure and Violent Crime," *American Sociological Review* 147 (1982): 114–129; Richard Block, "Community Environment and Violent Crime," *Criminology* 17 (1979): 46–57; Robert Sampson, "Structural Sources of Variation in Race-Age-Specific Rates of Offending across Major U.S. Cities," *Criminology* 23 (1985): 647–673.

77. Chin-Chi Hsieh and M. D. Pugh, "Poverty, Income Inequality, and Violent Crime: A Meta-Analysis of Recent Aggregate Data Studies," *Criminal Justice Review* 18 (1993): 182–199.

78. Richard Miech, Avshalom Caspi, Terrie Moffitt, Bradley Entner Wright, and Phil Silva, "Low Socioeconomic Status and Mental Disorders: A Longitudinal Study of Selection and Causation during Young Adulthood," *American Journal of Sociology* 104 (1999): 1,096–1,131; Marvin Krohn, Alan Lizotte, and Cynthia Perez, "The Interrelationship between Substance Use and Precocious Transitions to Adult Sexuality," *Journal of Health and Social Behavior* 38 (1997): 87–103, at 88; Richard Jessor, "Risk Behavior in Adolescence: A Psychosocial Framework for Understanding and Action," in *Adolescents at Risk: Medical and Social Perspectives*, eds. D. E. Rogers and E. Ginzburg (Boulder, CO: Westview, 1992).

79. Robert Agnew, "A General Strain Theory of Community Differences in Crime Rates," *Journal of Research in Crime and Delinquency* 36 (1999): 123–155.

80. Bonita Veysey and Steven Messner, "Further Testing of Social Disorganization Theory: An Elaboration of Sampson and Groves's Community Structure and Crime," *Journal of Research in Crime and Delinquency* 36 (1999): 156–174.

81. Lance Hannon and James DeFronzo, "Welfare and Property Crime," *Justice Quarterly* 15 (1998): 273–288.

82. Alan Lizotte, Terence Thornberry, Marvin Krohn, Deborah Chard-Wierschem, and David McDowall, "Neighborhood Context and Delinquency: A Longitudinal Analysis," in *Cross National Longitudinal Research on Human Development and Criminal Behavior*, eds. E. M. Weitekamp and H. J. Kerner (Stavernstr, Netherlands: Kluwer, 1994), pp. 217–227.

83. Travis Hirschi and Michael Gottfredson, "Age and the Explanation of Crime," *American Journal of Sociology* 89 (1983): 552–584, at 581.

84. Darrell Steffensmeier and Cathy Streifel, "Age, Gender, and Crime across Three Historical Periods: 1935, 1960 and 1985," *Social Forces* 69 (1991): 869–894.

85. For a comprehensive review of crime and the elderly, see Kyle Kercher, "Causes and Correlates of Crime Committed by the Elderly," in *Critical Issues in Aging Policy,* eds. E. Borgatta and R. Montgomery (Beverly Hills: Sage, 1987), pp. 254–306; Darrell Steffensmeier, "The Invention of the 'New' Senior Citizen Criminal," *Research on Aging* 9 (1987): 281–311.

86. Hirschi and Gottfredson, "Age and the Explanation of Crime."

87. Robert Agnew, "An Integrated Theory of the Adolescent Peak in Offending," *Youth and Society* 34 (2003): 263–302.

88. Margo Wilson and Martin Daly, "Life Expectancy, Economic Inequality, Homicide, and Reproductive Timing in Chicago Neighbourhoods," *British Journal of Medicine* 314 (1997): 1,271–1,274.

89. Edward Mulvey and John LaRosa, "Delinquency Cessation and Adolescent Development: Preliminary Data," *American Journal of Orthopsychiatry* 56 (1986): 212–224.

90. James Q. Wilson and Richard Herrnstein, *Crime and Human Nature* (New York: Simon & Schuster, 1985): 126–147.

91. Mulvey and LaRosa, "Delinquency Cessation and Adolescent Development: Preliminary Data," p. 219.

92. Erich Labouvie, "Maturing Out of Substance Use: Selection and Self-Correction," *Journal of Drug Issues* 26 (1996): 457–474.

93. Cesare Lombroso, *The Female Offender* (New York: Appleton, 1920), p. 122.

94. Otto Pollack, *The Criminality of Women* (Philadelphia: University of Pennsylvania, 1950).

95. For a review of this issue, see Darrell Steffensmeier, "Assessing the Impact of the Women's Movement on Sex-Based Differences in the Handling of Adult Criminal Defendants," *Crime and Delinquency* 26 (1980): 344–357.

96. Alan Booth and D. Wayne Osgood, "The Influence of Testosterone on Deviance in Adulthood: Assessing and Explaining the Relationship," *Criminology* 31 (1993): 93–118.

97. This section relies on the following sources: Kristen Kling, Janet Shibley Hyde, Carolin Showers, and Brenda Buswell, "Gender Differences in Self-Esteem: A Meta Analysis," *Psychological Bulletin* 125 (1999): 470–500; Rolf Loeber and Dale Hay, "Key Issues in the Development of Aggression and Violence from Childhood to Early Adulthood," *Annual Review of Psychology* 48 (1997): 371–410; Darcy Miller, Catherine Trapani, Kathy Fejes-Mendoza, Carolyn Eggleston, and Donna Dwiggins, "Adolescent Female Offenders: Unique Considerations," *Adolescence* 30 (1995): 429–435; John Mirowsky and Catherine Ross, "Sex Differences in Distress: Real or Artifact?" *American Sociological Review* 60 (1995): 449–468;

Anne Campbell, *Men, Women and Aggression* (New York: Basic Books, 1993); Ann Beutel and Margaret Mooney Marini, "Gender and Values," *American Sociological Review* 60 (1995): 436–448; John Gibbs, Velmer Burton, Francis Cullen, T. David Evans, Leanne Fiftal Alarid, and R. Gregory Dunaway, "Gender, Self-Control, and Crime," *Journal of Research in Crime and Delinquency* 35 (1998): 123–147; David Rowe, Alexander Vazsonyi, and Daniel Flannery, "Sex Differences in Crime: Do Means and Within-Sex Variation Have Similar Causes?" *Journal of Research in Crime and Delinquency* 32 (1995): 84–100.

98. Jean Bottcher, "Social Practices of Gender: How Gender Relates to Delinquency in the Everyday Lives of High-Risk Youths," *Criminology* 39 (2001): 893–932.

99. Daniel Mears, Matthew Ploeger, and Mark Warr, "Explaining the Gender Gap in Delinquency: Peer Influence and Moral Evaluations of Behavior," *Journal of Research in Crime and Delinquency* 35 (1998): 251–266.

100. Lisa Broidy, Elizabeth Cauffman, and Dorothy Espelage, "Sex Differences in Empathy and Its Relation to Juvenile Offending," *Violence and Victims* 18 (2003): 503–516.

101. Debra Kaysen, Miranda Morris, Shireen Rizvi, and Patricia Resick, "Peritraumatic Responses and Their Relationship to Perceptions of Threat in Female Crime Victims," *Violence Against Women* 11 (2005): 1,515–1,535.

102. Freda Adler, *Sisters in Crime* (New York: McGraw-Hill, 1975); Rita James Simon, *The Contemporary Woman and Crime* (Washington, DC: U.S. Government Printing Office, 1975).

103. Rowe, Vazsonyi, and Flannery, "Sex Differences in Crime: Do Mean and Within-Sex Variation Have Similar Causes?"; Michael Hindelang, "Age, Sex, and the Versatility of Delinquency Involvements," *Social Forces* 14 (1971): 525–534; Martin Gold, *Delinquent Behavior in an American City* (Belmont, CA: Brooks/Cole, 1970); Gary Jensen and Raymond Eve, "Sex Differences in Delinquency: An Examination of Popular Sociological Explanations," *Criminology* 13 (1976): 427–448.

104. Finn-Aage Esbensen and Elizabeth Piper Deschenes, "A Multisite Examination of Youth Gang Membership: Does Gender Matter?" *Criminology* 36 (1998): 799–828.

105. Darrell Steffensmeier and Renee Hoffman Steffensmeier, "Trends in Female Delinquency," *Criminology* 18 (1980): 62–85; see also Darrell Steffensmeier and Renee Hoffman Steffensmeier, "Crime and the Contemporary Woman: An Analysis of Changing Levels of Female Property Crime, 1960–1975," *Social Forces* 57 (1978): 566–584; Joseph Weis, "Liberation and Crime: The Invention of the New Female Criminal," *Crime and Social Justice* 1 (1976): 17–27; Carol Smart, "The New Female Offender: Reality or Myth," *British Journal of Criminology* 19 (1979): 50–59; Steven Box

and Chris Hale, "Liberation/ Emancipation, Economic Marginalization or Less Chivalry," *Criminology* 22 (1984): 473–478.

106. Anne Campbell, Steven Muncer, and Daniel Bibel, "Female-Female Criminal Assault: An Evolutionary Perspective," *Journal of Research in Crime and Delinquency* 35 (1998): 413–428.

107. Darrell Steffensmeier Jennifer Schwartz, Hua Zhong, and Jeff Ackerman, "An Assessment of Recent Trends in Girls' Violence Using Diverse Longitudinal Sources: Is the Gender Gap Closing?" *Criminology* 43 (2005): 355–406.

108. Susan Miller, Carol Gregory, and Leeann Iovanni, "One Size Fits All? A Gender-Neutral Approach to a Gender-Specific Problem: Contrasting Batterer Treatment Programs for Male and Female Offenders," *Criminal Justice Policy Review* 16 (2005): 336–359.

109. Leroy Gould, "Who Defines Delinquency: A Comparison of Self-Report and Officially Reported Indices of Delinquency for Three Racial Groups," *Social Problems* 16 (1969): 325–336; Harwin Voss, "Ethnic Differentials in Delinquency in Honolulu," *Journal of Criminal Law, Criminology, and Police Science* 54 (1963): 322–327; Ronald Akers, Marvin Krohn, Marcia Radosevich, and Lonn Lanza-Kaduce, "Social Characteristics and Self-Reported Delinquency," in *Sociology of Delinquency,* ed. Gary Jensen (Beverly Hills: Sage, 1981), pp. 48–62.

110. David Huizinga and Delbert Elliott, "Juvenile Offenders: Prevalence, Offender Incidence, and Arrest Rates by Race," *Crime and Delinquency* 33 (1987): 206–223. See also Dale Dannefer and Russell Schutt, "Race and Juvenile Justice Processing in Court and Police Agencies," *American Journal of Sociology* 87 (1982): 1,113–1,132.

111. Lloyd Johnston, Patrick O'Malley, and Jerald Bachman, *Monitoring the Future* (Ann Arbor, MI: Institute for Social Research, 2007).

112. Paul Tracy, "Race and Class Differences in Official and Self-Reported Delinquency," in *From Boy to Man, from Delinquency to Crime,* eds. Marvin Wolfgang, Terence Thornberry, and Robert Figlio (Chicago: University of Chicago Press, 1987), p. 120.

113. Miriam Sealock and Sally Simpson, "Unraveling Bias in Arrest Decisions: The Role of Juvenile Offender Type-Scripts," *Justice Quarterly* 15 (1998): 427–457.

114. Phillipe Rushton, "Race and Crime: An International Dilemma," *Society* 32 (1995): 37–42; for a rebuttal, see Jerome Neapolitan, "Cross-National Variation in Homicides: Is Race a Factor?" *Criminology* 36 (1998): 139–156.

115. "Law Enforcement Seeks Answers to 'Racial Profiling' Complaints," *Criminal Justice Newsletter* 29 (1998): 5.

116. Robin Shepard Engel and Jennifer Calnon, "Examining the Influence of Drivers' Characteristics during Traffic Stops with Police: Results from a National Survey," *Justice Quarterly* 21 (2004): 49–90.

117. Daniel Georges-Abeyie, "Definitional Issues: Race, Ethnicity and Official Crime/Victimization Rates," in *The Criminal Justice System and Blacks,* ed. D. Georges-Abeyie (New York: Clark Boardman, 1984), p. 12; Robert Sampson, "Race and Criminal Violence: A Demographically Disaggregated Analysis of Urban Homicide," *Crime and Delinquency* 31 (1985): 47–82.

118. Barry Sample and Michael Philip, "Perspectives on Race and Crime in Research and Planning," in *The Criminal Justice System and Blacks,* ed. Georges-Abeyie, pp. 21–36.

119. Candace Kruttschnitt, "Violence by and against Women: A Comparative and Cross-National Analysis," *Violence and Victims* 8 (1994): 4.

120. James Comer, "Black Violence and Public Policy," in *American Violence and Public Policy,* ed. Lynn Curtis (New Haven: Yale University Press, 1985), pp. 63–86.

121. Fox Butterfield, *All God's Children: The Bosket Family and the American Tradition of Violence* (New York: Avon, 1996).

122. Hubert Blalock, Jr., *Toward a Theory of Minority-Group Relations* (New York: Capricorn Books, 1967).

123. Karen Parker, Briam Stults, and Stephen Rice, "Racial Threat, Concentrated Disadvantage and Social Control: Considering the Macro-Level Sources of Variation in Arrests," *Criminology* 43 (2005): 1,111–1,134; Lisa Stolzenberg, J. Stewart D'Alessio, and David Eitle, "A Multilevel Test of Racial Threat Theory, *Criminology* 42 (2004) 673–698.

124. Michael Leiber and Kristan Fox, "Race and the Impact of Detention on Juvenile Justice Decision Making," *Crime and Delinquency* 51 (2005): 470–497; Traci Schlesinger, "Racial and Ethnic Disparity in Pretrial Criminal Processing," *Justice Quarterly* 22 (2005): 170–192.

125. Tracy Nobiling, Cassia Spohn, and Miriam DeLone, "A Tale of Two Counties: Unemployment and Sentence Severity," *Justice Quarterly* 15 (1998): 459–486.

126. Alexander Weiss and Steven Chermak, "The News Value of African-American Victims: An Examination of the Media's Presentation of Homicide," *Journal of Crime and Justice* 21 (1998): 71–84.

127. Jefferson Holcomb, Marian Williams, and Stephen Demuth, "White Female Victims and Death Penalty Disparity Research," *Justice Quarterly* 21 (2004): 877–902.

128. Jerome Miller, *Search and Destroy: African American Males in the Criminal Justice System* (New York: Cambridge University Press, 1996), p. 226.

129. *The Sentencing Project, Losing the Vote: The Impact of Felony Disenfranchisement Laws in the United States* (Washington, DC: Sentencing Project, 1998).

130. Ronald Weitzer and Steven Tuch, "Race, Class, and Perceptions of Discrimination by the Police," *Crime and Delinquency* 45 (1999): 494–507.

131. Joanne Kaufman, "Explaining the Race/Ethnicity–Violence Relationship: Neighborhood Context and Social Psychological Processes," *Justice Quarterly* 22 (2005): 224–251.

132. Karen Parker and Patricia McCall, "Structural Conditions and Racial Homicide Patterns: A Look at the Multiple Disadvantages in Urban Areas," *Criminology* 37 (1999): 447–469.

133. David Jacobs and Katherine Woods, "Interracial Conflict and Interracial Homicide: Do Political and Economic Rivalries Explain White Killings of Blacks or Black Killings of Whites?" *American Journal of Sociology* 105 (1999): 157–190.

134. Melvin Thomas, "Race, Class and Personal Income: An Empirical Test of the Declining Significance of Race Thesis, 1968–1988," *Social Problems* 40 (1993): 328–339.

135. Mallie Paschall, Robert Flewelling, and Susan Ennett, "Racial Differences in Violent Behavior among Young Adults: Moderating and Confounding Effects," *Journal of Research in Crime and Delinquency* 35 (1998): 148–165.

136. Gary LaFree and Richard Arum, "The Impact of Racially Inclusive Schooling on Adult Incarceration Rates among U.S. Cohorts of African Americans and Whites since 1930," *Criminology* 44 (2006): 73–103.

137. R. Kelly Raley, "A Shortage of Marriageable Men? A Note on the Role of Cohabitation in Black-White Differences in Marriage Rates," *American Sociological Review* 61 (1996): 973–983.

138. Julie Phillips, "Variation in African-American Homicide Rates: An Assessment of Potential Explanations," *Criminology* 35 (1997): 527–559.

139. Roy Austin, "Progress toward Racial Equality and Reduction of Black Criminal Violence," *Journal of Criminal Justice* 15 (1987): 437–459.

140. Reynolds Farley and William Frey, "Changes in the Segregation of Whites from Blacks during the 1980s: Small Steps toward a More Integrated Society," *American Sociological Review* 59 (1994): 23–45.

141. Marvin Wolfgang, Robert Figlio, and Thorsten Sellin, *Delinquency in a Birth Cohort* (Chicago: University of Chicago Press, 1972).

142. See Thorsten Sellin and Marvin Wolfgang, *The Measurement of Delinquency* (New York: Wiley, 1964), p. 120.

143. Paul Tracy and Robert Figlio, "Chronic Recidivism in the 1958 Birth Cohort," paper presented at the annual meeting of the American Society of Criminology, Toronto, October 1982; Marvin Wolfgang, "Delinquency in Two Birth Cohorts," in *Perspective Studies of Crime and Delinquency,* eds. Katherine Teilmann Van Dusen and Sarnoff Mednick (Boston: Kluwer-Nijhoff, 1983), pp. 7–17. The following sections rely heavily on these sources.

144. Lyle Shannon, *Criminal Career Opportunity* (New York: Human Sciences Press, 1988).

145. D. J. West and David P. Farrington, *The Delinquent Way of Life* (London: Hienemann, 1977).

146. Michael Schumacher and Gwen Kurz, *The 8% Solution: Preventing Serious Repeat Juvenile Crime* (Thousand Oaks, CA: Sage, 1999).

147. Peter Jones, Philip Harris, James Fader, and Lori Grubstein, "Identifying Chronic Juvenile Offenders," *Justice Quarterly* 18 (2001): 478–507.

148. Lila Kazemian and Marc LeBlanc, "Differential Cost Avoidance and Successful Criminal Careers," *Crime and Delinquency* 53 (2007): 38–63.

149. Rudy Haapanen, Lee Britton, and Tim Croisdale, "Persistent Criminality and Career Length," *Crime and Delinquency* 53 (2007): 133–155.

150. See generally Wolfgang, Thornberry, and Figlio, eds., *From Boy to Man, from Delinquency to Crime.*

151. Paul Tracy and Kimberly Kempf-Leonard, *Continuity and Discontinuity in Criminal Careers* (New York: Plenum Press, 1996).

152. Kimberly Kempf-Leonard, Paul Tracy, and James Howell, "Serious, Violent, and Chronic Juvenile Offenders: The Relationship of Delinquency Career Types to Adult Criminality," *Justice Quarterly* 18 (2001): 449–478.

153. R. Tremblay, R. Loeber, C. Gagnon, P. Charlebois, S. Larivee, and M. LeBlanc, "Disruptive Boys with Stable and Unstable High Fighting Behavior Patterns during Junior Elementary School," *Journal of Abnormal Child Psychology* 19 (1991): 285–300.

154. Jennifer White, Terrie Moffitt, Felton Earls, Lee Robins, and Phil Silva, "How Early Can We Tell? Predictors of Childhood Conduct Disorder and Adolescent Delinquency," *Criminology* 28 (1990): 507–535.

155. John Laub and Robert Sampson, "Unemployment, Marital Discord, and Deviant Behavior: The Long-Term Correlates of Childhood Misbehavior," paper presented at the annual meeting of the American Society of Criminology, Baltimore, November 1990; rev. version.

156. Michael Ezell and Amy D'Unger, "Offense Specialization among Serious Youthful Offenders: A Longitudinal Analysis of a California Youth Authority Sample" (Durham, NC: Duke University, 1998, unpublished report).

Victims and Victimization

CHAPTER OUTLINE

Problems of Crime Victims
Economic Loss
System Abuse
Long-Term Stress
Fear
Antisocial Behavior

The Nature of Victimization
The Social Ecology of Victimization
The Victim's Household
Victim Characteristics
Victims and Their Criminals

Theories of Victimization
Victim Precipitation Theory
Lifestyle Theory
Deviant Place Theory
Routine Activities Theory

The Criminological Enterprise: Crime and Everyday Life

Caring for the Victim
The Government's Response to Victimization
Victims and Self-Protection
Victims' Rights

PROFILES IN CRIME: Jesse Timmendequas
and Megan's Law

CHAPTER OBJECTIVES

1. Be familiar with the concept of victimization

2. Be familiar with the costs of victimization

3. Be able to discuss the problems of crime victims

4. Know the nature of victimization

5. Recognize that there are age, gender, and racial patterns in the victimization data

6. Be familiar with the term "victim precipitation"

7. Be able to discuss the association between lifestyle and victimization

8. List the routine activities associated with victimization risk

9. Be able to discuss the various victim assistance programs

© AP Images/Tina Fineberg

On February 25, 2006, Imette St. Guillen stopped in for a late night drink at The Falls bar, a popular New York City nightspot. Later that evening, the bar's manager asked the bouncer, Darryl Littlejohn, to escort Imette out after she stayed past the 4 A.M. closing time.[1] Later he recalled hearing the pair argue before they disappeared through a side door. Sometime during the next 17 hours, Imette was raped and killed and her bound body left on the side of a desolate Brooklyn roadway. Police investigators soon set their sights on Littlejohn, a felon with prior convictions for robbery, drugs, and gun possession. He was indicted for murder when blood found on plastic ties that were used to bind Imette's hands behind her back matched Littlejohn's DNA.

Imette St. Guillen was a brilliant and beautiful young woman loved by her family and friends. She attended the Boston Latin School in Massachusetts and graduated magna cum laude *from George Washington University in 2003 as a member of Phi Beta Kappa. At the time of her death, she was a graduate student at John Jay College of Criminal Justice in New York City, where she would have completed her master's degree in May 2006. "New York was Imette's home," her sister, Alejandra St. Guillen, told reporters. "She loved the city and its people . . . Imette was a good person, a kind person. Her heart was full of love. With Imette's death, the world lost someone very special too soon."[2]*

The St. Guillen murder case illustrates the importance of understanding the victim's role in the crime process. Why do people become targets of predatory criminals? Do people become victims because of their lifestyle and environment? Did Imette contribute to her attack by staying out late at night, drinking, and being alone? Imette's friends, who had been with her earlier in the evening, had left her in the early morning hours because they considered The Falls bar neighborhood safe. If Imette had been with friends to guard her, would she be alive today? And is this a matter of unfairly "blaming the victim" for her risky behavior? Can someone actually deflect or avoid criminal behavior or is it a matter of fate and chance? What can be done to protect victims, for instance, should a convicted criminal be employed in a bar and asked to escort patrons? And, failing that, what can be done to help them in the aftermath of crime?

Criminologists who focus their attention on crime victims refer to themselves as **victimologists**. This chapter examines victims and their relationship to the criminal process. First, using available victim data, we analyze the nature and extent of victimization. We then discuss the relationship between victims and criminal offenders. During this discussion, we look at the various theories of victimization that attempt to explain the victim's role in the crime problem. Finally, we examine how society has responded to the needs of victims and discuss the special problems they still face.

PROBLEMS OF CRIME VICTIMS

The National Crime Victimization Survey (NCVS) indicates that the annual number of victimizations in the United States is about 23 million.[3] Being the target or victim of a rape, robbery, or assault is a terrible burden that can have considerable long-term consequences.[4] The costs of victimization can include such things as damaged property, pain and suffering to victims, and the involvement of the police and other agencies of the justice system. In this section we explore some of the effects of these incidents.

Economic Loss

When the costs of goods taken during property crimes is added to productivity losses caused by injury, pain, and emotional trauma, the cost of victimization is estimated to be in the hundreds of billions of dollars.

System Costs Part of the economic loss due to victimization is the cost to American taxpayers of maintaining the justice system. Violent crime by juveniles alone costs the United States $158 billion each year.[5] This estimate includes some of the costs incurred by federal, state, and local governments to assist victims of juvenile violence, such as medical treatment for injuries and services for victims, which amounts to about $30 billion. The remaining $128 billion is due to losses suffered by victims, such as lost wages, pain, suffering, and reduced quality of life. Not included in these figures are the costs incurred trying to reduce juvenile violence, which include early prevention programs, services for juveniles, and the juvenile justice system.

Juvenile violence is only one part of the crime picture. If the cost of the justice system, legal costs, treatment costs, and so on are included, the total loss due to crime amounts to $450 billion annually, or about $1,800 per U.S. citizen. Crime produces social costs that must be paid by nonvictims as well. For example, each heroin addict is estimated to cost society more than $135,000 per year; an estimated half-million addicts cost society about $68 billion per year.[6]

Individual Costs In addition to these societal costs, victims may suffer long-term losses in earnings and occupational attainment. Victim costs resulting from an assault are as high as $9,400, and costs are even higher for rape and arson; the average murder costs around $3 million.[7] Research by Ross Macmillan shows that Americans who suffer a violent victimization during adolescence earn about $82,000 less than nonvictims; Canadian victims earn $237,000 less. Macmillan reasons that victims bear psychological and physical ills that inhibit first their academic achievement and later their economic and professional success.[8]

Some victims are physically disabled as a result of serious wounds sustained during episodes of random violence, including a growing number that suffer paralyzing spinal cord injuries. If victims have no insurance, the long-term effects of the crime may have devastating financial as well as emotional and physical consequences.[9]

System Abuse

The suffering endured by crime victims does not end when their attacker leaves the scene of the crime. They may suffer more **victimization** by the justice system.

While the crime is still fresh in their minds, victims may find that the police interrogation following the crime is handled callously, with innuendos or insinuations that they were somehow at fault. Victims have difficulty learning what is going on in the case; property is often kept for a long time as evidence and may never be returned.

The system can be especially harsh on rape victims, some of whom report that the treatment they receive from legal, medical, and mental health services is so destructive that they cannot help feeling "re-raped."[10] Research by Courtney Ahrens found that rape survivors who speak out about their assault experiences are often punished for doing so when they are subjected to negative reactions from people who were supposed to give them support, leading some rape survivors to stop talking about their experiences to anyone at all. Ahrens uncovered three routes to silence: (1) negative reactions from professionals led survivors to question whether future disclosures would be effective; (2) negative reactions from friends and family reinforced feelings of self-blame; and (3) negative reactions from either source reinforced uncertainty about whether their experiences qualified as rape.[11] But if the victim finds the justice system personnel sympathetic and responsive, she or he will develop confidence in the agencies of justice and be more willing to turn to them and report future victimizations.[12]

Long-Term Stress

Victims may suffer stress and anxiety long after the incident is over and the justice process has been completed. Posttraumatic stress disorder (PTSD)—a condition whose symptoms include depression, anxiety, and self-destructive behavior—is a common problem especially when the victim does not receive adequate support from family and friends.[13]

Adolescent Stress It is widely assumed that younger children are less likely to be injured in attacks than older teens and adults, but in fact the opposite may be true.[14] Recent research by David Finkelhor and his colleagues at the University of New Hampshire Crimes against Children Research Center found that younger children's victimization by peers and siblings was similar to that experienced by older youth. Both groups suffered similar injuries, were just as likely to be hit with an object that could cause injury, and were victimized on multiple occasions.[15]

These younger victims are also more prone to suffer stress. Adolescent victims are particularly at risk to PTSD.[16] Kids who have undergone traumatic sexual experiences later suffer psychological deficits.[17] Mark Shelvin and his associates found that a history of childhood trauma, including rape and molestation, was significantly associated with visual, auditory, and tactile hallucinations. Kids who were repeatedly traumatized increased their experience with the three types of hallucinations, clearly indicating that childhood abuse can have a devastating effect on long-term mental health.[18]

Many run away to escape their environment, which puts them at risk for juvenile arrest and involvement with the justice system.[19] Others suffer posttraumatic mental problems, including acute stress disorders, depression, eating disorders, nightmares, anxiety, suicidal ideation, and other psychological problems.[20] Stress, however, does not end in childhood. Children who are psychologically, sexually, or physically abused are more likely to suffer low self-esteem and be more suicidal as adults.[21] They are also placed at greater risk to be re-abused as adults than those who escaped childhood victimization.[22] The re-abused carry higher risks for psychological and physical problems, ranging from sexual promiscuity to increased HIV infection rates.[23] Abuse as a child may lead to despair, depression, and even homelessness as an adult. One study of homeless women found that they were much more likely than other women to report childhood physical abuse, childhood sexual abuse, adult physical assault, previous sexual assault in adulthood, and a history of mental health problems.[24]

Relationship Stress Spousal abuse takes a particularly heavy toll on victims. Numerous research efforts show that victims of spousal abuse suffer an extremely high prevalence of psychological problems, including but not limited to depression, generalized anxiety disorder (GAD), panic disorder, substance use disorders, borderline personality disorder, antisocial personality disorder, posttraumatic stress disorder (an emotional disturbance

following exposure to stresses outside the range of normal human experience), anxiety disorder, and obsessive-compulsive disorder (an extreme preoccupation with certain thoughts and compulsive performance of certain behaviors).[25] One reason may be that abusive spouses are as likely to abuse their victims psychologically with threats and intimidation as they are to use physical force; psychological abuse can lead to depression and other long-term disabilities.[26]

Fear

Many people fear crime, especially the elderly, the poor, and minority group members.[27] Their fear is escalated by lurid news accounts of crime and violence.[28] A recent study (2007) by Matthew Lee and Erica DeHart showed that news stories of a local serial killer can cause a chill felt throughout the city. About half the people they surveyed experienced an increase in their

Victims experience fear and suffer psychological pain long after their physical injuries have healed. Teacher Jose Rodriguez reads T-shirts designed by survivors of sexual abuse at the Denim Day in L.A. speak-out and rally in Los Angeles, California. The event, part of Sexual Assault Awareness Month, encourages sexual assault victims to break their silence and speak out about their experiences. Do you believe that going public about a sexual assault can assist the healing process?

fear of crime that prompted them to protect themselves and their family by implementing some sort of protective measure, such as carrying mace or pepper spray or adding a security device to their home.[29]

While hearing about crime causes fear, those who experience it are even more likely to be fearful and change their behaviors. Victims of violent crime are the most deeply affected, fearing a repeat of their attack. Many go through a fundamental life change, viewing the world more suspiciously and as a less safe, controllable, and meaningful place. Some develop a generalized fear of crime and worry about being revictimized. For example, if they have been assaulted, they may develop fears that their house will be burglarized.[30] These people are more likely to suffer psychological stress for extended periods of time.[31]

Crime can have devastating effects on its victims, who may take years to recover from the incident. In a moving book, *Aftermath: Violence and the Remaking of a Self*, rape victim Susan Brison recounts the difficult time she had recovering from her ordeal. The trauma disrupted her memory, cutting off events that happened before the rape from those that occurred afterward, and eliminated her ability to conceive of a happy or productive future. Although sympathizers encouraged her to forget the past, she found that confronting it could be therapeutic.[32]

Even if they have escaped attack themselves, hearing about another's victimization may make people timid and cautious.[33] If they don't fear for themselves, they become concerned for others—their wives or husbands, children, elderly parents, and siblings.[34]

Antisocial Behavior

There is growing evidence of a correlation between crime and victimization. Kids who are victims share many of the same characteristics as those who are delinquent, such as antisocial behavior tendencies and impulsive personalities.[35] As adults, victims are more likely to commit crimes themselves.[36] People who were physically or sexually abused, especially young males, are much more likely to smoke, drink, and take drugs than are nonabused youth. Incarcerated offenders report significant amounts of posttraumatic stress disorder as a result of prior victimization, which may in part explain their violent and criminal behaviors.[37]

Victims may seek revenge against the people who harmed them or who they believe are at fault for their problems. In some cases, these feelings become generalized to others who share the same characteristics of their attackers (e.g., men, Hispanics).[38] As a result their reactions become displaced, and they may lash out at people who are not their attackers.

The abuse–crime phenomenon is referred to as the **cycle of violence**.[39] Research shows that both boys and girls are more likely to engage in violent behavior if they were the targets of physical abuse and were exposed to violent behavior among adults they know or live with or were exposed to weapons.[40]

www The mission of the **National Center for Victims of Crime** is to help victims of crime rebuild their lives: "We are dedicated to serving individuals, families, and communities harmed by crime." Access their website at www.thomsonedu.com/criminaljustice/siegel.

THE NATURE OF VICTIMIZATION

How many crime victims are there in the United States, and what are the trends and patterns in victimization? According to the NCVS, about 23 million criminal victimizations occur each year.[41] While this total is significant, it represents a decade-long decline in criminal victimization that began in 1993. Since then the violent crime rate decreased 58 percent, from 50 to 21 victimizations per 1,000 persons age 12 or older (Figure 3.1). Property crime declined 52 percent, from 319 to 154 per 1,000 households (Figure 3.2).

> ### connections
>
> As discussed in Chapter 2, the NCVS is currently the leading source of information about the nature and extent of victimization. It employs a highly sophisticated and complex sampling methodology to collect data annually from thousands of citizens. Statistical techniques then estimate victimization rates, trends, and patterns that occur in the entire U.S. population.

While the number and rate of victimization have declined, patterns in the victimization survey findings are stable and repetitive, suggesting that victimization is not random but is a function of personal and ecological factors. The stability of these patterns allows us to make judgments about the nature of victimization;

Figure 3.1 Violent Crime Victimization Rates

The NCVS reveals long-term declines in victimization to the lowest per capita rates in 30 years.

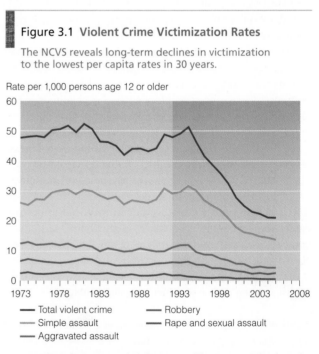

Rate per 1,000 persons age 12 or older

— Total violent crime   — Robbery
– Simple assault   — Rape and sexual assault
– Aggravated assault

Note: The violent crimes included are rape, robbery, aggravated and simple assault, and homicide. The NCVS redesign was implemented in 1993; the area with the lighter shading is before the redesign and the darker area after the redesign.

Source: Shannan Catalano, *Criminal Victimization 2005* (Washington, DC: Bureau of Justice Statistics, 2006).

Figure 3.2 Property Crime Victimization Rates

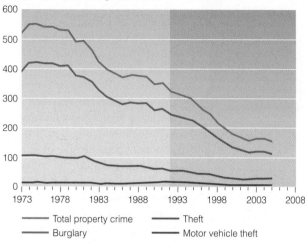

Rate per 1,000 persons age 12 or older

Total property crime
Burglary
Theft
Motor vehicle theft

Note: Property crimes include burglary, theft, and motor vehicle theft. The NCVS redesign was implemented in 1993; the area with the lighter shading is before the redesign and the darker area after the redesign.

Source: Shannan Catalano, *Criminal Victimization 2005* (Washington, DC: Bureau of Justice Statistics, 2006).

policies can then be created in an effort to reduce the victimization rate. Who are victims? Where does victimization take place? What is the relationship between victims and criminals? The following sections discuss some of the most important victimization patterns and trends.

The Social Ecology of Victimization

The NCVS shows that violent crimes are slightly more likely to take place in an open, public area (such as a street, a park, or a field), in a school building, or at a commercial establishment such as a tavern during the daytime or early evening hours than in a private home during the morning or late evening hours. The more serious violent crimes, such as rape and aggravated assault, typically take place after 6 P.M. Approximately two-thirds of rapes and sexual assaults occur at night—6 P.M. to 6 A.M. Less serious forms of violence, such as unarmed robberies and personal larcenies like purse snatching, are more likely to occur during the daytime. Neighborhood characteristics affect the chances of victimization. Those living in the central city have significantly higher rates of theft and violence than suburbanites; people living in rural areas have a victimization rate almost half that of city dwellers. The risk of murder for both men and women is significantly higher in disorganized inner-city areas where gangs flourish and drug trafficking is commonplace.

Not surprisingly, the chances of becoming a crime victim are most common in areas frequented by the most crime-prone elements of society. Since teenage males are the group most likely to engage in crime, schools unfortunately are the locale of a great

deal of victimization The most recent surveys of school crime show that while victim rates are declining, about 5 percent of students now experience a crime at school each year—about 4 percent reported a crime of theft and 1 percent reported having been a violence victim at school. This equals an estimated 1.2 million crimes of theft against students and about 740,000 violent crimes, including an estimated 150,000 of the most serious violent victimizations (rape, sexual assault, robbery, aggravated assault). Students also reported that about two-thirds of the serious violent crimes they experienced did not occur at school.[42] The risk of school victimization is not lost on students: about 6 percent of students age 12 to 18 reported that they avoided school activities or one or more places in school because they thought someone might attack or harm them.

The Victim's Household

The NCVS tells us that within the United States, larger, African American, western, and urban homes are the most vulnerable to crime. In contrast, rural, white homes in the Northeast are the least likely to contain crime victims or be the target of theft offenses, such as burglary or larceny. People who own their homes are less vulnerable than renters.

Recent population movement and changes may account for decreases in crime victimization. U.S. residents have become extremely mobile, moving from urban areas to suburban and rural areas. In addition, family size has been reduced; more people than ever before are living in single-person homes (about one-quarter of the population). It is possible that the decline in household victimization rates during the past decades can be explained by the fact that smaller households in less populated areas have a lower victimization risk.

Victim Characteristics

Social and demographic characteristics also distinguish victims and nonvictims. The most important of these factors are gender, age, social status, and race.

Gender Gender affects victimization risk. Males are more likely than females to be the victims of violent crime. Men are almost twice as likely as women to experience robbery and 50 percent more likely to be the victim of assault; women are much more likely than men to be victims of rape or sexual assault. For all crimes, males are more likely to be victimized than females. However, the gender differences in the violence victimization rate appear to be narrowing (Figure 3.3), a phenomenon related to increasing gender equality in contemporary society.[43]

Females are most often victimized by someone they know, whereas males are more likely to be victimized by a stranger. Of those offenders victimizing females, about two-thirds are described as someone the victim knows or is related to. In contrast, only about half of male victims are attacked by a friend, relative, or acquaintance.

Age Victim data reveal that young people face a much greater victimization risk than do older people. As Figure 3.4 shows,

Both personal characteristics and environmental factors influence victimization risk. Males, minority group members, and city dwellers have a greater chance of becoming victims than women, European Americans, and people living in rural areas. Living in a high-crime area also increases the likelihood of becoming a crime victim. Here, Kokomo, Indiana, police assist a victim of an attempted robbery. One man was wounded by police and another was arrested following a four-hour standoff at a local residence.

© AP Images/*Kokomo Tribune*/Tim Bath

victim risk diminishes rapidly after age 25 and becomes negligible after age 65.

The elderly, who are thought of as the helpless targets of predatory criminals, are actually much safer than their grandchildren. People over 65, who make up about 15 percent of the population, account for only 1 percent of violent victimizations; teens 12 to 19, who also make up 15 percent of the population, typically account for more than 30 percent of victimizations. Teens 16 to 19 suffer the most personal victimizations, at around 44 per 1,000, whereas people over 65 experience slightly more than 2.

Although the elderly are less likely to become crime victims than the young, they are most often the victims of a narrow band of criminal activities from which the young are more immune. Frauds and scams, purse snatching, pocket picking, stealing checks from the mail, and crimes committed in long-term care settings claim predominantly elderly victims. The elderly are especially susceptible to fraud schemes because they

have insurance, pension plans, proceeds from the sale of homes, and money from Social Security and savings that make them attractive financial targets. Because many elderly live by themselves and are lonely, they remain more susceptible to telephone and mail fraud. Unfortunately, once victimized the elderly have less opportunity to either recover their lost money or to earn enough to replace it.[44] **Elder abuse** is a particularly important issue because of shifts in the U.S. population; the Bureau of the Census predicts that by 2030 the population over age 65 will nearly triple to more than 70 million people, and older people will make up more than 20 percent of the population (up from 12.3 percent in 1990). The saliency of elder abuse is underscored by reports from the National Center on Elder Abuse, which show an increase of 150 percent in reported cases of elder abuse nationwide since 1986.[45]

connections

The association between age and victimization is undoubtedly tied to lifestyle: adolescents often stay out late at night, go to public places, and hang out with other kids who have a high risk of criminal involvement. Teens also face a high victimization risk because they spend a great deal of time in the most dangerous building in the community—the local school. As Chapter 2 indicated, adolescents have the highest crime rates. It is not surprising that people who associate with these high-crime-rate individuals (other adolescents) have the greatest victimization risk.

Social Status The poorest Americans are also the most likely victims of violent and property crime. For example, homeless people, who are among the poorest individuals in America, suffer very high rates of assault.[46] This association occurs across all gender, age, and racial groups. Although the poor are more likely to suffer violent crimes, the wealthy are more likely targets of personal theft crimes such as pocket picking and purse snatching. Perhaps the affluent—sporting more expensive attire and driving better cars—attract the attention of thieves.

Marital Status Marital status also influences victimization risk. Never-married males and females are victimized more often than married people. Widows and widowers have the lowest victimization risk. This association between marital status and victimization is probably influenced by age, gender, and lifestyle:

▍ Adolescence and teens who have the highest victimization risk, are too young to have been married.

Figure 3.3 Violent Crime Victimization and Gender

Rate per 1,000 persons age 12 or older

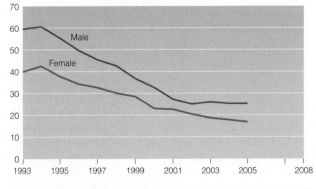

Source: Shannan Catalano, *Criminal Victimization 2005* (Washington, DC: Bureau of Justice Statistics, 2006).

Figure 3.4 **Age and Violent Crime Victimization**

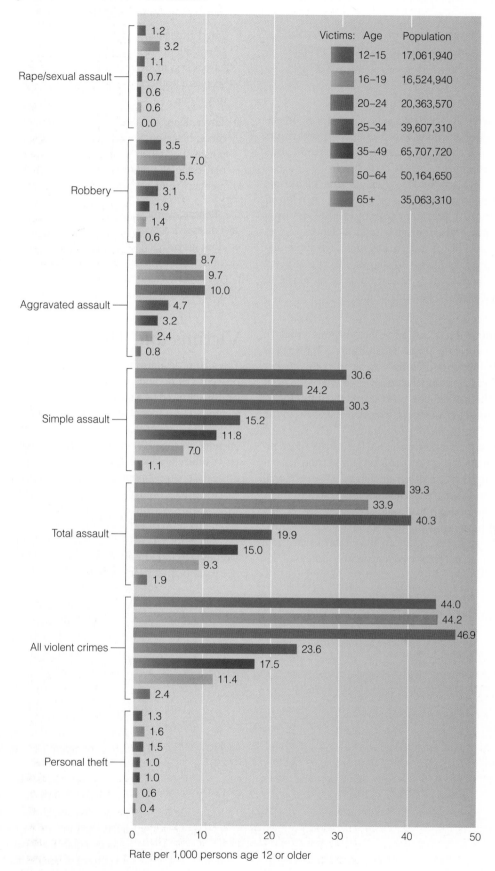

Rate per 1,000 persons age 12 or older

Source: Shannan Catalano, *Criminal Victimization 2005* (Washington, DC: Bureau of Justice Statistics, 2006).

- Young single people go out in public more often and sometimes interact with high-risk peers, increasing their exposure to victimization.

- Widows and widowers suffer much lower victimization rates because they are older, interact with older people, and are more likely to stay home at night and to avoid public places.

Race and Ethnicity As Figure 3.5 shows, (a) African Americans are more likely than whites to be victims of violent crime, and (b) serious violent crime rates have declined in recent years for both blacks and whites.

Why do these discrepancies exist? Because of income inequality, racial and minority group members are often forced to live in deteriorated urban areas beset by alcohol and drug abuse, poverty, racial discrimination, and violence. Consequently, their lifestyle places them in the most at-risk population group. However, as Figure 3.5 shows, the rate of black victimization has been in steep decline, and the racial gap in victimization rates seems to be narrowing.

Repeat Victimization Does prior victimization enhance or reduce the chances of future victimization? Individuals who have been crime victims have a significantly higher chance of future victimization than people who have not been victims.[47] Households that have experienced victimization in the past are the ones most likely to experience it again in the future.[48]

What factors predict chronic victimization? Most repeat victimizations occur soon after a previous crime has occurred, suggesting that repeat victims share some personal characteristic that makes them a magnet for predators.[49] For example, children who are shy, physically weak, or socially isolated may be prone to being bullied in the schoolyard.[50] David Finkelhor and Nancy Asigian have found that three specific types of characteristics increase the potential for victimization:

- *Target vulnerability.* The victims' physical weakness or psychological distress renders them incapable of resisting or deterring crime and makes them easy targets.

- *Target gratifiability.* Some victims have some quality, possession, skill, or attribute that an offender wants to obtain, use, have access to, or manipulate. Having attractive possessions such as a leather coat may make one vulnerable to predatory crime.

- *Target antagonism.* Some characteristics increase risk because they arouse anger, jealousy, or destructive impulses in potential offenders. Being gay or effeminate, for example, may bring on undeserved attacks in the street; being argumentative and alcoholic may provoke barroom assaults.[51]

Repeat victimization may occur when the victim does not take defensive action. For example, if an abusive husband finds out that his battered wife will not call the police, he repeatedly victimizes her; or if a hate crime is committed and the police do not respond to reported offenses, the perpetrators learn they have little to fear from the law.[52]

Victims and Their Criminals

The victim data also tell us something about the relationship between victims and criminals. Males are more likely to be violently victimized by a stranger, and females are more likely to be victimized by a friend, an acquaintance, or an intimate.

Victims report that most crimes are committed by a single offender over age 20. Crime tends to be intraracial: black offenders victimize blacks, and whites victimize whites. However, because the country's population is predominantly white, it stands to reason that criminals of all races will be more likely to target white victims. Victims report that substance abuse is involved in about one-third of violent crime incidents.[53]

On April 15, 2002, the body of Jackson Carr, a six-year-old boy, was found buried in mud in Lewisville, Texas; he had been stabbed to death. Later that day, Jackson's 15-year-old sister and 10-year-old brother confessed to the crime and were charged with murder.[54] (Sibling homicide is called siblicide.) Although many violent crimes are committed by strangers, a surprising number of violent crimes are committed by relatives or acquaintances of the victims. In fact, more than half of all nonfatal personal crimes are committed by people who are described as being known to the victim. Women are especially vulnerable to people they know. More than six in ten rape or sexual assault victims state the offender was an intimate, a relative, a friend, or an acquaintance. Women are more likely than men to be robbed by a friend or acquaintance; 74 percent of males and 43 percent of females state the individuals who robbed them were strangers.

Figure 3.5 Violent Crime Rates by Race of Victim

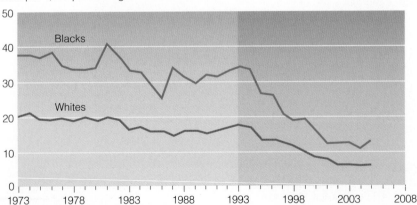

Rate per 1,000 persons age 12 and over

Source: Bureau of Justice Statistics, www.ojp.usdoj.gov/bjs/glance/race.htm.

THEORIES OF VICTIMIZATION

For many years criminological theory focused on the actions of the criminal offender; the role of the victim was virtually ignored. But more than 50 years ago scholars began to realize that the victim is not a passive target in crime but someone whose behavior can influence his or her own fate, someone who "shapes and molds the criminal."[55] These early works helped focus attention on the role of the victim in the crime problem and led to further research efforts that have sharpened the image of the crime victim. Today a number of different theories attempt to explain the cause of victimization; the most important are discussed here.

Victim Precipitation Theory

According to victim precipitation theory, some people may actually initiate the confrontation that eventually leads to their injury or death. Victim precipitation can be either active or passive.

Active precipitation occurs when victims act provocatively, use threats or fighting words, or even attack first.[56] In 1971, Menachem Amir suggested female victims often contribute to their attacks by dressing provocatively or pursuing a relationship with the rapist.[57] Although Amir's findings are controversial, courts have continued to return not-guilty verdicts in rape cases if a victim's actions can in any way be construed as consenting to sexual intimacy.[58]

In contrast, passive precipitation occurs when the victim exhibits some personal characteristic that unknowingly either threatens or encourages the attacker. The crime can occur because of personal conflict—for example, when two people compete over a job, promotion, love interest, or some other scarce and coveted commodity. A woman may become the target of intimate violence when she increases her job status, and her success results in a backlash from a jealous spouse or partner.[59] Although the victim may never have met the attacker or even know of his or her existence, the attacker feels menaced and acts accordingly.[60]

Passive precipitation may also occur when the victim belongs to a group whose mere presence threatens the attacker's reputation, status, or economic well-being. For example, hate crime violence may be precipitated by immigrant group members arriving in the community to compete for jobs and housing. Research indicates that passive precipitation is related to power: if the target group can establish themselves economically or gain political power in the community, their vulnerability will diminish. They are still a potential threat, but they become too formidable a target to attack; they are no longer passive precipitators.[61] By implication, economic power reduces victimization risk.

Lifestyle Theory

Some criminologists believe people may become crime victims because their lifestyle increases their exposure to criminal offenders. Victimization risk is increased by such behaviors as associating with young men, going out in public places late at night, and living in an urban area. Conversely, one's chances of victimization can be reduced by staying home at night, moving to a rural area, staying out of public places, earning more money, and getting married. The basis of lifestyle theory is that crime is not a random occurrence but rather a function of the victim's lifestyle. For example, due to their lifestyle and demographic makeup, college campuses contain large concentrations of young women who may be at greater risk for rape and other forms of sexual assault than women in the general population. Single women who drink frequently and have a prior history of being sexually assaulted are most likely to be assaulted on campus.[62]

High-Risk Lifestyles People who have high-risk lifestyles—drinking, taking drugs, getting involved in crime—maintain a much greater chance of victimization.[63] Groups that have an extremely risky life, such as young runaways living on the street, are at high risk for victimization; the more time they are exposed to street life, the greater their risk of becoming crime victims.[64] Teenage males have an extremely high victimization risk because their lifestyle places them at risk both at school and once they leave the school grounds.[65] They spend a great deal of time hanging out with friends and pursuing recreational fun.[66] Their friends may give them a false ID so they can go drinking in the neighborhood bar, or they may hang out in taverns at night, which places them at risk because many fights and assaults occur in places that serve liquor.

Exposure to violence and associating with violent peers enmeshes young men in a lifestyle that increases their victimization risk. One way for young males to avoid victimization is to choose their companions wisely. If they limit their male friends and hang out with girls they will lower their chances of victimization.[67] The perils of a deviant lifestyle do not end in adolescence and will haunt the risk taker into their adulthood. Kids who take drugs and carry weapons in their adolescence maintain a greater chance of being shot and killed as adults.[68]

Lifestyle risks continue into young adulthood. College students who spend several nights each week partying and who take recreational drugs are much more likely to suffer violent crime than those who avoid such risky academic lifestyles.[69] As adults, those who commit crimes increase their chances of becoming the victims of homicide.[70]

What lures victims into a high-risk lifestyle even though they realize it is fraught with danger? As you may recall, victims share personality traits also commonly found in law violators, namely impulsivity and low self-control. Perhaps their impetuous and reckless nature leads some people to seek out risky situations that put them in greater danger than they might have imagined.[71]

Victims and Criminals One element of lifestyle that may place people at risk for victimization is ongoing involvement in a criminal career. Analysis of data from the Rochester and Pittsburgh Youth Studies—two ongoing longitudinal surveys tracking thousands of at-risk youth—indicates that kids who became victims of serious crime were more likely than nonvictims to have participated in such criminal activities as gang/group fights, serious assaults, and drug dealing. They are also more likely to have associated with delinquent peers.

Carrying a weapon was another surefire way to become a crime victim. Males who carried weapons were approximately three times more likely to be victimized than those who did not carry weapons.[72] Another study of high school youth, conducted by Pamela Wilcox, David May, and Staci Roberts, also found that kids who carry weapons to school are much more likely to become crime victims than those who avoid weapons. They found that carrying a weapon may embolden youths and encourage them to become involved in risk-taking behavior that they would not have attempted otherwise. In short, while some kids carry weapons for self-defense, having a gun in their possession may actually increase the likelihood of their (a) getting involved in crime and (b) becoming a crime victim themselves.[73]

These data indicate that criminals and victims may not be two separate and distinct groups. Rather, the risk of victimization is directly linked to the high-risk lifestyle of young, weapon-toting gang boys.

Deviant Place Theory

According to deviant place theory, the greater their exposure to dangerous places, the more likely people will become victims of crime and violence.[74] Victims do not encourage crime but are victim prone because they reside in socially disorganized high-crime areas where they have the greatest risk of coming into contact with criminal offenders, irrespective of their own behavior or lifestyle.[75] The more often victims visit dangerous places, the more likely they will be exposed to crime and violence.[76] Neighborhood crime levels, then, may be more important for determining the chances of victimization than individual characteristics. Consequently, there may be little reason for residents in lower-class areas to alter their lifestyle or take safety precautions because personal behavior choices do not influence the likelihood of victimization.[77]

Deviant places are poor, densely populated, highly transient neighborhoods in which commercial and residential property exist side by side.[78] The commercial property provides criminals with easy targets for theft crimes, such as shoplifting and larceny. Successful people stay out of these stigmatized areas; they are homes for "demoralized kinds of people" who are easy targets for crime: the homeless, the addicted, the retarded, and the elderly poor.[79] People who live in more affluent areas and take safety precautions significantly lower their chances of becoming crime victims; the effect of safety precautions is less pronounced in poor areas. Residents of poor areas have a much greater risk of becoming victims because they live near many motivated offenders; to protect themselves, they have to try harder to be safe than the more affluent.[80]

Sociologist William Julius Wilson has described how people who can afford to leave dangerous areas do so. He suggests that affluent people realize that criminal victimization can be avoided by moving to an area with greater law enforcement and lower crime rates. Because there are significant interracial income differences, white residents are able to flee inner-city high-crime areas, leaving members of racial minorities behind to suffer high victimization rates.[81]

Routine Activities Theory

Routine activities theory was first articulated in a series of papers by Lawrence Cohen and Marcus Felson.[82] They concluded that the volume and distribution of predatory crime (violent crimes against a person and crimes in which an offender attempts to steal an object directly) are closely related to the interaction of three variables that reflect the routine activities of the typical American lifestyle (see Figure 3.6):

- The availability of suitable targets, such as homes containing easily salable goods
- The absence of capable guardians, such as police, homeowners, neighbors, friends, and relatives
- The presence of motivated offenders, such as a large number of unemployed teenagers

The presence of these components increases the likelihood that a predatory crime will take place. Targets are more likely to be victimized if they are poorly guarded and exposed to a large group of motivated offenders such as teenage boys.[83] As targets increase in value and availability, so too should crime rates. Conversely, as the resale value of formerly pricey goods such as iPods and cell phones declines, so too should burglary rates.[84]

Increasing the number of motivated offenders and placing them in close proximity to valuable goods will increase victimization levels. Even after-school programs, designed to reduce criminal activity, may produce higher crime rates because they lump together motivated offenders—teen boys with vulnerable victims (other teen boys).[85] Young women who drink to excess in bars and frat houses may elevate their risk of date rape because (a) they are perceived as easy targets, and (b) their attackers can rationalize the attack because they view intoxication as a sign of immorality ("She's loose, so I didn't think she'd care").[86] Conversely, people can reduce their chances of victimization if they adopt a lifestyle that limits their exposure to danger: by getting married, having children, and moving to a small town.[87]

Guardianship Even the most motivated offenders may ignore valuable targets if they are well guarded. Despite containing valuable commodities, private homes and/or public businesses may be considered off-limits by seasoned criminals if they are well protected by capable guardians and efficient security systems.[88]

Criminals are also aware of police guardianship. In order to convince them that "crime does not pay," more cops can be put on the street. Proactive, aggressive law enforcement officers who quickly get to the scene of the crime help deter criminal activities.[89]

Hot Spots Motivated people—such as teenage males, drug users, and unemployed adults—are the ones most likely to commit crime. If they congregate in a particular neighborhood, it becomes a "hot spot" for crime and violence. People who live in these hot

A young woman is carried out by emergency rescuers during the funeral service of Virginia Tech shooting victim Reema Samaha on April 23, 2007, in McLean, Virginia. Samaha graduated from Westfield High School, the same school attended by gunman Seung-Hui Cho. How would routine activities theory explain the Virginia Tech shooting? What aspects of the theory could be applied to such a seemingly senseless killing?

rip off an unoccupied home on the spur of the moment.[91] In hot spots for crime, therefore, an undefended yet attractive target becomes an irresistible objective for motivated criminals. Given these principles, it is not surprising that people who (a) live in high-crime areas and (b) go out late at night (c) carrying valuables such as an expensive watch and (d) engage in risky behavior such as drinking alcohol, (e) without friends or family to watch or help them, have a significant chance of becoming crime victims.[92]

Lifestyle, Opportunity, and Routine Activities Routine activities theory is bound up in opportunity and lifestyle. A person's living arrangements can affect victim risk; people who live in unguarded areas are at the mercy of motivated offenders. Lifestyle affects the opportunity for crime because it controls a person's proximity to criminals, time of exposure to criminals, attractiveness as a target, and ability to be protected.[93]

spots elevate their chances of victimization. For example, people who live in public housing projects may have high victimization rates because their fellow residents, mostly indigent, are extremely motivated to commit crime.[90] Yet motivated criminals must have the opportunity to find suitable undefended targets before they commit crime. Even the most desperate criminal might hesitate to attack a well-defended target, whereas a group of teens might

Criminal opportunities (such as suitable victims and targets) abound in urban environments where facilitators (such as guns and drugs) are also readily found. Environmental factors, such as physical layout and cultural style, may either facilitate or restrict criminal opportunity. Motivated offenders living in these urban hot spots continually learn about criminal opportunities from peers, the media, and their own perceptions; such information may either escalate their criminal motivation or warn them of its danger.[94]

Figure 3.6 Routine Activities Theory: The Interaction of Three Factors

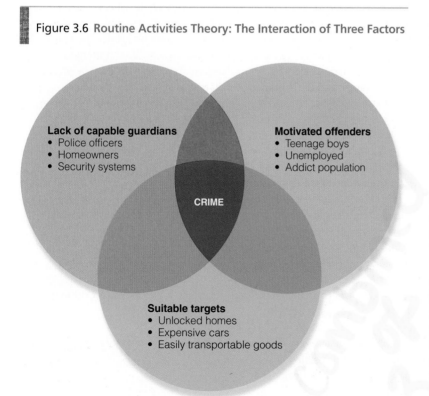

Lack of capable guardians
- Police officers
- Homeowners
- Security systems

Motivated offenders
- Teenage boys
- Unemployed
- Addict population

CRIME

Suitable targets
- Unlocked homes
- Expensive cars
- Easily transportable goods

Empirical Support Cohen and Felson argue that crime rates increased between 1960 and 1980 because the number of adult caretakers at home during the day (guardians) had decreased as a result of increased female participation in the workforce. While mothers are at work and children in daycare, homes are left unguarded. A recent study by Steven Messner and his associates found that between the years of 1967 and 1998, as unemployment rates increased, juvenile homicide arrest rates decreased, a finding that supports the effects of adult supervision on juvenile crime predicted by routine activities theory.[95]

Similarly, with the growth of suburbia during the 1960s, traditional urban neighborhoods were in transition and/or decline, and the number of such familiar guardians as family, neighbors, and friends had diminished. At the same time, the volume of easily transportable wealth increased, creating a greater number of available targets.[96] These structural changes in society led to 30 years of increasing

CRIME AND EVERYDAY LIFE

A core premise of routine activities theory is that all things being equal, the greater the opportunity to commit crime, the higher the crime and victimization rate. This thesis is cogently presented by Marcus Felson in *Crime and Everyday Life*. Using a routine activities perspective, Felson shows why he believes U.S. crime rates are so high and why U.S. citizens suffer such high rates of victimization.

According to Felson, there are always impulsive, motivated offenders who are willing to take the chance, if conditions are right, of committing crime for profit. Therefore, crime rates are a function of changing social conditions. Crime in the United States grew as the country changed from a nation of small villages and towns to one of large urban environments. In a village, not only could a thief be easily recognized, but the commodities stolen could be identified long after the crime occurred. Cities provided the critical population mass to allow predatory criminals to hide and evade apprehension. After the crime, criminals could blend into the crowd, disperse their loot, and make a quick escape using the public transportation system.

The modern-day equivalent of the urban center is the shopping mall. Here, strangers converge in large numbers and youths "hang out." The interior is filled with people, so drug deals can be concealed in the pedestrian flow. Stores have attractively displayed goods, which encourage shoplifting and employee pilferage. Substantial numbers of cars are parked in areas that make larceny and car theft virtually undetectable. Cars that carry away stolen merchandise have an undistinguished appearance. Who notices people placing items in a car in a shopping mall lot? Also, shoppers can be attacked in parking lots as people go in isolation to and from their cars.

EXHIBIT 3A

How Development of the Divergent Metropolis Has Increased Crime Levels

1. It has become more difficult to protect people from criminal entry because homes have been dispersed over larger areas, huge parking lots have been created, and building heights lowered.

2. There are fewer people in each household and consequently less intrapersonal and intrafamily supervision.

3. By spreading people and vehicles over larger areas as they travel and park, people are more exposed to attack.

4. As shopping, work, and socializing are spread further from home, people are forced to leave their immediate neighborhood, and, as strangers, they become more vulnerable to attack.

5. By spreading vast quantities of retail goods throughout huge stores and malls, with fewer employees to watch over them, the divergent metropolis creates a retail environment that invites people of all ages to shoplift.

6. Commuting to the inner city for work requires that millions of dollars' worth of vehicles be left in parking lots without supervision.

Felson believes these changes in the structure and function of society have been responsible for changes in the crime rates. He concludes that rather than change people, crime prevention strategies must be established to reduce the opportunity to commit crime.

Why did crime and delinquency rates increase dramatically between 1960 and 1990? According to Felson, structural changes in American society were the stimulus for increasing crime rates. During this period, suburbs grew in importance, and the divergent metropolis was created. Labor and family life began to be scattered away from the household, decreasing guardianship (see Exhibit 3A). The convenience of microwave ovens, automatic dishwashers, and increased emphasis on fast-food offerings freed adolescents from common household chores. Rather than help prepare the family dinner and wash dishes afterward, adolescents have the freedom to meet with their peers and avoid parental controls. As car ownership increased, teens had greater access to transportation outside of parental control. Greater mobility and access to transportation made it impossible for neighbors to know if a teen belonged in an area or is an intruder planning to commit a crime. As schools became larger and more complex, they provided ideal sites for crime. The many hallways and corridors prevented teachers from knowing who belongs where; spacious school grounds reduced teacher supervision. These structural changes helped produce a 30-year crime wave.

CRITICAL THINKING

1. What technological changes influence crime rates? The Internet? Video and computer games? Cell phones? ATM machines?

2. Would increased family contact decrease adolescent crime rates, or would it increase the opportunity for child abuse?

Source: Marcus Felson, *Crime and Everyday Life: Insights and Implications for Society* (Thousand Oaks, CA: Pine Forge Press, 1994; 3rd ed., 2002), Exhibit A at pp. 57–59.

violence shelters. Victims of child abuse and victims of domestic violence received most of the funds. VOCA money goes to support victims' medical expenses, gives them economic support for lost wages, helps to compensate for the death of loved ones, and provides mental health counseling.[110]

Victim Advocates Assuring victims' rights can involve an eclectic group of advocacy groups, some independent, others government sponsored, and some self-help. Advocates can be especially helpful when victims need to interact with the agencies of justice. For example, advocates can lobby police departments to keep investigations open as well as request the return of recovered stolen property. They can demand from prosecutors and judges protection from harassment and reprisals by, for example, making "no contact" a condition of bail. They can help victims make statements during sentencing hearings as well as probation and parole revocation procedures. Victim advocates can also interact with news media, making sure that reporting is accurate and that victim privacy is not violated. Victim advocates can be part of an independent agency similar to a legal aid society. If successful, top-notch advocates may eventually open private offices, similar to attorneys, private investigators, or jury consultants.

Some programs assign advocates to help victims understand the operations of the justice system and guide them through the process. Victims of sexual assault may be assigned the assistance of a rape victim advocate to stand by their side as they negotiate the legal and medical systems that must process their case. Research shows that rape survivors who had the assistance of an advocate were significantly more likely to have police reports taken, were less likely to be treated negatively by police officers, and reported less distress from their medical contact experiences.[111]

Court advocates prepare victims and witnesses by explaining court procedures: how to be a witness, how bail works, and what to do if the defendant makes a threat. Lack of such knowledge can cause confusion and fear, making some victims reluctant to testify in court procedures.

Many victim programs also provide transportation to and from court, and advocates may remain in the courtroom during hearings to explain procedures and provide support. Court escorts are particularly important for elderly and disabled victims, victims of child abuse and assault, and victims who have been intimidated by friends or relatives of the defendant. These types of services may be having a positive effect since recent research shows that victims may be now less traumatized by a court hearing than previously believed.[112]

Victim Counseling Numerous programs provide counseling and psychological support to help victims recover from the long-term trauma associated with a violent victimization. Clients are commonly referred to the local network of public and private social service agencies that can provide emergency and long-term assistance with transportation, medical care, shelter, food, and clothing. In addition, more than half of victim programs provide crisis intervention to victims, many of whom feel isolated, vulnerable, and in need of immediate services. Some programs counsel at their offices, and others visit victims' homes, the crime scene, or a hospital. Helping victims adjust is often a difficult process and recent research has found little evidence that counseling efforts are as successful as previously hoped.[113]

Public Education More than half of all victim programs include public education programs that help familiarize the general public with their services and with other agencies that assist crime victims. In some instances, these are primary education programs, which teach methods of dealing with conflict without resorting to violence. For example, school-based programs present information on spousal and dating abuse followed by discussions of how to reduce violent incidents.[114]

Victim-Offender Reconciliation Programs Victim–offender reconciliation programs (VORPs) use mediators to facilitate face-to-face encounters between victims and their attackers. The aim is to engage in direct negotiations that lead to restitution agreements and, possibly, reconciliation between the two parties involved.[115] Hundreds of programs are currently in operation, and they handle an many thousands of cases per year. Designed at first to address routine misdemeanors such as petty theft and vandalism, programs now commonly hammer out restitution agreements in more serious incidents such as residential burglary and even attempted murder.

Trisha Meili, author of *I Am the Central Park Jogger*, acknowledges the applause of people gathered in the Capitol Rotunda in Frankfort, Kentucky, after delivering a speech at the Crime Victims' Rights Day ceremony. Meili speaks to groups around the country about her recovery after a brutal attack while jogging in New York's Central Park in 1989. Educating people about how to avoid victimization may help them avoid similar attacks.

connections

Reconciliation programs are based on the concept of restorative justice, which rejects punitive correctional measures in favor of viewing crimes of violence and theft as interpersonal conflicts that need to be settled in the community through noncoercive means. See Chapter 8 for more on this approach.

Victim Impact Statements Most jurisdictions allow victims to make an impact statement before the sentencing judge. This gives the victim an opportunity to tell of his or her experiences and describe the ordeal; in the case of a murder trial, the surviving family can recount the effect the crime has had on their lives and well-being.[116] The effect of victim/witness statements on sentencing has been the topic of some debate. Some research finds that victim statements result in a higher rate of incarceration, but others find that the statements are insignificant.[117] Those who favor the use of impact statements argue that because the victim is harmed by the crime, the victim has a right to influence the outcome of the case. After all, the public prosecutor is allowed to make sentencing recommendations because the public has been harmed by the crime. Logically the harm suffered by the victim legitimizes his or her right to make sentencing recommendations.[118]

Victims and Self-Protection

Although the general public mostly approves of the police, fear of crime and concern about community safety have prompted some to become their own "police force," taking an active role in community protection and citizen crime control groups.[119] The more crime in an area, the greater the amount of fear and the more likely residents will be to engage in self-protective measures.[120]

Research indicates that a significant number of crimes may not be reported to police simply because victims prefer to take matters into their own hands.[121] One manifestation of this trend is the concept of target hardening, or making one's home and business crime-proof through locks, bars, alarms, and other devices.[122] Other commonly used crime prevention techniques include a fence or barricade at the entrance; a doorkeeper, guard, or receptionist in an apartment building; an intercom or phone to gain access to the building; surveillance cameras; window bars; warning signs; and dogs chosen for their ability to guard the house. The use of these measures is inversely proportional to perception of neighborhood safety: people who fear crime are more likely to use crime prevention techniques. Although the true relationship is still unclear, there is mounting evidence that people who protect their homes are less likely to be victimized by property crimes.[123] One study conducted in the Philadelphia area found that people who install burglar alarms are less likely to suffer burglary than those who forgo similar preventive measures.[124]

Fighting Back Some people take self-protection to its ultimate end by preparing to fight back when criminals attack them. How successful are victims when they resist? Research indicates that victims who fight back often frustrate their attackers but also face increased odds of being physically harmed during the attack.[125] In some cases, fighting back decreases the odds of a crime being completed but increases the victim's chances of injury.[126] Resistance may draw the attention of bystanders and make a violent crime physically difficult to complete, but it can also cause offenders to escalate their violence.[127]

What about the use of firearms for self-protection? Again, there is no clear-cut answer. Each year, 2.5 million times, victims use guns for defensive purposes, a number that is not surprising considering that about one-third of U.S. households contain guns.[128] Gary Kleck has estimated that armed victims kill between 1,500 and 2,800 potential felons each year and wound between 8,700 and 16,000. Kleck's research shows, ironically, that by fighting back victims kill far more criminals than the estimated 250 to 1,000 killed annually by police.[129] Kleck has found that the risk of collateral injury is relatively rare and that potential victims should be encouraged to fight back.[130] In a recent study conducted with colleague Jongyeon Tark, Kleck reviewed more than 27,000 contact crime incidents and found that when compared to nonresistance, self-protection significantly reduced the likelihood of property loss and injury and that the most forceful tactics, including resistance with a gun, appear to have the strongest effects in reducing the risk of injury. Importantly, the research indicated that resistance did not contribute to injury in any meaningful way. The conclusion: it is better to fight than flee.[131]

"Stand Your Ground" Should people carry guns for self-protection? The jury is still out on this issue so it depends on whom you ask! Nonetheless, 15 states have passed laws that allow crime victims to use deadly force in certain situations in which they might have formerly been charged with a crime.[132] Florida's law, enacted on October 1, 2005, allows the use of deadly force when a person reasonably believes it necessary to prevent the commission of a "forcible felony," including carjacking, robbery, or assault.

The traditional "castle doctrine" required that people could only use deadly force in their own home when they reasonably believed that their lives were in danger. The new law allows the average citizen to use deadly force when they reasonably believe that their homes or vehicles have been illegally invaded. The Florida law authorizes the use of defensive force by anyone "who is not engaged in an unlawful activity and who is attacked in any other place where he or she has a right to be." Furthermore, under the law, such a person has no duty to retreat and can stand his or her ground and meet force with force. The statute also grants civil and criminal immunity to anyone found to have had such a reasonable belief.[133]

Community Organization Not everyone is capable of buying a handgun or semiautomatic weapon and doing battle with predatory criminals. An alternative approach has been for communities to organize on the neighborhood level against crime. Citizens have been working independently and in co-operation with local police agencies in neighborhood patrol and block watch programs. These programs organize local citizens in urban areas to patrol neighborhoods, watch for suspicious people, help secure the neighborhood, lobby for improvements (such as increased lighting), report crime to police, put out community newsletters, conduct home security surveys, and serve as a source for crime information or tips.[134] Although such programs are welcome additions to police services, there is little evidence that they appreciably affect the crime rate. There is also concern that their effectiveness is spottier in low-income, high-crime areas, which need the most crime prevention assistance.[135] Block watches and neighborhood patrols seem more successful when they are part of general-purpose or multi-issue community groups rather than when they focus directly on crime problems.[136]

Victims' Rights

More than 20 years ago, legal scholar Frank Carrington suggested that crime victims have legal rights that should assure them of basic services from the government.[137] According to Carrington, just as the defendant has the right to counsel and a fair trial, society is also obliged to ensure basic rights for law-abiding citizens. These rights range from adequate protection from violent crimes to victim compensation and assistance from the criminal justice system.

Because of the influence of victims' rights advocates, every state now has a set of legal rights for crime victims in its code of laws, often called a Victims' Bill of Rights.[138] These generally include the right:

▪ To be notified of proceedings and the status of the defendant.

▪ To be present at criminal justice proceedings.

▪ To make a statement at sentencing, and to receive restitution from a convicted offender.

▪ To be consulted before a case is dismissed or a plea agreement entered.

▪ To a speedy trial.

▪ To keep the victim's contact information confidential.

Not only has the victims' rights movement caught on in the United States, it has also had an impact in Europe. The European Union member nations have agreed in principle to a set of rules that creates minimum standards for the protection of victims of crime. These guarantee that all victims should:

▪ Be treated with respect

▪ Have their entitlement to a real and appropriate role in criminal proceedings recognized

▪ Have the right to be heard during proceedings, and to supply evidence, safeguarded

▪ Receive information on: the type of support available; where and how to report an offence; criminal proceedings

and their role in them; access to protection and advice; entitlement to compensation; and, if they wish, the outcomes of their complaints including sentencing and release of the offender

▪ Have communication safeguards: that is, member states should take measures to minimize communication difficulties in criminal proceedings

▪ Have access to free legal advice concerning their role in the proceedings and, where appropriate, legal aid

▪ Receive payment of expenses incurred as a result of participation in criminal proceedings

▪ Receive reasonable protection, including protection of privacy

▪ Receive compensation in the course of criminal proceedings

▪ Receive penal mediation in the course of criminal proceedings where appropriate

▪ Benefit from various measures to minimize the difficulties faced where victims are resident in another member state, especially when organizing criminal proceedings[139]

A final, albeit controversial, element of the victims' rights movement is the development of offender registration laws that require that the name and sometimes addresses of known sex offenders be posted by law enforcement agencies. Today almost every state has adopted sex offender laws and the federal government runs a National Sex Offender Public Registry with links to every state.[140] Sex offender registration is indelibly linked to the death of Megan Kanka, an incident described in the Profiles in Crime feature "Jesse Timmendequas and Megan's Law."

www Go to www.thomsonedu.com/criminaljustice/siegel to learn more about the following services:

▪ It is the mission of the **Crime Victims Board of New York** to provide compensation to innocent victims of crime in a timely, efficient, and compassionate manner; to fund direct services to crime victims via a network of community-based programs; and to advocate for the rights and benefits of all innocent victims of crime. You can learn more about this program at.

▪ The **Office for Victims of Crime (OVC)** was established by the 1984 Victims of Crime Act (VOCA) to oversee diverse programs that benefit victims of crime. The OVC provides substantial funding to state victim assistance and compensation programs and supports training designed to educate criminal justice and allied professionals regarding the rights and needs of crime victims.

▪ The **Victim-Offender Reconciliation Program (VORP) Information and Resource Center** provides information on programs and training and provides technical assistance.

▪ The **National Organization for Victim Assistance** is a private, nonprofit organization of victim and witness assistance programs and practitioners, criminal justice agencies and professionals, mental health professionals, researchers, former victims and survivors, and others committed to the recognition and implementation of victim rights and services.

JESSE TIMMENDEQUAS AND MEGAN'S LAW

© AP Images/Charles Rex Arbogast

Richard and Maureen Kanka thought that their daughter Megan was safe in their quiet, suburban neighborhood in Hamilton Township, New Jersey. Then, on July 29, 1994, their lives were shattered when their 7-year-old daughter Megan went missing. Maureen Kanka searched the neighborhood and met 33-year-old Jesse Timmendequas, who lived across the street. Timmendequas told her that he had seen Megan earlier that evening while he was working on his car. The police were called in and soon focused their attention on Timmendequas's house when they learned that he and two other residents were convicted sex offenders who had met at a treatment center and decided to live together upon their release. Timmendequas, who appeared extremely nervous when questioned, was asked to accompany police back to their headquarters, where he confessed to luring Megan into his home by inviting her to see a puppy, then raping her and strangling her to death.

Timmendequas had served six years in prison for aggravated assault and attempted sexual assault on another child. The fact that a known sex offender was living anonymously in the Kankas' neighborhood turned Megan's death into a national crusade to develop laws that require sex offenders to register with local police when they move into a neighborhood and require local authorities to provide community notification of the sex offender's presence. New York State's Sex Offender Registration Act is typical of these efforts, commonly known as "Megan's Law." Becoming effective on January 21, 1996, the statute requires that sex offenders in New York are classified by the risk of reoffense. A court determines whether an offender is a level 1 (low risk), 2 (moderate risk), or 3 (high risk). The court also determines whether an offender should be given the designation of a sexual predator, sexually violent offender, or predicate sex offender. Offenders are required to be registered for 20 years or life. Level 1 offenders with no designation must register for 20 years. Level 1 offenders with a designation, as well as level 2 and level 3 offenders regardless of whether they have a designation, must register for life. Local law enforcement agencies are notified whenever a sex offender moves into their jurisdiction. That agency may notify schools and other "entities with vulnerable populations" about the presence of a level 2 or level 3 offender if the offender poses a threat to public safety. The act established a toll-free telephone information line that citizens can call to inquire whether a person is listed in the registry and access information on sex offenders living in their neighborhoods. On the federal level, the Jacob Wetterling Crimes Against Children Law, passed in May 1996, requires states to pass some version of "Megan's Law" or lose federal aid. At least 47 states plus the District of Columbia have complied. Jesse Timmendequas was sentenced to death on June 20, 1997, and is currently on death row.

The case of Megan Kanka illustrates both the risk children face from sexual predators and the efforts being made by the justice system to limit that risk. To some civil liberty groups, such as the American Civil Liberties Union, registration laws go too far because they will not prevent sex offenders from committing crimes and because they victimize rehabilitated ex-offenders and their families. Should the rights of the victim take precedent over the privacy of the offender?

Sources: New York State Sex Offender Registry and the Sex Offender Registration Act (SORA), http://criminaljustice.state.ny.us/nsor/ (accessed March 14, 2007), New York State Correction Law Article 6-C (Section 168 et seq.); CourtTV Library, *New Jersey v. Timmendequas*, www.courttv.com/archive/casefiles/verdicts/kanka.html (accessed March 14, 2007).

THINKING LIKE A CRIMINOLOGIST

The director of the state's department of human services has asked you to evaluate a self-report survey of adolescents age 10 to 18. She has provided you with the following information on physical abuse:

Adolescents experiencing abuse or violence are at high risk of immediate and lasting negative effects on health and well-being. Of the high school students surveyed, an alarming one in five (21 percent) said they had been physically abused. Of the older students, age 15 to 18, 29 percent said they had been physically abused. Younger students also reported significant rates of abuse: 17 percent responded "yes" when asked whether they had been physically abused. Although girls were far less likely to report abuse than boys, 12 percent said they had been physically abused. Most abuse occurs at home, occurs more than once, and the abuser is usually a family member. More than half of those physically abused had tried alcohol and drugs, and 60 percent had admitted to a violent act. Nonabused children were significantly less likely to abuse substances, and only 30 percent indicated they had committed a violent act.

Writing Exercise Write a brief paper (two double-spaced pages) explaining how you would interpret these data, what factors might influence their validity, and your interpretation of the association between abuse and delinquency.

Doing Research on the Web To help formulate your recommendations, review these Web-based resources:

▮ The National Council on Child Abuse and Family Violence (NCCAFV) maintains a website with links to documents on child abuse and violence.

▮ In Canada, the National Clearinghouse on Family Violence maintains information on abuse and violence.

These websites can be accessed via **www.thomsonedu.com/criminaljustice/siegel.**

SUMMARY

▮ Criminologists now consider victims and victimization a major focus of study. About 24 million U.S. citizens are victims of crime each year. Like the crime rate, the victimization rate has been in sharp decline.

▮ The social and economic costs of crime are in the billions of dollars. Victims suffer long-term consequences such as experiencing fear and posttraumatic stress disorder.

▮ Research shows that victims are more likely to engage in antisocial behavior than nonvictims.

▮ Like crime, victimization has stable patterns and trends. Violent-crime victims tend to be young, poor, single males living in large cities, although victims come in all ages, sizes, races, and genders.

▮ Females are more likely to be victimized by someone they know than are males.

▮ Adolescents maintain a high risk of being physically and sexually victimized. Their victimization has been linked to a multitude of subsequent social problems.

▮ Many victimizations occur in the home, and many victims are the target of relatives and loved ones.

▮ Victim precipitation theory holds that victims provoke criminals, through either active or passive precipitation.

▮ Lifestyle theory suggests that victims put themselves in danger by engaging in high-risk activities, such as going out late at night, living in a high-crime area, and associating with high-risk peers.

▮ Deviant place theory argues that victimization risk is related to neighborhood crime rates.

▮ The routine activities theory maintains that a pool of motivated offenders exists and that these offenders will take advantage of unguarded, suitable targets.

▮ Numerous programs help victims by providing court services, economic compensation, public education, and crisis intervention. Most states have created a Victims' Bill of Rights.

■ Rather than depend on the justice system, some victims have attempted to help themselves through community organization for self-protection.

■ **Thomson**NOW™ Maximize your study time by using ThomsonNOW's diagnostic study plan to help you review this chapter. The Personalized Study plan will help you identify areas on which you should concentrate; provide interactive exercises to help you master the chapter concepts; and provide a post-test to confirm you are ready to move on to the next chapter.

KEY TERMS

victimologists (66)
victimization (66)
posttraumatic stress disorder (PTSD) (67)
obsessive-compulsive disorder (67)
cycle of violence (68)
elder abuse (70)
chronic victimization (72)
siblicide (72)

victim precipitation theory (73)
active precipitation (73)
passive precipitation (73)
lifestyle theory (73)
deviant place theory (74)
routine activities theory (74)
suitable targets (74)
capable guardians (74)

motivated offenders (74)
date rape (74)
victim-witness assistance programs (78)
victim compensation (78)
crisis intervention (79)
restitution agreements (79)
target hardening (80)

CRITICAL THINKING QUESTIONS

1. Considering what we learned in this chapter about crime victimization, what measures can you take to better protect yourself from crime?

2. Do you agree with the assessment that schools are some of the most dangerous locations in the community? Did you find your high school to be a dangerous environment?

3. Does a person bear some of the responsibility for his or her victimization if the person maintains a lifestyle that contributes to the chances of becoming a crime victim? That is, should we "blame the victim"?

4. Have you ever experienced someone "precipitating" crime? If so, did you do anything to help the situation?

NOTES

1. New England News, "Authorities Develop Case Against Bouncer in Grad Student Slaying," 24 March 2006, www1.whdh.com/news/articles/local/BO16577/ (accessed May 9, 2007).
2. Ibid.
3. Shannan Catalano, *Criminal Victimization 2005* (Washington, DC: Bureau of Justice Statistics, 2006).
4. Arthur Lurigio, "Are All Victims Alike? The Adverse, Generalized, and Differential Impact of Crime," *Crime and Delinquency* 33 (1987): 452–467.
5. Children's Safety Network Economics and Insurance Resource Center, "State Costs of Violence Perpetrated by Youth," www.edarc.org/pubs/tables/youth-viol.htm (accessed March 14, 2007).
6. George Rengert, *The Geography of Illegal Drugs* (Boulder, CO: Westview, 1996), p. 5.
7. Ted R. Miller, Mark A. Cohen, and Brian Wiersema, *Victim Costs and Consequences: A New Look* (Washington, DC: National Institute of Justice, 1996), p. 9, table 2.
8. Ross Macmillan, "Adolescent Victimization and Income Deficits in Adulthood: Rethinking the Costs of Criminal Violence from a Life-Course Perspective," *Criminology* 38 (2000): 553–588.

9. James Anderson, Terry Grandison, and Laronistine Dyson, "Victims of Random Violence and the Public Health Implication: A Health Care or Criminal Justice Issue?" *Journal of Criminal Justice* 24 (1996): 379–393.
10. Rebecca Campbell and Sheela Raja, "Secondary Victimization of Rape Victims: Insights from Mental Health Professionals Who Treat Survivors of Violence," *Violence and Victims* 14 (1999): 261–274.
11. Courtney Ahrens, "Being Silenced: The Impact of Negative Social Reactions on the Disclosure of Rape," *American Journal of Community Psychology* 38 (2006): 263–274.
12. Min Xie, Greg Pogarsky, James Lynch, and David McDowall, "Prior Police Contact and Subsequent Victim Reporting: Results from the NCVS," *Justice Quarterly* 23 (2006): 481–501.
13. Angela Scarpa, Sara Chiara Haden, and Jimmy Hurley, "Community Violence Victimization and Symptoms of Posttraumatic Stress Disorder: The Moderating Effects of Coping and Social Support," *Journal of Interpersonal Violence* 21 (2006): 446–469.
14. Dean Kilpatrick, Benjamin Saunders, and Daniel Smith, *Youth Victimization:*

Prevalence and Implications (Washington, DC: National Institute of Justice, 2003.
15. David Finkelhor, Heather Turner, and Richard Ormrod, "Kid's Stuff: The Nature and Impact of Peer and Sibling Violence on Younger and Older Children," *Child Abuse and Neglect* 30 (2006): 1,401–1,421.
16. Catherine Grus, "Child Abuse: Correlations with Hostile Attributions," *Journal of Developmental and Behavioral Pediatrics* 24 (2003): 296–298.
17. Kim Logio, "Gender, Race, Childhood Abuse, and Body Image among Adolescents," *Violence Against Women* 9 (2003): 931–955.
18. Mark Shevlin, Martin Dorahy, and Gary Adamson, "Childhood Traumas and Hallucinations: An Analysis of the National Comorbidity Survey," *Journal of Psychiatric Research* 41 (2007): 222–228.
19. Jeanne Kaufman and Cathy Spatz Widom, "Childhood Victimization, Running Away, and Delinquency," *Journal of Research in Crime and Delinquency* 36 (1999): 347–370.
20. N. N. Sarkar and Rina Sarkar, "Sexual Assault on Woman: Its Impact on Her Life and Living in Society," *Sexual and Relationship Therapy* 20 (2005): 407–419.

21. Michael Wiederman, Randy Sansone, and Lori Sansone, "History of Trauma and Attempted Suicide among Women in a Primary Care Setting," *Violence and Victims* 13 (1998): 3–11; Susan Leslie Bryant and Lillian Range, "Suicidality in College Women Who Were Sexually and Physically Abused and Physically Punished by Parents," *Violence and Victims* 10 (1995): 195–215; William Downs and Brenda Miller, "Relationships between Experiences of Parental Violence During Childhood and Women's Self-Esteem," *Violence and Victims* 13 (1998): 63–78; Sally Davies-Netley, Michael Hurlburt, and Richard Hough, "Childhood Abuse as a Precursor to Homelessness for Homeless Women with Severe Mental Illness," *Violence and Victims* 11 (1996): 129–142.

22. Jane Siegel and Linda Williams, "Risk Factors for Sexual Victimization of Women," *Violence Against Women* 9 (2003): 902–930.

23. Michael Miner, Jill Klotz Flitter, and Beatrice Robinson, "Association of Sexual Revictimization with Sexuality and Psychological Function," *Journal of Interpersonal Violence* 21 (2006): 503–524.

24. Lana Stermac and Emily Paradis, "Homeless Women and Victimization: Abuse and Mental Health History among Homeless Rape Survivors," *Resources for Feminist Research* 28 (2001): 65–81.

25. Gregory Stuart, Todd M. Moore, Kristina Coop Gordon, Susan Ramsey, and Christopher Kahler, "Psychopathology in Women Arrested for Domestic Violence," *Journal of Interpersonal Violence* 21 (2006): 376–389; Caron Zlotnick, Dawn Johnson, and Robert Kohn, "Intimate Partner Violence and Long-Term Psychosocial Functioning in a National Sample of American Women," *Journal of Interpersonal Violence* 21 (2006): 262–275.

26. K. Daniel O'Leary, "Psychological Abuse: A Variable Deserving Critical Attention in Domestic Violence," *Violence and Victims* 14 (1999): 1–21.

27. Ron Acierno, Alyssa Rheingold, Heidi Resnick, and Dean Kilpatrick, "Predictors of Fear of Crime in Older Adults," *Journal of Anxiety Disorders* 18 (2004): 385–396.

28. Mirka Smolej and Janne Kivivuori, "The Relation Between Crime News and Fear of Violence," *Journal of Scandinavian Studies in Criminology and Crime Prevention* 7 (2006): 211–227.

29. Matthew Lee and Erica DeHart, "The Influence of a Serial Killer on Changes in Fear of Crime and the Use of Protective Measures: A Survey-Based Case Study of Baton Rouge," *Deviant Behavior* 28 (2007): 1–28.

30. Pamela Wilcox Rountree, "A Reexamination of the Crime–Fear Linkage," *Journal of Research in Crime and Delinquency* 35 (1998): 341–372.

31. Robert Davis, Bruce Taylor, and Arthur Lurigio, "Adjusting to Criminal Victimization: The Correlates of Postcrime Distress," *Violence and Victimization* 11 (1996): 21–34.

32. Susan Brison, *Aftermath: Violence and the Remaking of a Self* (Princeton, NJ: Princeton University Press, 2001).

33. Susan Popkin, Victoria Gwlasda, Dennis Rosenbaum, Jean Amendolla, Wendell Johnson, and Lynn Olson, "Combating Crime in Public Housing: A Qualitative and Quantitative Longitudinal Analysis of the Chicago Housing Authority's Anti-Drug Initiative," *Justice Quarterly* 16 (1999): 519–557.

34. Karen Snedker, "Altruistic and Vicarious Fear of Crime: Fear for Others and Gendered Social Roles," *Sociological Forum* 21 (2006): 163–195.

35. Jared Dempsey, Gary Fireman, and Eugene Wang, "Transitioning Out of Peer Victimization in School Children: Gender and Behavioral Characteristics," *Journal of Psychopathology and Behavioral Assessment* 28 (2006): 271–280.

36. Timothy Ireland and Cathy Spatz Widom, *Childhood Victimization and Risk for Alcohol and Drug Arrests* (Washington, DC: National Institute of Justice, 1995).

37. Brigette Erwin, Elana Newman, Robert McMackin, Carlo Morrissey, and Danny Kaloupek, "PTSD, Malevolent Environment, and Criminality among Criminally Involved Male Adolescents," *Criminal Justice and Behavior* 27 (2000): 196–215.

38. Ulrich Orth, Leo Montada, and Andreas Maercker, "Feelings of Revenge, Retaliation Motive, and Posttraumatic Stress Reactions in Crime Victims," *Journal of Interpersonal Violence* 21 (2006): 229–243.

39. Cathy Spatz Widom, *The Cycle of Violence* (Washington, DC: National Institute of Justice, 1992), p. 1.

40. Steve Spaccarelli, J. Douglas Coatsworth, and Blake Sperry Bowden, "Exposure to Serious Family Violence among Incarcerated Boys: Its Association with Violent Offending and Potential Mediating Variables," *Violence and Victims* 10 (1995): 163–180; Jerome Kolbo, "Risk and Resilience among Children Exposed to Family Violence," *Violence and Victims* 11 (1996): 113–127.

41. Victim data used in these sections are from Catalano, NVCS, 2005.

42. J. DeVoe, K. Peter, M. Noonan, T. Snyder, and K. Baum, *Indicators of School Crime and Safety: 2006*, U.S. Departments of Education and Justice (Washington, DC: U.S. Government Printing Office, 2006).

43. Victoria Titterington, "A Retrospective Investigation of Gender Inequality and Female Homicide Victimization," *Sociological Spectrum* 26 (2006): 205–231.

44. Lamar Jordan, "Law Enforcement and the Elderly: A Concern for the 21st Century," *FBI Law Enforcement Bulletin* 71 (2002): 20–24.

45. Robert C. Davis and Juanjo Medina-Ariza, *Results from an Elder Abuse Prevention Experiment in New York* (Washington, DC: National Institute of Justice, September 2001).

46. Tracy Dietz and James Wright, "Age and Gender Differences and Predictors of Victimization of the Older Homeless," *Journal of Elder Abuse and Neglect* 17 (2005): 37–59.

47. Karin Wittebrood and Paul Nieuwbeerta, "Criminal Victimization during One's Life Course: The Effects of Previous Victimization and Patterns of Routine Activities," *Journal of Research in Crime and Delinquency* 37 (2000): 91–122; Janet Lauritsen and Kenna Davis Quinet, "Repeat Victimizations among Adolescents and Young Adults," *Journal of Quantitative Criminology* 11 (1995): 143–163.

48. Denise Osborn, Dan Ellingworth, Tim Hope, and Alan Trickett, "Are Repeatedly Victimized Households Different?" *Journal of Quantitative Criminology* 12 (1996): 223–245.

49. Graham Farrell, "Predicting and Preventing Revictimization," in *Crime and Justice: An Annual Review of Research*, eds. Michael Tonry and David Farrington, vol. 20 (Chicago: University of Chicago Press, 1995), pp. 61–126.

50. Ibid., p. 61.

51. David Finkelhor and Nancy Asigian, "Risk Factors for Youth Victimization: Beyond a Lifestyles/Routine Activities Theory Approach," *Violence and Victimization* 11 (1996): 3–19.

52. Graham Farrell, Coretta Phillips, and Ken Pease, "Like Taking Candy: Why Does Repeat Victimization Occur?" *British Journal of Criminology* 35 (1995): 384–399.

53. Christopher Innes and Lawrence Greenfeld, *Violent State Prisoners and Their Victims* (Washington, DC: Bureau of Justice Statistics, 1990).

54. Associated Press, "Texas Siblings Accused of Killing 6-Year-Old Brother," *New York Times*, 16 April 2002.

55. Hans Von Hentig, *The Criminal and His Victim: Studies in the Sociobiology of Crime* (New Haven: Yale University Press, 1948), p. 384.

56. Marvin Wolfgang, *Patterns of Criminal Homicide* (Philadelphia: University of Pennsylvania Press, 1958).

57. Menachem Amir, *Patterns in Forcible Rape* (Chicago: University of Chicago Press, 1971).

58. Susan Estrich, *Real Rape* (Cambridge, MA: Harvard University Press, 1987).

59. Edem Avakame, "Female's Labor Force Participation and Intimate Femicide: An Empirical Assessment of the Backlash Hypothesis," *Violence and Victim* 14 (1999): 277–283.

60. Martin Daly and Margo Wilson, *Homicide* (New York: Aldine de Gruyter, 1988).

61. Rosemary Gartner and Bill McCarthy, "The Social Distribution of Femicide in Urban Canada, 1921–1988," *Law and Society Review* 25 (1991): 287–311.

62. Bonnie Fisher, Francis Cullen, and Michael Turner, *The Sexual Victimization of College Women* (Washington, DC: National Institute of Justice, 2001).

63. Lening Zhang, John W. Welte, and William F. Wieczorek, "Deviant Lifestyle and Crime Victimization," *Journal of Criminal Justice* 29 (2001): 133–143.

64. Dan Hoyt, Kimberly Ryan, and Mari Cauce, "Personal Victimizaton in a High-Risk Environment: Homeless and Runaway Adolescents," *Journal of Research in Crime and Delinquency* 36 (1999): 371–392.

65. See generally Gary Gottfredson and Denise Gottfredson, *Victimization in Schools* (New York: Plenum Press, 1985).

66. Gary Jensen and David Brownfield, "Gender, Lifestyles, and Victimization: Beyond Routine Activity Theory," *Violence and Victims* 1 (1986): 85–99.

67. Dana Haynie and Alex Piquero, "Pubertal Development and Physical Victimization in Adolescence," *Journal of Research in Crime and Delinquency* 43 (2006): 3–35.

68. Rolf Loeber, Mary DeLamatre, George Tita, Jacqueline Cohen, Magda Stouthamer-Loeber, and David Farrington, "Gun Injury and Mortality: The Delinquent Backgrounds of Juvenile Offenders," *Violence and Victim* 14 (1999): 339–351; Adam Dobrin, "The Risk of Offending on Homicide Victimization: A Case Control Study," *Journal of Research in Crime and Delinquency* 38 (2001): 154–173.

69. Bonnie Fisher, John Sloan, Francis Cullen, and Chunmeng Lu, "Crime in the Ivory Tower: The Level and Sources of Student Victimization," *Criminology* 36 (1998): 671–710.

70. Dobrin, "The Risk of Offending on Homicide Victimization."

71. Christopher Schreck, Eric Stewart, and Bonnie Fisher, "Self-control, Victimization, and Their Influence on Risky Lifestyles: A Longitudinal Analysis Using Panel Data," *Journal of Quantitative Criminology* 22 (2006): 319–340.

72. Rolf Loeber, Larry Kalb, and David Huizinga, *Juvenile Delinquency and Serious Injury Victimization* (Washington, DC: Office of Juvenile Justice and Delinquency Prevention, 2001).

73. Pamela Wilcox, David May, and Staci Roberts, "Student Weapon Possession and the 'Fear and Victimization Hypothesis': Unraveling the Temporal Order," *Justice Quarterly* 23 (2006): 502–529.

74. Maryse Richards, Reed Larson, and Bobbi Viegas Miller, "Risky and Protective Contexts and Exposure to Violence in Urban African American Young Adolescents," *Journal of Clinical Child and Adolescent Psychology* 33 (2004): 138–148.

75. James Garofalo, "Reassessing the Lifestyle Model of Criminal Victimization," in *Positive Criminology*, eds. Michael Gottfredson and Travis Hirschi (Newbury Park, CA: Sage, 1987), pp. 23–42.

76. Richards, Larson, and Miller, "Risky and Protective Contexts and Exposure to Violence in Urban African American Young Adolescents."

77. Terance Miethe and David McDowall, "Contextual Effects in Models of Criminal Victimization," *Social Forces* 71 (1993): 741–759.

78. Rodney Stark, "Deviant Places: A Theory of the Ecology of Crime," *Criminology* 25 (1987): 893–911.

79. Ibid., p. 902.

80. Pamela Wilcox Rountree, Kenneth Land, and Terance Miethe, "Macro–Micro Integration in the Study of Victimization: A Hierarchical Logistic Model Analysis across Seattle Neighborhoods," paper presented at the annual meeting of the American Society of Criminology, Phoenix, November 1993.

81. William Julius Wilson, *The Truly Disadvantaged* (Chicago: University of Chicago Press, 1990); see also Allen Liska and Paul Bellair, "Violent-Crime Rates and Racial Composition: Convergence over Time," *American Journal of Sociology* 101 (1995): 578–610.

82. Lawrence Cohen and Marcus Felson, "Social Change and Crime Rate Trends: A Routine Activities Approach," *American Sociological Review* 44 (1979): 588–608.

83. Teresa LaGrange, "The Impact of Neighborhoods, Schools, and Malls on the Spatial Distribution of Property Damage," *Journal of Research in Crime and Delinquency* 36 (1999): 393–422.

84. Melanie Wellsmith and Amy Burrell, "The Influence of Purchase Price and Ownership Levels on Theft Targets: The Example of Domestic Burglary," *British Journal of Criminology* 45 (2005): 741–764.

85. Denise Gottfredson and David Soulé, "The Timing of Property Crime, Violent Crime, and Substance Use among Juveniles," *Journal of Research in Crime and Delinquency* 42 (2005): 110–120.

86. Georgina Hammock and Deborah Richardson, "Perceptions of Rape: The Influence of Closeness of Relationship, Intoxication, and Sex of Participant," *Violence and Victimization* 12 (1997): 237–247.

87. Wittebrood and Nieuwbeerta, "Criminal Victimization during One's Life Course," pp. 112–113.

88. Brandon Welsh and David Farrington, "Surveillance for Crime Prevention in Public Space: Results and Policy Choices in Britain and America," *Criminology and Public Policy* 3 (2004): 701–730.

89. Richard Timothy Coupe and Laurence Blake, "The Effects of Patrol Workloads and Response Strength on Arrests at Burglary Emergencies," *Journal of Criminal Justice* 33 (2005): 239–255.

90. Don Weatherburn, Bronwyn Lind, and Simon Ku, "'Hotbeds of Crime?' Crime and Public Housing in Urban Sydney," *Crime and Delinquency* 45 (1999): 256–271.

91. Andy Hochstetler, "Opportunities and Decisions: Interactional Dynamics in Robbery and Burglary Groups," *Criminology* 39 (2001): 737–763.

92. Richard Felson, "Routine Activities and Involvement in Violence as Actor, Witness, or Target," *Violence and Victimization* 12 (1997): 209–223.

93. Terance Miethe and Robert Meier, *Crime and Its Social Context: Toward an Integrated Theory of Offenders, Victims, and Situations* (Albany: State University of New York Press, 1994).

94. Ronald Clarke, "Situational Crime Prevention," in *Building a Safer Society, Strategic Approaches to Crime Prevention,* vol. 19 of *Crime and Justice, A Review of Research,* eds. Michael Tonry and David Farrington (Chicago: University of Chicago Press, 1995), pp. 91–151.

95. Steven Messner, Lawrence Raffalovich, and Richard McMillan, "Economic Deprivation and Changes in Homicide Arrest Rates for White and Black Youths, 1967–1998: A National Time-Series Analysis," *Criminology* 39 (2001): 591–614.

96. Lawrence Cohen, Marcus Felson, and Kenneth Land, "Property Crime Rates in the United States: A Macrodynamic Analysis, 1947–1977, with Ex-Ante Forecasts for the Mid-1980s," *American Journal of Sociology* 86 (1980): 90–118.

97. Patrick Donnelly and Charles Kimble, "Community Organizing, Environmental Change, and Neighborhood Crime," *Crime and Delinquency* 43 (1997): 493–511.

98. Simha Landau and Daniel Fridman, "The Seasonality of Violent Crime: The Case of Robbery and Homicide in Israel," *Journal of Research in Crime and Delinquency* 30 (1993): 163–191.

99. Patricia Resnick, "Psychological Effects of Victimization: Implications for the Criminal Justice System," *Crime and Delinquency* 33 (1987): 468–478.

100. Dean Kilpatrick, Benjamin Saunders, Lois Veronen, Connie Best, and Judith Von, "Criminal Victimization: Lifetime Prevalence, Reporting to Police, and Psychological Impact," *Crime and Delinquency* 33 (1987): 479–489.

101. Cassidy Gutner, Shireen Rizvi, Candice Monson, and Patricia Resick, "Changes in Coping Strategies, Relationship to the Perpetrator, and Posttraumatic Distress in Female Crime Victims," *Journal of Traumatic Stress* 19 (2006): 813–823.

102. U.S. Department of Justice, *Report of the President's Task Force on Victims of Crime* (Washington, DC: U.S. Government Printing Office, 1983).

103. Ibid., pp. 2–10; and "Review on Victims—Witnesses of Crime," *Massachusetts Lawyers Weekly,* 25 April 1983, p. 26.

104. Robert Davis, *Crime Victims: Learning How to Help Them* (Washington, DC: National Institute of Justice, 1987).

105. Michael M. O'Hear, "Punishment, Democracy, and Victims," *Federal Sentencing Reporter* 19 (2006): 1.

106. Peter Finn and Beverly Lee, *Establishing a Victim-Witness Assistance Program* (Washington, DC: U.S. Government Printing Office, 1988).

107. This section leans heavily on Albert Roberts, "Delivery of Services to Crime Victims: A National Survey," *American Journal of Orthopsychiatry* 6 (1991): 128–137; see also Albert Roberts, *Helping Crime Victims: Research, Policy, and Practice* (Newbury Park, CA: Sage, 1990).

108. Randall Schmidt, "Crime Victim Compensation Legislation: A Comparative Study," *Victimology* 5 (1980): 428–437.

109. Ibid.

110. National Association of Crime Victim Compensation Boards, http://nacvcb.org/ (accessed May 9, 2007).

111. Rebecca Campbell, "Rape Survivors' Experiences with the Legal and Medical Systems: Do Rape Victim Advocates Make a Difference?" *Violence Against Women* 12 (2006): 30–45.

112. Ulrich Orth and Andreas Maercker, "Do Trials of Perpetrators Retraumatize Crime Victims?" *Journal of Interpersonal Violence* 19 (2004): 212–228.

113. Barbara Sims, Berwood Yost, and Christina Abbott, "The Efficacy of Victim Services Programs," *Criminal Justice Policy Review* 17 (2006): 387–406.

114. Pater Jaffe, Marlies Sudermann, Deborah Reitzel, and Steve Killip, "An Evaluation of a Secondary School Primary Prevention Program on Violence in Intimate Relationships," *Violence and Victims* 7 (1992): 129–145.

115. Andrew Karmen, "Victim–Offender Reconciliation Programs: Pro and Con," *Perspectives of the American Probation and Parole Association* 20 (1996): 11–14.

116. Rachelle Hong, "Nothing to Fear: Establishing an Equality of Rights for Crime Victims through the Victims' Rights Amendment," *Notre Dame Journal of Legal Ethics and Public Policy* (2002): 207–225; see also *Payne v. Tennessee*, 111 S.Ct. 2597, 115 L.Ed.2d 720 (1991).

117. Robert Davis and Barbara Smith, "The Effects of Victim Impact Statements on Sentencing Decisions: A Test in an Urban Setting," *Justice Quarterly* 11 (1994): 453–469; Edna Erez and Pamela Tontodonato, "The Effect of Victim Participation in Sentencing on Sentence Outcome," *Criminology* 28 (1990): 451–474.

118. Douglas E. Beloof, "Constitutional Implications of Crime Victims as Participants," *Cornell Law Review* 88 (2003): 282–305.

119. Sara Flaherty and Austin Flaherty, *Victims and Victims' Risk* (New York: Chelsea House, 1998).

120. Pamela Wilcox Rountree and Kenneth Land, "Burglary Victimization, Perceptions of Crime Risk, and Routine Activities: A Multilevel Analysis across Seattle Neighborhoods and Census Tracts," *Journal of Research in Crime and Delinquency* 33 (1996): 1,147–1,180.

121. Leslie Kennedy, "Going It Alone: Unreported Crime and Individual Self-Help," *Journal of Criminal Justice* 16 (1988): 403–413.

122. Ronald Clarke, "Situational Crime Prevention: Its Theoretical Basis and Practical Scope," in *Annual Review of Criminal Justice Research*, eds. Michael Tonry and Norval Morris (Chicago: University of Chicago Press, 1983).

123. See generally Dennis P. Rosenbaum, Arthur J. Lurigio, and Robert C. Davis, *The Prevention of Crime: Social and Situational Strategies* (Belmont, CA: Wadsworth, 1998).

124. Andrew Buck, Simon Hakim, and George Rengert, "Burglar Alarms and the Choice Behavior of Burglars," *Journal of Criminal Justice* 21 (1993): 497–507; for an opposing view, see James Lynch and David Cantor, "Ecological and Behavioral Influences on Property Victimization at Home: Implications for Opportunity Theory," *Journal of Research in Crime and Delinquency* 29 (1992): 335–362.

125. Alan Lizotte, "Determinants of Completing Rape and Assault," *Journal of Quantitative Criminology* 2 (1986): 213–217.

126. Polly Marchbanks, Kung-Jong Lui, and James Mercy, "Risk of Injury from Resisting Rape," *American Journal of Epidemiology* 132 (1990): 540–549.

127. Caroline Wolf Harlow, *Robbery Victims* (Washington, DC: Bureau of Justice Statistics, 1987).

128. Gary Kleck, "Guns and Violence: An Interpretive Review of the Field," *Social Pathology* 1 (1995): 12–45, at 17.

129. Ibid.

130. Gary Kleck, "Rape and Resistance," *Social Problems* 37 (1990): 149–162.

131. Jongyeon Tark and Gary Kleck, "Resisting Crime: The Effects of Victim Action on the Outcomes of Crimes," *Criminology* 42 (2004): 861–909.

132. Adam Liptak, "15 States Expand Right to Shoot in Self-Defense," *New York Times*, 7 August 2006, p. 1.

133. Patrik Jonsson, "Is Self-Defense Law Vigilante Justice? Some say proposed laws can help deter gun violence. Others worry about deadly confrontations," *Christian Science Monitor*, 24 February 2006.

134. James Garofalo and Maureen McLeod, *Improving the Use and Effectiveness of Neighborhood Watch Programs* (Washington, DC: National Institute of Justice, 1988).

135. Peter Finn, *Block Watches Help Crime Victims in Philadelphia* (Washington, DC: National Institute of Justice, 1986).

136. Ibid.

137. See Frank Carrington, "Victim's Rights Litigation: A Wave of the Future," in *Perspectives on Crime Victims*, eds. Burt Galaway and Joe Hudson (St. Louis: Mosby, 1981).

138. National Center for Victims of Crime, www.ncvc.org/policy/issues/rights/ (accessed March 14, 2007).

139. Council Framework Decision of 15 March 2001 on the Standing of Victims in Criminal Proceedings, http://eur-lex.europa.eu/smartapi/cgi/sga_doc?smartapi!celexapi!prod!CELEXnumdoc&lg=EN&numdoc=32001F0220&model=guichett (accessed March 14, 2007); Proposal for a Council Directive on Compensation to Crime Victims, http://europa.eu.int/eur-lex/en/com/pdf/2002/com2002_0562en01.pdf (accessed March 14, 2007).

140. U.S. Department of Justice, Dru Sjodin National Sex Offender Public Registry, www.nsopr.gov (accessed March 14, 2007).

PART TWO

THEORIES OF CRIME CAUSATION

An important goal of the criminological enterprise is to create valid and accurate theories of crime causation. A theory can be defined as an abstract statement that explains why certain things do (or do not) happen. A valid theory must have the ability to (a) predict future occurrences or observations of the phenomenon in question and (b) be validated or tested through experiment or some other form of empirical observation.

Criminologists have sought to collect vital facts about crime and interpret them in a scientifically meaningful fashion. By developing empirically verifiable statements, or hypotheses, and organizing them into theories of crime causation, they hope to identify the causes of crime.

Since the late nineteenth century, criminological theory has pointed to various underlying causes of crime. The earliest theories generally attributed crime to a single underlying cause: atypical body build, genetic abnormality, insanity, physical anomalies, or poverty. Later theories attributed crime causation to multiple factors: poverty, peer influence, school problems, and family dysfunction.

In this section, theories of crime causation are grouped into six chapters. Chapters 4 and 5 focus on theories that view crime as based on individual traits. They hold that crime is either a free will choice made by an individual, a function of personal psychological or biological abnormality, or both. Chapters 6, 7, and 8 investigate theories based in sociology and political economy. These theories portray crime as a function of the structure, process, and conflicts of social living. Chapter 9 is devoted to theories that combine or integrate these various concepts into a cohesive, complex, developmental view of crime.

CHAPTER 4
Rational Choice Theory

CHAPTER 5
Trait Theories

CHAPTER 6
Social Structure Theories

CHAPTER 7
Social Process Theories

CHAPTER 8
Social Conflict, Critical Criminology, and Restorative Justice

CHAPTER 9
Developmental Theories: Life Course and Latent Trait

Rational Choice Theory

CHAPTER OUTLINE

The Development of Rational Choice Theory
The Classical Theory of Crime
Contemporary Choice Theory Emerges

The Concepts of Rational Choice
Offense- and Offender-Specific Crimes
Structuring Criminality
PROFILES IN CRIME: Looting the Public Treasury
Structuring Crime

Is Crime Rational?
Is Theft Rational?
Is Drug Use Rational?
Is Violence Rational?

Eliminating Crime
Situational Crime Prevention
Comparative Criminology: CCTV or Not CCTV?
Comparing Situational Crime Prevention Efforts
in Great Britain and the United States
General Deterrence
The Criminological Enterprise: Does Capital
Punishment Deter Murder?
Specific Deterrence
Incapacitation

Public Policy Implications of Choice Theory
Just Desert

CHAPTER OBJECTIVES

1. Be familiar with the concept of rational choice

2. Know the work of Beccaria

3. Be familiar with the concept of offense-specific crime

4. Be familiar with the concept of offender-specific crime

5. Be able to discuss why violent and drug crimes are rational

6. Know the various techniques of situational crime prevention

7. Be able to discuss the association between punishment and crime

8. Be familiar with the concepts of certainty, severity, and speed of punishment

9. Know what is meant by specific deterrence

10. Be able to discuss the issues involving the use of incapacitation

11. Understand the concept of just desert

© David McNew/Getty Images

WANTED
BY THE FBI

JOHNNY RAY GASCA
Wanted on Charges of Criminal Copyright Infringement,
Conspiracy, Identity Theft, Witness Retaliation and Escape

DESCRIPTION

Date of Birth :   November 12, 1969
Place of Birth: New York
Race: White
Hair: Brown
Eyes: Brown
Height: 5'10"
Weight: 190 pounds
Nationality: American

CAUTION

GASKA HAS A VIOLENT CRIMINAL
HISTORY AND SHOULD BE CONSIDERED
ARMED AND DANGEROUS

IF YOU HAVE ANY INFORMATION CONCERNING THIS PERSON, PLEASE CONTACT YOUR
LOCAL FBI OFFICE OR THE NEAREST AMERICAN EMBASSY OR CONSULATE

IN LOS ANGELES, THE FBI CAN BE REACHED AT 310 477-6565

Johnny Ray Gasca was a native New Yorker with a track record of petty crime *when he moved to Hollywood in 2002 to seek his fortune in the movie business.[1] Given his criminal leanings, it comes as no surprise that Gasca was less interested in making movies than in stealing them!*

Gasca began to pose as a movie industry insider and would hang around theaters where advance screenings of feature films were scheduled. Once inside the theater, he would rig his camera to an armrest for stability and start filming when the lights went down. He used high-end sound and recording equipment that produced extraordinarily good quality master recordings. He would then mass produce the recordings on eleven interlinked VCRs and sell them over the Internet. By beating the public release of blockbuster films, he cleared as much as $4,500 a week from his illegal pirating scheme.

Though he was known as the "Prince of Pirates," Gasca had a bad habit of getting caught in the act. Police in Burbank, California, arrested him when he was filming the science fiction film The Core. *He was also arrested when he began filming* Anger Management *and* 8 Mile. *When Gasca's apartment was searched, federal agents found two video cameras, a microcamera built onto a trouser belt, two DVD recorders, the eleven linked VCRs, a stolen Social Security card, and his two diaries, which chronicled his exploits. While he was out on bail, Gasca threatened to sell up to twenty more unreleased movies online unless the Motion Picture Association of America (MPAA) helped him get his equipment back. In 2003, Gasca became the first person ever indicted on federal charges of movie piracy. Placed in his lawyer's custody, he disappeared without a trace until he was located two years later in Kissimmee, Florida, where, not surprisingly, he was supporting himself by illegally copying movies. On June 29, 2005, Gasca was found guilty of eight federal criminal charges, including three counts of copyright infringement.*

Criminals such as Johnny Ray Gasca carefully plan their criminal activities. They buy equipment, try to avoid detection, plot to sell their illegally gotten gains, and then attempt to squirrel their criminal profits in some hidden bank account. Their calculated actions suggest that the decision to commit crime can involve rational and detailed planning and decision making, designed to maximize personal gain and avoid capture and punishment. Some criminologists go as far as suggesting that the source of all criminal violations—committing a robbery, selling drugs, attacking a rival, or filing a false tax return—rests upon rational decision making. Such a decision may be based on a variety of personal reasons, including greed, revenge, need, anger, lust, jealousy, thrill-seeking, or vanity. But the final decision to commit a crime is only made after the potential offender carefully weighs the potential benefits and consequences of their planned action and decides that the benefits of crime are greater than its consequences. The jealous suitor concludes that the risk of punishment is worth the satisfaction of punching a rival in the nose. The greedy shopper considers the chance of apprehension by store detectives so small that she takes a "five-finger discount" on a new sweater. The drug dealer concludes that the huge profit from a single shipment of cocaine far outweighs the possible costs of apprehension. While we can easily assume that international drug dealers, white-collar criminals such as Johnny Ray, and organized crime figures use planning, organization, and rational decision making to commit their crimes, can we also assume that such common crimes as theft, fraud, and even murder are a function of detailed planning and decision making? Are these random senseless acts or a matter of personal choice, designed to maximize gain and minimize loss? Criminologists who would answer "yes" to these questions are known as rational choice theorists.

This chapter reviews the philosophical underpinnings of rational choice theory, tracing it back to the classical school of criminology. We then turn to more recent theoretical models that flow from the concept of choice. These models hold that because criminals are rational, their behavior can be controlled or deterred by the fear of punishment; desistance can then be explained by a growing and intense fear of criminal sanctions. These views include situational crime control, general deterrence theory, specific deterrence theory, and incapacitation. Finally, the chapter briefly reviews how choice theory has influenced criminal justice policy.

THE DEVELOPMENT OF RATIONAL CHOICE THEORY

Rational choice theory has its roots in the classical school of criminology developed by the Italian social thinker Cesare Beccaria.[2] As you may recall from Chapter 1, Beccaria and other utilitarian philosophers suggest that (a) people choose all behavior, including criminal behavior; (b) their choices are designed to bring them pleasure and reduce pain; (c) criminal choices can be controlled by fear of punishment; and (d) the more severe, certain, and swift the punishment, the greater its ability to control criminal behavior. In keeping with his utilitarian views, Beccaria called for fair and certain punishment to deter crime. He believed people are egotistical and self-centered, and therefore they must be motivated by the fear of punishment, which provides a tangible motive for them to obey the law and suppress the "despotic spirit" that resides in every person.[3]

Beccaria believed that, to deter people from committing more serious offenses, crime and punishment must be proportional; if not, people would be encouraged to commit more serious offenses. For example, if robbery, rape, and murder were all punished by death, robbers or rapists would have little reason to refrain from killing their victims to eliminate them as witnesses to the crime. Today, this is referred to as the concept of marginal deterrence—if petty offenses were subject to the same punishment as more serious crimes, offenders would choose the worse crime because the resulting punishment would be about the same.[4]

The Classical Theory of Crime

Beccaria's ideas and writings inspired social thinkers to believe that criminals choose to commit crime and that crime can be controlled by judicious punishment. His vision was widely accepted throughout Europe and the United States.[5]

In Britain, philosopher Jeremy Bentham (1748–1833) helped popularize Beccaria's views in his writings on utilitarianism. Bentham believed that people choose actions on the basis of whether they produce pleasure and happiness and help them avoid pain or unhappiness.[6] The purpose of law is to produce and support the total happiness of the community it serves. Because punishment is in itself harmful, its existence is justified only if it promises to prevent greater evil than it creates. Punishment, therefore, has four main objectives:

1. To prevent all criminal offenses

2. When it cannot prevent a crime, to convince the offender to commit a less serious crime

3. To ensure that a criminal uses no more force than is necessary

4. To prevent crime as cheaply as possible[7]

This vision was embraced by France's postrevolutionary Constituent Assembly (1789) in its Declaration of the Rights of Man:

> [T]he law has the right to prohibit only actions harmful to society. . . . The law shall inflict only such punishments as are strictly and clearly necessary . . . no person shall be punished except by virtue of a law enacted and promulgated previous to the crime and applicable to its terms.

Similarly, a prohibition against cruel and unusual punishment was incorporated in the Eighth Amendment to the U.S. Constitution.

Beccaria's writings have been credited as the basis of the elimination of torture and severe punishment in the nineteenth century. The practice of incarcerating criminals and structuring prison sentences to fit the severity of crime was a reflection of his classical criminology.

By the end of the nineteenth century, the popularity of the classical approach began to decline, and by the middle of the twentieth century, this perspective was neglected by mainstream criminologists. During this period, positivist criminologists focused on internal and external factors—poverty, IQ, education, home life—which were believed to be the true causes of criminality. Because these conditions could not be easily manipulated, the concept of punishing people for behaviors beyond their control seemed both foolish and cruel. Although classical principles still controlled the way police, courts, and correctional agencies operate, most criminologists rejected classical criminology as an explanation of criminal behavior.

Contemporary Choice Theory Emerges

Beginning in the mid-1970s, there was renewed interest in the classical approach to crime. First, the rehabilitation of known criminals—considered a cornerstone of positivist policy—came under attack. According to positivist criminology, if crime was caused by some social or psychological problem, such as poverty, then crime rates could be reduced by providing good jobs and economic opportunities. Despite some notable efforts to provide such opportunities, a number of national surveys (the best known being Robert Martinson's "What Works?") failed to find examples of rehabilitation programs that prevented future criminal activity.[8] A well-publicized book, *Beyond Probation*, by Charles Murray and Louis Cox, went as far as suggesting that punishment-oriented programs could suppress future criminality much more effectively than those that relied on rehabilitation and treatment efforts.[9]

A significant increase in the reported crime rate, as well as serious disturbances in the nation's prisons, frightened the general public. The media depicted criminals as callous and dangerous rather than as needy people deserving of public sympathy. Some criminologists began to suggest that it made more sense to frighten these cold calculators with severe punishments than to waste public funds by futilely trying to improve entrenched social conditions linked to crime, such as poverty.[10]

Thinking About Crime Beginning in the late 1970s, a number of criminologists began producing books and monographs expounding the theme that criminals are rational actors who plan their crimes, fear punishment, and deserve to be penalized for their misdeeds. In a 1975 book that came to symbolize renewed interest in classical views, *Thinking about Crime*, political scientist James Q. Wilson debunked the positivist view that crime was a function of external forces, such as poverty, that could be altered by government programs. Instead, he argued, efforts should be made to reduce criminal opportunity by deterring would-be offenders and incarcerating known criminals. People who are likely to commit crime, he maintained, lack inhibition against misconduct, value the excitement and thrills of breaking the law, have a low stake in conformity, and are willing to take

greater chances than the average person. If they could be convinced that their actions will bring severe punishment, only the totally irrational would be willing to engage in crime.[11] Wilson made this famous observation:

> *Wicked people exist. Nothing avails except to set them apart from innocent people. And many people, neither wicked nor innocent, but watchful, dissembling, and calculating of their chances, ponder our reaction to wickedness as a clue to what they might profitably do.*[12]

Here Wilson is saying that unless we react forcefully to crime, those "sitting on the fence" will get a clear message—crime pays.

Impact on Crime Control Coinciding with the publication of Wilson's book was a conservative shift in U.S. public policy, which resulted in Ronald Reagan's election to the presidency in 1980. Political decision makers embraced Wilson's ideas as a means to bring the crime rate down. Tough new laws were passed, creating mandatory prison sentences for drug offenders; the nation's prison population skyrocketed. Critics decried the disproportionate number of young minority men being locked up for drug law violations.[13] Despite liberal anguish, conservative views of crime control shaped criminal justice policy for the past two decades.[14] Many Americans, some of whom are passionate opponents of abortion on the grounds that it takes human life, became, ironically, ardent supporters of the death penalty![15] This "get tough" attitude was supported by the fact that while the prison population has grown to new heights, the crime rate has been in a steep decline.

From these roots, a more contemporary version of classical theory has evolved. It is based on intelligent thought processes and criminal decision making.[16] According to criminologists David Ward, Mark Stafford, and Louis Gray, this rational choice view is somewhat different from the original classical theory that portrayed criminals as people who tried to maximize their pleasure and minimize pain and suggested if people were caught committing crime it was because they were sloppy thinkers and imperfect in their decision making. The contemporary version now views the decision to commit crime as being shaped by human emotions and thought process. However, it recognizes that other influences have an impact on criminal decision making, including social relationships, individual traits and capabilities, and environmental characteristics. So, this new version of rational choice theory assumes that human behavior is both "willful and determined."[17]

 wwww Go to www.thomsonedu.com/criminaljustice/siegel to:

▌ Read about **Beccaria's life history and the formulation of his ideas**, as well as find some useful links.

▌ Read more about the life of **Jeremy Bentham**.

▌ Read a famous talk given by **James Wilson, "Two Nations,"** the 1997 Francis Boyer lecture delivered at the annual dinner of the American Enterprise Institute.

▌ Read what the American Civil Liberties Union has to say about the **death penalty**—even if it were an effective deterrent, some critics believe it presents ethical problems that make its use morally dubious.

THE CONCEPTS OF RATIONAL CHOICE

According to this contemporary rational choice approach, law-violating behavior occurs when an offender decides to risk breaking the law after considering both personal factors (such as the need for money, revenge, thrills, and entertainment) and situational factors (how well a target is protected and the efficiency of the local police force). Before choosing to commit a crime, the reasoning criminal evaluates the risk of apprehension, the seriousness of expected punishment, the potential value of the criminal enterprise, and his or her immediate need for criminal gain. They carefully choose targets and their behavior is systematic and selective. Burglars, for example, seem to choose targets based on their value, novelty, and resale potential. A relatively new piece of electronic gear, such as an Xbox 360, may be a prime target, because it has not yet saturated the market and still retains high value.[18] Conversely, the decision to forgo crime may be based on the criminal's perception that the economic benefits are no longer there or that the risk of apprehension is too great.[19]

Criminals then are people who share the same ambitions as conventional citizens but have decided to cut corners and use illegal means to achieve their goals (see the Profiles in Crime feature "Looting the Public Treasury"). Many criminal offenders retain conventional American values of striving for success, material attainment, and hard work.[20] When Philippe Bourgois studied crack dealers in East Harlem in New York City, he found that their motivations were not dissimilar from the "average citizen": They were upwardly mobile, scrambling around to obtain their "piece of the pie."[21] If they commit crime, it is because they have chosen an illegal path to obtain the goals that might otherwise have been out of reach.

connections

Lack of conventional opportunity is a persistent theme in sociological theories of crime. The frustration caused by a perceived lack of opportunity explains the high crime rates in lower-class areas. Chapter 6 discusses strain and cultural deviance theories, which provide alternative explanations of how lack of opportunity is associated with crime.

Offense- and Offender-Specific Crimes

Rational choice theorists view crime as both offense- and offender-specific.[22] That a crime is offense-specific means that offenders will react selectively to the characteristics of particular offenses. Take for instance the decision to commit the crime of burglary. The thought process might include:

- Evaluating the target yield
- Probability of security devices
- Police patrol effectiveness
- Availability of a getaway car
- Ease of selling stolen merchandise
- Presence of occupants
- Neighbors who might notice a break-in
- Presence of guard dogs
- Presence of escape routes
- Entry points and exits

The fact that a crime is offender-specific means that criminals are not simply automatons who, for one reason or another, engage in random acts of antisocial behavior. Before deciding to commit crime, individuals must decide whether they have the prerequisites to commit a successful criminal act. These might include evaluation of:

- Whether they possess the necessary skills to commit the crime
- Their need for money or other valuables
- Whether legitimate financial alternatives to crime exist
- Whether they have available resources to commit the crime
- Their fear of expected punishment
- Option of alternative criminal acts, such as selling drugs
- Physical ability and dexterity
- Health and strength

Criminal acts might be ruled out if potential offenders perceive that they can reach a desired personal goal through legitimate means or if they are too afraid of getting caught.[23]

Note the distinction made here between crime and criminality.[24] Crime is an event; criminality is a personal trait. Professional criminals do not commit crime all the time, and even ordinary citizens may, on occasion, violate the law. Some people considered "high risk" because they are indigent or disturbed may never violate the law, whereas others who are seemingly affluent and well adjusted may risk criminal behavior given enough provocation and/or opportunity. What conditions promote crime and enhance criminality?

Structuring Criminality

A number of personal factors condition people to choose crime. Among the more important factors are economic opportunity, learning and experience, and knowledge of criminal techniques.

Economic Opportunity In a recent issue of *Boston Magazine*, a university lecturer with a master's degree from Yale and a doctorate in cultural anthropology wrote a first-person account of how she took another job to pay the bills: call girl.[25] Rather than living on the meager teaching salary she was offered, she chose to take the tax-free $140 per hour for her services (she charged $200, handing over $60 to the escort service that arranged her dates). She left the "business" when she became financially self-sufficient.

PROFILES IN CRIME

LOOTING THE PUBLIC TREASURY

After graduating from UCLA, Albert Robles served terms as mayor, councilman, and deputy city manager of South Gate, California, an industrial community about 12 miles outside downtown Los Angeles. Soon after Robles became city treasurer in 1997, he plotted to rule the city purely for his own benefit. He even proclaimed himself "King of South Gate" and referred to the city as his "fiefdom." Once in power, Robles got involved in a number of convoluted illegal schemes, including:

▮ Using the city's treasury as his "private piggy bank for himself, his family, and his friends" (according to acting U.S. Attorney George Cardona), costing South Gate more than $35 million and bringing it to the verge of bankruptcy

▮ Firing city hall employees at will, replacing them with supporters who had little experience

▮ Recruiting and bankrolling unqualified local supporters for city council until he controlled the council

▮ Threatening anyone who stood in his way (suspiciously, one of his adversaries on the city council was shot in the head)

Robles and his corrupt cronies then cooked up schemes to line their own pockets with the public's cash. In one such scheme, Robles coerced businesses to hire a financial consultant named Edward Espinoza in order to win various city contracts, including senior housing and sewer rehabilitation projects. As part of this plan, Robles and Espinoza set up a shell corporation that raked in some $2.4 million—more than $1.4 million of which went straight into Robles's pockets.

He used part of the money to buy a $165,000 beach condo in Baja for his mother; he also forked over $55,000 for "platinum membership" in a motivational group. In another scheme, Robles steered a $48 million refuse and recycling contract to a company in exchange for more than $30,000 in gifts and campaign contributions.

In February 2003, Robles was targeted by a federal grand jury looking into the handling of federal loans and grants. FBI and IRS investigators poured over city records to uncover his illegal schemes. The citizens of South Gate ultimately voted Robles and his cronies out of office (but not before he racked up huge legal bills at the city's expense), and he was convicted at trial in July 2005. Two of his business associates—including Espinoza—also went to prison.

Robles's illegal acts were the product of careful plotting and planning. They were motivated by greed and not need. To some criminologists stories like these confirm the fact that many crimes are a matter of rational choice.

Sources: Federal Bureau of Investigation, "Corruption in City Hall: The Crooked Reign of 'King' Albert," January 8, 2007, www.fbi.gov/page2/jan07/cityhall010807.htm (accessed March 15, 2007); Hector Becerra, "Robles Sentenced to 10 Years," *Los Angeles Times*, 29 November 2006, p. 1.

The Ivy League hooker is not alone. Perceptions of economic opportunity influence the decision to commit crime. Sociologists Christopher Uggen and Melissa Thompson found that people who begin taking hard drugs also increase their involvement in crime, taking in from $500 to $700 per month. Once they become cocaine and heroin users, the benefits of other criminal enterprise become overwhelmingly attractive.[26]

Crime also becomes attractive when an individual becomes convinced that it will result in excessive profits with few costs. Research shows that criminals may be motivated to commit crime when they know others who have made "big scores" and are quite successful at crime. Although the prevailing wisdom is that crime does not pay, a small but significant subset of criminals actually enjoy earnings of close to $50,000 per year from crime, and their success may help motivate

other would-be offenders.[27] However, offenders are likely to desist from crime if they believe that their future criminal earnings will be relatively low and that attractive and legal opportunities to generate income are available.[28] In this sense, rational choice is a function of a person's perception of conventional alternatives and opportunities.

connections

The role of economic needs in the motivation of white-collar criminals is discussed in Chapter 12. Research shows that even consistently law-abiding people may turn to criminal solutions when faced with overwhelming economic needs. They make the rational decision to commit crimes to solve some economic crisis.

Some people choose to commit crime because it can pay so much! Even highly paid corporate execs can succumb to the lure of ill-gotten gains. Here, former Enron CFO Andrew Fastow is led from the courthouse after sentencing from his conviction related to the collapse of Enron. Fastow testified against his former bosses Kenneth Lay and Jeff Skilling and received a six-year sentence. Fastow—who played a huge role in the Enron scandal, which triggered one of the largest bankruptcy cases in U.S. history—made more than $30 million managing Enron-owned partnerships and embezzled millions more.

Learning and Experience Learning and experience may be important elements in structuring the choice of crime.[29] Career criminals may learn the limitations of their powers; they know when to take a chance and when to be cautious. Experienced criminals may turn from a life of crime when they develop a belief that the risk of crime is greater than its potential profit.[30] Patricia Morgan and Karen Ann Joe's three-city study (San Francisco, San Diego, and Honolulu) of female drug abusers found that experience helped dealers avoid

detection. One dealer, earning $50,000 per year, explained her strategy this way:

I stayed within my goals, basically . . . I don't go around doing stupid things. I don't walk around telling people I have drugs for sale. I don't have people sitting out in front of my house. I don't have traffic in and out of my house . . . I control the people I sell to.[31]

Morgan and Joe found that these female dealers consider drug distribution a positive experience that gives them economic independence, self-esteem, increased ability to function, professional pride, and the ability to maintain control over their lives. These women often seemed more like yuppies opening a boutique than out-of-control addicts:

I'm a good dealer. I don't cut my drugs, I have high-quality drugs insofar as it's possible to get high-quality drugs. I want to be known as somebody who sells good drugs, but doesn't always have them, as opposed to someone who always has them and sometimes the drugs are good.[32]

Here we see how experience in the profession shapes criminal decision making.

Knowledge of Criminal Techniques Criminals report learning techniques that help them avoid detection, a sure sign of rational thinking and planning. In his studies of drug dealers, criminologist Bruce Jacobs found that crack dealers learn how to stash crack cocaine in some undisclosed location so that they are not forced to carry large amounts of product on their persons. Dealers carefully evaluate the security of their sales area before setting up shop.[33] Most consider the middle of a long block the best place for drug deals because they can see everything in both directions; police raids can be spotted before they develop.[34] If a buyer seems dangerous or unreliable, the dealer would require that they do business in spaces between apartment buildings or in back lots. Although dealers lose the tactical edge of being on a public street, they gain a measure of protection because their associates can watch over the deal and come to the rescue if the buyer tries to "pull something."[35] Similar detection avoidance schemes were found by Gordon Knowles in his study of crack dealers in Honolulu, Hawaii. Knowles found that drug dealers often use pornographic film houses as their base of operations because they offer both privacy and convenience.[36]

When Jacobs, along with Jody Miller, studied female crack dealers, they discovered a variety of defensive moves used by the dealers to avoid detection.[37] One of these techniques, called stashing, involved learning how to hide drugs on their person, on the street, or at home. One dealer told Jacobs and Miller how she hid drugs in the empty shaft of a curtain rod; another wore hollow earmuffs to hide crack. Because a female officer is required to conduct body cavity searches on women, the dealers had time to get rid of their drugs before they got to the station house. Dealers are aware of legal definitions of possession. One said she stashed her drugs 250 feet from her home because that was beyond the distance (150 feet) police considered a person legally to be in "constructive possession" of drugs.

© Dave Einsel/Getty Images

Criminals who learn the proper techniques may be able to prolong their criminal careers. Jacobs found that these offenders use specific techniques to avoid being apprehended by police. They play what they call the "peep game" before dealing drugs, scoping out the territory to make sure the turf is free from anything out of place that could be a potential threat (such as police officers or rival gang members).[38] One crack dealer told Jacobs:

> There was this red Pontiac sittin' on the corner one day with two white guys inside. They was just sittin' there for an hour, not doin' nothin'. Another day, diff'rent people be walkin' up and down the street you don't really recognize. You think they might be kin of someone but then you be askin' around and they [neighbors] ain't never seen them before neither. When ya' see strange things like that, you think somethin' be goin' on [and you don't deal].[39]

Drug dealers told Jacobs that they also carefully consider whether they should deal alone or in groups; large groups draw more attention from police but can offer more protection. Drug-dealing gangs and groups can help divert the attention of police: if their drug dealing is noticed by detectives, a dealer can slyly walk away or dispose of evidence while confederates distract the cops.[40]

connections

Rational choice theory dovetails with routine activities theory, which you learned about in Chapter 3. Although not identical, these approaches both claim that crime rates are a normal product of criminal opportunity. Both suggest that criminals consider such elements as guardianship and target attractiveness before they decide to commit crimes. The routine activities and rational choice views also agree that criminal opportunity is a key element in the criminal process. The overlap between these two viewpoints may help criminologists suggest means for effective crime control.

Structuring Crime

Not only do criminals structure their careers, but they rationally choose where and when to commit crime and whom to target. According to the rational choice approach, the decision to commit crime is structured by analysis of (a) the type of crime, (b) the time and place of crime, and (c) the target of crime.

Choosing the Type of Crime Some criminals are specialists, for example, professional car thieves. Others are generalists who sell drugs one day and commit burglaries the next. Their choice of crime may be dictated by a rational analysis of market conditions. For example, they may rob the elderly on the first of the month when they know that Social Security checks have been cashed.

Sometimes the choice of crime is structured by the immediacy of the need for funds. Eric Baumer and his associates found that cities with greater levels of crack cocaine often experience an increase in robbery and a corresponding decrease in burglary rates. Baumer reasons that crack users need a quick influx of cash to purchase drugs and are in no position to plan a burglary and take the time to sell their loot; street robberies are designed to provide a quick influx of cash that meets their lifestyle needs.[41]

Choosing the Time and Place of Crime There is evidence of rationality in the way criminals choose the time and place of their crimes. Burglars seem to prefer "working" between 9 A.M. and 11 A.M. and in mid-afternoon, when parents are either working or dropping off or picking up kids at school.[42] Burglars avoid Saturdays because most families are at home; Sunday morning during church hours is considered a prime time for weekend burglaries.[43] Some find out which families have star high school athletes because those that do are sure to be at the weekend game, leaving their houses unguarded.[44]

Evidence of rational choice may also be found in the way criminals choose target locations. Thieves seem to avoid free-standing buildings because they can more easily be surrounded by police; they like to select targets that are known to do a primarily cash business, such as bars, supermarkets, and restaurants.[45] Burglars appear to monitor car and pedestrian traffic and avoid selecting targets on heavily traveled streets.[46] Corner homes, usually near traffic lights or stop signs, are the ones most likely to be burglarized: stop signs give criminals a legitimate reason to stop their cars and look for an attractive target.[47] Secluded homes, such as those at the end of a cul-de-sac or surrounded by wooded areas, make suitable targets.[48] Thieves also report being concerned about target convenience. They are more apt to choose familiar burglary sites that are located in easily accessible and open areas.[49]

Because criminals often go on foot or use public transportation, they are unlikely to travel long distances to commit crimes and are more likely to drift toward the center of a city than move toward outlying areas.[50] Some may occasionally commute to distant locations to commit crimes, but most prefer to stay in their own neighborhood where they are familiar with the terrain. They will only travel to unfamiliar areas if they believe the new location contains a worthy target and lax law enforcement. They may be encouraged to travel when the police are cracking down in their own neighborhood and the "heat is on."[51] Evidence is accumulating that predatory criminals are in fact aware of law enforcement capabilities and consider them closely before deciding to commit crimes. Communities with the reputation of employing aggressive "crime-fighting" cops are less likely to attract potential offenders than areas perceived to have passive law enforcers.[52]

The Target of Crime Criminals may also be well aware of target vulnerability. For example, there is evidence that people engaging in deviant or antisocial behaviors are also the most likely to become crime victims.[53] Perhaps predatory criminals sense that people with "dirty hands" make suitable targets because they are unlikely to want to call police or get entangled with the law.

Criminals tend to shy away from victims who are perceived to be armed and potentially dangerous.[54] In a series of interviews with career property offenders, Kenneth Tunnell found that burglars avoid targets if they feel there are police in the area or if "nosy neighbors" might be suspicious and cause trouble.[55]

IS CRIME RATIONAL?

It is relatively easy to show that some crimes are the product of rational, objective thought, especially when they involve an ongoing criminal conspiracy centered on economic gain. When prominent bankers in the savings and loan industry were indicted for criminal fraud, their elaborate financial schemes exhibited not only signs of rationality but brilliant, though flawed, financial expertise.[56] The stock market manipulations of Enron and WorldCom executives, the drug dealings of international cartels, and the gambling operations of organized crime bosses all demonstrate a reasoned analysis of market conditions, interests, and risks. Even small-time wheeler-dealers, such as the female drug dealers discussed earlier in the chapter, are guided by their rational assessment of the likelihood of apprehension and take pains to avoid detection. But what about common crimes of theft and violence? Are these rational acts or unplanned, haphazard, and spontaneous?

Is Theft Rational?

Common theft-related crimes—burglaries, larcenies, shoplifting, purse snatchings—seem more likely to be random acts of criminal opportunity than well-thought-out conspiracies. However, there is evidence that even these seemingly unplanned events may be the product of careful risk assessment, including environmental, social, and structural factors. For example, there are professional shoplifters, referred to as boosters, who use complex methods in order to avoid detection. They steal with the intention of reselling stolen merchandise to professional fences, another group of criminals who use cunning and rational decision making in their daily activities.

Burglars also seem to use skill and knowledge when choosing targets. Experienced burglars report having to learn detection avoidance techniques. Some check to make sure that no one is home, either by calling ahead or ringing the doorbell, preparing to claim they had the wrong address if someone answers. Others seek unlocked doors and avoid the ones with deadbolts; houses with dogs are usually considered off limits.[57] Most burglars prefer to commit crimes in permeable neighborhoods with a greater than usual number of access streets from traffic arteries into the neighborhood.[58] These areas are chosen for theft and break-ins because they are familiar and well traveled, they appear more open and vulnerable, and they offer more potential escape routes.[59]

American burglars are not alone in using rational choice. English authorities report that carefully planned burglaries seem to be on the decline presumably because goods that were the target a few years back—video recorders and DVD players—are now so cheap that they are not worth stealing; in English terms, they are barely worth *nicking*. Televisions may be valuable, but those that are the most valuable have become so large that they are impractical to steal.[60] As a result, the planned professional burglary is on a decline in Britain at the same time that street muggings are on the rise.

Is Drug Use Rational?

Did actor Robert Downey, Jr., make an objective, rational choice to abuse drugs and potentially sabotage his career? Did Lindsay Lohan make a rational choice when she abused alcohol and other substances to the point where she had to enter rehab? What was Paris Hilton thinking when she violated her probation by drinking and driving and was forced to do jail time? Is it possible that substance users and dealers, a group not usually associated with clear thinking, make rational choices?

Research does in fact show that from its onset drug use is controlled by rational decision making. Users report that they begin taking drugs when they believe that the benefits of substance abuse outweigh its costs (for example, they believe that drugs will provide a fun, exciting, thrilling experience). Their entry into substance abuse is facilitated by their perception that valued friends and family members endorse and encourage drug use and abuse substances themselves.[61]

In adulthood, heavy drug users and dealers show signs of rationality and cunning in their daily activity, approaching drug dealing as a business proposition. Research conducted by Leanne Fiftal Alarid and her partners provides a good illustration of this phenomenon because it focused on how women drawn into dealing drugs learn the trade in a businesslike manner. One young dealer told them how she learned the techniques of the trade from an older male partner:

> He taught me how to "recon" [reconstitute] cocaine, cutting and repacking a brick from 91 proof to 50 proof, just like a business. He treats me like an equal partner, and many of the friends are business associates. I am a catalyst. . . . I even get guys turned on to drugs.[62]

Note the business terminology used. This coke dealer could be talking about taking a computer training course at a major corporation! If criminal acts are treated as business decisions, in which profit and loss potential must be carefully calculated, then crime must indeed be a rational event.

Is Violence Rational?

Brandon Wilson, 21, slashed the throat of Matthew Cecchi, a nine-year-old California boy, then stabbed him in the back and left him to bleed to death. After his conviction on murder charges, Wilson told the jury that he would "do it again in a second if I had the chance." When the jury later met to consider the death penalty, Wilson told them, "My whole purpose in life is to help destroy your society. You people are here as representatives of that society. As such, you should do everything in your power to rid the world of me, execute me." Granting his wish, the jury foreman told reporters, "If there was ever a case that deserved the death penalty, this one fits."[63] Though seemingly a demented child killer, Brandon Wilson's statements indicate that he is a rational and calculating killer who may have carefully chosen his victim. Is it possible that violent acts, through which the offender gains little material benefit, are the product of reasoned decision making? Could the violent acts of seemingly demented Virginia Tech killer Seung-Hui Cho have been motivated by some

Brandon Wilson, the accused killer of 9-year-old Matthew Cecchi, stands handcuffed in felony arraignment court in Vista, California. Can such violent acts ever be considered "rational"? Before you answer, remember that Wilson could have attacked a Marine, police officer, or kung fu expert, but instead "chose" a defenseless child.

elements of rational choice and not merely the product of irrational mental instability?

Yes, it is possible, according to crime experts such as Richard Felson, who argues that violence is a matter of choice and serves specific goals:

▎ *Control.* The violent person may want to control their victim's behavior and life.

▎ *Retribution.* The perpetrator may want to punish someone without calling the police or using the justice system to address their grievances. They take the law into their own hands.

▎ *Deterrence.* The attacker may want to stop someone from repeating acts that they consider hostile or provocative.

▎ *Reputation.* An attack may be motivated by the need to enhance reputation and create self-importance in the eyes of others.

Felson also recognizes that the violent act may have multiple goals. But in any case, it is a product of rational decision making.[64]

Rational Robbers Street robbers also are likely to choose victims who are vulnerable, have low coercive power, and do not pose any threat.[65] In their survey of violent felons, James Wright and Peter Rossi found that robbers avoid victims who

may be armed and dangerous. About three-fifths of all felons interviewed were more afraid of armed victims than of police; about two-fifths had avoided a victim because they believed the victim was armed; and almost one-third reported that they had been scared off, wounded, or captured by armed victims.[66] It comes as no surprise that cities with higher than average gun-carrying rates generally have lower rates of unarmed robbery.[67]

Robbers also tend to pick the time and day of crimes carefully. When they rob a commercial establishment, they choose the time when there is the most cash on hand to increase their take from the crime. For example, robbery rates increase in the winter partly because the Christmas shopping season means more money in the cash registers of potential targets.[68] Targets are generally found close to robbers' homes or in areas in which they routinely travel. Familiarity with the area gives them ready knowledge of escape routes; this is referred to as their "awareness space."[69] A familiar location allows them to blend in, not look out of place, and not get lost when returning home with their loot.[70]

Robbers may be wary of people who are watching the community for signs of trouble: research by Paul Bellair shows that robbery levels are relatively low in neighborhoods where residents keep a watchful eye on their neighbors' property.[71] Robbers avoid buildings that can be easily surrounded by police; they also prefer to rob businesses that deal primarily with cash.[72] Their activities show clear signs of rational choice.

Rational Killers? Hollywood likes to portray deranged people killing innocent victims at random, but people who carry guns and are ready to use them typically do so for more rational reasons. They may perceive that they live in a dangerous environment and carry a weapon for self-protection.[73] Some are involved in dangerous illegal activities such as drug dealing and carry weapons as part of the job.[74] Even in apparently senseless killings among strangers, the conscious motive is typically revenge for a prior dispute or disagreement among the parties involved or their families.[75] Many homicides are motivated by offenders' desire to avoid retaliation from a victim they assaulted or to avoid future prosecutions by getting rid of witnesses.[76] Although some killings are the result of anger and aggression, others are the result of rational planning.

Even serial murderers, outwardly the most irrational of all offenders, tend to pick their targets with care. Most choose victims who are defenseless or who cannot count on police protection: prostitutes, gay men, hitchhikers, children, hospital patients, the elderly, and the homeless. Rarely do serial killers target weightlifters, martial arts experts, or any other potentially powerful group.[77] Even mass killings show elements of rationality. While Virginia Tech killer Seung-Hui Cho's behavior seems essentially irrational, he did purchase a gun and ammunition while hiding his prior mental problems, brought chains to lock the doors of the classroom building where most of the murders occurred, and had the presence of mind to write notes and make videotapes explaining his actions.

Rational Sex Criminals? One might think that sex crimes are highly irrational, motivated by hate, lust, revenge, emotions that defy rational planning. But sex criminals report using rational thought and planning when carrying out their crimes. Serial rapists rationally choose their targets. They travel, on average, three miles from their homes to commit their crimes in order to avoid victims who might recognize them later. The desire to avoid detection supersedes the wish to obtain a victim with little effort. Older, more experienced rapists who have extensive criminal histories are willing to travel further; younger rapists who have less experience committing crimes travel less and are therefore more at risk of detection.[78]

Child molesters/rapists report that they volunteer or seek employment in day care centers and other venues where victims can be found. They use their status to gain the trust of children and to be seen as nonthreatening to the child. Within the context of this work environment they can then use subtle strategies of manipulation, such as giving love and attention to gain their victims' trust (e.g., spending a lot of time with them), and they can gradually desensitize the children and gain their cooperation in sexual activity (e.g., through nonsexual touching).[79] These efforts obviously display planning and rationality.

Rational Airplane Hijackers? Certainly the activities of people who hijack airplanes can't be called rational. Or can they? In a recent study, Laura Dugan, Gary Lafree, and Alex Piquero found that even airplane hijackers, a rather unique sort of violent criminal, may be rational decision makers. Hijacking rates declined when airlines employed measures to make it more difficult to commit crime (for example, using metal detectors in airports) or to increase the cost of crime (for example, boosting the punishments for hijacking). Dugan and her associates found that hijacking rates significantly increased soon after a spate of successful hijackings and decreased when antihijacking policies were implemented. The fact that hijackers were deterred by the threat of apprehension and punishment and encouraged by others' success is surely a sign of rational decision making.[80]

For many people, then, crime is attractive; it brings rewards, excitement, prestige, or other desirable outcomes without lengthy work or effort.[81] Whether it is violent or profit oriented, crime has an allure that some people cannot resist. Crime may produce a natural high and other positive sensations that are instrumental in maintaining and reinforcing criminal behavior.[82] Some law violators describe the adrenaline rush that comes from successfully executing illegal activities in dangerous situations. This has been described as edgework, the "exhilarating, momentary integration of danger, risk, and skill" that motivates people to try a variety of dangerous criminal and noncriminal behaviors.[83] Crime is not some random act but a means that can provide both pleasure and solutions to vexing personal problems.

ELIMINATING CRIME

If crime is rational and people choose to commit crime, then it follows that crime can be controlled or eradicated by convincing potential offenders that crime is a poor choice that will not bring them rewards but pain, hardship, and deprivation instead. Evidence shows that jurisdictions with relatively low incarceration rates also experience the highest crime rates.[84] As we have seen, according to rational choice theory, street-smart offenders know which areas offer the least threat and plan their crimes accordingly. Strategies for crime control based on this premise are illustrated in Concept Summary 4.1. The following sections discuss each of these crime reduction or control strategies.

Situational Crime Prevention

Desperate people may contemplate crime, but only the truly irrational would attack a well-defended, inaccessible target and risk strict punishment. Crime prevention can be achieved by reducing the opportunities people have to commit particular crimes, a practice known as situational crime prevention. According to this concept, in order to reduce criminal activity, planners must be aware of the characteristics of sites and situations that are at risk to crime; the things that draw or push people toward these sites and situations; what equips potential criminals to take advantage of illegal opportunities offered by these sites and situations; and what constitutes the immediate triggers for criminal actions.[85] Criminal acts will be avoided if (a) potential targets are guarded securely, (b) the means to commit crime are controlled, and (c) potential offenders are carefully monitored.

Situational crime prevention was first popularized in the United States in the early 1970s by Oscar Newman, who coined the term defensible space. This term signifies that crime can be prevented or displaced through the use of residential architectural designs that reduce criminal opportunity, such as well-lit housing projects that maximize surveillance.[86] C. Ray Jeffery wrote *Crime Prevention through Environmental Design*, which extended Newman's concepts and applied them to nonresidential areas, such as schools and factories.[87] According to this view, mechanisms such as security systems, deadbolt locks, high-intensity street lighting, and neighborhood watch patrols should reduce criminal opportunity.[88] The subway system in Washington, D.C., has used some of these environmental crime reduction techniques to control crime since it began operations in 1976.

In 1992 Ronald Clarke published *Situational Crime Prevention*, which compiled the best-known strategies and tactics to reduce criminal incidents.[89] Criminologists have suggested using a number of situational crime prevention efforts that might reduce crime rates. One approach is not to target a specific crime but to create an environment that can reduce the overall crime rate by limiting the access to tempting targets for a highly motivated offender group (such as high school students).[90]

Targeting Specific Crimes Situational crime prevention can also involve developing tactics to reduce or eliminate a specific crime problem (such as shoplifting in an urban mall or street-level drug dealing). According to Derek Cornish and Ronald Clarke, situational crime prevention efforts may be divided into five strategies:[91]

▍ Increase the effort needed to commit crime

▍ Increase the risks of committing crime

EXHIBIT 4.1

Crime Discouragers

Types of Supervisors and Objects of Supervision

Level of Responsibility	Guardians (monitoring suitable targets)	Handlers (monitoring likely offenders)	Managers (monitoring amenable places)
Personal (owners, family, friends)	Student keeps eye on own book bag	Parent makes sure child gets home	Homeowner monitors area near home
Assigned (employees with specific assignment)	Store clerk monitors jewelry	Principal sends kids back to school	Doorman protects building
Diffuse (employees with general assignment)	Accountant notes shoplifting	School clerk discourages truancy	Hotel maid impairs trespasser
General (strangers, other citizens)	Bystander inhibits shoplifting	Stranger questions boys at mall	Customer observes parking structure

Source: Marcus Felson, "Those Who Discourage Crime," in John Eck and David Weisburd, *Crime and Place* (Monsey, NY: Criminal Justice Press, 1995), p. 59. Reprinted by permission.

▌ Reduce the rewards for committing crime

▌ Reduce provocation/induce guilt or shame for committing crime

▌ Reduce excuses for committing crime

Increase Efforts Some of the tactics to increase efforts include target-hardening techniques such as putting unbreakable glass on storefronts, locking gates, and fencing yards. Technological advances can make it more difficult to commit crimes; having an owner's photo on credit cards should reduce the use of stolen cards. The development of new products, such as steering locks on cars, can make it more difficult to commit crimes. Empirical evidence indicates that steering locks have helped reduce car theft in the United States, Britain, and Germany.[92] Installing a locking device on cars that prevents inebriated drivers from starting the vehicle (breath-analyzed ignition interlock device) significantly reduces drunk-driving rates among people with a history of driving while intoxicated.[93] Removing visibility-blocking signs from store windows, installing brighter lights, and instituting a pay-first policy can help reduce thefts from gas stations and convenience stores.[94]

Another way to increase effort is to reduce opportunities for criminal activity. Many cities have established curfew laws in an effort to limit the opportunity juveniles have to engage in antisocial behavior.[95] However, curfew laws have not met with universal success.[96] So another approach has been to involve kids in after-school programs that take up their time and reduce their opportunity to get in trouble. An example of this type of program is the Doorsteps Neighbourhood Program in Toronto, Ontario, which is designed to help children in high-risk areas complete their schoolwork as well as providing them with playtime that helps improve their literacy and communication skills. Children who are part of this program enter into routines that increase the effort they must make if they want to get involved in after-school crime and nuisance activities.[97]

Reduce Rewards Target reduction strategies are designed to reduce the value of crime to the potential criminal. These include making car radios removable so they can be kept in the home at night, marking property so that it is more difficult to sell when stolen, and having gender-neutral phone listings to discourage obscene phone calls. Tracking systems, such as those made by the Lojack Corporation, help police locate and return stolen vehicles.

Increase Risk If criminals believe that committing crime is very risky, only the most foolhardy would attempt to commit criminal acts. Managing crime falls into the hands of people Marcus Felson calls crime discouragers.[98] These discouragers can be grouped into three categories: guardians, who monitor targets (such as store security guards); handlers, who monitor potential offenders (such as parole officers and parents); and managers, who monitor places (such as homeowners and doorway attendants). If crime discouragers do their job correctly, the potential criminal will be convinced that the risk of crime outweighs any potential gains.[99]

Crime discouragers have different levels of responsibility, ranging from highly personal involvement, such as the homeowner protecting her house and the parent controlling his children, to the most impersonal general involvement, such as a stranger who stops someone from shoplifting in the mall (Exhibit 4.1).

Research indicates that crime discouragers can have an impact on crime rates. An evaluation of a police initiative in Oakland, California, found that an active working partnership with residents and businesspeople who have a stake in maintaining order in their places of work or residences can reduce levels of drug dealing while at the same time increasing civil behavior. Collective action and cooperation in solving problems were effective in controlling crime, whereas individual action (such as calling 911) seemed to have little effect.[100]

In addition to crime discouragers, it may be possible to raise the risks of committing crime by creating mechanical devices that increase the likelihood that a criminal will be observed and captured. The Comparative Criminology feature, "CCTV or Not CCTV?" discusses a recent evaluation of such methods in Great Britain and the United States.

Increase Shame/Reduce Provocation Inducing guilt or shame might include such techniques as setting strict rules to embarrass offenders. Publishing "John lists" in the newspaper shames those arrested for soliciting prostitutes. Facilitating compliance by providing trash bins might shame chronic litterers into using them. Ronald Clarke shows how caller ID in New Jersey resulted in significant reductions in the number of obscene phone calls. Caller ID displays the telephone number of the party placing the call; the threat of exposure had a deterrent effect on the number of obscene calls reported to police.[101]

Some crimes are the result of extreme provocation (e.g., road rage). It might be possible to reduce provocation by creating programs that reduce conflict. Creating an early closing time in local bars and pubs might limit assaults that are the result of late night drinking, such as conflicts in pubs at closing time. Posting guards outside of schools at recess might prevent childish taunts from escalating into full-blown brawls. Antibullying programs that have been implemented in schools are another method of reducing provocation.

Remove Excuses Crime may be reduced by making it difficult for people to excuse their criminal behavior by saying things like "I did not know that was illegal" or "I had no choice." Some municipalities have set up roadside displays that electronically flash cars' speed rate as they drive by, so that when stopped by police, drivers cannot say they did not know how fast they were going. Litter boxes, brightly displayed, can eliminate the claim that "I just did not know where to throw my trash." Reducing or eliminating excuses also makes it physically easy for people to comply with laws and regulations, thereby reducing the likelihood they will choose crime.

Situational Crime Prevention: Costs and Benefits Some attempts at situational crime prevention have proven highly successful while others have not met their goals. However, it is now apparent that the approach brings with it certain nontransparent or hidden costs and benefits that can either increase effectiveness or undermine success. Before the overall success of this approach can be evaluated, these costs and benefits must be considered. Among the hidden benefits of situational crime control efforts are:

▌ *Diffusion.* Sometimes efforts to prevent one crime help prevent another; in other instances, crime control efforts in one locale reduce crime in another area.[102] This effect is referred to as diffusion of benefits. Diffusion may be produced by two independent effects. Crime control efforts may deter criminals by causing them to fear apprehension. Video cameras set up in a mall to reduce shoplifting can also reduce property damage because would-be vandals

fear they will be caught on camera. One recent police program targeting drugs in areas of Jersey City, New Jersey, also reduced public morals crimes because potential offenders were aware of increased police patrols.[103]

▌ *Discouragement.* Sometimes crime control efforts targeting a particular locale help reduce crime in surrounding areas and populations; this is referred to as discouragement. In her study of the effects of the SMART program (a drug enforcement program in Oakland, California, that enforces municipal codes and nuisance abatement laws), criminologist Lorraine Green found that not only did drug dealing decrease in targeted areas but improvement was found in adjacent areas as well. She suggests that the program most likely discouraged buyers and sellers who saw familiar hangouts closed. This sign that drug dealing would not be tolerated probably decreased the total number of people involved in drug activity even though they did not operate in the targeted areas.[104] Another example of this effect can be found in evaluations of the Lojack auto protection system. Lojack uses a hidden radio transmitter to track stolen cars. As the number of Lojack installations rises, police notice that the sale of stolen auto parts declines. It appears that people in the illegal auto parts business (that is, chop shops) close down because they fear that the stolen cars they buy might contain Lojack.[105] A device designed to protect cars from theft also has the benefit of disrupting the sale of stolen car parts.

While there are hidden benefits to situational crime prevention, there may also be costs that limit their effectiveness:

▌ *Displacement.* A program that seems successful because it helps lower crime rates at specific locations or neighborhoods may simply be redirecting offenders to alternative targets; crime is not prevented but deflected or displaced.[106] Beefed-up police patrols in one area may shift crimes to a more vulnerable neighborhood.[107] Sometimes crime prevention efforts may backfire and create even greater problems. When Edward Powers and Janet Wilson studied the effect of banning alcohol sales in some Arkansas counties, they found that the "dry" jurisdictions had the same rate of DUI arrests as "wet" ones. One unforeseen effect of going "dry": because people are forced to travel outside the county to buy liquor they may drink while driving home with their purchase![108] Although in this instance a crime displacement effort may have gone awry, under some circumstances deflection seems to reduce the frequency of crime and may produce less serious offense patterns.[109]

▌ *Extinction.* Sometimes crime reduction programs may produce a short-term positive effect, but benefits dissipate as criminals adjust to new conditions. They learn to dismantle alarms or avoid patrols; they may try new offenses they had previously avoided. And elimination of one crime may encourage commission of another: if every residence in a neighborhood has a foolproof burglar alarm system, motivated offenders may be forced to turn to armed robbery, a riskier and more violent crime.

180. Greg Pogarsky and Alex R. Piquero, "Can Punishment Encourage Offending? Investigating the 'Resetting' Effect," *Journal of Research in Crime and Delinquency* 40 (2003): 92–117.

181. Doris Layton MacKenzie and Spencer De Li, "The Impact of Formal and Informal Social Controls on the Criminal Activities of Probationers," *Journal of Research in Crime and Delinquency* 39 (2002): 243–276.

182. Lawrence Sherman and Richard Berk, "The Specific Deterrent Effects of Arrest for Domestic Assault," *American Sociological Review* 49 (1984): 261–272.

183. Christopher Maxwell, Joel H. Garner, and Jeffrey A. Fagan, *The Effects of Arrest in Intimate Partner Violence: New Evidence from the Spouse Assault Replication Program* (Washington, DC: National Institute of Justice, 2001); J. David Hirschel, Ira Hutchison, and Charles Dean, "The Failure of Arrest to Deter Spouse Abuse," *Journal of Research in Crime and Delinquency* 29 (1992): 7–33; Franklyn Dunford, David Huizinga, and Delbert Elliott, "The Role of Arrest in Domestic Assault: The Omaha Experiment," *Criminology* 28 (1990): 183–206.

184. Charles Murray and Louis Cox, *Beyond Probation* (Beverly Hills: Sage, 1979); Perry Shapiro and Harold Votey, "Deterrence and Subjective Probabilities of Arrest: Modeling Individual Decisions to Drink and Drive in Sweden," *Law and Society Review* 18 (1984): 111–149; Douglas Smith and Patrick Gartin, "Specifying Specific Deterrence: The Influence of Arrest on Future Criminal Activity," *American Sociological Review* 54 (1989): 94–105.

185. Eleni Apospori and Geoffrey Alpert, "Research Note: The Role of Differential Experience with the Criminal Justice System in Changes in Perceptions of Severity of Legal Sanctions over Time," *Crime and Delinquency* 39 (1993): 184–194.

186. Bobby Caina Calvan, "Calif. Initiative Seeks to Rewrite Three-Strikes Law," *Boston Globe*, 12 July 2004, p. 1.

187. David Greenberg and Nancy Larkin, "The Incapacitation of Criminal Opiate Users," *Crime and Delinquency* 44 (1998): 205–228.

188. Reuel Shinnar and Shlomo Shinnar, "The Effects of the Criminal Justice System on the Control of Crime: A Quantitative Approach," *Law and Society Review* 9 (1975): 581–611.

189. Steven Levitt, "Why Do Increased Arrest Rates Appear to Reduce Crime: Deterrence, Incapacitation, or Measurement Error?" *Economic Inquiry* 36 (1998): 353–372; see also Thomas Marvell and Carlisle Moody, "The Impact of Prison Growth on Homicide," *Homicide Studies* 1 (1997): 205–233.

190. Marc Mauer, testimony before the U.S. Congress, House Judiciary Committee, on "Three Strikes and You're Out," 1 March 1994.

191. John Wallerstedt, *Returning to Prison, Bureau of Justice Statistics Special Report* (Washington, DC: U.S. Department of Justice, 1984).

192. James Marquart, Victoria Brewer, Janet Mullings, and Ben Crouch, "The Implications of Crime Control Policy on HIV/AIDS-Related Risk among Women Prisoners," *Crime and Delinquency* 45 (1999): 82–98.

193. Jose Canela-Cacho, Alfred Blumstein, and Jacqueline Cohen, "Relationship between the Offending Frequency of Imprisoned and Free Offenders," *Criminology* 35 (1997): 133–171.

194. Kate King and Patricia Bass, "Southern Prisons and Elderly Inmates: Taking a Look Inside," paper presented at the annual meeting of the American Society of Criminology, San Diego, November 1997.

195. James Lynch and William Sabol, "Prisoner Reentry in Perspective," Urban Institute: www.urban.org/publications/410213.html (accessed March 15, 2007).

196. Rudy Haapanen, Lee Britton, and Tim Croisdale, "Persistent Criminality and Career Length," *Crime and Delinquency* 53 (2007): 133–155.

197. Stephen Markman and Paul Cassell, "Protecting the Innocent: A Response to the Bedeau-Radelet Study," *Stanford Law Review* 41 (1988): 121–170, at 153.

198. James Stephan and Tracy Snell, *Capital Punishment, 1994* (Washington, DC: Bureau of Justice Statistics, 1996), p. 8.

199. Andrew Von Hirsch, *Doing Justice* (New York: Hill and Wang, 1976).

200. Ibid., pp. 15–16.

201. Ibid.

CHAPTER 5

Trait Theories

CHAPTER OUTLINE

Foundations of Trait Theory
Sociobiology
Modern Trait Theories

Biosocial Trait Theories
Biochemical Conditions and Crime

Comparative Criminology: Diet and Crime:
An International Perspective

Neurophysiological Conditions and Crime
Arousal Theory
Genetics and Crime
Evolutionary Theory
Evaluation of the Biosocial Branch of Trait Theory

Psychological Trait Theories
Psychodynamic Theory

PROFILES IN CRIME: Andrea Yates

Behavioral Theory
Cognitive Theory

The Criminological Enterprise: The Media
and Violence

Psychological Traits and Characteristics
Personality and Crime
Intelligence and Crime

The Criminological Enterprise: The Antisocial Personality

Public Policy Implications of Trait Theory

CHAPTER OBJECTIVES

1. Be familiar with the concept of sociobiology
2. Know what is meant by the term "equipotentiality"
3. Be able to discuss the relationship between diet and crime
4. Be familiar with the association between hormones and crime
5. Be able to discuss why violent offenders may suffer from neurological problems
6. Know the factors that make up the ADHD syndrome
7. Be able to discuss the role genetics plays in violent behavior
8. Be familiar with the concepts of evolutionary theory
9. Be able to discuss the psychodynamics of criminality
10. Understand the association between media and crime
11. Discuss the role of personality and intelligence in antisocial behaviors

© AP Images/Amy Sancetta

In the aftermath of the Virginia Tech massacre, psychologists and mental health experts quickly began to diagnose the killer, Seung-hui Cho, concluding that he was a deeply disturbed young man who left behind a shocking and horrifying video that revealed his twisted fantasies. His behavior seemed similar to Columbine High School killers Eric Harris and Dylan Klebold, who also left behind rage-filled statements. Cho even refers to the Columbine perpetrators as "martyrs." These killers may have other common characteristics, such as feelings of rejection: in his video, Cho says: "You have vandalized my heart, raped my soul, and tortured my conscience. You thought it was one more pathetic life you were extinguishing. Thanks to you, I die like Jesus Christ to inspire generations of the weak and the defenseless people." Cho also had a fascination with guns and explosives and a preoccupation with death. While no one expected his rampage, he had previously been accused of stalking two female students and in 2005 had been taken to a mental health facility. There were also concerns at the time that he was suicidal. Other diagnoses suggested that Cho could have been suffering from some severe psychological disorder, possibly bipolar depression or even schizophrenia.[1]

How can we explain the bizarre behavior of Seung-hui Cho? Why would a young college student gun down helpless classmates he barely knew? Could his acts possibly be the result of calculation and planning, or are they the product of some mental aberration or personality disturbance? What drives people who seem to have everything to commit bizarre crimes? Could it be some aberration in their physical or mental makeup?

The image of a disturbed, mentally ill offender seems plausible because a generation of Americans has grown up on films and TV shows that portray violent criminals as mentally deranged and physically abnormal. Beginning with Alfred Hitchcock's film *Psycho*, producers have made millions depicting the ghoulish acts of people who at first seem normal and even friendly but turn out to be demented and dangerous. Lurking out there are crazed babysitters (*The Hand that Rocks the Cradle*), frenzied airline passengers (*Red Eye; Turbulence*), deranged roommates (*Single White Female*), cracked neighbors (*Disturbia*), psychotic tenants (*Pacific Heights*), demented secretaries (*The Temp*), unhinged police (*Maniac Cop*), mad cab drivers (*The Bone Collector*), irrational fans (*The Fan; Misery*), abnormal girlfriends (*Fatal Attraction*) and boyfriends (*Fear*), unstable husbands (*Enough; Sleeping with the Enemy*) and wives (*Black Widow*), loony fathers (*The Stepfather*), mothers (*Friday the 13th, Part 1*), and grandmothers (*Hush*), and entire families (*Texas Chainsaw Massacre*). People are routinely menaced by unbalanced crime victims (*I Know What You Did Last Summer*), maniacal children (*The Good Son; Children of the Corn*), lunatic high school friends (*Scream*) and college classmates (*Scream II*), possessed dolls (*Child's Play 1–5*) and their mates (*Bride of Chucky*), and nutsy teenaged admirers (*The Crush*). Sometimes they even try to kill each other (*Freddy vs. Jason*). No one can ever be safe when the psychologists and psychiatrists who should be treating these disturbed people turn out to be demonic murderers themselves (*Hannibal, Silence of the Lambs*). Is it any wonder that we respond to a particularly horrible crime by saying of the perpetrator, "That guy must be crazy" or "She is a monster!"

The view that criminals bear physical and/or mental traits that make them different and abnormal is not restricted to the moviegoing public. Since the nineteenth century, some criminologists have suggested that biological and psychological traits may influence behavior. Some people may develop physical or mental traits at birth or soon after that affect their social functioning over the life course and influence their behavior choices. Low-birthweight babies have been found to suffer poor educational achievement later in life. Academic deficiency has been linked to delinquency and drug abuse, so it is possible that a condition present at birth (such as low birth weight) will influence antisocial behavior during later adolescence.[2] Possessing these personal differences explains why, when faced with the same life situations, one person commits crime and becomes a chronic offender, whereas another attends school, church, and neighborhood functions and obeys the laws of society. To understand this view of crime causation, we begin with a brief review of the development of trait theories.

FOUNDATIONS OF TRAIT THEORY

As you may recall, Cesare Lombroso's work on the "born criminal" identified the primitive, atavistic anomalies that he believed were the direct cause of crime. Lombroso was not alone in his views on the biological basis of crime. A contemporary, Raffaele Garofalo (1852–1934), shared the belief that certain physical characteristics indicate a criminal nature: "a lower degree of sensibility to physical pain seems to be demonstrated by the readiness with which prisoners submit to the operation of tattooing."[3] Enrico Ferri (1856–1929) added a social dimension to Lombroso's work and argued that criminals should not be held personally or morally responsible for their actions because forces outside their control caused criminality.[4]

Advocates of the inheritance school such as Henry Goddard, Richard Dugdale and Arthur Estabrook traced several generations of crime-prone families (referred to by pseudonyms the "Jukes" and the "Kallikaks"), finding evidence that criminal tendencies were based on genetics.[5] Their conclusion: traits deemed socially inferior could be passed down from generation to generation through inheritance. Modern scholars point out that these families lived in severe poverty so that social rather than biological factors may have been at the root of their problems.[6]

The body build or somatotype school, developed more than 50 years ago by William Sheldon, held that criminals manifest distinct physiques that make them susceptible to particular types of antisocial behavior. Three types of body builds were identified:

▌ *Mesomorphs* have well-developed muscles and an athletic appearance. They are active, aggressive, sometimes violent, and the most likely to become criminals.

▌ *Endomorphs* have heavy builds and are slow moving. They are known for lethargic behavior rendering them unlikely to commit violent crime and more willing to engage in less strenuous criminal activities such as fencing stolen property.

▌ *Ectomorphs* are tall, thin, and less social and more intellectual than the other types.[7]

The work of Lombroso and his contemporaries is regarded today as a historical curiosity, not scientific fact. Their research methodology has been discredited because they did not use control groups from the general population to compare results. Many of the traits they assumed to be inherited are not really genetically determined but could be caused by deprivation in surroundings and diet. Even if most criminals shared some biological traits, they might be products not of heredity but of some environmental condition, such as poor nutrition or health care. Unusual appearance, and not behavior, may have prompted people to be labeled and punished by the justice system. In his later writings, even Lombroso admitted that the born criminal was just one of many criminal types.

Because of these deficiencies the validity of biological/psychological explanations of criminality became questionable and, for a time, disregarded by the criminological mainstream. At midcentury, sociology dominated the study of crime and scholarship and any suggestion that antisocial behavior may have an individual-level cause was treated with enmity.[8] Some criminologists have gone as far as to label this position as biophobia, the view that no serious consideration should be given to biological factors when attempting to understand human nature.[9]

Sociobiology

What seems no longer tenable at this juncture is any theory of human behavior which ignores biology and relies exclusively on socio-cultural learning. . . . Most social scientists have been wrong in their dogmatic rejection and blissful ignorance of the biological parameters of our behavior.[10]

In the early 1970s, spurred by the publication of *Sociobiology*, by biologist Edmund O. Wilson, the biological basis for crime once again emerged into the limelight.[11] Sociobiology differs from earlier theories of behavior in that it stresses that biological and genetic conditions affect how social behaviors are learned and perceived. These perceptions, in turn, are linked to existing environmental structures. Sociobiologists view the gene as the ultimate unit of life that controls all human destiny. Although they believe environment and experience also have an impact on behavior, their main premise is that most actions are controlled by a person's "biological machine." Most important, people are controlled by the innate need to have their genetic material survive and dominate others. Consequently, they do everything in their power to ensure their own survival and that of others who share their gene pool (relatives, fellow citizens, and so forth). Even when they come to the aid of others, which is called reciprocal altruism, people are motivated by the belief that their actions will be reciprocated and that their gene survival capability will be enhanced.

The study of sociobiology revived interest in finding a biological basis for crime and delinquency. If, as it suggests, biological (genetic) makeup controls human behavior, it follows that it should also be responsible for determining whether a person chooses law-violating or conventional behavior. This view of crime causation is referred to as trait theory.

Modern Trait Theories

Trait theorists today do not suggest that a single biological or psychological attribute is thought to adequately explain all criminality. Rather, each offender is considered unique, physically and mentally; consequently, there must be different explanations for each person's behavior. Some may have inherited criminal tendencies, others may be suffering from nervous system (neurological) problems, and still others may have a blood chemistry disorder that heightens their antisocial activity. Criminologists who focus on the individual see many explanations for

crime, because, in fact, there are many differences among criminal offenders.

Trait theorists are not overly concerned with legal definitions of crime; they do not try to explain why people violate particular statutory laws such as car theft or burglary. To them, these are artificial legal concepts based on arbitrary boundaries (i.e., speeding may be arbitrarily defined as exceeding 65 miles per hour in some areas, 70 in others). Instead, trait theorists focus on basic human behavior and drives—aggression, violence, impulsivity—that are linked to antisocial behavior patterns. They also recognize that human traits alone do not produce criminality and that crime-producing interactions involve both personal traits—such as intelligence, personality, and chemical and genetic makeup—and environmental factors, such as family life, educational attainment, economic factors, and neighborhood conditions. Physical or mental traits are, therefore, but one part of a large pool of environmental, social, and personal factors that account for criminality. Some people may have a predisposition toward aggression, but environmental stimuli can either suppress or trigger antisocial acts.

Even the most committed trait theorists recognize that environmental conditions in disadvantaged inner-city areas may have a powerful influence on antisocial behavior. Many people who reside in these areas experience poverty, racism, frustration, and anger, yet relatively few become delinquents and even fewer mature into adult criminals. Because not all humans are born with equal potential to learn and achieve (equipotentiality), the combination of physical traits and the environment produces individual behavior patterns. There is a significant link between behavior patterns and physical or chemical changes in the brain, autonomic nervous system, and central nervous system.[12] Trait theorists argue that those who do become chronic offenders suffer some biological/psychological condition or trait that renders them incapable of resisting social pressures and problems.[13] As biocriminologists Anthony Walsh and Lee Ellis conclude, "If there is one take-away lesson from studying biological bases of behavior, it is that the more we study them the more we realize how important the environment is."[14]

Trait theories have gained recent prominence because of what is now known about chronic recidivism and the development of criminal careers. If only a small percentage of all offenders go on to become persistent repeaters, then it is possible that what sets them apart from the criminal population is an abnormal biochemical makeup, brain structure, or genetic constitution.[15] Even if criminals do "choose crime," the fact that some repeatedly make that choice could well be linked to their physical and mental makeup. All people may be aware of and even fear the sanctioning power of the law, but some are unable to control their urges and passions.

Trait theories can be divided into two major subdivisions: one that stresses psychological functioning and another that stresses biological makeup. Although there is often overlap between these views (i.e., brain functioning may have a biological basis), each branch has its unique characteristics and will be discussed separately.

BIOSOCIAL TRAIT THEORIES

Rather than view the criminal as a person whose behavior is controlled by biological conditions determined at birth, biosocial theorists believe physical, environmental, and social conditions work in concert to produce human behavior. Biosocial theory has several core principles.[16] First, it assumes that genetic makeup contributes significantly to human behavior. Further, it contends that not all humans are born with equal potential to learn and achieve (equipotentiality). Biosocial theorists argue that no two people are alike (with rare exceptions, such as identical twins) and that the combination of human genetic traits and the environment produces individual behavior patterns (Figure 5.1). In contrast, social theorists suggest, either explicitly or implicitly, that all people are born equal and that thereafter behavior is controlled by social forces (parents, schools, neighborhoods, and friends).

The following subsections will examine some of the more important schools of thought within biosocial theory.[17] First, we look at the biochemical factors that are believed to affect behavior. Then the relationship of brain function and crime will be considered, followed by an analysis of genetics and crime. Finally, evolutionary views of crime causation are evaluated.

Biochemical Conditions and Crime

Some trait theorists believe biochemical conditions, including both those that are genetically predetermined and those acquired through diet and environment, control and influence antisocial behavior.[18] The influence of damaging chemical and biological contaminants may begin before birth: maternal alcohol abuse and or smoking during gestation has long been linked to prenatal damage and subsequent antisocial behavior in adolescence.[19] Exposure to harmful chemicals and poor diet may then affect people throughout their life course. Some of the more important biochemical factors that have been linked to criminality are set out in detail here.

Chemical and Mineral Influences Biosocial criminologists maintain that minimum levels of minerals and chemicals are needed for normal brain functioning and growth, especially in the early years of life. Research conducted over the past decade shows that an over- or undersupply of certain chemicals and minerals—including sodium, mercury potassium, calcium, amino acids, monoamines, and peptides—can lead to depression, mania, cognitive problems, memory loss, and abnormal sexual activity.[20] Common food additives such as calcium propionate, which is used to preserve bread, have been linked to problem behaviors.[21] Even some commonly used medicines may have detrimental side effects. There has been recent research linking sildenafil, more commonly known as Viagra, with aggressive and violent behavior. While the cause is still unknown, it is possible that sildenafil exerts various biochemical and physiologic effects in the brain and that it affects information processing.[22]

In some instances the influence of chemicals and minerals is direct. Research now shows that people who start drinking by the age of 14 are five times more likely to become alcoholics than people who hold off on drinking until the age of 21. It is possible that early exposure of the brain to alcohol may short-circuit the growth of brain cells, impairing the learning and memory processes that protect against addiction. Thus, early ingestion of alcohol will have a direct influence on behavior.[23]

In other cases, the relationship between biochemical makeup and antisocial behavior is indirect. Chemical and mineral imbalance leads to cognitive and learning deficits and problems, and these factors in turn are associated with antisocial behaviors.[24] Research shows that excessive intake of certain metals such as iron and manganese may be linked to neurological dysfunctions such as intellectual impairment and attention deficit hyperactivity disorder (ADHD). These neurological conditions are believed to be a precursor of delinquent and criminal behaviors.[25]

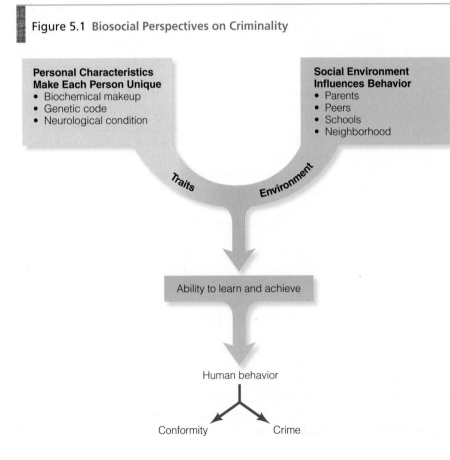

Figure 5.1 Biosocial Perspectives on Criminality

Personal Characteristics Make Each Person Unique
- Biochemical makeup
- Genetic code
- Neurological condition

Social Environment Influences Behavior
- Parents
- Peers
- Schools
- Neighborhood

Traits   Environment

Ability to learn and achieve

Human behavior

Conformity   Crime

Benita Nahimana (foreground left), 3, plays with her sister Sophia and neighbor Gloria on the chipped-paint wood floor in their old apartment as parents Regina and Razaro watch. Now in a new home, Benita is still recovering from being exposed to lead poisoning in the apartment. Some criminologists believe that early and prolonged exposure to lead is related to antisocial behavior in adolescence.

criminologists have found that areas with the highest concentrations of lead also reported the highest levels of homicide.[70] On a micro-level, research finds that delinquents are almost four times more likely to have high bone lead levels than children in the general population.[71] Criminologist Deborah Denno investigated the behavior of more than 900 African American youth and found that lead poisoning was one of the most significant predictors of male delinquency and persistent adult criminality.[72] Herbert Needleman and his associates have conducted a number of studies indicating that youths who had high lead concentrations in their bones were much more likely to report attention problems, delinquency, and aggressiveness than those who were lead free.[73] High lead ingestion is related to lower IQ scores, a factor linked to aggressive behavior.[74] There is also evidence linking lead exposure to mental illnesses, such as schizophrenia, which have been linked to antisocial behaviors.[75]

The CDC survey found that among children ages 1 to 5, the average blood lead level was about 2.2 percent, which was down from 4.4 percent a decade ago. While the improvement is welcome, exposure of children to lead in homes containing lead-based paint and lead-contaminated dust remains a serious public health concern.[76] Research also shows that lead effects may actually begin in the womb due to the mother's dietary consumption of foods, such as seafood, that are high in lead content.[77] Improved prenatal care may help mothers avoid the danger of lead exposure and reduce long-term crime rates.

Neurophysiological Conditions and Crime

Some researchers focus their attention on neurophysiology, the study of brain activity.[78] They believe neurological and physical abnormalities are acquired as early as the fetal or prenatal stage or through birth delivery trauma and that they control behavior throughout the life span.[79]

Studies conducted in the United States and in other nations have indicated that the relationship between impairment in executive brain functions (such as abstract reasoning, problem-solving skills, and motor behavior skills) and aggressive behavior is significant.[80] Children who suffer from measurable neurological deficits at birth are believed to also suffer from a number of antisocial traits throughout their life course, ranging from habitual lying to antisocial violence.[81]

The association between neurological deficits has been linked to chronic violent offending.[82] Clinical analysis of convicted murderers by Peer Briken and colleagues found that a significant number (31 percent) showed evidence of brain abnormalities, including epilepsy, traumatic brain injury, childhood encephalitis or meningitis causing brain damage, genetic disorders, and unspecified brain damage.[83] In addition, the subjects with brain abnormalities were significantly more likely to commit multiple murders.

The association between brain dysfunction and antisocial behavior may also have a social component. An important study by Adrian Raine examined the medical histories of 4,269 Danish males born between 1959 and 1961. By age 18, boys whose mothers had experienced birth complications and who had also experienced maternal rejection later in life were more than twice as likely to commit a violent crime than boys who did not experience birth trauma and maternal rejection. Raine concluded that birth complications and maternal rejection seemed to predispose offenders to criminal offending.[84]

Measuring Neurological Impairment There are numerous ways to measure neurological functioning, including memorization and visual awareness tests, short-term auditory memory tests, and verbal IQ tests. These tests have been found to distinguish criminal offenders from noncriminal control groups.[85]

Traditionally, the most important measure of neurophysiological functioning is the electroencephalograph (EEG), which records the electrical impulses given off by the brain.[86] It represents a signal composed of various rhythms and transient electrical discharges, commonly called brain waves, which can be recorded by electrodes placed on the scalp. The frequency is given in cycles per second, measured in hertz (Hz), and usually ranges from 0.5 to 30 Hz. Studies using the EEG find that violent criminals have far higher levels of abnormal EEG recordings than nonviolent or one-time offenders.[87] Although about 5 percent of the general population have abnormal EEG readings, about 50 to 60 percent of adolescents with known behavior disorders display abnormal recordings.[88] Behaviors highly correlated with abnormal EEG included poor impulse control, inadequate social adaptation, hostility, temper tantrums, and destructiveness.[89] Studies of adults have associated slow and bilateral brain waves with hostile, hypercritical, irritable, nonconforming, and impulsive behavior.[90]

Newer brain scanning techniques, using electronic imaging such as positron emission tomography (PET), brain electrical activity mapping (BEAM), and the superconducting quantum interference device (SQUID), have made it possible to assess which areas of the brain are directly linked to antisocial behavior.[91] Violent criminals have been found to have impairment in the prefrontal lobes, thalamus, hypothalamus, medial temporal lobe, superior parietal, and left angular gyrus areas of the brain.[92] For example, some research using PET shows that domestic violence offenders have lower metabolism in the right hypothalamus and decreased correlations between cortical and subcortical brain structures than a group of control subjects.[93]

It is possible that antisocial behavior is influenced by what is referred to as prefrontal dysfunction, a condition that occurs when demands on brain activity overload the prefrontal cortex and result in a lack of control over antisocial behaviors. Because the prefrontal lobes have not fully developed in adolescence, they may become overwhelmed at times; it is not surprising that violent behavior peaks in late adolescence.[94]

Minimal Brain Dysfunction (MBD) MBD is related to an abnormality in cerebral structure. It has been defined as an abruptly appearing, maladaptive behavior that interrupts an individual's lifestyle and life flow. In its most serious form, MBD has been linked to serious antisocial acts, an imbalance in the urge-control mechanisms of the brain, and chemical abnormality. Included in the category of minimal brain dysfunction are several abnormal behavior patterns: dyslexia, visual perception problems, hyperactivity, poor attention span, temper tantrums, and aggressiveness. One type of minimal brain dysfunction is manifested through episodic periods of explosive rage. This form of the disorder is considered an important cause of such behavior as spouse beating, child abuse, suicide, aggressiveness, and motiveless homicide. One perplexing feature of this syndrome is that people who are afflicted with it often maintain warm and pleasant personalities between episodes of violence. Some studies measuring the presence of MBD in offender populations have found that up to 60 percent exhibit brain dysfunction on psychological tests.[95] Criminals have been characterized as having a dysfunction of the dominant hemisphere of the brain.[96] Researchers using brain wave data have predicted with 95 percent accuracy the recidivism of violent criminals.[97] More sophisticated brain scanning techniques, such as PET, have also shown that brain abnormality is linked to violent crime.[98]

Attention Deficit Hyperactivity Disorder (ADHD) Many parents have noticed that their children do not pay attention to them—they run around and do things in their own way. Sometimes this inattention is a function of age; in other instances, it is a symptom of **attention deficit hyperactivity disorder (ADHD)**, in which a child shows a developmentally inappropriate lack of

---

EXHIBIT 5.1

Symptoms of Attention Deficit Hyperactivity Disorder (ADHD)

Lack of Attention

- Frequently fails to finish projects
- Does not seem to pay attention
- Does not sustain interest in play activities
- Cannot sustain concentration on schoolwork or related tasks
- Is easily distracted

Impulsivity

- Frequently acts without thinking
- Often "calls out" in class
- Does not want to wait his or her turn in lines or games
- Shifts from activity to activity
- Cannot organize tasks or work
- Requires constant supervision

Hyperactivity

- Constantly runs around and climbs on things
- Shows excessive motor activity while asleep
- Cannot sit still; is constantly fidgeting
- Does not remain in his or her seat in class
- Is constantly on the go like a "motor"

Source: Adapted from American Psychiatric Association, *Diagnostic and Statistical Manual of Mental Disorders,* 4th ed. (Washington, DC: American Psychiatric Press, 1994).

---

attention, impulsivity, and hyperactivity. The various symptoms of ADHD are described in Exhibit 5.1.

About 3 percent of U.S. children (most often boys, but the condition can also affect girls) are believed to suffer from this disorder, and it is the most common reason children are referred to mental health clinics.[99] ADHD has been associated with poor school performance, grade retention, placement in special needs classes, bullying, stubbornness, and lack of response to discipline.[100] Although the origin of ADHD is still unknown, suspected causes include neurological damage, prenatal stress, and even reactions to food additives and chemical allergies. Some psychologists believe that the syndrome is essentially a chemical problem, specifically, an impairment in the chemical system that supports rapid and efficient communication in the brain's management system.[101]

There are also ties to family turmoil: parents of ADHD children are more likely to be divorced or separated, and ADHD children are much more likely to move to new locales than non-ADHD children.[102] It may be possible then that emotional turmoil either produces symptoms of ADHD or, if they already exist, causes them to intensify.

A series of research studies now links ADHD to the onset and sustenance of a delinquent career.[103] Children with ADHD are more likely to use illicit drugs, alcohol, and cigarettes in adolescence; to be arrested; to be charged with a felony; and to have

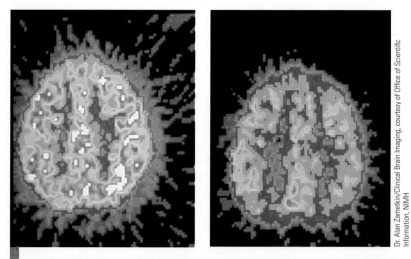

This scan compares a normal brain (left) and an ADHD brain (right). Areas of orange and white demonstrate a higher rate of metabolism, while areas of blue and green represent an abnormally low metabolic rate. Why is ADHD so prevalent in the United States today? Some experts believe that our immigrant forebears, risk takers who impulsively left their homelands for life in a new world, may have brought with them a genetic predisposition for ADHD.

multiple arrests than non-ADHD youths. There is some evidence that ADHD youths who also exhibit early signs of MBD and conduct disorder (e.g., fighting) are the most at risk for persistent antisocial behaviors continuing into adulthood.[104] Many ADHD children also suffer from conduct disorder (CD) and continually engage in aggressive and antisocial behavior in early childhood. The disorders are sustained over the life course: children diagnosed as ADHD are more likely to be suspended from school and engage in criminal behavior as adults. This ADHD–crime association is important because symptoms of ADHD seem stable through adolescence into adulthood.[105] Hyperactive/ADHD children are at greater risk for adolescent antisocial activity and drug use/abuse that persists into adulthood.[106]

How is ADHD treated? Today, the most typical treatment is doses of stimulants, such as Ritalin, which ironically help control emotional and behavioral outbursts. Other therapies, such as altering diet and food intake, are now being investigated.[107] However, treatment is not always effective. While some treated children with ADHD improve, many do not and continue to show a greater occurrence of externalizing ("acting-out") behaviors and significant deficits in areas such as social skills, peer relations, and academic performance over the life course. A recent study by Stephen Hinshaw and his associates compared groups of ADHD and non-ADHD girls and found that even after treatment about four-fifths of the ADHD girls required social services such as special education, tutoring, or psychotherapy, compared to only one-seventh of the comparison girls; 50 percent of the ADHD girls exhibited oppositional defiant disorder, compared to only 7 percent of the control group.[108]

Tumors, Lesions, Injury, and Disease The presence of brain tumors and lesions has also been linked to a wide variety of psychological problems, including personality changes, hallucinations, and psychotic episodes.[109] Persistent criminality has been linked to lesions in the frontal and temporal regions of the brain, which play an important role in regulating and inhibiting human behavior, including formulating plans and controlling intentions.[110] Clinical evaluation of depressed and aggressive psychopathic subjects showed a significant number (more than 75 percent) had dysfunction of the temporal and frontal regions of the brain.[111]

There is evidence that people with tumors are prone to depression, irritability, temper outbursts, and even homicidal attacks. Clinical case studies of patients suffering from brain tumors indicate that previously docile people may undergo behavior changes so great that they attempt to seriously harm their families and friends. When the tumor is removed, their behavior returns to normal.[112] In addition to brain tumors, head injuries caused by accidents, such as falls or auto crashes, have been linked to personality reversals marked by outbursts of antisocial and violent behavior.[113]

A variety of central nervous system diseases have also been linked to personality changes. Some of these conditions include cerebral arteriosclerosis, epilepsy, senile dementia, Wernicke-Korsakoff's syndrome, and Huntington's chorea. Associated symptoms of these diseases are memory deficiency, orientation loss, and affective (emotional) disturbances dominated by rage, anger, and increased irritability.[114]

Brain Chemistry Neurotransmitters are chemical compounds that influence or activate brain functions. Those studied in relation to aggression include dopamine, norepinephrine, serotonin, monoamine oxidase, and GABA.[115] Evidence exists that abnormal levels of these chemicals are associated with aggression. For example, several researchers have reported inverse correlations between serotonin concentrates in the blood and impulsive and/or suicidal behavior.[116] Recent studies of habitually violent Finnish criminals show that low serotonin (5-hydroxytryptamine, 5-HT) levels are associated with poor impulse control and hyperactivity. In addition, a relatively low concentration of 5-hydroxyindoleactic acid (5-HIAA) is predictive of increased irritability, sensation seeking, and impaired impulse control.[117]

What is the link between brain chemistry and crime? Prenatal exposure of the brain to high levels of androgens can result in a brain structure that is less sensitive to environmental inputs. Affected individuals seek more intense and varied stimulation and are willing to tolerate more adverse consequences than individuals not so affected.[118] Such exposure also results in a rightward shift in (brain) hemispheric functioning and a concomitant diminution of cognitive and emotional tendencies. One result of this tendency is that left-handers are disproportionately represented in the criminal population since the movement of each hand tends to be controlled by the hemisphere of the brain on the opposite side of the body.

Dr. Alan Zametkin/Clinical Brain Imaging, courtesy of Office of Scientific Information, NIMH

It has also been suggested that individuals with a low supply of the enzyme monoamine oxidase (known either by the acronym MOMA and/or MAO) engage in behaviors linked with violence and property crime, including defiance of punishment, impulsivity, hyperactivity, poor academic performance, sensation seeking and risk taking, and recreational drug use.[119] Abnormal levels of MAO may explain both individual and group differences in the crime rate. For example, females have higher levels of MAO than males, a condition that may explain gender differences in the crime rate.[120]

The brain and neurological system can produce natural or endogenous opiates that are chemically similar to the narcotics opium and morphine. It has been suggested that the risk and thrills involved in crime cause the neurological system to produce increased amounts of these natural narcotics. The result is an elevated mood state, perceived as an exciting and rewarding experience that acts as a positive reinforcement for crime.[121] The brain then produces its own natural high as a reward for risk-taking behavior. Some people achieve this high by rock climbing and skydiving; others engage in crimes of violence.

Because this linkage has been found, it is not uncommon for violence-prone people to be treated with antipsychotic drugs such as Haldol, Stelazine, Prolixin, and Risperdal, which help control levels of neurotransmitters (such as serotonin/dopamine); these are sometimes referred to as chemical restraints or chemical straitjackets.

Arousal Theory

It has long been suspected that obtaining thrills is a crime motivator. Adolescents may engage in crimes such as shoplifting and vandalism simply because they offer the attraction of "getting away with it"; from this perspective, delinquency is a thrilling demonstration of personal competence. According to sociologist Jack Katz, there are immediate gratifications from criminality, which he labels the "seductions of crime." These are situational inducements that directly precede the commission of a crime and draw offenders into law violations. For example, someone challenges their authority and they vanquish their opponent with a beating; or they want to do something exciting, so they break into and vandalize a school building.

According to Katz, choosing crime can help satisfy personal needs for thrills and excitement. For some people, shoplifting and vandalism are attractive because getting away with crime is a thrilling demonstration of personal competence; Katz calls this "sneaky thrills." Even murder can have an emotional payoff. Killers behave like the avenging gods of mythology, choosing to have life-or-death control over their victims.[122]

According to arousal theory, for a variety of genetic and environmental reasons, some people's brains function differently in response to environmental stimuli. All of us seek to maintain a preferred or optimal level of arousal: too much stimulation leaves us anxious and stressed out; too little makes us feel bored and weary. There is, however, variation in the way people's brains process sensory input. Some nearly always feel comfortable with little stimulation, whereas others require a high degree of environmental input to feel comfortable. The latter are "sensation seekers," who seek out stimulating activities, which may include aggressive, violent behavior patterns.[123]

Evidence that some people may have lower levels of arousal comes from studies on resting heart rate levels conducted by Adrian Raine and his associates, who found that antisocial children have lower resting heart rates than the general population. Raine speculates that some people lack fear and are nonresponsive to the threat of punishment, a condition that allows them to feel relatively comfortable while engaging in antisocial encounters. People who have low arousal levels will seek out risky situations and become more involved with criminal behavior as an avenue toward thrill-seeking. Because lack of fear and thrill-seeking behavior are characteristics of adult psychopaths, antisocial children might therefore develop into psychopaths as adults.[124]

The factors that determine a person's level of arousal are not fully determined, but suspected sources include brain chemistry (for example, serotonin levels) and brain structure. Some people have brains with many more nerve cells with receptor sites for neurotransmitters than others. Another view is that people with low heartbeat rates are more likely to commit crime because they seek stimulation to increase their feelings of arousal to normal levels.[125]

Genetics and Crime

Early biological theorists believed that criminality ran in families. Although research on deviant families is not taken seriously today, modern biosocial theorists are still interested in the role of genetics. Some believe antisocial behavior characteristics and mental disorders may be inherited. According to this view, (a) antisocial behavior is inherited, (b) the genetic makeup of parents is passed on to children, and (c) genetic abnormality is linked to a variety of antisocial behaviors.

This view, while controversial, is not strange or unusual. There is evidence that animals can be bred to have aggressive traits: pit bull dogs, fighting bulls, and fighting cocks have been selectively mated to produce superior predators. Although no similar data exist with regard to people, a growing body of research is focusing on the genetic factors associated with human behavior.[126] There is evidence that personality traits including extraversion, openness, agreeableness, and conscientiousness are genetically determined.[127] There are also data suggesting that human traits associated with criminality have a genetic basis.[128] Personality conditions linked to aggression (such as psychopathy, impulsivity, and neuroticism) and psychopathology (such as schizophrenia) may be heritable.[129]

This line of reasoning was cast in the spotlight in the 1970s when genetic testing showed that Richard Speck, the convicted killer of eight nurses in Chicago, allegedly had an abnormal XYY chromosomal structure (XY is normal in males). There was much public concern that all people with XYYs were potential killers and should be closely controlled. Civil libertarians expressed fear that all XYYs could be labeled dangerous and violent regardless of whether they had engaged in violent activities.[130] When it was disclosed that neither Speck nor most violent offenders actually had an extra Y chromosome, interest in the XYY theory dissipated.[131] However, the Speck case drew researchers' attention to looking for a genetic basis of crime.

Researchers have carefully explored the heritability of criminal tendencies by looking at a variety of factors. Some of the most important are described here.

Parental Deviance If criminal tendencies are inherited, then it stands to reason that the children of criminal parents should be more likely to become law violators than the offspring of conventional parents. A number of studies have found that parental criminality and deviance do, in fact, have a powerful influence on delinquent behavior.[132] Some of the most important data on parental deviance were gathered by Donald J. West and David P. Farrington as part of a long-term study of English youth called the Cambridge Study in Delinquent Development (CSDD). Now directed by Dr. Farrington, this research has followed a group of about 1,000 males from the time they were 8 years old until today when many are in their 30s and older. The boys in the study have been repeatedly interviewed and their school and police records evaluated. These cohort data indicate that a significant number of delinquent youths have criminal fathers.[133] While 8.4 percent of the sons of noncriminal fathers eventually became chronic offenders, about 37 percent of youths with criminal fathers were multiple offenders.[134] More recent analysis of the data confirms that delinquent youth grow up to become the parents of antisocial children.[135]

In another important analysis, Farrington found that one type of parental deviance, schoolyard aggression or bullying, may be both inter- and intragenerational. Bullies have children who bully others, and these "second-generation bullies" grow up to become the fathers of children who are also bullies, in a never-ending cycle.[136] Farrington's findings are supported by some recent research data from the Rochester Youth Development Study (RYDS), a longitudinal analysis that has been monitoring the behavior of 1,000 area youths since 1988. Though their data does not allow them to definitively determine whether it is a result of genetics or socialization, the RYDS researchers have also found an intergenerational continuity in antisocial behavior.[137]

The cause of intergenerational deviance is still uncertain. It is possible that environmental, genetic, psychological, or childrearing factors are responsible for the linkage between generations. The link might also have some biological basis. Research on the sons of alcoholic parents shows that these boys suffer many neurological impairments related to chronic delinquency.[138] These results may indicate (a) that prolonged parental alcoholism causes genetic problems related to developmental impairment or (b) that the children of substance-abusing parents are more prone to suffer neurological impairment before, during, or after birth.

The quality of family life may be key in determining children's behavior. Criminal parents should be the ones least likely to have close, intimate relationships with their offspring. Research shows that substance-abusing and/or criminal parents are the ones most likely to use harsh and inconsistent discipline, a factor closely linked to delinquent behavior.[139]

There is no certainty about the nature and causal relationship between parental and child deviance. Data from the CSDD may help shed some light on the association. Recent analysis shows that parental conflict and authoritarian parenting were related to early childhood conduct problems in two successive generations. In addition, males who were poorly supervised by their parents were themselves poor supervisors as fathers. These findings indicate that parenting styles may help explain antisocial behavior in children and that style is passed down from one generation to the next. In addition, CSDD data found that antisocial males tend to partner with antisocial female peers and breed antisocial children. In sum then, the CSDD data indicate that the intergenerational transmission of antisocial behaviors may have both genetic and experiential dimensions.[140] Nonetheless, recent evidence indicates that at least part of the association is genetic in nature.[141] It is also possible that the association is related to the labeling process and family stigma: social control agents may be quick to fix a delinquent label on the children of known law violators; "the acorn," the reasoning goes, "does not fall far from the tree."[142]

wwww To learn more about the **Rochester Youth Development Study (RYDS)**, go to www.thomsonedu.com/criminaljustice/siegel.

Sibling Similarities It stands to reason that if the cause of crime is in part genetic, then the behavior of siblings should be similar because they share genetic material. Research does show that if one sibling engages in antisocial behavior, so do his/her brothers and sisters. The effect is greatest among same-sex siblings.[143] Sibling pairs who report warm, mutual relationships and share friends are the most likely to behave in a similar fashion; those who maintain a close relationship also have similar rates of crime and drug abuse.[144]

While the similarity of siblings' behavior seems striking, what appears to be a genetic effect may also be explained by other factors:

- Siblings who live in the same environment are influenced by similar social and economic factors.

- Deviant siblings may grow closer because of shared interests.

- Younger siblings who admire their older siblings may imitate the elders' behavior.

- The deviant sibling forces or threatens the brother or sister into committing criminal acts.

- Siblings living in a similar environment may develop similar types of friends; it is peer behavior that is the critical influence. The influence of peers may negate any observed interdependence of sibling behavior.[145]

Twin Behavior As mentioned above, because siblings are usually brought up in the same household and share common life experiences, any similarity in their antisocial behavior might be a function of environmental influences and experiences and not genetics at all. To guard against this, biosocial theorists have compared the behavior of same-sex twins and again found concordance in their behavior patterns.[146]

However, an even more rigorous test of genetic theory involves comparison of the behavior of identical monozygotic (MZ) twins with fraternal dizygotic (DZ) twins; while the former have an identical genetic makeup, the latter share only about 50 percent of their genetic combinations. Research has shown that MZ twins are significantly closer in their personal characteristics, such as intelligence, than are DZ twins.[147]

The earliest studies conducted on the behavior of twins detected a significant relationship between the criminal activities of MZ twins and a much lower association between those of DZ twins. A review of relevant studies conducted between 1929 and 1961 found that 60 percent of MZ twins shared criminal behavior patterns (if one twin was criminal, so was the other), whereas only 30 percent of DZ twin behavior was similarly related.[148] These findings may be viewed as powerful evidence that a genetic basis for criminality exists.

There have been several research efforts confirming the significant correspondence of twin behavior in activities ranging from frequency of sexual activity to crime.[149] David Rowe and D. Wayne Osgood analyzed the factors that influence self-reported delinquency in a sample of twin pairs and concluded that genetic influences actually have significant explanatory power: if one member of a twin pair was delinquent, so was the other, and the effect was greater among MZ twins.[150] In another recent study, Sara Jaffee and colleagues found a strong genetic association in the development of conduct disorder—for example, persistent lying, bullying, violence, physical cruelty, and stealing. There was significantly more concordance among MZ twins than DZ twins.[151]

Other relevant findings include:

▍ There is a significantly higher risk for suicidal behavior among monozygotic twin pairs than dizygotic twin pairs.[152]

▍ Differences in concordance between MZ and DZ twins have been found in tests measuring psychological dysfunctions, such as conduct disorders, impulsivity, and antisocial behavior.[153]

▍ MZ twins are closer than DZ twins in such crime relevant measures as level of aggression and verbal skills.[154]

▍ Both members of MZ twin pairs who suffer child abuse are more likely to engage in later antisocial acivity more often than DZ pairs.[155]

▍ Insensitive, unemotional traits in very young children can be a warning sign for future antisocial behavior. Using samples of same-sex twin pairs, psychiatrist Essi Viding and colleagues found a powerful hereditary influence on levels of callous, unemotional behavior in children.[156]

One famous study of twin behavior still underway is the Minnesota Study of Twins Reared Apart (now called the Minnesota Twin Family Study). This research compares the behavior of MZ and DZ twin pairs who were raised together with others who were separated at birth and in some cases did not even know of each other's existence. The study shows some striking similarities in behavior and ability for twin pairs raised apart. An MZ twin reared away from a co-twin has about as good a chance of being similar to the co-twin in terms of personality, interests,

EXHIBIT 5.2

Findings from the Minnesota Twin Family Study

▍ MZ twins become *more* similar with respect to abilities such as vocabularies and arithmetic scores as they age. As DZ (fraternal) twins get older they become less similar with respect to vocabularies and arithmetic scores.

▍ A P300 is a tiny electrical response (a few millionths of a volt) that occurs in the brain when a person detects something that is unusual or interesting. For example, if a person were shown nine circles and one square, a P300 brain response would appear after seeing the square because it's different. Identical (MZ) twin children have very similar looking P300s. By comparison, children who are fraternal (DZ) twins do not show as much similarity in their P300s. These results indicate that the way the brain processes information may be greatly influenced by genes.

▍ An EEG is a measure of brain activity or brain waves that can be used to monitor a person's state of arousal. MZ twins tend to produce strikingly similar EEG spectra; DZ twins show far less similarity.

▍ MZ twins tend to have more similar ages at the time of death than DZ twins do. That is, MZ twins are more likely to die at about the same age, and DZ twins are more likely to die at different ages.

Source: Minnesota Twin Family Study, www.psych.umn.edu/psylabs/mtfs/special.htm (accessed June 2, 2007).

and attitudes as one who has been reared with his or her co-twin. The conclusion: similarities between twins are due to genes, not the environment. Because twins reared apart are so similar, the environment, if anything, makes them different (see Exhibit 5.2).[157]

Some experts, including David Rowe, conclude that individuals who share genes are alike in personality regardless of how they are reared; in contrast, environment induces little or no personality resemblance on twin pairs.[158]

Evaluating Genetic Research Twin studies also have their detractors. Some opponents suggest that available evidence provides little conclusive proof that crime is genetically predetermined. Not all research efforts have found that MZ twin pairs are more closely related in their criminal behavior than DZ or ordinary sibling pairs, and some that have found an association note that it is at best "modest."[159] Those who oppose the genes–crime relationship point to the inadequate research designs and weak methodologies of supporting research. The newer, better-designed research studies, critics charge, provide less support than earlier, less methodically sound studies.[160]

Even if the behavior similarities between MZ twins are greater than those between DZ twins, the association may be explained by environmental factors. MZ twins are more likely to look alike and to share physical traits than DZ twins, and they are more likely to be treated similarly. Similarities in their shared behavior patterns may therefore be a function of socialization and/or environment and not heredity.[161]

It is also possible that what appears to be a genetic effect picked up by the twin research is actually the effect of sibling influence on criminality referred to as the contagion effect: genetic predispositions and early experiences make some people, including twins, susceptible to deviant behavior, which is transmitted by the presence of antisocial siblings in the household.[162]

The contagion effect may explain in part the higher concordance of deviant behaviors found in identical twins as compared to fraternal twins or mere siblings. The relationship between identical twins may be stronger and more enduring than other sibling pairs so that contagion and not genetics explains their behavioral similarities. According to Marshall Jones and Donald Jones, the contagion effect may also help explain why the behavior of twins is more similar in adulthood than adolescence.[163] Youthful misbehavior is influenced by friends and peer group relationships. As adults, the influence of peers may wane as people marry and find employment. In contrast, twin influence is everlasting; if one twin is antisocial, it legitimizes and supports the criminal behavior in his or her co-twin. This effect may grow even stronger in adulthood because twin relations are more enduring than any other. What seems to be a genetic effect may actually be the result of sibling interaction with a brother or sister who engages in antisocial activity.

Adoption Studies One way of avoiding the pitfalls of twin studies is to focus attention on the behavior of adoptees. It seems logical that if the behavior of adopted children is more closely aligned to that of their biological parents than to that of their adoptive parents, then the idea of a genetic basis for criminality would be supported. If, on the other hand, adoptees are more closely aligned to the behavior of their adoptive parents than their biological parents, an environmental basis for crime would seem more valid.

Several studies indicate that some relationship exists between biological parents' behavior and the behavior of their children, even when their contact has been nonexistent.[164] In what is considered the most significant study in this area, Barry Hutchings and Sarnoff Mednick analyzed 1,145 male adoptees born in Copenhagen, Denmark, between 1927 and 1941. Of these, 185 had criminal records.[165] After following 143 of the criminal adoptees and matching them with a control group of 143 noncriminal adoptees, Hutchings and Mednick found that the criminality of the biological father was a strong predictor of the child's criminal behavior. When both the biological and the adoptive fathers were criminals, the probability that the youth would engage in criminal behavior greatly increased: 24.5 percent of the boys whose adoptive and biological fathers were criminals had been convicted of a criminal law violation. Only 13.5 percent of those whose biological and adoptive fathers were not criminals had similar conviction records.[166]

A more recent analysis of Swedish adoptees also found that genetic factors are highly significant, accounting for 59 percent of the variation in their petty crime rates. Boys who had criminal parents were significantly more likely to violate the law. Environmental influences and economic status were significantly less important, explaining about 19 percent of the variance in crime. Nonetheless, having a positive environment, such as being adopted into a more affluent home, helped inhibit genetic predisposition.[167]

The genes–crime relationship is controversial because it implies that the propensity to commit crime is present at birth and cannot be altered. It raises moral dilemmas. If *in utero* genetic testing could detect a gene for violence, and a violence gene was found to be present, what could be done as a precautionary measure?

Evolutionary Theory

Some criminologists believe the human traits that produce violence and aggression are produced through the long process of human evolution.[168] According to this evolutionary view, the competition for scarce resources has influenced and shaped the human species. Over the course of human existence, people whose personal characteristics enable them to accumulate more than others are the most likely to breed and dominate the species. People have been shaped to engage in actions that promote their well-being and ensure the survival and reproduction of their genetic line. Males who are impulsive risk-takers may be able to father more children because they are reckless in their social relationships and have sexual encounters with numerous partners. If, according to evolutionary theories, such behavior patterns are inherited, impulsive behavior becomes intergenerational, passed down from father to son. It is not surprising then that human history has been marked by war, violence, and aggression.

Violence and Evolution In their classic book *Homicide*, Martin Daly and Margo Wilson suggest that violent offenses are often driven by evolutionary and reproductive factors. High rates of spouse abuse in modern society may be a function of aggressive men seeking to control and possess mates. When females are murdered by their spouses, the motivating factor is typically fear of infidelity and the threat of attachment to a new partner. Infidelity challenges male dominance and future reproductive rights. It comes as no surprise that in some cultures, including our own, sexual infidelity discovered in progress by the aggrieved husband is viewed legally as a provocation that justifies retaliatory killing.[169] Men who feel most threatened over the potential of losing mates to rivals are the ones most likely to engage in sexual violence. Research shows that women in common-law marriages, especially those who are much younger than their husbands, are at greater risk than older married women. Abusive males may fear the potential loss of their younger mates, especially if they are not bound by a marriage contract, and may use force for purposes of control and possession.[170] Armed robbery is another crime that may have evolutionary underpinnings. Though most robbers are caught and severely punished, it remains an alluring pursuit for men who want to both show their physical prowess and display resources with which to conquer rivals and attract mates. Violent episodes are far more common among men who are unemployed and unmarried—in other words, those who may want to demonstrate their allure to the opposite sex but who are without the benefit of position or wealth.[171]

Gender and Evolution Evolutionary concepts have been linked to gender-based differences in the crime rate. To ensure survival of the gene pool (and the species), it is beneficial for a male of any species to mate with as many suitable females as possible since each can bear his offspring. In contrast, because of the long period of gestation, females require a secure home and a single, stable nurturing partner to ensure their survival. Because of these differences in mating patterns, the most aggressive males mate most often and have the greatest number of offspring. Therefore, over the history of the human species, aggressive males have had the greatest impact on the gene pool. The descendants of these aggressive males now account for the disproportionate amount of male aggression and violence.[172]

Crime rate differences between the genders, then, may be less a matter of socialization than inherent differences in mating patterns that have developed over time.[173] Among young men, reckless, life-threatening "risk-proneness" is especially likely to evolve in cultures that force males to find suitable mates to ensure their ability to reproduce. Unless they are aggressive with potential mates and potential rivals for those suitable mates, they are doomed to remain childless.[174]

Other evolutionary factors may have influenced gender differences. With the advent of agriculture and trade in prehistory, feminists have suggested that women were forced into a position of high dependence and limited power. They began to compete among themselves to secure partners who could provide necessary resources. As a result of these early evolutionary developments, intergender competition became greatest during periods of resource deprivation—times when women become most dependent on a male for support. These trends can still be observed. For example, during times of high female unemployment, female–female aggression rates increase as women compete with each other for men who can provide them with support. In contrast, as rates of social welfare increase, female–female aggression rates diminish because the state serves as a readily available substitute for a male breadwinner.[175]

Evaluation of the Biosocial Branch of Trait Theory

Biosocial perspectives on crime have raised some challenging questions. Critics find some of these theories to be racist and dysfunctional. If there are biological explanations for street crimes, such as assault, murder, or rape, the argument goes, and if, as the official crime statistics suggest, the poor and minority-group members commit a disproportionate number of such acts, then by implication biological theory says that members of these groups are biologically different, flawed, or inferior.

Some biological explanations for the geographic, social, and temporal patterns in the crime rate are problematic. Furthermore, biological theory seems to divide people into criminals and noncriminals on the basis of their genetic and physical makeup, ignoring self-reports indicating that almost everyone has engaged in some type of illegal activity during his or her lifetime.

Biosocial theorists counter that their views should not be confused with Lombrosian, deterministic biology. Rather than suggest that there are born criminals and noncriminals, they maintain that some people carry the potential to be violent or antisocial and that environmental conditions can sometimes trigger antisocial responses.[176] This would explain why some otherwise law-abiding citizens engage in a single, seemingly unexplainable antisocial act, and conversely, why some people with long criminal careers often engage in conventional behavior. It also explains why there are geographic and temporal patterns in the crime rate: people who are predisposed to crime may simply have more opportunities to commit illegal acts in the summer in Los Angeles and Atlanta than in the winter in Bedford, New Hampshire, and Minot, North Dakota, or perhaps their hormonal levels become activated as the temperature rises.

The biosocial view is that behavior is a product of interacting biological and environmental events.[177] Physical impairments may make some people "at risk" to crime, but it is when they are linked to social and environmental problems, such as family dysfunction, that they trigger criminal acts.[178] For example, Avshalom Caspi and his associates found that girls who reach physical maturity at an early age are the ones most likely to engage in delinquent acts. This finding might suggest a relationship between biological traits (hormonal activity) and crime. However, the Caspi research found that the association may also have an environmental basis. Physically mature girls are the ones most likely to have prolonged contact with a crime-prone group: older adolescent boys.[179] Here, the combination of biological change, social relationships, and routine opportunities may predict crime rates.

The most significant criticism of biosocial theory has been the lack of adequate empirical testing. In most research efforts, sample sizes are relatively small and nonrepresentative. A great deal of biosocial research is conducted with samples of adjudicated offenders who have been placed in clinical treatment settings. Methodological problems make it impossible to determine whether findings apply only to offenders who have been convicted of crimes and placed in treatment or to the population of criminals as a whole.[180] More research is needed to clarify the relationships proposed by biosocial researchers and to silence critics.

Concept Summary 5.1 summarizes the various biosocial theories of crime.

PSYCHOLOGICAL TRAIT THEORIES

The second branch of trait theories focuses on the psychological aspects of crime, including the associations among intelligence, personality, learning, and criminal behavior.

Psychological theories of crime have a long history. In *The English Convict*, Charles Goring (1870–1919) studied the mental characteristics of 3,000 English convicts.[181] He found little

CONCEPT SUMMARY 5.1

BIOSOCIAL THEORIES OF CRIME

Biochemical

- The major premise of the theory is that crime, especially violence, is a function of diet, vitamin intake, hormonal imbalance, or food allergies.

- The strengths of the theory are that it explains irrational violence; it shows how the environment interacts with personal traits to influence behavior.

- The research focuses of the theory are diet, hormones, enzymes, environmental contaminants, and lead intake.

Neurological

- The major premise of the theory is that criminals and delinquents often suffer brain impairment, as measured by the EEG. Attention deficit hyperactivity disorder and minimal brain dysfunction are related to antisocial behavior.

- The strengths of the theory are that it explains irrational violence; it shows how the environment interacts with personal traits to influence behavior.

- The research focuses of the theory are ADD, ADHD, learning disabilities, brain injuries, and brain chemistry.

Genetic

- The major premise of the theory is that criminal traits and predispositions are inherited. The criminality of parents can predict the delinquency of children.

- The strengths of the theory are that it explains why only a small percentage of youth in high-crime areas become chronic offenders.

- The research focuses of the theory are twin behavior, sibling behavior, and parent–child similarities.

Evolutionary

- The major premise of the theory is that as the human race evolved, traits and characteristics have become ingrained. Some of these traits make people aggressive and predisposed to commit crime.

- The strengths of the theory are that it explains high violence rates and aggregate gender differences in the crime rate.

- The research focuses of the theory are gender differences and understanding human aggression.

difference in the physical characteristics of criminals and noncriminals, but he uncovered a significant relationship between crime and a condition he referred to as **defective intelligence**, which involves such traits as feeblemindedness, epilepsy, insanity, and defective social instinct.[182] Goring believed criminal behavior was inherited and could, therefore, be controlled by regulating the reproduction of families who produced mentally defective children.

Gabriel Tarde (1843–1904) is the forerunner of modern-day learning theorists.[183] Tarde believed people learn from one another through a process of imitation. Tarde's ideas are similar to modern social learning theorists who believe that both interpersonal and observed behavior, such as a movie or television, can influence criminality.

Since the pioneering work of people like Tarde and Goring, psychologists, psychiatrists, and other mental health professionals have long played an active role in formulating criminological theory. In their quest to understand and treat all varieties of abnormal mental conditions, psychologists have encountered clients whose behavior falls within categories society has labeled as criminal, deviant, violent, and antisocial.

This section is organized along the lines of the predominant psychological views most closely associated with the causes of criminal behavior. Some psychologists view antisocial behavior from a **psychoanalytic** or **psychodynamic perspective**. Their focus is on early childhood experience and its effect on personality. In contrast, **behaviorism** stresses social learning and behavior modeling as the keys to criminality. **Cognitive theory** analyzes human perception and how it affects behavior.

Psychodynamic Theory

Psychodynamic (or psychoanalytic) psychology was originated by Viennese psychiatrist Sigmund Freud (1856–1939) and has since remained a prominent segment of psychological theory.[184] Freud believed that we all carry with us residue of the most significant emotional attachments of our childhood, which then guide future interpersonal relationships. Today the term "psychodynamic" refers to a broad range of theories that focus on the influence of instinctive drives and forces and the importance of developmental processes in shaping personality. Contemporary psychodynamic theory places greater emphasis on conscious experience and its interaction with the unconscious, in addition to the role that social factors play in development. Nonetheless, it still focuses on the influence of early childhood experiences on the development of personality, motivation, and drives.

connections

Chapter 1 discussed how some of the early founders of psychiatry, including Philippe Pinel and Benjamin Rush, tried to develop an understanding of the "criminal mind." Later theories suggested that mental illness and insanity were inherited and that deviants were inherently mentally damaged by reason of their inferior genetic makeup.

Elements of Psychodynamic Theory According to the classic version of the theory, the human personality contains a three-part structure. The **id** is the primitive part of an individual's mental makeup present at birth. It represents unconscious biological drives for sex, food, and other life-sustaining necessities. The id follows the **pleasure principle**: it requires instant gratification without concern for the rights of others.

The **ego** develops early in life, when a child begins to learn that his or her wishes cannot be instantly gratified. The ego is

EXHIBIT 5.3

Freud's Model of the Personality Structure

Personality Structure	Guiding Principle	Description
Id	Pleasure principle	Unconscious biological drives; requires instant gratification
Ego	Reality principle	Helps the personality refine the demands of the id; helps person adapt to conventions
Superego	The conscience	The moral aspect of the personality

that part of the personality that compensates for the demands of the id by helping the individual guide his or her actions to remain within the boundaries of social convention. The ego is guided by the reality principle: it takes into account what is practical and conventional by societal standards.

The superego develops as a result of incorporating within the personality the moral standards and values of parents, community, and significant others. It is the moral aspect of an individual's personality; it passes judgments on behavior. The superego is divided into two parts: conscience and ego ideal. Conscience tells what is right and wrong. It forces the ego to control the id and directs the individual into morally acceptable and responsible behaviors, which may not be pleasurable. Exhibit 5.3 summarizes Freud's personality structure.

Psychosexual Stages of Human Development The most basic human drive present at birth is eros, the instinct to preserve and create life. The other is the death instinct (thanatos), which is expressed as aggression.

Eros is expressed sexually. Consequently, very early in their development, humans experience sexuality, which is expressed by seeking pleasure through various parts of the body. During the first year of life, a child attains pleasure by sucking and biting; Freud called this the oral stage. During the second and third years of life, the focus of sexual attention is on the elimination of bodily wastes—the anal stage. The phallic stage occurs during the third year when children focus their attention on their genitals. Males begin to have sexual feelings for their mothers (the Oedipus complex) and girls for their fathers (the Electra complex). Latency begins at age 6. During this period, feelings of sexuality are repressed until the genital stage begins at puberty; this marks the beginning of adult sexuality.

If conflicts are encountered during any of the psychosexual stages of development, a person can become fixated at that point. This means, as an adult, the fixated person will exhibit behavior traits characteristic of those encountered during infantile sexual development. For example, an infant who does not receive enough oral gratification during the first year of life is likely as an adult to engage in such oral behavior as smoking, drinking, or drug abuse or to be clinging and dependent in

personal relationships. Thus, according to Freud, the roots of adult behavioral problems can be traced to problems developed in the earliest years of life.

The Psychodynamics of Antisocial Behavior Psychologists have long linked criminality to abnormal mental states produced by early childhood trauma. For example, Alfred Adler (1870–1937), the founder of individual psychology, coined the term inferiority complex to describe people who have feelings of inferiority and compensate for them with a drive for superiority. Controlling others may help reduce personal inadequacies. Erik Erikson (1902–1984) described the identity crisis—a period of serious personal questioning people undertake in an effort to determine their own values and sense of direction. Adolescents undergoing an identity crisis might exhibit out-of-control behavior and experiment with drugs and other forms of deviance.

The psychoanalyst whose work is most closely associated with criminality is August Aichorn.[185] After examining many delinquent youths, Aichorn concluded that societal stress, though damaging, could not alone result in a life of crime unless a predisposition existed that psychologically prepared youths for antisocial acts. This mental state, which he labeled latent delinquency, is found in youngsters whose personality requires them to act in these ways:

▌ Seek immediate gratification (to act impulsively)

▌ Consider satisfying their personal needs more important than relating to others

▌ Satisfy instinctive urges without considering right and wrong (that is, they lack guilt)

The psychodynamic model of the criminal offender depicts an aggressive, frustrated person dominated by events that occurred early in childhood. Perhaps because they may have suffered unhappy experiences in childhood or had families that could not provide proper love and care, criminals suffer from weak or damaged egos that make them unable to cope with conventional society. Weak egos are associated with immaturity, poor social skills, and excessive dependence on others. People with weak egos may be easily led into crime by antisocial peers and drug abuse. Some offenders have underdeveloped superegos and consequently lack internalized representations of those behaviors that are punished in conventional society. They commit crimes because they have difficulty understanding the consequences of their actions.[186]

Offenders may suffer from a garden variety of mood and/or behavior disorders. They may be histrionic, depressed, antisocial, or narcissistic.[187] They may suffer from conduct disorders, which include long histories of antisocial behavior, or mood disorders characterized by disturbance in expressed emotions. Among the latter is bipolar disorder, in which moods alternate between periods of wild elation and deep depression.[188] Some offenders are driven by an unconscious desire to be punished for prior sins, either real or imaginary. As a result, they may violate the law to gain attention or to punish their parents.

According to this view, crime is a manifestation of feelings of oppression and people's inability to develop the proper

self-assertiveness	sadism
defiance	lack of concern for others
extroversion	feeling unappreciated
ambivalence	distrust of authority
impulsiveness	poor personal skills
narcissism	mental instability
suspicion	hostility
destructiveness	resentment[253]

connections

The Glueck research is representative of the view that antisocial people maintain a distinct set of personal traits, which makes them particularly sensitive to environmental stimuli. Once dismissed by mainstream criminologists, the section on life course theories in Chapter 9 shows how the Gluecks' views still influence contemporary criminological theory.

Psychologist Hans Eysenck linked personality to crime when he identified two traits that he associated with antisocial behavior: *extroversion-introversion* and *stability-instability*. Extreme introverts are overaroused and avoid sources of stimulation; in contrast, extreme extroverts are unaroused and seek sensation. Introverts are slow to learn and be conditioned; extroverts are impulsive individuals who lack the ability to examine their own motives and behaviors. Those who are unstable, a condition Eysenck calls "neuroticism," are anxious, tense, and emotionally unstable.[254] People who are both neurotic and extroverted lack self-insight and are impulsive and emotionally unstable; they are unlikely to have reasoned judgments of life events. While extrovert neurotics may act self-destructively (e.g., abusing drugs), more stable people will be able to reason that such behavior is ultimately harmful and life threatening. Eysenck believes that personality is controlled by genetic factors and is heritable.

A number of research efforts have found an association between the personality traits identified by Eysenck and repeat and chronic criminal offending.[255] Other suspected traits include impulsivity, hostility, and aggressiveness.[256] Callous, unemotional traits in very young children can be a warning sign for future psychopathy and antisocial behavior.[257] Personality defects have been linked not only to aggressive antisocial behaviors such as assault and rape, but also to white-collar and business crimes.[258]

According to this view, the personality is the key to understanding antisocial behavior. The more severe the disorder, the greater the likelihood that the individual will engage in serious and repeat antisocial acts.[259]

As a group, people who suffer the most severe personality disturbance are referred to as *antisocial, sociopathic,* or *psychopathic*. Though these terms are often used interchangeably, some psychologists distinguish between sociopaths and psychopaths, suggesting that the former are a product of a destructive home environment whereas the latter are a product of a defect or aberration within themselves.[260] This condition is discussed in The Criminological Enterprise feature "The Antisocial Personality."

Research on Personality Since maintaining a deviant personality has been related to crime and delinquency, numerous attempts have been made to devise accurate measures of personality and determine whether they can predict antisocial behavior. One of the most widely used psychological tests is the Minnesota Multiphasic Personality Inventory, commonly called the MMPI. This test has subscales designed to measure many different personality traits, including psychopathic deviation (Pd scale), schizophrenia (Sc), and hypomania (Ma).[261] Research studies have detected an association between scores on the Pd scale and criminal involvement.[262] Another frequently administered personality test, the California Personality Inventory (CPI), has also been used to distinguish deviants from nondeviant groups.[263] The Multidimensional Personality Questionnaire (MPQ) allows researchers to assess such personality traits as control, aggression, alienation, and well-being.[264] Evaluations using this scale indicate that adolescent offenders who are crime prone maintain "negative emotionality," a tendency to experience aversive affective states, such as anger, anxiety, and irritability. They also are predisposed to weak personal constraints, and they have difficulty controlling impulsive behavior urges. Because they are both impulsive and aggressive, crime-prone people are quick to take action against perceived threats.

Evidence that personality traits predict crime and violence is important because it suggests that the root cause of crime can be found in the forces that influence human development at an early stage of life. If these results are valid, rather than focus on job creation and neighborhood improvement, crime control efforts might be better focused on helping families raise children who are reasoned and reflective and enjoy a safe environment.

Intelligence and Crime

Though many early criminologists believed there was a link between intelligence and crime, in 1931, Edwin Sutherland evaluated IQ studies of criminals and delinquents and noted significant variation in the findings, which disproved Goddard's notion that criminals were "feebleminded."[265] Goddard attributed discrepancies to testing and scoring methods rather than to differences in the mental ability of criminals. Sutherland's research all but put an end to the belief that crime was caused by "feeblemindedness"; the IQ–crime link was all but forgotten in the criminological literature.

Rediscovering IQ and Criminality In a widely read paper Travis Hirschi and Michael Hindelang reexamined existing research data, and concluded that the weight of evidence shows that IQ is a more important factor than race and socioeconomic class for predicting criminal and delinquent involvement.[266] Rejecting the notion that IQ tests are race and class biased, they concluded that major differences exist between criminals and noncriminals within similar racial and socioeconomic class categories. They proposed the idea that low IQ increases the likelihood of criminal behavior through its effect on school performance. That is, youths with low IQs do poorly in school, and school failure and academic incompetence are highly related to delinquency and later to adult criminality.

THE ANTISOCIAL PERSONALITY

Some violent offenders may have a disturbed character structure commonly and interchangeably referred to as psychopathy, sociopathy, or antisocial personality. Psychopaths exhibit a low level of guilt and anxiety and persistently violate the rights of others. Although they may exhibit superficial charm and above-average intelligence, this often masks a disturbed personality that makes them incapable of forming enduring relationships with others and continually involves them in such deviant behaviors as violence, risk taking, substance abuse, and impulsivity.

From an early age, many psychopaths have had home lives that were filled with frustrations, bitterness, and quarreling. Antisocial youths exhibit low levels of guilt and anxiety and persistently violate the rights of others. Their intelligence may alter their criminal career development, and render it quite different from that of nonpsychopathic criminals; high intelligence appears to enhance the destructive potential of a psychopath while intelligence may mediate the criminality of the nonpsychopath.

As a result of this instability and frustration, these individuals developed personalities that became unreliable, unstable, demanding, and egocentric. Most psychopaths are risk-taking, sensation seekers who are constantly involved in a garden variety of antisocial behaviors. Some may become almost addicted to thrill seeking, resulting in repeated and dangerous risky behaviors. They are often described as grandiose, egocentric, manipulative, forceful, and cold-hearted, with shallow emotions and the inability to feel remorse, empathy with others, or anxiety over their misdeeds.

Hervey Cleckley, a leading authority on psychopathy, described them as follows:

> [Psychopaths are] chronically antisocial individuals who are always in trouble, profiting neither from experience nor punishment, and maintaining no real loyalties to any person, group, or code. They are frequently callous and hedonistic, showing marked emotional immaturity, with lack of responsibility, lack of judgment and an ability to rationalize their behavior so that it appears warranted, reasonable and justified.

Considering these personality traits, it is not surprising that research studies show that people evaluated as psychopaths are significantly more prone to criminal and violent behavior when compared to nonpsychopathic control groups. Psychopaths tend to continue their criminal careers long after other offenders burn out or age out of crime. They are continually in trouble with the law and, therefore, are likely to wind up in penal institutions. Criminologists estimate that 10 percent or more of all prison inmates display psychopathic tendencies.

The Cause of Psychopathy

Though psychologists are still not certain of the cause of psychopathy, a number of factors are believed to contribute to its development.

Traumatic Socialization

Some explanations focus on family experiences, suggesting that the influence of an unstable parent, parental rejection, lack of love during childhood, and inconsistent discipline may be related to psychopathy. Children who lack the opportunity to form an attachment to a mother figure in the first three years of life, who suffer sudden separation from the mother figure, or who see changes in the mother figure are most likely to develop psychopathic personalities. According to this view, the path runs from antisocial parenting to psychopathy to criminality. Psychologist

---

Hirschi and Hindelang's inferences have been supported by research conducted by both U.S. and international scholars.[267] *The Bell Curve*, Richard Herrnstein and Charles Murray's influential albeit controversial book on intelligence, comes down firmly for an IQ–crime link. Their extensive review of the available literature shows that people with lower IQs are more likely to commit crime, get caught, and be sent to prison.[268]

Some studies have found a direct IQ–delinquency link among samples of adolescent boys.[269] When Alex Piquero examined violent behavior among groups of children in Philadelphia, he found that scores on intelligence tests were the best predictors of violent behavior and could be used to distinguish between groups of violent and nonviolent offenders.[270] Others find that the IQ–crime link is an indirect one: low intelligence leads to poor school performance, which enhances the chances of criminality.[271] The IQ–crime relationship has also been found in cross-national studies conducted in a number of countries, including Sweden, Denmark, and Canada.[272]

IQ and Crime Reconsidered The Hirschi-Hindelang research increased interest and research on the association between IQ and crime, but the issue is far from settled and is still a matter of significant debate. A number of recent studies find that IQ level has negligible influence on criminal behavior.[273] An evaluation of existing knowledge on intelligence conducted by the American Psychological Association concluded that the strength of an IQ–crime link was "very low."[274]

It is unlikely that the IQ–crime debate will be settled in the near future. Any perceived association is beset by many methodological problems. The well-documented criticisms suggesting that IQ tests are race and class biased would certainly influence the testing of the criminal population who are besieged with a multitude of social and economic problems. The

David Lykken suggests that psychopaths have an inherited "low fear quotient," which inhibits their fear of punishment. All people have a natural or innate fear of certain stimuli, such as spiders, snakes, fires, or strangers. Psychopaths, as a rule, have few fears. Normal socialization processes depend on punishing antisocial behavior to inhibit future transgressions. Someone who does not fear punishment is simply harder to socialize.

Neurological Disorder

Psychopaths may suffer from lower than normal levels of arousal. Research studies show that psychopaths have lower skin conductance levels and fewer spontaneous responses than normal subjects. There may be a link between psychopathy and autonomic nervous system (ANS) dysfunction. The ANS mediates physiological activities associated with emotions and is manifested in such measurements as heartbeat rate, blood pressure, respiration, muscle tension, capillary size, and electrical activity of the skin (called galvanic skin resistance). Psychopaths may be less capable of regulating their activities than other people. While some people may become anxious and afraid when facing the prospect of

committing a criminal act, psychopaths in the same circumstances feel no such fear. James Ogloff and Stephen Wong conclude that their reduced anxiety levels result in behaviors that are more impulsive and inappropriate and in deviant behavior, apprehension, and incarceration.

Another view is that psychopathy is caused by some form of brain abnormality. Some research has linked psychopathy to a dysfunction of the limbic inhibitory system manifested through damage to the frontal and temporal lobes of the brain. Consequently, psychopaths may need greater than average stimulation to bring them up to comfortable levels (similar to arousal theory, discussed earlier).

Chronic Offending

The antisocial personality concept seems to jibe with what is known about chronic offending. As many as 80 percent of these high-end chronic offenders exhibit sociopathic behavior patterns. Though comprising about 4 percent of the total male population and less than 1 percent of the total female population, they are responsible for half of all serious felony offenses committed annually. Not all high-rate chronic offenders are sociopaths, but enough are to support a

strong link between personality dysfunction and long-term criminal careers.

CRITICAL THINKING

1. Should people diagnosed as psychopaths be separated and treated even if they have not yet committed a crime?

2. Should psychopathic murderers be spared the death penalty because they lack the capacity to control their behavior?

Sources: Gisli Gudjonsson, Emil Einarsson, Ólafur Örn Bragason, and Jon Fridrik Sigurdsson, "Personality Predictors of Self-Reported Offending in Icelandic Students," *Psychology, Crime and Law* 12 (2006): 383–393; Sue Kellett and Harriet Gross, "Addicted to Joyriding? An Exploration of Young Offenders' Accounts of Their Car Crime," *Psychology, Crime and Law* 12 (2006): 39–59; Peter Johansson and Margaret Kerr, "Psychopathy and Intelligence: A Second Look," *Journal of Personality Disorders* 19 (2005): 357–369; Kent Kiehl, Andra Smith, Adrianna Mendrek, Bruce Forster, Robert Hare, and Peter F. Liddle, "Temporal Lobe Abnormalities in Semantic Processing by Criminal Psychopaths as Revealed by Functional Magnetic Resonance Imaging," *Psychiatry Research: Neuroimaging* 130 (2004): 27–42; Grant Harris, Marnie Rice, and Martin Lalumiere, "Criminal Violence: The Roles of Psychopathy, Neurodevelopmental Insults, and Antisocial Parenting," *Criminal Justice and Behavior* 28 (2001): 402–415; David Lykken, "Psychopathy, Sociopathy, and Crime," *Society* 34 (1996): 30–38; Hervey Cleckley, "Psychopathic States," in *American Handbook of Psychiatry,* ed. S. Aneti (New York: Basic Books, 1959), pp. 567–569.

measurement of intelligence is often varied and haphazard and results may depend on the particular method used. The correlation between intelligence and antisocial behavior using IQ tests as a measure of aptitude is slight; it is stronger if attendance in special programs or special schools is used as an indicator of intellectual ability.[275] There is also evidence that low IQ may influence some criminal patterns, such as arson and sex crimes, but not others, further clouding the waters.[276] And even if it can be shown that known offenders have lower IQs than the general population, it is difficult to explain many patterns in the crime rate: Why are there more male than female criminals? (Are females smarter than males?) Why do crime rates vary by region, time of year, and even weather patterns? Why does aging out occur? IQs do not increase with age, so why should crime rates fall?

The various psychological perspectives, characteristics, and attributes are outlined in Figure 5.2.

🖱 **www** To read all about **IQ testing and intelligence,** go to www.thomsonedu.com/criminaljustice/siegel.

PUBLIC POLICY IMPLICATIONS OF TRAIT THEORY

For most of the twentieth century, biological and psychological views of criminality have influenced crime control and prevention policy. The result has been front-end or **primary prevention programs** that seek to treat personal problems before they manifest themselves as crime. To this end, thousands of family therapy organizations, substance abuse clinics, and mental

While some research shows that people who act aggressively in social settings also have lower IQ scores than their peers, other findings suggest that the association between intelligence and crime is insignificant. Should mentally challenged offenders be punished in the same manner as those who are nonintellectually impaired? Here, Daryl Atkins walks into the York-Poquoson Courtroom in York, Virginia. Atkins, whose case led the U.S. Supreme Court to bar execution of the mentally retarded as unconstitutionally cruel, remained on death row years after the landmark ruling.

© AP Images/*Daily Press*/Sangjib Min

Figure 5.2 Psychological Perspectives on Criminality

Theory	Cause
PSYCHODYNAMIC (psychoanalytic)	**Intrapsychic processes** • Unconscious conflicts • Mood disorders • Psychosis • Anger • Sexuality
BEHAVIORAL	**Learning processes** • Learning experiences • Stimulus • Rewards and punishments • Direct/indirect observation
COGNITIVE	**Information processing** • Thinking • Planning • Memory • Perception • Ethical values

Characteristic	Cause
PERSONALITY	**Personality processes** • Antisocial personality • Sociopath/psychopath temperament • Abnormal affect, lack of emotional depth
INTELLIGENCE	**Intellectual processes** • Low IQ • Poor school performance • Decision-making ability

health associations operate throughout the United States. Teachers, employers, relatives, welfare agencies, and others make referrals to these facilities. These services are based on the premise that if a person's problems can be treated before they become overwhelming, some future crimes will be prevented. Secondary prevention programs provide treatment such as psychological counseling to youths and adults who are at risk for law violation. Tertiary prevention programs may be a requirement of a probation order, part of a diversionary sentence, or aftercare at the end of a prison sentence.

Biologically oriented therapy is also being used in the criminal justice system. Programs have altered diets, changed lighting, compensated for learning disabilities, treated allergies, and so on.[277] More controversial has been the use of mood-altering chemicals, such as lithium, pemoline, imipramine, phenytoin, and benzodiazepines, to control behavior. Another practice that has elicited concern is the use of psychosurgery (brain surgery) to control antisocial behavior. Surgical procedures have been used to alter the brain structure of convicted sex offenders in an effort to eliminate or control their sex drives. Results are still preliminary, but some critics argue that these procedures are without scientific merit.[278]

Numerous psychologically based treatment methods range from individual counseling to behavior modification. For example, treatment based on how people process information takes into account that people are more likely to respond aggressively to provocation if thoughts intensify the insult or otherwise stir feelings of anger. Cognitive therapists attempt to teach explosive people to control aggressive impulses by viewing social provocations as problems demanding a solution rather than retaliation. Therapeutic interventions designed to make people better problem solvers may involve measures that enhance

▌ Coping and problem-solving skills

▌ Relationships with peers, parents, and other adults

▌ Conflict resolution and communication skills, and methods for resisting peer pressure related to drug use and violence

▌ Consequential thinking and decision-making abilities

▌ Prosocial behaviors, including cooperation with others, self-responsibility, respecting others, and public-speaking efficacy

▌ Empathy[279]

While it is often difficult to treat people with severe mental and personality disorders, there is evidence that positive outcomes can be achieved with the right combination of treatment modalities.[280]

THINKING LIKE A CRIMINOLOGIST

The American Psychiatric Association believes a person should not be held legally responsible for a crime if his or her behavior meets the following standard developed by legal expert Richard Bonnie:

> *A person charged with a criminal offense should be found not guilty by reason of insanity if it is shown that as a result of mental disease or mental retardation he was unable to appreciate the wrongfulness of his conduct at the time of the offense.*

As used in this standard, the terms "mental disease" and "mental retardation" include only those severely abnormal mental conditions that grossly and demonstrably impair a person's perception or understanding of reality and that are not attributable primarily to the voluntary ingestion of alcohol or other psychoactive substances.

Writing Exercise As a criminologist with expertise on trait theories of crime, do you agree with this standard? Write a brief paper (two pages double-spaced) explaining your view of the APA's standard, and what modifications, if any, you suggest to include other categories of offenders who are not excused by this definition.

Doing Research on the Web To give you more data on trait theories of crime, review these Web-based resources:

- Visit the American Psychiatric Association and see what their position is on the insanity defense.
- Learn more about the structure of mental illness and how it relates to crime, at the Health Canada website.

These websites can be accessed via **www.thomsonedu.com/criminaljustice/siegel.**

SUMMARY

- The earliest positivist criminologists were biologists. Led by Cesare Lombroso, these early researchers believed that some people manifested primitive traits that made them born criminals. Today their research is debunked because of poor methodology, testing, and logic.

- Biological views fell out of favor in the early twentieth century. In the 1970s, spurred by the publication of Edmund O. Wilson's *Sociobiology*, several criminologists again turned to the study of the biological basis of criminality. For the most part, the effort has focused on the cause of violent crime.

- One area of interest is biochemical factors, such as diet, allergies, hormonal imbalances, and environmental contaminants (such as lead). The conclusion is that crime, especially violence,

is a function of diet, vitamin intake, hormonal imbalance, or food allergies.

- Neurophysiological factors, such as brain disorders, ADHD, EEG abnormalities, tumors, and head injuries, have been linked to crime. Criminals and delinquents often suffer brain impairment, as measured by the EEG. Attention deficit hyperactivity disorder and minimal brain dysfunction are related to antisocial behavior.

- Some biocriminologists believe that the tendency to commit violent acts is inherited. Research has been conducted with twin pairs and adopted children to determine whether genes are related to behaviors.

- An evolutionary branch holds that changes in the human condition, which have taken millions of years to evolve,

may help explain crime rate differences. As the human race evolved, traits and characteristics have become ingrained.

- There are also psychologically based theories of crime. The psychodynamic view, developed by Sigmund Freud, links aggressive behavior to personality conflicts arising from childhood. According to psychodynamic theory, unconscious motivations developed early in childhood propel some people into destructive or illegal behavior. The development of the unconscious personality early in childhood influences behavior for the rest of a person's life. Criminals have weak egos and damaged personalities. According to some psychoanalysts, psychotics are aggressive, unstable people who can easily become involved in crime.

- Behaviorists view aggression as a learned behavior. Children who are exposed to violence and see it rewarded may become violent as adults. People commit crime when they model their behavior after others they see being rewarded for the same acts. Behavior is reinforced by rewards and extinguished by punishment.

- Learning may be either direct and experiential or observational, such as watching TV and movies.

- Cognitive psychology is concerned with human development and how people perceive the world. Cognitive theory stresses knowing and perception. Some people have a warped view of the world.

- Criminality is viewed as a function of improper information processing. Individual reasoning processes influence behavior. Reasoning is influenced by the way people perceive their environment.

- There is evidence that people with abnormal or antisocial personalities are crime prone.

- Psychological traits such as personality and intelligence have been linked to criminality. One important area of study has been the antisocial personality, a person who lacks emotion and concern for others.

- While some criminologists find a link between intelligence and crime, others

dispute any linkage between IQ level and law-violating behaviors.

- The controversial issue of the relationship of IQ to criminality has been resurrected once again with the publication of research studies purporting to show that criminals have lower IQs than noncriminals.

- **ThomsonNOW** Maximize your study time by using ThomsonNOW's diagnostic study plan to help you review this chapter. The Personalized Study plan will help you identify areas on which you should concentrate; provide interactive exercises to help you master the chapter concepts; and provide a post-test to confirm you are ready to move on to the next chapter.

KEY TERMS

inheritance school (122)
somatotype (122)
biophobia (123)
reciprocal altruism (123)
trait theory (123)
equipotentiality (123)
hypoglycemia (125)
androgens (125)
testosterone (126)
neocortex (128)
premenstrual syndrome (PMS) (128)
cerebral allergies (128)
neuroallergies (128)
neurophysiology (129)
electroencephalograph (EEG) (129)
attention deficit hyperactivity disorder (ADHD) (130)
conduct disorder (CD) (131)
chemical restraints (132)
chemical straitjackets (132)
arousal theory (132)
contagion effect (135)
defective intelligence (137)

psychoanalytic or psychodynamic perspective (137)
behaviorism (137)
cognitive theory (137)
id (137)
pleasure principle (137)
ego (138)
reality principle (138)
superego (138)
conscience (138)
ego ideal (138)
eros (138)
thanatos (138)
oral stage (138)
anal stage (138)
phallic stage (138)
Oedipus complex (138)
Electra complex (138)
latency (138)
fixated (138)
inferiority complex (138)
identity crisis (138)
latent delinquency (138)

bipolar disorder (138)
alexithymia (139)
psychosis (139)
disorders (139)
schizophrenia (139)
paranoid schizophrenic (139)
social learning (141)
behavior modeling (141)
moral development (142)
humanistic psychology (142)
information processing (142)
personality (146)
Minnesota Multiphasic Personality Inventory (MMPI) (147)
California Personality Inventory (CPI) (147)
Multidimensional Personality Questionnaire (MPQ) (147)
primary prevention programs (149)
secondary prevention programs (150)
tertiary prevention programs (150)

CRITICAL THINKING QUESTIONS

1. What should be done with the young children of violence-prone criminals if in fact research could show that the tendency to commit crime is inherited?

2. After considering the existing research on the subject, would you recommend that young children be forbidden from eating foods with a heavy sugar content?

3. Knowing what you do about trends and patterns in crime, how would you counteract the assertion that people who commit crime are physically or mentally abnormal? For example, how would you explain the fact that crime is more likely to occur in western and urban areas than in eastern or rural areas?

4. Aside from becoming a criminal, what other career paths are open to psychopaths?

5. Research shows that kids who watch a lot of TV in adolescence are more likely to behave aggressively in adulthood. This has led some to conclude that TV watching is responsible for adult violence. Can this relationship be explained in another way?

NOTES

1. Kathryn Westcott, "Cho Fits Pattern of Campus Killers," BBC News, http://news.bbc.co.uk/2/hi/americas/6567143.stm (accessed June 4, 2007).

2. Dalton Conley and Neil Bennett, "Is Biology Destiny? Birth Weight and Life Chances," *American Sociological Review* 654 (2000): 458–467.

3. Raffaele Garofalo, *Criminology*, trans. Robert Miller (Boston: Little, Brown, 1914), p. 92.

4. Enrico Ferri, *Criminal Sociology* (New York: D. Appleton, 1909).

5. See Richard Dugdale, *The Jukes* (New York: Putnam, 1910); Arthur Estabrook, *The Jukes in 1915* (Washington, DC: Carnegie Institute of Washington, 1916); Henry H. Goddard, *The Kallikak Family: A Study in the Heredity of Feeble-Mindedness* (New York: Macmillan, 1912).

6. Stephen Jay Gould, *The Mismeasure of Man*, rev. ed. (New York: Norton, 1996).

7. William Sheldon, *Varieties of Delinquent Youth* (New York: Harper Bros., 1949).

8. John Laub and Robert Sampson, "The Sutherland-Glueck Debate: On the Sociology of Criminological Knowledge," *American Journal of Sociology* 96 (1991): 1,402–1,440.

9. Lee Ellis, "A Discipline in Peril: Sociology's Future Hinges on Curing Biophobia," *American Sociologist* 27 (1996): 21–41.

10. Pierre van den Bergle, "Bringing the Beast Back In: Toward a Biosocial Theory of Aggression," *American Sociological Review* 39 (1974): 779.

11. Edmund O. Wilson, *Sociobiology* (Cambridge, MA: Harvard University Press, 1975).

12. See generally Lee Ellis, *Theories of Rape* (New York: Hemisphere Publications, 1989).

13. Anthony Walsh, "Behavior Genetics and Anomie/Strain Theory," *Criminology* 38 (2000): 1,075–1,108.

14. Anthony Walsh and Lee Ellis, "Shoring Up the Big Three: Improving Criminological Theories with Biosocial Concepts," paper presented at the annual meeting of the American Society of Criminology, San Diego, November 1997, p. 16.

15. Israel Nachshon, "Neurological Bases of Crime, Psychopathy and Aggression," in *Crime in Biological, Social and Moral Contexts,* eds. Lee Ellis and Harry Hoffman (New York: Praeger, 1990), p. 199. Herein cited as *Crime in Biological Contexts.*

16. See generally Lee Ellis, "Introduction: The Nature of the Biosocial Perspective," in *Crime in Biological Contexts,* pp. 3–18.

17. Leonard Hippchen, "Some Possible Biochemical Aspects of Criminal Behavior," *Journal of Behavioral Ecology* 2 (1981): 1–6; Sarnoff Mednick and Jan Volavka, "Biology and Crime," in *Crime and Justice,* eds. Norval Morris and Michael Tonry (Chicago: University of Chicago Press, 1980), pp. 85–159; Saleem Shah and Loren Roth, "Biological and Psychophysiological Factors in Criminality," in *Handbook of Criminology,* ed. Daniel Glazer (Chicago: Rand McNally, 1974), pp. 125–140.

18. See generally Adrian Raine, *The Psychopathology of Crime* (San Diego: Academic Press, 1993); see also Leonard Hippchen, *The Ecologic-Biochemical Approaches to Treatment of Delinquents and Criminals* (New York: Van Nostrand Reinhold, 1978).

19. Lauren Wakschlag, Kate Pickett, Kristen Kasza, and Rolf Loeber, "Is Prenatal Smoking Associated with a Developmental Pattern of Conduct Problems in Young Boys?" *Journal of the American Academy of Child and Adolescent Psychiatry* 45 (2006): 461–467; "Diet and the Unborn Child: The Omega Point," *The Economist,* January 19, 2006.

20. K. Murata, P. Weihe, E. Budtz-Jorgensen, P. J. Jorgensen, and P. Grandjean, "Delayed Brainstem Auditory Evoked Potential Latencies in 14-Year-Old Children Exposed to Methylmercury," *Journal of Pediatrics* 144 (2004): 177–183; Eric Konofal, Samuele Cortese, Michel Lecendreux, Isabelle Arnulf, and Marie Christine Mouren, "Effectiveness of Iron Supplementation in a Young Child with Attention-Deficit/Hyperactivity Disorder," *Pediatrics* 116 (2005): 732–734.

21. Sue Dengate and Alan Ruben, "Controlled Trial of Cumulative Behavioural Effects of a Common Bread Preservative," *Journal of Pediatrics and Child Health* 38 (2002): 373–376.

22. Harold Milman and Suzanne Arnold, "Neurologic, Psychological, and Aggressive Disturbances with Sildenafil," *Annals of Pharmacotherapy* 36 (2002): 1,129–1,134.

23. F. T. Crews, A. Mdzinarishvili, D. Kim, J. He, and K. Nixon, "Neurogenesis in Adolescent Brain Is Potently Inhibited by Ethanol," *Neuroscience* 137 (2006): 437–445.

24. G. B. Ramirez, O. Pagulayan, H. Akagi, A. Francisco Rivera, L. V. Lee, A. Berroya, M. C. Vince Cruz, and D. Casintahan, "Tagum Study II: Follow-Up Study at Two Years of Age after Prenatal Exposure to Mercury," *Pediatrics* 111 (2003): 289–295.

25. Gail Wasserman, Xinhua Liu, Faruque Parvez, Habibul Ahsan, Diane Levy, Pam Factor-Litvak, Jennie Kline, Alexander van Geen, Vesna Slavkovich, Nancy J. Lolacono, Zhongqi Cheng, Yan Zheng, and Joseph Graziano, "Water Manganese Exposure and Children's Intellectual Function in Araihazar, Bangladesh," *Environmental Health Perspectives* 114 (2006): 124–129; Eric Konofal, Michel Lecendreux, Isabelle Arnulf, and Marie-Christine Mouren, "Iron Deficiency in Children with Attention-Deficit/Hyperactivity Disorder," *Archives of Pediatric and Adolescent Medicine* 158 (2004): 1,113–1,115; Eric Konofal, Samuele Cortese, Michel Lecendreux, Isabelle Arnulf, and Marie Christine Mouren, "Effectiveness of Iron Supplementation in a Young Child with Attention-Deficit/Hyperactivity Disorder," *Pediatrics* 116 (2005): 732–734.

26. Alexandra Richardson and Paul Montgomery, "The Oxford-Durham Study: A Randomized Controlled Trial of Dietary Supplementation with Fatty Acids in Children with Developmental Coordination Disorder," *Pediatrics* 115 (2005): 1,360–1,366.

27. Ronald Prinz and David Riddle, "Associations between Nutrition and Behavior in 5-Year-Old Children," *Nutrition Reviews Supplement* 44 (1986): 151–158.

28. Karen Lau, W. Graham McLean, Dominic P. Williams, and C. Vyvyan Howard "Synergistic Interactions between Commonly Used Food Additives in a Developmental Neurotoxicity Test," *Toxicological Science* 90 (2006): 178–187.

29. M. Mousain-Bosc, M. Roche, A. Polge, D. Pradai-Prat, J. Rapin, and J. P. Bali, "Improvement of Neurobehavioral Disorders in Children Supplemented with Magnesium-Vitamin B6, Part I, Attention Deficit Hyperactivity Disorder," *Magnesium Research* 19 (2006): 46–52.

30. J. Kershner and W. Hawke, "Megavitamins and Learning Disorders: A Controlled Double-Blind Experiment," *Journal of Nutrition* 109 (1979): 819–826.

31. Stephen Schoenthaler and Walter Doraz, "Types of Offenses which Can Be Reduced in an Institutional Setting Using Nutritional Intervention," *International Journal of Biosocial Research* 4 (1983): 74–84; and Schoenthaler and Doraz, "Diet and Crime," *International Journal of Biosocial Research* 4 (1983): 74–84. See also A. G. Schauss, "Differential Outcomes among Probationers Comparing Orthomolecular Approaches to Conventional Casework Counseling," paper presented at the annual meeting of the American Society of Criminology, Dallas, November 9, 1978; A. Schauss and C. Simonsen, "A Critical Analysis of the Diets of Chronic Juvenile Offenders, Part I," *Journal of Orthomolecular Psychiatry* 8 (1979): 222–226; A. Hoffer, "Children with Learning and Behavioral Disorders," *Journal of Orthomolecular Psychiatry* 5 (1976): 229.

32. H. Bruce Ferguson, Clare Stoddart, and Jovan Simeon, "Double-Blind Challenge Studies of Behavioral and Cognitive Effects of Sucrose-Aspartame Ingestion in Normal Children," *Nutrition Reviews Supplement* 44 (1986): 144–158; Gregory Gray, "Diet, Crime and Delinquency: A Critique," *Nutrition Reviews Supplement* 44 (1986): 89–94.

33. Mark Wolraich, Scott Lindgren, Phyllis Stumbo, Lewis Steginck, Mark Appelbaum, and Mary Kiritsy, "Effects of Diets High in Sucrose or Aspartame on the Behavior and Cognitive Performance of Children," *The New England Journal of Medicine* 330 (1994): 303–306.

34. Dian Gans, "Sucrose and Unusual Childhood Behavior," *Nutrition Today* 26 (1991): 8–14.

35. Diana Fishbein, "Neuropsychological Function, Drug Abuse, and Violence, a Conceptual Framework," *Criminal Justice and Behavior* 27 (2000): 139–159.

36. D. Hill and W. Sargent, "A Case of Matricide," *Lancet* 244 (1943): 526–527.

37. E. Podolsky, "The Chemistry of Murder," *Pakistan Medical Journal* 15 (1964): 9–14.

38. J. A. Yaryura-Tobias and F. Neziroglu, "Violent Behavior, Brain Dysrhythmia and Glucose Dysfunction: A New Syndrome," *Journal of Orthopsychiatry* 4 (1975): 182–188.

39. Matti Virkkunen, "Reactive Hypoglycemic Tendency among Habitually Violent Offenders," *Nutrition Reviews Supplement* 44 (1986): 94–103.

40. James Q. Wilson, *The Moral Sense* (New York: Free Press, 1993).

41. Walter Gove, "The Effect of Age and Gender on Deviant Behavior: A Biopsychosocial Perspective," in *Gender and the Life Course,* ed. A. S. Rossi (New York: Aldine, 1985), pp. 115–144.

42. A. Maras, M. Laucht, D. Gerdes, C. Wilhelm, S. Lewicka, D. Haack, L. Malisova, and M. H. Schmidt, "Association of Testosterone and Dihydrotestosterone with Externalizing Behavior in Adolescent Boys and Girls," *Psychoneuroendocrinology* 28 (2003): 932–940; Alan Booth and D. Wayne Osgood, "The Influence of Testosterone on Deviance in Adulthood: Assessing and Explaining the Relationship," *Criminology* 31 (1993): 93–118.

43. Anthony Walsh, "Genetic and Cytogenetic Intersex Anomalies: Can They Help Us to Understand Gender Differences in Deviant Behavior?" *International Journal of Offender Therapy and Comparative Criminology* 39 (1995): 151–166.

44. Christy Miller Buchanan, Jacquelynne Eccles, and Jill Becker, "Are Adolescents the Victims of Raging Hormones? Evidence for Activational Effects of Hormones on Moods and Behavior at Adolescence," *Psychological Bulletin* 111 (1992): 62–107.

45. Alex Piquero and Timothy Brezina, "Testing Moffitt's Account of Adolescent-Limited Delinquency," *Criminology* 39 (2001): 353–370.

46. Booth and Osgood, "The Influence of Testosterone on Deviance in Adulthood."

47. Walsh, "Genetic and Cytogenetic Intersex Anomalies: Can They Help Us to Understand Gender Differences in Deviant Behavior?"

48. Celina Cohen-Bendahan, Jan Buitelaar, Stephanie van Goozen, Jacob Orlebeke, and Peggy Cohen-Kettenis, "Is There an Effect of Prenatal Testosterone on Aggression and Other Behavioral Traits? A Study Comparing Same-Sex and Opposite-Sex Twin Girls," *Hormones and Behavior* 47 (2005): 230–237; Albert Reiss and Jeffrey Roth, eds., *Understanding and Preventing Violence* (Washington, DC: National Academy Press, 1993), p. 118.

49. John Simister and Cary Cooper, "Thermal Stress in the U.S.A.: Effects on Violence and on Employee Behaviour," *Stress and Health: Journal of the International Society for the Investigation of Stress* 21 (2005): 3–15.

50. Lee Ellis, "Evolutionary and Neurochemical Causes of Sex Differences in Victimizing Behavior: Toward a Unified Theory of Criminal Behavior and Social Stratification," *Social Science Information* 28 (1989): 605–636.

51. For a general review, see Lee Ellis and Phyllis Coontz, "Androgens, Brain Functioning, and Criminality: The Neurohormonal Foundations of Antisociality," in *Crime in Biological Contexts,* pp. 162–193.

52. Ibid., p. 181.

53. Robert Rubin, "The Neuroendocrinology and Neuro-Chemistry of Antisocial Behavior," in *The Causes of Crime, New Biological Approaches,* eds. Sarnoff Mednick, Terrie Moffitt, and Susan Stack (Cambridge: Cambridge University Press, 1987), pp. 239–262.

54. J. Money, "Influence of Hormones on Psychosexual Differentiation," *Medical Aspects of Nutrition* 30 (1976): 165.

55. Mednick and Volavka, "Biology and Crime."

56. For a review of this concept, see Anne E. Figert, "The Three Faces of PMS: The Professional, Gendered, and Scientific Structuring of a Psychiatric Disorder," *Social Problems* 42 (1995): 56–72.

57. Katharina Dalton, *The Premenstrual Syndrome* (Springfield, IL: Charles C Thomas, 1971).

58. M. S. Zeedyk and F. E. Raitt, "Biology in the Courtroom: PMS in Legal Defenses," *Psychology, Evolution and Gender* 1 (1999): 123–143.

59. Julie Horney, "Menstrual Cycles and Criminal Responsibility," *Law and Human Nature* 2 (1978): 25–36.

60. Diana Fishbein, "Selected Studies on the Biology of Antisocial Behavior," in *New Perspectives in Criminology,* ed. John Conklin (Needham Heights, MA: Allyn & Bacon, 1996), pp. 26–38.

61. Ibid.; Karen Paige, "Effects of Oral Contraceptives on Affective Fluctuations Associated with the Menstrual Cycle," *Psychosomatic Medicine* 33 (1971): 515–537.

62. H. E. Amos and J. J. P. Drake, "Problems Posed by Food Additives," *Journal of Human Nutrition* 30 (1976): 165.

63. Ray Wunderlich, "Neuroallergy as a Contributing Factor to Social Misfits: Diagnosis and Treatment," in *Ecologic-Biochemical Approaches to Treatment of Delinquents and Criminals,* ed. Leonard Hippchen (New York: Von Nostrand Reinhold, 1978), pp. 229–253.

64. See, for example, Paul Marshall, "Allergy and Depression: A Neurochemical Threshold Model of the Relation between the Illnesses," *Psychological Bulletin* 113 (1993): 23–39.

65. A. R. Mawson and K. J. Jacobs, "Corn Consumption, Tryptophan, and Cross-National Homicide Rates," *Journal of Orthomolecular Psychiatry* 7 (1978): 227–230.

66. Centers for Disease Control, "CDC Releases Most Extensive Assessment Ever of Americans' Exposure to Environmental Chemicals," Centers for Disease Control press release, 31 January 2003.

67. Alexander Schauss, *Diet, Crime, and Delinquency* (Berkeley: Parker House, 1980).

68. John Ott, "The Effects of Light and Radiation on Human Health and Behavior," in *Ecologic-Biochemical Approaches to Treatment of Delinquents and Criminals,* ed. Leonard Hippchen (New York: Von Nostrand Reinhold, 1978), pp. 105–83. See also A. Kreuger and S. Sigel, "Ions in the Air," *Human Nature* (July 1978): 46–47; Harry Wohlfarth, "The Effect of Color Psychodynamic Environmental Modification on Discipline Incidents in Elementary Schools over One School Year: A Controlled Study," *International Journal of Biosocial Research* 6 (1984): 44–53.

69. David C. Bellinger, "Lead," *Pediatrics* 113 (2004): 1,016–1,022.

70. Paul Stretesky and Michael Lynch, "The Relationship between Lead Exposure and Homicide," *Archives of Pediatric Adolescent Medicine* 155 (2001): 579–582.

71. Jeff Evans, "Asymptomatic, High Lead Levels Tied to Delinquency," *Pediatric News* 37 (2003): 13.

72. Deborah Denno, "Considering Lead Poisoning as a Criminal Defense," *Fordham Urban Law Journal* 20 (1993): 377–400.

73. Herbert Needleman, Christine McFarland, Roberta Ness, Stephen Fienberg, and Michael Tobin, "Bone Lead Levels in Adjudicated Delinquents: A Case Control Study," *Neurotoxicology and Teratology* 24 (2002): 711–717; Herbert Needleman, Julie Riess, Michael Tobin, Gretchen Biesecker, and Joel Greenhouse, "Bone Lead Levels and Delinquent Behavior," *Journal of the American Medical Association* 275 (1996): 363–369.

74. Neisser et al., "Intelligence: Knowns and Unknowns."

75. Mark Opler, Alan Brown, Joseph Graziano, Manisha Desai, Wei Zheng, Catherine Schaefer, Pamela Factor-Litvak, and Ezra S. Susser, "Prenatal Lead Exposure, Δ-Aminolevulinic Acid, and Schizophrenia," *Environmental Health Perspectives* 112 (2004): 548–553.

76. Centers for Disease Control, "CDC Releases Most Extensive Assessment Ever of Americans' Exposure to Environmental Chemicals."

77. Emily Oken, Robert O. Wright, Ken P. Kleinman, David Bellinger, Chitra J. Amarasiriwardena, Howard Hu, Janet W. Rich-Edwards, and Matthew W. Gillman, "Maternal Fish Consumption, Hair Mercury, and Infant Cognition in a U.S. Cohort," *Environmental Health Perspectives* 113 (2005): 1,376–1,380.

78. Terrie Moffitt, "The Neuropsychology of Juvenile Delinquency: A Critical Review," in *Crime and Justice, An Annual Review,* vol. 12, eds. Norval Morris and Michael Tonry (Chicago: University of Chicago Press, 1990), pp. 99–169.

79. Terrie Moffitt, Donald Lynam, and Phil Silva, "Neuropsychological Tests Predicting Persistent Male Delinquency," *Criminology* 32 (1994): 277–300; Elizabeth Kandel and

Sarnoff Mednick, "Perinatal Complications Predict Violent Offending," *Criminology* 29 (1991): 519–529; Sarnoff Mednick, Ricardo Machon, Matti Virkkunen, and Douglas Bonett, "Adult Schizophrenia Following Prenatal Exposure to an Influenza Epidemic," *Archives of General Psychiatry* 44 (1987): 35–46; C. A. Fogel, S. A. Mednick, and N. Michelson, "Hyperactive Behavior and Minor Physical Anomalies," *Acta Psychiatrica Scandinavia* 72 (1985): 551–556.

80. Jean Seguin, Robert Pihl, Philip Harden, Richard Tremblay, and Bernard Boulerice, "Cognitive and Neuropsychological Characteristics of Physically Aggressive Boys," *Journal of Abnormal Psychology* 104 (1995): 614–624; Deborah Denno, "Gender, Crime and the Criminal Law Defenses," *Journal of Criminal Law and Criminology* 85 (1994): 80–180.

81. Yaling Yang, Adrian Raine, Todd Lencz, Susan Bihrle, Lori Lacasse, and Patrick Colletti, "Prefrontal White Matter in Pathological Liars," *British Journal of Psychiatry* 187 (2005): 320–325.

82. Pallone and Hennessy, "Brain Dysfunction and Criminal Violence," p. 25.

83. Peer Briken, Niels Habermann, Wolfgang Berner, and Andreas Hill, "The Influence of Brain Abnormalities on Psychosocial Development, Criminal History and Paraphilias in Sexual Murderers," *Journal of Forensic Sciences* 50 (2005): 1–5.

84. Adrian Raine, P. Brennan, and S. Mednick, "Interaction Between Birth Complications and Early Maternal Rejection in Predisposing to Adult Violence: Specificity to Serious, Early Onset Violence," *American Journal of Psychiatry* 154 (1997): 1265–1271.

85. Deborah Denno, *Biology, Crime and Violence: New Evidence* (Cambridge: Cambridge University Press, 1989).

86. Diana Fishbein and Robert Thatcher, "New Diagnostic Methods in Criminology: Assessing Organic Sources of Behavioral Disorders," *Journal of Research in Crime and Delinquency* 23 (1986): 240–267.

87. See generally David Rowe, *Biology and Crime* (Los Angeles: Roxbury Press, 2001).

88. Lorne Yeudall, "A Neuropsychosocial Perspective of Persistent Juvenile Delinquency and Criminal Behavior," paper presented at the New York Academy of Sciences, September 26, 1979.

89. R. W. Aind and T. Yamamoto, "Behavior Disorders of Childhood," *Electroencephalography and Clinical Neurophysiology* 21 (1966): 148–156.

90. See generally Jan Volavka, "Electroencephalogram among Criminals," in *The Causes of Crime, New Biological Approaches,* eds. Sarnoff Mednick, Terrie Moffitt, and Susan Stack (Cambridge: Cambridge University Press, 1987), pp. 137–145; Z. A. Zayed, S. A. Lewis, and R. P. Britain, "An Encephalographic and Psychiatric Study of 32 Insane Murderers," *British Journal of Psychiatry* 115 (1969): 1115–1124.

91. Nathaniel Pallone and James Hennessy, "Brain Dysfunction and Criminal Violence," *Society* 35 (1998): 21–27; P. F. Goyer, P. J. Andreason, and W. E. Semple, "Positronic Emission Tomography and Personality Disorders," *Neuropsychopharmacology* 10 (1994): 21–28.

92. Adrian Raine, Monte Buchsbaum, and Lori LaCasse, "Brain Abnormalities in Murderers Indicated by Positron Emission Tomography," *Biological Psychiatry* 42 (1997): 495–508.

93. David George, Robert Rawlings, Wendol Williams, Monte Phillips, Grace Fong, Michael Kerich, Reza Momenan, John Umhau, and Daniel Hommer, "A Select Group of Perpetrators of Domestic Violence: Evidence of Decreased Metabolism in the Right Hypothalamus and Reduced Relationships between Cortical/Subcortical Brain Structures in Positron Emission Tomography," *Psychiatry Research: Neuroimaging* 130 (2004): 11–25.

94. Adrian Raine, "The Role of Prefrontal Deficits, Low Autonomic Arousal, and Early Health Factors in the Development of Antisocial and Aggressive Behavior in Children," *Journal of Child Psychology and Psychiatry* 43 (2002): 417–434.

95. D. R. Robin, R. M. Starles, T. J. Kenney, B. J. Reynolds, and F. P. Heald, "Adolescents Who Attempt Suicide," *Journal of Pediatrics* 90 (1977): 636–638.

96. R. R. Monroe, *Brain Dysfunction in Aggressive Criminals* (Lexington, MA: D.C. Heath, 1978).

97. L. T. Yeudall, *Childhood Experiences as Causes of Criminal Behavior* (Senate of Canada, Issue no. 1, Thirteenth Parliament, Ottawa, 1977).

98. Raine, Buchsbaum, and LaCasse, "Brain Abnormalities in Murderers Indicated by Positron Emission Tomography."

99. National Institute of Mental Health, "Attention Deficit Hyperactivity Disorder," www.nimh.nih.gov/publicat/adhd.cfm (accessed July 11, 2007).

100. Leonore Simon, "Does Criminal Offender Treatment Work?" *Applied and Preventive Psychology* (summer 1998); Stephen Faraone et al., "Intellectual Performance and School Failure in Children with Attention Deficit Hyperactivity Disorder and Their Siblings," *Journal of Abnormal Psychology* 102 (1993): 616–623.

101. Thomas Brown, *Attention Deficit Disorder: The Unfocused Mind in Children and Adults* . (New Haven, CT: Yale University Press, 2005).

102. Simon, "Does Criminal Offender Treatment Work?"

103. Terrie Moffitt and Phil Silva, "Self-Reported Delinquency, Neuropsychological Deficit, and History of Attention Deficit Disorder," *Journal of Abnormal Child Psychology* 16 (1988): 553–569.

104. Molina Pelham, Jr., "Childhood Predictors of Adolescent Substance Use in a Longitudinal Study of Children with ADHD," *Journal of Abnormal Psychology* 112 (2003): 497–507; Peter Muris and Cor Meesters, "The Validity of Attention Deficit Hyperactivity and Hyperkinetic Disorder Symptom Domains in Nonclinical Dutch Children," *Journal of Clinical Child and Adolescent Psychology* 32 (2003): 460–466.

105. Elizabeth Hart et al., "Criterion Validity of Informants in the Diagnosis of Disruptive Behavior Disorders in Children: A Preliminary Study," *Journal of Consulting and Clinical Psychology* 62 (1994): 410–414.

106. Russell Barkley, Mariellen Fischer, Lori Smallish, and Kenneth Fletcher, "Young Adult Follow-Up of Hyperactive Children: Antisocial Activities and Drug Use," *Journal of Child Psychology and Psychiatry* 45 (2004): 195–211.

107. Karen Harding, Richard Judah, and Charles Gant, "Outcome-Based Comparison of Ritalin® versus Food-Supplement Treated Children with AD/HD," *Alternative Medicine Review* 8 (2003): 319–330.

108. Stephen Hinshaw, Elizabeth Owens, Nilofar Sami, and Samantha Fargeon, "Prospective Follow-Up of Girls with Attention-Deficit/Hyperactivity Disorder into Adolescence: Evidence for Continuing Cross-Domain Impairment," *Journal of Consulting and Clinical Psychology* 74 (2006): 489–499.

109. Rita Shaughnessy, "Psychopharmacotherapy of Neuropsychiatric Disorders," *Psychiatric Annals* 25 (1995): 634–640.

110. Yeudall, "A Neuropsychosocial Perspective of Persistent Juvenile Delinquency and Criminal Behavior," p. 4; F. A. Elliott, "Neurological Aspects of Antisocial Behavior," in *The Psychopath: A Comprehensive Study of Antisocial Disorders and Behaviors,* ed. W. H. Reid (New York: Brunner/Mazel, 1978), pp. 146–189.

111. Ibid., p. 177.

112. H. K. Kletschka, "Violent Behavior Associated with Brain Tumor," *Minnesota Medicine* 49 (1966): 1,853–1,855.

113. V. E. Krynicki, "Cerebral Dysfunction in Repetitively Assaultive Adolescents," *Journal of Nervous and Mental Disease* 166 (1978): 59–67.

114. C. E. Lyght, ed., *The Merck Manual of Diagnosis and Therapy* (West Point, FL: Merck, 1966).

115. Reiss and Roth, *Understanding Violence,* p. 119.

116. M. Virkkunen, M. J. DeJong, J. Bartko, and M. Linnoila, "Psychobiological Concomitants of History of Suicide Attempts among Violent Offenders and Impulsive Fire Starters," *Archives of General Psychiatry* 46 (1989): 604–606.

117. Matti Virkkunen, David Goldman, and Markku Linnoila, "Serotonin in Alcoholic Violent Offenders," *The Ciba Foundation Symposium, Genetics of Criminal and Antisocial Behavior* (Chichester, England: Wiley, 1995).

118. Lee Ellis, "Left- and Mixed-Handedness and Criminality: Explanations for a Probable

118. Relationship," in *Left-Handedness, Behavioral Implications and Anomalies,* ed. S. Coren (Amsterdam: Elsevier, 1990): 485–507.

119. M. Skondras, M. Markianos, A. Botsis, E. Bistolaki, and G. Christodoulou, "Platelet Monoamine Oxidase Activity and Psychometric Correlates in Male Violent Offenders Imprisoned for Homicide or Other Violent Acts," *European Archives of Psychiatry and Clinical Neuroscience* 254 (2004): 380–386.

120. Lee Ellis, "Monoamine Oxidase and Criminality: Identifying an Apparent Biological Marker for Antisocial Behavior," *Journal of Research in Crime and Delinquency* 28 (1991): 227–251.

121. Walter Gove and Charles Wilmoth, "Risk, Crime and Neurophysiologic Highs: A Consideration of Brain Processes that May Reinforce Delinquent and Criminal Behavior," in *Crime in Biological Contexts,* pp. 261–293.

122. Jack Katz, *Seduction of Crime: Moral and Sensual Attractions of Doing Evil* (New York: Basic Books, 1988), pp. 12–15.

123. Lee Ellis, "Arousal Theory and the Religiosity-Criminality Relationship," in *Contemporary Criminological Theory,* eds., Peter Cordella and Larry Siegel (Boston, MA: Northeastern University Press, 1996), pp. 65–84.

124. Adrian Raine, Patricia Brennan, and Sarnoff Mednick, "The Interaction between Birth Complications and Early Maternal Rejection in Predisposing to Adult Violence: Specificity to Serious, Early Onset Violence," *American Journal of Psychiatry* 154 (1997): 1265–1271.

125. Adrian Raine, Peter Venables, and Sarnoff Mednick, "Low Resting Heart Rate at Age 3 Years Predisposes to Aggression at Age 11 Years: Evidence from the Mauritius Child Health Project," *Journal of the American Academy of Adolescent Psychiatry* 36 (1997): 1,457–1,464.

126. Anita Thapar, Kate Langley, Tom Fowler, Frances Rice, Darko Turic, Naureen Whittinger, John Aggleton, Marianne Van den Bree, Michael Owen, and Michael O'Donovan, "Catechol O-methyltransferase Gene Variant and Birth Weight Predict Early-Onset Antisocial Behavior in Children with Attention-Deficit/Hyperactivity Disorder," *Archives of General Psychiatry* 62 (2005) 1,275–1,278.

127. Kerry Jang, W. John Livesley, and Philip Vernon, "Heritability of the Big Five Personality Dimensions and Their Facets: A Twin Study," *Journal of Personality* 64 (1996): 577–589.

128. David Rowe, "As the Twig Is Bent: The Myth of Child-Rearing Influences on Personality Development," *Journal of Counseling and Development* 68 (1990): 606–611; David Rowe, Joseph Rogers, and Sylvia Meseck-Bushey, "Sibling Delinquency and the Family Environment: Shared and Unshared Influences," *Child Development* 63 (1992): 59–67.

129. Gregory Carey and David DiLalla, "Personality and Psychopathology: Genetic Perspectives," *Journal of Abnormal Psychology* 103 (1994): 32–43.

130. T. R. Sarbin and L. E. Miller, "Demonism Revisited: The XYY Chromosome Anomaly," *Issues in Criminology* 5 (1970): 195–207.

131. Mednick and Volavka, "Biology and Crime," p. 93.

132. For an early review, see Barbara Wooton, *Social Science and Social Pathology* (London: Allen & Unwin, 1959); John Laub and Robert Sampson, "Unraveling Families and Delinquency: A Reanalysis of the Gluecks' Data," *Criminology* 26 (1988): 355–380.

133. D. J. West and D. P. Farrington, eds., "Who Becomes Delinquent?" in *The Delinquent Way of Life* (London: Heinemann, 1977); D. J. West, *Delinquency, Its Roots, Careers, and Prospects* (Cambridge, MA: Harvard University Press, 1982).

134. West, *Delinquency,* p. 114.

135. Carolyn Smith and David Farrington, "Continuities in Antisocial Behavior and Parenting across Three Generations," *Journal of Child Psychology and Psychiatry* 45 (2004): 230–247.

136. David Farrington, "Understanding and Preventing Bullying," in *Crime and Justice,* vol. 17, ed. Michael Tonry (Chicago: University of Chicago Press, 1993), pp. 381–457.

137. Terence Thornberry, Adrienne Freeman-Gallant, Alan Lizotte, Marvin Krohn, and Carolyn Smith, "Linked Lives: The Intergenerational Transmission of Antisocial Behavior," *Journal of Abnormal Child Psychology* 31 (2003): 171–185.

138. Philip Harden and Robert Pihl, "Cognitive Function, Cardiovascular Reactivity, and Behavior in Boys at High Risk for Alcoholism," *Journal of Abnormal Psychology* 104 (1995): 94–103.

139. Laub and Sampson, "Unraveling Families and Delinquency," p. 370.

140. Smith and Farrington, "Continuities in Antisocial Behavior and Parenting across Three Generations."

141. David Rowe and David Farrington, "The Familial Transmission of Criminal Convictions," *Criminology* 35 (1997): 177–201.

142. D. P. Farrington, Gwen Gundry, and D. J. West, "The Familial Transmission of Criminality," in *Crime and the Family,* eds. Alan Lincoln and Murray Straus (Springfield, IL: Charles C Thomas, 1985), pp. 193–206.

143. Abigail Fagan and Jake Najman, "Sibling Influences on Adolescent Delinquent Behaviour: An Australian Longitudinal Study," *Journal of Adolescence* 26 (2003): 547–559.

144. David Rowe and Bill Gulley, "Sibling Effects on Substance Use and Delinquency," *Criminology* 30 (1992): 217–232; see also David Rowe, Joseph Rogers, and Sylvia Meseck-Bushey, "Sibling Delinquency and the Family Environment: Shared and Unshared Influences," *Child Development* 63 (1992): 59–67.

145. Dana Haynie and Suzanne Mchugh, "Sibling Deviance in the Shadows of Mutual and Unique Friendship Effects?" *Criminology* 41 (2003): 355–393.

146. Louise Arseneault, Terrie Moffitt, Avshalom Caspi, Alan Taylor, Fruhling Rijsdijk, Sara Jaffee, Jennifer Ablow, and Jeffrey Measelle, "Strong Genetic Effects on Cross-Situational Antisocial Behaviour among 5-Year-Old Children According to Mothers, Teachers, Examiner-Observers, and Twins' Self-Reports," *Journal of Child Psychology and Psychiatry* 44 (2003): 832–848.

147. David Rowe, "Sibling Interaction and Self-Reported Delinquent Behavior: A Study of 265 Twin Pairs," *Criminology* 23 (1985): 223–240; Nancy Segal, "Monozygotic and Dizygotic Twins: A Comparative Analysis of Mental Ability Profiles," *Child Development* 56 (1985): 1051–1058.

148. Ibid.

149. Michael Lyons, Karestan Koenen, Francisco Buchting, Joanne Meyer, Lindon Eaves, Rosemary Toomey, Seth Eisen, Jack Goldberg, Stephen Faraone, Rachel Ban, Beth Jerskey, and Ming Tsuang, "A Twin Study of Sexual Behavior in Men," *Archives of Sexual Behavior* 33 (2004): 129–136.

150. David Rowe, "Genetic and Environmental Components of Antisocial Behavior: A Study of 265 Twin Pairs," *Criminology* 24 (1986): 513–532; David Rowe and D. Wayne Osgood, "Heredity and Sociological Theories of Delinquency: A Reconsideration," *American Sociological Review* 49 (1984): 526–540.

151. Sara Jaffee, Avshalom Caspi, Terrie Moffitt, Kenneth Dodge, Michael Rutter, Alan Taylor, and Lucy Tully, "Nature × Nurture: Genetic Vulnerabilities Interact with Physical Maltreatment to Promote Conduct Problems," *Development and Psychopathology,* 17 (2005): 67–84.

152. Ping Qin, "The Relationship of Suicide Risk to Family History of Suicide and Psychiatric Disorders," *Psychiatric Times* 20 (2003): 13. Available at: www.psychiatrictimes.com/p031262.html (accessed March 15, 2007).

153. Jane Scourfield, Marianne Van den Bree, Neilson Martin, and Peter McGuffin, "Conduct Problems in Children and Adolescents: A Twin Study," *Archives of General Psychiatry* 61 (2004): 489–496; Jeanette Taylor, Bryan Loney, Leonardo Bobadilla, William Iacono, and Matt McGue, "Genetic and Environmental Influences on Psychopathy Trait Dimensions in a Community Sample of Male Twins," *Journal of Abnormal Child Psychology* 31 (2003): 633–645.

154. Ginette Dionne, Richard Tremblay, Michel Boivin, David Laplante, and Daniel Perusse, "Physical Aggression and Expressive Vocabulary in 19-Month-Old Twins," *Developmental Psychology* 39 (2003): 261–273.

155. Jaffee et al., "Nature × Nurture: Genetic Vulnerabilities Interact with Physical Maltreatment to Promote Conduct Problems."

156. Essi Viding, James Blair, Terrie Moffitt, and Robert Plomin, "Evidence for Substantial Genetic Risk for Psychopathy in 7-Year-Olds," *Journal of Child Psychology and Psychiatry* 46 (2005): 592–597.

157. Thomas Bouchard, "Genetic and Environmental Influences on Intelligence and Special Mental Abilities," *American Journal of Human Biology* 70 (1998): 253–275; some findings from the Minnesota study can be accessed from the website: www.psych.umn.edu/psylabs/mtfs/ (accessed March 15, 2007).

158. David Rowe, *The Limits of Family Influence: Genes, Experiences and Behavior* (New York: Guilford Press, 1995), p. 64.

159. Gregory Carey, "Twin Imitation for Antisocial Behavior: Implications for Genetic and Family Environment Research," *Journal of Abnormal Psychology* 101 (1992): 18–25; David Rowe and Joseph Rodgers, "The Ohio Twin Project and ADSEX Studies: Behavior Genetic Approaches to Understanding Antisocial Behavior," paper presented at the annual meeting of the American Society of Criminology, Montreal, Canada, November 1987.

160. Glenn Walters, "A Meta-Analysis of the Gene–Crime Relationship," *Criminology* 30 (1992): 595–613.

161. Alice Gregory, Thalia Eley, and Robert Plomin, "Exploring the Association between Anxiety and Conduct Problems in a Large Sample of Twins Aged 2–4," *Journal of Abnormal Child Psychology* 32 (2004): 111–123.

162. Marshall Jones and Donald Jones, "The Contagious Nature of Antisocial Behavior," *Criminology* 38 (2000): 25–46.

163. Jones and Jones, "The Contagious Nature of Antisocial Behavior," p. 31.

164. R. J. Cadoret, C. Cain, and R. R. Crowe, "Evidence for a Gene–Environment Interaction in the Development of Adolescent Antisocial Behavior," *Behavior Genetics* 13 (1983): 301–310.

165. Barry Hutchings and Sarnoff A. Mednick, "Criminality in Adoptees and Their Adoptive and Biological Parents: A Pilot Study," in *Biological Bases in Criminal Behavior,* eds. S. A. Mednick and K. O. Christiansen (New York: Gardner Press, 1977).

166. For similar results, see Sarnoff Mednick, Terrie Moffitt, William Gabrielli, and Barry Hutchings, "Genetic Factors in Criminal Behavior: A Review," in *Development of Antisocial and Prosocial Behavior,* ed. Dan Olweus (New York: Academic Press, 1986), pp. 3–50; Sarnoff Mednick, William Gabrielli, and Barry Hutchings, "Genetic Influences in Criminal Behavior: Evidence from an Adoption Cohort," in *Perspective Studies of Crime and Delinquency,* eds. Katherine Teilmann Van Dusen and Sarnoff Mednick (Boston: Kluver-Nijhoff, 1983), pp. 39–57; Michael Bohman, "Predisposition to Criminality: Swedish Adoption Studies in Retrospect," in *Genetics of Criminal and Antisocial Behavior,* pp. 99–114.

167. Lawrence Cohen and Richard Machalek, "A General Theory of Expropriative Crime: An Evolutionary Ecological Approach," *American Journal of Sociology* 94 (1988): 465–501.

168. For a general review, see Martin Daly and Margo Wilson, "Crime and Conflict: Homicide in Evolutionary Psychological Theory," in *Crime and Justice, An Annual Edition,* ed. Michael Tonry (Chicago: University of Chicago Press, 1997), pp. 51–100.

169. Martin Daly and Margo Wilson, *Homicide* (New York: Aldine de Gruyter, 1988), p. 194.

170. Margo Wilson, Holly Johnson, and Martin Daly, "Lethal and Nonlethal Violence against Wives," *Canadian Journal of Criminology* 37 (1995): 331–361.

171. Daly and Wilson, *Homicide,* pp. 172–173.

172. Lee Ellis, "The Evolution of Violent Criminal Behavior and Its Nonlegal Equivalent," in *Crime in Biological, Social, and Moral Contexts,* eds. Lee Ellis and Harry Hoffman (New York: Praeger, 1990), pp. 63–65.

173. David Rowe, Alexander Vazsonyi, and Aurelio Jose Figuerdo, "Mating-Effort in Adolescence: A Conditional Alternative Strategy," *Personal Individual Differences* 23 (2002): 105–115.

174. Ibid.

175. Anne Campbell, Steven Muncer, and Daniel Bibel, "Female–Female Criminal Assault: An Evolutionary Perspective," *Journal of Research in Crime and Delinquency* 35 (1998): 413–429.

176. Deborah Denno, "Sociological and Human Developmental Explanations of Crime: Conflict or Consensus," *Criminology* 23 (1985): 711–741.

177. Israel Nachshon and Deborah Denno, "Violence and Cerebral Function," in *The Causes of Crime, New Biological Approaches,* eds. Sarnoff Mednick, Terrie Moffitt, and Susan Stack (Cambridge: Cambridge University Press, 1987), pp. 185–217.

178. Raine, Brennan, Mednick, and Mednick, "High Rates of Violence, Crime, Academic Problems, and Behavioral Problems in Males with Both Early Neuromotor Deficits and Unstable Family Environments."

179. Avshalom Caspi, Donald Lynam, Terrie Moffitt, and Phil Silva, "Unraveling Girls' Delinquency: Biological, Dispositional, and Contextual Contributions to Adolescent Misbehavior," *Developmental Psychology* 29 (1993): 283–289.

180. Glenn Walters and Thomas White, "Heredity and Crime: Bad Genes or Bad Research," *Criminology* 27 (1989): 455–486, at 478.

181. Charles Goring, *The English Convict: A Statistical Study, 1913* (Montclair, NJ: Patterson Smith, 1972).

182. Edwin Driver, "Charles Buckman Goring," in *Pioneers in Criminology,* ed. Hermann Mannheim (Montclair, NJ: Patterson Smith, 1970), p. 440.

183. Gabriel Tarde, *Penal Philosophy,* trans. R. Howell (Boston: Little, Brown, 1912).

184. See generally Donn Byrne and Kathryn Kelly, *An Introduction to Personality* (Englewood Cliffs, NJ: Prentice Hall, 1981).

185. August Aichorn, *Wayward Youth* (New York: Viking Press, 1935).

186. See generally D. A. Andrews and James Bonta, *The Psychology of Criminal Conduct* (Cincinnati, OH: Anderson, 1994), pp. 72–75.

187. Paige Crosby Ouimette, "Psychopathology and Sexual Aggression in Nonincarcerated Men," *Violence and Victimization* 12 (1997): 389–397.

188. Robert Krueger, Avshalom Caspi, Phil Silva, and Rob McGee, "Personality Traits Are Differentially Linked to Mental Disorders: A Multitrait-Multidiagnosis Study of an Adolescent Birth Cohort," *Journal of Abnormal Psychology* 105 (1996): 299–312.

189. Seymour Halleck, *Psychiatry and the Dilemmas of Crime* (Berkeley: University of California Press, 1971).

190. Jeffrey Burke, Rolf Loeber, and Boris Birmaher, "Oppositional Defiant Disorder and Conduct Disorder: A Review of the Past 10 Years, Part II," *Journal of the American Academy of Child and Adolescent Psychiatry* 41 (2002): 1275–1294.

191. Ellen Kjelsberg, "Gender and Disorder Specific Criminal Career Profiles in Former Adolescent Psychiatric In-Patients," *Journal of Youth and Adolescence* 33 (2004): 261–270.

192. Richard Rowe, Julie Messer, Robert Goodman, and Howard Meltzer, "Conduct Disorder and Oppositional Defiant Disorder in a National Sample: Developmental Epidemiology," *Journal of Child Psychology and Psychiatry and Allied Disciplines* 45 (2004): 609–621.

193. Paul Rohde, Gregory N. Clarke, David E. Mace, Jenel S. Jorgensen, and John R. Seeley, "An Efficacy/Effectiveness Study of Cognitive-Behavioral Treatment for Adolescents with Comorbid Major Depression and Conduct Disorder," *Journal of the American Academy of Child and Adolescent Psychiatry* 43 (2004): 660–669.

194. Minna Ritakallio, Riittakerttu Kaltiala-Heino, Janne Kivivuori, Tiina Luukkaala, and Matti Rimpelä, "Delinquency and the Profile of Offences among Depressed and Non-Depressed Adolescents," *Criminal Behaviour and Mental Health* 16 (2006): 100–110.

195. Grégoire Zimmermann, "Delinquency in Male Adolescents: The Role of Alexithymia and Family Structure," *Journal of Adolescence* 29 (2006): 321–332.

196. Ching-hua Ho, J. B Kingree, and Martie Thompson, "Associations between Juvenile Delinquency and Weight-Related Variables: Analyses from a National Sample of High School Students," *International Journal of Eating Disorders* 39 (2006): 477–483.

197. Michael Pullmann, Jodi Kerbs, Nancy Koroloff, Ernie Veach-White, Rita Gaylor,

and DeDe Sieler, "Juvenile Offenders with Mental Health Needs: Reducing Recidivism Using Wraparound," *Crime and Delinquency* 52 (2006): 375–397; Jennifer Beyers and Rolf Loeber, "Untangling Developmental Relations between Depressed Mood and Delinquency in Male Adolescents," *Journal of Abnormal Child Psychology* 31 (2003): 247–267.

198. Dorothy Espelage, Elizabeth Cauffman, Lisa Broidy, Alex Piquero, Paul Mazerolle, and Hans Steiner, "A Cluster-Analytic Investigation of MMPI Profiles of Serious Male and Female Juvenile Offenders," *Journal of the American Academy of Child and Adolescent Psychiatry* 42 (2003): 770–777.

199. Richard Famularo, Robert Kinscherff, and Terence Fenton, "Psychiatric Diagnoses of Abusive Mothers, A Preliminary Report," *Journal of Nervous and Mental Disease* 180 (1992): 658–660.

200. James Sorrells, "Kids Who Kill," *Crime and Delinquency* 23 (1977): 312–320.

201. Richard Rosner, "Adolescents Accused of Murder and Manslaughter: A Five-Year Descriptive Study," *Bulletin of the American Academy of Psychiatry and the Law* 7 (1979): 342–351.

202. Richard Wagner, Dawn Taylor, Joy Wright, Alison Sloat, Gwynneth Springett, Sandy Arnold, and Heather Weinberg, "Substance Abuse among the Mentally Ill," *American Journal of Orthopsychiatry* 64 (1994): 30–38.

203. Susan Phillips, Alaattin Erkanli, Gordon Keeler, Jane Costello, Adrian Angold, "Disentangling the Risks: Parent Criminal Justice Involvement and Children's Exposure to Family Risks," *Criminology and Public Policy* 5 (2006): 677–702.

204. Bruce Link, Howard Andrews, and Francis Cullen, "The Violent and Illegal Behavior of Mental Patients Reconsidered," *American Sociological Review* 57 (1992): 275–292; Ellen Hochstedler Steury, "Criminal Defendants with Psychiatric Impairment: Prevalence, Probabilities and Rates," *Journal of Criminal Law and Criminology* 84 (1993): 354–374.

205. Richard Friendman, " Violence and Mental Illness—How Strong Is the Link?" *New England Journal of Medicine* 355 (2006): 2064–2066.

206. Henrik Belfrage, "A Ten-Year Follow-Up of Criminality in Stockholm Mental Patients: New Evidence for a Relation between Mental Disorder and Crime," *British Journal of Criminology* 38 (1998): 145–155.

207. C. Wallace, P. Mullen, P. Burgess, S. Palmer, D. Ruschena, and C. Browne, "Serious Criminal Offending and Mental Disorder. Case Linkage Study," *British Journal of Psychiatry* 174 (1998): 477–484.

208. Patricia Brennan, Sarnoff Mednick, and Sheilagh Hodgins, "Major Mental Disorders and Criminal Violence in a Danish Birth Cohort," *Archives of General Psychiatry* 57 (2000): 494–500.

209. Stefan Watzke, Simone Ullrich, and Andreas Marneros, "Gender- and Violence-Related Prevalence of Mental Disorders in Prisoners," *European Archives of Psychiatry and Clinical Neuroscience* 256 (2006): 414–421.

210. Robert Vermeiren, "Psychopathology and Delinquency in Adolescents: A Descriptive and Developmental Perspective," *Clinical Psychology Review* 23 (2003): 277–318.

211. John Monahan, *Mental Illness and Violent Crime* (Washington, DC: National Institute of Justice, 1996).

212. Robin Shepard Engel and Eric Silver, "Policing Mentally Disordered Suspects: A Reexamination of the Criminalization Hypothesis," *Criminology* 39 (2001): 225–352; Marc Hillbrand, John Krystal, Kimberly Sharpe, and Hilliard Foster, "Clinical Predictors of Self-Mutilation in Hospitalized Patients," *Journal of Nervous and Mental Disease* 182 (1994): 9–13.

213. James Bonta, Moira Law, and Karl Hanson, "The Prediction of Criminal and Violent Recidivism among Mentally Disordered Offenders: A Meta-Analysis," *Psychological Bulletin* 123 (1998): 123–142.

214. Eric Silver, "Mental Disorder and Violent Victimization: The Mediating Role of Involvement in Conflicted Social Relationships," *Criminology* 40 (2002): 191–212.

215. Eric Silver, "Extending Social Disorganization Theory: A Multilevel Approach to the Study of Violence among Persons with Mental Illness," *Criminology* 38 (2000): 1043–1074.

216. Stacy DeCoster and Karen Heimer, "The Relationship between Law Violation and Depression: An Interactionist Analysis," *Criminology* 39 (2001): 799–837.

217. Alexander McFarlane, Geoff Schrader, Clara Bookless, and Derek Browne, "Prevalence of Victimization, Posttraumatic Stress Disorder and Violent Behaviour in the Seriously Mentally Ill," *Australian and New Zealand Journal of Psychiatry* 40 (2006): 1,010–1,015

218. B. Lögdberg, L. L. Nilsson, M. T. Levander, and S. Levander, "Schizophrenia, Neighbourhood, and Crime," *Acta Psychiatrica Scandinavica* 110 (2004): 92–97.

219. Courtenay Sellers, Christopher Sullivan, Bonita Veysey, and Jon Shane, "Responding to Persons with Mental Illnesses: Police Perspectives on Specialized and Traditional Practices," *Behavioral Sciences and the Law* 23 (2005): 647–657.

220. Paul Hirschfield, Tina Maschi, Helene Raskin White, Leah Goldman Traub, and Rolf Loeber, "Mental Health and Juvenile Arrests: Criminality, Criminalization, or Compassion?" *Criminology* 44 (2006): 593–630.

221. Jeffrey Wanson, Randy Borum, Marvin Swartz, Virginia Hidaym, H. Ryan Wagner, and Barbara Burns, "Can Involuntary Outpatient Commitment Reduce Arrests among Persons with Severe Mental Illness?" *Criminal Justice and Behavior* 28 (2001): 156–189.

222. This discussion is based on three works by Albert Bandura: *Aggression: A Social Learning Analysis* (Englewood Cliffs, NJ: Prentice Hall, 1973); *Social Learning Theory* (Englewood Cliffs, NJ: Prentice Hall, 1977); and "The Social Learning Perspective: Mechanisms of Aggression," in *Psychology of Crime and Criminal Justice,* ed. Hans Toch (New York: Holt, Rinehart & Winston, 1979), pp. 198–236.

223. David Phillips, "The Impact of Mass Media Violence on U.S. Homicides," *American Sociological Review* 48 (1983): 560–568.

224. See generally Jean Piaget, *The Moral Judgment of the Child* (London: Kegan Paul, 1932).

225. Lawrence Kohlberg, *Stages in the Development of Moral Thought and Action* (New York: Holt, Rinehart & Winston, 1969).

226. L. Kohlberg, K. Kauffman, P. Scharf, and J. Hickey, *The Just Community Approach in Corrections: A Manual* (Niantic: Connecticut Department of Corrections, 1973).

227. Scott Henggeler, *Delinquency in Adolescence* (Newbury Park, CA: Sage, 1989), p. 26.

228. Carol Veneziano and Louis Veneziano, "The Relationship between Deterrence and Moral Reasoning," *Criminal Justice Review* 17 (1992): 209–216.

229. Quinten Raaijmakers, Rutger Engels, and Anne Van Hoof, "Delinquency and Moral Reasoning in Adolescence and Young Adulthood," *International Journal of Behavioral Development* 29 (2005): 247–258; Scott Henggeler, *Delinquency in Adolescence* (Newbury Park, CA: Sage, 1989), p. 26.

230. K. A. Dodge, "A Social Information Processing Model of Social Competence in Children," in *Minnesota Symposium in Child Psychology,* vol. 18, ed. M. Perlmutter (Hillsdale, NJ: Erlbaum, 1986), pp. 77–125.

231. Adrian Raine, Peter Venables, and Mark Williams, "Better Autonomic Conditioning and Faster Electrodermal Half-Recovery Time at Age 15 Years as Possible Protective Factors against Crime at Age 29 Years," *Developmental Psychology* 32 (1996): 624–630.

232. Jean Marie McGloin and Travis Pratt, "Cognitive Ability and Delinquent Behavior among Inner-City Youth: A Life-Course Analysis of Main, Mediating, and Interaction Effects," *International Journal of Offender Therapy and Comparative Criminology* 47 (2003): 253–271.

233. Elizabeth Cauffman, Laurence Steinberg, and Alex Piquero, "Psychological, Neuropsychological, and Physiological Correlates of Serious Antisocial Behavior in Adolescence: The Role of Self-Control," *Criminology* 43 (2005): 133–176.

234. Donald Lynam and Joshua Miller, "Personality Pathways to Impulsive Behavior and Their Relations to Deviance: Results from Three Samples," *Journal of Quantitative Criminology* 20 (2004): 319–341.

235. Shadd Maruna, "Desistance from Crime and Explanatory Style: A New Direction in the Psychology of Reform," *Journal of*

Contemporary Criminal Justice 20 (2004): 184–200.

236. Tony Ward and Claire Stewart, "The Relationship Between Human Needs and Criminogenic Needs," *Psychology, Crime and Law* 9 (2003): 219–225.

237. David Ward, Mark Stafford, and Louis Gray, "Rational Choice, Deterrence, and Theoretical Integration," *Journal of Applied Social Psychology* 36 (2006): 571–585.

238. Coralijn Nas, Bram Orobio de Castro, and Willem Koops, "Social Information Processing in Delinquent Adolescents," *Psychology, Crime and Law* 11 (2005): 363–375.

239. Elizabeth Kubik and Jeffrey Hecker, "Cognitive Distortions About Sex and Sexual Offending: A Comparison of Sex Offending Girls, Delinquent Girls, and Girls from the Community" *Journal of Child Sexual Abuse* 14 (2005): 43–69.

240. L. Huesman and L. Eron, "Individual Differences and the Trait of Aggression," *European Journal of Personality* 3 (1989): 95–106.

241. Rolf Loeber and Dale Hay, "Key Issues in the Development of Aggression and Violence from Childhood to Early Adulthood," *Annual Review of Psychology* 48 (1997): 371–410.

242. Judith Baer and Tina Maschi, "Random Acts of Delinquency: Trauma and Self-Destructiveness in Juvenile Offenders," *Child and Adolescent Social Work Journal* 20 (2003): 85–99.

243. J. E. Lochman, "Self and Peer Perceptions and Attributional Biases of Aggressive and Nonaggressive Boys in Dyadic Interactions," *Journal of Consulting and Clinical Psychology* 55 (1987): 404–410.

244. Kathleen Cirillo, B. E. Pruitt, Brian Colwell, Paul M. Kingery, Robert S. Hurley, and Danny Ballard, "School Violence: Prevalence and Intervention Strategies for At-Risk Adolescents," *Adolescence* 33 (1998): 319–331.

245. Leilani Greening, "Adolescent Stealers' and Nonstealers' Social Problem-Solving Skills," *Adolescence* 32 (1997): 51–56.

246. D. Lipton, E. C. McDonel, and R. McFall, "Heterosocial Perception in Rapists," *Journal of Consulting and Clinical Psychology* 55 (1987): 17–21.

247. Vincent Marziano, Tony Ward, Anthony Beech, and Philippa Pattison, "Identification of Five Fundamental Implicit Theories Underlying Cognitive Distortions in Child Abusers: A Preliminary Study," *Psychology, Crime and Law* 12 (2006): 97–105.

248. *Understanding Violence,* p. 389.

249. Cirillo, Pruitt, Colwell, Kingery, Hurley, and Ballard, "School Violence."

250. See generally Walter Mischel, *Introduction to Personality,* 4th ed. (New York: Holt, Rinehart & Winston, 1986).

251. D. A. Andrews and J. Stephen Wormith, "Personality and Crime: Knowledge and Construction in Criminology," *Justice Quarterly* 6 (1989): 289–310; Donald Gibbons, "Comment—Personality and Crime: Non-Issues, Real Issues, and a Theory and Research Agenda," *Justice Quarterly* (1989): 311–324.

252. Sheldon Glueck and Eleanor Glueck, *Unraveling Juvenile Delinquency* (Cambridge, MA: Harvard University Press, 1950).

253. See generally Hans Eysenck, *Personality and Crime* (London: Routledge and Kegan Paul, 1977).

254. Hans Eysenck and M. W. Eysenck, *Personality and Individual Differences* (New York: Plenum, 1985).

255. Catrien Bijleveld and Jan Hendriks, "Juvenile Sex Offenders: Differences between Group and Solo Offenders," *Psychology, Crime and Law* 9 (2003): 237–246; Joshua Miller and Donald Lynam, "Personality and Antisocial Behavior," *Criminology* 39 (2001): 765–799; Edelyn Verona and Joyce Carbonell, "Female Violence and Personality," *Criminal Justice and Behavior* 27 (2000): 176–195.

256. Hans Eysenck and M. W. Eysenck, *Personality and Individual Differences* (New York: Plenum, 1985).

257. Essi Viding, James Blair, Terrie Moffitt, and Robert Plomin, "Evidence for Substantial Genetic Risk for Psychopathy in 7-Year-Olds," *Journal of Child Psychology and Psychiatry* 46 (2005): 592–597.

258. Gerhard Blickle, Alexander Schlegel, Pantaleon Fassbender, and Uwe Klein, "Some Personality Correlates of Business White-Collar Crime," *Applied Psychology: An International Review* 55 (2006): 220–233.

259. Andreas Hill, Niels Habermann, Wolfgang Berner, and Peer Briken, "Sexual Sadism and Sadistic Personality Disorder in Sexual Homicide," *Journal of Personality Disorders* 20 (2006): 671–684.

260. See generally R. Starke Hathaway and Elio Monachesi, *Analyzing and Predicting Juvenile Delinquency with the MMPI* (Minneapolis: University of Minnesota Press, 1953).

261. R. Starke Hathaway, Elio Monachesi, and Lawrence Young, "Delinquency Rates and Personality," *Journal of Criminal Law, Criminology, and Police Science* 51 (1960): 443–460; Michael Hindelang and Joseph Weis, "Personality and Self-Reported Delinquency: An Application of Cluster Analysis," *Criminology* 10 (1972): 268; Spencer Rathus and Larry Siegel, "Crime and Personality Revisited," *Criminology* 18 (1980): 245–251.

262. See generally Edward Megargee, *The California Psychological Inventory Handbook* (San Francisco: Jossey-Bass, 1972).

263. Avshalom Caspi, Terrie Moffitt, Phil Silva, Magda Stouthamer-Loeber, Robert Krueger, and Pamela Schmutte, "Are Some People Crime-Prone? Replications of the Personality–Crime Relationship across Countries, Genders, Races and Methods," *Criminology* 32 (1994): 163–195.

264. Edwin Sutherland, "Mental Deficiency and Crime," in *Social Attitudes,* ed. Kimball Young (New York: Henry Holt, 1931).

265. Travis Hirschi and Michael Hindelang, "Intelligence and Delinquency: A Revisionist Review," *American Sociological Review* 42 (1977): 471–586.

266. Ibid.

267. Donald Lynam, Terrie Moffitt, and Magda Stouthamer-Loeber, "Explaining the Relation between IQ and Delinquency: Class, Race, Test Motivation, School Failure or Self-Control," *Journal of Abnormal Psychology* 102 (1993): 187–196.

268. Susan Pease and Craig T. Love, "Optimal Methods and Issues in Nutrition Research in the Correctional Setting," *Nutrition Reviews Supplement* 44 (1986): 122–131.

269. Alex Piquero, "Frequency, Specialization, and Violence in Offending Careers," *Journal of Research in Crime and Delinquency* 37 (2000): 392–418.

270. James Q. Wilson and Richard Herrnstein, *Crime and Human Nature* (New York: Simon & Schuster, 1985), p. 148.

271. Ibid., p. 171.

272. Lorne Yeudall, Delee Fromm-Auch, and Priscilla Davies, "Neuropsychological Impairment of Persistent Delinquency," *Journal of Nervous and Mental Diseases* 170 (1982): 257–265; Hakan Stattin and Ingrid Klackenberg-Larsson, "Early Language and Intelligence Development and Their Relationship to Future Criminal Behavior," *Journal of Abnormal Psychology* 102 (1993): 369–378; H. D. Day, J. M. Franklin, and D. D. Marshall, "Predictors of Aggression in Hospitalized Adolescents," *Journal of Psychology* 132 (1998): 427–435;

273. Camilla Hagelstam and Helinä Häkkänen, "Adolescent Homicides in Finland: Offence and Offender Characteristics," *Forensic Science International* 164 (2006): 110–115.

274. Richard Herrnstein and Charles Murray, *The Bell Curve, Intelligence and Class Structure in American Life* (New York: Free Press, 1994).

275. M. K. Simpson and J. Hogg, "Patterns of Offending among People with Intellectual Disability: A Systematic Review Part I: Methodology and Prevalence Data," *Journal of Intellectual Disability Research* 45 (2001): 384–396.

276. Ibid.

277. Mark O'Callaghan and Douglas Carroll, "The Role of Psychosurgical Studies in the Control of Antisocial Behavior," in *The Causes of Crime: New Biological Approaches,* ed. Sarnoff Mednick, Terrie Moffitt, and Susan Stack (Cambridge: Cambridge University Press, 1987), pp. 312–328.

278. Reiss and Roth, *Understanding and Preventing Violence,* p. 389.

279. Cirillo, Pruitt, Colwell, Kingery, Hurley, and Ballard, "School Violence."

280. Martin Olsson, Kjell Hansson, and Marianne Cederblad, "A Long-Term Follow-Up of Conduct Disorder Adolescents into Adulthood," *Nordic Journal of Psychiatry* 60 (2006): 469–479.

Social Structure Theories

CHAPTER OUTLINE

Socioeconomic Structure and Crime
The Underclass
Child Poverty
Minority Group Poverty

Race, Culture, Gender, and Criminology:
There Goes the Neighborhood

Social Structure Theories
Social Disorganization Theory
The Social Ecology School
Collective Efficacy

Strain Theories
The Concept of Anomie
Merton's Theory of Anomie
Macro-Level Theory: Institutional Anomie Theory
Micro-Level Theory: General Strain Theory
Sources of Strain
Coping with Strain
Evaluating GST

Cultural Deviance Theories
Conduct Norms
Focal Concerns
Theory of Delinquent Subcultures

PROFILES IN CRIME: A Life in the Drug Trade

Race, Culture, Gender, and Criminology:
The Code of the Streets

Theory of Differential Opportunity
Evaluating Social Structure Theories

Public Policy Implications of Social Structure Theory

CHAPTER OBJECTIVES

1. Be familiar with the concept of social structure

2. Have knowledge of the socioeconomic structure of American society

3. Be able to discuss the concept of social disorganization

4. Be familiar with the works of Shaw and McKay

5. Know the various elements of ecological theory

6. Be able to discuss the association between collective efficacy and crime

7. Know what is meant by the term "anomie"

8. Be familiar with the concept of strain

9. Understand the concept of cultural deviance

10. Explain the meaning of the terms "focal concerns" and "conduct norms"

© AP Images/Edgard Garrido

The tiny country of El Salvador (population 6.6 million) is home to more than 40,000 gang members. Rather than being a homegrown phenomenon, gangs are actually a U.S import. How did this happen? In the early 1990s, hundreds of members of two of Los Angeles's largest gangs, the 18th Street Gang and the MS-13 gang, who had illegally made their home in the United States, were deported back to El Salvador. The deportees brought L.A. gang culture with them to a country already swamped with weapons from an ongoing civil war. Now on their home turf, gang boys recruited thousands of local teenagers into their reconstituted gangs. Joining a gang gave these poor, urban teenagers a powerful sense of identity and belonging. They were also free now to show their courage and manhood by engaging in a never-ending turf war with one another.

Ironically, both gangs were started in Los Angeles by Salvadorans fleeing a civil war. When they first arrived in L.A. they were preyed upon by preexisting Mexican gangs. The MS-13 gang was formed as a means of self-protection. The gang's name— Mara Salvatrucha—most likely refers to a mara, slang for "army ant," and salvatrucha, local slang for tough, streetwise Salvadorans; the "13" is a common L.A. gang reference. Over time, both gangs' ranks grew and members entered a variety of rackets, from extortion to drug trafficking. When law enforcement cracked down and deported members, the deportees quickly created outposts in El Salvador and throughout Central America. The Salvadoran government has responded by criminalizing gang membership and arresting thousands. But government efforts have not stemmed the tide of recruitment and the gangs appear to be more popular than ever.[1] Gang membership has continued to grow and the gangs have returned to set up branches in the United States. Some experts believe that the 10,000-member MS-13 is now the nation's most dangerous gang, while the 18th Street Gang, with over 20,000 members, is the largest.

Both MS-13 and the 18th Street Gang are part of a significant national gang population. The federal government sponsors the National Youth Gang Survey (NYGS) to measure gang activity around the United States. The most recent NYGS found that a significant majority of urban areas report the presence of gangs and that gangs exist in all levels of the social strata, from rural counties to metropolitan areas.[2] The most recent count found an estimated 760,000 gang members, and 24,000 gangs were active in more than 2,900 jurisdictions around the United States.

Teen gangs have become an ever-present fixture of the American urban experience. Gang members are heavily armed, dangerous, and more violent than nonmembers. They are about ten times more likely to carry handguns than nongang members, and gun-toting gang members commit about ten times more violent crimes than nonmembers; gang homicides seem to be on an upswing. Nowhere is the gang problem more serious than in Los Angeles, where a single gang can have up to 20,000 members.

To criminologists it comes as no surprise that gangs develop in poor, deteriorated urban neighborhoods. Many kids in these areas grow up hopeless and alienated, believing that they have little chance of being part of the American Dream.[3] Joining a gang holds the promise of economic rewards and status enhancements, which the conventional world simply cannot provide.

This association between social conditions and crime is not lost on criminologists, many of whom conclude that criminals are indigent and desperate people rather than abnormal, calculating, or evil. Raised in deteriorated parts of town, they lack the social support and economic resources available to more affluent members of society. According to this view, it is *social forces*—and not individual traits—that cause crime. To understand criminal behavior, we must analyze the influence of these destructive social forces.

As you may recall (Chapter 1), the social environment and its influence on human behavior has been the primary focus of criminology since the early twentieth century, when sociologists Robert Ezra Park (1864–1944), Ernest W. Burgess (1886–1966), Louis Wirth (1897–1952), and their colleagues were teaching and conducting criminological research in the sociology department at the University of Chicago. Their influence was such that most criminologists have been trained in sociology, and criminology courses are routinely taught in departments of sociology. What is their vision and how do they connect criminality with a person's place in the social structure?

connections

Concern about the ecological distribution of crime, the effect of social change, and the interactive nature of crime itself has made sociology the foundation of modern criminology. This chapter reviews sociological theories that emphasize the relationship between social status and criminal behavior. In Chapter 7 the focus shifts to theories that emphasize socialization and its influence on crime and deviance; Chapter 8 covers theories based on the concept of social conflict.

Table 6.1 Mean and Share of Household Income

	Mean Household Income	Share of Household Income
Lowest fifth	$10,655	3.4%
Second fifth	27,357	8.6
Third fifth	46,301	14.6
Fourth fifth	72,825	23.0
Highest fifth	159,583	50.4

Source: Income, Poverty and Health Insurance in the United States: 2005 (P60-231) (Washington, DC: U.S. Census Department, 2006), www.census.gov/prod/2006pubs/p60-231.pdf (accessed June 3, 2007).

SOCIOECONOMIC STRUCTURE AND CRIME

People in the United States live in a stratified society. Social strata are created by the unequal distribution of wealth, power, and prestige. Social classes are segments of the population whose members have a relatively similar portion of desirable things and who share attitudes, values, norms, and an identifiable lifestyle. In U.S. society, it is common to identify people as upper-, middle-, and lower-class citizens, with a broad range of economic variations existing within each group. The upper-upper class is reserved for a small number of exceptionally well-to-do families who maintain enormous financial and social resources. Today, the poorest fifth (20 percent) of all U.S. households earn about $10,000 per year and receive only 3 percent of the country's aggregate income, the smallest share ever (see Table 6.1). In contrast, the top fifth (20 percent) of households earn more than $150,000 per year, a record high; the top 20 percent collect more than 50 percent of all household income, the most in history.[4]

Nor is the wealth concentration effect unique to the United States; it is a worldwide phenomenon. According to the most recent World Wealth Report, there are about 8 million high net worth individuals in the world today (people with more than $1 million in assets excluding their primary residence); they have a net worth of more than $30.8 trillion, and their numbers are steadily growing.[5]

In contrast, the indigent have scant, if any, resources and suffer socially and economically as a result. And while the United States is the richest country in the world, the most recent federal data indicate that the number and rate of people living in poverty has risen since 2000[6] (Figure 6.1). More than 37 million Americans now live in poverty.

Lower-class areas are scenes of inadequate housing and health care, disrupted family lives, underemployment, and despair. Members of the lower class also suffer in other ways. They are more prone to depression, less likely to have achievement motivation, and less likely to put off immediate gratification for future gain. For example, they may be less willing to stay in

THERE GOES THE NEIGHBORHOOD

William Julius Wilson, one of the nation's most prominent sociologists, has produced an impressive body of work that details racial problems and racial politics in American society. In 1987, he provided a description of the plight of the lowest levels of the underclass, which he labeled the truly disadvantaged. Wilson portrayed members of this group as socially isolated people who dwell in urban inner cities, occupy the bottom rung of the social ladder, and are the victims of discrimination. They live in areas in which the basic institutions of society—family, school, housing—have long since declined. Their decline triggers similar breakdowns in the strengths of inner-city areas, including the loss of community cohesion and the ability of people living in the area to control the flow of drugs and criminal activity. For example, in a more affluent area, neighbors might complain to parents that their children were acting out. In distressed areas, this element of informal social control may be absent because parents are under stress or all too often absent. These effects magnify the isolation of the underclass from mainstream society and promote a ghetto culture and behavior.

Because the truly disadvantaged rarely come into contact with the actual source of their oppression, they direct their anger and aggression at those with whom they are in close and intimate contact, such as neighbors, businesspeople, and landlords. Members of this group, plagued by under- or unemployment, begin to lose self-confidence, a feeling supported by the plight of kin and friendship groups who also experience extreme economic marginality. Self-doubt is a neighborhood norm, overwhelming those forced to live in areas of concentrated poverty.

In his important book, *When Work Disappears*, Wilson assesses the effect of joblessness and underemployment on residents in poor neighborhoods on Chicago's south side. He argues that for the first time since the nineteenth century, most adults in inner-city ghetto neighborhoods are not working during a typical week. He finds that inner-city life is only marginally affected by the surge in the nation's economy, which has been brought about by new industrial growth connected with technological development. Poverty in these inner-city areas is eternal and unchanging and, if anything, worsening as residents are further shut out of the economic mainstream.

Wilson focuses on the plight of the African American community, which had enjoyed periods of relative prosperity in the 1950s and 1960s. He suggests that as difficult as life was in the 1940s and 1950s for African Americans, they at least had a reasonable hope of steady work. Now, because of the globalization of the economy, those opportunities have evaporated. Though in the past racial segregation had limited opportunity, growth in the manufacturing sector fueled upward mobility and provided the foundation of today's African American middle class. Those opportunities no longer exist as manufacturing plants have moved to inaccessible rural and overseas locations where the cost of doing business is lower. With manufacturing opportunities all but obsolete in the United States, service and retail establishments, which depended on blue-collar spending, have similarly disappeared, leaving behind an economy based on welfare and government supports. In less than 20 years, formerly active African American communities have become crime-infested inner-city neighborhoods.

The hardships faced by residents in Chicago's south side are not unique to that community. Beyond sustaining inner-city poverty, the absence of employment opportunities has torn at the social fabric of the nation's inner-city neighborhoods. Work helps socialize young people into the wider society, instilling in them such desirable values as hard work, caring, and respect for others. When work becomes scarce, however, the discipline and structure it provides are absent. Community-wide underemployment destroys social cohesion, increasing the presence of neighborhood social problems ranging from drug use to educational failure. Schools in these areas are unable to teach basic skills and because desirable employment is lacking, there are few adults to serve as role models. In contrast to more affluent suburban households where daily life is organized around job and career demands, children in inner-city areas are not socialized in the workings of the mainstream economy.

In *The Bridge over the Racial Divide: Rising Inequality and Coalition Politics*, Wilson expands on his views of race in contemporary society. He argues that despite economic gains, there is a growing inequality in American society, and ordinary families, of all races and ethnic origins, are suffering. Whites, Latinos, African Americans, Asians, and Native Americans must therefore begin to put aside their differences and concentrate more on what they have in common—their aspirations, problems, and hopes. There needs to be mutual cooperation across racial lines.

One reason for this set of mutual problems is that the government tends to aggravate rather than ease the financial stress being placed on ordinary families. Monetary policy, trade policy, and tax policy are harmful to working-class families. A multiracial citizens' coalition could pressure national public officials to focus on the interests of ordinary people. As long as middle- and working-class groups are fragmented along racial lines, such pressure is impossible.

Wilson finds that racism is becoming more subtle and harder to detect. Whites believe that blacks are responsible for their inferior economic status because of their cultural traits. Because even affluent whites fear corporate downsizing, they are unwilling to vote for governmental assistance to the poor because it means

(continued)

(continued)
more taxes and lower corporate profits, a condition that threatens their jobs. Whites are continuing to be suburban dwellers, further isolating poor minorities in central cities and making their problems distant and unimportant. Wilson continues to believe that the changing marketplace, with its reliance on sophisticated computer technologies, is continually decreasing demand for low-skilled workers, which impacts African Americans more negatively than other better educated and affluent groups.

Wilson argues for a cross-race, class-based alliance of working- and middle-class Americans to pursue policies that will benefit them rather than the affluent. These include full employment, programs to help families and workers in their private lives, and a reconstructed "affirmative opportunity" program that benefits African Americans without antagonizing whites.

In his most recent work, *There Goes the Neighborhood*, Wilson, along with Richard P. Taub, assesses racial relations

in four Chicago neighborhoods. The picture he paints is quite bleak. He finds that racism is still an active part of people's lives though its motif is changing. People are unusually hostile when outsiders move into their enclave. If they have a choice they move, if not they are angry and sullen. In a white middle-class neighborhood, people are angry when black and Latino newcomers arrive, believing they threaten property values and neighborhood stability. Whites and Latinos are able to reach common ground on only one social issue: preventing kids from being bused to a black school district. People seem unfazed about using offensive racist language to express their feelings and feel superior to other groups and races. Racism seems to cloak social anxiety: people worried about jobs and health care take their frustrations out on others. Wilson as always comes up with a prescription for positive change: strengthen neighborhood social organizations and people will be less likely to flee. Race relations can be improved if people from diverse backgrounds can

come together to reach common goals such as school improvement. Society as a whole must be willing to help out and repair inner-city ghetto areas. Without such help, racial and class tensions spread throughout the city.

CRITICAL THINKING

1. Is it unrealistic to assume that a government-sponsored public works program can provide needed jobs in this era of budget cutbacks?

2. What are some of the hidden costs of unemployment in a community setting?

3. How would a biocriminologist explain Wilson's findings?

Sources: William Julius Wilson and Richard Taub, *There Goes the Neighborhood: Racial, Ethnic, and Class Tensions in Four Chicago Neighborhoods and Their Meaning for America* (New York: Knopf, 2006); William Julius Wilson, *The Truly Disadvantaged* (Chicago: University of Chicago Press, 1987); *When Work Disappears: The World of the Urban Poor* (New York: Alfred Knopf, 1996); *The Bridge over the Racial Divide: Rising Inequality and Coalition Politics* (Wildavsky Forum Series, 2) (Berkeley: University of California Press, 1999).

SOCIAL STRUCTURE THEORIES

The problems caused by poverty and income inequality are not lost on criminologists. They recognize that the various sources of crime data show that crime rates are highest in neighborhoods characterized by poverty and social disorder. Although members of the middle and upper classes sometimes engage in crime, these are generally nonviolent acts, such as embezzlement and fraud, which present little danger to the general public. In contrast, lower-class crime is often the violent, destructive product of youth gangs and marginally and underemployed young adults. The real crime problem is essentially a lower-class phenomenon, which breeds criminal behavior that begins in youth and continues into young adulthood. Kids growing up poor and living in households that lack economic resources are much more likely to get involved in serious crime than their wealthier peers.[23] To explain this phenomenon, criminologists have formulated social structure theories. As a group, they suggest that social and economic forces operating in deteriorated lower-class areas are the

key determinant of criminal behavior patterns. Social forces begin to affect people while they are relatively young and continue to influence them throughout their lives. Though not all youthful offenders become adult criminals, those who are exposed to a continual stream of violence in deteriorated inner-city neighborhoods are the ones most likely to persist in their criminal careers.[24]

Social structure theorists challenge those who suggest that crime is an expression of some personal trait or individual choice. They argue that people living in equivalent social environments tend to behave in a similar, predictable fashion. If the environment did not influence human behavior, then crime rates would be distributed equally across the social structure, which they are not.[25] Because crime rates are higher in lower-class urban centers than in middle-class suburbs, social forces must be operating in blighted urban areas that influence or control behavior.[26]

There are three independent yet overlapping branches within the social structure perspective—social disorganization, strain theory, and cultural deviance theory (outlined in Figure 6.3):

▌ Social disorganization theory focuses on the conditions within the urban environment that affect crime rates. A disorganized area is one in which institutions of social

Figure 6.3 The Three Branches of Social Structure Theory

Social disorganization theory focuses on conditions in the environment:
- Deteriorated neighborhoods
- Inadequate social control
- Law-violating gangs and groups
- Conflicting social values

Strain theory focuses on conflict between goals and means:
- Unequal distribution of wealth and power
- Frustration
- Alternative methods of achievement

Cultural deviance theory combines the other two:
- Development of subcultures as a result of disorganization and stress
- Subcultural values in opposition to conventional values

CRIME

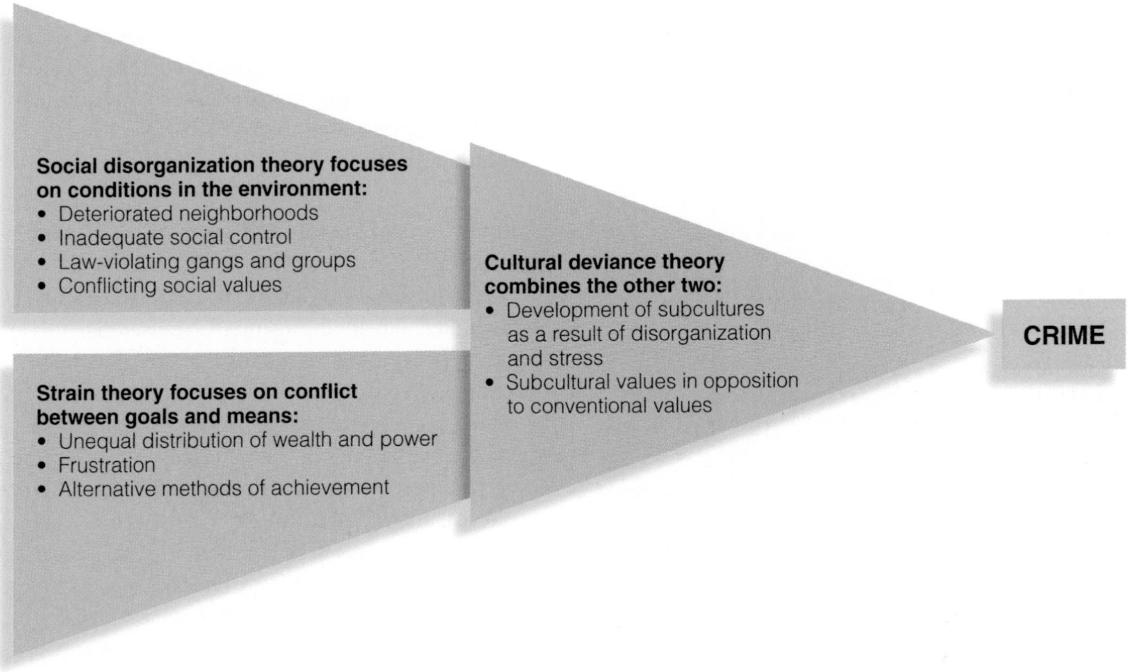

control—such as the family, commercial establishments, and schools—have broken down and can no longer carry out their expected or stated functions. Indicators of social disorganization include high unemployment, school dropout rates, deteriorated housing, low-income levels, and large numbers of single-parent households. Residents in these areas experience conflict and despair, and, as a result, antisocial behavior flourishes.

Strain theory holds that crime is a function of the conflict between the goals people have and the means they can use to obtain them legally. Most people in the United States desire wealth, material possessions, power, prestige, and other life comforts. And although these social and economic goals are common to people in all economic strata, strain theorists insist that the ability to obtain these goals is class dependent. Members of the lower class are unable to achieve these symbols of success through conventional means. Consequently, they feel anger, frustration, and resentment, which is referred to as strain. Lower-class citizens can either accept their condition and live out their days as socially responsible, if unrewarded, citizens, or they can choose an alternative means of achieving success, such as theft, violence, or drug trafficking.

Cultural deviance theory, the third variation of structural theory, combines elements of both strain and social disorganization. According to this view, because of strain and social isolation, a unique lower-class culture develops in disorganized neighborhoods. These independent subcultures maintain a unique set of values and beliefs that are in conflict with conventional social norms. Criminal behavior is an expression of conformity to lower-class subcultural values

and traditions and not a rebellion from conventional society. Subcultural values are handed down from one generation to the next in a process called cultural transmission.

Although each of these theories is distinct in critical aspects, each approach has at its core the view that socially isolated people, living in disorganized neighborhoods, are the ones most likely to experience crime-producing social forces. Each branch of social structure theory will now be discussed in some detail.

Social Disorganization Theory

Social disorganization theory links crime rates to neighborhood ecological characteristics. Communities where the fabric of social life has become frayed and torn are unable to provide essential services to their residents, such as education, health care, and proper housing. Residents in these crime-ridden neighborhoods want to leave the community at the earliest opportunity. Because they want out, they become uninterested in community matters. As a result, these neighborhoods are destabilized. There is constant population turnover; people are not interested in investing in these communities. Because housing is deteriorated the neighborhood becomes mixed-use (i.e., residential and commercial property exist side by side).

Because the area is undergoing stress, the normal sources of *social control* common to most neighborhoods—the family, school, personal ties, interest of the business community, law enforcement, and social service agencies—become weak and disorganized. Personal relationships are strained because neighbors are constantly relocating to better areas. Resident turnover further weakens communication and blocks the establishment

Figure 6.4 Social Disorganization Theory

Poverty
- Development of isolated lower-class areas
- Lack of conventional social opportunities
- Racial and ethnic discrimination

∨

Social disorganization
- Breakdown of social institutions and organizations such as school and family
- Lack of informal and formal social control

∨

Breakdown of traditional values
- Development of law violating gangs and groups
- Deviant values replace conventional values and norms

∨

Criminal areas
- Neighborhood becomes crime prone
- Stable pockets of crime develop
- Lack of external support and investment

∨

Cultural transmission
Adults pass norms (focal concerns) to younger generation, creating stable lower-class culture

∨

Criminal careers
Most youths age out of delinquency, marry, and raise families, but some remain in life of crime

A policewoman searches the schoolbag of a young girl in the graffiti-covered Cabrini Green Housing Project. Because socially disorganized areas are undergoing stress, the normal sources of social control common to most neighborhoods—the family, school, personal ties, interest of the business community, law enforcement, and social service agencies—become weak and disorganized. When social control can be maintained, the likelihood of crime and violence decreases.

of common goals. The result: any attempt at community-level problem solving ends in frustration.[27]

The problems encountered in this type of disorganized area take the form of a contagious disease, destroying the inner workings that enable neighborhoods to survive; the community becomes "hollowed out."[28] Crime and violence take the form of a "slow epidemic," spreading to surrounding areas and infecting them with inner-city problems.[29] The elements of social disorganization theory are shown in Figure 6.4.

Foundations of Social Disorganization Theory Social disorganization theory was first popularized by the work of two Chicago sociologists, Clifford R. Shaw and Henry D. McKay, who linked life in disorganized, transitional urban areas to neighborhood crime rates. Shaw and McKay began their pioneering work on crime in Chicago during the early 1920s while working as researchers for a state-supported social service agency.[30] They were heavily influenced by Chicago School sociologists Ernest Burgess and Robert Park, who had pioneered the ecological analysis of urban life.

Shaw and McKay began their analysis during a period in the city's history that was fairly typical of the transition that was taking place in many other urban areas. Chicago had experienced a mid-nineteenth-century population expansion, fueled by a dramatic influx of foreign-born immigrants and, later, migrating southern families. Congregating in the central city, the newcomers occupied the oldest housing areas and therefore faced numerous health and environmental hazards.

Sections of the city started to physically deteriorate. This condition prompted the city's wealthy, established citizens to become concerned about the moral fabric of Chicago society. The belief was widespread that immigrants from Europe and the rural South were crime prone and morally dissolute. In fact, local groups were created with the very purpose of "saving" the children of poor families from moral decadence.[31] It was popular to view crime as the property of inferior racial and ethnic groups.

Transitional Neighborhoods Shaw and McKay explained crime and delinquency within the context of the changing urban environment and ecological development of the city. They saw that Chicago had developed into distinct neighborhoods (natural areas), some affluent and others wracked by extreme poverty. These poverty-ridden, **transitional neighborhoods** suffered high rates of population turnover and were incapable of inducing residents to remain and defend the neighborhoods against criminal groups.

Low rents in these areas attracted groups with different racial and ethnic backgrounds. Newly arrived immigrants from Europe and the South congregated in these transitional neighborhoods. Their children were torn between assimilating into a new culture and abiding by the traditional values of their parents. They soon found that informal social control mechanisms

© Ralf-Finn Hestoft/Corbis

that had restrained behavior in the "old country" or rural areas were disrupted. These urban areas were believed to be the spawning grounds of young criminals.

In transitional areas, successive changes in the population composition, disintegration of traditional cultures, diffusion of divergent cultural standards, and gradual industrialization of the area result in dissolution of neighborhood culture and organization. The continuity of conventional neighborhood traditions and institutions is broken, leaving children feeling displaced and without a strong or definitive set of values.

Concentric Zones Shaw and McKay identified the areas in Chicago that had excessive crime rates. Using a model of analysis pioneered by Ernest Burgess, they noted that distinct ecological areas had developed in the city, comprising a series of five concentric circles, or zones, and that there were stable and significant differences in interzone crime rates (Figure 6.5). The areas of heaviest concentration of crime appeared to be the transitional inner-city zones, where large numbers of foreign-born citizens had recently settled.[32] The zones furthest from the city's center had correspondingly lower crime rates.

Analysis of these data indicated a surprisingly stable pattern of criminal activity in the various ecological zones over a 65-year period. Shaw and McKay concluded that, in the transitional neighborhoods, multiple cultures and diverse values, both conventional and deviant, coexist. Children growing up in the street culture often find that adults who have adopted a deviant lifestyle are the most financially successful people in the neighborhood: for example, the gambler, the pimp, or the drug dealer. Required to choose between conventional and deviant lifestyles, many inner-city kids saw the value in opting for the latter. They join with other like-minded youths and form law-violating gangs and cliques. The development of teenage law-violating groups is an essential element of youthful misbehavior in lower-class areas. The values that inner-city youths adopt are often in conflict with existing middle-class norms, which demand strict obedience to the legal code. Consequently, a value conflict occurs that sets the delinquent youth and his or her peer group even further apart from conventional society. The result is a more solid embrace of deviant goals and behavior. To justify their choice of goals, these youths seek support by recruiting new members and passing on the delinquent tradition.

Shaw and McKay's statistical analysis confirmed their theoretical suspicions. Even though crime rates changed, they found that the highest rates were always in Zones I and II (central city and a transitional area). The areas with the highest crime rates retained high rates even when their ethnic composition changed (in the areas Shaw and McKay examined, from German and Irish to Italian and Polish).[33]

The Legacy of Shaw and McKay Social disorganization concepts articulated by Shaw and McKay have remained a prominent fixture of criminological scholarship and thinking for more than 75 years. While cultural and social conditions have changed and American society today is much more heterogeneous and mobile than during Shaw and McKay's time, the most important elements of their findings still hold up:[34]

Figure 6.5 Shaw and McKay's Concentric Zones Map of Chicago

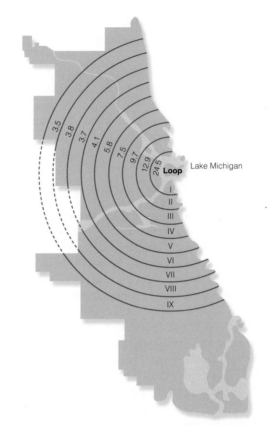

Note: Arabic numerals represent the rate of male delinquency.

Source: Clifford R. Shaw, et al., *Delinquency Areas* (Chicago: University of Chicago Press, 1929), p. 99.

■ Crime rates are sensitive to the destructive social forces operating in lower-class urban neighborhoods.

■ Environmental factors, rather then individual differences, are the root cause of crime. Personal abnormality or inferiority has little to do with crime rates.

■ Crime is a constant fixture in poverty areas regardless of racial and/or ethnic makeup.

■ Neighborhood disintegration and the corresponding erosion of social control are the primary causes of criminal behavior; community values, norms, and cohesiveness affect individual behavior choices.

Despite these noteworthy achievements, the validity of some of Shaw and McKay's positions have been challenged. Some critics have faulted their assumption that neighborhoods are essentially stable, suggesting that there is a great deal more fluidity and transition than assumed by Shaw and McKay.[35] There is also concern about their reliance on police records to calculate neighborhood crime rates. Relying on official data means that findings may be more sensitive to the validity of police-generated data than they are true interzone crime rate differences. Numerous studies indicate that police use extensive discretion when arresting people and that social status is one factor that influences their decisions.[36] It is possible that people in middle-class neighborhoods commit many criminal acts that never show up in official statistics, whereas people in lower-class areas face a far greater chance of arrest and court adjudication.[37] The relationship between ecology and crime rates, therefore, may reflect police behavior more than criminal behavior.

These criticisms aside, the concept of social disorganization provides a valuable contribution to our understanding of the causes of criminal behavior. By introducing a new variable—the ecology of the city—to the study of crime, Shaw and McKay paved the way for a whole generation of criminologists to focus on the social influences of criminal and delinquent behavior.

The Social Ecology School

Beginning in the 1980s, a group of criminologists began to study the ecological conditions that support criminality, changing the direction of social disorganization theory.[38] Contemporary social ecologists developed a "purer" form of structural theory that emphasizes the association of community deterioration and economic decline to criminality but places less emphasis on the value and norm conflict that lay at the core of Shaw and McKay's vision. According to this more contemporary view, living in deteriorated, crime-ridden neighborhoods exerts a powerful influence over behavior that is strong enough to neutralize the positive effects of a supportive family and close social ties. As sociologist Stacy De Coster and her associates point out, if individual or family status influence criminality and violence it is because of the nature of the communities in which disadvantaged persons and families reside and not the strength of family relationships themselves.[39] In the following sections, some of the more recent social ecological research is discussed in detail.

Community Deterioration Social ecologists have focused their attention on the association between crime rates and community deterioration: disorder, poverty, alienation, disassociation, and fear of crime.[40] They find that neighborhoods with a high percentage of deserted houses and apartments experience high crime rates; abandoned buildings serve as a "magnet for crime."[41] Areas in which houses are in poor repair, boarded up, and burned out, and whose owners are best described as "slumlords," are also the location of the highest violence rates and gun crime.[42] These are neighborhoods in which retail establishments often go bankrupt, are abandoned, and deteriorate physically.[43]

Poverty becomes "concentrated" in deteriorated areas.[44] As working- and middle-class families flee, elements of the most disadvantaged population are consolidated within inner-city poverty areas. As the working and middle classes move out, they take with them their financial and institutional resources and support. Businesses are disinclined to locate in poverty areas; banks become reluctant to lend money for new housing or businesses.[45] Areas of poverty concentration experience significant income and wealth disparities, nonexistent employment opportunities, inferior housing patterns, and unequal access to health care; not surprisingly, they also experience high rates of crime.[46]

Minority group members living in these areas are hit particularly hard. They are also exposed to race-based disparity such as income inequality and institutional racism.[47] Black crime rates, more so than white, seem to be influenced by the shift of high-paid manufacturing jobs overseas and their replacement with lower-paid service sector jobs. Both African American men and women seem less able to prosper in a service economy than white men and women, and over time the resulting economic disadvantage translates into increased levels of violence.[48] In desperation, some turn to armed robbery as a means of economic survival. More often than not, these desperate acts go awry, and the result is gun play and death. And because victims may be white there appears to be a racial motivation. However, what appear to be racially motivated crimes may be more a function of economic factors (i.e., the shift of jobs overseas) rather than interracial hate or antagonism.[49]

Chronic Unemployment The association between unemployment and crime is still unsettled: aggregate crime rates and aggregate unemployment rates seem weakly related. In other words, crime rates sometimes rise during periods of economic prosperity and fall during periods of economic decline.[50] Yet, as Shaw and McKay claimed, neighborhoods that experience chronic unemployment also encounter social disorganization and crime.[51] How can these divergent trends be explained?

One possibility is that even though short-term national economic trends may have little effect on crime, long-term *local unemployment* rates may have a more significant impact on conditions at the community or neighborhood level.[52] Take the situation in Milwaukee.[53] Since 1998, Wisconsin has lost nearly 90,000 manufacturing jobs and the city of Milwaukee has suffered the brunt of the slowdown. The unemployment rate hovers around 7 percent, up from 2.6 percent in 1998, and nearly double the national average. In inner-city neighborhoods, nearly 60 percent of working-age males are without jobs. With only half of adults earning more than a high school diploma, the city's residents aren't well matched for the white-collar positions most common today. During this period of economic transition, the city has experienced a significant increase in violent crime, especially murder. Hopefully, as the economy evolves and expands, crime rates may be reduced.

How does job loss lead to crime? Unemployment destabilizes households, and unstable families are the ones most likely to produce children who put a premium on violence and aggression as a means of dealing with limited opportunity. This lack of opportunity perpetuates higher crime rates, especially when large groups or cohorts of people of the same age compete for relatively scant resources.[54]

Limited employment opportunities also reduce the stabilizing influence of parents and other adults, who may have once been able to counteract the allure of youth gangs. Sociologist Elijah Anderson's analysis of Philadelphia neighborhood life found that "old heads" (i.e., respected neighborhood residents) who at one time played an important role in socializing youth have been displaced by younger street hustlers and drug dealers. While the old heads complain that these newcomers may not have earned or worked for their fortune in the "old-fashioned way," the old heads also admire and envy these kids whose gold chains and luxury cars advertise their wealth amid poverty.[55] The old heads may admire the fruits of crime, but they disdain the violent manner in which they were acquired.

Community Fear In neighborhoods where people help one another, residents are less likely to fear crime and be afraid of becoming a crime victim.[56] People feel safe in neighborhoods that are orderly and in repair.[57] In contrast, those living in neighborhoods that suffer social and physical incivilities—rowdy youth, trash and litter, graffiti, abandoned storefronts, burned-out buildings, littered lots, strangers, drunks, vagabonds, loiterers, prostitutes, noise, congestion, angry words, dirt, and stench—are much more likely to be fearful. Put another way, disorder breeds fear.[58] Fear is based on experience. Residents who have already been victimized are more fearful of the future than those who have escaped crime.[59] People become afraid when they are approached by someone in the neighborhood selling drugs. They become afraid when they see neighborhood kids hanging out in community parks and playgrounds or when gangs proliferate in the neighborhood.[60] They may fear that their children will also be approached and seduced into the drug life.[61] The presence of such incivilities, especially when accompanied by relatively high crime rates, convinces residents that their neighborhood is dangerous; becoming a crime victim seems inevitable.[62] Eventually they become emotionally numb, and as their exposure to crime increases, they experience indifference to the suffering of others.[63]

Fear can become contagious. People tell others when they have been victimized, spreading the word that the neighborhood is getting dangerous and that the chances of future victimization are high.[64] They dread leaving their homes at night and withdraw from community life.

> **connections**
>
> Fear of repeat victimization may be both instinctual and accurate. Remember that in Chapter 3 we discussed the fact that some people may be "victim prone" and fated to suffer repeated victimization over the life course.

When people live in areas where the death rates are high and life expectancies are short, they may alter their behavior out of fear. They may feel, "Why plan for the future when there is a significant likelihood that I may never see it?" In such areas, young boys and girls may psychologically assimilate by taking risks and discounting the future. Teenage birthrates soar and so do violence rates.[65] For these children, the inevitability of death skews their perspective of how they live their lives.

When fear grips a neighborhood, business conditions begin to deteriorate, population mobility increases, and a "criminal element" begins to drift into the area.[66] In essence, the existence of fear incites more crime, increasing the chances of victimization, producing even more fear, in a never-ending loop.[67] Fear is often associated with other community-level factors:

1. *Race and fear.* Fear of crime Is also bound up in anxiety over racial and ethnic conflicts. Fear becomes most pronounced in areas undergoing rapid and unexpected racial and age-composition changes, especially when they are out of proportion to the rest of the city.[68] Whites become particularly fearful when they sense that they are becoming a racial minority in their neighborhood.[69]

   The fear experienced by whites may be based on racial stereotypes, but it may also be caused by the premonition that they will become less well protected because police do not provide adequate services in predominantly African American neighborhoods.[70]

   Whites are not the only group to experience race-based fear. Minority group members may experience greater levels of fear than whites, perhaps because they may have fewer resources to address ongoing social problems.[71] Fear can be found among other racial and ethnic groups, especially when they believe they are in the minority and vulnerable to attack. In their study of race relations in Florida, Ted Chiricos and his associates found that whites feel threatened by Latinos and blacks but only in South Florida where whites are outnumbered by those two groups; in contrast, Latinos are threatened by blacks but only outside of South Florida where Latinos are the minority.[72]

2. *Gangs and fear.* Gangs flourish in deteriorated neighborhoods with high levels of poverty, lack of investment, high unemployment rates, and population turnover.[73] Unlike any other crime, however, gang activity is frequently undertaken out in the open, on the public ways, and in full view of the rest of the community.[74] Brazen criminal activity undermines community solidarity because it signals that the police must be either corrupt or inept. The fact that gangs are willing to openly engage in drug sales and other types of criminal activity shows their confidence that they have silenced or intimidated law-abiding people in their midst. The police and the community alike become hopeless about their ability to restore community stability, producing greater levels of community fear.

3. *Mistrust and fear.* People who report living in neighborhoods with high levels of crime and civil disorder become suspicious and mistrusting.[75] They develop a sense of powerlessness, which amplifies the effect of neighborhood disorder and increases levels of mistrust. Some residents become so suspicious of authority that they develop a siege mentality in which the outside world is considered the enemy out to destroy the neighborhood. Elijah Anderson found that residents in the African American neighborhoods he studied believed in the existence of a secret plan to eradicate the population by such strategies as permanent unemployment, police brutality, imprisonment, drug distribution, and AIDS.[76] White officials and political leaders were believed to have hatched this conspiracy, and it was demonstrated by the lax law enforcement efforts in poor areas. Residents felt that police cared little about black-on-black crime because it helped reduce the population. Rumors abounded that federal government agencies, such as the CIA, controlled the drug trade and used profits to fund illegal overseas operations.

This siege mentality results in mistrust of critical social institutions, including business, government, and schools. Government officials seem arrogant and haughty. Residents become self-conscious, worried about garnering any respect, and are particularly attuned to anyone who disrespects them. Considering this feeling of mistrust, when police ignore crime in poor areas or, conversely, when they are violent and corrupt, anger flares, and people take to the streets and react in violent ways.[77]

Community Change In our postmodern society, urban areas undergoing rapid structural changes in racial and economic composition also seem to experience the greatest change in crime rates. In contrast, stable neighborhoods, even those with a high rate of poverty, experience relatively low crime rates and have the strength to restrict substance abuse and criminal activity.[78]

Recent studies recognize that change, not stability, is the hallmark of inner-city areas. A neighborhood's residents, wealth, density, and purpose are constantly evolving. Even disorganized neighborhoods acquire new identifying features. Some may become multiracial, while others become racially homogeneous. Some areas become stable and family oriented, while in others, mobile, never-married people predominate.[79]

As areas decline, residents flee to safer, more stable localities. Those who can move to more affluent neighborhoods find that their lifestyles and life chances improve immediately and continue to do so over their life span.[80] Those who cannot leave because they cannot afford to live in more affluent communities face an increased risk of victimization.

High population turnover can have a devastating effect on community culture because it thwarts communication and information flow.[81] In response to this turnover, a culture may develop that dictates standards of dress, language, and behavior to neighborhood youth that are in opposition to those of conventional society. All these factors are likely to produce increased crime rates.

The Cycles of Community Change During periods of population turnover, communities may undergo changes that undermine their infrastructure. Urban areas seem to have life cycles, which begin with building residential dwellings and are followed by a period of decline, with marked decreases in socioeconomic status and increases in population density.[82] Later stages in this life cycle include changing racial or ethnic makeup, population thinning, and finally, a renewal stage in which obsolete housing is replaced and upgraded (i.e., **gentrification**). Areas undergoing such change seem to experience an increase in their crime rates.[83]

As communities go through cycles, neighborhood deterioration precedes increasing rates of crime and delinquency.[84] Neighborhoods most at risk for crime rate increases contain large numbers of single-parent families and unrelated people living together, have gone from having owner-occupied to renter-occupied units, and have an economic base that has lost semi-skilled and unskilled jobs (indicating a growing residue of discouraged workers who are no longer seeking employment).[85] These ecological disruptions strain existing social control mechanisms and inhibit their ability to control crime and delinquency.

Community change may also have racial overtones. Because of racial differences in economic well-being, those "left behind" are all too often minority citizens.[86] Those who cannot move find themselves surrounded by a constant influx of new residents. Whites may feel threatened as the number of minorities in the population increases and competes with them for jobs and political power.[87] According to the racial threat hypothesis as the percentage of minority group members in the population increases, so too does the crime rate. Why does this phenomenon occur? In changing neighborhoods, adults may actually encourage the law-violating behavior of youths. They may express attitudes that justify violence as a means of protecting their property and way of life by violently resisting newcomers.[88] They may also demand more money be spent on police and other justice agencies. As racial prejudice increases, the call for law and order aimed at controlling the minority population grows louder.[89]

Collective Efficacy

Cohesive communities, whether urban or rural, with high levels of social control and social integration, where people know one another and develop interpersonal ties, may also develop **collective efficacy**: mutual trust, a willingness to intervene in the supervision of children, and the maintenance of public order.[90] It is the cohesion among neighborhood residents combined with shared expectations for informal social control of public space that promotes collective efficacy.[91] Residents in these areas are able to enjoy a better life because the fruits of cohesiveness can be better education, health care, and housing opportunities.[92]

In contrast, residents of socially disorganized neighborhoods find that efforts at social control are weak and attenuated. People living in economically disadvantaged areas are significantly more likely to perceive their immediate surroundings in more negative terms (i.e., higher levels of incivilities) than those living in areas that maintain collective efficacy.[93] When community social control efforts are blunted, crime rates increase, further weakening neighborhood cohesiveness.[94]

There are actually three forms of collective efficacy:

1. *Informal social control.* Some elements of collective efficacy operate on the primary or private level and involve peers, families, and relatives. These sources exert informal control by either awarding or withholding approval, respect, and admiration. Informal control mechanisms include direct criticism, ridicule, ostracism, desertion, or physical punishment.[95]

   The most important wielder of informal social control is the family, which may keep at-risk kids in check through such mechanisms as corporal punishment, withholding privileges, or ridiculing lazy or disrespectful behavior. The importance of the family to apply informal social control takes on greater importance in neighborhoods with few social ties among adults and limited collective efficacy. In these areas parents cannot call upon neighborhood resources to take up the burden of controlling children and face the burden of providing adequate supervision.[96]

The family is not the only force of informal social control. In some neighborhoods, people are committed to preserving their immediate environment by confronting destabilizing forces such as teen gangs.[97] By helping neighbors become more resilient and self-confident, adults in these areas provide the external support systems that enable youth to desist from crime. Residents teach one another that they have moral and social obligations to their fellow citizens; children learn to be sensitive to the rights of others and to respect differences.

In some areas, neighborhood associations and self-help groups form.[98] The threat of skyrocketing violence rates may draw people together to help each other out. While criminologists believe that crime rates are lower in cohesive neighborhoods, it is also possible that an escalating crime rate may bring people closer together to fight a common problem.[99] Some neighbors may get involved in informal social control through surveillance practices, for example, by keeping an eye out for intruders when their neighbors go out of town. Informal surveillance has been found to reduce the levels of some crimes such as street robberies; however, if robbery rates remain high, surveillance may be terminated because people become fearful for their safety.[100]

2. *Institutional social control.* Social institutions such as schools and churches cannot work effectively in a climate of alienation and mistrust. Unsupervised peer groups and gangs, which flourish in disorganized areas, disrupt the influence of those neighborhood control agents that do exist.[101]

People who reside in these neighborhoods find that involvement with conventional social institutions, such as schools and afternoon programs, is often attenuated or blocked.[102] Children are at risk for recruitment into gangs and law-violating groups when there is a lack of effective public services. Gangs become an attractive alternative when adolescents have little to do after school and must rely on out-of-home care rather than more structured school-based programs.[103] As a result, crime may flourish and neighborhood fear increases, conditions that decrease a community's cohesion and thwart the ability of its institutions to exert social control over its residents.[104]

To combat these influences, communities that have collective efficacy attempt to utilize their local institutions to control crime. Sources of institutional social control include businesses, stores, schools, churches, and social service and volunteer organizations.[105] When these institutions are effective, crime rates decline.[106] Some institutions, such as recreation centers for teens, have been found to lower crime rates because they exert a positive effect; others, such as taverns and bars, can help destabilize neighborhoods and increase the rate of violent crimes such as rape and robbery.[107]

3. *Public social control.* Stable neighborhoods are also able to arrange for external sources of social control. If they can draw on outside help and secure external resources—a process referred to as public social control—they are better able to reduce the effects of disorganization and maintain lower levels of crime and victimization.[108] Racial differences in crime and violence rates may be explained in part by the ability of citizens in affluent, predominantly white neighborhoods to use their economic resources, and the political power they bring, to their own advantage. They demand and receive a level of protection in their communities that is not enjoyed in less affluent minority communities.[109]

The level of policing, one of the primary sources of public social control, may vary from neighborhood to neighborhood. The police presence is typically greatest when community organizations and local leaders have sufficient political clout to get funding for additional law enforcement personnel. An effective police presence sends a message that the area will not tolerate deviant behavior. Because they can respond vigorously to crime, the police prevent criminal groups from gaining a toehold in the neighborhood.[110] Criminals and drug dealers avoid such areas and relocate to easier and more appealing targets.[111] In contrast, crime rates are highest in areas where police are mistrusted because they engage in misconduct, for example, use of excessive force, or because they are seemingly indifferent to neighborhood problems.[112]

In more disorganized areas, the absence of political powerbrokers limits access to external funding and protection.[113] Without outside funding, a neighborhood may lack the ability to get back on its feet.[114] In these areas there are fewer police, and those that do patrol the area are less motivated and their resources are stretched tighter. These communities cannot mount an effective social control effort because as neighborhood disadvantage increases, its level of informal social control decreases.[115]

The government can also reduce crime by providing economic and social supports through publicly funded social support and welfare programs. Though welfare is often criticized by conservative politicians as being a government handout, there is evidence of a significant negative association between the amount of welfare money people receive and crime rates.[116] Government assistance may help people improve their social status by providing them with the financial resources to clothe, feed, and educate their children while at the same time reducing stress, frustration, and anger. Using government subsidies to reduce crime is controversial and not all research has found that it actually works as advertised.[117]

People living in disorganized areas may also be able to draw on resources from their neighbors in more affluent surrounding communities, helping to keep crime rates down.[118] This phenomenon may explain, in part, why violence rates are high in poor African American neighborhoods cut off from outside areas for support.[119]

The Effect of Collective Efficacy The ramifications of having adequate controls are critical. In areas where collective efficacy remains high, children are less likely to become involved with deviant peers and engage in problem behaviors.[120] In these more stable areas, kids are able to use their wits to avoid violent confrontations and to feel safe in their own neighborhood, a

SOCIAL DISORGANIZATION THEORIES

Theory	Major Premise	Strengths	Research Focus
Shaw and McKay's Concentric Zones Theory	Crime is a product of transitional neighborhoods that manifest social disorganization and value conflict.	Identifies why crime rates are highest in slum areas. Points out the factors that produce crime. Suggests programs to help reduce crime.	Poverty; disorganization, gangs, neighborhood change; community context of crime.
Social Ecology Theory	The conflicts and problems of urban social life and communities, including fear, unemployment, deterioration, and siege mentality, influence crime rates.	Accounts for urban crime rates and trends. Identifies community-level factors that produce high crime rates.	Social control; fear; collective efficacy; unemployment.

concept referred to as street efficacy.[121] In contrast, adolescents who live in neighborhoods with concentrated disadvantage and low collective efficacy, lose confidence in their ability to avoid violence. And as research by sociologist Patrick Sharkey has shown, this is important because adolescents with high levels of street efficacy are less likely to resort to violence themselves or to associate with delinquent peers.[122]

Collective efficacy has other benefits. When residents are satisfied that their neighborhoods are good places to live they feel a sense of obligation to maintain order and are more willing to work hard to encourage informal social control. In areas where social institutions and processes—such as police protection—are working adequately, residents are willing to intervene personally to help control unruly children and uncivil adults.[123]

In contrast, in disorganized areas, the population is transient and people want to leave as soon as they can afford to find better housing. Interpersonal relationships remain superficial, and people are less willing to help out neighbors or exert informal controls over their own or neighbors' children. Social institutions such as schools and churches cannot work effectively in a climate of alienation and mistrust.[124] Children who live in these neighborhoods find that involvement with conventional social institutions, such as schools and afternoon programs, is blocked; they are instead at risk for recruitment into gangs.[125] These problems are stubborn and difficult to overcome. And even when an attempt is made to revitalize a disorganized neighborhood by creating institutional support programs such as community centers and better schools, the effort may be countered by the ongoing drain of deep-rooted economic and social deprivation.[126]

According to the social ecology school, then, the quality of community life, including levels of change, fear, incivility, poverty, and deterioration, has a direct influence on an area's crime rate. It is not some individual property or trait that causes people to commit crime but the quality and ambience of the community in which they reside. Conversely, in areas that have high levels of social control and collective efficacy, crime rates have been shown to decrease—no matter what the economic situation. Concept Summary 6.1 sets out the features of social disorganization theory.

wwww Go to www.thomsonedu.com/criminaljustice/siegel to read:

- A famous *Atlantic Magazine* article titled "Broken Windows," which discusses the concept of **community deterioration and crime**.

- An article showing the association between **collective efficacy and crime**.

STRAIN THEORIES

As a group, strain theorists believe that most people share similar values and goals. They want to earn money, have a nice home, drive a great car, and wear stylish clothes. They also want to care for their families and educate their children. Unfortunately, the ability to achieve these personal goals is stratified by socioeconomic class. While the affluent may live out the American Dream, the poor are shut out from achieving their goals. Because they can't always get what they want, they begin to feel frustrated and angry; a condition which is referred to as strain.

Strain is related to criminal motivation. People who feel economically and socially humiliated may perceive the right to humiliate others in return.[127] Psychologists warn that under these circumstances those who consider themselves "losers" begin to fear and envy "winners" who are doing very well at their expense. If they fail to take risky aggressive tactics, they are surely going to lose out in social competition and have little chance of future success.[128] These generalized feelings of relative deprivation are precursors to high crime rates.[129]

According to the strain view, sharp divisions between the rich and poor create an atmosphere of envy and mistrust that may lead to violence and aggression.[130] People who feel deprived because of their race or economic class standing eventually develop a sense of injustice and discontent. The less fortunate begin to distrust the society that has nurtured social inequality and obstructed their chances of progressing

adult role models are absent, and young criminals have few opportunities to join established gangs or to learn the fine points of professional crime. Cloward and Ohlin's most important finding, then, is that all opportunities for success, both illegal and conventional, are closed for the most "truly disadvantaged" youth.

Because of differential opportunity, kids are likely to join one of three types of gangs:

- *Criminal gangs.* Criminal gangs exist in stable lower-class areas in which close connections among adolescent, young adult, and adult offenders create an environment for successful criminal enterprise.[199] Youths are recruited into established criminal gangs that provide a training ground for a successful criminal career. Gang membership provides a learning experience in which the knowledge and skills needed for success in crime are acquired. During this "apprenticeship stage," older, more experienced members of the criminal subculture hold youthful "trainees" on tight reins, limiting activities that might jeopardize the gang's profits (for example, engaging in nonfunctional, irrational violence). Over time, new recruits learn the techniques and attitudes of the criminal world and how to "cooperate successfully with others in criminal enterprises."[200] To become a fully accepted member of the criminal gang, novices must prove themselves reliable and dependable in their contacts with their criminal associates.

- *Conflict gangs.* Conflict gangs develop in communities unable to provide either legitimate or illegitimate opportunities. These highly disorganized areas are marked by transient residents and physical deterioration. Crime in this area is "individualistic, unorganized, petty, poorly paid, and unprotected."[201] There are no successful adult criminal role models from whom youths can learn criminal skills. When such severe limitations on both criminal and conventional opportunity intensify frustrations of the young, violence is used as a means of gaining status. The image of the conflict gang member is the swaggering, tough adolescent who fights with weapons to win respect from rivals and engages in unpredictable and destructive assaults on people and property. Conflict gang members must be ready to fight to protect their own and their gang's integrity and honor. By doing so, they acquire a "rep," which provides them with a means for gaining admiration from their peers and consequently helps them develop their own self-image. Conflict gangs, according to Cloward and Ohlin, "represent a way of securing access to the scarce resources for adolescent pleasure and opportunity in underprivileged areas."[202]

- *Retreatist gangs.* Retreatists are double failures, unable to gain success through legitimate means and unwilling to do so through illegal ones. Some retreatists have tried crime or violence but are too clumsy, weak, or scared to be accepted in criminal or violent gangs. They then retreat into a role on the fringe of society. Members of the retreatist subculture constantly search for ways of getting high—alcohol, pot, heroin, unusual sexual experiences, music. They are always "cool," detached from relationships with the conventional

world. To feed their habit, retreatists develop a "hustle"—pimping, conning, selling drugs, and committing petty crimes. Personal status in the retreatist subculture is derived from peer approval.

Evaluating Social Structure Theories

The social structure approach has significantly influenced both criminological theory and crime prevention strategies. Its core concepts seem to be valid in view of the relatively high crime and delinquency rates and gang activity occurring in the deteriorated inner-city areas of the nation's largest cities.[203] The public's image of the disorganized inner city includes roaming bands of violent teenage gangs, drug users, prostitutes, muggers, and similar frightening examples of criminality. All of these are present today in inner-city areas.

Critics of the approach charge that we cannot be sure that it is lower-class culture itself that promotes crime and not some other force operating in society. They deny that residence in urban areas alone is sufficient to cause people to violate the law.[204] It is possible, they counter, that lower-class crime rates may be an artifact of bias in the criminal justice system. Lower-class areas seem to have higher crime rates because residents are arrested and prosecuted by agents of the justice system who, as members of the middle class, exhibit class bias.[205] Class bias is often coupled with discrimination against minority group members, who have long suffered at the hands of the justice system.

Even if the higher crime rates recorded in lower-class areas are valid, it is still true that most members of the lower class are not criminals. The discovery of the chronic offender indicates that a significant majority of people living in lower-class environments are not criminals and that a relatively small proportion of the population commits most crimes. If social forces alone could be used to explain crime, how can we account for the vast number of urban poor who remain honest and law abiding? Given these circumstances, law violators must be motivated by some individual mental, physical, or social process or trait.[206]

It is also questionable whether a distinct lower-class culture actually exists. Several researchers have found that gang members and other delinquent youths seem to value middle-class concepts, such as sharing, earning money, and respecting the law, as highly as middle-class youths. Criminologists contend that lower-class youths also value education as highly as middle-class students do.[207] Public opinion polls can also be used as evidence that a majority of lower-class citizens maintain middle-class values. National surveys find that people in the lowest income brackets want tougher drug laws, more police protection, and greater control over criminal offenders.[208] These opinions seem similar to conventional middle-class values rather than representative of an independent, deviant subculture. While this evidence contradicts some of the central ideas of social structure theory, the discovery of stable patterns of lower-class crime, the high crime rates found in disorganized inner-city areas, and the rise of teenage gangs and groups support a close association between

CULTURAL DEVIANCE THEORIES

Theory	Major Premise	Strengths	Research Focus
Miller's Focal Concern Theory	Citizens who obey the street rules of lower-class life (focal concerns) find themselves in conflict with the dominant culture.	Identifies the core values of lower-class culture and shows their association to crime.	Cultural norms; focal concerns.
Cohen's Theory of Delinquent Gangs	Status frustration of lower-class boys, created by their failure to achieve middle-class success, causes them to join gangs.	Shows how the conditions of lower-class life produce crime. Explains violence and destructive acts. Identifies conflict of lower class with middle class.	Gangs; culture conflict; middle-class measuring rods; reaction formation.
Cloward and Ohlin's Theory of Opportunity	Blockage of conventional opportunities causes lower-class youths to join criminal, conflict, or retreatist gangs.	Shows that even illegal opportunities are structured in society. Indicates why people become involved in a particular type of criminal activity. Presents a way of preventing crime.	Gangs; cultural norms; culture conflict; effects of blocked opportunity.

crime rates and social class position. Concept Summary 6.3 sets out the features of cultural deviance theories.

PUBLIC POLICY IMPLICATIONS OF SOCIAL STRUCTURE THEORY

Social structure theory has had a significant influence on public policy. If the cause of criminality is viewed as a schism between lower-class individuals and conventional goals, norms, and rules, it seems logical that alternatives to criminal behavior can be provided by giving inner-city dwellers opportunities to share in the rewards of conventional society.

One approach is to give indigent people direct financial aid through welfare and Aid to Dependent Children (ADC). Although welfare has been curtailed through the Federal Welfare Reform Act of 1996, research shows that crime rates decrease when families receive supplemental income through public assistance payments.[209]

There are also efforts to reduce crime by improving the community structure in high-crime inner-city areas. Crime prevention efforts based on social structure precepts can be traced back to the Chicago Area Project, supervised by Clifford R. Shaw. This program attempted to organize existing community structures to develop social stability in otherwise disorganized lower-class neighborhoods. The project sponsored recreation programs for children in the neighborhoods, including summer camping. It campaigned for community improvements in such areas as education, sanitation, traffic safety, physical conservation, and law enforcement. Project members also worked with police and court agencies to supervise and treat gang youth and adult

offenders. In a 25-year assessment of the project, Solomon Kobrin found that it was successful in demonstrating the feasibility of creating youth welfare organizations in high-delinquency areas.[210] Kobrin also discovered that the project made a distinct contribution to ending the isolation of urban males from the mainstream of society.

Social structure concepts, especially Cloward and Ohlin's views, were a critical ingredient in the Kennedy and Johnson administrations' "War on Poverty," begun in the early 1960s. Rather than organizing existing community structures, as Shaw's Chicago Area Project had done, this later effort called for an all-out attack on the crime-producing structures of inner-city areas. War on Poverty programs included the Job Corps, VISTA (the urban Peace Corps), Head Start and Upward Bound (educational enrichment programs), Neighborhood Legal Services, and the largest community organizing effort, the Community Action Program. War on Poverty programs were sweeping efforts to change the social structure of the inner-city area. They sought to reduce crime by developing a sense of community pride and solidarity in poverty areas and by providing educational and job opportunities for crime-prone youths. Some War on Poverty programs—Head Start, Neighborhood Legal Services, and the Community Action Program—have continued to help people.

Today Operation Weed and Seed is the foremost structural theory based crime reduction strategy. Its aim is to prevent, control, and reduce violent crime, drug abuse, and gang activity in targeted high-crime neighborhoods across the country. Weed and Seed sites range in size from several neighborhood blocks to 15 square miles.[211] The strategy involves a two-pronged approach. First, law enforcement agencies and prosecutors cooperate in "weeding out" criminals who participate in violent crime and drug abuse and attempt to prevent their return to the targeted area. Then, participating agencies begin "seeding," which brings human services to the area,

177. Teresa LaGrange and Robert Silverman, "Investigating the Interdependence of Strain and Self-Control," *Canadian Journal of Criminology and Criminal Justice* 45 (2003): 431–464.

178. Christopher Browning, Seth Feinberg, and Robert D. Dietz, "The Paradox of Social Organization: Networks, Collective Efficacy, and Violent Crime in Urban Neighborhoods," *Social Forces* 83 (2004): 503–534.

179. Thorsten Sellin, *Culture Conflict and Crime,* Bulletin No. 41 (New York: Social Science Research Council, 1938).

180. Ibid., p. 22.

181. Ibid., p. 29.

182. Ibid., p. 68.

183. Walter Miller, "Lower-Class Culture as a Generating Milieu of Gang Delinquency," *Journal of Social Issues* 14 (1958): 5–19.

184. Ibid., pp. 14–17.

185. Fred Markowitz and Richard Felson, "Social-Demographic Attitudes and Violence," *Criminology* 36 (1998): 117–138.

186. Jeffrey Fagan, *Adolescent Violence: A View from the Street,* NIJ Research Preview (Washington, DC: National Institute of Justice, 1998).

187. Albert Cohen, *Delinquent Boys* (New York: Free Press, 1955).

188. Ibid., p. 25.

189. Ibid., p. 28.

190. Ibid.

191. Clarence Schrag, *Crime and Justice American Style* (Washington, DC: U.S. Government Printing Office, 1971), p. 74.

192. Cohen, *Delinquent Boys,* p. 30.

193. Ibid., p. 31.

194. Ibid., p. 133.

195. J. Johnstone, "Social Class, Social Areas, and Delinquency," *Sociology and Social Research* 63 (1978): 49–72; Joseph Harry, "Social Class and Delinquency: One More Time," *Sociological Quarterly* 15 (1974): 294–301.

196. Richard Cloward and Lloyd Ohlin, *Delinquency and Opportunity* (New York: Free Press, 1960).

197. Ibid., p. 7.

198. Ibid., p. 85.

199. Ibid., p. 171.

200. Ibid., p. 23.

201. Ibid., p. 73.

202. Ibid., p. 24.

203. Finn-Aage Esbensen and David Huizinga, "Gangs, Drugs and Delinquency in a Survey of Urban Youth," *Criminology* 31 (1993): 565–587.

204. For a general criticism, see Kornhauser, *Social Sources of Delinquency*.

205. Charles Tittle, "Social Class and Criminal Behavior: A Critique of the Theoretical Foundations," *Social Forces* 62 (1983): 334–358.

206. James Q. Wilson and Richard Herrnstein, *Crime and Human Nature* (New York: Simon & Schuster, 1985).

207. Kenneth Polk and F. Lynn Richmond, "Those Who Fail," in *Schools and Delinquency,* eds. Kenneth Polk and Walter Schafer (Englewood Cliffs, NJ: Prentice Hall, 1974), p. 67.

208. Kathleen Maguire and Ann Pastore, *Sourcebook of Criminal Justice Statistics, 1996* (Washington, DC: U.S. Government Printing Office, 1996), pp. 150–166.

209. James DeFronzo, "Welfare and Burglary," *Crime and Delinquency* 42 (1996): 223–230.

210. Solomon Kobrin, "The Chicago Area Project—25-Year Assessment," *Annals of the American Academy of Political and Social Science* 322 (1959): 20–29.

211. Community Capacity Development Office website: www.ojp.usdoj.gov/ccdo/nonflash.html (accessed April 23, 2007).

CHAPTER 7

Social Process Theories

CHAPTER OUTLINE

Socialization and Crime
Family Relations
Educational Experience
Peer Relations
Institutional Involvement and Belief
The Effects of Socialization on Crime

Social Learning Theory
Differential Association Theory
Differential Reinforcement Theory
Neutralization Theory
Are Learning Theories Valid?

The Criminological Enterprise: When Being
Good Is Bad

Social Control Theory
Self-Concept and Crime
Hirschi's Social Bond Theory

PROFILES IN CRIME: Alpha Dog

Social Reaction Theory
Interpreting Crime
Differential Enforcement
Consequences of Labeling
Primary and Secondary Deviance
Research on Social Reaction Theory
Is Labeling Theory Valid?

Evaluating Social Process Theories
Public Policy Implications of Social Process Theory

The Criminological Enterprise: Storylines

CHAPTER OBJECTIVES

1. Be familiar with the concept of socialization
2. Discuss the effect of schools, family, and friends on crime
3. Be able to discuss the differences between the concepts of social learning, social control, and social reaction
4. Be familiar with the concept of differential association
5. Be able to discuss what is meant by a definition toward criminality
6. Understand the concept of neutralization
7. Be able to discuss the relationship between self-concept and crime
8. Know the elements of the social bond
9. Describe the labeling process and how it leads to criminal careers
10. Be familiar with the concepts of primary and secondary deviance
11. Show how the process of labeling leads to criminal careers

© AP Images/John Bazemore

Teenager Genarlow Wilson was an honor student and a gifted athlete, attractive, popular, and outgoing. He had a 3.2 grade point average, was all-conference in football, voted 11th-grade prom prince, and his senior year was capped off with a special honor when he was elected Douglas County High's first-ever homecoming king. Genarlow is now serving a sentence in a Georgia prison. His crime: Engaging in consensual sex when he was 17 years old with a girl two years younger. Wilson was convicted of aggravated child molestation even though he and the girl were both minors at the time and the sex was clearly consensual.

Wilson engaged in oral sex with the girl during a wild party involving a bunch of kids, marijuana, and alcohol, all captured on videotape. The tapes made it clear the sex was voluntary and not coerced. Though the prosecutor favored leniency, Wilson refused a plea bargain because it would mean admitting he was a sexual predator, a charge he vehemently denied and that no one, including the prosecutor, believed was true. Ironically, if the couple had had sexual intercourse, it would have been considered a misdemeanor, but since oral sex was involved, the crime was considered a felony. An additional irony in the case: After Wilson was convicted the Georgia law was changed, making consensual oral sex between minors a misdemeanor as well. But the new law did not apply retroactively. Instead of using his college scholarship, Wilson was sent to prison.[1]

Genarlow Wilson's case shows how social interactions and process shape crime. He did not consider himself a criminal and even in court denied his culpability. Here is an exchange he had with the prosecutor during the trial:

Genarlow: *. . . Aggravated child molestation is when like a 60-year–some old man likes messing with 10-year-old girls. I'm 17, the girl was 15, sir. You call that child molestation, two years apart?*

Barker: *I didn't write the law.*

Genarlow: *I didn't write the law, either.*

Barker: *That's what the law states is aggravated child molestation, Mr. Wilson, not me.*

Genarlow: *Well, sir, I understand you're just doing your job. I don't blame you. . . . But do you think it's fair? . . . Would you want your son on trial for something like this?[2]*

Should Genarlow Wilson have been labeled a "sexual predator"? If he had engaged in a different type of sex act, the case would never have been made public. The law itself was designed to protect young girls from being abused by much older men, and not members of their own peer group with whom they were socializing freely. And if the act itself was so bad, why was it decriminalized a short time later? The bottom line: if the party had occurred a few months later, Genarlow Wilson would have been playing football at Georgia State University, and not sent to Georgia State Prison!

Genarlow Wilson was in fact labeled a sexual predator and sent to prison because those in power, who define the law and control its process, decided that his behavior constituted a serious crime, a felony. They could have just as easily ignored the action and let him go. It would have been just another case of teens behaving badly. But even powerful decision makers can change their minds and reassess labels. On June 9, 2007, a Georgia judge threw out Genarlow's 10-year sentence and amended it to misdemeanor aggravated child molestation with a 12-month term, plus credit for time served. Under the ruling, Genarlow, who has been behind bars for more than two years, would not be required to register as a sex offender. In making his decision, the Georgia judge stated:

> If this court or any court cannot recognize the injustice of what has occurred here, then our court system has lost sight of the goal our judicial system has always strived to accomplish . . . justice being served in a fair and equal manner . . . . The fact that Genarlow Wilson has spent two years in prison for what is now classified as a misdemeanor, and without assistance from this court, will spend eight more years in prison, is a grave miscarriage of justice.[3]

So now Genarlow Wilson, imprisoned for years after he was labeled as a dangerous sexual predator, has been relabeled as a *victim* of the same justice process that had destroyed his life and reputation.

SOCIALIZATION AND CRIME

To some criminologists, an individual's relationship with critical elements of the social process is the key to understanding the onset and continuation of a criminal career. They believe that criminality is a function of socialization, the interactions people have with various organizations, institutions, and processes of society. Most people are influenced by their family relationships, peer group associations, educational experiences, and interactions with authority figures, including teachers, employers, and agents of the justice system. If these relationships are positive and supportive, people can succeed within the rules of society; if these relationships are dysfunctional and destructive, conventional success may be impossible, and criminal solutions may become a feasible alternative. Taken together, this view of crime is referred to as social process theory.

The influence of social process theories has endured because the relationship between social class and crime is still

uncertain. Most residents of inner-city areas refrain from criminal activity, and few of those who do commit crimes remain persistent chronic offenders into their adulthood. If poverty were the sole cause of crime, then indigent adults would be as criminal as indigent teenagers. The association between economic status and crime has been called problematic because class position alone cannot explain crime rates.[4] Today, more than 37 million Americans live below the poverty line. Even if we were to assume that all criminals come from the lower class—which they do not—it is evident that the great majority of the most indigent Americans do not commit criminal acts even though they may have a great economic incentive to do so. Relatively few people living in the most deteriorated areas become persistent offenders, and most who do desist from crime despite the continuing pressure of poverty and social decay. Some other force, then, must be at work to explain why the majority of at-risk individuals do not become persistent criminal offenders and to explain why some who have no economic or social reason to commit crime do so anyway.

Criminologists have long studied the critical elements of socialization to determine how they contribute to a burgeoning criminal career. Prominent among these elements are the family, the peer group, and the school.

Family Relations

For some time, family relationships have been considered a major determinant of behavior.[5] In fact, there is abundant evidence that parenting factors, such as the ability to communicate and to provide proper discipline, may play a critical role in determining whether people misbehave as children and even later as adults.

Youth who grow up in households characterized by conflict and tension, and where there is a lack of familial love and support, are susceptible to the crime-promoting forces in the environment.[6] Even those children living in so-called high-crime areas will be better able to resist the temptations of the streets if they receive fair discipline, care, and support from parents who provide them with strong, positive role models. Nonetheless, living in a disadvantaged neighborhood places terrific strain on family functioning, especially in single-parent families that experience social isolation from relatives, friends, and neighbors. Children who are raised within such distressed families are at risk for delinquency.[7]

The relationship between family structure and crime is critical when the high rates of divorce and single parents are considered. Table 7.1 shows that today about 32 percent of children live in single-family homes and that there are significant racial differences in family structure.[8] Family disruption or change can have a long-lasting impact on children. Research conducted in both the United States and abroad shows that children raised in homes with one or both parents absent may be prone to antisocial behavior.[9] It is not surprising that the number of single-parent households in the population is significantly related to arrest rates.[10]

The Effects of Divorce Why is the effect of divorce or separation so devastating? Even if single mothers (or fathers) can make

Table 7.1 Children in Single-Parent Families, by Race

United States

Non-Hispanic White	23%
Black or African American	65%
American Indian	49%
Asian and Pacific Islander	17%
Hispanic or Latino	36%
Total	32%

Source: Annie E. Casey Foundation, Kids Count, 2006, www.kidscount.org/sld/compare_results.jsp?i=722 (accessed June 9, 2007).

up for the loss of a second parent, it is difficult to do so and the chances of failure increase. Single parents may find it difficult to provide adequate supervision, exposing kids to the negative effects of antisocial peers.[11] Poorly supervised kids may be more prone to act impulsively and are therefore less able to employ self-control to restrain their activities.[12]

Living in a single-parent household has been linked to educational failure. Kids living with a single parent may receive less encouragement and less help with schoolwork. Poor school achievement and limited educational aspirations have been associated with delinquent behavior. Also, because they are receiving less attention as a result of having just one parent, these children may be more prone to rebellious acts, such as running away and truancy.[13] Children in two-parent households, on the other hand, are more likely to want to go on to college than kids in single-parent homes.[14]

Because their incomes may decrease substantially in the aftermath of marital breakup, some divorced mothers are forced to move to residences in deteriorated neighborhoods that may place children at risk of crime and drug abuse. In poor neighborhoods single parents cannot call upon neighborhood resources to take up the burden of controlling children, and, as a result, a greater burden is placed on families to provide adequate supervision.[15] Some groups (i.e., Hispanics, Asians) have been raised in cultures where divorce is rare and parents have less experience in developing child-rearing practices that buffer the effects of family breakup on adolescent problem behavior.[16]

When a mother remarries, it does not seem to mitigate the effects of divorce on youth. Children living with a stepparent exhibit as many problems as youth in single-parent families and considerably more problems than those who are living with both biological parents.[17]

Family Deviance A number of studies have found that parental deviance has a powerful influence on children's future behavior. Kids look up to and are influenced by their parents, so it comes as no surprise that they are willing to model their behavior along parental lines.[18] When parents drink, take drugs, and commit crimes, the effects can be both devastating and long term. In fact, research shows the effect is intergenerational: the children of deviant parents produce delinquent children themselves.[19]

Some of the most important data on the influence of parental deviance were gathered by British criminologist David Farrington, whose longitudinal research data were gathered in the long-term Cambridge Study in Delinquent Development (CSDD). Some of the most important results include:

- A significant number of delinquent youths have criminal fathers. About 8 percent of the sons of noncriminal fathers became chronic offenders, compared to 37 percent of youths with criminal fathers.[20]

- School yard bullying may be both inter- and intragenerational. Bullies have children who bully others, and these "second-generation bullies" grow up to become the fathers of children who are also bullies (see Chapter 9 for more on bullying in the school yard).[21] Thus, one family may have a grandfather, father, and son who are or were school yard bullies.[22]

- Kids whose parents go to prison are much more likely to be at risk for delinquency than children of nonincarcerated parents.[23]

connections

Sampson and Laub's research will be discussed more fully in Chapter 9. Although deviant parents may encourage offending, Sampson and Laub believe that life experiences can either encourage crime-prone people to offend or conversely aid them in their return to a conventional lifestyle.

Parental Efficacy While poor parenting and parental deviance may increase exposure to criminality, children raised by parents who have excellent parenting skills, who are supportive and can effectively control their children in a noncoercive fashion, are more insulated from crime-producing forces in society.[24] Effective parenting can help neutralize the effect of both individual (e.g., emotional problems) and social (e.g., delinquent peers) forces that promote delinquent behaviors.[25] Even kids who are at risk to delinquency because of personality problems or neurological syndromes, such as ADHD, have a much better prognosis if they receive effective, supportive parenting.[26]

Research shows that antisocial behavior will be reduced if parents provide the type of structure that integrates children into families, while giving them the ability to assert their individuality and regulate their own behavior—a phenomenon referred to as parental efficacy.[27] In some cultures emotional support from the mother is critical, whereas in others the father's support remains the key factor.[28]

A number of studies support the link between the quality of family life and delinquency. Children who feel inhibited with their parents and refuse to discuss important issues with them are more likely to engage in deviant activities. Kids who report having troubled home lives also exhibit lower levels of self-esteem and are more prone to antisocial behaviors.[29] One reason for poor communication is parents who rely on authoritarian disciplinary practices, holding a "my way or the

Children raised by parents who have excellent parenting skills, who are supportive, and who can effectively control their children in a noncoercive fashion are more insulated from crime-producing forces in society. Effective parenting can help neutralize the effect of both individual and social forces that promote delinquent behaviors. Parental efficacy means that parents provide the type of structure that integrates children into families, while giving them the ability to assert their individuality and regulate their own behavior.

© AP Images/Steve Helber

EXHIBIT 7.1

The Chicken or the Egg?

Which comes first, bad parents or bad kids? Does poor parenting cause delinquency or do delinquents undermine their parents' supervisory abilities? In a recent survey, David Huh and colleagues questioned 500 adolescent girls from eight different schools to determine their perceived parental support and control and whether they engage in problem behaviors such as lying, stealing, running away, or substance abuse. Huh and his colleagues found little evidence that poor parenting is a direct cause of children's misbehavior problems or that it escalates misbehavior. Rather, their results suggest that children's problem behaviors undermine parenting effectiveness. *Increases* in adolescent behavior problems, such as substance abuse, result in a *decrease* in parental control and support. Parental control actually played a small role in influencing children's behavior problems.

Huh suggests it is possible that the parents of adolescents who consistently misbehave may become more tolerant of their behavior and give up on attempts at control. As their kids' behaviors become increasingly threatening and unruly, parents may simply detach from and reject their kids. So in the final analysis, the egg may control the chicken and not vice versa.

Source: David Huh, Jennifer Tristan, Emily Wade, and Eric Stice, "Does Problem Behavior Elicit Poor Parenting? A Prospective Study of Adolescent Girls," *Journal of Adolescent Research* 21 (2006): 185–204.

---

highway" orientation. Telling kids that "as long as you live in my house you will obey my rules" does little to improve communications and may instead produce kids who are rebellious and crime prone.[30]

While the prevailing wisdom is that bad parents produce bad kids, some recent research by David Huh and his colleagues found that the relationship may not be what it seems. To find out what he discovered, read Exhibit 7.1.

Child Abuse and Crime There is also a suspected link between crime and child abuse, neglect, and sexual abuse.[31] Numerous studies conducted in the United States and abroad show that there is a significant association between child maltreatment and serious self-reported and official delinquency, even when taking into account gender, race, and class.[32] Children, both males and females, black or white, who experience abuse, neglect, or sexual abuse are believed to be more crime prone and suffer from other social problems such as depression, suicide attempts, substance abuse, and self-injurious behaviors.[33]

Educational Experience

The educational process and adolescent achievement in school have been linked to criminality. Studies show that children who do poorly in school, lack educational motivation, and feel alienated are the most likely to engage in criminal acts.[34] Children who fail in school have been found to offend more frequently than those who are successful in school. These children commit more serious and violent offenses and persist in their offending into adulthood.[35]

Schools contribute to criminality when they label problem youths and set them apart from conventional society. One way in which schools perpetuate this stigmatization is the "track system," which identifies some students as college bound and others as academic underachievers or potential dropouts.[36] Those children placed in tracks labeled advanced placement, college prep, or honors will develop positive self-images and achievement motivation, whereas those assigned to lower level or general courses of study may believe academic achievement is closed to someone of their limited skills.

Another significant educational problem is that many students leave high school without gaining a diploma. According to a recent report by the nonprofit Urban Institute, the national graduation rate is 68 percent, with nearly one-third of all public high school students failing to graduate. Institute researchers found tremendous racial gaps in graduation rates. Students from historically disadvantaged minority groups (American Indian, Latino, African American) have little more than a 50-50 chance of finishing high school with a diploma; by comparison, graduation rates for whites and Asians are 75 and 77 percent nationally.[37] These results are disturbing because research indicates that many school dropouts, especially those who have been expelled, face a significant chance of entering a criminal career.[38] In contrast, doing well in school and developing attachments to teachers have been linked to crime resistance.[39]

Peer Relations

Psychologists have long recognized that the peer group has a powerful effect on human conduct and can have a dramatic influence on decision making and behavior choices.[40] Peer influence on behavior has been recorded in different cultures and may be a universal norm.[41]

Though experts have long debated the exact relationship between peer group interaction and delinquency, there is little question that some kids are particularly susceptible to peer influence.[42] The more antisocial the peer group, the more likely its members will engage in delinquency; nondelinquent friends will help moderate delinquency.[43] One recent study found that kids involved in delinquency are five times more likely than nonoffenders to associate with delinquent peers.[44]

While there is agreement that the association between peers and criminality exists, there is some debate over the path of the relationship:

▮ Delinquent friends cause law-abiding youth to get in trouble. Kids who fall in with a bad crowd are at risk for delinquency.[45] For girls, a "bad crowd" usually means teenage boys! It may not be surprising that delinquent girls are significantly more likely than their nondelinquent peers to identify males as their closest friends.[46] For girls, hanging out with males may be a precursor to antisocial behavior.[47]

▮ Antisocial youths seek out and join up with like-minded friends; deviant peers sustain and amplify delinquent careers.[48] Those who choose aggressive or violent friends are more likely to begin engaging in antisocial behavior themselves and suffer psychological deficits.[49] A number of research efforts have found that boys who go through puberty at an early age are more likely to later engage in violence, property crimes, drug use, and precocious sexual behavior.[50] The boys who mature early are the most likely to develop strong attachments to delinquent friends and to be influenced by peer pressure.[51]

▮ As children move through their life course, antisocial friends help youths maintain delinquent careers and obstruct the aging-out process.[52] In contrast, noncriminal friends moderate criminality.[53] When (and if) adulthood brings close and sustaining ties to conventional friends, marriage, and family, levels of deviant behavior decline.[54]

Troubled kids choose delinquent peers out of necessity rather than desire. The social baggage they cart around prevents them from developing associations with conventional peers. Because they are impulsive, they may join cliques whose members are dangerous and get them into trouble.[55] Deviant peers do not cause straight kids to go bad, but they amplify the likelihood of a troubled kid getting further involved in antisocial behaviors.[56]

Many kids have religious affiliations or belong to other institutions that teach moral values that may help shield them from delinquency. Here, Natalie Kruger (15) gives a high-five to youth leader Adrian Martin at a food distribution center in Stone Mountain, Georgia, as other teenagers from Eastminster Presbyterian Church gather around them after the group finished stocking items they brought from their church. The teens joined their peers nationwide for "World Vision," a 30-hour fast during which they also donated food and necessities to organizations that distribute them to the needy.

© AP Images/John Amis

Institutional Involvement and Belief

Peers, schools, and family are not the only sources of socialization. Many kids have religious affiliations or belong to other institutions that teach moral values. It follows that people who hold high moral values and beliefs, who have learned to distinguish "right from wrong," and who regularly attend religious services should also eschew crime and other antisocial behaviors. Religion binds people together and forces them to confront the consequences of their behavior. Committing crimes would violate the principles of all organized religions.

Sociologists Travis Hirschi and Rodney Stark found in a classic study that, contrary to expectations, the association between religious attendance and belief and delinquent behavior patterns is negligible and insignificant.[57] However, some research efforts have reached an opposite conclusion, finding that attending religious services significantly helps reduce crime.[58] Kids living in disorganized high-crime areas who attend religious services are better able to resist illegal drug use.[59]

Interestingly, participation seems to be a more significant inhibitor of crime than merely having religious beliefs and values.[60]

The Effects of Socialization on Crime

To many criminologists, the elements of socialization described up to this point are the chief determinants of criminal behavior. According to this view, people living in even the most deteriorated urban areas can successfully resist inducements to crime if they have a positive self-image, learn moral values, and have the support of their parents, peers, teachers, and neighbors. The girl with a positive self-image who is chosen for a college scholarship has the warm, loving support of her parents and is viewed by friends and neighbors as someone who is "going places." She is less likely to adopt a criminal way of life than another adolescent who is abused at home, lives with criminal parents, and whose bond to her school and peer group is shattered because she is labeled a troublemaker.[61] The boy who has learned criminal behavior from his parents and siblings and then joins a neighborhood gang is much more likely to become an adult criminal than his next-door neighbor who idolizes his hardworking, deeply religious parents. It is socialization, not the social structure, which determines life chances. The more social problems encountered during the socialization process, the greater the likelihood that youths will encounter difficulties and obstacles as they mature, such as being unemployed or becoming a teenage mother.

Theorists who believe that an individual's socialization determines the likelihood of criminality adopt the social process approach to human behavior. The social process approach has several independent branches (Figure 7.1):

▌ Social learning theory suggests that people learn the techniques and attitudes of crime from close and intimate relationships with criminal peers; crime is a learned behavior.

▌ Social control theory maintains that everyone has the potential to become a criminal but that most people are controlled by their bonds to society. Crime occurs when the forces that bind people to society are weakened or broken.

▌ Social reaction theory (labeling theory) says people become criminals when significant members of society label them as such, and they accept those labels as a personal identity.

Put another way, social learning theory assumes people are born good and learn to be bad; social control theory assumes people are born bad and must be controlled in order to be good; social reaction theory assumes that, whether good or bad, people are controlled by the reactions of others. Each of these independent branches will be discussed separately.

Figure 7.1 The Social Processes That Control Human Behavior

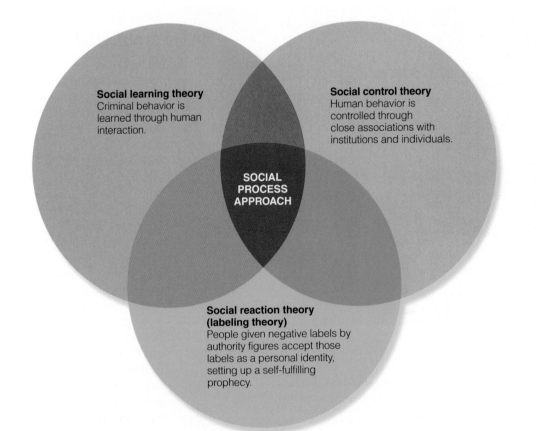

Social learning theory
Criminal behavior is learned through human interaction.

Social control theory
Human behavior is controlled through close associations with institutions and individuals.

SOCIAL PROCESS APPROACH

Social reaction theory (labeling theory)
People given negative labels by authority figures accept those labels as a personal identity, setting up a self-fulfilling prophecy.

www Go to www.thomsonedu.com/criminaljustice/siegel to access the following:

▮ The **Institute for Child and Family**, whose goal is to stimulate and coordinate the cross-disciplinary work required to make progress on the most difficult child and family policy issues facing the United States.

▮ **United Family Services**, a website devoted to family issues of all types.

SOCIAL LEARNING THEORY

Social learning theorists believe crime is a product of learning the norms, values, and behaviors associated with criminal activity. Social learning can involve the actual techniques of crime—how to hot-wire a car or roll a joint—as well as the psychological aspects of criminality—how to deal with the guilt or shame associated with illegal activities. This section briefly reviews the three most prominent forms of social learning theory: differential association theory, differential reinforcement theory, and neutralization theory.

Differential Association Theory

One of the most prominent social learning theories is Edwin H. Sutherland's **differential association theory**. Often considered the preeminent U.S. criminologist, Sutherland first put forth his theory in his 1939 text, *Principles of Criminology*.[62] The final version of the theory appeared in 1947. When Sutherland died in 1950, Donald Cressey, his long-time associate, continued his work. Cressey was so successful in explaining and popularizing his mentor's efforts that differential association remains one of the most enduring explanations of criminal behavior.

Sutherland's research on white-collar crime, professional theft, and intelligence led him to dispute the notion that crime was a function of the inadequacy of people in the lower classes.[63] To Sutherland, criminality stemmed neither from individual traits nor from socioeconomic position; instead, he believed it to be a function of a learning process that could affect any individual in any culture. Acquiring a behavior is a social learning process, not a political or legal process. Skills and motives conducive to crime are learned as a result of contacts with procrime values, attitudes, and definitions and other patterns of criminal behavior.

Principles of Differential Association The basic principles of differential association are explained as follows:[64]

▮ *Criminal behavior is learned.* This statement differentiates Sutherland's theory from prior attempts to classify criminal behavior as an inherent characteristic of criminals. By suggesting that delinquent and criminal behavior is learned, Sutherland implied that it can be classified in the same manner as any other learned behavior, such as writing, painting, or reading.

▮ *Learning is a by-product of interaction.* Criminal behavior is learned as a by-product of interacting with others. Sutherland believed individuals do not start violating the law simply by living in a criminogenic environment or by manifesting personal characteristics, such as low IQ or family problems, associated with criminality. People actively participate in the learning process as they interact with other individuals. Romantic partners who engage in antisocial activities may influence their partner's behavior, suggesting that partners learn from one another.[65] Thus, criminality cannot occur without the aid of others; it is a function of socialization.

▮ *Learning occurs within intimate groups.* Learning criminal behavior occurs within intimate personal groups. People's contacts with their most intimate social companions—family, friends, peers—have the greatest influence on their deviant behavior and attitude development. Relationships with these influential individuals color and control the way people interpret everyday events. For example, research shows that children who grow up in homes where parents abuse alcohol are more likely to view drinking as being socially and physically beneficial.[66] The intimacy of these associations far outweighs the importance of any other form of communication—for example, movies or television. Even on those rare occasions when violent motion pictures seem to provoke mass criminal episodes, these outbreaks can be more readily explained as a reaction to peer group pressure than as a reaction to the films themselves.

▮ *Criminal techniques are learned.* Learning criminal behavior involves acquiring the techniques of committing the crime, which are sometimes very complicated and sometimes very simple. This requires learning the specific direction of motives, drives, rationalizations, and attitudes. Some kids may meet and associate with criminal "mentors" who teach them how to be successful criminals and gain the greatest benefits from their criminal activities.[67] They learn the proper way to pick a lock, shoplift, and obtain and use narcotics. In addition, novice criminals learn to use the proper terminology for their acts and then acquire "proper" reactions to law violations. For example, getting high on marijuana and learning the proper way to smoke a joint are behavior patterns usually acquired from more experienced companions. Moreover, criminals must learn how to react properly to their illegal acts, such as when to defend them, rationalize them, or show remorse for them.

▮ *Perceptions of legal code influence motives and drives.* The specific direction of motives and drives is learned from perceptions of various aspects of the legal code as being favorable or unfavorable. The reaction to social rules and laws is not uniform across society, and people constantly come into contact with others who maintain different views on the utility of obeying the legal code. Some people they admire may openly disdain or flout the law or ignore its substance. People experience what Sutherland calls *culture conflict* when they are exposed to different and opposing attitudes toward what is right and wrong, moral and immoral.

The conflict of social attitudes and cultural norms is the basis for the concept of differential association.

■ *Differential associations may vary in frequency, duration, priority, and intensity.* Whether a person learns to obey the law or to disregard it is influenced by the quality of social interactions. Those of lasting *duration* have greater influence than those that are brief. Similarly, *frequent* contacts have greater effect than rare and haphazard contacts. Sutherland did not specify what he meant by *priority*, but Cressey and others have interpreted the term to mean the age of children when they first encounter definitions of criminality. Contacts made early in life probably have a greater and more far-reaching influence than those developed later on. Finally, *intensity* is generally interpreted to mean the importance and prestige attributed to the individual or groups from whom the definitions are learned. For example, the influence of a father, mother, or trusted friend far outweighs the effect of more socially distant figures.

■ *The process of learning criminal behavior by association with criminal and anticriminal patterns involves all of the mechanisms involved in any other learning process.* This suggests that learning criminal behavior patterns is similar to learning

nearly all other patterns and is not a matter of mere imitation.

■ *Criminal behavior is an expression of general needs and values, but it is not excused by those general needs and values because noncriminal behavior is also an expression of those same needs and values.* This principle suggests that the motives for criminal behavior cannot logically be the same as those for conventional behavior. Sutherland rules out such motives as desire to accumulate money or social status, personal frustration, or low self-concept as causes of crime because they are just as likely to produce noncriminal behavior, such as getting a better education or working harder on a job. It is only the learning of deviant norms through contact with an excess of definitions favorable toward criminality that produces illegal behavior.

A person becomes a criminal when he or she perceives more favorable than unfavorable consequences to violating the law (Figure 7.2). According to Sutherland's theory, individuals become law violators when they are in contact with people, groups, or events that produce an excess of definitions favorable toward criminality and are isolated from counteracting forces. A definition favorable toward criminality occurs, for example,

Figure 7.2 Differential Associations

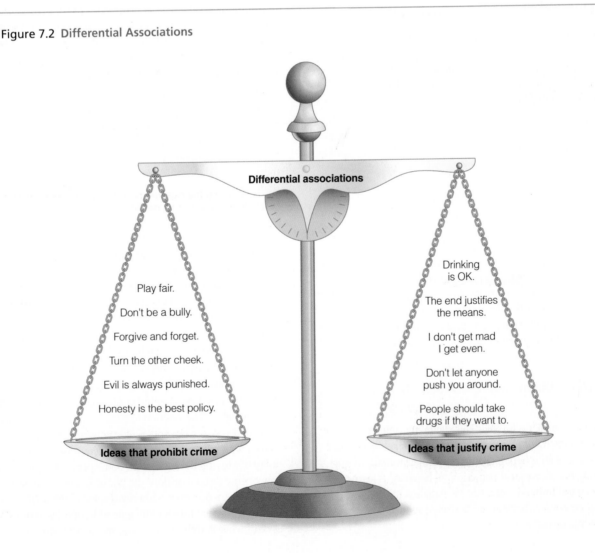

leads to relationship problems, depression, tendency to commit suicide, and poor health in adulthood.[44] Males seem to be more deeply influenced by an early history of childhood aggression: males who exhibited chronic physical aggression during the elementary school years exhibit the risk of continued physical violence and delinquency during adolescence; there is less evidence of a linkage between childhood physical aggression and adult aggression among females.[45]

Adolescent-Limiteds and Life Course Persisters

But not all persistent offenders begin at an early age: some begin their journey at different times. Some are precocious, beginning their criminal careers early and persisting into adulthood.[46] Others stay out of trouble in adolescence and do not violate the law until their teenage years. Some offenders may peak at an early age, whereas others persist into adulthood. Some youth maximize their offending rates at a relatively early age and then reduce their criminal activity; others persist into their 20s. Some are high-rate offenders, whereas others offend at relatively low rates.[47] While some kids begin their deviant life course at an early age, others do not. However, some late starters may "catch up" later in their adolescence.

According to psychologist Terrie Moffitt, most young offenders follow one of two paths: **adolescent-limited offenders** may be considered "typical teenagers" who get into minor scrapes and engage in what might be considered rebellious teenage behavior with their friends.[48] As they reach their mid-teens, adolescent-limited delinquents begin to mimic the antisocial behavior of more troubled teens, only to reduce the frequency of their offending as they mature to around age 18.[49] So while it may be cool for some kids to swagger around and get into trouble during their teenage years, they are ready to settle down and assume more conventional roles as they enter young adulthood.

The second path is the one taken by a small group of **life course persisters** who begin their offending career at a very early age and continue to offend well into adulthood.[50] Moffitt finds that the seeds of life course persistence are planted early in life and may combine the effects of abnormal traits, such as neurological deficits, with severe family dysfunction. Life course persisters are more likely to manifest abnormal personal traits such as low verbal ability, impaired reasoning skills, limited learning ability, and weak spatial and memory functions than adolescent-limited offenders.[51] Individual traits rather than environment seem to have the greatest influence on life course persistence.[52]

It is not surprising, then, that many life course persisters display elements of problem behavior syndrome, including mental health problems, psychiatric pathologies, limited school achievement, ADHD, and health issues.[53]

Research shows that the persistence patterns predicted by Moffitt are valid and accurate.[54] Life course persisters offend more frequently and engage in a greater variety of antisocial acts than other offenders; they also manifest significantly more mental health problems, including psychiatric pathologies, than adolescent-limited offenders.[55]

connections

Moffitt views adolescent-limited kids as following the social learning perspective discussed in Chapter 7. Kids learn that violating the norms of society is an act of independence; some such actions, like smoking and drinking, may be efforts at gaining a pseudomaturity. These acts are neither serious nor violent.

THEORIES OF THE CRIMINAL LIFE COURSE

A number of systematic theories have been formulated that account for onset, continuance, and desistance from crime. As a group they integrate societal level variables such as measures of social control, social learning, and structural models. It is not uncommon for life course theories to interconnect *personal factors* such as personality and intelligence, *social factors* such as

According to life course theory, people who engage in antisocial behavior in their adolescence are the ones most likely to persist in that behavior in their adulthood. Here, Quentin Simeon, four-time winner in the Alaska Native Oratory Society annual competition, speaks during the University of Alaska, Anchorage, commencement ceremony on May 7, 2006. Simeon, who was raised in rural Alaska, had been a depressed and troubled teen. He graduated from the honors program with a bachelor's degree as his wife and two daughters watched from the audience. Does his success undermine the validity of the life course view? What factors allow offenders to desist and age out of crime?

© AP Images/Anchorage Daily News/Bill Roth

EXHIBIT 9.2

Principal Life Course Theories

Name Social Development Model (SDM)

Principal Theorists J. David Hawkins, Richard Catalano

Major Premise Community-level risk factors make some people susceptible to antisocial behaviors. Preexisting risk factors are either reinforced or neutralized by socialization. To control the risk of antisocial behavior, a child must maintain prosocial bonds. Over the life course involvement in prosocial or antisocial behavior determines the quality of attachments. Commitment and attachment to conventional institutions, activities, and beliefs insulate youths from the criminogenic influences in their environment. The prosocial path inhibits deviance by strengthening bonds to prosocial others and activities. Without the proper level of bonding, adolescents can succumb to the influence of deviant others.

Name Interactional Theory

Principle Theorists Terence Thornberry and Marvin Krohn, Alan Lizotte, Margaret Farnworth

Major Premise The onset of crime can be traced to a deterioration of the social bond during adolescence, marked by weakened attachment to parents, commitment to school, and belief in conventional values. The cause of crime and delinquency is bidirectional: weak bonds lead kids to develop friendships with deviant peers and get involved in delinquency. Frequent delinquency involvement further weakens bonds and makes it difficult to reestablish conventional ones. Delinquency-promoting factors tend to reinforce one another and sustain a chronic criminal career. Kids who go through stressful life events such as a family financial crisis are more likely to later get involved in antisocial behaviors and vice versa. Criminality is a developmental process that takes on different meaning and form as a person matures. During early adolescence, attachment to the family is critical; by mid-adolescence, the influence of the family is replaced by friends, school, and youth culture; by adulthood, a person's behavioral choices are shaped by his or her place in conventional society and his or her own nuclear family. Although crime is influenced by these social forces, it also influences these processes and associations. Therefore, crime and social processes are interactional.

Name General Theory of Crime and Delinquency (GTCD)

Primary Theorist Robert Agnew

Major Premise Crime and social relations are reciprocal. Family relationships, work experiences, school performance, and peer relations influence crime. In turn, antisocial acts have a significant impact on family relationships, work experiences, school performance, and peer relations. Engaging in crime leads to a weakened bond with significant others and strengthens the association with criminal peers. Close ties to criminal peers weakens bonds to conventional society.

Crime is most likely to occur when the constraints against crime (e.g., fear of punishment, stake in conformity, self-control) are low and the motivations for crime (e.g., beliefs favorable to crime, exposure to criminals, criminal learning experiences) are high. The way an individual reacts to constraints and motivations is shaped by five key elements of human development, called life domains:

1. *Self.* Irritability and/or low self-control.

2. *Family.* Poor parenting and no marriage or a bad marriage.

3. *School.* Negative school experiences and limited education.

4. *Peers.* Delinquent friends.

5. *Work.* Unemployment or having a bad job.

The structure and impact of each of the life domains are continuously evolving; each has an influence over the other; they are mutually interdependent.

Sources: Robert Agnew, *Why Do Criminals Offend? A General Theory of Crime and Delinquency* (Los Angeles: Roxbury Publishing, 2005); Terence Thornberry, "Toward an Interactional Theory of Delinquency," *Criminology* 25 (1987): 863–891; Richard Catalano, and J. David Hawkins, "The Social Development Model: A Theory of Antisocial Behavior," in *Delinquency and Crime: Current Theories*, ed. J. David Hawkins (New York: Cambridge University Press, 1996): pp. 149–197.

---

income and neighborhood, *socialization factors* such as marriage and military service, *cognitive factors* such as information processing and attention/perception, and *situational factors* such as criminal opportunity, effective guardianship, and apprehension risk into complex multifactor explanations of human behavior. In this sense they are integrated theories because they incorporate social, personal, and developmental factors into complex explanations of human behavior. They do not focus on the relatively simple question—why do people commit crime?—but on more complex issues: Why do some offenders persist in criminal careers while others desist from or alter their criminal activity as they mature?[56] Why do some people continually escalate their criminal involvement, whereas others slow down and turn their lives around? Are all criminals similar in their offending patterns, or are there different types of offenders and

paths to offending? Life course theorists want to know not only why people enter a criminal way of life but why, once they do, they are able to alter the trajectory of their criminal involvement. One of the more important life course theories, Sampson and Laub's age-graded theory is set out below in some detail. Exhibit 9.2 outlines the principles of some other important life course theories.

Sampson and Laub: Age-Graded Theory

If there are various pathways to crime and delinquency, are there trails back to conformity? In an important 1993 work, *Crime in the Making*, Robert Sampson and John Laub formulated

Figure 9.3 Sampson and Laub's Age-Graded Theory

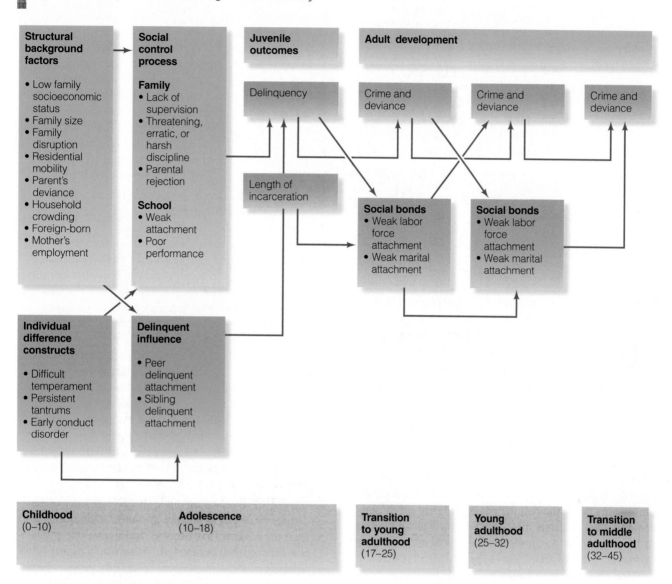

Source: Robert Sampson and John Laub, *Crime in the Making: Pathways and Turning Points through Life* (Cambridge, MA: Harvard University Press, 1993), pp. 244–245.

what they called an *age-graded theory of informal social control* (Figure 9.3). In their pioneering research, Laub and Sampson reanalyzed the data originally collected by the Gluecks more than 40 years before. Using modern statistical analysis, Laub and Sampson relied on this data to formulate a life course/developmental view of crime.[57] Some of the principles of age-graded theory are listed below:

▊ Individual traits and childhood experiences are important to understand the onset of delinquent and criminal behavior. But these alone cannot explain the continuity of crime into adulthood.

▊ Experiences in young adulthood and beyond can redirect criminal trajectories or paths. In some cases people can be turned in a positive direction, while in others negative life experiences can be harmful and injurious.

▊ Repeat negative experiences create a condition called **cumulative disadvantage**. Serious problems in adolescence undermine life chances and reduce employability and social relations. People who increase their cumulative disadvantage risk continued offending.

▊ Positive life experiences and relationships can help a person become reattached to society and allow them to *knife off* from a criminal career path.

▊ Positive life experiences such as gaining employment, getting married, or joining the military create informal social control mechanisms that limit criminal behavior opportunities. These elements of informal social control are called *turning points in crime.*

▊ Two critical elements of informal social control/turning points are marriage and career. Adolescents who are at risk for crime can live conventional lives if they can find good jobs, achieve successful military careers, or enter into a successful marriage. Turning points may be serendipitous and unexpected: success may hinge on a lucky break; someone takes a chance on them; they win the lottery.

- Another vital feature that helps people desist from crime is "human agency" or the purposeful execution of choice and free will. Former delinquents may choose to go straight and develop a new sense of self and an identity. They can choose to desist from crime and become family men and hard workers.[58]

- While some people persist in crime simply because they find it lucrative or perhaps because it serves as an outlet for their frustrations, others choose not to participate because as human beings they find other, more conventional paths more beneficial and rewarding. Human choice cannot be left out of the equation.

Social Capital Social scientists recognize that people build social capital—positive relations with individuals and institutions that are life sustaining. Laub and Sampson view the development of social capital as essential for desistance. In the same manner that building financial capital improves the chances for personal success, building social capital supports conventional behavior and inhibits deviant behavior. A successful marriage creates social capital when it improves a person's stature, creates feelings of self-worth, and encourages people to trust the individual. A successful career inhibits crime by creating a stake in conformity; why commit crime when you are doing well at your job? The relationship is reciprocal. If people are chosen to be employees, they return the favor by doing the best job possible; if they are chosen as spouses, they blossom into devoted partners. In contrast, people who fail to accumulate social capital are more prone to commit criminal acts.[59]

The fact that social capital influences the trajectory of a criminal career underscores the life course view that events that occur in later adolescence and adulthood do in fact influence behavior choices. Life events that occur in adulthood can help either terminate or sustain deviant careers.

Testing Age-Graded Theory There have been a number of research efforts that have supported the basic assumptions of age-graded theory:

- Empirical research now shows that, as predicted by Sampson and Laub, people change over the life course and that the factors that predict delinquency in adolescence, such as a weak bond to parents, may have less of an impact on adult crime when other factors, such as marriage and family, take on greater importance.[60]

- Criminality appears to be dynamic and is affected both by the erosion of informal social control and by interaction with antisocial influences. For example, accumulating deviant peers helps sustain criminality: the more deviant friends one accumulates over time, the more likely one is to maintain a criminal career.[61]

- As levels of cumulative disadvantage increase, crime-resisting elements of social life are impaired. Adolescents who are convicted of crime at an early age are more likely to develop antisocial attitudes later in life. They later develop low educational achievement, declining occupational status, and unstable employment records.[62] People who get involved with the justice system as adolescents may find that their career paths are blocked well into adulthood.[63] The relationship is reciprocal: men who are unemployed or underemployed report higher criminal participation rates than employed men.[64]

- Evidence is also available that confirms Sampson and Laub's suspicion that criminal career trajectories can be reversed if life conditions improve and they gain social capital.[65] Kids who have long-term exposure to poverty find that their involvement in crime escalates. Those, however, whose life circumstances improve because their parents are able to escape poverty and move to more attractive environments find that they can be released from criminal trajectories. Relocating may place them in better educational environments where they can have a positive high school experience, facilitated by occupationally oriented course work, small class size, and positive peer climates. Such children are less likely to become incarcerated as adults than those who do not enjoy these social benefits.[66] Research by Ross Macmillan and his colleagues shows that children whose mothers were initially poor but escaped from poverty were no more likely to develop behavior problems than children whose mothers were never poor.

- Gaining social capital later in life helps erase some of the damage caused by its absence in youth.[67] Delinquents who enter the military, serve overseas, and receive veterans' benefits enhance their occupational status (social capital) while reducing criminal involvement.[68] Similarly, people who are fortunate enough to obtain high-quality jobs are likely to reduce their criminal activities even if they had a prior history of offending.[69]

The Marriage Factor When they achieve adulthood, adolescents who had significant problems with the law are able to desist from crime if they can establish meaningful social ties that provide informal social control. Of these, none is more important than a successful marriage. People who cannot sustain secure marital relations are less likely to desist from crime. People who can find a spouse who supports them despite knowing about their past misdeeds are the ones most likely to steer away from the path of crime. Marriage both transforms people and reduces their opportunity to commit crimes. It helps cut off a person's past, provides new relationships, creates new levels of supervision, and helps the former offender develop structured routines focused on family life. Happy marriages are life sustaining, and marital quality can even improve over time (as people work less and have fewer parental responsibilities).[70] Spending

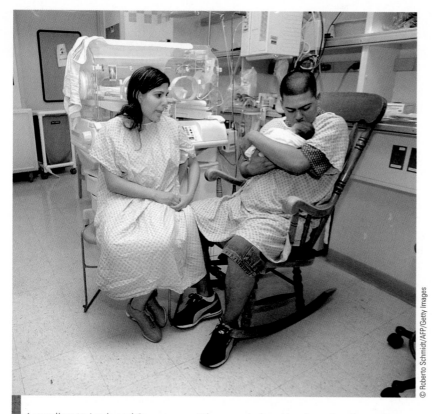

© Roberto Schmidt/AFP/Getty Images

According to Laub and Sampson, getting married and having a family are key elements of social capital and informal social control that allow prior offenders to knife off from crime and live a more conventional lifestyle.

2 percent other races.[75] The research team found former offenders were far less likely to return to crime if they settled down into the routines of a solid marriage. Common-law marriages or living with a partner did not have the same crime-reducing effect as did traditional marriages in which the knot is tied, the union is registered at the court-house, and there is a general expectation to lead a steady life. Among non-Caucasians, parolees cohabiting without the benefit of marriage actually increased their recidivism rates.

Piquero explains his findings by suggesting that

People who are married often have schedules where they work nine-to-five jobs, come home for dinner, take care of children if they have them, watch television, go to bed, and repeat that cycle over and over again. People who are not married have a lot of free rein to do what they want, especially if they are not employed. There's something about crossing the line of getting married that helps these men stay away from crime. If they don't cross that line, they can continue their lifestyles, which are pretty erratic.[76]

time in marital and family activities also reduces exposure to deviant peers, which in turn reduces the opportunity to become involved in criminal activities.[71] As Mark Warr states:

For many individuals, it seems, marriage marks a transition from heavy peer involvement to a preoccupation with one's spouse. That transition is likely to reduce interaction with former friends and accomplices and thereby reduce the opportunities as well as the motivation to engage in crime.[72]

Even people who have histories of criminal activity and have been convicted of serious offenses reduce the frequency of their offending if they live with spouses and maintain employment when they are in the community.[73] The marriage benefit may also be intergenerational: children who grow up in two-parent families are more likely to later have happy marriages themselves than children who are the product of divorced or never-married parents.[74] If people with marital problems are more crime prone, their children will also suffer a greater long-term risk of marital failure and antisocial activity.

One important new research study further confirms the benefits of marriage as a crime-reducing social event. Researchers Alex Piquero, John MacDonald, and Karen Parker tracked 524 men in their late teens and early 20s for a seven-year period after they were paroled from the California Youth Authority during the 1970s and 1980s. The sample of men, who had been incarcerated for lengthy periods of time, was 48 percent white, 33 percent black, 17 percent Latino, and

While the Piquero research is persuasive, some important questions still need to be answered: Why do some people enter strong marriages while others fail? Does the influence of marriage have an equal effect on men and women? Research by Ronald Simons and his associates found that while marriage significantly improves a woman's life chances, it has less impact on men.[77] However, for both males and females, having an antisocial romantic partner as a young adult increased the likelihood of later criminal behavior, a finding that supports Laub and Sampson.

Future Research Directions Although age-graded theory has received enormous attention, there are still many research questions left unanswered. For example, what is it about a military career that helps reduce future criminality? Does the connection between military service and desistance suggest universal military service as a crime prevention alternative? Why are some troubled youth able to conform to the requirements of a job or career while others cannot? If acquiring social capital—family, friends, education, marriage, and employment—aids in the successful recovery from crime, does the effect produce an actual change in the propensity to commit crime or merely the reduction of criminal opportunity?[78]

Probably the most important issue that must be addressed is whether the relationships that underpin age-graded theory are still valid today. Laub and Sampson's theory relies heavily on the Glueck data collected more than 50 years ago. The Glueck sample lived in a world that was quite

SHARED BEGINNINGS, DIVERGENT LIVES

Why are some delinquents destined to become persistent criminals as adults? John Laub and Robert Sampson have conducted a follow-up to their reanalysis of Sheldon Glueck and Eleanor Glueck's study that matched 500 delinquent boys with 500 nondelinquents. The individuals in the original sample were re-interviewed by the Gluecks at ages 25 and 32. Sampson and Laub located and interviewed the survivors of the delinquent sample, the oldest 70 years old and the youngest 62.

Persistence and Desistance

Laub and Sampson find that delinquency and other forms of antisocial conduct in childhood are strongly related to adult delinquency and drug and alcohol abuse. Former delinquents also suffer consequences in other areas of social life, such as school, work, and family life. For example, delinquents are far less likely to finish high school than are nondelinquents and subsequently are more likely to be unemployed, receive welfare, and experience separation or divorce as adults.

In their latest research, Laub and Sampson address one of the key questions posed by life course theories: is it possible for former delinquents to turn their lives around as adults? They find that most antisocial children do not remain antisocial as adults. For example, of men in the study cohort who survived to age 50, 24 percent had no arrests for delinquent acts of violence and property after age 17 (6 percent had no arrests for total delinquency); 48 percent had no arrests for predatory delinquency after age 25 (19 percent for total delinquency); 60 percent had no arrests for predatory delinquency after age 31 (33 percent for total delinquency); and 79 percent had no arrests for predatory delinquency after age 40 (57 percent for total delinquency). They conclude that desistance from delinquency is the norm and that most, if not all, serious delinquents desist from delinquency.

Why Do Delinquents Desist?

Laub and Sampson's earlier research indicated that building social capital through marriage and jobs were key components of desistance from delinquency. However, in this new round of research, Laub and Sampson were able to find out more about long-term desistance by interviewing 52 men as they approached age 70. The follow-up showed a dramatic drop in criminal activity as the men aged. Between the ages of 17 and 24, 84 percent of the subjects had committed violent crimes; in their 30s and 40s, that number dropped to 14 percent; it fell to just 3 percent as the men reached their 60s and 70s. Property crimes and alcohol- and drug-related crimes also showed significant decreases. They found that men who desisted from crime were rooted in structural routines and had strong social ties to family and community. Drawing on the men's own words, they found that one important element for "going straight" is the "knifing off" of individuals from their immediate environment and offering the men a new script for the future. Joining the military can provide this knifing-off effect, as does marriage or changing one's residence. One former delinquent (age 69) told them:

I'd say the turning point was, number one, the Army. You get into an outfit, you had a sense of belonging, you made your friends. I think I became a pretty good judge of character. In the Army, you met some good ones, you met some foul balls. Then I met the wife. I'd say probably that would be the turning point. Got married, then naturally, kids come. So now you got to get a better job, you got to make more money. And that's how I got to the Navy Yard and tried to improve myself.

Former delinquents who "went straight" were able to put structure into their lives. Structure often led the men to

different from contemporary society: they did not watch violent video games or TV shows; they used alcohol but were not part of a drug culture; marriage was the norm and the divorce rate was much lower; globalization and job loss were not issues. An important research task is to determine whether the theory's basic premises are still valid considering these structural changes in society. Recent research by Ryan Schroeder and his colleagues show that getting involved in the drug culture has a much more damaging effect on marriage and employment than heavy alcohol abuse.[79] Similarly, joining the military today may have a significantly different meaning and produce significantly different effects than it did for the men in the Glueck sample: recent research indicates that the 12-month prevalence of common mental illnesses in the United States military is estimated to be 26 percent, far above the level in the civilian population. Considering this condition, it is difficult to believe that serving in the military today has the same effect it did 60 years ago.[80]

To answer some of these questions, Laub and Sampson contacted the surviving members of the Glueck cohort. Some of their findings are discussed in The Criminological Enterprise feature "Shared Beginnings, Divergent Lives."

www To read an **assessment of age-graded theory** by Sampson, Laub, and Gary Sweeten, and also one by Laub and Sampson, go to www.thomsonedu.com/criminaljustice/siegel.

disassociate from delinquent peers, reducing the opportunity to get into trouble. Getting married, for example, may limit the number of nights men can "hang with the guys." As one wife of a former delinquent said, "It is not how many beers you have, it's who you drink with." Even multiple offenders who did time in prison were able to desist with the help of a stabilizing marriage.

Former delinquents who can turn their life around, who have acquired a degree of maturity by taking on family and work responsibilities, and who have forged new commitments are the ones most likely to make a fresh start and find new direction and meaning in life. It seems that men who desisted changed their identity as well, and this, in turn, affected their outlook and sense of maturity and responsibility. The ability to change did not reflect delinquency "specialty": violent offenders followed the same path as property offenders.

While many former delinquents desisted from delinquency, they still faced the risk of an early and untimely death. Thirteen percent (N=62) of the delinquent as compared to only 6 percent (N=28) of the nondelinquent subjects died unnatural deaths such as violence, cirrhosis of the liver caused by alcoholism, poor self-care, suicide, and so on. By age 65, 29 percent (N=139) of the delinquent and 21 percent (N=95) of the

nondelinquent subjects had died from natural causes. Frequent delinquent involvement in adolescence and alcohol abuse were the strongest predictors of an early and unnatural death. So while many troubled youth are able to reform, their early excesses may haunt them across their life span.

Policy Implications

Laub and Sampson find that youth problems—delinquency, substance abuse, violence, dropping out, teen pregnancy—often share common risk characteristics. Intervention strategies, therefore, should consider a broad array of antisocial, criminal, and deviant behaviors and not limit the focus to just one subgroup or delinquency type. Because criminality and other social problems are linked, early prevention efforts that reduce delinquency will probably also reduce alcohol abuse, drunk driving, drug abuse, sexual promiscuity, and family violence. The best way to achieve these goals is through four significant life-changing events: marriage, joining the military, getting a job, and changing one's environment or neighborhood. What appears to be important about these processes is that they all involve, to varying degrees, the following items: a knifing off of the past from the present; new situations that provide both supervision and monitoring as well as new

opportunities of social support and growth; and new situations that provide the opportunity for transforming identity. Prevention of delinquency must be a policy at all times and at all stages of life.

CRITICAL THINKING

1. Do you believe that the factors that influenced the men in the original Glueck sample are still relevant for change? For example, considering the high current divorce rate, is marriage still a stabilizing force?

2. Recent reports show that male U.S. veterans are twice as likely to die by suicide than people with no military service, and are more likely to kill themselves with a gun than others who commit suicide. Considering this recent finding, do you agree with Laub and Sampson that military service might be beneficial and help troubled kids turn their lives around?

Sources: John Laub and Robert Sampson, *Shared Beginnings, Divergent Lives: Delinquent Boys to Age 70* (Cambridge, MA: Harvard University Press, 2003); John Laub and Robert Sampson, "Understanding Desistance from Delinquency," in *Delinquency and Justice: An Annual Review of Research*, vol. 28, ed. Michael Tonry (Chicago: University of Chicago Press, 2001), pp. 1–71; John Laub and George Vaillant, "Delinquency and Mortality: A 50-Year Follow-Up Study of 1,000 Delinquent and Nondelinquent Boys," *American Journal of Psychiatry* 157 (2000): 96–102.

LATENT TRAIT THEORIES

In a critical 1990 article, David Rowe, D. Wayne Osgood, and W. Alan Nicewander proposed the concept of latent traits to explain the flow of crime over the life cycle. Their model assumes that a number of people in the population have a personal attribute or characteristic that controls their inclination or propensity to commit crimes.[81] This disposition, or latent trait, may be either present at birth or established early in life, and it can remain stable over time. Suspected latent traits include defective intelligence, damaged or impulsive personality, genetic abnormalities,

the physical-chemical functioning of the brain, and environmental influences on brain function such as drugs, chemicals, and injuries.[82]

Regardless of gender or environment, those who maintain one of these suspect traits may be at risk to crime and in danger of becoming career criminals; those who lack the traits have a much lower risk.[83] Because latent traits are stable, people who are antisocial during adolescence are the most likely to persist in crime. The positive association between past and future criminality detected in the cohort studies of career criminals reflects the presence of this underlying stable criminal propensity. That is, if an impulsive personality contributes to delinquency in childhood, it should

EXHIBIT 9.3

Some Important Latent Trait Theories

Name Integrated Cognitive Antisocial Potential (ICAP) Theory

Principal Theorist David Farrington

Latent Trait Antisocial potential

Major Premise People maintain a range of *antisocial potential* (AP), the potential to commit antisocial acts. AP can be viewed as both a long- and short-term phenomenon. Those with high levels of long-term AP are at risk for offending over the life course; those with low AP levels live more conventional lives. Though AP levels are fairly consistent over time, they peak in the teenage years because of the effects of maturational factors—such as increase in peer influence and decrease in family influence—that directly affect crime rates. Long-term AP can be reduced by life-changing events such as marriage. There is also short-term AP when immediate life events may increase a personal antisocial potential so that, in the immediate moment, people may advance their location on the AP continuum. For example, a person with a relatively low long-term AP may suffer a temporary amplification if he is bored, angry, drunk, or frustrated. According to the ICAP theory, the commission of offenses and other types of antisocial acts depends on the interaction between the individual (with his immediate level of AP) and the social environment (especially criminal opportunities and victims).

Name Differential Coercion Theory

Principal Theorist Mark Colvin

Latent Trait Perceptions of coercion

Major Premise Perceptions of coercion begin early in life when children experience punitive forms of discipline—both physical attacks and psychological coercion, including negative commands, critical remarks, teasing, humiliation, whining, yelling, and threats. Through these destructive family interchanges, coercion becomes ingrained and guides reactions to adverse situations that arise in both family and nonfamily settings.

There are two sources of coercion: interpersonal and impersonal. Interpersonal coercion is direct, involving the use or threat of force and intimidation from parents, peers, and significant others. Impersonal coercion involves pressures beyond individual control, such as economic and social pressure caused by unemployment, poverty, or competition among businesses or other groups. High levels of coercion produce criminality, especially when the episodes of coercive behavior are inconsistent and random, because this teaches people that they cannot control their lives. Chronic offenders grew up in homes where parents used erratic control and applied it in an inconsistent fashion.

Name Control Balance Theory

Principal Theorist Charles Tittle

Latent Trait Control/balance

Major Premise The concept of control has two distinct elements: the amount of control one is subject to by others and the amount of control one can exercise over others. Conformity results when these two elements are in balance; control imbalances produce deviant and criminal behaviors.

Those people who sense a deficit of control turn to three types of behavior to restore balance:

1. *Predation* involves direct forms of physical violence, such as robbery, sexual assault, or other forms of assault.

2. *Defiance* challenges control mechanisms but stops short of physical harm: for example, vandalism, curfew violations, and unconventional sex.

3. *Submission* involves passive obedience to the demands of others, such as submitting to physical or sexual abuse without response.

An excess of control can result in crimes of (1) *exploitation,* which involves using others to commit crimes, such as contract killers or drug runners, (2) *plunder,* which involves using power without regard for others, such as committing a hate crime or polluting the environment, or (3) *decadence,* which involves spur of the moment, irrational acts such as child molesting.

Sources: David P. Farrington, "Developmental and Life-Course Criminology: Key Theoretical and Empirical Issues," Sutherland Award address presented at the annual meeting of the American Society of Criminology, Chicago, November 2002, revised March 2003; Charles Tittle, *Control Balance: Toward a General Theory of Deviance* (Boulder, CO: Westview Press, 1995); Mark Colvin, *Crime and Coercion: An Integrated Theory of Chronic Criminality* (New York: Palgrave Press, 2000).

---

also cause the same people to offend as adults because personality traits remain stable over the life span.

But how then can the aging out process be explained? People do commit less crime as they mature. However, declining criminal activity may not be a valid indicator of real behavioral change. Why does this illusion exist? Whereas the propensity to commit crime is stable, the opportunity to commit crime fluctuates over time. People may appear to age out of crime as they mature and develop, simply because there are fewer opportunities to commit crimes and greater inducements to remain "straight." They may marry, have children, and obtain jobs. The former delinquents' newfound adult responsibilities leave them little time to hang with their friends, abuse substances, and get into scrapes with the law. So while their propensity to commit crime remains stable, their opportunity to commit crime has changed.

To understand this concept of stable criminal propensity better, assume that intelligence as measured by IQ tests is a stable latent trait associated with crime. Intelligence remains stable and unchanging over the life course but crime rates decline with age. How can latent trait theory explain this phenomenon? Teenagers have more opportunity to commit crime than adults, so at every level of intelligence, adolescent crime rates will be higher. As they mature, however, teens with both high and low IQs will commit less crime because their adult responsibilities provide them with fewer criminal opportunities. They may get married and raise a family, get a job and buy a home. And like most people, as they age they lose strength and vigor, qualities necessary to commit crime. Though their IQ remains stable and their propensity to commit crime is unchanged, their living environment and biological condition have undergone radical change. Even if they wanted to engage in criminal activities, the former delinquents may lack the opportunity and energy to do so.

Crime and Human Nature

Latent trait theorists were encouraged when two prominent social scientists, James Q. Wilson and Richard Herrnstein, published *Crime and Human Nature* in 1985 and suggested that personal traits—such as genetic makeup, intelligence, and body build—may outweigh the importance of social variables as predictors of criminal activity.[84]

According to Wilson and Herrnstein, all human behavior, including criminality, is determined by its perceived consequences. A criminal incident occurs when an individual chooses criminal over conventional behavior (referred to as *noncrime*) after weighing the potential gains and losses of each: "The larger the ratio of net rewards of crime to the net rewards of noncrime, the greater the tendency to commit the crime."[85]

Wilson and Herrnstein's model assumes that both biological and psychological traits influence the crime–noncrime choice. They see a close link between a person's decision to choose crime and such biosocial factors as low intelligence, mesomorphic body type, genetic influences (parental criminality), and possessing an autonomic nervous system that responds too quickly to stimuli. Psychological traits, such as an impulsive or extroverted personality or generalized hostility, also determine the potential to commit crime.

In their focus on the association between these constitutional and psychological factors and crime, Wilson and Herrnstein seem to be suggesting the existence of an elusive latent trait that predisposes people to commit crime.[86] Their vision helped inspire other criminologists to identify the elusive latent trait that causes criminal behavior. The most prominent latent trait theory is Gottfredson and Hirschi's **General Theory of Crime (GTC)**. Exhibit 9.3 discusses some other important contributions to the latent trait model.

General Theory of Crime

In their important work, *A General Theory of Crime,* Michael Gottfredson and Travis Hirschi modified and redefined some of the principles articulated in Hirschi's original social control theory by adding elements of trait and rational choice theories and shifting the focus from social control to **self-control**.[87]

According to Gottfredson and Hirschi the propensity to commit crime is tied directly to a person's level of self-control. People with limited self-control tend to be impulsive; they are insensitive to other people's feelings, physical (rather than mental), risk-takers, shortsighted, and nonverbal.[88] They have a here-and-now orientation and refuse to work for distant goals; they lack diligence, tenacity, and persistence. People lacking self-control tend to be adventuresome, active, physical, and self-centered. As they mature, they often have unstable marriages, jobs, and friendships.[89] They are less likely to feel shame if they engage in deviant acts and are more likely to find them pleasurable.[90] They are also more likely to engage in dangerous

According to the General Theory of Crime, people who are impulsive and lack self-control are the ones most likely to engage in risky behavior, even if it is not always illegal per se.

behaviors such as drinking, smoking, and reckless driving; all of these behaviors are associated with criminality.[91]

Because those with low self-control enjoy risky, exciting, or thrilling behaviors with immediate gratification, they are more likely to enjoy criminal acts, which require stealth, agility, speed, and power, than conventional acts, which demand long-term study and cognitive and verbal skills. As Gottfredson and Hirschi put it, they derive satisfaction from "money without work, sex without courtship, revenge without court delays."[92]

Gottfredson and Hirschi suggest that crime is not the only outlet for people with an impulsive personality. Even if they do not engage in antisocial behaviors, impulsive people enjoy other risky behaviors such as smoking, drinking, gambling, and illicit sexuality.[93] Although these acts are not illegal, they provide immediate, short-term gratification. It is not surprising then, considering their risky lifestyle, that impulsive people are more prone to be crime victims themselves than their less impulsive peers.[94] Exhibit 9.4 lists the elements of impulsivity.

Low self-control develops early in life and remains stable into and through adulthood.[95] Considering the continuity of criminal motivation, Hirschi and Gottfredson have questioned the utility of the juvenile justice system and of giving more lenient treatment to young delinquent offenders. Why separate youthful and adult offenders legally when the source of their criminality (i.e., impulsivity) is essentially the same?[96]

© Gabriele Stabile/Getty Image

EXHIBIT 9.4

The Elements of Impulsivity: Signs that a Person Has Low Self-Control

- Insensitive
- Physical
- Shortsighted
- Nonverbal
- Here-and-now orientation
- Unstable social relations
- Enjoys deviant behaviors
- Risk-taker
- Refuses to work for distant goals
- Lacks diligence
- Lacks tenacity
- Adventuresome
- Self-centered
- Shameless
- Imprudent
- Lacks cognitive and verbal skills
- Enjoys danger and excitement

connections

In his original version of control theory, discussed in Chapter 7, Hirschi focused on the social controls that attach people to conventional society and insulate them from criminality. In this newer work, he concentrates on self-control as a stabilizing force. While both views talk about control, they are actually quite different in their concept of control and its formation.

What Causes Impulsivity? Gottfredson and Hirschi trace the root cause of poor self-control to inadequate childrearing practices that begin soon after birth and can influence neural development. Once experiences are ingrained, the brain establishes a pattern of electrochemical activation that remains for life.[97] Parents who refuse or are unable to monitor a child's behavior, to recognize deviant behavior when it occurs, and to punish that behavior will produce children who lack self-control. Children who are not attached to their parents, who are poorly supervised, and whose parents are criminal or deviant themselves are the most likely to develop poor self-control. In a sense, lack of self-control occurs naturally when steps are not taken to stop its development.[98]

While Gottfredson and Hirschi believe that parenting, not heredity, shapes self-control, some recent research efforts do show that an impulsive personality may have physical or social roots, or perhaps both. Children who suffer anoxia (i.e., oxygen starvation) during the birthing process are the ones most likely to lack self-control later in life, suggesting that impulsivity may have a biological basis.[99]

Crime Rate Variations? If individual differences are stable over the life course, how come crime rates vary? Why do people commit less crime as they age? Why are some regions more crime prone than others? Why are some groups more crime prone than others? Does that mean there are between-group differences in self-control? If male crime rates are higher than female rates does that mean men are more impulsive and lacking in self-control? How does the GTC address these issues?

Gottfredson and Hirschi remind us that criminal propensity and criminal acts are separate concepts (Figure 9.4). On one hand, criminal acts, such as robberies or burglaries, are illegal events or deeds that offenders engage in when they perceive them to be advantageous. Burglaries are typically committed by young males looking for cash, liquor, and entertainment; the crime provides "easy, short-term gratification."[100] Crime is rational and predictable; people commit crime when it promises rewards with minimal threat of pain; the threat of punishment can deter crime. If targets are well guarded, crime rates diminish. Only the truly irrational offender would dare to strike under those circumstances.

On the other hand, while criminal offenders are people predisposed to commit crimes, they are not robots who commit crime without restraint; their days are also filled with conventional

Figure 9.4 Gottfredson and Hirschi's General Theory of Crime

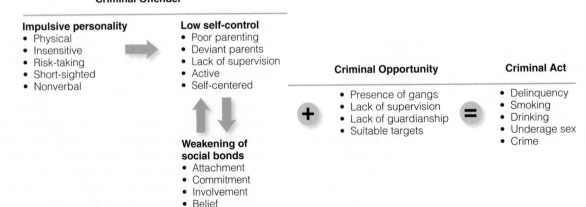

behaviors, such as going to school, parties, concerts, and church. But given the same set of criminal opportunities, such as having a lot of free time for mischief and living in a neighborhood with unguarded homes containing valuable merchandise, crime-prone people have a much higher probability of violating the law than do noncriminals. The propensity to commit crimes remains stable throughout a person's life. Change in the frequency of criminal activity is purely a function of change in criminal opportunity.

If we accept this provision of the GTC, then both criminal propensity and criminal opportunity must be considered to explain criminal participation. So if males and females are equally impulsive but their crime rates vary, the explanation is that males have more opportunity to commit crime. Young teenage girls may be more closely monitored by their parents and therefore lack the freedom to offend. Girls are also socialized to have more self-control than boys: Although females get angry as often as males, many have been taught to blame themselves for such feelings. Females are socialized to fear that anger will harm relationships; males are encouraged to react with "moral outrage," blaming others for their discomfort.[101]

Opportunity can also be used to explain ecological variation in the crime rate. How does the GTC explain the fact that crime rates are higher in the summer than the winter? The number of impulsive people lacking in self-control is no higher in August than it is in December. Gottfredson and Hirschi would argue that seasonal differences are explained by opportunity: during the summer kids are out of school and have more opportunity to commit crime. Similarly, if crime rates are higher in Los Angeles than Minneapolis, it is because either there are more criminal opportunities in this Western city, or because the fast-paced life of L.A. attracts more impulsive people than the laid-back Midwest.

Self-Control and Crime Gottfredson and Hirschi claim that the principles of self-control theory can explain all varieties of criminal behavior and all the social and behavioral correlates of crime. That is, such widely disparate crimes as burglary, robbery, embezzlement, drug dealing, murder, rape, and insider trading all stem from a deficiency of self-control. Likewise, gender, racial, and ecological differences in crime rates can be explained by discrepancies in self-control.

Unlike other theoretical models that explain only narrow segments of criminal behavior (i.e., teenage gang formation), Gottfredson and Hirschi argue that self-control applies equally to all crimes, ranging from murder to corporate theft. White-collar crime rates remain low, they claim, because people who lack self-control rarely attain the positions necessary to commit those crimes. However, the relatively few white-collar criminals lack self-control to the same degree and in the same manner as criminals such as rapists and burglars (see the Profiles in Crime feature "James Paul Lewis, Jr.: 'Crimes Against Humanity,'" for an account of someone who may fit this description).

Support for GTC Since the publication of *A General Theory of Crime*, numerous researchers have attempted to test the validity of Gottfredson and Hirschi's theoretical views and a great many research efforts using a variety of methodologies and subject groups have found empirical support for the basic assumptions of the GTC.[102] The general consensus of this research is that people with low self-control and poor impulse control are the most likely to engage in serious crime.[103] Gottfredson and Hirschi's view has become a cornerstone of contemporary criminological theory.

Importantly, the self-control–crime association has been found across different cultures, nationalities, and ethnicities, supporting its universal status.[104] When Alexander Vazsonyi and his associates analyzed self-control and deviant behavior with samples drawn from a number of different countries including Hungary, Switzerland, the Netherlands, the United States, and Japan, they found that low self-control was significantly related to antisocial behavior and that the association can be seen regardless of culture or national settings.[105] Showing that the self-control–crime association is invariant across cultures is a significant contribution to supporting its validity.

Analyzing the General Theory of Crime By integrating the concepts of socialization and criminality, Gottfredson and Hirschi help explain why some people who lack self-control can escape criminality, and, conversely, why some people who have self-control might not escape. People who are at risk because they have impulsive personalities may forgo criminal careers because there are no criminal opportunities that satisfy their impulsive needs; instead, they may find other outlets for their impulsive personalities. In contrast, if the opportunity is strong enough, even people with relatively strong self-control may be tempted to violate the law; the incentives to commit crime may overwhelm self-control.

Integrating criminal propensity and criminal opportunity can explain why some children enter into chronic offending while others living in similar environments are able to resist criminal activity. It can also help us understand why the corporate executive with a spotless record gets caught up in business fraud. Even a successful executive may find self-control inadequate if the potential for illegal gain is large. The driven executive, accustomed to both academic and financial success, may find that the fear of failure can overwhelm self-control. During tough economic times, the impulsive manager who fears dismissal may be tempted to circumvent the law to improve the bottom line.[106]

Although the General Theory seems persuasive, several questions and criticisms remain unanswered. Among the most important are the following:

▌ *Tautological.* Some critics argue that the theory is tautological or involves circular reasoning: How do we know when people are impulsive? When they commit crimes! Are all criminals impulsive? Of course, or else they would not have broken the law![107]

Gottfredson and Hirschi counter by saying that impulsivity is not itself a propensity to commit crime but a condition that inhibits people from appreciating the long-term consequences of their behavior. Consequently, if given the opportunity, they are more likely to indulge in criminal acts than their nonimpulsive

PROFILES IN CRIME

JAMES PAUL LEWIS, JR.: "CRIMES AGAINST HUMANITY"

On May 26, 2006, James Paul Lewis, Jr., the former director of Orange County, California–based Financial Advisory Consultants (FAC), was sentenced to 30 years in federal prison for running a massive Ponzi scheme that raised more than $300 million and caused more than 1,600 victims to lose more than $156 million of their hard-earned money.

What exactly did James Lewis do to earn a 30-year prison sentence? He offered investors opportunities to invest in two mutual funds. Through false and fraudulent brochures and other promotional material issued by FAC, he told investors that they would earn annual rates of return of up to 18 percent in an Income Fund, which claimed to generate revenue from the leasing of medical equipment, commercial lending, and financing insurance premiums, and 40 percent annual returns in a Growth Fund, which claimed to generate revenue through the purchase and sale of distressed businesses. Instead of investing the investors' money as promised, Lewis used the funds to purchase homes in Villa Park, Laguna Niguel, Palm Desert, San Diego, and Greenwich, Connecticut. He also used investors' money to purchase luxury automobiles for himself, his wife, and his girlfriend. Among other schemes, he used investor money to trade currency futures, managing to lose at least $22 million. To conceal the scheme at FAC, Lewis ran a Ponzi scheme: he took the money of new investors (and new purchases of those who had already bought into the funds) to pay the rates of return promised to investors.

In other words, he used the principal to pay the interest! That is, until the money ran out. At one point nearly 3,300 investors had a total balance of $813,932,080 in the funds, but FAC and Lewis's bank accounts held only slightly more than $2 million.

At Lewis's sentencing hearing, United States District Judge Cormac J. Carney ordered him to pay $156 million in restitution. Because many of this victims were elderly, Judge Carney described the scheme as a "crime against humanity." Several victims told the court about their losses, which included life savings and college funds. Many victims described being forced back to work after losing their retirement savings in the scheme.

How would Gottfredson and Hirschi explain Lewis's ongoing criminal activities? Can someone so calculating lack self-control?

Sources: Department of Justice press release, "Operator of Orange County–Based Ponzi Scheme that Caused More than $150 Million in Losses Sentenced to 30 Years in Federal Prison," May 30, 2006, http://losangeles.fbi.gov/dojpressrel/pressrel06/la053006usa.htm (accessed July 20, 2007); Gillian Flaccus, "California Man Gets 30 Years for Ponzi Scheme," *Washington Post,* 27 May 2006, www.washingtonpost.com/wp-dyn/content/article/2006/05/27/AR2006052700250.html (accessed July 20, 2007).

---

counterparts.[108] According to Gottfredson and Hirschi, impulsivity and criminality are neither identical nor equivalent. Some impulsive people may channel their reckless energies into noncriminal activity, such as trading on the commodities markets or real estate speculation, and make a legitimate fortune for their efforts.

■ *Different classes of criminals.* As you may recall, Moffitt has identified two classes of criminals—adolescent-limited and life course persistent.[109] Other researchers have found that there may be different criminal paths or trajectories. People offend at a different pace, commit different kinds of crimes, and are influenced by different external forces.[110] For example, most criminals tend to be "generalists" who engage in a garden variety of criminal acts. However, some people "specialize" in violent crimes and others in theft offenses, and these two groups seem quite different in personality and temperament.[111] This would contradict the GTC vision that a single factor causes crime and that there is a single class of offender.

■ *Ecological differences.* The GTC also fails to address individual and ecological patterns in the crime rate. If crime rates are higher in Los Angeles than in Albany, New York, can it be assumed that residents of Los Angeles are more impulsive than residents of Albany? There is little evidence of regional differences in impulsivity or self-control. Can these differences be explained solely by variation in criminal opportunity? Few researchers have tried to account for the influence of culture, ecology, economy, and so on. Gottfredson and Hirschi might counter that crime rate differences may reflect criminal opportunity: one area may have more effective law enforcement, more draconian laws, and higher levels of guardianship. In their view, opportunity is controlled by economy and culture.

■ *Racial and gender differences.* Although distinct gender differences in the crime rate exist, there is little evidence that males are more impulsive than females (although females and males differ in many other personality traits).[112] Some research efforts have found gender differences in the association between self-control and crime; the theory predicts no such difference should occur.[113]

One criticism of the General Theory of Crime is that people actually do change over their lifetimes. Here, pictures of cofounder of the Crips gang Stanley "Tookie" Williams show him at an early age. Sentenced to prison for the 1979 murders of four people, Williams spent several years involved with violent activities in prison, but around 1993 changed his behavior and became an antigang activist. Williams coauthored such books as *Life in Prison*, which encourages kids to stay out of gangs, and his memoir *Blue Rage, Black Redemption*. Williams was nominated for the Nobel Peace Prize for his efforts. Do you believe that a gang leader like Tookie Williams can really change, or did his changing life circumstances (i.e., being incarcerated) simply prevent him from committing violent criminal acts? Williams was executed in 2005.

Looking at this relationship from another perspective, males who persist in crime exhibit characteristics that are different than female persisters. Women seem to be influenced by their place of residence, childhood and recent abuses, living with a criminal partner, selling drugs, stress, depression, fearfulness, their romantic relationships, their children, and whether they have suicidal thoughts. In contrast, men are more likely to persist because of their criminal peer associations, carrying weapons, alcohol abuse, and aggressive feelings. Impulsivity alone may not be able to explain why males and females persist or desist.[114]

Similarly, Gottfredson and Hirschi explain racial differences in the crime rate as a failure of childrearing practices in the African American community.[115] In so doing, they overlook issues of institutional racism, poverty, and relative deprivation, which have been shown to have a significant impact on crime rate differentials.

▌ *Moral beliefs.* The General Theory also ignores the moral concept of right and wrong, or "belief," which Hirschi considered a cornerstone in his earlier writings on the social bond.[116] Does this mean that learning and assimilating moral values has little effect on criminality? Belief may be the weakest of the bonds associated with crime, and the General Theory reflects this relationship.[117]

▌ *Peer influence.* A number of research efforts show that the quality of peer relations either enhances or controls criminal behavior and that these influences vary over time.[118] As children mature, peer influence continues to grow.[119] Research shows that kids who lack self-control also have trouble maintaining relationships with law-abiding peers. They may either choose or be forced to seek out friends who are similarly limited in their ability to maintain self-control. Similarly, as they mature they may seek out romantic relationships with law-violating boyfriends or girlfriends and these entanglements enhance the likelihood that they will get further involved in crime (girls seem more deeply influenced by their delinquent boyfriends than boys by their delinquent girlfriends).[120] This finding contradicts the GTC, which suggests the influence of friends should be stable and unchanging and that a relationship established later in life (making deviant friends) should not influence criminal propensity. Gottfredson and Hirschi might counter that it should come as no surprise that impulsive kids, lacking in self-control, seek out peers with similar personality characteristics.

▌ *People change.* One of the most important questions raised about the GTC concerns its assumption that criminal propensity does not change. Is it possible that human personality and behavior patterns remain unaltered over the life course? Research shows that changing life circumstances, such as starting and leaving school, abusing substances and then "getting straight," and starting or ending personal relationships, all influence the frequency of offending.[121] Involvement in organized activities such as karate that teach self-discipline and self-regulation have been shown to improve personality traits in at-risk kids, even those diagnosed with oppositional defiance disorder.[122] As people mature, they may be better able to control their impulsive behavior and reduce their criminal activities.[123]

▌ *Effective parenting.* Gottfredson and Hirschi propose that children either develop self-control by the end of early childhood or fail to develop it at all, Research shows, however, that some kids who are predisposed toward delinquency may find their life circumstances improved and their involvement with antisocial behavior diminished if they are exposed to positive and effective parenting that appears later in life.[124] Parenting can influence self-control in later adolescence and kids who receive improved parenting may improve their self-control much later in the life course than predicted by the GTC.[125]

Some of the most significant research on this topic has been conducted by Ronald Simons and his colleagues. Simons has found that boys who were involved in deviant and oppositional behavior during childhood were able to turn their lives around if they later experienced improved parenting, increased school commitment, and/or reduced involvement with deviant peers. So while early childhood antisocial behavior may increase the chances of later criminality, even the most difficult children are at no greater risk for delinquency than are their conventional counterparts if they later experience positive changes in their daily lives and increased ties with significant others and institutions.[126]

▪ *Modest relationship.* Some research results support the proposition that self-control is a causal factor in criminal and other forms of deviant behavior but that the association is at best quite modest.[127] This would indicate that other forces influence criminal behavior and that low self-control alone cannot predict the onset of a criminal or deviant career. Perhaps antisocial behavior is best explained by a condition that either develops subsequent to the development of self-control or is independent of a person's level of impulsivity.[128] This alternative quality, which may be the real stable latent trait, is still unknown.

▪ *Cross-cultural differences.* There is some evidence that criminals in other countries do not lack self-control, indicating that the GTC may be culturally limited. Otwin Marenin and Michael Resig actually found equal or higher levels of self-control in Nigerian criminals than in noncriminals.[129] Behavior that may be considered imprudent in one culture may be socially acceptable in another and therefore cannot be viewed as "lack of self-control."[130] There is, however, emerging evidence that the GTC may have validity in predicting criminality abroad.[131]

▪ *Misreads human nature.* According to Francis Cullen, John Paul Wright, and Mitchell Chamlin, the GTC makes flawed assumptions about human character.[132] It assumes that people are essentially selfish, self-serving, and hedonistic and must therefore be controlled lest they gratify themselves at the expense of others. A more plausible view is that humans are inherently generous and kind; selfish hedonists may be a rare exception.

▪ *One of many causes.* Research shows that even if lack of self-control is a prerequisite to crime so are other social, neuropsychological, and physiological factors.[133] Social cultural factors have been found to make an independent contribution to criminal offending patterns.[134] Among the many psychological characteristics that set criminals apart from the general population is their lack of self-direction; their behavior has a here-and-now orientation rather than being aimed at providing long-term benefits.[135] Law violators also exhibit lower resting heart rates and perform poorly on tasks that trigger cognitive functions.[136]

▪ *Some criminals are not impulsive.* Gottfredson and Hirshi assume that criminals are impatient or "present-oriented." They choose to commit crime because the rewards can be enjoyed immediately while the costs or punishments come later or may not come at all. As long as the gains from crime are immediate while the costs of crime are delayed, impulsive present-oriented individuals will commit crimes even if they are not obviously lucrative. However, not all research efforts support this position. As you may recall (Chapter 4), Steven Levitt and Sudhir Alladi Venkatesh found that many young gang boys are willing to wait years to "rise through the ranks" before earning high wages. Their stay in the gang is fueled by the promises of future compensation, a fact that contradicts the GTC. Levitt and Venkatesh conclude that the economic aspects of the decision to join the gang can be viewed as a tournament in which participants vie for large awards that only a small fraction will eventually obtain. Members of the gang accept low wages in the present in the hope that they will advance in the gang and earn well above market wages in the future.[137]

Moreover, gang members seem acutely aware that they are making an investment in the future by foregoing present gains. As one noted:

> You think I wanta be selling drugs on the street my whole life? No way, but I know these n— [above me] are making more money . . . . So you know, I figure I got a chance to move up. But if not, s——, I get me a job doin' something else.[138]

This quotation does not comport with the notion of a super-impulsive young criminal. Even though few gang recruits will ever become gang leaders, they are willing to take the risk in order to earn a future benefit. This finding contradicts Gottfredson and Hirschi's vision of an impulsive criminal who lives for today without worrying about tomorrow.

▪ *Self-control may waiver.* Gottfredson and Hirschi assume that impulsivity is a singular construct—one is either impulsive or not. However, there may be more than one kind of impulsive personality and it may waiver over time. Some people may be impulsive because they are sensation seekers who are constantly looking for novel experiences, while others lack deliberation and rarely think through problems. Some may give up easily while others act without thinking. Some people may have the ability to persist in self-control while others "get tired" and eventually succumb to their impulses.[139] Think of it this way: a dieter ogles the cheesecake in the fridge all day but has the self-control not to take a slice. Then he wakes hungry in the middle of the night and makes his way into the kitchen, thinking "a little piece of cheesecake won't hurt me." His self-control slips, and his diet goes out the window.

Although questions like these remain, the strength of the GTC lies in its scope and breadth: it attempts to explain all forms of crime and deviance, from lower-class gang delinquency to sexual harassment in the business community.[140] By integrating concepts of criminal choice, criminal

DEVELOPMENTAL THEORIES

Theory	Major Premise	Strengths	Research Focus
LIFE COURSE THEORIES	As people go through the life course, social and personal traits undergo change and influence behavior.	Explains why some at-risk children desist from crime.	Identify critical moments in a person's life course that produce crime.
Interactional Theory	Criminals go through lifestyle changes during their offending career. Crime influences lifestyle and changing lifestyle influences crime.	Combines sociological and psychological theories.	Identify crime-producing interpersonal interactions and their reciprocal effects.
General Theory of Crime and Delinquency (GTCD)	Five critical life domains shape criminal behavior and are shaped by criminal behavior.	Shows that crime and other aspects of social life are interactive and developmental.	Measure the relationship between life domains and crime.
Age-Graded Theory	As people mature, the factors that influence their propensity to commit crime change. In childhood, family factors are critical; in adulthood, marital and job factors are key.	Shows how crime is a developmental process that shifts in direction over the life course.	Identify critical points in the life course that produce crime. Analyze the association between social capital and crime.
LATENT TRAIT THEORIES	A master trait controls human development.	Explains the continuity of crime and chronic offending.	Identify master trait that produces crime.
Integrated Cognitive Antisocial Potential (ICAP) Theory	People with antisocial potential (AP) are at risk to commit antisocial acts. AP can be viewed as both a long- and short-term phenomenon.	Identifies different types of criminal propensity and shows how they may influence behavior in both the short and long term.	Identify the components of long- and short-term AP.
General Theory of Crime	Crime and criminality are separate concepts. People choose to commit crime when they lack self-control. People lacking self-control will seize criminal opportunities.	Integrates choice and social control concepts. Identifies the difference between crime and criminality.	Measure association among impulsivity, low self-control, and criminal behaviors.
Differential Coercion Theory	Individuals exposed to coercive environments develop social-psychological deficits that enhance their probability of engaging in criminal behavior.	Explains why feeling of coercion is a master trait that determines behavior.	Measuring the sources of coercion.
Control Balance Theory	A person's "control ratio" influences his or her behavior.	Explains how the ability to control one's environment is a master trait.	Measuring control balance and imbalance.

opportunity, socialization, and personality, Gottfredson and Hirschi make a plausible argument that all deviant behaviors may originate at the same source. Continued efforts are needed to test the GTC and establish the validity of its core concepts. It remains one of the key developments of modern criminological theory.

A number of other theories have been formulated that propose a master trait controls human development and the propensity to commit crime. Some of the most prominent ones are summarized in Concept Summary 9.2.

wwww To read an article by Bruce J. Arneklev, Lori Elis, and Sandra Medlicott that **tests the General Theory of Crime**, go to www.thomsonedu.com/criminaljustice/siegel.

EVALUATING DEVELOPMENTAL THEORIES

Although the differences between the views presented in this chapter may seem irreconcilable, they in fact share some common ground. They indicate that a criminal career must be understood as a passage along which people travel, that it has a beginning and an end, and that events and life circumstances influence the journey. The factors that affect a criminal career may include structural factors, such as income and status; socialization factors, such as family and peer relations; biological factors, such as size and strength; psychological factors, including intelligence and personality; and opportunity factors, such as free time, inadequate police protection, and a supply of easily stolen merchandise.

Life course theories emphasize the influence of changing interpersonal and structural factors (that is, people change along with the world they live in). Latent trait theories place more emphasis on the fact that behavior is linked less to personal change and more to changes in the surrounding world.

These perspectives differ in their view of human development. Do people constantly change, as life course theories suggest, or are they stable, constant, and changeless, as the latent trait view indicates? Are the factors that produce criminality different at each stage of life, as the life course view suggests, or does a master trait—such as control balance, self-control, or coercion—steer the course of human behavior?

It is also possible that these two positions are not mutually exclusive, and each may make a notable contribution to understanding the onset and continuity of a criminal career. In other words, stable individual characteristics—latent traits—may interact with or modify the effects of life course varying social factors to increase their effect and shape the direction of criminal careers.[141] Needless to say, measuring these effects is quite complex and relies on sophisticated research techniques. One research effort by Bradley Entner Wright and his associates found evidence supporting both latent trait and life course theories.[142] Their research, conducted with subjects in New Zealand, indicates that low self-control in childhood predicts disrupted social bonds and criminal offending later in life, a finding that supports latent trait theory. They also found that maintaining positive social bonds helps reduce criminality and that maintaining prosocial bonds could even counteract the effect of low self-control. Latent traits are an important influence on crime, but their findings indicate that social relationships that form later in life appear to influence criminal behavior "above and beyond" individuals' preexisting characteristics.[143] This finding may reflect the fact that there are two classes of criminals: a less serious group who are influenced by life events, and a more chronic group whose latent traits insulate them from any positive prosocial relationships.[144]

PUBLIC POLICY IMPLICATIONS OF DEVELOPMENTAL THEORY

There have been a number of policy-based initiatives based on premises of developmental theory. These typically feature multisystemic treatment efforts designed to provide at-risk kids with personal, social, educational, and family services. For example, one program found that an intervention that promotes academic success, social competence, and educational enhancement during the elementary grades can reduce risky sexual practices and their accompanying health consequences in early adulthood.[145]

Other programs are now employing multidimensional strategies and are aimed at targeting children in preschool through the early elementary grades in order to alter the direction of their life course. Many of the most successful programs are aimed at strengthening children's social-emotional competence and positive coping skills and suppressing the development of antisocial, aggressive behavior.[146] Research evaluations indicate that the most promising multicomponent crime and substance abuse prevention programs for youths, especially those at high risk, are aimed at improving their developmental skills. They may include a school component, an after-school component, and a parent-involvement component. All of these components have the common goal of increasing protective factors and decreasing risk factors in the areas of the family, the community, the school, and the individual.[147] The Boys and Girls Clubs and School Collaborations' Substance Abuse Prevention Program includes a school component called SMART (skills mastery and resistance training) Teachers, an after-school component called SMART Kids, and a parent-involvement component called SMART Parents. Each component is designed to reduce specific risk factors in the children's school, family, community, and personal environments.[148]

Another successful program, Fast Track, is designed to prevent serious antisocial behavior and related adolescent problems in high-risk children entering first grade. The intervention is guided by a developmental approach that suggests that antisocial behavior is the product of the interaction of multiple social and psychological influences:

▌ Residence in low-income, high-crime communities places stressors and influences on children and families that increase their risk levels. In these areas, families characterized by marital conflict and instability make consistent and effective parenting difficult to achieve, particularly with children who are impulsive and of difficult temperament.

▌ Children of high-risk families usually enter the education process poorly prepared for its social, emotional, and cognitive demands. Their parents often are unprepared to relate effectively with school staff, and a poor home–school bond often aggravates the child's adjustment problems. They may be grouped with other children who are similarly unprepared. This peer group may be negatively influenced by disruptive classroom contexts and punitive teachers.

▌ Over time, aggressive and disruptive children are rejected by families and peers and tend to receive less support from teachers. All of these processes increase the risk of antisocial behaviors, in a process that begins in elementary school and lasts throughout adolescence. During this period, peer influences, academic difficulties, and dysfunctional personal identity development can contribute to serious conduct problems and related risky behaviors.[149]

Compared with children in the control group, children in the intervention group displayed significantly less aggressive behavior at home, in the classroom, and on the playground.

THINKING LIKE A CRIMINOLOGIST

Gary L. Sampson, 41, addicted to alcohol and cocaine, was a deadbeat dad, a two-bit thief, and a bank robber with a long history of violence. On August 1, 2001, he turned himself in to the Vermont State Police after fleeing from a string of three murders he committed in Massachusetts and New Hampshire.

Those who knew Sampson speculated that his murders were a desperate finale to a troubled life. During his early life in New England, he once bound, gagged, and beat three elderly women in a candy store, hijacked cars at knifepoint, and had been medically diagnosed as schizophrenic. In 1977, he married a 17-year-old girl he had impregnated; two months later he was arrested and charged with rape for having "unnatural intercourse with a child under 16." Although he was acquitted of that charge, his wife noticed that Sampson was developing a hair-trigger temper and had become increasingly violent; their marriage soon ended. As the years passed, Sampson had at least four failed marriages, was an absentee father to two children, and became an alcoholic and a drug user; he spent nearly half of his adult life behind bars.

Jumping bail after being arrested for theft from an antique store, he headed south to North Carolina and took on a new identity: Gary Johnson, a construction worker. He took up with Ricki Carter, a transvestite, but their relationship was anything but stable. Sampson once put a gun to Carter's head, broke his ribs, and threatened to kill his family. After his breakup with Carter, Sampson moved in with a new girlfriend, Karen Anderson, and began pulling bank jobs. When the police closed in, Sampson fled north. Needing transportation, he carjacked three vehicles and killed the drivers, one a 19-year-old college freshman who had stopped to give Sampson a hand. In December 2003, Sampson received a death sentence from a jury who was not swayed by his claim that he was mentally unfit.

The governor is unsettled by the verdict. She wants to grant clemency in the case and reduce Sampson's sentence to life in prison. She asks you to help her make the judgment.

Writing Exercise Write a paper (about 400 words) explaining what advice you would give the governor regarding granting Sampson's clemency. Were his crimes a product of his impaired development? Should he be spared death?

Doing Research on the Web Before writing your paper, review these Web-based resources:

▪ Read analyses about using the death penalty for criminals like Sampson in the articles "Science and the Death Penalty" by James P. Rooney and "Give 'Em a Fair Trial . . . Then Hang 'Em" by Colin Kingsbury.

▪ Also read what U.S. District Court Judge Mark L. Wolf had to say when he sentenced Sampson to death.

▪ For a conservative take on this issue, go to the National Center for Policy Analysis.

All of these websites can be accessed via **www.thomsonedu.com/criminaljustice/siegel.**

By the end of the third grade, 37 percent of the intervention group had become free of conduct problems, in contrast with 27 percent of the control group. By the end of elementary school, 33 percent of the intervention group had a developmental trajectory of decreasing conduct problems, as compared with 27 percent of the control group. Furthermore, placement in special education by the end of elementary school was about one-fourth lower in the intervention group than in the control group.

Group differences continued through adolescence. Court records indicate that by eighth grade, 38 percent of the intervention group boys had been arrested, in contrast with 42 percent of the control group. Finally, psychiatric interviews after ninth grade indicate that the Fast Track intervention has reduced serious conduct disorder by over a third, from 27 percent to 17 percent. These effects generalized across gender and ethnic groups and across the wide range of child and family characteristics measured by Fast Track.

SUMMARY

- Life course theories argue that events that take place over the life course influence criminal choices.

- The cause of crime constantly changes as people mature. At first, the nuclear family influences behavior; during adolescence, the peer group dominates; in adulthood, marriage and career are critical.

- There are a variety of pathways to crime: some kids are sneaky, others hostile, and still others defiant.

- Crime may be part of a variety of social problems, including health, physical, and interpersonal troubles.

- The social development model finds that living in a disorganized area helps weaken social bonds and sets people off on a delinquent path.

- According to interactional theory, crime influences social relations, which in turn influence crime; the relationship is interactive. The sources of crime evolve over time.

- Agnew's General Theory of Crime and Delinquency revolves around five life domains that interact with social factors to produce crime and, in turn, are influenced by crime.

- Sampson and Laub's age-graded theory holds that the social sources of behavior change over the life course. People who develop social capital are best able to avoid antisocial entanglements. There are important life events or turning points that enable adult offenders to desist from crime. Among the most important are getting married and serving in the military. Laub and Sampson have found that while many criminals desist from crime, they still face other risks such as an untimely death.

- Latent trait theories hold that some underlying condition present at birth or soon after controls behavior. Suspect traits include low IQ, impulsivity, and personality structure. This underlying trait explains the continuity of offending because, once present, it remains

with a person throughout his or her life. Opportunity to commit crime varies; latent traits remain stable.

- The General Theory of Crime, developed by Gottfredson and Hirschi, integrates choice theory concepts. People with latent traits choose crime over noncrime; the opportunity for crime mediates their choice.

- Impulsive people have low self-control and a weak bond to society; they often cannot resist criminal opportunities.

- Programs that are based on developmental theory are typically multidimensional and multifaceted.

- **ThomsonNOW** Maximize your study time by using ThomsonNOW's diagnostic study plan to help you review this chapter. The Personalized Study plan will help you identify areas on which you should concentrate; provide interactive exercises to help you master the chapter concepts; and provide a post-test to confirm you are ready to move on to the next chapter.

KEY TERMS

desist (260)
developmental theories (260)
life course theories (260)
latent trait theories (260)
problem behavior syndrome (PBS) (262)
authority conflict pathway (263)

covert pathway (263)
overt pathway (263)
adolescent-limited offenders (265)
life course persisters (265)
integrated theories (266)
age-graded theory (266)

cumulative disadvantage (267)
social capital (268)
latent trait (271)
General Theory of Crime (GTC) (273)
self-control (273)
self-control theory (275)

CRITICAL THINKING QUESTIONS

1. Do you consider yourself to have social capital? If so, what form does it take?

2. Someone you know gets a perfect score on the SAT. What personal, family, and social characteristics do you think this individual has? Another person becomes a serial killer. Without knowing this person, what personal, family, and social

characteristics do you think this individual has? If "bad behavior" is explained by multiple problems, is "good behavior" explained by multiple strengths?

3. Do you believe it is a latent trait that makes a person crime prone, or is crime a function of environment and socialization?

4. Do you agree with Loeber's multiple pathways model? Do you know people who have traveled down those paths?

5. Do people really change, or do they stay the same but appear to be different because their life circumstances have changed?

NOTES

1. Fox News, "Xbox Slayings Ringleader Has Criminal History," August 11, 2004, www.foxnews.com/story/0,2933,128674,00.html (accessed June 9, 2007).

2. See generally Sheldon Glueck and Eleanor Glueck, *500 Criminal Careers* (New York: Knopf, 1930); Glueck and Glueck, *One Thousand Juvenile Delinquents* (Cambridge, MA: Harvard University Press, 1934); Glueck and Glueck, *Predicting Delinquency and Crime* (Cambridge, MA: Harvard University Press, 1967), pp. 82–83; Glueck and Glueck, *Unraveling Juvenile Delinquency* (Cambridge, MA: Harvard University Press, 1950).

3. See generally John Laub and Robert Sampson, "The Sutherland–Glueck Debate: On the Sociology of Criminological Knowledge," *American Journal of Sociology* 96 (1991): 1,402–1,440; John Laub and Robert Sampson, "Unraveling Families and Delinquency: A Reanalysis of the Gluecks' Data," *Criminology* 26 (1988): 355–380.

4. Marvin E. Wolfgang, Robert M. Figlio, and Thorsten Sellin, *Delinquency in a Birth Cohort* (Chicago: University of Chicago Press, 1972).

5. Rolf Loeber and Marc LeBlanc, "Toward a Developmental Criminology," in *Crime and Justice,* vol. 12, eds. Norval Morris and Michael Tonry (Chicago: University of Chicago Press, 1990), pp. 375–473; Loeber and LeBlanc, "Developmental Criminology Updated," in *Crime and Justice,* vol. 23, ed. Michael Tonry (Chicago: University of Chicago Press, 1998), pp. 115–198.

6. Marvin Krohn, Alan Lizotte, and Cynthia Perez, "The Interrelationship between Substance Use and Precocious Transitions to Adult Sexuality," *Journal of Health and Social Behavior* 38 (1997): 87–103, at 88.

7. Jennifer M. Beyers and Rolf Loeber, "Untangling Developmental Relations between Depressed Mood and Delinquency in Male Adolescents,"*Journal of Abnormal Child Psychology* 31 (2003): 247–266.

8. Stephanie Milan and Ellen Pinderhughes, "Family Instability and Child Maladjustment Trajectories during Elementary School," *Journal of Abnormal Child Psychology* 34 (2006): 43–56.

9. Bradley Entner Wright, Avshalom Caspi, Terrie Moffitt, and Phil Silva, "The Effects of Social Ties on Crime Vary by Criminal Propensity: A Life-Course Model of Interdependence," *Criminology* 39 (2001): 321–352.

10. Joan McCord, "Family Relationships, Juvenile Delinquency, and Adult Criminality," *Criminology* 29 (1991): 397–417.

11. Paul Mazerolle, "Delinquent Definitions and Participation Age: Assessing the Invariance Hypothesis," *Studies on Crime and Crime Prevention* 6 (1997): 151–168.

12. Peggy Giordano, Stephen Cernkovich, and Jennifer Rudolph, "Gender, Delinquency, and Desistance: Toward a Theory of Cognitive Transformation?" *American Journal of Sociology* 107 (2002): 990–1,064.

13. John Hagan and Holly Foster, "S/He's a Rebel: Toward a Sequential Stress Theory of Delinquency and Gendered Pathways to Disadvantage in Emerging Adulthood," *Social Forces* 82 (2003): 53–86.

14. G. R. Patterson, Barbara DeBaryshe, and Elizabeth Ramsey, "A Developmental Perspective on Antisocial Behavior," *American Psychologist* 44 (1989): 329–335.

15. Robert Sampson and John Laub, "Crime and Deviance in the Life Course," *American Review of Sociology* 18 (1992): 63–84.

16. David Farrington, Darrick Jolliffe, Rolf Loeber, Magda Stouthamer-Loeber, and Larry Kalb, "The Concentration of Offenders in Families, and Family Criminality in the Prediction of Boys' Delinquency," *Journal of Adolescence* 24 (2001): 579–596.

17. Raymond Paternoster, Charles Dean, Alex Piquero, Paul Mazerolle, and Robert Brame, "Generality, Continuity, and Change in Offending," *Journal of Quantitative Criminology* 13 (1997): 231–266.

18. Magda Stouthamer-Loeber and Evelyn Wei, "The Precursors of Young Fatherhood and Its Effect on Delinquency of Teenage Males," *Journal of Adolescent Health* 22 (1998): 56–65; Richard Jessor, John Donovan, and Francis Costa, *Beyond Adolescence: Problem Behavior and Young Adult Development* (New York: Cambridge University Press, 1991); Xavier Coll, Fergus Law, Aurelio Tobias, Keith Hawton, and Joseph Tomas, "Abuse and Deliberate Self-Poisoning in Women: A Matched Case-Control Study," *Child Abuse and Neglect* 25 (2001): 1,291–1,293.

19. Richard Miech, Avshalom Caspi, Terrie Moffitt, Bradley Entner Wright, and Phil Silva, "Low Socioeconomic Status and Mental Disorders: A Longitudinal Study of Selection and Causation during Young Adulthood," *American Journal of Sociology* 104 (1999): 1,096–1,131; Krohn, Lizotte, and Perez, "The Interrelationship between Substance Use and Precocious Transitions to Adult Sexuality," p. 88; Richard Jessor, "Risk Behavior in Adolescence: A Psychosocial Framework for Understanding and Action," in *Adolescents at Risk: Medical and Social Perspectives,* eds. D. E. Rogers and E. Ginzburg (Boulder, CO: Westview Press, 1992).

20. Deborah Capaldi and Gerald Patterson, "Can Violent Offenders Be Distinguished from Frequent Offenders? Prediction from Childhood to Adolescence," *Journal of Research in Crime and Delinquency* 33 (1996): 206–231; D. Wayne Osgood, "The Covariation among Adolescent Problem Behaviors," paper presented at the annual meeting of the American Society of Criminology, Baltimore, November 1990.

21. For an analysis of more than 30 studies, see Mark Lipsey and James Derzon, "Predictors of Violent or Serious Delinquency in Adolescence and Early Adulthood: A Synthesis of Longitudinal Research," in *Serious and Violent Juvenile Offenders: Risk Factors and Successful Interventions,* eds. Rolf Loeber and David Farrington (Thousand Oaks, CA: Sage, 1998).

22. Gina Wingood, Ralph DiClemente, Rick Crosby, Kathy Harrington, Susan Davies, and Edward Hook III, "Gang Involvement and the Health of African American Female Adolescents," *Pediatrics* 110 (2002): 57.

23. David Husted, Nathan Shapira, and Martin Lazoritz, "Adolescent Gambling, Substance Use, and Other Delinquent Behavior," *Psychiatric Times* 20 (2003): 52–55.

24. Krohn, Lizotte, and Perez, "The Interrelationship between Substance Use and Precocious Transitions to Adult Sexuality," p. 88; Richard Jessor, "Risk Behavior in Adolescence: A Psychosocial Framework for Understanding and Action," in *Adolescents at Risk: Medical and Social Perspectives,* ed. D. E. Rogers and E. Ginzburg (Boulder, CO: Westview, 1992).

25. Terence Thornberry, Carolyn Smith, and Gregory Howard, "Risk Factors for Teenage Fatherhood," *Journal of Marriage and the Family* 59 (1997): 505–522; Todd Miller, Timothy Smith, Charles Turner, Margarita Guijarro, and Amanda Hallet, "A Meta-Analytic Review of Research on Hostility and Physical Health," *Psychological Bulletin* 119 (1996): 322–348; Marianne Junger, "Accidents and Crime," in *The Generality of Deviance,* eds. T. Hirschi and M. Gottfredson (New Brunswick, NJ: Transaction Books, 1993).

26. James Marquart, Victoria Brewer, Patricia Simon, and Edward Morse, "Lifestyle Factors among Female Prisoners with Histories of Psychiatric Treatment," *Journal of Criminal Justice* 29 (2001): 319–328; Rolf Loeber, David Farrington, Magda Stouthamer-Loeber, Terrie Moffitt, Avshalom Caspi, and Don Lynam, "Male Mental Health Problems, Psychopathy, and Personality Traits: Key Findings from the First 14 Years of the Pittsburgh Youth Study," *Clinical Child and Family Psychology Review* 4 (2002): 273–297.

27. Robert Johnson, S. Susan Su, Dean Gerstein, Hee-Choon Shin, and John Hoffman, "Parental Influences on Deviant Behavior in Early Adolescence: A Logistic Response Analysis of Age and Gender-Differentiated Effects," *Journal of Quantitative Criminology* 11 (1995): 167–192; Judith Brooks, Martin Whiteman, and Patricia Cohen, "Stage of Drug Use, Aggression, and Theft/Vandalism," in *Drugs, Crime and Other Deviant Adaptations: Longitudinal Studies,* ed. Howard Kaplan (New York: Plenum Press, 1995), pp. 83–96.

28. Helene Raskin White, Peter Tice, Rolf Loeber, and Magda Stouthamer-Loeber, "Illegal Acts Committed by Adolescents under the Influence of Alcohol and Drugs," *Journal of Research in Crime and Delinquency* 39

(2002): 131–153; Candace Kruttschnitt, Jane McLeod, and Maude Dornfeld, "The Economic Environment of Child Abuse," *Social Problems* 41 (1994): 299–312.

29. David Fergusson, L. John Horwood, and Elizabeth Ridder, "Show Me the Child at Seven, II: Childhood Intelligence and Later Outcomes in Adolescence and Young Adulthood," *Journal of Child Psychology and Psychiatry and Allied Disciplines* 46 (2005): 850–859.

30. Margit Wiesner and Ranier Silbereisen, "Trajectories of Delinquent Behaviour in Adolescence and Their Covariates: Relations with Initial and Time-Averaged Factors," *Journal of Adolescence* 26 (2003): 753–771.

31. Rolf Loeber, Phen Wung, Kate Keenan, Bruce Giroux, Magda Stouthamer-Loeber, Wemoet Van Kammen, and Barbara Maughan, "Developmental Pathways in Disruptive Behavior," *Development and Psychopathology* (1993): 12–48.

32. Sheila Royo Maxwell and Christopher Maxwell, "Examining the 'Criminal Careers' of Prostitutes within the Nexus of Drug Use, Drug Selling, and Other Illicit Activities," *Criminology* 38 (2000): 787–809.

33. Alex R. Piquero and He Len Chung, "On the Relationships between Gender, Early Onset, and the Seriousness of Offending," *Journal of Criminal Justice* 29 (2001): 189–206.

34. David Nurco, Timothy Kinlock, and Mitchell Balter, "The Severity of Preaddiction Criminal Behavior among Urban, Male Narcotic Addicts and Two Nonaddicted Control Groups," *Journal of Research in Crime and Delinquency* 30 (1993): 293–316.

35. Hanno Petras, Nicholas Alongo, Sharon Lambert, Sandra Barrueco, Cindy Schaeffer, Howard Chilcoat, and Sheppard Kellam, "The Utility of Elementary School TOCA-R Scores in Identifying Later Criminal Court Violence Among Adolescent Females," *Journal of the American Academy of Child and Adolescent Psychiatry* 44 (2005): 790–797; Hanno Petras, Howard Chilcoat, Philip Leaf, Nicholas Ialongo, and Sheppard Kellam, "Utility of TOCA-R Scores During the Elementary School Years in Identifying Later Violence among Adolescent Males," *Journal of the American Academy of Child and Adolescent Psychiatry* J43 (2004): 88–96.

36. W. Alex Mason, Rick Kosterman, J. David Hawkins, Todd Herrenkohi, Liliana Lengua, and Elizabeth McCauley, "Predicting Depression, Social Phobia, and Violence in Early Adulthood from Childhood Behavior Problems," *Journal of the American Academy of Child and Adolescent Psychiatry* 43 (2004): 307–315; Rolf Loeber and David Farrington, "Young Children Who Commit Crime: Epidemiology, Developmental Origins, Risk Factors, Early Interventions, and Policy Implications," *Development and Psychopathology* 12 (2000): 737–762; Patrick Lussier, Jean Proulx, and Marc LeBlanc, "Criminal Propensity, Deviant Sexual Interests and Criminal Activity of Sexual Aggressors Against Women:

A Comparison of Explanatory Models," *Criminology* 43 (2005): 249–281.

37. Dawn Jeglum Bartusch, Donald Lynam, Terrie Moffitt, and Phil Silva, "Is Age Important? Testing a General versus a Developmental Theory of Antisocial Behavior," *Criminology* 35 (1997): 13–48.

38. Daniel Nagin and Richard Tremblay, "What Has Been Learned from Group-Based Trajectory Modeling? Examples from Physical Aggression and Other Problem Behaviors," *The Annals of the American Academy of Political and Social Science* 602 (2005): 82–117.

39. Mason, Kosterman, Hawkins, Herrenkohi, Lengua, McCauley, "Predicting Depression, Social Phobia, and Violence in Early Adulthood from Childhood Behavior Problems"; Ronald Prinz and Suzanne Kerns, "Early Substance Use by Juvenile Offenders," *Child Psychiatry and Human Development* 33 (2003): 263–268.

40. Glenn Clingempeel and Scott Henggeler, "Aggressive Juvenile Offenders Transitioning into Emerging Adulthood: Factors Discriminating Persistors and Desistors," *American Journal of Orthopsychiatry* 73 (2003): 310–323.

41. David Gadd and Stephen Farrall, "Criminal Careers, Desistance and Subjectivity: Interpreting Men's Narratives of Change," *Theoretical Criminology* 8 (2004): 123–156.

42. G. R. Patterson, L. Crosby, and S. Vuchinich, "Predicting Risk for Early Police Arrest," *Journal of Quantitative Criminology* 8 (1992): 335–355.

43. Holly Hartwig and Jane Myers, "A Different Approach: Applying a Wellness Paradigm to Adolescent Female Delinquents and Offenders," *Journal of Mental Health Counseling* 25 (2003): 57–76.

44. Terrie Moffitt, Avshalom Caspi, Michael Rutter, and Phil Silva, *Sex Differences in Antisocial Behavior: Conduct Disorder, Delinquency, and Violence in the Dunedin Longitudinal Study* (London: Cambridge University Press, 2001).

45. Lisa Broidy, Richard Tremblay, Bobby Brame, David Fergusson, John Horwood, Robert Laird, Terrie Moffitt, Daniel Nagin, John Bates, Kenneth Dodge, Rolf Loeber, Donald Lynam, Gregory Pettit, and Frank Vitaro, "Developmental Trajectories of Childhood Disruptive Behaviors and Adolescent Delinquency: A Six-Site, Cross-National Study," *Developmental Psychology* 39 (2003): 222–245.

46. Ick-Joong Chung, Karl G. Hill, J. David Hawkins, Lewayne Gilchrist, and Daniel Nagin, "Childhood Predictors of Offense Trajectories," *Journal of Research in Crime and Delinquency* 39 (2002): 60–91.

47. Amy D'Unger, Kenneth Land, Patricia McCall, and Daniel Nagin, "How Many Latent Classes of Delinquent/Criminal Careers? Results from Mixed Poisson Regression Analyses," *American Journal of Sociology* 103 (1998): 1,593–1,630.

48. Alex Piquero and Timothy Brezina, "Testing Moffitt's Account of Adolescent-Limited Delinquency," *Criminology* 39 (2001): 353–370.

49. Terrie Moffitt, "Adolescence-Limited and Life-Course Persistent Antisocial Behavior: A Developmental Taxonomy," *Psychological Review* 100 (1993): 674–701.

50. Terrie Moffitt, "Natural Histories of Delinquency," in *Cross-National Longitudinal Research on Human Development and Criminal Behavior,* eds. Elmar Weitekamp and Hans-Jurgen Kerner (Dordrecht, Netherlands: Kluwer, 1994), pp. 3–65.

51. Adrian Raine, Rolf Loeber, Magda Stouthamer-Loeber, Terrie Moffitt, Avshalom Caspi, and Don Lynam, "Neurocognitive Impairments in Boys on the Life-Course Persistent Antisocial Path," *Journal of Abnormal Psychology* 114 (2005): 38–49.

52. Per-Olof Wikstrom and Rolf Loeber, "Do Disadvantaged Neighborhoods Cause Well-Adjusted Children to Become Adolescent Delinquents? A Study of Male Juvenile Serious Offending, Individual Risk and Protective Factors, and Neighborhood Context," *Criminology* 38 (2000): 1,109–1,142.

53. Alex Piquero, Leah Daigle, Chris Gibson, Nicole Leeper Piquero, and Stephen Tibbetts, "Are Life-Course-Persistent Offenders at Risk for Adverse Health Outcomes?" *Journal of Research in Crime & Delinquency* 44 (2007): 185–207.

54. Andrea Donker, Wilma Smeenk, Peter van der Laan, and Frank Verhulst, "Individual Stability of Antisocial Behavior from Childhood to Adulthood: Testing the Stability Postulate of Moffitt's Developmental Theory," *Criminology* 41 (2003): 593–609.

55. Robert Vermeiren, "Psychopathology and Delinquency in Adolescents: A Descriptive and Developmental Perspective," *Clinical Psychology Review* 23 (2003): 277–318; Paul Mazerolle, Robert Brame, Ray Paternoster, Alex Piquero, and Charles Dean, "Onset Age, Persistence, and Offending Versatility: Comparisons across Sex," *Criminology* 38 (2000): 1,143–1,172.

56. Stephen Farrall and Benjamin Bowling, "Structuration, Human Development, and Desistance from Crime," *British Journal of Criminology* 39 (1999): 253–268.

57. Robert Sampson and John Laub, *Crime in the Making: Pathways and Turning Points through Life* (Cambridge, MA: Harvard University Press, 1993); John Laub and Robert Sampson, "Turning Points in the Life Course: Why Change Matters to the Study of Crime," paper presented at the annual meeting of the American Society of Criminology, New Orleans, November 1992.

58. Robert Sampson and John Laub, "A Life-Course View of the Development of Crime," *The Annals of the American Academy of Political and Social Science* 602 (2005): 12–45.

59. Daniel Nagin and Raymond Paternoster, "Personal Capital and Social Control: The Deterrence Implications of a Theory of Criminal Offending," *Criminology* 32 (1994): 581–606.

60. Leonore M. J. Simon, "Social Bond and Criminal Record History of Acquaintance and Stranger Violent Offenders," *Journal of Crime and Justice* 22 (1999): 131–146.

61. Raymond Paternoster and Robert Brame, "Multiple Routes to Delinquency? A Test of Developmental and General Theories of Crime," *Criminology* 35 (1997): 49–84.

62. Spencer De Li, "Legal Sanctions and Youths' Status Achievement: A Longitudinal Study," *Justice Quarterly* 16 (1999): 377–401.

63. Shawn Bushway, "The Impact of an Arrest on the Job Stability of Young White American Men," *Journal of Research on Crime and Delinquency* 35 (1999): 454–479.

64. Candace Kruttschnitt, Christopher Uggen, and Kelly Shelton, "Individual Variability in Sex Offending and Its Relationship to Informal and Formal Social Controls," paper presented at the annual meeting of the American Society of Criminology, San Diego, November 1997; Mark Collins and Don Weatherburn, "Unemployment and the Dynamics of Offender Populations," *Journal of Quantitative Criminology* 11 (1995): 231–245.

65. Robert Hoge, D. A. Andrews, and Alan Leschied, "An Investigation of Risk and Protective Factors in a Sample of Youthful Offenders," *Journal of Child Psychology and Psychiatry* 37 (1996): 419–424.

66. Richard Arum and Irenee Beattie, "High School Experience and the Risk of Adult Incarceration," *Criminology* 37 (1999): 515–540.

67. Ross Macmillan, Barbara J. McMorris, and Candace Kruttschnitt, "Linked Lives: Stability and Change in Maternal Circumstances and Trajectories of Antisocial Behavior in Children," *Child Development* 75 (2004): 205–220.

68. Robert Sampson and John Laub, "Socioeconomic Achievement in the Life Course of Disadvantaged Men: Military Service as a Turning Point, circa 1940–1965," *American Sociological Review* 61 (1996): 347–367.

69. Christopher Uggen, "Ex-Offenders and the Conformist Alternative: A Job Quality Model of Work and Crime," *Social Problems* 46 (1999): 127–151.

70. Terri Orbuch, James House, Richard Mero, and Pamela Webster, "Marital Quality over the Life Course," *Social Psychology Quarterly* 59 (1996): 162–171; Lee Lillard and Linda Waite, "'Til Death Do Us Part: Marital Disruption and Mortality," *American Journal of Sociology* 100 (1995): 1,131–1,156.

71. Mark Warr, "Life-Course Transitions and Desistance from Crime," *Criminology* 36 (1998): 183–216.

72. Ibid.

73. Doris Layton MacKenzie and Spencer De Li, "The Impact of Formal and Informal Social Controls on the Criminal Activities of Probationers," *Journal of Research in Crime and Delinquency* 39 (2002): 243–278.

74. Pamela Webster, Terri Orbuch, and James House, "Effects of Childhood Family Background on Adult Marital Quality and Perceived Stability," *American Journal of Sociology* 101 (1995): 404–432.

75. Alex Piquero, John MacDonald, and Karen Parker, "Race, Local Life Circumstances, and Criminal Activity over the Life-Course," *Social Science Quarterly* 83 (2002): 654–671.

76. Personal communication with Alex Piquero, September 24, 2002.

77. Ronald Simons, Eric Stewart, Leslie Gordon, Rand Conger, and Glen Elder, Jr., "Test of Life-Course Explanations for Stability and Change in Antisocial Behavior from Adolescence to Young Adulthood," *Criminology* 40 (2002): 401–435.

78. Dunlop and Johnson, "Family and Human Resources in the Development of a Female Crack-Seller Career."

79. Ryan Schroeder, Peggy Giordano, and Stephen Cernkovich, "Drug Use and Desistance Processes," *Criminology* 45 (2007): 191–222.

80. James Ridde et al., "Millennium Cohort: The 2001–2003 Baseline Prevalence of Mental Disorders in the U.S. Military," *Journal of Clinical Epidemiology* 60 (2007): 192–201.

81. David Rowe, D. Wayne Osgood, and W. Alan Nicewander, "A Latent Trait Approach to Unifying Criminal Careers," *Criminology* 28 (1990): 237–270.

82. Lee Ellis, "Neurohormonal Bases of Varying Tendencies to Learn Delinquent and Criminal Behavior," in *Behavioral Approaches to Crime and Delinquency*, eds. E. Morris and C. Braukmann (New York: Plenum, 1988), pp. 499–518.

83. David Rowe, Alexander Vazsonyi, and Daniel Flannery, "Sex Differences in Crime: Do Means and Within-Sex Variation Have Similar Causes?" *Journal of Research in Crime and Delinquency* 32 (1995): 84–100.

84. James Q. Wilson and Richard Herrnstein, *Crime and Human Nature* (New York: Simon & Schuster, 1985).

85. Ibid., p. 44.

86. Ibid., p. 171.

87. Michael Gottfredson and Travis Hirschi, *A General Theory of Crime* (Stanford, CA: Stanford University Press, 1990).

88. Gottfredson and Hirschi, *A General Theory of Crime*, p. 90.

89. Ibid., p. 89.

90. Alex Piquero and Stephen Tibbetts, "Specifying the Direct and Indirect Effects of Low Self-Control and Situational Factors in Offenders' Decision Making: Toward a More Complete Model of Rational Offending," *Justice Quarterly* 13 (1996): 481–508.

91. David Forde and Leslie Kennedy, "Risky Lifestyles, Routine Activities, and the General Theory of Crime," *Justice Quarterly* 14 (1997): 265–294.

92. Gottfredson and Hirschi, *A General Theory of Crime*, p. 112.

93. Ibid.

94. Christopher Schreck, Eric Stewart, and Bonnie Fisher, "Self-Control, Victimization, and their Influence on Risky Lifestyles: A Longitudinal Analysis Using Panel Data," *Journal of Quantitative Criminology* 22 (2006): 319–340.

95. Robert Agnew, "The Contribution of Social-Psychological Strain Theory to the Explanation of Crime and Delinquency," *Anomie Theory: Advances in Criminological Theory*, vol. 6, eds. Freda Adler and William Laufer (New Brunswick, NJ: Transaction Books, 1995), pp. 81–96.

96. Travis Hirschi and Michael Gottfredson, "Rethinking the Juvenile Justice System," *Crime and Delinquency* 39 (1993): 262–271.

97. Anthony Walsh and Lee Ellis, "Shoring Up the Big Three: Improving Criminological Theories with Biosocial Concepts," paper presented at the annual meeting of the American Society of Criminology, San Diego, November 1997, p. 15.

98. Dennis Giever, "An Empirical Assessment of the Core Elements of Gottfredson and Hirschi's General Theory of Crime," paper presented at the annual meeting of the American Society of Criminology, Boston, November 1995.

99. Kevin Beaver and John Paul Wright, "Evaluating the Effects of Birth Complications on Low Self-Control in a Sample of Twins," *International Journal of Offender Therapy and Comparative Criminology* 49 (2005): 450–472.

100. Gottfredson and Hirschi, *A General Theory of Crime*, p. 27.

101. For a review of this issue, see Anne Campbell, *Men, Women, and Aggression* (New York: Basic Books, 1993).

102. David Brownfield and Ann Marie Sorenson, "Self-Control and Juvenile Delinquency: Theoretical Issues and an Empirical Assessment of Selected Elements of a General Theory of Crime," *Deviant Behavior* 14 (1993): 243–264; Harold Grasmick, Charles Tittle, Robert Bursik, and Bruce Arneklev, "Testing the Core Empirical Implications of Gottfredson and Hirschi's General Theory of Crime," *Journal of Research in Crime and Delinquency* 30 (1993): 5–29; John Cochran, Peter Wood, and Bruce Arneklev, "Is the Religiosity–Delinquency Relationship Spurious? A Test of Arousal and Social Control Theories," *Journal of Research in Crime and Delinquency* 31 (1994): 92–123; Marc LeBlanc, Marc Ouimet, and Richard Tremblay, "An Integrative Control Theory of Delinquent Behavior: A Validation 1976–1985," *Psychiatry* 51 (1988): 164–176.

103. Daniel Nagin and Greg Pogarsky, "Time and Punishment: Delayed Consequences and Criminal Behavior," *Journal of Quantitative Criminology* 20 (2004): 295–317.

104. Gregory Morris, Peter Wood, and Gregory Dunaway, "Self-Control, Native Traditionalism, and Native American Substance Use: Testing the Cultural Invariance of a General Theory of Crime," *Crime and Delinquency* 52 (2006): 572–598.

105. Alexander Vazsonyi, Janice Clifford Wittekind, Lara Belliston, Timothy Van Loh, "Extending the General Theory of Crime to 'The East': Low Self-Control in Japanese Late Adolescents," *Journal of Quantitative Criminology* 20 (2004): 189–216; Alexander Vazsonyi, Lloyd Pickering, Marianne Junger, and Dick Hessing, "An Empirical Test of a General Theory of Crime: A Four-Nation Comparative Study of Self-Control and the Prediction

of Deviance," *Journal of Research in Crime and Delinquency* 38 (2001): 91–131.

106. Michael Benson and Elizabeth Moore, "Are White-Collar and Common Offenders the Same? An Empirical and Theoretical Critique of a Recently Proposed General Theory of Crime," *Journal of Research in Crime and Delinquency* 29 (1992): 251–272.

107. Ronald Akers, "Self-Control as a General Theory of Crime," *Journal of Quantitative Criminology* 7 (1991): 201–211.

108. Gottfredson and Hirschi, *A General Theory of Crime*, p. 88.

109. Moffitt, "Adolescence-Limited and Life-Course Persistent Antisocial Behaviors."

110. Alex Piquero, Robert Brame, Paul Mazerolle, and Rudy Haapanen, "Crime in Emerging Adulthood," *Criminology* 40 (2002): 137–170.

111. Donald Lynam, Alex Piquero, and Terrie Moffitt, "Specialization and the Propensity to Violence: Support from Self-Reports but Not Official Records," *Journal of Contemporary Criminal Justice* 20 (2004): 215–228.

112. Alan Feingold, "Gender Differences in Personality: A Meta Analysis," *Psychological Bulletin* 116 (1994): 429–456.

113. Charles Tittle, David Ward, and Harold Grasmick, "Gender, Age, and Crime/Deviance: A Challenge to Self-Control Theory," *Journal of Research in Crime and Delinquency* 40 (2003): 426–453.

114. Brent Benda, "Gender Differences in Life-Course Theory of Recidivism: A Survival Analysis," *International Journal of Offender Therapy and Comparative Criminology* 49 (2005): 325–342.

115. Gottfredson and Hirschi, *A General Theory of Crime*, p. 153.

116. Ann Marie Sorenson and David Brownfield, "Normative Concepts in Social Control," paper presented at the annual meeting of the American Society of Criminology, Phoenix, November 1993.

117. Brent Benda, "An Examination of Reciprocal Relationship between Religiosity and Different Forms of Delinquency within a Theoretical Model," *Journal of Research in Crime and Delinquency* 34 (1997): 163–186.

118. Delbert Elliott and Scott Menard, "Delinquent Friends and Delinquent Behavior: Temporal and Developmental Patterns," in *Crime and Delinquency: Current Theories*, ed. J. David Hawkins (Cambridge: Cambridge University Press, 1996).

119. Graham Ousey and David Aday, "The Interaction Hypothesis: A Test Using Social Control Theory and Social Learning Theory," paper presented at the annual meeting of the American Society of Criminology, Boston, November 1995.

120. Dana Haynie, Peggy Giordano, Wendy Manning, and Monica Longmore, "Adolescent Romantic Relationships and Delinquency Involvement," *Criminology* 43 (2005): 177–210.

121. Julie Horney, D. Wayne Osgood, and Ineke Haen Marshall, "Criminal Careers in the Short-Term: Intra-Individual Variability in Crime and Its Relations to Local Life Cir-

cumstances," *American Sociological Review* 60 (1995): 655–673; Martin Daly and Margo Wilson, "Killing the Competition," *Human Nature* 1 (1990): 83–109.

122. Mark Palermo, Massimo Di Luigi, Gloria Dal Forno, Cinzia Dominici, David Vicomandi, Augusto Sambucioni, Luca Proietti, and Patrizio Pasqualetti, "Externalizing and Oppositional Behaviors and Karate-do: The Way of Crime Prevention," *International Journal of Offender Therapy and Comparative Criminology* 50 (2006): 654–660.

123. Charles R. Tittle and Harold G. Grasmick, "Criminal Behavior and Age: A Test of Three Provocative Hypotheses," *Journal of Criminal Law and Criminology* 88 (1997): 309–342.

124. Callie Harbin Burt, Ronald Simons, and Leslie Simons, "A Longitudinal Test of the Effects of Parenting and the Stability of Self-Control: Negative Evidence for the General Theory of Crime," *Criminology* 44 (2006): 353–396.

125. Carter Hay and Walter Forrest, "The Development of Self-Control: Examining Self-Control Theory's Stability Thesis," *Criminology* 44 (2006): 739–774.

126. Ronald Simons, Christine Johnson, Rand Conger, and Glen Elder, "A Test of Latent Trait versus Life-Course Perspectives on the Stability of Adolescent Antisocial Behavior," *Criminology* 36 (1998): 217–244.

127. Carter Hay, "Parenting, Self-Control, and Delinquency: A Test of Self-Control Theory," *Criminology* 39 (2001): 707–736; Douglas Longshore, "Self-Control and Criminal Opportunity: A Prospective Test of the General Theory of Crime," *Social Problems* 45 (1998): 102–114; Finn-Aage Esbensen and Elizabeth Piper Deschenes, "A Multisite Examination of Youth Gang Membership: Does Gender Matter?" *Criminology* 36 (1998): 799–828.

128. Raymond Paternoster and Robert Brame, "The Structural Similarity of Processes Generating Criminal and Analogous Behaviors," *Criminology* 36 (1998): 633–670.

129. Otwin Marenin and Michael Resig, "A General Theory of Crime and Patterns of Crime in Nigeria: An Exploration of Methodological Assumptions," *Journal of Criminal Justice* 23 (1995): 501–518.

130. Bruce Arneklev, Harold Grasmick, Charles Tittle, and Robert Bursik, "Low Self-Control and Imprudent Behavior," *Journal of Quantitative Criminology* 9 (1993): 225–246.

131. Peter Muris and Cor Meesters, "The Validity of Attention Deficit Hyperactivity and Hyperkinetic Disorder Symptom Domains in Nonclinical Dutch Children," *Journal of Clinical Child and Adolescent Psychology* 32 (2003): 460–466.

132. Francis Cullen, John Paul Wright, and Mitchell Chamlin, "Social Support and Social Reform: A Progressive Crime Control Agenda," *Crime and Delinquency* 45 (1999): 188–207.

133. Alex Piquero, John MacDonald, Adam Dobrin, Leah Daigle, and Francis Cullen, "Self-Control, Violent Offending, and Homicide Victimization: Assessing the

General Theory of Crime," *Journal of Quantitative Criminology* 21 (2005): 55–71.

134. Ibid.

135. Richard Wiebe, "Reconciling Psychopathy and Low Self-Control," *Justice Quarterly* 20 (2003): 297–336.

136. Elizabeth Cauffman, Laurence Steinberg, and Alex Piquero, "Psychological, Neuropsychological and Physiological Correlates of Serious Antisocial Behavior in Adolescence: The Role of Self-Control," *Criminology* 43 (2005): 133–176.

137. Steven Levitt and Sudhir Alladi Venkatesh, "An Economic Analysis of a Drag-Selling Gang's Finances," *Quarterly Journal of Economics* 13 (2000): 755–789.

138. Ibid.

139. Mark Muraven, Greg Pogarsky, and Dikla Shmueli, "Self-Control Depletion and the General Theory of Crime," *Journal of Quantitative Criminology* 22 (2006): 263–277.

140. Kevin Thompson, "Sexual Harassment and Low Self-Control: An Application of Gottfredson and Hirschi's General Theory of Crime," paper presented at the annual meeting of the American Society of Criminology, Phoenix, November 1993.

141. Graham Ousey and Pamela Wilcox, "The Interaction of Antisocial Propensity and Life-Course Varying Predictors of Delinquent Behavior: Differences by Method of Estimation and Implications for Theory," *Criminology* 45 (2007): 313–354.

142. Bradley Entner Wright, Avashalom Caspi, Terrie Moffitt, and Phil Silva, "Low Self-Control, Social Bonds, and Crime: Social Causation, Social Selection, or Both?" *Criminology* 37 (1999): 479–514.

143. Ibid., p. 504.

144. Stephen Cernkovich and Peggy Giordano, "Stability and Change in Antisocial Behavior: The Transition from Adolescence to Early Adulthood," *Criminology* 39 (2001): 371–410.

145. Heather Lonczk, Robert Abbott, J. David Hawkins, Rick Kosterman, and Richard Catalano, "Effects of the Seattle Social Development Project on Sexual Behavior, Pregnancy, Birth, and Sexually Transmitted Disease Outcomes by Age 21 Years," *Archive of Pediatrics and Adolescent Medicine* 156 (2002): 438–447.

146. Kathleen Bodisch Lynch, Susan Rose Geller, and Melinda G. Schmidt, "Multi-Year Evaluation of the Effectiveness of a Resilience-Based Prevention Program for Young Children," *Journal of Primary Prevention* 24 (2004): 335–353.

147. This section leans on Thomas Tatchell, Phillip Waite, Renny Tatchell, Lynne Durrant, and Dale Bond, "Substance Abuse Prevention in Sixth Grade: The Effect of a Prevention Program on Adolescents' Risk and Protective Factors," *American Journal of Health Studies* 19 (2004): 54–61.

148. Nancy Tobler and Howard Stratton, "Effectiveness of School Based Drug Prevention Programs: A Meta-Analysis of the Research," *Journal of Primary Prevention* 18 (1997): 71–128.

PART THREE

CRIME TYPOLOGIES

Criminologists group criminal offenders and/or criminal behaviors into categories or typologies so they may be more easily studied and understood. Are there common traits or characteristics that link offenders together and make them distinct from nonoffenders? Are there common areas between seemingly different acts such as murder and rape?

In this section, we focus on crime typologies. They are clustered into six groups: violent crime (Chapter 10), political crime and terrorism (Chapter 11), economic crimes involving common theft offenses (Chapter 12), enterprise crimes involving white-collar and organized criminals (Chapter 13), public order crimes, such as prostitution and drug abuse (Chapter 14), and cyber crimes (Chapter 15). This format groups criminal behaviors by their focus and consequence: bringing physical harm to others; misappropriating other people's property; violating laws designed to protect public morals; and using technology to commit crime.

Typologies can be useful in classifying large numbers of criminal offenses or offenders into easily understood categories. This text has grouped offenses and offenders on the basis of their legal definitions and their collective goals, objectives, and consequences.

CHAPTER 10
Interpersonal Violence

CHAPTER 11
Political Crime
and Terrorism

CHAPTER 12
Property Crime

CHAPTER 13
Enterprise Crime:
White-Collar and
Organized Crime

CHAPTER 14
Public Order Crime

CHAPTER 15
Cyber Crime and
Technology

Interpersonal Violence

CHAPTER OUTLINE

The Causes of Violence
Psychological/Biological Abnormality
Evolutionary Factors/Human Instinct
Substance Abuse
Socialization and Upbringing
Exposure to Violence
Cultural Values/Subculture of Violence
Comparative Criminology: The Honor Killing
of Women and Girls

Forcible Rape
History of Rape
Rape and the Military
Incidence of Rape
Types of Rape and Rapists
The Causes of Rape
Rape and the Law

Murder and Homicide
Degrees of Murder
The Nature and Extent of Murder
Murderous Relations
Serial Murder
Mass Murderers

Assault and Battery
Nature and Extent of Assault
Assault in the Home

Robbery
Acquaintance Robbery
Rational Robbery

Emerging Forms of Interpersonal Violence
Hate Crimes
Workplace Violence
Stalking

CHAPTER OBJECTIVES

1. Be familiar with the various causes of violent crime
2. Know the concept of the brutalization process
3. Be able to discuss the history of rape and know the different types of rape
4. Be able to discuss the legal issues in rape prosecution
5. Recognize that there are different types of murder
6. Be able to discuss the differences among serial killing, mass murder, and spree killing
7. Be familiar with the nature of assault in the home
8. Understand the careers of armed robbers
9. State the arguments for and against creating a special legal category for hate crimes.
10. Be able to discuss newly emerging forms of violence such as stalking, hate crimes, and workplace violence

One of the most notorious incidents of the past decade began on March 13, 2006, when after a "performance" at a private residence, three members of Duke University's men's lacrosse team alledgedly raped one of two strippers who had been hired to entertain the team. The three players, David Evans, Reade Seligmann, and Collin Finnerty, were charged with first-degree forcible rape, first-degree sexual offense, and kidnapping.

Media outlets had a field day with the case because the young woman was African American and the players white. The event soon drew national media attention and highlighted racial tensions not only in Durham, North Carolina, where the crime took place, but across the entire nation. The accused boys were wealthy, attractive, and successful. Did they actually believe they could rape a poor young minority woman and get away with the crime because of their power and position? Members of the community demanded justice, the public voiced its outrage, and school officials suspended the accused students and cancelled the lacrosse team's season.

Despite initial shock, public sentiment began to shift as the facts of the case were leaked to the press. There was a lack of physical evidence, the victim's story constantly changed, her character was questioned, there were changes to and inconsistencies her story, the second stripper did not back up her story, and most damaging, the press got hold of testimony by a lab director that the prosecutor, Durham District Attorney Mike Nifong, deliberately withheld evidence from the defense that might have cleared the suspects (i.e., DNA from other men but not the Duke players were found on the victim's body). On December 22, 2006, Nifong dropped the rape charges against the three indicted players. After ethics charges were filed against him, Nifong asked to be taken off the case, and on January 13, 2007, North Carolina Attorney General Roy Cooper agreed to take over. Soon after, Duke University announced that Collin Finnerty and Reade Seligmann had been invited to return to school while they awaited trial and were eligible to rejoin the team (David Evans had already graduated). On April 11, 2007, all remaining charges were dropped against the three players and in an ironic turnabout, Nifong was brought up on misconduct charges, during which he abruptly resigned his post; he was later stripped of his law license.[1]

The Duke case illustrates the toll violent crime takes on American society. It can divide a community, damage reputations, and cause lifelong harm. It tells people that no matter where they go, they may encounter violent acts. And if the Duke case was a matter of false accusation and overzealous prosecution, it still sends the message that anyone can be accused of violent crime. It may also make it tougher to get a conviction when an actual crime takes place.

Millions of violent crimes occur each year. Some are expressive violence—acts that vent rage, anger, or frustration—and some are instrumental violence—acts designed to improve the financial or social position of the criminal, for example, through an armed robbery or murder for hire. No matter its cause, interpersonal violence takes a terrible toll. It causes people to live in fear, staying home at night and avoiding dangerous neighborhoods. It can also take a toll on communities, disrupting services and driving down real estate values, further destabilizing areas already reeling from the shock of violent crimes.[2]

This chapter explores the concept of violence in some depth. First, it reviews the suggested causes of violent crime. Then it focuses on specific types of interpersonal violence—rape, homicide, assault, robbery, and newly recognized types of interpersonal violence such as stalking and workplace violence. Finally, it briefly examines political violence and terrorism.

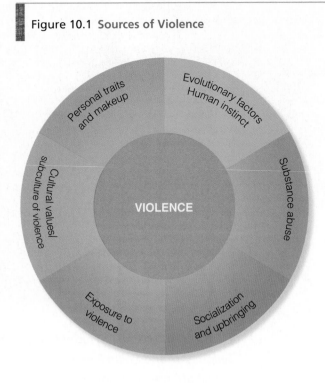

Figure 10.1 Sources of Violence

THE CAUSES OF VIOLENCE

What sets off a violent person? Criminologists have a variety of views on this subject. Some believe that violence is a function of human traits and makeup. Others point to improper socialization and upbringing. Violent behavior may be culturally determined and relate to dysfunctional social values.[3] The various sources of violence are set out in Figure 10.1.

Psychological/Biological Abnormality

On March 13, 1995, an ex–Boy Scout leader named Thomas Hamilton took four high-powered rifles into the primary school of the peaceful Scottish town of Dunblane and slaughtered 16 kindergarten children and their teacher. This horrific crime shocked the British Isles into implementing strict controls on all guns.[4] Bizarre outbursts such as Hamilton's support a link between violence and some sort of mental or biological abnormality.

As you may recall (Chapter 5), some criminologists believe that a significant number of people who are involved in violent episodes may be suffering from severe mental abnormalities.[5] In a classic work, psychologist Dorothy Otnow Lewis shows that kids who kill may be suffering from multiple symptoms of psychological abnormality: neurological impairment (e.g., abnormal EEGs, multiple psychomotor impairments, and severe seizures), low intelligence, and psychotic symptoms such as paranoia,

illogical thinking, and hallucinations.[6] In her book *Guilty by Reason of Insanity*, Lewis finds that death row inmates have a history of mental impairment and intellectual dysfunction.[7]

Lewis's research is not unique. Abnormal personality structures, including such traits as depression, impulsivity, aggression, dishonesty, pathological lying, lack of remorse, borderline personality syndrome, and psychopathology, have all been associated with various forms of violence.[8] It comes as no surprise to psychologists that many murderers kill themselves shortly after committing their crime.[9]

There is also evidence that personality disturbance is linked to some physical trait or characteristic. Neuroscientists claim to have found differences in both the limbic system and the prefrontal cortex of the brain that separates aggressive, violent people from the more level-headed and reasonable. According to this view, if some defect or injury impairs communication between the limbic system and the frontal cortex, a person might not be entirely able to moderate his or her emotional reactions.[10]

Evolutionary Factors/ Human Instinct

Sigmund Freud believed that human behavior is shaped by two instinctual drives: eros, the life instinct, which drives people toward self-fulfillment and enjoyment; and thanatos, the death instinct, which produces self-destruction. Thanatos can be expressed externally (e.g., violence and sadism) or internally (e.g., suicide, alcoholism, or other self-destructive habits).[11]

While rates of violent crime are higher in the United States than in most other Western nations, violence abroad is not unknown. One of the most catastrophic incidents occurred in the village of Dunblane, Scotland, on July 8, 1996, when heavily armed Thomas Hamilton walked onto the grounds of St. Luke's Infant School and began to methodically shoot children in this kindergarten class. Sixteen children and their teacher were killed. The Dunblane massacre prompted the passage of legislation to control handguns in Scotland and England, which failed to please some critics who felt there should be an outright ban on the possession of guns.

© AP Images/Gwen Mayor

found between community levels of crack cocaine and heroin use and the incidence of street robberies.[15] High use areas may also face social disorganization, poverty, and unemployment, factors that further escalate violence rates.[16]

The link between substance abuse and violence appears in three different formats:[17]

1. *Psychopharmacological relationship.* Violence may be the direct consequence of ingesting mood-altering substances. Experimental evidence shows that high doses of drugs such as PCP and amphetamines produce violent, aggressive behavior.[18] For example, binge drinking has been closely associated with violent crime rates.[19] Heavy drinking reduces cognitive ability, information processing skills, and the ability to process and react to verbal and nonverbal behavior. As a result, miscommunication becomes more likely and the capacity for rational dialogue is compromised.[20] It is not surprising that males involved in sexual assaults often claim that they were drinking and misunderstood their victims' intentions.[21] Drinking becomes particularly dangerous when abusers have access to firearms; guns and alcohol do not mix well.[22]

2. *Economic compulsive behavior.* Drug users resort to violence to obtain the financial resources to support their habit. Studies conducted in the United States and Europe show that addicts commit hundreds of crimes each year.[23]

3. *Systemic link.* Violence escalates when drug-dealing gangs flex their muscle to dominate territory and drive out rivals. Studies of gangs that sell drugs show that their violent activities may result in a significant proportion of all urban homicides.[24]

In his celebrated book *On Aggression*, anthropologist Konrad Lorenz argued that aggressive energy is produced by inbred instincts that are independent of environmental forces.[12] In the animal kingdom, aggression usually serves a productive purpose—for example, it leads members of grazing species such as zebras and antelopes to spread out over available territory to ensure an ample food supply and the survival of the fittest. Lorenz found that humans possess some of the same aggressive instincts as animals. But among lower species, aggression is rarely fatal; when a conflict occurs, the winner is determined through a test of skill or endurance. This inhibition against killing members of their own species protects animals from self-extinction. Humans, lacking this inhibition against fatal violence, are capable of killing their own kind in war or as a result of interpersonal conflicts such as those arising over finding suitable mates.[13]

Lorenz feared that as technology develops and more lethal weapons are produced, the extinction of the human species becomes a significant possibility.

Substance Abuse

Substance abuse has been associated with violence on both the individual and social levels: substance abusers have higher rates of violence than nonabusers; neighborhoods with high levels of substance abuse have higher violence rates when compared to areas with low use rates.[14] A direct association has been

Socialization and Upbringing

Another view is that improper socialization and upbringing are responsible for the onset of violent acts. Absent or deviant parents, inconsistent discipline, physical abuse, and lack of supervision have all been linked to persistent violent offending.[25]

Although infants demonstrate individual temperaments, who they become may have a lot to do with how they are treated during their early years. Some children are harder to soothe than others; in some cases, difficult infant temperament has been associated with later aggression and behavioral problems.[26] Parents who fail to set adequate limits or to use proper, consistent discipline reinforce a child's coercive behavior.[27] The effects of inadequate parenting and early rejection may affect violent behavior throughout life.[28] There is evidence that children who are maltreated and neglected in early childhood are the ones most likely to be initiated into criminality and thereafter continue or persist in a criminal career.[29]

There are also indications that children who are subject to even minimal amounts of physical punishment may be more likely one day to use violence themselves.[30] Sociologist Murray Straus reviewed the concept of discipline in a series of surveys and found a powerful relationship between exposure to physical punishment and later aggression.[31] The effect of physical punishment may be mediated or neutralized to some extent if parents also provide support, warmth, and care. When kids experience physical punishment in the absence of parental involvement, they feel angry and unjustly treated and are more willing to defy their parents and engage in antisocial behavior.[32]

Abused Children A number of research studies have found that children who are clinically diagnosed as abused later engage in delinquent behaviors, including violence, at a rate significantly greater than that of children who were not abused.[33] Samples of convicted murderers reveal a high percentage of seriously abused youth.[34] The abuse–violence association has been established in many cases in which parents have been killed by their children; sexual abuse is also a constant factor in father (patricide) and mother (matricide) killings.[35] Lewis found in her study of juvenile death row inmates that all had long histories of intense child abuse.[36]

Abuse may have the greatest effect if it is persistent and extends from childhood to adolescence.[37] Children who are physically punished by their parents are likely to physically abuse a sibling and later engage in spouse abuse and other forms of criminal violence.[38] There is evidence that spousal batterers received significantly less love and more punishment from their mothers than did men in a general population comparison group. Abusive childhood experiences may be a key factor in the later development of relationship aggression.[39] Lonnie Athens, a well-known criminologist who links violence to early experiences with child abuse, has coined the phrase violentization process to describe how abused kids are turned into aggressive adults.[40] The stages of this process are described in Exhibit 10.1. Athens recognizes that abuse alone is not a sufficient condition to cause someone to become a dangerous violent criminal. One must complete the full cycle of the "violentization process"—brutalization, belligerence, violent performances, and virulency—to become socialized into violence. Many brutalized children do not go on to become violent criminals, and some later reject the fact that they were abused as youths and redefine their early years as normative.

Exposure to Violence

People who are constantly exposed to violence in the environment may adopt violent methods themselves. Children living in areas marked by extreme violence may eventually

EXHIBIT 10.1

Stages in the Violentization Process

1. **Brutalization Stage.** During this phase of the violentization process, a young victim develops a belligerent, angry demeanor as a result of being mistreated by abusive parents or caretakers. Brutalization can be broader than parental physical or sexual abuse and can result from violent coaching by peers, neighbors, and schoolmates. Although most brutalization occurs early in life, some people can be brutalized as they mature. There are a number of facets in the brutalization stage:

   ■ *Violent subjugation.* A person is coerced into compliance by physical or verbal force. Coercive violence ends at submission, but retaliatory violence continues regardless of submission, with the goal of gaining long-term submission.

   ■ *Personal horrification.* An individual is exposed to violence directed at someone else close to them, leading to inner conflict and guilt associated with their helplessness to do anything about the abuse.

   ■ *Violent coaching.* A brutalizer, through ridicule, threats, or coercion, advises the brutalized individual to depend only on his or her self, encourages defensiveness, and insists that they have a personal responsibility to commit violence.

2. **Belligerency Stage.** During this stage, the target of brutalization begins to understand their dilemma. At first they may wonder, "Why can't I stop this violence and brutalization?" Then they begin a cognitive process in which they conclude that sometimes violence is a necessary evil in the world. They think, "Why have I not done anything to stop my own and my intimates' violent subjugation?" Resorting to violence is sometimes necessary in this world.

3. **Violent Performance Stage.** Brutalized youth may become belligerent and angry. When confronted at home, school, or on the street, these belligerent youth respond with violent performances of angry, hostile behavior. The success of their violent confrontations provides them with a sense of power and achievement.

4. **Virulency Stage.** The emerging criminal develops a violent identity that makes them feared; they enjoy intimidating others. Filled with feelings of exultancy, the brutalized person believes that can perform even more impressive violent feats in the future. They believe they are now invincible. This process takes violent youths full circle from being the victims of aggression to its initiators; they are now the same person they grew up despising, ready to begin the process with their own children.

Source: Lonnie Athens, *The Creation of Dangerous Violent Criminals* (Urbana: University of Illinois Press, 1992), pp. 27–80.

become desensitized to the persistent brutality.[41] Much of the differences in violent crime rates between whites and racial minorities can be explained by the fact that the latter are often forced to live in high-crime neighborhoods, which increases their risk of exposure to violence.[42] Areas where people have little confidence in the police and are therefore reluctant to call for help, a condition common in the minority community, may also experience higher levels of violent behavior.[43]

Social scientist Felton Earls and his associates conducted the Project on Human Development in Chicago Neighborhoods—a government-funded longitudinal study of pathways to violence among 7,000 Chicago area people in eighty different, randomly selected neighborhoods.[44] Interviews with youths aged 9 to 15 show that large numbers of these children have been victims of or witnesses to violence and that many carry weapons.

Between 30 and 40 percent of the children who reported exposure to violence also displayed significant violent behavior themselves. Earls finds that young teens who witness gun violence are more than twice as likely as nonwitnesses to commit violent crime themselves in the following years.[45] Even a single exposure to firearm violence doubles the chance that a young person will later engage in violent behavior.

Children living in these conditions become "crusted over": they do not let people inside, nor do they express their feelings. They exploit others and in turn are exploited by those older and stronger; as a result, they develop a sense of hopelessness. They find that parents and teachers focus on their failures and problems, not their achievements. Consequently, they are vulnerable to the lure of delinquent gangs and groups.[46]

Cultural Values/Subculture of Violence

Violence may be the product of cultural beliefs, values, and behaviors that develop in poor and disorganized neighborhoods.[47] To explain this phenomenon, criminologists Marvin Wolfgang and Franco Ferracuti formulated the famous concept that some areas contain an independent subculture of violence.[48]

The subculture of violence's norms are separate from society's central, dominant value system. In this subculture, a potent theme of violence influences lifestyles, the socialization process, and interpersonal relationships. Even though the subculture's members share some of the dominant culture's values, they expect that violence will be used to solve social conflicts and dilemmas. In some cultural subgroups, then, violence has become legitimized by custom and norms. It is considered appropriate behavior within culturally defined conflict situations in which an individual who has been offended by a negative outcome in a dispute seeks reparations through violent means—a concept referred to as disputatiousness.[49]

There is evidence that a subculture of violence may be found in areas that experience concentrated poverty and social disorganization.[50] Though most people abhor violence, income inequality and racial disparity may help instill a sense of hopelessness that nourishes pro-violence norms and values.[51] In these areas people are more likely to carry weapons and use them in assaults and robberies. Victims are aware of these tactics and are less likely to fight back forcibly when attacked.[52] However, when pressed to the limit even passive victims may eventually fight back. When Charis Kubrin and Ronald Weitzer studied homicide in St. Louis, Missouri, they discovered that a certain type of killing referred to as *cultural retaliatory homicide* is common in neighborhoods that suffer economic disadvantage. In these areas, residents resolve interpersonal conflicts informally—without calling the police—even if it means killing their opponent; neighbors understand and support their violent methods.[53] Because police and other agencies of formal social control are viewed as weak and devalued, understaffed and/or corrupt, people are willing to take matters into their own hands and violence rates increase accordingly.[54]

Peer Group Influences Empirical evidence shows that violence rates are highest in urban areas where subcultural values support teenage gangs whose members typically embrace the use of violence.[55] Gang boys are more likely to own guns and other weapons than non–gang members. They are also more likely to have peers who are gun owners and are more likely to carry guns outside the home.[56] Ominously, major metropolitan areas such as Los Angeles and Chicago are now reporting a significant increase in the number of street gang–related killings.[57]

The association between gang membership and violence has a number of roots. It can result from drug-trafficking activities and turf protection but also stems from personal vendettas and a perceived need for self-protection.[58] Gang boys are much more likely to own guns and associate with violent peers than nonmembers.[59] Those who choose aggressive or violent friends are more likely to begin engaging in antisocial behavior themselves and suffer psychological deficits.[60] The risky gang lifestyle increases the likelihood that boys will themselves become a victim of violent crime. Experiencing victimization brings on retaliation, creating a never-ending cycle of violence begetting even more violence.[61]

While many boys are predisposed toward violence before joining a gang, research shows that once in gangs their violent behavior quickly escalates; after they leave, it significantly declines.[62]

National Values Some nations—including the United States, Sri Lanka, Angola, Uganda, and the Philippines—have relatively high violence rates; others are much more peaceful. According to research by sociologist Jerome Neapolitan, a number of national characteristics are predictive of violence, including a high level of social disorganization, economic stress, high child abuse rates, approval of violence by the government, political corruption, and an inefficient justice system.[63] Children in high-violence nations are likely to be economically deprived and socially isolated, exposed to constant violence, and lacking in hope and respect for the law. Guns are common in these nations because, lacking an efficient justice system, people arm themselves or hire private security forces for protection.[64] In contrast, nations such as Japan have relatively low violence rates because of cultural and economic strengths. Japan boasts a system of exceptionally effective informal social controls that help reduce crime. It also has had a robust economy that may alleviate the stresses that produce violence.[65] The Comparative Criminology feature "The Honor Killing of Women and Girls" discusses one type of culturally based violent crime.

Does the United States maintain values that promote violence? According to historian David Courtwright, relatively high

THE HONOR KILLING OF WOMEN AND GIRLS

Honor killing and honor crime involve violence against women and girls, including such acts as beating, battering, or killing, by a family member or relative. The attacks are provoked by the belief or perception that an individual's or family's honor has been threatened because of the actual or perceived sexual misconduct of the female. Honor killings are most common in traditional societies in the Middle East, Southwest Asia, India, China, and Latin America.

Honor killing of a woman or girl by her father, brother, or other male relative may occur because of a suspicion that she engaged in sexual activities before or outside marriage and thus has dishonored the family. Even when rape of a woman or girl has occurred this may be seen as violation of the honor of the family for which the female must be killed. Wives' adultery and daughters'

premarital "sexual activity," including rape, are seen as extreme violations of the codes of behavior and thus may result in the death of the female through this so-called "honor" killing. Honor killing/crime is based on the shame that a loss of control of the woman or girl brings to the family and to the male heads of the family.

According to criminologist Linda Williams, men consider honor killings culturally necessary, because any suspicion of sexual activity or suspicion that a girl or a woman was touched by another in a sexual manner is enough to raise questions about the family's honor. Consequently, strict control of women and girls within the home and outside the home is justified. Women are restricted in their activities in the community, religion, and politics. These institutions, in turn, support the control of females. Williams believes that the existence of honor killing is designed for maintaining male dominance. Submissiveness may be seen as a sign of sexual purity and a woman's or girl's attempts to assert her rights can

be seen as a violation of the family's honor that needs to be redressed. Rules of honor and threats against females who "violate" such rules reinforce the control of women and have a powerful impact on their lives. Honor killings/crimes serve to keep women and girls from "stepping out of line." The manner in which such behaviors silence women and kill their spirit has led some to label honor killings/crimes more broadly as "femicide."

CRITICAL THINKING

While we may scoff at honor killings, are there elements of American culture and life that you consider harmful to women yet are still tolerated? What can be done to change them?

Sources: Linda M. Williams, "Honor Killings," in *Encyclopedia of Interpersonal Violence*, eds. Claire M. Renzetti and Jeffrey I. Edelson (Thousand Oaks, CA: Sage Publications, 2007); Dan Bilefsky, "How to Avoid Honor Killing in Turkey? Honor Suicide," *New York Times*, 16 July 2006, p. 3; Nadera Shalhoub-Kevorkian, "Reexamining Femicide: Breaking the Silence and Crossing 'Scientific' Borders," *Signs* 28 (2003): 581–608.

---

violence rates in the United States can be traced to a frontier culture that was characterized by racism and preoccupation with personal honor.[66] Westerners drank heavily and frequented saloons and gambling halls, where petty arguments could become lethal because most patrons carried guns and knives. Violent acts often went unpunished because law enforcement agencies were unable or unwilling to take action. The population of the frontier was mostly young bachelors who were sensitive about honor, heavy drinkers, morally indifferent, heavily armed, and unchecked by adequate law enforcement. Many died from disease, but others succumbed to drink and violence. Smoking, gambling, and heavy drinking became a cultural imperative, and those who were disinclined to indulge were considered social outcasts. Courtwright claims that over time gender ratios equalized as more men brought families to the frontier and children of both sexes were born. Many men died, returned home, or drifted elsewhere. By the mid-twentieth century, America's overall male surplus was disappearing, and a balanced population helped bring down the crime rate, but remnants of the frontier mentality still exist in contemporary American society.

www Go to www.thomsonedu.com/criminaljustice/siegel to:

▌ Read more about the **Dunblane massacre**.

▌ Read the **autobiography of Konrad Lorenz**, who won the Nobel Prize in medicine in 1973.

▌ Visit the **Project on Human Development in Chicago Neighborhoods** website.

FORCIBLE RAPE

Rape (from the Latin *rapere*, to take by force) is defined in common law as "the carnal knowledge of a female forcibly and against her will."[67] It is one of the most loathed, misunderstood, and frightening crimes. Under traditional common-law definitions, rape involves nonconsensual sexual intercourse that a male performs against a female he is neither married to nor cohabiting with.[68] There are of course other forms of sexual assault, including male on male, female on female, and female on male sexual assaults, but these are

ALDRICH HAZEN AMES

Aldrich Hazen Ames was arrested by the FBI in Arlington, Virginia, on espionage charges on February 24, 1994. At the time of his arrest, Ames was a 31-year veteran of the Central Intelligence Agency (CIA) who had been spying for the Russians since 1985. Arrested with him was his wife, Rosario Ames, who had aided and abetted his espionage activities.

Ames was a CIA case officer who spoke Russian and specialized in the Russian intelligence services, including the KGB, the USSR's foreign intelligence service. His initial overseas assignment was in Ankara, Turkey, where he targeted Russian intelligence officers for recruitment. Later, he worked in New York City and Mexico City. On April 16, 1985, while assigned to the CIA's Soviet/East European Division at CIA Headquarters in Langley, Virginia, he secretly volunteered to KGB officers at the USSR Embassy in Washington, D.C. Shortly thereafter, the KGB paid him $50,000. During the summer of 1985, Ames met several times with a Russian diplomat to whom he passed classified information about CIA and FBI human sources, as well as technical operations targeting the Soviet Union. In December 1985, Ames met with a Moscow-based KGB officer in Bogota, Colombia. In July 1986, Ames was transferred to Rome.

In Rome, Ames continued his meetings with the KGB, including a Russian diplomat assigned to Rome and a Moscow-based KGB officer. At the conclusion of his assignment in Rome, Ames received instructions from the KGB regarding clandestine contacts in the Washington, D.C., area, where he would next be assigned. In the four years since he first volunteered, the KGB had paid Ames $1.88 million.

Upon his return to Washington, D.C., in 1989, Ames continued to pass classified documents to the KGB, using "dead drops" or prearranged hiding places where he would leave the documents to be picked up later by KGB officers from the USSR Embassy in Washington. In return, the KGB left money and instructions for Ames, usually in other dead drops.

In the meantime, the CIA and FBI learned that Russian officials who had been recruited by them were being arrested and executed. These human sources had provided critical intelligence information about the USSR, which was used by U.S. policymakers in determining U.S. foreign policy. Following analytical reviews and receipt of information about Ames's unexplained wealth, the FBI opened an investigation in May 1993.

FBI special agents and investigative specialists conducted intensive physical and electronic surveillance of Ames during a 10-month investigation. Searches of Ames's residence revealed documents and other information linking Ames to the Russian foreign intelligence service. On October 13, 1993, investigative specialists observed a chalk mark Ames made on a mailbox confirming to the Russians his intention to meet them in Bogota, Colombia. On November 1, special agents observed him and, separately, his Russian handler in Bogota. When Ames planned foreign travel, including a trip to Moscow, as part of his official duties, a plan to arrest him was approved.

Following guilty pleas by both Ames and his wife on April 28, 1994, Ames was sentenced to incarceration for life without the possibility of parole. Rosario Ames was sentenced on October 20, 1994, to 63 months in prison. Ames also forfeited his assets to the United States, and $547,000 was turned over to the Justice Department's Victims Assistance Fund. Ames is serving his sentence in the federal prison system. Rosario Ames completed her sentence and was released.

Source: FBI, "Famous Cases: Aldrich Hazen Ames," www.fbi.gov/libref/historic/famcases/ames/ames.htm (accessed April 24, 2007).

It is possible to divide state political crimes into five varieties:[16]

1. *Political corruption.* This violation of citizen trust can involve nonviolent crimes such as soliciting bribes (usually money or some other economic benefit, like a gift or service). Politicians, judges, police, and government regulators all engage in corruption that damages public trust in the government and its process. And unfortunately, when corruption is uncovered and the perpetrator brought to justice it is difficult to determine whether a real criminal has been caught or a political opponent framed and punished.

2. *Illegal domestic surveillance.* This occurs when government agents listen in on telephone conversations or intercept e-mails without proper approval in order to stifle dissent and monitor political opponents. Sometimes the true purpose of the surveillance is masked by the need for national security while in reality it is illegal organizational policy and practice that has in some cases been sanctioned by heads of state for political purposes.

3. *Human rights violations.* States may treat their citizens in such a fashion as to deny them basic civil rights. Correctional systems have long been suspected of depriving people of civil rights. While prison conditions are notorious in third-world nations and inmates are deprived of basic necessities, such human rights violations have also occurred in industrial societies such as the United States. The use of secret prisons to detain terror suspects without trial or indictment might be considered by critics such as the American Civil Liberties Union a human rights violation, and so would be the use of illegal interrogations to obtain confessions or information from suspected terrorists.[17]

4. *State violence.* Sometimes state action involves violence (state-sponsored terror is discussed later in the chapter). While the use of torture and illegal imprisonment is notorious in third-world countries, police violence and use of deadly force is not uncommon in Western industrialized nations. In some nations, such as the Russian province of Chechnya, almost all political detainees are subjected to torture, including electric shocks, burnings, and severe beating with boots, sticks, plastic bottles filled with water or sand, and heavy rubber-coated cables. The rest are subject to psychological pressure, coercion, execution, as well as threats to harm their relatives.[18]

5. *State-corporate crime.* This type of political crime is committed by individuals who abuse their state authority or who fail to exercise it when working with people and organizations in the private sector. These crimes may occur when state institutions such as an environmental agency fails to enforce laws, resulting in the pollution of public waterways. This type of crime is particularly alarming, considering that regulatory law aimed at controlling private corporations are being scaled back while globalization has made corporations worldwide entities both in production and in advancing the consumption of their products.[19]

Using Torture On February 23, 2007, Osama Hassan Mustafa Nasr, an Egyptian cleric, made worldwide headlines when he claimed that he had been kidnapped in Italy by American CIA agents and sent to Egypt for interrogation as part of the CIA's "extraordinary rendition." Nasr claimed, "I was subjected to the worst kind of torture in Egyptian prisons. I have scars of torture all over my body." Italy indicted 26 Americans and five Italian agents accused of seizing him and sending him to Egypt without trial or due process.[20]

Of all state political crimes, the use of torture to gain information from suspected political criminals is perhaps the most notorious. Can the torture of a suspected terrorist determined to destroy the government and harm innocent civilians ever be permissible or is it always an example of state sponsored political crime? While most people loathe the thought of torturing anyone, some experts argue that torture can sometimes be justified in what they call the ticking bomb scenario: suppose the government found out that a captured terrorist knew the whereabouts of a dangerous explosive device that was set to go

off and kill thousands of innocent people. Would it be permissible to engage in the use of torture on this single suspect if it would save the population of a city? While the ticking bomb scenario has appeal (see The Criminological Enterprise feature "Want to Torture? Get a Warrant"), opponents of torture believe that even imminent danger does not justify state violence. There is a danger that such state sponsored violence would become calculated and premeditated; torturers would have to be trained, ready, and in place for the ticking bomb argument to work. We couldn't be running around looking for torturers with a bomb set to go off, could we? Because torturers would be part of the government bureaucracy, there is no way to ensure that they would only use their skills in certain morally justifiable cases.[21] What happens if a superior officer tells them to torture someone, but they believe the order is unjustified? Should they follow orders or risk a court-martial for being disobedient? Furthermore, there is very little empirical evidence suggesting that torture provides any real benefits and much more that suggests it can create serious problems. It can damage civil rights and democratic institutions and cause the general public to have sympathy for the victims of torture no matter their evil intent.[22]

Legal scholars have complained that agencies of the government that use torture, such as the Central Intelligence Agency (CIA), do so without legal authority. Despite its illegality, enemy agents have been detained and physically abused in secret prisons around the world without the benefit of due process. In some cases suspects have been held in foreign countries simply because their governments are not squeamish about using torture during interrogations. Shocking photo evidence of torture from the Abu Ghraib prison in Iraq and detention facilities at the Guantánamo base in Cuba support their charges. Legal scholars have argued that these tactics violate both international treaties and domestic statutes prohibiting torture. Some maintain that the U.S. Constitution limits the authority of an executive agency like the CIA to act against foreigners abroad and also limits physical coercion by the government under the Fifth Amendment Due Process and Self-Incrimination Clauses and the Eighth Amendment prohibition against cruel and unusual punishments. Legally, it is impermissible for United States authorities to engage in indefinite detention or torture regardless of the end, the place, or the victim.[23]

www Go to www.thomsonedu.com/criminaljustice/siegel to learn more about the following topics:

▌ **Vote fraud and election fairness**

▌ **Important espionage cases**

TERRORISM

The political crime that many people are most concerned with is terrorism, and the remainder of this chapter focuses on the history, nature, and extent of terrorism and the methods being employed for its control. Despite its long history, it is often difficult

The Criminological Enterprise

WANT TO TORTURE? GET A WARRANT

According to the ticking bomb scenario, torture can be justified in order to force a political criminal to reveal the location of an explosive device before it can go off and kill many people. While a number of legal and social scholars have debated whether torture can ever be justified in a moral society no matter what the intent, famed social commentator and legal scholar Alan Dershowitz disagrees. He argues that torture can be justified under some circumstances, especially to prevent damaging terror attacks. Moreover, he believes that the "vast majority" of Americans would expect law enforcement agents to engage in time-honored methods of "loosening tongues" if the circumstances demanded it even though international bodies such as the UN forbid its use no matter how exigent the circumstances. To ensure that torture is not used capriciously, Dershowitz proposes the creation of a "torture warrant" that can only be issued by a judge in cases where (a) there is an absolute need to obtain immediate information in order to save lives and (b) there is probable cause that the suspect has such information and is unwilling to reveal it to law enforcement agents. The suspect would be given immunity from prosecution based on information elicited by the torture; it would only be to save lives. The warrant would limit the torture to nonlethal means, such as sterile needles being inserted beneath the nails to cause excruciating pain without endangering life.

While Dershowitz recognizes that it may sound both awful and absurd for a judge to be issuing a warrant to torture a suspect, in truth every democracy, including our own, has employed torture outside of the law. It is routine for police officers to put tremendous pressure on suspects in order to get them to talk. The "third degree" is all too common, not only on TV shows, but in the back rooms of real police station houses. If it is already used, would it not be better to have it regulated and controlled by the rule of law? If it isn't, law enforcement agents would continue to use torture anyway, only it would fall "below the radar screen of accountability." Which would be more consistent with democratic values?

Dershowitz recognizes that those opposed to the idea of a torture warrant argue that establishing such a precedent would legitimize torture and make it easier to use under any circumstances. But he believes that the opposite would be true: by expressly limiting the use of torture only to the "ticking bomb case" and by requiring an objective and reasoned judge to approve, limit, and monitor the torture, it will be far more difficult to justify its extension to other institutions. The goal of the warrant would be to reduce and limit the amount of torture that would, in fact, be used in an emergency.

Not everyone agrees that in some extreme cases the "ends justify the means." Human Rights Watch, an international group dedicated to protecting the human rights of people around the world, counters Dershowitz by pointing out that while the ticking bomb scenario makes for great philosophical discussion, it rarely arises in real life. Except in movies and TV, interrogators rarely learn that a suspect in custody knows of a particular, imminent terrorist bombing and that they have the knowledge to prevent a catastrophe. Intelligence is rarely, if ever, good enough to provide such specific advance warning. If terrorists knew their plan could be foiled by information provided by a prisoner, why would they not change the plan? While not practical, the ticking bomb scenario can be dangerous because it expands the use of torture to anyone who might have knowledge of unspecified future terrorist attacks: Why are only the victims of an imminent terrorist attack deserving of protection by torture? Why not also use torture to prevent a terrorist attack tomorrow or next week or next year? And why stop with the alleged terrorists themselves? Why not also torture their families or associates— anyone who might provide life-saving information? The slope is very slippery, Human Rights Watch claims.

CRITICAL THINKING

You are a government agent holding a prisoner who has been arrested on suspicion of being a terrorist. You get a call stating that there is a credible threat that a bomb will go off in two hours unless it can be found and defused. The prisoner has knowledge of the bomb's location. How would you get him to reveal the location? Would you consider using torture? Is there a better method?

Sources: Alan M. Dershowitz, *Shouting Fire: Civil Liberties in a Turbulent Age* (New York: Little, Brown, 2002); Dershowitz, "Want to Torture? Get a Warrant," *San Francisco Chronicle*, 22 January 2002; Human Rights Watch, "The Twisted Logic of Torture," January 2005, http://hrw.org/wr2k5/darfurandabughraib/6.htm (accessed April 24, 2007).

---

to precisely define terrorism (from the Latin *terrere*, which means to frighten) and to separate terrorist acts from interpersonal crimes of violence. For example, if a group robs a bank to obtain funds for its revolutionary struggles, should the act be treated as terrorism or as a common bank robbery? In this instance, defining a crime as terrorism depends on the kind of legal response the act evokes from those in power. To be considered terrorism, which is a political crime, an act must carry with it the intent to disrupt and change the government and must not be merely a common-law crime committed for greed or egotism.

Because of its complexity, an all-encompassing definition of terrorism is difficult to formulate, although most experts agree that it generally involves the illegal use of force against innocent people to achieve a political objective. According to the U.S. State Department, the term "terrorism" means premeditated, politically motivated violence perpetrated against non-combatant targets by subnational groups or clandestine agents, usually intended to influence an audience. The term "international terrorism" means terrorism involving citizens or the territory of more than one country. A terrorist group is any group practicing, or that has significant subgroups that practice, international terrorism.[24] Exhibit 11.2 sets out a number of definitions of terrorism drafted or used by prominent governmental agencies or organizations.

Terrorism usually involves a type of political crime that emphasizes violence as a mechanism to promote change. Whereas some political criminals may sell secrets, spy, and the like, terrorists systematically murder and destroy or threaten such violence to terrorize individuals, groups, communities, or governments into conceding to the terrorists' political demands.[25] Because terrorists lack large armies and formidable weapons, their use of subterfuge, secrecy, and hit-and-run tactics is designed to give them a psychological advantage and the power to neutralize the physical superiority of their opponents.

However, it may be erroneous to equate terrorism with political goals, because not all terrorist actions are aimed at political change. Some terrorists may try to bring about what they consider to be economic or social reform—for example, by attacking women wearing fur coats or sabotaging property during a labor dispute. Terrorism must also be distinguished from conventional warfare, because it requires secrecy and clandestine operations to exert social control over large populations.[26]

Terrorist and Guerilla

The word "terrorist" is often used interchangeably with the term "guerilla," but the terms are quite different. Guerilla comes from the Spanish term meaning "little war," which developed out of the Spanish rebellion against French troops after Napoleon's 1808 invasion of the Iberian Peninsula.[27] Terrorists have an urban focus. Operating in small bands, or cadres, of three to five members, they target the property or persons of their enemy, such as members of the ruling class.[28] Guerillas, on the other hand, are located in rural areas and attack the military, the police, and government officials. Their organizations can grow quite large and eventually take the form of a conventional military force. However, guerilas can infiltrate urban areas in small bands, and terrorists can make forays into the countryside; consequently, the terms are sometimes used interchangeably.

Terrorist and Insurgent

During the Iraq war, the term insurgent began to be used to describe the forces opposed to American involvement. As commonly used, an insurgency is somewhat different from both guerilla warfare and terrorism. The typical goal of an

EXHIBIT 11.2

Definitions of Terrorism

1. **League of Nations Convention (1937)**

   All criminal acts directed against a State and intended or calculated to create a state of terror in the minds of particular persons or a group of persons or the general public.

2. **UN resolution language (1999)**

   1. *Strongly condemns* all acts, methods and practices of terrorism as criminal and unjustifiable, wherever and by whomsoever committed;

   2. *Reiterates* that criminal acts intended or calculated to provoke a state of terror in the general public, a group of persons or particular persons for political purposes are in any circumstance unjustifiable, whatever the considerations of a political, philosophical, ideological, racial, ethnic, religious or other nature that may be invoked to justify them. (GA Res. 51/210, "Measures to Eliminate International Terrorism")

3. **Short legal definition proposed by A. P. Schmid to United Nations Crime Branch (1992)**

   Act of Terrorism = Peacetime Equivalent of War Crime

4. **Academic consensus definition used by the UN**

   Terrorism is an anxiety-inspiring method of repeated violent action, employed by (semi-) clandestine individual, group or state actors, for idiosyncratic, criminal or political reasons, whereby—in contrast to assassination—the direct targets of violence are not the main targets. The immediate human victims of violence are generally chosen randomly (targets of opportunity) or selectively (representative or symbolic targets) from a target population, and serve as message generators. Threat- and violence-based communication processes between terrorist (organization), (imperiled) victims, and main targets are used to manipulate the main target (audience[s]), turning it into a target of terror, a target of demands, or a target of attention, depending on whether intimidation, coercion, or propaganda is primarily sought"

5. **United States Department of State**

   The term "terrorism" means premeditated, politically motivated violence perpetrated against noncombatant (1) targets by subnational groups or clandestine agents, usually intended to influence an audience.

   The term "international terrorism" means terrorism involving citizens or the territory of more than one country.

   The term "terrorist group" means any group practicing, or that has significant subgroups that practice, international terrorism.

Sources: Patterns of Global Terrorism (Washington: Department of State, 2001): vi; United Nations Office on Drugs and Crime, www.unodc.org/unodc/terrorism_definitions.html (accessed June 13, 2007).

insurgency is to confront the existing government for control of all or a portion of its territory, or force political concessions in sharing political power.[29] While terrorists are inherently violent, insurgents do not necessarily need to use terror or violence to meet their aims but can also use nonviolent methods or political tactics. For example, they may set up food distribution centers and schools in areas in which they gain control in order to provide the population with needed services while contrasting their benevolent rule with the government's incompetence and corruption.

When insurgents use violence, it is designed to inspire support and gain converts while at the same time destroying the government's ability to resist. It is easy to recruit supporters once the population believes that the government is incapable of fighting back. On the other hand, some members of the insurgency might shun violence and eventually break away from the mainstream, creating nonviolent splinter groups that operate within the mainstream. They can then operate openly, claiming to sympathize with the violent wing of their organization but just not being part of its structure.

Insurgents, unlike terrorists, require support of a significant portion of the population. While terrorists may operate in small bands with a narrow focus, such as ending the use of animals in medical research, insurgents represent a popular movement and may also seek external support from other nations to bring pressure on the government. A terror group, in contrast, neither requires nor has active support or sympathy from a large percentage of the population.

Terrorist and Revolutionary

A revolution (from the Latin *revolutio*, "a revolving," and *revolvere*, "turn, roll back") is generally seen as a civil war fought between nationalists and a sovereign power that holds control of the land, or between the existing government and local groups over issues of ideology and power. Historically, the American Revolution may be considered an example of a struggle between nationalistic groups and an imperialistic overseas government. Classic examples of ideological rebellions are the French Revolution, which pitted the middle class and urban poor against the aristocracy, and the Russian Revolution of 1917 during which the Czarist government was toppled by the Bolsheviks. More recent ideological revolutions have occurred in China, Cuba, Nicaragua, and Chile, to name but a few.

While some revolutions (such as the American, French, and Russian) rely on armed force, terror activities, and violence, others can be nonviolent, depending on large urban protests and threats. Such was the case when the Shah Mohammad Reza Pahlavi was toppled in Iran after a slew of nonviolent demonstrations which ended in the 1979 revolution that transformed Iran from a constitutional monarchy into an Islamic republic or theocracy under the rule of Ayatollah Ruhollah Khomeini.

A BRIEF HISTORY OF TERRORISM

Acts of terrorism have been known throughout history. The assassination of Julius Caesar on March 15, 44 BCE, is considered an act of terrorism. Terrorism became widespread at the end of the Middle Ages, when political leaders were frequently subject to assassination by their enemies.

Religious Roots

The first terrorist activities were committed by members of minority religious groups who engaged in violence to (a) gain the right to practice their own form of religion, (b) establish the supremacy of their own religion over others, or (c) meet the requirements of the bloodthirsty gods they worshipped.[30]

In some instances, a conquered people used force and violence to maintain their right to worship in their own faith. Zealots, Hebrew warrior groups, were active during the Roman occupation of Palestine during the first century CE. A subgroup of the Zealots, the Sciari (literally translated as *daggermen*), were so named after the long curved knives they favored as a weapon to assassinate Romans or their sympathizers. The Zealots carried out their attacks in broad daylight, typically with witnesses around, in order to send a message that the Roman authorities and those Jews who collaborated with them would not be safe. Ironically, this tactic is still being used by contemporary terrorists. The Zealots and Sciari led the revolt in 66 CE against Roman occupation of the Holy Land, during which they occupied the fortress of Masada. Here they held out for more than seven months before engaging in mass suicide rather than surrender to the Roman legions. The revolt ended badly and the Romans destroyed the Jewish temple and sent the population into exile.

Some religious terrorists want to promote the supremacy of their own sect over a rival group. The (Shi'ite) Muslim Order of the Assassins (*assassin* literally means "hashish-eater," a reference to the commonly held belief that gang members engaged in acts of ritual intoxication and smoked hashish just prior to undertaking their missions) was active in Persia, Syria, and Palestine from 1090 to 1272, killing a great number of their enemies, mainly Sunnis whom they considered apostates, but also Christians who were then the rulers of the kingdom of Jerusalem.[31] The Assassins also were prone to stabbing their victims in an effort to spread their vision of Islam, and carried out missions in public places on holy days in order to publicize their cause. Successful assassinations guaranteed them a place in heaven.

Another form of religious terror is inspired by the requirements of belief. Some religious beliefs have focused on violence, the gods demanding the death of nonbelievers. In India, members of the Thugee cult (from which the modern term "thug" was derived) were devoted to Kali, the goddess of death and destruction. The thugs believed each murder prevented Kali's arrival for 1,000 years, thus sparing the nation from her death and destruction. The thugs traveled in gangs of up to 100 with each member having a defined role—some lured unwary travelers, while others strangled the chosen victim. The gang used secret argot and jargon which only they could understand and signs so that members could recognize each other even in the most remote parts of India. Cult members may have killed hundreds of thousands of victims over a 300-year span. They would attach themselves to travelers and when the opportunity arose, strangle them with a noose around their necks, steal their money, and bury their bodies. The killings were highly ritualistic and involved religious rites and prayers. By the mid-nineteenth century the

British made it a policy to end Thugee activities, hanged nearly 4,000, and all but eradicated the cult. Thugees represented the last serious religion-inspired terrorist threat until the emergence of Islamic terrorism in the 1980s.

Political Roots

When rulers had absolute power, terrorist acts were viewed as one of the only means of gaining political rights. At times European states encouraged terrorist acts against their enemies. In the sixteenth century, Queen Elizabeth I empowered her naval leaders, including famed captains John Hawkins and Francis Drake, to attack the Spanish fleet and take prizes. These privateers would have been considered pirates had they not operated with government approval. American privateers attacked the British during the Revolutionary War and the War of 1812 and were considered heroes for their actions against the British Navy.

The term "terrorist" first became popular during the French Revolution. Use of the word "terrorism" began in 1795 in reference to the Reign of Terror initiated by the revolutionary government during which agents of the Committee of Public Safety and the National Convention were referred to as terrorists. In response, royalists and opponents of the Revolution employed terrorist tactics in resistance to the Revolutionists. The widespread use of the guillotine is an infamous reminder of the revolutionary violence; urban mobs demanded blood and many government officials and aristocrats were beheaded in gruesome public spectacles. From the fall of the Bastille on July 14, 1789, until July 1794, thousands suspected of counterrevolutionary activity were killed on the guillotine. Here again, the relative nature of political crime is documented: most victims of the French Reign of Terror were revolutionaries who had been denounced by rival factions, whereas thousands of the hated nobility lived in relative tranquility. The end of the terror was signaled by the death of its prime mover, Maximilien Robespierre, on July 28, 1794, as the result of a successful plot to end his rule. He was executed on the same guillotine to which he had sent almost 20,000 people.

In the hundred years following the French Revolution, terrorism continued to be a political tool around the world. Terrorist acts became the preferred method of political action for national groups in the early years of the twentieth century. In eastern Europe the Internal Macedonian Revolutionary Organization campaigned against the Turkish government, which controlled its homeland (Macedonia became part of the former Yugoslavia). Similarly, the protest of the Union of Death Society, or Black Hand, against the Austro-Hungarian Empire's control of Serbia led to the group's assassination of Archduke Franz Ferdinand, which started World War I. Russia was the scene of left-wing revolutionary activity, which killed the czar in 1917 and gave birth to the Marxist state.

After the war ended, the Treaty of Versailles restructured Europe and broke up the Austro-Hungarian Empire. The result was a hodgepodge of new nations controlled by majority ethnic groups. Self-determination was limited to European nations and ethnic groups and denied to others, especially the colonial possessions of the major European powers, creating bitterness and setting the stage for the long conflicts of the anticolonial period. The Irish Republican Army, established around 1916, steadily battled British forces from 1919 to 1923, culminating in the Republic of Ireland gaining independence.

Between the world wars, right-wing terrorism existed in Germany, Spain, and Italy. One source of tension, according to author Michael Kellogg, was the virulently anti-Communist exiles who fled Russia after the 1917 Revolution (called White Russians) and took up residence in Germany and other Western nations. According to Kellogg, between 1920 and 1923, Adolf Hitler was deeply influenced by the *Aufbau* (Reconstruction), the émigrés' organization. Members of the Aufbau allied with the Nazis to overthrow the legitimate German government and thwart German communists from seizing power. The White Russians deep-seated anti-Semitism may have inspired Hitler to go public with his campaign to kill the European Jews, prompting both the Holocaust and the invasion of Russia, which spelled the eventual doom of Hitler and National Socialism.[32]

During World War II, resistance to the occupying German troops was common throughout Europe. The Germans considered the resistors to be terrorists, but the rest of the world considered them heroes. Meanwhile, in Palestine, Jewish terrorist groups—the Haganah, Irgun, and Stern Gang, whose leaders included Menachem Begin, who later became Israel's prime minister—waged war against the British to force them to allow Jewish survivors of the Holocaust to settle in their traditional homeland. Today, of course, many of these alleged terrorists are considered freedom fighters who laid down their lives for a just cause.

After the war, Arab nationalists felt that they had been betrayed. Believing they were promised postwar independence, they were doubly disappointed; first when the French and British were given authority over their lands, and then especially when the British allowed Zionist immigration into Palestine in keeping with a promise contained in the Balfour Declaration.

Since the end of World War II, terrorism has accelerated its development into a major component of contemporary conflict. Primarily in use immediately after the war as a subordinate element of anticolonial insurgencies, it expanded beyond that role. In the service of various ideologies and aspirations, terrorism sometimes supplanted other forms of conflict completely. It became a far-reaching weapon capable of effects no less global than the intercontinental bomber or missile. It has also proven to be a significant tool of diplomacy and international power for states inclined to use it.

CONTEMPORARY FORMS OF TERRORISM

Today the term "terrorism" encompasses many different behaviors and goals. Some of the more common forms are briefly described here.

EXHIBIT 11.4

Breeding Ranches and Animal Liberation

A common misconception about fur "ranches" is that the animals do not suffer. This is entirely untrue. These animals suffer a life of misery and frustration, deprived of their most basic needs. They are kept in wire-mesh cages that are tiny, overcrowded, and filthy. Here they are malnourished, suffer contagious diseases, and endure severe stress.

On these farms, the animals are forced to forfeit their natural instincts. Beavers, who live in water in the wild, must exist on cement floors. Minks in the wild, too, spend much of their time in water, which keeps their salivation, respiration, and body temperature stable. They are also, by nature, solitary animals. However, on these farms, they are forced to live in close contact with other animals. This often leads to self-destructive behavior, such as pelt and tail biting. They often resort to cannibalism.

The methods used on these farms reflect not the interests and welfare of the animals but the furriers' primary interest—profit. The end of the suffering of these animals comes only with death, which, in order to preserve the quality of the fur, is inflicted with extreme cruelty and brutality. Engine exhaust is often pumped into a box of animals. This exhaust is not always lethal, and the animals sometimes writhe in pain as they are skinned alive. Another common execution practice, often used on larger animals, is anal electrocution. The farmers attach clamps to an animal's lips and insert metal rods into its anus. The animal is then electrocuted. Decompression chambers, neck snapping, and poison are also used.

Source: Animal Liberation Front, http://animalliberationfront.com/Practical/Fishing—Hunting/FishHuntFAQ.htm (accessed April 24, 2007).

level Spanish officials. In 1973, the group assassinated Admiral Luis Carrero Blanco, the heir apparent to Franco. Spanish King Juan Carlos was also the target of an unsuccessful plot. In addition, the group has targeted lower-level officials, journalists, and businessmen.

In the Middle East, terrorist activities have been linked to the Palestinians' desire to wrest their former homeland from Israel. At first, the Palestinian Liberation Organization (PLO), led by Yassir Arafat, directed terrorist activities against Israel. Now the group Hamas is perpetuating the conflict with Israel and is behind a spate of suicide bombings and terrorist attacks designed to elicit a sharp response from Israel and set back any chance for peace in the region. Hundreds on both sides of the conflict have been killed during terrorist attacks and reprisals. In Lebanon, Hezbollah, an Iranian supported group, is dedicated to fighting Israel and seizing control of the government. Their activities are described in Exhibit 11.5.

The Middle East is not the only source of nationalistic terrorism. The Chinese government has been trying to suppress separatist groups fighting for an independent state in the northwestern province of Xinjiang. The rebels are drawn from the region's Uyghur people, most of whom practice Sufi Islam, speak a Turkic language, and wish to set up a Muslim state called Eastern Turkistan. During the past decade the Uyghur separatists have organized demonstrations, bombings, and political assassinations. The province has witnessed more than 200

EXHIBIT 11.5

Hezbollah

Hezbollah (from the Arabic, meaning "party of God") is a Lebanese Shi'ite Islamist organization founded in 1982 in response to the presence of Israeli forces in southern Lebanon. At inception, its goals were to both drive Israeli troops out of Lebanon and to form a Shi'ite Islamic republic in Lebanon. Taking its inspiration from Iran, Hezbollah members follow a distinct version of Shia ideology developed by Ayatollah Ruhollah Khomeini, leader of the Islamic Revolution in Iran. Hezbollah has received arms and financial support from Iran, and some observers believe that it is actually a proxy Iranian paramilitary force. Hezbollah is anti-West and anti-Israel and has engaged in a series of terrorist actions including kidnappings, car bombings, and airline hijackings. Some of its most notable attacks directed at U.S. citizens and others include:

- The suicide truck bombings that killed more than 200 U.S. Marines at their barracks in Beirut, Lebanon, in 1983
- The 1985 hijacking of TWA flight 847
- Two major 1990s attacks in Argentina—the 1992 bombing of the Israeli Embassy (killing 29) and the 1994 bombing of a Jewish community center (killing 95)
- A July 2006 raid on a border post in northern Israel in which two Israeli soldiers were taken captive, an action which sparked an Israeli military incursion into Lebanon and the firing of rockets by Hezbollah across the Lebanese border into Israel.

In addition to its military/terror campaigns, Hezbollah has attempted to win the hearts and minds of the Lebanese Shi'ite community by providing social services and food to the population. It has also entered the political world, and its candidates have won seats in Lebanon's parliament.

The public face of Hezbollah is Hassan Nasrallah, the group's senior political leader. Originally a military commander, Nasrallah's military and religious training makes him a unique leader. His leadership of Hezbollah's resistance to the Israeli army in the summer of 2006 made him one of the most popular leaders in the Middle East.

Source: Council on Foreign Relations, Hezbollah, www.cfr.org/publication/9155/ (accessed June 13, 2007).

attacks since 1990, causing more than 150 deaths.[38] In Russia, Chechen terrorists have been intent on creating a free Chechen homeland and have been battling the Russian government to achieve their goal.

Retributive Terrorism

Some terrorist groups are not nationalist, political, or revolutionary organizations. They do not wish to set up their own homeland or topple a government but rather want to impose their social and religious code on others.[39] Retributive terrorists have a number of characteristics that are unique and separate them from guerrillas, revolutionaries, and other terrorists:[40]

- Violence is used as a method of influence, persuasion, or intimidation. The true target of the terrorist act extends far beyond those directly affected by the attack and is designed to lead to some desired behavior on the part of the larger target population or government.

■ Victims are usually selected for their maximum propaganda value, usually ensuring a high degree of media coverage. The message is that the target population had better comply with their demands because the terrorists are desperate enough to "do anything." Sometimes this may backfire if the attack results in the death of innocents, especially children, along with the symbolic targets

■ Unconventional military tactics are used, especially secrecy and surprise, as well as targeting civilians, including women and children. Because the goal is to inflict maximum horror, it makes sense to choose targets that contain the largest number of victims from all walks of life. The message: Everyone is a target; no one is safe.

Al-Qaeda is essentially a retributive terror organization. Rather than fighting for a homeland, its message is a call to take up a cause: there is a war of civilizations in which "Jews and Crusaders" want to destroy Islam and must therefore be defeated. Armed jihad is the individual obligation of every Muslim; terrorism and violence are appropriate methods for defeating even the strongest powers. One way of defeating the enemy is to attack their economy, which is the vulnerable "center of gravity" of Western nations.[41] These themes are preached in schools, on the Internet, and disseminated in books, cassette tapes, and pamphlets. Videotapes are distributed in which al-Qaeda's leaders expound on political topics, going as far as calling Western leaders liars and drunkards. As a result of this media strategy, al-Qaeda's messages have penetrated deeply into Muslim communities around the world, finding a sympathetic response among many Muslims who have a sense of helplessness both in the Arab world and in the Western Muslim diaspora. Al-Qaeda appears to have had an impact by offering a sense of empowerment to young men who feel lost in their adopted cultures.[42]

Today the retributive terrorists can be categorized into four main groups:

1. Al-Qaeda, including the group's strategy, ideology, operations, tactics, finances, changing character, and possible future.

2. Terrorist groups that have adopted al-Qaeda's worldview and concept of mass-casualty terrorist attacks, even if the groups are not formally part of al-Qaeda.

3. Violent Islamist and non-Islamist terrorist and insurgent groups without known links to al-Qaeda that threaten United States interests, friends, and allies. These include Hezbollah and Hamas, along with insurgencies in Iraq, the Philippines, and other countries.

4. The nexus between terrorism and organized crime, including the terrorists and insurgents that use criminal organizations and connections to finance their activities. Such actions also tend to weaken and corrupt political and social institutions.[43]

Osama bin Laden and al-Qaeda are the paradigm of the new retributive terrorist organization. His masterminding of the 9/11 bombing was not designed to restore his homeland or bring about a new political state but to have his personal value structure adopted by Muslim nations. His attack may have been designed to create a military invasion of Afghanistan, which he hoped to exploit for his particular brand of revolution, a plan that has succeeded. According to Michael Scott Doran, bin Laden believed his acts would reach the audience that concerned him the most: the *umma*, or universal Islamic community.[44] The media would show Americans killing innocent civilians in Afghanistan, and the *umma* would find it shocking how Americans nonchalantly caused Muslims to suffer and die. The ensuing outrage would open a chasm between the Muslim population of the Middle East and the ruling governments in states such as Saudi Arabia, which were allied with the West. On October 7, 2001, bin Laden made a broadcast in which he said that the Americans and the British "have divided the entire world into two regions—one of faith, where there is no hypocrisy, and another of infidelity, from which we hope God will protect us."

State-Sponsored Terrorism

State-sponsored terrorism occurs when a repressive government regime forces its citizens into obedience, oppresses minorities, and stifles political dissent. Death squads and the use of government troops to destroy political opposition parties are often associated with political terrorism. Much of what we know about state-sponsored terrorism comes from the efforts of human rights groups such as London-based Amnesty International, whose research shows that tens of thousands of people continue to become victims of security operations that result in disappearances and executions. Political prisoners are now being tortured in about 100 countries, people have disappeared or are being held in secret detention in about 20 countries, and government-sponsored death squads have been operating in more than 35 countries. Countries known for encouraging violent control of dissidents include Brazil, Colombia, Guatemala, Honduras, Peru, Iraq, and the Sudan.

State-sponsored terrorism became a world issue when South and Central American dictatorships in the 1970s and 1980s unleashed state violence against political dissidents through forced disappearance, political imprisonment, torture, blacklisting, and massive exile. The region-wide state repression in this period emerged in response to the rise of the 1960s radical movements, which demanded public reforms and programs to help the lower classes in urban areas and agricultural workers in the countryside. Local authoritarian governments, which used repression to take control of radical political groups, were given financial support by the economic elites who dominated Latin American politics and were fearful of a socialist revolution.[45]

Cult Terrorism

In 1995 members of Aum Shinrikyo, a radical religious cult, set off poison gas in a Tokyo subway, killing 12 and injuring more than 3,000. Cult members found modern society too complex to understand, with few clear-cut goals and values.[46]

Some cults like Aum Shinrikyo may be classified as terror groups because their leaders demand that followers prove their loyalty through violence or intimidation.[47] These destructive cults are willing to have members commit violence, including murder. Members typically follow a charismatic leader who may be viewed as having godlike powers or even being the reincarnation of an important religious figure. The leader and his or her lieutenants commonly enforce loyalty by severe discipline and by physically preventing members from leaving the group. They may go through doomsday drills and maintain a siege mentality, fearing attacks from the government. It is not uncommon for cult terror groups to begin stockpiling weapons and building defensive barricades. The cult may openly or tacitly endorse individual killings or mass murder, which may be accompanied by mass suicide, either as a further symbolic instrument of their cause or, more commonly, as what they perceive to be justified self-defense, a last resort when the hostile world starts closing in and the leader's authority is threatened.[48]

Criminal Terrorism

Sometimes terrorist groups become involved in common-law crimes such as drug dealing and kidnapping, even selling nuclear materials. According to terrorism expert Chris Dishman, these illegal activities may on occasion become so profitable that they replace the group's original focus. Burmese insurgents continue to actively cultivate, refine, and traffic opium and heroin out of the Golden Triangle (the border between Myanmar [Burma], Thailand, and Laos), and some have even moved into the methamphetamine market.

In December 2001, six men were arrested by Russian security forces as they were making a deal for weapons-grade uranium. Some of the men were members of the Balashikha criminal gang, and they were in possession of two pounds of top-grade radioactive material, which can be used to build weapons. They were asking $30,000 for the deadly merchandise.[49] Since 1990 there have been a half-dozen cases involving theft and transportation of nuclear material and other cases involving people who offered to sell agents material not yet in their possession. These are the known cases; it is impossible to know if client states have already purchased enriched uranium or plutonium.

In some cases there has been close cooperation between organized criminal groups and guerillas. In other instances the relationship is more superficial. For example, the Revolutionary Armed Forces of Colombia (FARC) imposes a tax on Colombian drug producers, but evidence indicates that the group cooperates with Colombia's top drug barons in running the trade. In some instances, the line between being a terrorist organization with political support and vast resources and being an organized criminal group engaging in illicit activities for profit becomes blurred. What appears to be a politically motivated action, such as the kidnapping of a government official for ransom, may turn out to be merely a crime for profit.[50]

www Check out the **Animal Liberation Front** website via www.thomsonedu.com/criminaljustice/siegel.

HOW ARE TERROR GROUPS ORGANIZED?

Terror groups tend to be networked or hierarchical. Newer terrorist organizations tend to be formed as networks, loosely organized groups located in different parts of the city, state, or country (or world) that share a common theme or purpose, but have a diverse leadership and command structure and are only in intermittent communication with one another. While there may be a variety of antigovernment groups operating in the United States there is little evidence that they share a single command structure or organizational fabric. These groups have few resources and little experience, so it is critical that they operate under cover and with as little public exposure as possible.

When needed, networked groups can pull factions together for larger scale operations, such as an attack on a military headquarters, or conversely, they can readily splinter off into smaller groups to avoid detection when a counterterrorism operation is underway. The advent of the Internet has significantly improved communications among networked terror groups.

As terror organizations evolve and expand they may eventually develop a hierarchical organization with a commander at the top of the organization, captains, local area leaders, and so on. Ideological and religious groups tend to gravitate toward this model since a common creed/dogma controls their operations and a singular leader may be needed to define and disseminate group principles and maintain discipline. In a hierarchical model, the leader has the power to increase or decrease levels of violence for political purposes (i.e., they may order their followers to initiate a bombing campaign to influence an election). Schools may be off limits so that the population is not antagonized, or schools may become a target to show that the government cannot protect their children.

Terror Cells Regardless of what organizational structure is used, most groups subdivide their affiliates into terror cells for both organizational and security purposes. To enhance security, each cell may be functionally independent so that each member has little knowledge of other cells, their members, locations, and so on. However, individual cell members provide emotional support to one another and maintain loyalty and dedication. Because only the cell leader knows how to communicate with other cells and/or a central command, capture of one cell does not then compromise other group members.

Terrorist cell formations may be based on location, employment, or family membership. Some are formed on the basis of function: some are fighters, others political organizers. The number of cells and their composition depend on the size of the terrorist group: local or national groups will have fewer cells than international terrorist groups that may operate in several countries such as the al-Qaeda group.

WHAT MOTIVATES THE TERRORIST?

Before terrorism can be effectively fought, controlled, and eradicated, it is important to understand something about the kind of people who become terrorists, what motivates their behavior, and how their ideas are formed. Unfortunately, this is not an easy task. Terrorism researchers have generally concluded that there is no single personality trait or behavior pattern that distinguishes the majority of terrorists or sets them apart so they can be easily identified and apprehended. Some seem truly disturbed whereas many others have not suffered long-term mental illness or displayed sociopathic traits and/or tendencies; if that were so, bizarre or violent behavior in their early childhood would be a giveaway.[51] As such, there have been a number of competing visions of why terrorists engage in criminal activities such as bombings, shootings, and kidnappings to achieve a political end. Four stand out.

Psychological View

While not all terrorists suffer from psychological deficits, enough do so that the typical terrorist can be described as an emotionally disturbed individual who acts out his or her psychoses within the confines of violent groups. According to this view, terrorist violence is not so much a political instrument as an end in itself; it is the result of compulsion or psychopathology. Terrorists do what they do because of garden variety emotional problems, including but not limited to self-destructive urges and disturbed emotions combined with problems with authority.[52] As terrorism expert Jerrold M. Post puts it, "Political terrorists are driven to commit acts of violence as a consequence of psychological forces, and . . . their special psychology is constructed to rationalize acts they are psychologically compelled to commit."[53]

The view that terrorists suffer psychological abnormality is quite controversial and some critics suggest that it is spurious. It is also possible that engaging in stressful terrorist activity results in the development of mental disorders and not vice versa.[54] Charles Ruby reviewed the literature on the psychology of terrorists and found little evidence that terrorists are psychologically dysfunctional or pathological. Ruby claims that terrorism is a form of politically motivated violence that is carried out by rational, lucid people who have valid motives; if they had more resources, terrorists would be military officers.[55]

Socialization View

According to this view, if terrorists suffer psychological deficiencies it is because they have been poorly and improperly socialized.[56] Many have been raised to hate their opponents and learn at an early age that they have been victimized by some oppressor. Often, this socialization occurs in dysfunctional families in which the father was absent or, even if present, was a distant and cold figure.[57] Ironically, many terrorists appear to be educated members of the upper class. Osama bin Laden was a multimillionaire and at least some of his followers were highly educated and trained. The acts of the modern terrorist—using the Internet; organizing logistically complex and expensive assaults; and writing and disseminating formal critiques, manifestos, and theories—require the training and education of the social elite, not the poor and oppressed.

Terrorists report that they were estranged from their fathers, whom they viewed as economically, socially, or politically weak and ineffective. Because of this family estrangement the budding terrorist may have been swayed to join a group or cult by a charismatic leader who serves as an alternative father figure. In this sense, terror groups, similar to what happens in urban street gangs, provide a substitute family-like environment, which can nurture a heretofore emotionally underprivileged youth.

Ideological View

Another view is that terrorists hold extreme ideological beliefs that prompt their behavior. At first they have heightened perceptions of oppressive conditions, believing that they are being victimized by some group or government. Once these potential terrorists recognize that these conditions can be changed by an active governmental reform effort that has not happened, they conclude that they must resort to violence to encourage change. The violence need not be aimed at a specific goal. Rather, terror tactics must help set in motion a series of events that enlists others in the cause and leads to long-term change. "Successful" terrorists believe that their "self-sacrifice" outweighs the guilt created by harming innocent people. Terrorism, therefore, requires violence without guilt; the cause justifies the violence.

Alienation View

Terrorist operatives are not poor or lacking in education. And yet lack of economic opportunity and recessionary economies are positively correlated with terrorism.[58] Terrorists may be motivated by feelings of alienation and failure to maintain the tools to compete in a post-technological society. Many are relatively "ordinary" people who, alienated from modern society, believe that a suicide mission will cleanse them from the corruption of the modern world.[59]

Explaining State Terrorism

How can state sponsored terror be explained? After all, these violent acts are not directed at a foreign government or overseas adversaries but against natives of one's own country. In her book *Reigns of Terror*, Patricia Marchak finds that people willing to kill or maim their fellow countrymen are likely to be highly susceptible to unquestioning submission to authority. They are conformists who want to be part of the central group and who are quite willing to be part of a state regime. They are vulnerable to ideology that dehumanizes their targets and can utilize propaganda to distance themselves psychologically from those they are terrorizing.[60] So the Nazis had little trouble recruiting people to carry out horrific acts during the Holocaust because many

Germans wanted to be part of the popular social/political movement and were easily indoctrinated by the Nazi propaganda that branded Jews as subhuman. Stalin was able to carry out his reign of terror in Russia because his victims were viewed as state enemies who were trying to undermine the Communist regime. How can these tendencies be neutralized? Marchak sees little benefit to international intervention which results in after-the-fact punishment of the perpetrators, a course of action that was attempted in the former Yugoslavia after death squads had performed "ethnic cleansing" of undesirables. Instead she argues for a prevention strategy that involves international aid and economic development by industrialized nations to those in the third world that are on the verge of becoming collapsed states, the construction of social welfare systems, and the acceptance of international legal norms and standards of human rights.[61]

RESPONSE TO TERRORISM

After the 9/11 attacks, agencies of the criminal justice system began to focus their attention on combating the threat of terror. Even local police agencies created anti-terror programs designed to protect their communities from the threat of attack. How should the nation best prepare itself to thwart potential attacks? The National Commission on Terrorist Attacks Upon the United States (also known as the 9/11 Commission), an independent, bipartisan commission, was created in late 2002 and given the mission of preparing an in-depth report of the events leading up to the 9/11 attacks. Part of their goal was to create a comprehensive plan to ensure that no further attacks of that magnitude take place.

To monitor the more than 500 million people who cross into America, the commission recommended that a single agency should be created to screen border crossings. They also recommended creation of an investigative agency to monitor all aliens in the United States and to gather intelligence on the way terrorists travel across borders. The commission suggested that people who wanted passports be tagged with biometric measures to make them easily identifiable.

In response to the commission report, a **Director of National Intelligence (DNI)** was created and charged with coordinating data from the nation's primary intelligence-gathering agencies. The DNI serves as the principal intelligence adviser to the president and the statutory intelligence advisor to the National Security Council.

On February 17, 2005, President George W. Bush named U.S. Ambassador to Iraq John Negroponte to be the first person to hold the post; he was confirmed on April 21, 2005; the current director is Mike McConnell, a former admiral and Director of the National Security Agency.

Among the agencies reporting to the DNI is the staff of the newly created National Counterterrorism Center (NCTC), which is staffed by terrorism experts from the CIA, FBI, and the Pentagon; the Privacy and Civil Liberties Board; and the National Counterproliferation Center. The NCTC serves as the primary organization in the United States government for analyzing and integrating all intelligence possessed or acquired by the government pertaining to terrorism and counterterrorism, excepting purely domestic counterterrorism information.

While the 9/11 Commission report outlines what has already been done, what has not been done, and what needs to be done, agencies of the justice system have begun to respond to the challenge.

Fighting Terrorism with Law Enforcement

In the aftermath of the September 11, 2001, attacks, even before the 9/11 Commission made its report, it became obvious that the nation was not prepared to deal adequately with the threat of terrorism. One reason is the very nature of American society. Because we live in a free and open nation, it is extremely difficult to seal the borders and prevent the entry of terrorist groups. In his book *Nuclear Terrorism*, Graham Allison, an expert on nuclear weapons and national security, describes the almost superhuman effort it would take to seal the nation's borders from nuclear attack. Every day, 30,000 trucks, 6,500 rail cars, and 140 ships deliver more than 50,000 cargo containers into the United States. And while fewer than 5 percent ever get screened, those that do are given inspections using external detectors, which may not detect nuclear weapons or fissile material. The potential for terrorists to obtain bombs is significant: there are approximately 130 nuclear research reactors in 40 countries. Two dozen of these have enough highly enriched uranium for one or more nuclear bombs. If terrorists can get their hands on fissile material from these reactors, they could build a crude but working nuclear bomb within a year. But they may not have to build their own bomb. They may be able to purchase an intact device on the black market. Russia alone has thousands of nuclear warheads and material for many thousands of additional weapons; all of these remain vulnerable to theft. Terrorists may also be able to buy the knowledge to construct bombs. In one well-known incident, Pakistan's leading nuclear scientist, A. Q. Khan, sold comprehensive "nuclear starter kits" that included advanced centrifuge components, blueprints for nuclear warheads, uranium samples in quantities sufficient to make a small bomb, and even provided personal consulting services to assist nuclear development.[62]

Recognizing this problem, law enforcement agencies around the country began to realign their resources to combat future terrorist attacks. In response to 9/11, law enforcement agencies undertook a number of steps: increasing the number of personnel engaged in emergency response planning; updating response plans for chemical, biological, or radiological attacks; and reallocating internal resources or increasing departmental spending to focus on terrorism preparedness.[63] Actions continue to be taken on the federal, state, and local levels.

Federal Law Enforcement One of the most significant changes has been a realignment of the Federal Bureau of Investigation (FBI), the federal government's main law enforcement agency. The FBI has already announced a reformulation of its priorities, making protecting the United States from terrorist attack its number one commitment. It is now charged with coordinating intelligence collection with the Border Patrol, Secret Service, and the CIA. The FBI must also work with and share intelligence with the National Counterterrorism Center (NCTC).

To carry out its newly formulated mission, the FBI is expanding its force of agents. In addition to recruiting candidates with the traditional background in law enforcement, law, and accounting, the Bureau is concentrating on hiring agents with scientific and technological skills as well as foreign-language proficiency in priority areas such as Arabic, Farsi, Pashtun, Urdu, all dialects of Chinese, Japanese, Korean, Russian, Spanish, and Vietnamese, and with other priority backgrounds such as foreign counterintelligence, counterterrorism, and military intelligence. Besides helping in counterterrorism activities, these agents will staff the Cyber Division, which was created in 2001 to coordinate, oversee, and facilitate FBI investigations in which the Internet, online services, and computer systems and networks are the principal instruments or targets of terrorists.

connections

The FBI and its duties will be discussed more fully in Chapter 17 along with other federal law enforcement agencies.

Department of Homeland Security (DHS) Soon after the 2001 attack, President George W. Bush proposed the creation of a new cabinet-level agency called the Department of Homeland Security (DHS) and assigned it the following mission:

▌ Preventing terrorist attacks within the United States

▌ Reducing America's vulnerability to terrorism

▌ Minimizing the damage and recovering from attacks that do occur

On November 19, 2002, Congress passed legislation authorizing the creation of the DHS and assigned it the mission of providing intelligence analysis and infrastructure protection, strengthening the borders, improving the use of science and technology to counter weapons of mass destruction, and creating a comprehensive response and recovery division.

Rather than work from ground up, the DHS combined a number of existing agencies into a superagency that carried out the following missions:

▌ *Border and transportation security.* The Department of Homeland Security is responsible for securing our nation's borders and transportation systems, which include 350 ports of entry. The department manages who and what enters the country, and works to prevent the entry of terrorists and the instruments of terrorism while simultaneously ensuring the speedy flow of legitimate traffic. The DHS also is in charge of securing territorial waters, including ports and waterways.

▌ *Emergency preparedness and response.* The Department of Homeland Security ensures the preparedness of emergency response professionals, provides the federal government's response, and aids America's recovery from terrorist attacks and natural disasters. The department is responsible for reducing the loss of life and property and protecting institutions from all types of hazards through an emergency management program of preparedness, mitigation, response, and recovery.

▌ *Chemical, biological, radiological, and nuclear countermeasures.* The department leads the federal government's efforts in preparing for and responding to the full range of terrorist threats involving weapons of mass destruction. To do this, the department sets national policy and establishes guidelines for state and local governments. It directs exercises and drills for federal, state, and local chemical, biological, radiological, and nuclear (CBRN) response teams and plans. The department is assigned to prevent the importation of nuclear weapons and material.

▌ *Information analysis and infrastructure protection.* The department analyzes information from multiple available sources, including the CIA and FBI, in order to assess the dangers facing the nation. It also analyzes law enforcement and intelligence information.[64]

The DHS has numerous and varied duties. It is responsible for port security and transportation systems and manages airport security with its Transportation Security Administration (TSA). It has its own intelligence section, and it covers every special event in the United States including political conventions.

State Law Enforcement Efforts to Combat Terrorism In the wake of the 9/11 attacks, a number of states have beefed up their intelligence-gathering capabilities and aimed them directly at homeland security. California has introduced the California Anti-Terrorism Information Center (CATIC), a statewide intelligence system designed to combat terrorism. It divides the state into operational zones, and links federal, state, and local information services in one system. Trained intelligence analysts operate within civil rights guidelines and utilize information in a secure communications system; information is analyzed daily.[65] CATIC combines machine-intelligence with information coming from a variety of police agencies. The information is correlated and organized by analysts looking for trends. Rather than simply operating as an information-gathering unit, CATIC is a synthesizing process. It combines open-source public information with data on criminal trends and possible terrorist activities. Processed intelligence is designed to produce threat assessments for each area and to project trends outside the jurisdiction. The CATIC system attempts to process multiple sources of information to predict threats. By centralizing the collection and analytical sections of a statewide system, California's Department of Justice may have developed a method for moving offensively against terrorism.

Local Law Enforcement Federal and state law enforcement agencies are not alone in responding to the threat of terrorism. And, of course, nowhere is the threat of terrorism being taken more seriously than in New York City, one of the main targets of the 9/11 attacks, which has established a new Counterterrorism Bureau.[66] Teams within the bureau have been trained to examine potential targets in the city and are now attempting to insulate them from possible attack. Viewed as prime targets are the city's

29. Terrorism Research, "Differences between Terrorism and Insurgency," www.terrorismresearch.com/insurgency/ (accessed July 23, 2007).

30. Walter Laqueur, *The New Terrorism: Fanaticism and the Arms of Mass Destruction Terrorism and History* (New York: Oxford University Press, 1999).

31. This section relies heavily on Friedlander, *Terrorism*, pp. 8–20.

32. Michael Kellogg, *The Russian Roots of Nazism: White Russians and the Making of National Socialism, 1917–1945* (New York: Cambridge University Press, 2005).

33. Associated Press, "Malaysia Arrests Five Militants," *New York Times*, 15 October 2002, p. A2.

34. Jocelyn Parker, "Vehicles Burn at Dealership: SUV Attacks Turn Violent," *Detroit Free Press*, 23 August 2003, p. 1.

35. "Brutal Elves in the Woods," *The Economist* 359 (2001): 28–30.

36. Fiona Proffitt, "Costs of Animal Rights Terror," *Science* 304 (2004): 1,731–1,739.

37. Department of Justice, "Eleven Defendants Indicted on Domestic Terrorism Charges: Group Allegedly Responsible for Series of Arsons in Western States, Acting on Behalf of Extremist Movements," January 20, 2006, www.usdoj.gov/opa/pr/2006/January/06_crm_030.html (accessed July 23, 2007).

38. Chung Chien-Peng, "China's War on Terror," *Foreign Affairs* 81 (2002): 8–13.

39. Angel Rabasa, Peter Chalk, Kim Cragin, Sara A. Daly, Heather S. Gregg, Theodore W. Karasik, Kevin A. O'Brien, and William Rosenau, *Beyond al-Qaeda, Part 1, The Global Jihadist Movement* and *Part 2, The Outer Rings of the Terrorist Universe* (Santa Monica, CA: Rand Corporation, 2006).

40. Lawrence Miller, "The Terrorist Mind: A Psychological and Political Analysis, Part I," *International Journal of Offender Therapy and Comparative Criminology* 50 (2006): 121–138.

41. Rabasa et al., *Beyond al-Qaeda: The Global Jihadist Movement*.

42. Ibid.

43. Mark Mazzetti and David Rohde, "Al Qaeda Chiefs Are Seen to Regain Power," *New York Times*, 19 February 2007, p.1; Sanjeev Gupta, Benedict Clements, Rina Bhattacharya, and Shamit Chakravarti, "Fiscal Consequences of Armed Conflict and Terrorism in Low- and Middle-Income Countries," *European Journal of Political Economy* 20 (2004): 403–421.

44. Michael Scott Doran, "Somebody Else's Civil War," *Foreign Affairs* 81 (January–February 2002): 22–25.

45. Gabriela Fried, "Piecing Memories Together after State Terror and Policies of Oblivion in Uruguay: The Female Political Prisoner's Testimonial Project (1997–2004)," *Social Identities* 12 (2006): 543–562.

46. Haruki Murakami, *Underground* (New York: Vintage Books, 2001).

47. Lawrence Miller, "The Terrorist Mind: A Psychological and Political Analysis, Part II," *International Journal of Offender Therapy and Comparative Criminology* 50 (2006): 255–268.

48. Ibid.

49. Jeffrey Kluger, "The Nuke Pipeline: The Trade in Nuclear Contraband Is Approaching Critical Mass. Can We Turn Off the Spigot?" *Time*, 17 December 2001, p. 40.

50. Chris Dishman, "Terrorism, Crime, and Transformation," *Studies in Conflict and Terrorism* 24 (2001): 43–56.

51. Stephen J. Morgan, *The Mind of a Terrorist Fundamentalist: The Psychology of Terror Cults* (Awe-Struck E-Books, 2001); Martha Crenshaw, "The Psychology of Terrorism: An Agenda for the 21st Century," *Political Psychology*, vol. 21, no. 2, June 2000, 405–420.

52. Andrew Silke, "Courage in Dark Places: Reflections on Terrorist Psychology," *Social Research* 71 (2004): 177–198.

53. Jerrold M. Post, "Terrorist Psycho-Logic: Terrorist Behavior as a Product of Psychological Forces," in *Origins of Terrorism: Psychologies, Ideologies Theologies, States of Mind*, ed. Walter Reich (Cambridge: Cambridge University Press, 1990), p. 12.

54. David Weatherston and Jonathan Moran, "Terrorism and Mental Illness: Is There a Relationship?" *International Journal of Offender Therapy and Comparative Criminology* 47 (2003): 698–711.

55. Charles Ruby, "Are Terrorists Mentally Deranged?" *Analyses of Social Issues and Public Policy* 2 (2002): 15–26.

56. Jerrold Post, "When Hatred Is Bred in the Bone: Psycho-cultural Foundations of Contemporary Terrorism," *Political Psychology* 25 (2005): 615–637.

57. This section leans heavily on Anthony Stahelski, "Terrorists Are Made, Not Born: Creating Terrorists Using Social Psychological Conditioning," *Journal of Homeland Security*, March 2004.

58. Ethan Bueno de Mesquita, "The Quality of Terror," *American Journal of Political Science* 49 (2005): 515–530.

59. Murakami, *Underground*.

60. Patricia Marchak, *Reigns of Terror* (Montreal: McGill-Queen's University Press, 2003).

61. Ibid., pp. 153–155.

62. Graham Allison, *Nuclear Terrorism: The Ultimate Preventable Catastrophe* (New York: Times Books, 2004)

63. Rand Corporation, "How Prepared Are State and Local Law Enforcement for Terrorism?" www.rand.org/publications/RB/RB9093/ (accessed July 23, 2007).

64. White House press release, November 11, 2002, www.whitehouse.gov/news/releases/2002/11/20021119–4.html (accessed July 23, 2007). The section on homeland security relies heavily on "The Department of Homeland Security," www.whitehouse.gov/infocus/homeland/ (accessed July 23, 2007).

65. California Anti-Terrorism Information Center (CATIC), www.ag.ca.gov/antiterrorism/ (accessed July 23, 2007).

66. William K. Rashbaum, "Terror Makes All the World a Beat for New York Police," *New York Times*, 15 July 2002, B1; Al Baker, "Leader Sees New York Police in Vanguard of Terror Fight," *New York Times*, 6 August 2002, A2; Stephen Flynn, "America the Vulnerable," *Foreign Affairs* 81 (January–February 2002): 60.

67. U.S. House of Representatives Committee on the Judiciary, http://judiciary.house.gov/Printshop.aspx?Section=232 (accessed July 23, 2007).

68. Rabasa et al., *Beyond al-Qaeda*, Parts 1 and 2.

Property Crime

CHAPTER OUTLINE

A Brief History of Theft
Theft in the Nineteenth Century: Train Robbery and Safecracking

Contemporary Theft
Occasional Thieves
Professional Thieves
Sutherland's Professional Criminal
The Professional Fence

The Criminological Enterprise: Confessions of a Dying Thief

The Occasional Fence

Larceny/Theft
Larceny Today

PROFILES IN CRIME: Invasion of the Body Snatchers

Shoplifting
Bad Checks
Credit Card Theft

PROFILES IN CRIME: Credit Card Con

Auto Theft
False Pretenses or Fraud
Confidence Games
Embezzlement

Burglary
The Nature and Extent of Burglary
Planning to Burgle
Commercial Burglary

Race, Culture, Gender, and Criminology:
Are There Gender Differences in Burglary?

Careers in Burglary

Arson
The Juvenile Fire Starter
Professional Arson

CHAPTER OBJECTIVES

1. Be familiar with the history of theft offenses
2. Recognize the differences between professional and amateur thieves
3. Know the similarities and differences between the various types of larceny
4. Understand the different forms of shoplifting
5. Be able to discuss the concept of fraud
6. Know what is meant by a confidence game
7. Understand what it means to burgle a home
8. Know what it takes to be a good burglar
9. Understand the concept of arson

© AP Images/Bob Child

For seven years, dozens of rare maps—often hundreds of years old— were mysteriously disappearing from prestigious libraries around the world. The thefts went unsolved—and in most cases, undetected—until one morning when the head of public services for Yale University's Beinecke Rare Book and Manuscript Library in New Haven, Connecticut, happened to notice an X-Acto knife blade on the floor in the rare documents room. Spotting a man in the stacks, she hurriedly got his name from the library's sign-in register. He was Edward Forbes Smiley III, a well-known rare maps dealer. Yale police conducted video surveillance, and when Smiley left the library, he was followed and arrested at the Yale Center for the British Arts. A search of Smiley's personal property revealed seven rare maps worth more than $700,000. One was a 1614 map that had been removed from the book Advertisements for the Unexperienced Planters of New England, or Anywhere *by Captain John Smith, founder of Jamestown. Another was a "Septentrio vniuersalis descripto" authored by Richard Hakluyt (1552–1616) that had a comparable value of $500,000.*

When interrogated by federal law enforcement agents Smiley admitted stealing and selling 97 rare maps from numerous collections worldwide, worth an estimated $3 million. He was able to lead investigators to most of the dealers and collectors who originally purchased them, but precise identification proved difficult. Many of the libraries weren't even aware they were missing any items since they didn't inventory their books very often. After much painstaking work, 86 of the maps were recovered. On June 29, 2006, Smiley pleaded guilty to numerous charges of art theft. Standing before Judge Janet Bond Arterton, Smiley said he "knowingly and willfully" removed five maps from the Beinecke Library. "I concealed them in my briefcase with the intention of removing them from the library," he said, adding that he knew at the time that his actions were wrong. "I very much regret my actions and apologize to the court and to all the institutions that have been harmed by my conduct." On September 27, 2006, he was sentenced to 42 months in prison and ordered to pay nearly $2 million in restitution. The court left the issue of restitution open in case more maps are found and identified.[1]

Though average citizens may be puzzled and enraged by violent crimes, believing them to be both senseless and cruel, they often view economic crimes with a great deal more ambivalence. Society generally disapproves of crimes involving theft and corruption, but the public seems quite tolerant of the "gentleman bandit," such as Edward Forbes Smiley III, even to the point of admiring such figures. They pop up as characters in popular myths and legends—such as the famed English outlaw Robin Hood—and in films such as *Ocean's Eleven* (2001) and *Ocean's Twelve* (2004), and *Ocean's Thirteen* (2007) in which a suave George Clooney and roguish Brad Pitt lead a band of thieves who loot hundreds of millions of dollars from casinos, galleries, and so on.

How can such ambivalence toward thievery be explained? For one thing, if self-report surveys are accurate, national tolerance toward economic criminals may be prompted by the fact that almost every U.S. citizen has at some time been involved in economic crime. Even those among us who would never consider ourselves lawbreakers may have at one time engaged in petty theft, cheated on our income tax, stolen a textbook from a college bookstore, or pilfered from our place of employment. Consequently, it may be difficult for society to condemn economic criminals without feeling hypocritical.

People may also be somewhat more tolerant of economic crimes because they never seem to seriously hurt anyone— banks are insured, large businesses pass along losses to consumers, stolen cars can be easily replaced and, in most cases, are insured. The true pain of economic crime often goes unappreciated. Convicted offenders, especially businesspeople who commit white-collar crimes involving millions of dollars, often are punished rather lightly.

This chapter is the first of two that reviews the nature and extent of economic crime in the United States. It is divided into two principal sections. The first deals with the concept of professional crime and focuses on different types of professional criminals, including the fence, a buyer and seller of stolen merchandise. The chapter then turns to a discussion of common theft-related offenses or street crime. Included within these general offense categories are such common crimes as auto theft, shoplifting, and credit card fraud. Next, the chapter discusses a more serious form of theft, burglary, which involves forcible entry into a person's home or place of work for the purpose of theft. Finally, the crime of arson is discussed briefly. In Chapter 13 attention will be given to white-collar crimes and economic crimes that involve organizations devoted to criminal enterprise.

A BRIEF HISTORY OF THEFT

As a group, economic crime can be defined as acts in violation of the criminal law designed to bring financial reward to an offender. In U.S. society, the range and scope of criminal activity motivated by financial gain is tremendous: self-report studies show that property crime is widespread among the young in every social class. National surveys of criminal behavior indicate that millions of personal and household thefts occur annually, including auto thefts, shoplifting incidents, embezzlements, burglaries, and larcenies.

Theft, however, is not a phenomenon unique to modern times; the theft of personal property has been known throughout recorded history. The Crusades of the eleventh century inspired peasants and downtrodden noblemen to leave the shelter of their estates to prey on passing pilgrims.[2] Crusaders felt it within their rights to appropriate the possessions of any infidels—Greeks, Jews, or Muslims—they happened to encounter during their travels.

By the thirteenth century, returning pilgrims, not content to live as serfs on feudal estates, gathered in the forests of England and the Continent to poach on game that was the rightful property of their lord or king and, when possible, to steal from passing strangers. By the fourteenth century, many such highwaymen and poachers were full-time livestock thieves, stealing great numbers of cattle and sheep.[3] The fifteenth and sixteenth centuries brought hostilities between England and France in what has come to be known as the Hundred Years' War. Foreign mercenary troops fighting for both sides roamed the countryside; loot and pillage were viewed as a rightful part of their pay. As cities developed and a permanent class of propertyless urban poor was established,[4] theft became more professional. By the eighteenth century, three separate groups of property criminals were active: skilled thieves, smugglers, and poachers.

- **Skilled thieves** typically worked in the larger cities, such as London and Paris. This group included pickpockets, forgers, and counterfeiters, who operated freely. They congregated in flash houses—public meeting places, often taverns, that served as headquarters for gangs. Here, deals were made, crimes were plotted, and the sale of stolen goods was negotiated.[5]

- **Smugglers** were the second group of thieves. They moved freely in sparsely populated areas and transported goods, such as spirits, gems, gold, and spices, without bothering to pay tax or duty.

- **Poachers**, the third type of thief, typically lived in the country and supplemented their diet and income with game that belonged to a landlord.

Professional thieves in the larger cities had banded together into gangs to protect themselves, increase the scope of their activities, and help dispose of stolen goods. Jack Wild, perhaps London's most famous thief, perfected the process of buying and selling stolen goods and gave himself the title of Thief-Taker General of Great Britain and Ireland. Before he was hanged, Wild controlled numerous gangs and dealt harshly with any thief who violated his strict code of conduct.[6] During this period, individual theft-related crimes began to be defined by the common law. The most important of these categories are still used today.

When compliance fails, and businesspeople violate the law, the institution rather than its individual employees are punished. In 2006, for example, employees of the Longley Jones real estate management company illegally removed and disposed of asbestos in 98 buildings they owned or managed. Longley Jones was charged with one count of conspiracy and seven counts of violating the Clean Air Act. The sentence: the company paid a $3,200 special assessment and a $4 million fine, $3 million of which was suspended if it cleaned up the asbestos at various Longley Jones facilities.[101] Compliance rather than punishment is the goal of the court order.

Another compliance approach is to force corporate boards to police themselves and take more oversight responsibility. In the wake of the Enron and WorldCom debacles, the federal government enacted the Sarbanes-Oxley (SOX) legislation in 2002 to combat fraud and abuse in publicly traded companies.[102] This law limits the nonaudit services auditing firms can perform for publicly traded companies in order to make sure accounting firms do not fraudulently collude with corporate officers; as well, it places greater responsibilities on boards to preserve an organization's integrity and reputation, primarily for U.S. publicly traded companies. It also penalizes any attempts to alter or falsify company records in order to delude shareholders:

> Sec. 802(a) Whoever knowingly alters, destroys, mutilates, conceals, covers up, falsifies, or makes a false entry in any record, document, or tangible object with the intent to impede, obstruct, or influence the investigation or proper administration of any matter within the jurisdiction of any department or agency of the United States or any case filed under title 11, or in relation to or contemplation of any such matter or case, shall be fined under this title, imprisoned not more than 20 years, or both.

In sum, compliance strategies attempt to create a marketplace incentive to obey the law. Compliance strategies avoid punishing, stigmatizing, and shaming businesspeople by focusing on the act, rather than the actor, in white-collar crime.[103]

Deterrence Strategies Some criminologists say that the punishment of white-collar crimes should include a retributive component similar to that used in common-law crimes. White-collar crimes, after all, are immoral activities that have harmed social values and deserve commensurate punishment.[104] Even the largest fines and penalties are no more than a slap on the wrist to multibillion-dollar companies. Corporations can get around economic sanctions by moving their rule-violating activities overseas, where legal controls over injurious corporate activities are lax or nonexistent.[105] They argue that the only way to limit white-collar crime is to deter potential offenders through fear of punishment.

Deterrence strategies involve detecting criminal violations, determining who is responsible, and penalizing the offenders to deter future violations.[106] Deterrence systems are oriented toward apprehending violators and punishing them rather than creating conditions that induce conformity to the law.

Deterrence strategies should work—and they have—because white-collar crime by its nature is a rational act whose perpetrators are extremely sensitive to the threat of criminal sanctions. Perceptions of detection and punishment for white-collar crimes appear to be powerful deterrents to future law violations. Although deterrence strategies may prove effective, federal agencies have traditionally been reluctant to throw corporate executives in jail. The government seeks criminal indictments in corporate violations only in "instances of outrageous conduct of undoubted illegality," such as price fixing.[107] The government has also been lenient with companies and individuals that cooperate voluntarily after an investigation has begun; leniency is not given as part of a confession or plea arrangement. Those who comply with the leniency policy are charged criminally for the activity reported.[108]

Is the Tide Turning?

Despite years of neglect, there is growing evidence that white-collar crime deterrence strategies have become normative. In one important case, Adelphia cable operator John Rigas was sentenced to 15 years in prison for bank and securities fraud and his son Timothy Rigas was sentenced to 20 after their conviction on charges that they used company funds to support their extravagant lifestyle. John Rigas took advantage of a shared line of credit with Adelphia, using the company's money—stockholder's money—for personal extravagances.[109]

This get-tough deterrence approach appears to be affecting all classes of white-collar criminals. Although many people believe affluent corporate executives usually avoid serious punishment, public displeasure with such highly publicized white-collar crimes may be producing a backlash that is resulting in more frequent use of prison sentences.[110] With the Enron scandal depriving so many people of their life savings, the general public has become educated as to the damage caused by white-collar criminals and may now consider white-collar crimes as more serious offenses than common-law theft offenses.[111]

Considering this changing vision, it is not surprising that the U.S Department of Justice Anti-Trust Division is now vigorously pursuing increased jail time for violators as well as more punitive financial penalties. As Figure 13.2 shows, the division has significantly increased the amount of fines it has collected, from $75 million in 2002 to almost $500 million in 2006.

Some commentators now argue that the government may actually be going overboard in its efforts to punish white-collar criminals, especially for crimes that are the result of negligent business practices rather than intentional criminal conspiracy.[112] The U.S. Sentencing Commission has voted to increase penalties for high-dollar fraud and theft offenses.[113] While the Sherman Antitrust Act caps fines at $10 million, the commission's penalties are far more severe. Under these guidelines, corporations convicted of antitrust felonies may result in fines equal to the greater of twice the corporation's illegal financial gain or twice the victim's loss. Both fines and penalties have been increasing, and in one case a food company executive was sentenced to serve more than five years in prison for his role in a

Figure 13.2 Fines in Antitrust Cases Collected by U.S. Department of Justice

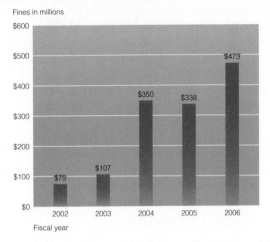

Fines in millions

Source: Anti-Trust Division U.S. Department of Justice, www.usdoj.gov/atr/public/press_releases/2006/220465a.htm (accessed June 20, 2007).

bid-rigging scheme; it was the longest single prison sentence ever obtained for an antitrust violation.[114]

www Since 1999, Florida's Department of Environmental Protection has fielded a multiagency Strike Force—led by the department's Division of Law Enforcement—to **investigate pollutant discharges and the release of hazardous material statewide**. Check it out at www.thomsonedu.com/criminaljustice/siegel.

ORGANIZED CRIME

Organized crime involves ongoing criminal enterprise groups whose ultimate purpose is personal economic gain through illegitimate means. Here a structured enterprise system is set up to continually supply consumers with merchandise and services banned by criminal law but for which a ready market exists: prostitution, pornography, gambling, and narcotics. The system may resemble a legitimate business run by an ambitious chief executive officer, his or her assistants, staff attorneys, and accountants, with thorough, efficient accounts receivable and complaint departments.[115]

Because of its secrecy, power, and fabulous wealth, a great mystique has grown up about organized crime. Its legendary leaders—Al Capone, Meyer Lansky, Lucky Luciano—have been the subjects of books and films. The famous *Godfather* films popularized and humanized organized crime figures; the media often glamorize organized crime figures.[116] Watching the exploits of Tony Soprano and his family life became a national craze.

Most citizens believe organized criminals are capable of taking over legitimate business enterprises if given the opportunity. Almost everyone is familiar with such terms as mob, underworld, Mafia, wise guys, syndicate, or Cosa Nostra, which refer to organized crime. Although most of us have neither met nor seen members of organized crime families, we feel sure that they exist, and we fear them. This section briefly defines organized crime, reviews its history, and discusses its economic effect and control.

Characteristics of Organized Crime

A precise description of the characteristics of organized crime is difficult to formulate, but here are some of its general traits:[117]

▌ Organized crime is a conspiratorial activity, involving the coordination of numerous people in the planning and execution of illegal acts or in the pursuit of a legitimate objective by unlawful means (e.g., threatening a legitimate business to get a stake in it).

▌ It involves continuous commitment by primary members, although individuals with specialized skills may be brought in as needed. Organized crime is usually structured along hierarchical lines—a chieftain supported by close advisers, lower subordinates, and so on.

▌ Organized crime has economic gain as its primary goal, although power and status may also be motivating factors. Economic gain is achieved through maintenance of a near-monopoly on illegal goods and services, including drugs, gambling, pornography, and prostitution.

▌ Its activities are not limited to providing illicit services. They include such sophisticated activities as laundering illegal money through legitimate businesses, land fraud, and computer crime.

▌ Organized crime employs predatory tactics, such as intimidation, violence, and corruption. It appeals to greed to accomplish its objectives and preserve its gains.

▌ By experience, custom, and practice, organized crime's conspiratorial groups are usually very quick and effective in controlling and disciplining their members, associates, and victims. The individuals involved know that any deviation from the rules of the organization will evoke a prompt response from the other participants. This response may range from a reduction in rank and responsibility to a death sentence.

▌ Organized crime is not synonymous with the Mafia, which is really a common stereotype of organized crime. Although several families in the organization called the Mafia are important components of organized crime activities, they do not hold a monopoly on underworld activities.

▌ It does not include terrorists dedicated to political change. Although violent acts are a major tactic of organized crime, the use of violence does not mean that a group is part of a confederacy of organized criminals.

Activities of Organized Crime

What are the main activities of organized crime? The traditional sources of income are derived from providing illicit materials and using force to enter into and maximize profits in legitimate businesses.[118] Most organized crime income comes from narcotics distribution, loan sharking (lending money at illegal rates), and prostitution. However, additional billions come from gambling, theft rings, pornography, and other illegal enterprises. Organized criminals have infiltrated labor unions and taken control of their pension funds and dues.[119] Hijacking of shipments and cargo theft are other sources of income. Underworld figures fence high-value items and maintain international sales territories. In recent years they have branched into computer crime and other white-collar activities. Organized crime figures have also kept up with the information age by using computers and the Internet to sell illegal material such as pornography.

Organized crime figures are also involved in stock market manipulation. The FBI notes that organized crime groups target "small cap" or "micro cap" stocks, over-the-counter stocks, and other types of thinly traded stocks that can be easily manipulated and sold to elderly or inexperienced investors. The conspirators use offshore bank accounts to conceal their participation in the fraud scheme and to launder the illegal proceeds in order to avoid paying income tax.[120]

© AP Photo/Mike Derer, Pool

Though the mob has been diminished in size and power, it is still flourishing. Michael Coppola, a captain of the Genovese crime family, looks around the court in Somerville, New Jersey, on March 13, 2007, where he faces a first-degree murder charge in connection with the 1977 shooting of John "Johnny Coca Cola" Lardiere. Coppola was on the lam for nearly 11 years, but it now appears he was hiding in plain sight—living the life of a well-heeled gangster, maintaining apartments in New York and San Francisco, and generating income through gambling, extortion, loan sharking, and possibly murder. Authorities allege that Coppola, then a young up-and-comer in the Genovese crime family, was the triggerman who blew away Lardiere in the parking lot of the Red Bull Inn in Somerset County on Easter Sunday morning 30 years ago.

The Concept of Organized Crime

The term "organized crime" conjures up images of strong men in dark suits, machine gun–toting bodyguards, rituals of allegiance to secret organizations, professional "gangland" killings, and meetings of "family" leaders who chart the course of crime much as the board members at General Motors decide on the country's transportation needs. These images have become part of what criminologists refer to as the alien conspiracy theory concept of organized crime. According to this vision, organized crime is a direct offshoot of a criminal society—the Mafia—that first originated in Italy and Sicily and is still involved in racketeering in major U.S. cities. A major premise of the alien conspiracy theory is that the Mafia is centrally coordinated and the various gangs work cooperatively to settle disputes, dictate policy, and assign territory.[121]

The Mob: Cosa Nostra

To some alien conspiracy theorists, "real" organized crime is made up of a national syndicate of 25 or so Italian-dominated crime families that call themselves Cosa Nostra. The major families have a total membership of about 1,000 to 2,000 "made men," who have been inducted into organized crime families, and another 17,000 "associates," who are criminally involved with syndicate members. The families control crime in distinct geographic areas. New York City, the most important organized crime area, alone contains five families—the Gambino, Columbo (formerly Profaci), Lucchese, Bonanno, and Genovese families—named after their founding "godfathers"; in contrast, Chicago contains a single mob organization called the "outfit," which also influences racketeering in such cities as Milwaukee, Kansas City, and Phoenix.[122] The families are believed to be ruled by a "commission" made up of the heads of the five New York families and bosses from Detroit, Buffalo, Chicago, and Philadelphia, which settles personal problems and jurisdictional conflicts and enforces rules that allow members to gain huge profits through the manufacture and sale of illegal goods and services.

Contemporary Organized Crime Groups

A more contemporary vision of organized crime views these groups and gangs as a loose confederation of ethnic and regional crime groups, bound together by a commonality of economic and political objectives.[123] Some of these groups are located in fixed geographical areas. Chicano crime families are found in areas with significant Latino populations, such as California and Arizona. Others are involved in national and even cross-national criminal enterprise. The Hell's Angels motorcycle club is now believed to be one of the leading distributors of narcotics in the United States. Some Italian and Cuban groups operate internationally. Some have preserved their past identity, whereas others are constantly changing organizations. There are several trends among these emerging criminal enterprise groups. First, it is more common to see criminal groups cooperate across ethnic and racial heritage lines. Also, some gangs and criminal enterprises have begun to structure their groups in a hierarchical fashion to be more competitive, and the criminal activities they engage in have become globalized. Finally, more of these criminal enterprises are engaging in white-collar crimes and are co-mingling their illegal activities with legitimate business ventures.[124] As law enforcement pressure has been put on traditional organized crime figures and Mafia dons given long prison sentences, other groups have filled the vacuum.[125]

▌ Middle Eastern organized criminals, natives of Lebanon, Egypt, Syria, and other nations in the region, have been active in the United States since the 1970s. These gangs have been known to engage in automobile theft, financial fraud, money laundering, interstate transportation of stolen property, smuggling, drug trafficking, document fraud, health care fraud, identity fraud, cigarette smuggling, and the theft and redistribution of infant formula. Their enterprises rely on extensive networks of international criminal associates and can be highly sophisticated in their criminal operations.

▌ Chinese criminal gangs have taken over the dominant role in New York City's heroin market from the traditional Italian-run syndicates. In the United States, Asian criminal enterprises have been identified in more than 50 metropolitan areas. They are most prevalent in Boston, Chicago, Honolulu, Las Vegas, Los Angeles, New Orleans, New York, Newark, Philadelphia, Portland, San Francisco, Seattle, and Washington, D.C.

▌ African criminal enterprises have developed quickly since the 1980s and are now targeting international victims and developing criminal networks within more prosperous countries and regions. They are active in several major metropolitan areas in the United States, but are most prevalent in Atlanta, Baltimore, Chicago, Dallas, Houston, Milwaukee, Newark, New York, and Washington, D.C. Of these, Nigerian criminal enterprises are the most commonplace and operate in more than 80 other countries of the world. Engaged in money laundering, drug trafficking, and financial frauds, they specialize in delivering heroin from Southeast and Southwest Asia into Europe and the U.S. and cocaine from South America into Europe and South Africa. The associated money laundering has helped establish Nigerian criminal enterprises on every populated continent of the world.

▌ Balkan criminal organizations whose members hale from Serbia, Croatia, Albania, and other nations in southeastern Europe have been active in the United States since the mid-1980s. The various Balkan groups are active in gambling, money laundering, drug trafficking, human smuggling, extortion, violent witness intimidation, robbery, attempted murder, and murder. Balkan organized crime groups have recently expanded into more sophisticated crimes including real estate fraud.

▌ Eastern Europe has been the scene of a massive buildup in organized crime since the fall of the Soviet Union. Trading in illegal arms, narcotics, pornography, and prostitution, they operate a multibillion-dollar transnational crime cartel. Some of these groups prey upon women in the poorest areas of Europe—Romania, the Ukraine, Bosnia—and sell them into virtual sexual slavery. Many of these women are transported as prostitutes around the world, some ending up in the United States.

Intensive European enforcement operations conducted with American assistance have helped eliminate some of the major players in the international sex trade. However, it is estimated that 700,000 women are still transported, mostly involuntarily, over international borders each year for the sex trade. One reason for the difficulty in creating effective enforcement is the complicity of local authorities with criminal organizations.[126]

Since 1970, Russian and other eastern European groups have been operating on U.S. soil. Some groups are formed by immigrants from former satellites of the Soviet Union. The FBI established the Yugoslavian/Albanian/Croatian/Serbian (YACS) Crime Group initiative as a response to the increasing threat of criminal activity by people originating from these areas. YACS gangs focus on highly organized and specialized thefts from ATM machines in the New York City area.[127]

In addition, thousands of Russian immigrants are believed to be involved in criminal activity, primarily in Russian enclaves in New York City. Beyond extortion from immigrants, Russian organized crime groups have cooperated with Mafia families in narcotics trafficking, fencing stolen property, money laundering, and other traditional organized crime schemes.[128]

For more on the Russian mob, see the Comparative Criminology feature "Russian Organized Crime."

Controlling Organized Crime

George Vold has argued that the development of organized crime parallels early capitalist enterprises. Organized crime employs ruthless monopolistic tactics to maximize profits; it is also secretive, protective of its operations, and defensive against any outside intrusion.[129] Consequently, controlling its activities is extremely difficult.

Federal and state governments actually did little to combat organized crime until fairly recently. One of the first measures aimed directly at organized crime was the Interstate and Foreign Travel or Transportation in Aid of Racketeering Enterprises Act (Travel Act).[130] The Travel Act prohibits travel in interstate commerce or use of interstate facilities with the intent to promote, manage, establish, carry on, or facilitate an unlawful activity; it also prohibits the actual or attempted engagement in these activities. In 1970 Congress passed the Organized Crime Control Act. Title IX of the act, probably

RUSSIAN ORGANIZED CRIME

In the decade since the collapse of the Soviet Union, criminal organizations in Russia and other former Soviet republics such as the Ukraine have engaged in a variety of crimes: drugs and arms trafficking, stolen automobiles, trafficking in women and children, and money laundering. No area of the world seems immune to this menace, especially not the United States. America is the land of opportunity for unloading criminal goods and laundering dirty money.

Unlike Colombian, Italian, Mexican, or other well-known forms of organized crime, Russian organized crime is not primarily based on ethnic or family structures. Instead, Russian organized crime is based on economic necessity that was nurtured by the oppressive Soviet regime. Here, a professional criminal class developed in Soviet prisons during the Stalinist period that began in 1924—the era of the gulag. These criminals adopted behaviors, rules, values, and sanctions that bound them together in what was called the thieves' world, led by the elite *vory v zakone*, criminals who lived according to the "thieves' law." This thieves' world, and particularly the *vory*, created and maintained the bonds and climate of trust necessary for carrying out organized crime.

The following are some specific characteristics of Russian organized crime in the post-Soviet era:

▪ Russian criminals make extensive use of the state governmental apparatus to protect and promote their criminal activities. For example, most businesses in Russia—legal, quasilegal, and illegal—must operate with the protection of a *krysha* (roof). The protection is often provided by police or security officials employed outside their "official" capacities for this purpose. In other cases, officials are "silent partners" in criminal enterprises that they, in turn, protect.

▪ The criminalization of the privatization process has resulted in the massive use of state funds for criminal gain. Valuable properties are purchased through insider deals for much less than their true value and then resold for lucrative profits.

▪ Criminals have been able to directly influence the state's domestic and foreign policy to promote the interests of organized crime, either by attaining public office themselves or by buying public officials.

Beyond these particular features, organized crime in Russia shares other characteristics that are common to organized crime elsewhere in the world:

▪ Systematic use of violence, including both the threat and the use of force

▪ Hierarchical structure

▪ Limited or exclusive membership

▪ Specialization in types of crime and a division of labor

▪ Military-style discipline, with strict rules and regulations for the organization as a whole

▪ Possession of high-tech equipment, including military weapons

Threats, blackmail, and violence are used to penetrate business management and assume control of commercial enterprises or, in some instances, to found their own enterprises with money from their criminal activities. As a result of these activities:

▪ Russia has high rates of homicide that are now more than 20 times those in western Europe and approximately three times the rates recorded in the United States. The rates more closely resemble those of a country engaged in civil war or in conflict than those of a country 10 years into a transition.

▪ Corruption and organized crime are globalized. Russian organized crime is active in Europe, Africa, Asia, and North and South America.

▪ Massive money laundering is now common. It allows Russian and foreign organized crime to flourish. In some cases, it is tied to terrorist funding.

The organized crime threat to Russia's national security is now becoming a global threat. Russian organized crime operates both on its own and in cooperation with foreign groups. The latter cooperation often comes in the form of joint money laundering ventures. Russian criminals have become involved in killings for hire in central and western Europe, Israel, Canada, and the United States.

However, in the United States, with the exception of extortion and money laundering, Russians have had little or no involvement in some of the more traditional types of organized crime, such as drug trafficking, gambling, and loan sharking. Instead, these criminal groups are extensively engaged in a broad array of frauds and scams, including health care fraud, insurance scams, stock frauds, antiquities swindles, forgery, and fuel tax evasion schemes. Recently, for example, Russians have become the main purveyors of credit card fraud in the United States. Legitimate businesses, such as the movie business and textile industry, have become targets of criminals from the former Soviet Union, and they are often used for money laundering.

CRITICAL THINKING

The influence of new immigrant groups in organized crime seems to suggest that illegal enterprise is a common practice among "new" Americans. Do you believe that there is some aspect of American culture that causes immigrants to choose a criminal lifestyle? Or does our open culture encourage criminal activities that may have been incubating in people's native lands?

Sources: Louise I. Shelley, "Crime and Corruption: Enduring Problems of Post-Soviet Development," *Demokratizatsiya* 11 (2003): 110–114; James O. Finckenauer and Yuri A. Voronin, *The Threat of Russian Organized Crime* (Washington, DC: National Institute of Justice, 2001).

its most effective measure, has been called the Racketeer Influenced and Corrupt Organization Act (RICO).[131]

RICO did not create new categories of crimes but rather new categories of offenses in racketeering activity, which it defined as involvement in two or more acts prohibited by twenty-four existing federal and eight state statutes. The offenses listed in RICO include state-defined crimes (such as murder, kidnapping, gambling, arson, robbery, bribery, extortion, and narcotic violations) and federally defined crimes (such as bribery, counterfeiting, transmission of gambling information, prostitution, and mail fraud). RICO is designed to limit patterns of organized criminal activity by prohibiting involvement in acts intended to

▮ Derive income from racketeering or the unlawful collection of debts and use or invest such income

▮ Acquire through racketeering an interest in or control over any enterprise engaged in interstate or foreign commerce

▮ Conduct business through a pattern of racketeering

▮ Conspire to use racketeering as a means of making income, collecting loans, or conducting business

An individual convicted under RICO is subject to 20 years in prison and a $25,000 fine. Additionally, the accused must forfeit to the U.S. government any interest in a business in violation of RICO. These penalties are much more potent than simple conviction and imprisonment.

RICO's success has shaped the way the FBI attacks organized crime groups. They now use the enterprise theory of investigation (ETI) model as their standard investigative tool. Rather than investigate crimes after they are committed, under the ETI model the focus is on criminal enterprise and investigation attacks on the structure of the criminal enterprise rather than on criminal acts viewed as isolated incidents.[132] For example, a drug trafficking organization must get involved in such processes as transportation and distribution of narcotics, finance such as money laundering, and communication with clients and dealers. The ETI identifies and then targets each of these areas simultaneously, focusing on the subsystems that are considered the most vulnerable.

The Future of Organized Crime

Joseph Massino's nickname was "the Last Don." The name seemed quite apropos when in 2004 this boss of New York's Bonanno crime family was convicted on charges of murder and racketeering and ordered to pay fines of $9 million and given two consecutive life sentences. Massino's greatest sin, however, may have been violating the Mafia's rule of *omerta*, the traditional "code of silence." While in prison, Massino cooperated with prosecutors, secretly taping a conversation with family *capo* Vincent "Vinnie Gorgeous" Basciano, who was outlining a plan to kill lead prosecutor Greg Andres. Massino's current circumstances are not unique. The heads of the four other New York Mafia families—Lucchese, Colombo, Gambino, and Genovese—also have been convicted and sentenced to prison terms.[133]

The successful prosecution of Massino and other high-ranking organized crime figures are indications that the traditional organized crime syndicates are in decline. Law enforcement officials in Philadelphia, New Jersey, New England, New Orleans, Kansas City, Detroit, and Milwaukee all report that years of federal and state interventions have severely eroded the Mafia organizations in their areas.

What has caused this alleged erosion of Mafia power? First, a number of the reigning family heads are quite old, in their 80s and older, prompting some law enforcement officials to dub them "the Geritol gang."[134] A younger generation of mob leaders is stepping in to take control of the families, and they seem to lack the skill and leadership of the older bosses. In addition, active government enforcement policies have halved what the estimated mob membership was 25 years ago, and a number of the highest-ranking leaders have been imprisoned.

Additional pressure comes from newly emerging ethnic gangs that want to muscle in on traditional syndicate activities, such as drug sales and gambling. For example, Chinese Triad gangs in New York and California have been active in the drug trade, loan sharking, and labor racketeering. Other ethnic crime groups include black and Colombian drug cartels and the Sicilian Mafia, which operates independently of U.S. groups.

The Mafia has also been hurt by changing values in U.S. society. White, ethnic, inner-city neighborhoods, which were the locus of Mafia power, have been shrinking as families move to the suburbs. (It comes as no surprise that fictional character Tony Soprano lived in suburban New Jersey and his daughter went to Columbia.) Organized crime groups have consequently lost their political and social base of operations. In addition, the code of silence that protected Mafia leaders is now broken regularly by younger members who turn informer rather than face prison terms. It is also possible that their success has hurt organized crime families: younger members are better educated than their forebears and are equipped to seek their fortunes through legitimate enterprise.[135]

If traditional organized gangs are in decline, that does not mean the end of organized crime. Russian, Caribbean, and Asian gangs seem to be thriving, and there are always new opportunities for illegal practices. Law enforcement officials believe that Internet gambling sites are tempting targets for enterprise criminals. It is not surprising then that Illinois, Louisiana, Nevada, Oregon, and South Dakota have recently passed laws specifically banning Internet gambling.[136] It is unlikely, considering the demand for illegal goods and services and the emergence of newly constituted crime families, that organized criminal behavior will ever be eradicated.

www Go to www.thomsonedu.com/criminaljustice/siegel to:

▮ Learn more about *The Sopranos*.

▮ Read about **organized crime** and access links to informative sites.

THINKING LIKE A CRIMINOLOGIST

As a criminologist and expert on white-collar crime you are asked to help a legal defense team prepare a sentencing statement in support of Anthony J. Facciabrutto, 33, recently convicted of numerous federal charges.

In 2003, Facciabrutto was charged with mail fraud, money laundering, telemarketing fraud against the elderly, and securities fraud. Facciabrutto owned and operated Facciabrutto Holdings, Inc., a telemarketing company in the Los Angeles area, from 1994 through February 1999. Facciabrutto Holdings, Inc., raised approximately $31 million from more than 800 victims across the United States. Facciabrutto's investors received only a fraction of their total investment in the company. One victim invested in excess of $400,000 and received less than $10,000 in return.

It is alleged that Facciabrutto and the telemarketers he employed sold investments in restaurants and what were marketed as luxury resorts, which never generated profits. The telemarketing operation was, according to the indictment, a scheme where earlier investors were paid "dividend payments" derived from funds obtained from later investors.

Facciabrutto was the chief executive officer for Facciabrutto Holdings, Inc., and is alleged to have paid himself a 40 percent sales commission. Sales managers were paid 25 percent of total sales and salespersons received a 25 percent commission. Facciabrutto allegedly misrepresented sales commissions and made false guarantees to customers. Facciabrutto misrepresented the company's imminent initial public offering, which never occurred. The SEC conducted a civil investigation into Facciabrutto during 1999 and as a result, Facciabrutto was ordered to pay a $3 million judgment. This was his first offense and he claims that overwhelming personal problems drove him to commit crime. Facciabrutto had big personal debts and had borrowed heavily from organized crime figures.

Writing Exercise Write a brief paper (200 words) explaining how, as a criminologist consulting for his attorney, you would save Facciabrutto from prison.

Doing Research on the Web Visit www.thomsonedu.com/criminaljustice/siegel for information on lawyers in white-collar cases, to read an article on deterring white-collar crime, and to check out Cornell University's Legal Information page.

SUMMARY

- Enterprise crime involves illicit entrepreneurship and commerce.

- White-collar and organized crime are linked together because they involve entrepreneurship. Losses from enterprise crime may far outstrip any other type of crime.

- Enterprise crime involves criminal acts that twist the legal rules of commercial enterprise for criminal purposes.

- There are various types of white-collar crime. Stings and swindles involve long-term efforts to cheat people out

of their money; chiseling involves regular cheating of an organization or its customers; exploitation involves coercing victims (clients) into paying for services for which they are entitled by threatening consequences if they refuse; influence peddling and bribery involve demanding payment for a service for which the payer is clearly not entitled (the victim here is the organization).

- Embezzlement and employee fraud occur when a person uses a position of trust to steal from an organization.

- Client fraud involves theft from an organization that advances credit, covers losses, or reimburses for services.

- Corporate crime involves various illegal business practices such as price fixing, restraint of trade, and false advertising.

- There are numerous explanations for white-collar crime: some offenders are motivated by greed; others offend due to personal problems.

- Corporate culture theory suggests that some businesses actually encourage employees to cheat or cut corners.

- The self-control view is that white-collar criminals are like any other law violators: impulsive people who lack self-control.

- Little has been done in the past to combat white-collar crime. Most offenders do not view themselves as criminals and therefore do not seem to be deterred by criminal statutes.

- Although thousands of white-collar criminals are prosecuted each year, their numbers are insignificant compared with the magnitude of the problem.

- The government has used various law enforcement strategies to combat white-collar crime. Some involve deterrence, which uses punishment to frighten potential abusers. Others involve economic or compliance strategies, which create economic incentives to obey the law.

- Organized crime supplies gambling, drugs, prostitutes, and pornography to the public. It is immune from prosecution because of public apathy and because of its own strong political connections.

- Organized criminals used to be "white" ethnics, but today other groups have become involved in organized crime activities. The old-line "families" are now more likely to use their criminal wealth and power to buy into legitimate businesses.

- There is debate over the control of organized crime. Some experts believe a national crime cartel controls all activities. Others view organized crime as a group of disorganized, competing gangs dedicated to extortion or to providing illegal goods and services. Efforts to control organized crime have been stepped up. The federal government has used antiracketeering statutes to arrest syndicate leaders. But as long as huge profits can be made, illegal enterprises will continue to flourish.

- **ThomsonNOW** Maximize your study time by using ThomsonNOW's diagnostic study plan to help you review this chapter. The Personalized Study plan will help you identify areas on which you should concentrate; provide interactive exercises to help you master the chapter concepts; and provide a post-test to confirm you are ready to move on to the next chapter.

KEY TERMS

enterprise crime (372)
white-collar crime (372)
organized crime (372)
corporate crime (373)
sting or swindle (374)
chiseling (375)
insider trading (376)
exploitation (376)

influence peddling (377)
payola (377)
pilferage (380)
organizational crime (382)
actual authority (383)
apparent authority (383)
Sherman Antitrust Act (384)
alien conspiracy theory (391)

Mafia (391)
racketeering (391)
Cosa Nostra (391)
Racketeer Influenced and Corrupt Organization Act (RICO) (394)
enterprise theory of investigation (ETI) (394)

CRITICAL THINKING QUESTIONS

1. How would you punish a corporate executive whose product killed people if the executive had no knowledge that the product was potentially lethal? What if the executive did know?

2. Is organized crime inevitable as long as immigrant groups seek to become part of the American Dream?

3. Does the media glamorize organized crime? Does it paint an inaccurate picture of noble crime lords fighting to protect their families?

4. Apply traditional theories of criminal behavior to white-collar and organized crime. Which one seems to best predict why someone would engage in these behaviors?

NOTES

1. Department of Justice press release, "Five Arrested in Health Care Fraud Scheme that Collected at Least $20 Million from Medicare Program," March 21, 2006, http://losangeles.fbi.gov/dojpressrel/ pressrel06/la032106usa.htm (accessed April 26, 2007).
2. John Locker and Barry Godfrey, "Ontological Boundaries and Temporal Watersheds in the Development of White-Collar Crime," *British Journal of Criminology* 46 (2006): 976–999.
3. Nikos Passas and David Nelken, "The Thin Line between Legitimate and Criminal Enterprises: Subsidy Frauds in the European

Community," *Crime, Law, and Social Change* 19 (1993): 223–243.

4. For a thorough review, see David Friedrichs, *Trusted Criminals* (Belmont, CA: Wadsworth, 1996).

5. Kitty Calavita and Henry Pontell, "Savings and Loan Fraud as Organized Crime: Toward a Conceptual Typology of Corporate Illegality," *Criminology* 31 (1993): 519–548.

6. Mark Haller, "Illegal Enterprise: A Theoretical and Historical Interpretation," *Criminology* 28 (1990): 207–235.

7. Nancy Frank and Michael Lynch, *Corporate Crime, Corporate Violence* (Albany, NY: Harrow & Heston, 1992), p. 7.

8. Edward Alsworth Ross, *Sin and Society: An Analysis of Latter-Day Iniquity* (Boston: Houghton Mifflin Company, 1907): 45–71.

9. Edwin Sutherland, *White-Collar Crime: The Uncut Version* (New Haven, CT: Yale University Press, 1983).

10. Edwin Sutherland, "White-Collar Criminality," *American Sociological Review* 5 (1940): 2–10.

11. David Weisburd and Kip Schlegel, "Returning to the Mainstream," in *White-Collar Crime Reconsidered*, eds. Kip Schlegel and David Weisburd (Boston: Northeastern University Press, 1992), pp. 352–365.

12. Ronald Kramer and Raymond Michalowski, "State-Corporate Crime," paper presented at the annual meeting of the American Society of Criminology, Baltimore, November 1990.

13. Elizabeth Moore and Michael Mills, "The Neglected Victims and Unexamined Costs of White-Collar Crime," *Crime and Delinquency* 36 (1990): 408–418.

14. National Public Survey on White Collar Crime, www.nw3c.org/research/national_public_survey.cfm (accessed April 26, 2007).

15. Natalie Taylor, "Under-Reporting of Crime against Small Business: Attitudes Towards Police and Reporting Practices," *Policing and Society* 13 (2003): 79–90.

16. Gilbert Geis, "White-Collar and Corporate Crime," in *Major Forms of Crime*, ed. Robert Meier (Beverly Hills: Sage, 1984), p. 145.

17. Marshall Clinard and Richard Quinney, *Criminal Behavior Systems: A Typology* (New York: Holt, Rinehart & Winston, 1973), p. 117; Mark Moore, "Notes Toward a National Strategy to Deal with White-Collar Crime," in *A National Strategy for Containing White-Collar Crime*, eds. Herbert Edelhertz and Charles Rogovin (Lexington, MA: Lexington Books, 1980), pp. 32–44.

18. David Firestone, "In Racketeering Trial, Well-Dressed Strip Club Takes the Stage," *New York Times*, 5 May 2001, p. 3.

19. Federal Bureau of Investigation, Operation Bullpen, www.fbi.gov/hq/cid/fc/ec/sm/smoverview.htm (accessed April 26, 2007).

20. Nikos Passas, "Structural Sources of International Crime: Policy Lessons from the BCCI Affair," *Crime, Law and Social Change* 19 (1994): 223–231.

21. Nikos Passas, "Accounting for Fraud: Auditors' Ethical Dilemmas in the BCCI Affair," in *The Ethics of Accounting and Finance*, eds. W. Michael Hoffman, Judith Brown Kamm, Robert Frederick, and Edward Petry (Westport, CT: Quorum Books, 1996), pp. 85–99.

22. Washington State Department of Financial Institutions press release, "Beware of Oil and Gas Schemes, State Securities Regulators Warn Investors, Con Artists May Seek to Exploit Fears over Mideast, Oil Supply," www.dfi.wa.gov/news/oil_gasnr.pdf (accessed April 26, 2007).

23. Earl Gottschalk, "Churchgoers Are the Prey as Scams Rise," *Wall Street Journal* 7 August 1989, p. C1.

24. FBI, "Empty Promises, Empty Cradles: Adoption Scams Bilk Victims, Break Hearts," August 28, 2006, www.fbi.gov/page2/aug06/adoptscams082806.htm (accessed March 26, 2007).

25. Associated Press, "NYC Cab Scam Warning Given," *Boston Globe*, 19 September 1997, p. 13.

26. Richard Pérez-Peña, "Indictments Charge 4 Racetrack Tellers with Laundering Money at Betting Windows," *New York Times*, 20 July 2001, p. A4.

27. Richard Quinney, "Occupational Structure and Criminal Behavior: Prescription Violation of Retail Pharmacists," *Social Problems* 11 (1963): 179–185; see also John Braithwaite, *Corporate Crime in the Pharmaceutical Industry* (London: Routledge and Kegan Paul, 1984).

28. Pam Belluck, "Prosecutors Say Greed Drove Pharmacist to Dilute Drugs" *New York Times*, 18 August 2001, p. 3.

29. Press release, April 22, 2002, Kansas City Division, Federal Bureau of Investigation.

30. U.S. Department of Justice, "Two Men Arraigned in Fraud Scheme that Cost Victims Nearly $1.7 Million," September 7, 2005, www.usdoj.gov/usao/cac/news/pr2005/126.html (accessed April 25, 2007).

31. Anish Vashista, David Johnson, and Muhtashem Choudhury, "Securities Fraud," *American Criminal Law Review* 42 (2005): 877–942.

32. James Armstrong, et al., "Securities Fraud," *American Criminal Law Review* 33 (1995): 973–1,016.

33. Scott McMurray, "Futures Pit Trader Goes to Trial," *Wall Street Journal*, 8 May 1990, p. C1; Scott McMurray, "Chicago Pits' Dazzling Growth Permitted a Free-for-All Mecca," *Wall Street Journal*, 3 August 1989, p. A4.

34. Securities and Exchange Commission press release, "Ten of Nation's Top Investment Firms Settle Enforcement Actions Involving Conflicts of Interest Between Research and Investment Banking. Historic Settlement Requires Payments of Penalties of $487.5 Million, Disgorgement of $387.5 Million, Payments of $432.5 Million to Fund Independent Research, and Payments of $80 Million to Fund Investor Education and Mandates Sweeping Structural Reforms," April 28, 2003.

35. *Carpenter v. United States* 484 U.S. 19 (1987); also see John Boland, "The SEC Trims the First Amendment," *Wall Street Journal*, 4 December 1986, p. 28.

36. The Associated Press, "Prosecutors Crack Insider-Trading Ring" *New York Times*, 2 March 2007.

37. Kevin Sack, "49ers Owner Pleads Guilty in Louisiana Casino Case," *New York Times*, 7 October 1998, p. 1.

38. Charles V. Bagli, "Kickback Investigation Extends to Middle-Class Buildings in New York," *New York Times*, 14 October 1998, p. A19.

39. Press Release, FBI National Press Office, August, 19, 1999.

40. Charles R. Babcock and Jonathan Weisman, "Congressman Admits Taking Bribes, Resigns," *Washington Post*, 29 November 2005, p. 1.

41. Monica Davey and John O'Neil, "Ex-Governor of Illinois Is Convicted on All Charges," *New York Times*, 18 April 2006, p. 1.

42. "DeLay Indicted, Steps Down as Majority Leader," *CNN*, 29 September 2005, www.cnn.com/2005/POLITICS/09/28/delay.indict/index.html (accessed April 26, 2007).

43. *The Knapp Commission Report on Police Corruption* (New York: George Braziller, 1973), pp. 1–3, 170–182.

44. David Kocieniewski and David M. Halbfinger, "New York's Most Respected Officers Led Precinct Where Sex Scandal Festered," *New York Times*, 20 July 1998, p. 1.

45. Disclosure of payments to individuals connected with broadcasts, United States Criminal Code, Title 47, Chapter 5, Subchapter V § 508.

46. Marshall Clinard and Peter Yeager, *Corporate Crime* (New York: Free Press, 1980), p. 67.

47. Carter Dougherty, "Germany Battling Rising Tide of Corporate Corruption," *New York Times*, 15 February 2007.

48. PL No. 95-213, 101-104, 91 Stat. 1494.

49. Thomas Burton, "The More Baxter Hides Its Israeli Boycott Role, the More Flak It Gets," *Wall Street Journal*, 25 April 1991, p. 1.

50. Foreign Corrupt Practices Act Update, "Schering-Plough Settles FCPA Case with SEC for Payments to Charity Headed by Government Official," http://wilmer.admin.hubbardone.com/files/tbl_s29Publications%5CFileUpload5665%5C4421%5CFCPA%2006-30-04.pdf (accessed April 26, 2007).

51. Terence O'Hara, "Chrysler Probe Reflects Trend, U.S. More Vigilant Against Domestic, Foreign Bribery," *Washington Post*, 6 August 2005, p. D01.

52. Adrian Cho, "Hey Buddy . . . Wanna Buy a Moon Rock?" *Science Now*, 7 July 2002, p. 1.

53. Charles McCaghy, *Deviant Behavior* (New York: Macmillan, 1976), p. 178.

54. Hayes International, Highlights from Jack L. Hayes International, Inc.'s 18th Annual Retail Theft Survey," www.hayesinternational.com/thft_srvys.html (accessed April 26, 2007).

55. J. Sorenson, H. Grove, and T. Sorenson, "Detecting Management Fraud: The Role of the Independent Auditor," in *White-Collar Crime, Theory and Research*, eds. G. Geis and E. Stotland (Beverly Hills: Sage, 1980), pp. 221–251.

56. National Health Care Anti-Fraud Association, "About Health Care Fraud," www.nhcaa.org/about_health_care_fraud/ (accessed March 1, 2007).

57. Ibid.

58. Michael Luo and Clifford Levy, "As Medicaid Balloons, Watchdog Force Shrinks," *New York Times*, 19 July 2005, p. A1.

59. National Health Care Anti-Fraud Association, "About Health Care Fraud."

60. Kurt Eichenwald, "Hospital Chain Cheated U.S. on Expenses, Documents Show," *New York Times*, 18 December 1997, p. B1.

61. Health Insurance Portability and Accountability Act of 1996 (HIPAA), United States Code, Title 18, Section 1347.

62. FBI, Financial Crime Report to the Public, 2005, www.fbi.gov/publications/financial/fcs_report052005/fcs_report052005.htm#c1 (accessed March 1, 2007).

63. 18 U.S.C. section 1344 (1994).

64. FBI, Financial Crime Report to the Public, 2006, www.fbi.gov/publications/financial/fcs_report052005/fcs_report052005.htm#c1 (accessed March 1, 2007).

65. *United States v. Bishop*, 412 U.S. 346 (1973).

66. David Cay Johnston, "Departing Chief Says I.R.S. Is Losing War on Tax Cheats," *New York Times*, 5 November 2002, p. 1.

67. Cited in Frank and Lynch, *Corporate Crime, Corporate Violence*, pp. 12–13.

68. Sutherland, "White-Collar Criminality," pp. 2–10.

69. Joseph S. Hall, "Corporate Criminal Liability," *American Criminal Law Review* 35 (1998): 549–560.

70. Kylie Cooper and Adrienne Dedjinou, "Antitrust Violations," *American Criminal Law Review* 42 (2005): 179–221.

71. 15 U.S.C. section 1 (1994).

72. 15 U.S.C. 1–7 (1976).

73. *Northern Pacific Railways v. United States*, 356 U.S. 1 (1958).

74. Tim Carrington, "Federal Probes of Contractors Rise for Year," *Wall Street Journal*, 23 February 1987, p. 50.

75. Ibid.

76. *Illinois Ex Rel. Madigan v. Telemarketing Associates, Inc., et al.* No. 01-1806 (2003).

77. Environmental Protection Agency, Criminal Investigation Division, www.epa.gov/compliance/criminal/index.html (accessed April 26, 2007).

78. Andrew Oliveira, Christopher Schenck, Christopher Cole, and Nicole Janes, "Environmental Crimes (Annual Survey of White Collar Crime)," *American Criminal Law Review* 42 (2005): 347–380.

79. Belluck, "Prosecutors Say Greed Drove Pharmacist to Dilute Drugs," p. 3.

80. Kathleen Daly, "Gender and Varieties of White-Collar Crime," *Criminology* 27 (1989): 769–793.

81. Quoted in Tim Metz and Michael Miller, "Boesky's Rise and Fall Illustrate a Compulsion to Profit by Getting Inside Track on Market," *Wall Street Journal*, 17 November 1986, p. 28.

82. Donald Cressey, *Other People's Money: A Study of the Social Psychology of Embezzlement* (Glencoe, IL: Free Press, 1973), p. 96.

83. Rhonda Evans and Dianne Porche, "The Nature and Frequency of Medicare/Medicaid Fraud and Neutralization Techniques among Speech, Occupational, and Physical Therapists," *Deviant Behavior* 26 (2005): 253–271.

84. Herbert Edelhertz and Charles Rogovin, eds., *A National Strategy for Containing White-Collar Crime* (Lexington, MA: Lexington Books, 1980), Appendix A, pp. 122–123.

85. Mandeep Dhami, "White-Collar Prisoners' Perceptions of Audience Reaction," *Deviant Behavior* 28 (2007): 57–77.

86. Nicole Leeper Piquero, Stephen Tibbetts, and Michael Blankenship, "Examining the Role of Differential Association and Techniques of Neutralization in Explaining Corporate Crime," *Deviant Behavior* 26 (2005): 159–188.

87. John A. Byrne, "At Enron, the Environment Was Ripe for Abuse," *BusinessWeek*, 25 February 2002, p. 14.

88. Travis Hirschi and Michael Gottfredson, "Causes of White-Collar Crime," *Criminology* 25 (1987): 949–974.

89. Michael Gottfredson and Travis Hirschi, *A General Theory of Crime* (Stanford, CA: Stanford University Press, 1990), p. 191.

90. This section relies heavily on Daniel Skoler, "White-Collar Crime and the Criminal Justice System: Problems and Challenges," in *A National Strategy for Containing White-Collar Crime*, eds. Herbert Edelhertz and Charles Rogovin (Lexington, MA: Lexington Books, 1980), pp. 57–76.

91. Theodore Hammett and Joel Epstein, *Prosecuting Environmental Crime: Los Angeles County* (Washington, DC: National Institute of Justice, 1993).

92. Information provided by Los Angeles County District Attorney's Office, April 2003.

93. Ronald Burns, Keith Whitworth, and Carol Thompson, "Assessing Law Enforcement Preparedness to Address Internet Fraud," *Journal of Criminal Justice* 32 (2004): 477–493.

94. Michael Benson, Francis Cullen, and William Maakestad, "Local Prosecutors and Corporate Crime," *Crime and Delinquency* 36 (1990): 356–372.

95. Ibid., pp. 369–370.

96. David Simon and D. Stanley Eitzen, *Elite Deviance* (Boston: Allyn & Bacon, 1982), p. 28.

97. Stuart P. Green, *Lying, Cheating, and Stealing: A Moral Theory of White Collar Crime* (London: Oxford University Press, 2006).

98. Michael Lynch, Paul Stretesky, and Ronald Burns, "Slippery Business," *Journal of Black Studies* 34 (2004): 421–440.

99. This section relies heavily on Albert Reiss, Jr., "Selecting Strategies of Social Control over Organizational Life," in *Enforcing Regulation*, eds. Keith Hawkins and John M. Thomas (Boston: Kluwer Publications, 1984), pp. 25–37.

100. John Braithwaite, "The Limits of Economism in Controlling Harmful Corporate Conduct," *Law and Society Review* 16 (1981–1982): 481–504.

101. Environmental Protection Agency, Office of Criminal Enforcement, Forensics and Training, September 30, 2006, www.epa.gov/compliance/resources/cases/criminal/highlights/2006/longleyjones.pdf (accessed March 7, 2007).

102. Sarbanes-Oxley Act, H.R. 3763-2 (2002).

103. Michael Benson, "Emotions and Adjudication: Status Degradation among White-Collar Criminals," *Justice Quarterly* 7 (1990): 515–528; John Braithwaite, *Crime, Shame, and Reintegration* (Sydney: Cambridge University Press, 1989).

104. Kip Schlegel, "Desert, Retribution and Corporate Criminality," *Justice Quarterly* 5 (1988): 615–634.

105. Raymond Michalowski and Ronald Kramer, "The Space between Laws: The Problem of Corporate Crime in a Transnational Context," *Social Problems* 34 (1987): 34–53.

106. Ibid.

107. Christopher M. Brown and Nikhil S. Singhvi, "Antitrust Violations," *American Criminal Law Review* 35 (1998): 467–501.

108. Howard Adler, "Current Trends in Criminal Antitrust Enforcement," *Business Crimes Bulletin* (April 1996): 1.

109. CNNMoney, "Adelphia Founder Sentenced to 15 Years: John and Timothy Rigas Are Sentenced to Prison Nearly a Year After Their Convictions," 20 June 2005, http://money.cnn.com/2005/06/20/news/newsmakers/rigas_sentencing/index.htm (accessed April 26, 2007).

110. David Weisburd, Elin Waring, and Stanton Wheeler, "Class, Status, and the Punishment of White-Collar Criminals," *Law and Social Inquiry* 15 (1990): 223–243.

111. Sean Rosenmerkel, "Wrongfulness and Harmfulness as Components of Seriousness of White-Collar Offenses," *Journal of Contemporary Criminal Justice* 17 (2001): 308–328.

112. Mark Cohen, "Environmental Crime and Punishment: Legal/Economic Theory and Empirical Evidence on Enforcement of Federal Environmental Statutes," *Journal of*

Criminal Law and Criminology 82 (1992): 1,054–1,109.

113. Russell Mokhiber, "White Collar Crime Penalties," *Multinational Monitor* 22 (2001): 30.

114. Jonathan Lechter, Daniel Posner, and George Morris, "Antitrust Violations," *American Criminal Law Review* 39 (2002): 225–273.

115. See generally President's Commission on Organized Crime, *Report to the President and the Attorney General, The Impact: Organized Crime Today* (Washington, DC: U.S. Government Printing Office, 1986). Herein cited as *Organized Crime Today*.

116. Frederick Martens and Michele Cunningham-Niederer, "Media Magic, Mafia Mania," *Federal Probation* 49 (1985): 60–68.

117. *Organized Crime Today*, pp. 7–8.

118. Alan Block and William Chambliss, *Organizing Crime* (New York: Elsevier, 1981).

119. Alan Block, *East Side/West Side* (New Brunswick, NJ: Transaction Books, 1983), pp. vii, 10–11.

120. Statement for the record of Thomas V. Fuentes, Chief, Organized Crime Section, Criminal Investigative Division, Federal Bureau of Investigation, "Organized Crime before the House Subcommittee on Finance and Hazardous Materials." September 13, 2000.

121. Donald Cressey, *Theft of the Nation* (New York: Harper & Row, 1969).

122. Stanley Einstein, and Menachem Amir, *Organized Crime: Uncertainties and Dilemmas* (Chicago: University of Illinois at Chicago, Office of International Criminal Justice, 1999); William Kleinknecht, *The New Ethnic Mobs: The Changing Face of Organized Crime in America* (New York: Free Press, 1996); Don Liddick, *An Empirical, Theoretical, and Historical Overview of Organized Crime* (Lewiston, NY: Edwin Mellen Press, 1999); Maria Minniti, "Membership Has Its Privileges: Old and New Mafia Organizations," *Comparative Economic Studies* 37 (1995): 31–47.

123. *Organized Crime Today*, p. 11.

124. FBI, "Organized Crime Today," February 20, 2007, www.fbi.gov/page2/feb07/orgcrime022007.htm (accessed April 26, 2007).

125. Ibid.

126. David Binder, "In Europe, Sex Slavery Is Thriving Despite Raids," *New York Times*, 19 October 2002, p. A3.

127. Richard A. Ballezza, "YACS Crime Groups: An FBI Major Crime Initiative," *FBI Law Enforcement Bulletin* 67 (1998): 7–13.

128. Omar Bartos, "Growth of Russian Organized Crime Poses Serious Threat," *CJ International* 11 (1995): 8–9.

129. George Vold, *Theoretical Criminology*, 2nd ed., rev. Thomas Bernard (New York: Oxford University Press, 1979).

130. 18 U.S.C. 1952 (1976).

131. PL 91-452, Title IX, 84 Stat. 922 (1970) (codified at 18 U.S.C. 1961–68, 1976).

132. Richard McFeely, "Enterprise Theory of Investigation," *FBI Law Enforcement Bulletin* 70 (2001): 19–26.

133. National Legal Policy Center, "Bonanno Crime Boss Gets Two Life Terms," August 17, 2005, www.nlpc.org/view.asp?action=viewArticle&aid=975 (accessed April 26, 2007).

134. Selwyn Raab, "A Battered and Ailing Mafia Is Losing Its Grip on America," *New York Times*, 22 October 1990, p. 1.

135. Ibid., p. B7.

136. Rebecca Porter, "Prosecutors, Plaintiffs Aim to Curb Internet Gambling," *Trial* 40 (August 2004): 14.

Public Order Crime

CHAPTER OUTLINE

Law and Morality
Debating Morality
Social Harm
Moral Crusades and Crusaders
Moral Crusades Today

Sexually Related Offenses
Paraphilias
Prostitution
PROFILES IN CRIME: John Evander Couey
and the Jessica Lunsford Murder Case

Incidence of Prostitution

Comparative Criminology: International
Trafficking in Prostitution

International Sex Trade
Types of Prostitutes
Becoming a Prostitute
Controlling Prostitution
Legalize Prostitution?

Pornography
Child Pornography
Does Pornography Cause Violence?
Pornography and the Law
Controlling Pornography

Substance Abuse
When Did Drug Use Begin?
Alcohol and Its Prohibition
The Extent of Substance Abuse
AIDS and Drug Use
What Causes Substance Abuse?
Is There a Drug Gateway?
Types of Drug Users
Drugs and Crime
Drugs and the Law
Drug Control Strategies

Policy and Practice in Criminology: Drug
Abuse Resistance Education

Drug Legalization

CHAPTER OBJECTIVES

1. Be familiar with the association between law and morality
2. Be able to discuss moral crusades and crusaders
3. Know what is meant by paraphilias
4. Be able to discuss the various types of prostitution
5. Describe the relationship between obscenity and pornography
6. Know the various techniques being used to control pornography
7. Discuss the history and extent of drug abuse
8. Be able to discuss the cause of substance abuse
9. Describe the different types of drug users
10. Identify the various drug control strategies

© AP Images/Bill Habor

On February 17, 2006, the front page of the Dallas Morning News *announced, "Candidate Worked as Prostitute."[1] The story concerned* Tom Malin's campaign for district 108 of the Texas House of Representatives. The 37-year-old Malin had been running as an openly gay candidate in the Democratic primary. A Dallas native, community activist, and successful businessman (sales director for Mary Kay cosmetics), Malin lived in a fashionable high-rise with his partner, a philanthropist and businessman.

Before the scandal made headlines, Malin seemed to have the race in hand. He had secured endorsements from the Dallas Stonewall Democrats, Dallas Tejano Democrats (a Latino political group), and the Morning News. His issues were school financing, crime, the economy, and tax and ethics reform. Then the story broke that he had been an escort on and off until 2001—mostly while a struggling actor in New York and Los Angeles. He gave a statement to the Morning News: "I've made mistakes in my life, and I've stood before my creator and I've accepted responsibility for my behavior. I've also accepted his grace and his redemption and his love and his forgiveness, and that's what's important."[2] Nonetheless, Malin's campaign never recovered. On March 7, 2006, he lost the primary 55 percent to 45 percent. In the aftermath, The Advocate, a national gay and lesbian newsmagazine, issued the following statement:

> Even among many gays and lesbians—and certainly in mainstream culture—sex for pay remains the irredeemable sin. The president can be a recovering alcoholic with a DUI arrest; the vice president can accidentally shoot a man—all is forgiven. But if a person takes money for sex, the taint may be inescapable. Forget about running for office. Forget about a high-profile business career. Forget about acting, modeling, or MTV. It's over. Even many gays will prefer that you take a hike.

Tom Malin's experience illustrates the concern the public and the media have with issues of morality and values. It is ironic that Malin could be a successful candidate for public office as an openly gay man, something that would have been unthinkable 50 years ago, yet his career was destroyed by his involvement in sex for hire. Although one act considered a violation of social norms only a few years ago is now accepted, another is still prohibited and shunned by "polite society." Who decides what is acceptable behavior, what is not, and how we distinguish between them are still matters of great concern to criminologists.

Societies have long banned or limited behaviors believed to run contrary to social norms, customs, and values. These behaviors are often referred to as **public order crimes** or **victimless crimes**, although the latter term can be misleading.[3] Public order crimes involve acts that interfere with the operations of society and the ability of people to function efficiently. Put another way, whereas such common-law crimes as rape or robbery are considered inherently wrong and damaging, other behaviors are outlawed because they conflict with social policy, prevailing moral rules, and current public opinion.

Statutes designed to uphold public order usually prohibit the manufacture and distribution of morally questionable goods and services such as erotic material, commercial sex, and mood-altering drugs. They may also ban acts that a few people holding political power consider morally tinged, such as homosexual solicitation in public places. Statutes like these are controversial in part because millions of otherwise law-abiding citizens often engage in these outlawed activities and consequently become criminals. These statutes are also controversial because they selectively prohibit desired goods, services, and behaviors; in other words, they outlaw sin and vice.

This chapter covers these public order crimes; it first briefly discusses the relationship between law and morality. Next the chapter addresses public order crimes of a sexual nature: paraphilias, prostitution, and pornography. The chapter concludes by focusing on the abuse of drugs and alcohol.

With a thoughtful look on her face, UN special ambassador and Somalian model Waris Dirie answers questions from journalists during a press conference in Hamburg, Germany. Born into a nomadic tribe in Somalia, at age five her mother held her down while a local woman cut away her genitals. Afterwards, she was stitched up tightly, leaving a hole the diameter of a matchstick and making it nearly impossible to walk. Although Dirie survived the procedure, her sister and two cousins did not. Should local customs such as female genital mutilation be respected or are some too barabaric to condone? Who defines morality? Waris has devoted her life to ending the practice.

LAW AND MORALITY

Legislation of moral issues has continually frustrated lawmakers. There is little debate that the purpose of criminal law is to protect society and reduce social harm. When a store is robbed or a child assaulted, it is relatively easy to see and condemn the harm done the victim. It is, however, more difficult to sympathize with or even identify the victims of immoral acts, such as pornography or prostitution, where the parties involved may be willing participants. If there is no victim, can there be a crime?

To answer this question, we might first consider whether there is actually a victim in so-called victimless crimes. Some participants may have been coerced into their acts; they are therefore its victims. Opponents of pornography, such as Andrea Dworkin, charge that women involved in adult films, far from being highly paid stars, are "dehumanized—turned into objects and commodities."[4] Research on prostitution shows that many young runaways and abandoned children are coerced into a life on the streets, where they are cruelly treated and held as virtual captives.[5]

Even if public order crimes do not actually harm their participants, perhaps society as a whole should be considered the victim of these crimes. Is the community harmed when an adult bookstore opens or a brothel is established? Does this signal that a neighborhood is in decline? Does it teach children that deviance is to be tolerated and profited from?

Debating Morality

Some scholars argue that acts like pornography, prostitution, and drug use erode the moral fabric of society and therefore should be prohibited and punished. They are crimes, according to the great legal scholar Morris Cohen, because "it is one

© Jeff Greenberg/PhotoEdit

On March 12, 2007, a federal grand jury in Omaha, Nebraska, indicted Jaisankar Marimuthu, 32, and Chockalingam Ramanathan, 33, residents of Chennai, India, and Thirugnanam Ramanathan, 34, a resident of Malaysia, on charges of conspiracy, fraud, and aggravated identity theft stemming from a high-tech, international fraud scheme designed to hijack online brokerage accounts for profit. The indictment marked the first time that individuals were arrested overseas in connection with an online brokerage intrusion scheme perpetrated in the United States.

According to the indictment, the defendants, operating primarily from Thailand and India, used their personal online brokerage accounts to purchase shares of several thinly traded stocks. They then hacked into online brokerage accounts of others using stolen usernames and passwords or established new brokerage accounts using stolen identities. Using these accounts, the three allegedly made scores of unauthorized purchases of the same stocks to drive up the market price. Once the share prices were artificially inflated, the defendants sold their own shares for a substantial profit. This "hack, pump, and dump" scheme netted the three more than $2 million.

The defendants used this type of scheme with various stocks between July and November 2006. Because of the scheme's sophistication, the investigation required a cooperative effort of the U.S. Justice Department's Criminal Division, the FBI, and the Securities and Exchange Commission working with international law enforcement. The conspiracy and computer fraud charges in this case each carry a maximum sentence of five years in prison. Wire fraud and securities fraud carry maximum sentences of 20 and 15 years, respectively. Each count of aggravated identity theft adds two years in prison.[1]

This complex, global criminal enterprise could not have existed 20 years ago. Innovation brings change and with it new opportunities to commit crime. The technological revolution has provided new tools to misappropriate funds, damage property, and sell illicit material. It has created cyber crime, a new breed of offenses that can be singular or ongoing but typically involves the theft and/or destruction of information, resources, or funds utilizing computers, computer networks, and the Internet.

> ### connections
>
> Chapter 13 reviewed the concept of enterprise crime and its motivations. Cyber crime can be viewed as a type of enterprise crime employing sophisticated technology to achieve illegal profits. The Internet enables these ploys to be used on a global scale.

Cyber crime presents a compelling challenge for the justice system because (a) it is rapidly evolving with new schemes being created daily, (b) it is difficult to detect through traditional law enforcement channels, and (c) its control demands that agents of the justice system develop technical skills that match those of the perpetrators.[2]

Why has cyber crime become so important? The widespread use of computers and the Internet has ushered in the age of information technology (IT) and made it an intricate part of daily life in most industrialized societies. IT involves computer networking, the Internet, and advanced communications. It is the key to the economic system and will become more important as major industries shift their manufacturing plants to areas of the world where production is much cheaper. IT is responsible for the globalization phenomenon or the process of creating transnational markets, politics, and legal systems—in other words, creating a global economy. The Internet coupled with ever more powerful computers is now the chosen medium to provide a wide range of global services, ranging from entertainment and communication to research and education.

The cyber age has also generated an enormous amount of revenue. Spending on IT and telecommunications will grow by more than 6 percent each year, soon reaching about $2 trillion.[3] Today more than 1 billion people are using e-mail and 240 million are mobile Internet users. Magnifying the importance of the Internet is the fact that many critical infrastructure functions are now being conducted online, ranging from banking to control of shipping on the Mississippi River.[4]

This vast network has become a target for illegal activities and enterprise. As a group, these activities are referred to as cyber crime—any criminal act that involves communication, computer and Internet networks. Some cyber criminals use modern technology to accumulate goods and services. Cyber theft schemes range from illegal copying of copyrighted material to using technology to commit traditional theft-based offenses such as larceny and fraud.

Another type of cyber criminal is motivated less by profit and more by the urge to commit cyber vandalism or technological destruction. They aim their malicious attacks at

CONCEPT SUMMARY 15.1

TYPES OF CYBER CRIME

Crime	Definition	Examples
Cyber theft	Use of cyberspace to either distribute illegal goods and services or to defraud people for quick profits	Illegal copyright infringement, identity theft, Internet securities fraud, warez
Cyber vandalism	Use of cyberspace for revenge, destruction, and to achieve a malicious intent	Website defacement, worms, viruses, cyber stalking, cyber bullying
Cyber terrorism	An effort by covert forces to disrupt the intersection where the virtual electronic reality of computers meets the physical world	Logic bombs used to disrupt or destroy "secure" systems or network, Internet used to communicate covertly with agents around the world

disrupting, defacing, and destroying technology that they find offensive.

A third type of cyber crime is cyber terrorism, acts aimed at undermining the social, economic, and political system of an enemy nation by destroying its electronic infrastructure and disrupting its economy.

In sum, some cyber criminals are high-tech thieves while others are high-tech vandals; the property they destroy is electronic rather then physical. And some may combine theft and vandalism in cyber terror attacks (see Concept Summary 15.1). This chapter reviews the various forms of cyber crime. It also looks at how law enforcement agencies are beginning to fight back against cyber criminals and learning to apply some of the emerging technology to deal with traditional crime problems.

CYBER THEFT: CYBER CRIMES FOR PROFIT

It is ironic that technological breakthroughs since the dawn of the Industrial Revolution—such as telephones and automobiles—not only brought with them dramatic improvements for society but also created new opportunities for criminal wrongdoing: criminals use the telephone to place bets or threaten victims; cars can be stolen and sold for big profits.[5] The same pattern is now occurring during the IT revolution. The computer and Internet provide opportunities for socially beneficial endeavors—such as education, research, commerce, and entertainment—while at the same time serving as a tool to facilitate illegal activity. The new computer-based technology allows criminals to operate in a more efficient and effective manner. Cyber thieves now have the luxury of remaining anonymous, living in any part of the world (such as the three hackers discussed above), conducting their business during the day or in the evening, working alone or in a group, while at the same time reaching a much wider number of potential victims than ever before. No longer is the con artist or criminal entrepreneur limited to fleecing victims in a particular geographic locale; the whole world can be their target. The technology revolution has opened novel methods for cyber theft that heretofore were nonexistent, ranging from the unlawful distribution of computer software to Internet security fraud.

Cyber thieves conspire to use cyberspace to either distribute illegal goods and services or to defraud people for quick profits. Some of the most common methods are discussed here.

Computer Fraud

In 2004 Jessica Sabathia, a 31-year-old California woman, pleaded guilty to counts of computer fraud for embezzling more than $875,000 from North Bay Health Care Group. Sabathia, an accounts payable clerk for North Bay, used her computer to access North Bay's accounting software without the authority of her employer and issued approximately 127 checks payable to herself and others. To conceal the fraud, she then altered the electronic check register to make it appear that the checks had been payable to North Bay's vendors. Jessica cashed several of the checks, and many were deposited into her bank account and the bank accounts of others and used for personal expenses.[6]

Jessica's crime falls under the general category of computer fraud, not a unique offense but rather a common-law crime committed using contemporary technology. Consequently, many computer crimes are prosecuted under such traditional criminal statutes as larceny or fraud. However, not all computer crimes fall under common-law statutes because the property stolen may be intangible (electronic and/or magnetic impulse). Some of these crimes are listed in Exhibit 15.1.

There are a number of recent trends in computer frauds. Internal attacks are now outgrowing external attacks at the world's largest financial institutions. According to a recent global security survey (2006), 57 percent of U.S. companies report being hit by viruses in the past year; computer network attacks were experienced by 9 percent. Almost 48 percent of the 2,193 security professionals and business technology managers surveyed said that managing the complexity of security is their top challenge.[7]

There has also been a growing trend to commit fraud using devices that rely on IT for their operations. For example, **automatic teller machines (ATMs)** are now attracting the attention of cyber criminals looking for easy profits.[8] One approach is to use a thin, transparent-plastic overlay on an ATM keypad that captures a user's identification code as it is

---

EXHIBIT 15.1

Examples of Computer Fraud

Theft of Information
The unauthorized obtaining of information from a computer (hacking), including software that is copied for profit.

The "Salami" Fraud
With this type of fraud the perpetrator carefully skims small sums from the balances of a large number of accounts in order to bypass internal controls and escape detection.

Software Theft
The comparative ease of making copies of computer software has led to a huge illegal market, depriving authors of very significant revenues.

Manipulation of Accounts/Banking Systems
Similar to a "Salami" fraud, but on a much larger and usually more complex scale. Sometimes perpetrated as a "one-off kamikaze" fraud.

Corporate Espionage
Trade secrets are stolen by a company's competitors, which can be either domestic or foreign. The goal is to increase the rival company's (or nation's) competitive edge in the global marketplace.

Source: Clive Carmichael-Jones, "The Enemy Within," VoGon International, www.vogon-international.com/literature/international/EnemyWithin.pdf (accessed March 20, 2007).

---

entered. Though the plastic covering looks like some sort of cover to protect the keys, in fact, microchips in the device record every keystroke. Another transparent device inside the card slot captures card data. While the client completes the transaction, a computer attached to the overlay records all the data necessary to clone the card. Rather than rob an ATM user at gunpoint the cyber criminal relies on stealth and technological skill to commit the crime.

Distributing Illegal Sexual Material

The IT revolution has revitalized the porn industry. The Internet is an ideal venue for selling and distributing obscene material; the computer is an ideal device for storage and viewing. It is difficult to estimate the vast number of websites featuring sexual content, including nude photos, videos, live sex acts, and webcam strip sessions among other forms of "adult entertainment."[9] There are some indicators that show the extent of the industry:[10]

▌ 89 percent of porn is created in the United States

▌ About $3 billion in revenue is generated from U.S. porn sites each year, compared to $9 billion for all movie box office sales

▌ $89/second is spent on porn

▌ 72 percent of porn viewers are men

▌ 260 new porn sites go online daily[11]

The number of visits to pornographic sites surpasses those made to Internet search engines; some individual sites report as many as 50 million hits per year.

How do adult sites make their profits?[12]

▪ A large firm sells annual subscriptions in exchange for unlimited access to content.

▪ Password services charge an annual fee to deliver access to hundreds of small sites, which share the subscription revenues.

▪ Large firms provide free content to smaller affiliate sites. The affiliates post the free content and then try to channel visitors to the large sites, which give the smaller sites a percentage of the fees paid by those who sign up.

▪ Webmasters forward traffic to another porn site in return for a small per-consumer fee. In many cases, the consumer is sent to the other sites involuntarily, which is known in the industry as *mousetrapping*. Web surfers who try to close out a window after visiting an adult site are sent to another web page automatically. This can repeat dozens of times, causing users to panic and restart their computers in order to escape.

▪ Adult sites cater to niche audiences looking for specific kinds of adult content.

While some sites cater to adult tastes, others cross the legal border by peddling access to obscene material or even kiddie porn. Despite some successful prosecutions, it has been difficult to control Internet pornography. Various federal legislative efforts, including the Communications Decency Act (1996), the Child Online Protection Act (1998), and the Children's Internet Protection Act (2000), have been successfully challenged in the courts under the First Amendment. Filtering devices used extensively in schools and libraries fail to block out a lot of obscene material, giving youngsters the opportunity to use computers away from home to surf the net for adult content. It is unlikely that any law enforcement efforts will put a dent in the Internet porn industry.

> **connections**
>
> Pornography was discussed more fully in Chapter 14. The ability to access pornographic material over the Internet has helped expand the sale of sexually related material. People wishing to purchase sexually related material no longer face the risk of public exposure in adult book stores or movie theaters. Sellers of adult films and photos can now reach a much wider international audience.

Denial-of-Service Attack

A **denial-of-service attack** is characterized as an attempt to extort money from legitimate users of an Internet service by threatening to prevent the user having access to the service.[13] Examples include:

▪ Attempts to flood a computer network, thereby preventing legitimate network traffic

▪ Attempts to disrupt connections within a computer network, thereby preventing access to a service

▪ Attempts to prevent a particular individual from accessing a service

▪ Attempts to disrupt service to a specific system or person

A denial-of-service attack may involve threatening or actually flooding an Internet site with millions of bogus messages or orders so that the services will be tied up and unable to perform as promised. Unless the site operator pays extortion, the attackers threaten to keep up the interference until real consumers become frustrated and abandon the site. Even so-called respectable businesspeople have been accused of launching denial-of-service attacks against rival business interests.[14]

Online gambling casinos—a $7 billion a year industry—have proven particularly vulnerable to attack. Hundreds of attacks have been launched against online casinos located in Costa Rica, the Caribbean, and Great Britain. If the attack coincides with a big sporting event such as the Super Bowl, the casinos may give in and make payments rather than lose revenue and fray customer relations.[15]

Illegal Copyright Infringement

For the past decade, groups of individuals have been working together to illegally obtain software and then "crack" or "rip" its copyright protections, before posting it on the Internet for other members of the group to use; this is called **warez**.

Frequently, these new pirated copies reach the Internet days or weeks before the legitimate product is commercially available. The government has actively pursued members of the warez community, and some have been charged and convicted under the Computer Fraud and Abuse Act (CFAA), which criminalizes accessing computer systems without authorization to obtain information,[16] and the Digital Millennium Copyright Act (DMCA), which makes it a crime to circumvent antipiracy measures built into most commercial software and also outlaws the manufacture, sale, or distribution of code-cracking devices used to illegally copy software.[17]

File Sharing Another form of illegal copyright infringement involves file-sharing programs that allow Internet users to download music and other copyrighted material without paying the artists and record producers their rightful royalties. Theft through the illegal reproduction and distribution of movies, software, games, and music is estimated to cost U.S. industries $19 billion worldwide each year. Although some students routinely share files and download music, criminal copyright infringement represents a serious economic threat. The United States Criminal Code provides penalties for a first-time offender of five years incarceration and a fine of $250,000.[18] Other provisions provide for the forfeiture and destruction of infringing copies and all equipment used to make the copies.[19]

On June 27, 2005, copyright protection of music and other types of entertainment distributed via the Internet was upheld by the Supreme Court in the case of *MGM Studios, Inc. v. Grokster*, 125 S. Ct. 2764 (2005). The Court unanimously held that software distributors such as Grokster could be sued for inducing copyright infringement if they market file-sharing software that might induce people to illegally copy protected material even if that software could also be used for legitimate purposes. Justice Souter wrote:

> We hold that one who distributes a device with the object of promoting its use to infringe copyright, as shown by the clear expression or other affirmative steps taken to foster infringement, is liable for the resulting acts of infringement by third parties.

As a result of the opinion, on November 7, 2005, Grokster, announced that it would suspend its file-sharing service; it was also forced to pay $50 million to the music and recording industries.

Internet Securities Fraud

Fifteen-year-old Jonathan Lebed was charged with securities fraud by the SEC after he repeatedly bought low-cost, thinly traded stocks and then spread hundreds of false and misleading messages concerning them—generally baseless price predictions. After their values were artificially inflated, Lebed sold the securities at an inflated price. His smallest one-day gain was $12,000 and one day he made $74,000. Lebed agreed to findings of fraud but later questioned whether he had done anything wrong; he was forced to hand over his illicit gains, plus interest, which came to $285,000.[20]

Though he might not agree, young Lebed's actions are considered Internet fraud because they involve using the Internet to intentionally manipulate the securities marketplace for profit. There are three major types of Internet securities fraud today:

- *Market manipulation.* Stock market manipulation occurs when an individual tries to control the price of stock by interfering with the natural forces of supply and demand. There are two principal forms of this crime: the "pump and dump" (described in the opening vignette) and the "cyber smear." In a pump and dump scheme, erroneous and deceptive information is posted online to get unsuspecting investors interested in a stock while those spreading the information sell previously purchased stock at an inflated price. The cyber smear is a reverse pump and dump: negative information is spread online about a stock, driving down its price and enabling people to buy it at an artificially low price before rebuttals by the company's officers reinflate the price.[21]

- *Fraudulent offerings of securities.* Some cyber criminals create websites specifically designed to fraudulently sell securities. To make the offerings look more attractive than they are, assets may be inflated, expected returns overstated, and risks understated. In these schemes, investors are promised abnormally high profits on their investments. No investment is actually made. Early investors are paid returns with the investment money received from the later investors. The system usually collapses, and the later investors do not receive dividends and lose their initial investment. For

example, the Tri-West Investment Company solicited investments in "prime bank notes."[22] Visitors to their website were promised an annualized rate of return of 120 percent plus return of their principal at the end of a year, as well as substantial referral fees of 15 percent on all referred investments. The website, which contained alleged testimonials describing instant wealth from early investors, also told visitors that their investments were "guaranteed." Investors contributed $60 million in funds to Tri-West, and some "dividends" were paid. However, no money was actually invested, the dividends were paid from new investments, and most of the cash was siphoned off by the schemers.

- *Illegal touting.* This crime occurs when individuals make securities recommendations and fail to disclose that they are being paid to disseminate their favorable opinions. Section 17(b) of the Securities Act of 1933 requires that paid touters disclose the nature, source, and amount of their compensation. If those who tout stocks fail to disclose their relationship with the company, information misleads investors into believing that the speaker is objective and credible rather than bought and paid for.

Identity Theft

Identity theft occurs when a person uses the Internet to steal someone's identity and/or impersonate the victim to open a new credit card account or conduct some other financial transaction. It is a type of cyber crime that has grown at surprising rates over the past few years.[23]

Identity theft can destroy a person's life by manipulating credit records or stealing from their bank accounts. Identity thieves use a variety of techniques to steal information. They may fill out change of address cards at the post office and obtain people's credit card bills and bank statements. They may then call the credit card issuer and, pretending to be the victim, ask for a change in address on the account. They can then charge numerous items over the Internet and have the merchandise sent to the new address. It may take months for the victim to realize the fraud because the victim is not getting bills from the credit card company.

Some identity theft schemes are extremely elaborate. In one recent scheme, 19 people were indicted on charges that they had created an organization called Shadowcrew to provide stolen credit card numbers and identity documents through an online marketplace. The stolen account numbers were contributed by approved "vendors" who had been granted permission to sell on the Shadowcrew site after being vetted through a complex review process. Shadowcrew members allegedly trafficked in at least 1.7 million stolen credit card numbers and caused total losses in excess of $4 million.[24]

Phishing Some identity thieves create false e-mails or websites that look legitimate but are designed to gain illegal access to a victim's personal information; this is known as phishing (also known as *carding* and *spoofing*).

Some phishers send out e-mails that look like they come from a credit card company or online store telling the victim there is a problem with their account credit or balance. To fix the problem and update their account they are asked to submit their name, address, phone numbers, personal information, credit card account numbers, and Social Security number (SSN). Or the e-mail may direct them to a phony website that purports to be a legitimate company or business enterprise. Once a victim accesses the website they are asked to provide personal information or financial account information to the website so that the problem can be fixed.

Once phishers have a victim's personal information they can do three things. They can gain access to preexisting accounts, banking, credit cards, and buy things using those accounts. Phishers can also use the information to open brand new banking accounts and credit cards without the victim's knowledge. Finally, the phishers can implant viruses into their software that forwards the phishing e-mail to other recipients once one person responds to the original e-mail, thereby luring more potential victims into his or her net. Some common phisher scams are listed in Exhibit 15.2.

Phishing e-mails and websites have become even more of a problem now that cyber criminals can easily copy brand names, logos, and corporate personnel insignia directly into the e-mail. The look is so authentic that victims believe the e-mail comes from the advertised company. Most phishers send out spam e-mails to a large number of recipients knowing that some of those recipients will have accounts with the company that they are impersonating.

To meet the increasing threat of phishing and identity theft, Congress passed the Identity Theft and Assumption Deterrence Act of 1998 (Identity Theft Act) to make it a federal crime when anyone:

> Knowingly transfers or uses, without lawful authority, a means of identification of another person with the intent to commit, or to aid or abet, any unlawful activity that constitutes a violation of Federal law, or that constitutes a felony under any applicable State or local law.[25]

Violations of the act are investigated by federal investigative agencies such as the U.S. Secret Service, the FBI, and the U.S. Postal Inspection Service. In 2004 the Identity Theft Penalty Enhancement Act was signed into law; the act increases existing penalties for the crime of identity theft, establishes aggravated identity theft as a criminal offense, and establishes mandatory penalties for aggravated identity theft. According to the new law, anyone who knowingly "transfers, possesses, or uses, without lawful authority" someone else's identification will be sentenced to an extra prison term of two years with no possibility of probation. Committing identity fraud while engaged in crimes associated with terrorism—such as aircraft destruction, arson, airport violence, or kidnapping top government officials—will receive a mandatory sentence enhancement of five years.[26]

Vishing Voice over Internet Protocol (VoIP) is a technology that allows people to make voice calls using a broadband Internet connection instead of a regular (or analog) phone

EXHIBIT 15.2

Common Phishing Scams

▪ *Account verification scams.* Individuals purchase domain names that are similar to those of legitimate companies, such as *Amazon.Accounts.net*. The real company is Amazon, but it does not have *Accounts* in its domain name. These con artists then send out millions of e-mails asking consumers to verify account information and request Social Security numbers. The victim is directed to a bogus website by clicking the legitimate-looking address.

▪ *Sign-in rosters.* There are some companies and governmental agencies (colleges, EDD, state-sponsored programs) that ask you to put your name and SSN on a sign-in roster. Identity thieves may sign up toward the end of a page so that they can copy and collect personal identifying information.

▪ *"Help move money from my country," aka Nigerian 419 scam.* A bogus e-mail is sent from an alleged representative of a foreign government asking the victim to help move money from one account to another. Some forms include requests to help a dying woman or free a political prisoner. Some claim that the victim has been the recipient of a legacy or a winning lottery ticket. Nigerian money offers now account for about 12 percent of all Internet scams.

▪ *Canadian/Netherlands lottery.* Originating from the Netherlands and other foreign countries, these scams usually ask for money to hold the prize until the victim can collect in person.

▪ *"Free credit report."* Almost all "free credit report" e-mails are scams. Either the person is trying to find out the victim's Social Security number or the victim is billed for services later on.

▪ *"You have won a free gift."* The victim receives an e-mail about a free gift or prize. They just have to send their credit card info to take care of shipping and handling. Responding may result in hundreds of spams or telemarketing calls.

▪ *E-mail chain letters/pyramid schemes.* Victims are sent an official looking e-mail requesting cooperation by sending a report to five friends or relatives. Those who respond are then contacted for money in order to keep the chain going.

▪ *"Find out everything on anyone."* This e-mail is trying to solicit money by offering a CD or program that victims can use to find out personal information on another person. This information is always a matter of public record and may be accessed for personal use.

▪ *Job advertisement scams.* Phishers spoofing legitimate Internet job websites (for instance, Monster.com) contact a victim promising a high paying job. They solicit personal information, including Social Security numbers.

▪ *VISA/MasterCard scam.* A VISA or MasterCard "employee" sends an e-mail asking to confirm unusual spending activity and asks the victim for the code on the back of their credit card.

Source: Identity Theft Resource Center (ITRC), "Scams and Consumer Alerts," www.idtheftcenter.org (accessed June 20, 2007).

line.[27] Some VoIP services only allow subscribers to call other people using the same service, but others allow you to call anyone who has a telephone number—including local, long distance, mobile, and international numbers. Also, while some VoIP services only work over a computer or a special VoIP phone, others allow traditional phone hookups connected to a VoIP adapter. Cyber thieves have already employed this technology in identity theft schemes.

EXHIBIT 15.5

Key Provisions of the National Information Infrastructure Protection Act (NIIPA)

■ The NIIPA makes it a crime to access computer files without authorization, or in excess of authorization, and subsequently to transmit classified government information.

■ The act criminalizes gaining information without access, or in excess of authorized access, from financial institutions, the U.S. government, or private sector computers used in interstate commerce.

■ The act proscribes intentionally accessing a U.S. department or agency nonpublic computer without authorization. If the government or a government agency does not use the computer exclusively, the illegal access must affect the government's use.

■ The act prohibits accessing a protected computer, without or beyond authorization, with the intent to defraud and obtain something of value. There is an exception if the defendant only obtained computer time with a value less than $5,000 per year.

■ The act extends the protection against computer hacking by including interstate, government, and financial institution computers as "protected" computers. It prohibits unauthorized access that causes damage regardless of whether or not the damage was "recklessly caused."

■ The act criminalizes knowingly causing the transmission of a program, code, or command, and as a result, intentionally causing damage to a protected computer (without regard as to authorization to access the computer). Company employees and other authorized users can be culpable for intentional damage to a protected computer.

■ The act makes unauthorized users, such as hackers, who cause the transmission of viruses responsible even if the transmission was not intentional because it was only reckless or negligent.

■ The act prohibits one with intent to defraud from trafficking in passwords, which either would permit unauthorized access to a government computer or affect interstate or foreign commerce.

■ The act makes it illegal to transmit in interstate or foreign commerce any threat to cause damage to a protected computer with intent to extort something of value. For example, hackers threatening to crash a system if not given system privileges or encrypting a company's data and demanding money for the key would be held criminally liable.

Source: Public Law 104-294, Title II, [sections] 201, 110 Stat. 3488, 3491–94 (1996).

files, and access to computers operated for the government. The act was supplemented in 1996 by the National Information Infrastructure Protection Act (NIIPA), which significantly broadens the scope of the law. The key provisions of this act are set out in Exhibit 15.5.

Because cyber crime is new, existing laws sometimes are inadequate to address the problem. Therefore new legislation has been drafted to protect the public from this new breed of cyber criminal. For example, before October 30, 1998, when the Identity Theft and Assumption Deterrence Act of 1998 became law, there was no federal statute that made identity theft a crime. Today, federal prosecutors are making substantial use of the statute and are actively prosecuting cases of identity theft.[83] Since then all states except Vermont and the District of Columbia have passed laws related to identity theft.

In the wake of the 9/11 attacks, the NIIPA has been amended by sections of the USA Patriot Act to make it easier to enforce crimes by terrorists and other organized enemies against the nation's computer systems. Subsection 1030(a)(5)(A)(i) of the act criminalizes knowingly causing the transmission of a program, code, or command, and as a result, intentionally causing damage to a protected computer. This section applies regardless of whether the user had authorization to access the protected computer; company insiders and authorized users can be culpable for intentional damage to a protected computer. The act also prohibits intentional access without authorization that results in damage but does not require intent to damage; the attacker can merely be negligent or reckless.

In addition to these main acts, computer-related crimes can also be charged under at least 40 different federal statutes. Supplementing some of the statutes discussed earlier in the chapter, these include the Copyright Act and Digital Millennium Copyright Act, the National Stolen Property Act, the mail and wire fraud statutes, the Electronic Communications Privacy Act, the Communications Decency Act of 1996, the Child Online Protection Act, the Child Pornography Prevention Act of 1996, and the Internet False Identification Prevention Act of 2000.[84] Movie pirates who use the Internet to sell illegally copied films have led the federal government to create the Family Entertainment and Copyright Act of 2005. One part of that statute, known as the ART Act (Artists' Rights and Theft Prevention Act of 2005), criminalizes the use of recording equipment to make copies of films while in movie theaters. The statute also makes it illegal to make a copy of a work in production and put it on the Internet so it will be accessible to members of the public when the individual making the copy knew or should have known the work was intended for commercial distribution.[85]

International Treaties

Because cyber crime is essentially global, international cooperation is required for its control. The Convention on Cybercrime, ratified by the U.S. Senate in August 2006, is the first international treaty that addresses the definition and enforcement of cyber crime. Now signed by 43 nations, it focuses on improving investigative techniques and increasing cooperation among nations. The Convention includes a list of crimes that each signatory state must incorporate into their own law, including such cyber offenses as hacking, distribution of child pornography, and protection of intellectual property rights. It also allows law enforcement agencies new powers, including the ability to require that an Internet service provider monitor a person's online viewing and search choices in real time. The Convention also requires signatory states to cooperate whenever possible in the investigations and prosecution of cyber criminals. The vision is

A number of nations have entered into international agreements as they attempt to scuttle software piracy. Here, a steamroller crushes thousands of pirated compact disks and video- and audiotapes during an antipiracy crackdown in Miyun, north of Beijing. The U.S. government had threatened sanctions to punish what it viewed as China's failure to comply with international agreements to curtail rampant piracy of U.S. films, music, and computer software, and the Chinese government responded with a big stick.

that a common legal framework will eliminate jurisdictional hurdles to facilitate the law enforcement of borderless cyber crimes.[86]

Carrying out this mandate may be difficult to achieve given the legal rights afforded U.S. citizens that may not be realized by residents of other nations. For example, First Amendment protections that restrict the definition of pornography and obscenity in this country may not apply overseas. It is not surprising that watchdog institutions such as the ACLU have condemned the treaty and campaigned against U.S. participation.[87]

Cyber Crime Enforcement Agencies

To enforce cyber laws, the federal government is now operating a number of organizations to control cyber fraud. One approach is to create working groups that coordinate the activities of numerous agencies involved in investigating cyber crime. For example, the Interagency Telemarketing and Internet Fraud Working Group brings together representatives of numerous U.S. attorneys' offices, the FBI, the Secret Service, the Postal Inspection Service, the Federal Trade Commission, the Securities and Exchange Commission, and other law enforcement and regulatory agencies to share information about trends and patterns in Internet fraud schemes.[88]

Specialized enforcement agencies have been created. The Internet Fraud Complaint Center, based in Fairmont, West Virginia, is run by the FBI and the National White-Collar Crime Center. It brings together about 1,000 state and local law enforcement officials and regulators. Its goal is to analyze fraud-related complaints in order to find distinct patterns, develop information on particular cases, and send investigative packages to law enforcement authorities in the jurisdiction that appears likely to have the greatest investigative interest in the matter. The Center now receives more than 200,000 complaints each year, including auction fraud, nondelivery, and credit/debit card fraud, as well as nonfraudulent complaints, such as computer intrusions, spam/unsolicited e-mail, and child pornography.[89] Law enforcement has made remarkable strides in dealing with identity theft as a crime problem over the last several years.

One of the most successful federal efforts is the New York Electronic Crimes Task Force (NYECTF), a partnership between the U.S. Secret Service and a host of other public safety agencies and private corporations. Today, the task force consists of over 250 individual members representing federal, state, and local law enforcement, the private sector, and computer science specialists from 18 different universities. Since 1995, the New York task force has charged over 1,000 individuals with electronic crime losses exceeding $1.0 billion. It has trained over 60,000 law enforcement personnel, prosecutors, and private industry representatives in cyber crime prevention. Its success has prompted similar electronic crime task forces to be set up in Boston, Miami, Charlotte, Chicago, Las Vegas, San Francisco, Los Angeles, and Washington, D.C.[90]

Local Enforcement Efforts

Local police departments are now creating special units to crack down on cyber criminals. In Toronto, Canada, the police department's child-exploitation section concentrates on cracking high profile and difficult cases of Internet child pornography, using inventive and aggressive investigative methods. They estimate there are perhaps 100,000 children depicted in as many as 1 million pictures that circulate via the Internet. The efforts of the four-year-old Toronto police unit have led to 300 arrests so far, and only half have been made in the Toronto area. The unit looks for even the smallest clues to lead them to perpetrators. In one well-known case, investigators homed in on a computer keyboard where the character ñ—unique to Spanish—was visible. In the same series of pictures, they noticed a train ticket that appeared to be European in a child's hand. Sharing the information with Interpol, the international police consortium led to the break-up of a sadistic child-porn ring operating south of Madrid led by a man who had been using his position as a babysitter to gain access to small children.[91]

📎 **WWW** To access the Council of Europe's website and to read more about the **Convention on Cyber Crime**, go to www.thomsonedu.com/criminaljustice/siegel.

INFORMATION TECHNOLOGY IN CRIMINAL JUSTICE

Not only have computers and the Internet been used by criminals and scam artists to fleece the public, but criminal justice agencies are turning the tables by using modern technology to increase their own effectiveness. Information technology now plays a significant role in law enforcement. This effort was given a jump start in 1998, when the federal government, recognizing the vital role information, identification, and communication technologies could and must play in the criminal justice system, enacted the Crime Identification Technology Act of 1998 (CITA), which provided more than a billion dollars in grants to the states to upgrade their IT capabilities in areas such as criminal history record and identification systems and to promote the compatibility and integration of national, state, and local computer systems. The areas that CITA aided are set out in Exhibit 15.6.

Another innovation that pits technology against crime is biometric identification. The Policy and Practice in Criminology feature "Biometric Technology" discusses this new technique.

IT, CRIME, AND CIVIL LIBERTIES

Though the new IT techniques provide the opportunity to increase effectiveness and efficiency within criminal agencies, they come with a price. Some critics believe that they can compromise the privacy and liberty of U.S citizens who have not engaged in any form of illegal activity. Wary of "Big Brother," the American Civil Liberties Union (ACLU) warns that we are turning into a surveillance society, constantly watched by a plethora of computers, cameras, sensors, wireless communication, GPS, biometrics, and other technologies. And, they warn, there are new technologies on the horizon that can threaten privacy, such as implantable microchips that monitor behavior.[92]

Privacy concerns often focus on the new surveillance techniques, ranging from traditional closed circuit surveillance cameras to more recent ones such as biometrics. Critics believe

---

EXHIBIT 15.6

The Areas for Criminal Justice Improvement Designated by the Crime Identification Technology Act of 1998 (CITA)

▪ Improving adult and juvenile criminal history record information systems

▪ Creating automated fingerprint identification systems that are compatible with standards established by the Commerce Department's National Institute of Standards and Technology (NIST) and are interoperable with the Federal Bureau of Investigation (FBI) Integrated Automated Fingerprint System

▪ Establishing finger imaging, live scan, and other automated systems to digitize and communicate fingerprints consistent with NIST standards and ensure interoperability with print systems operated by the states and the FBI

▪ Augmenting state and local participation in the Interstate Identification Index of the National Crime Information System

▪ Improving systems to allow any compact relating to the Interstate Identification Index to participate fully in the National Crime Information System

▪ Enhancing systems to improve state and local participation in the FBI's National Instant Check System (NICS), which was authorized with the creation of the Brady Handgun Violence Prevention Act

▪ Creating an integrated criminal justice system, so that law enforcement agencies, courts, prosecutors, and corrections agencies have access to the same information

▪ Improving criminal history record information to determine eligibility to purchase firearms under NICS

▪ Developing court-based criminal justice information systems that integrate with other criminal justice information systems and promote the reporting of dispositions to central state repositories and to the FBI

▪ Accessing ballistics identification programs and technology that are compatible with the Bureau of Alcohol, Tobacco, Firearms, and Explosives' National Integrated Ballistics Network

▪ Enhancing the capabilities of forensic science laboratories and medical examiner programs

▪ Improving sex offender identification, tracking, and registration systems

▪ Creating systems to track and share information about domestic violence offenders

▪ Supporting fingerprint-supported background checks for noncriminal justice purposes

▪ Developing criminal justice information systems that provide research and statistical analysis

▪ Establishing multiagency, multijurisdictional communications systems among the states to share information among federal, state, and local law enforcement agencies

▪ Enhancing the capability of the criminal justice system to deliver timely, accurate, and complete criminal record information to child welfare agencies, organizations, and programs that are engaged in the assessment of risk and other activities related to the protection of children, including protection against child sexual abuse, and placement of children in foster care

Source: Office of Justice Programs Crime Identification Technology Act, http://it.ojp.gov/fund/files/cita.html#17%20Purposes (accessed April 26, 2007).

Policy and Practice in Criminology

BIOMETRIC TECHNOLOGY

Since the terrorist attacks on September 11, 2001, added security measurements have been installed to help protect the country's citizens. Biometrics, the science of using digital technology to identify individuals, has been implemented in many facets of the country's security system. Biometric technology has been installed in both airports and immigration centers to ensure that people are not using fake identities for illegal behavior.

Airports

Airports have started to implement the use of biometrics into their systems to prevent nonemployees from entering secured locations. The most popular type of biometrics being used in airports is iris scanning. While you are looking into a camera, a computer scans your eye, records information regarding your iris, and stores the information into a database. Once your eye has been scanned, you are then permitted onto the plane.

In order to depart from the plane at your destination, your iris scan must match the one in the database to ensure that you are the person who is supposed to be departing the plane. For those who travel frequently this procedure has proved effective, as it does not require the individual to continuously stop at checkpoints and have his or her identification checked. The person simply looks into a camera and within seconds is permitted to pass through all the checkpoints.

In addition, an airport in Charlotte, North Carolina, has used the system to keep unwanted individuals from entering secure facilities. With the prior use of swipe cards and/or codes, unauthorized people were able to walk in behind personnel to gain entry into an area; however, this is no longer a problem with the use of biometrics. Employees of the Charlotte airport have their irises scanned and the information gained remains in a database. In order to access the secured areas, personnel must look into a tube and have their match confirmed to be

allowed entrance. Although fingerprints have also been used for this purpose, an iris scan can match over 400 different points of identification compared to that of only 60 to 70 points of a fingerprint.

Other airports have incorporated another type of biometric technology within their security system: facial recognition. Facial recognition systems measure facial features of people, noting the distance of one feature from another, along with sizes of features, and so on. An airport in Florida uses a facial recognition system that contains images of the FBI's top ten most wanted criminals, along with other sought-after individuals. Passengers are required to look into cameras to verify that they do not match any of the images in the system. If no matches are found, passengers are permitted to pass through and board their airplane. There is hope that with the continued success of this system, facial recognition systems will help locate fugitives, terrorists, and abducted children who are passing through transportation terminals.

that an identification system based on face-recognition technology poses several threats to civil liberties, the most telling being false positives where a person is falsely identified and then investigated, a process which unfairly impinges on the privacy of innocent people. Biometrics can also be used to locate and physically track people, prying into their movements that may have little to do with any crime or terrorist activity.[93] As a result, people, wary of being watched and recorded by the government, will alter their activities and actions, and in so doing, lose the right to self-determination of their own behavior.[94]

There are also concerns about the linkage of surveillance information to fast and inexpensive data processing and storage systems. The result is a permanent record that is easily accessed. Every move an individual makes over the course of a day—from using their E-ZPass at a particular exit on the throughway to the items they bought at the drugstore—can be tied across various databases to create a detailed dossier on daily activities.[95] Who should have access to this information and for what purpose is a critical issue.

While these intrusions are troubling, people also want to be protected from harmful criminal activity, ranging from identity theft to terrorism. Protection of civil liberties is important, but so is protection from civil dangers. The level of intrusion and surveillance people will tolerate may depend in large part on their assessment of the risks they face and their willingness to sacrifice civil liberties to reduce these risks. [96] As the threat of terrorism and cyber crime grows, so too may tolerance for invasions of privacy. A number of beliefs seem to sway public opinion about IT. Some justify the use of IT in law enforcement while others are voiced by people who wish to restrict its use:

1. *Not much to fear.* Is the government really intent on keeping the public under surveillance? Some commentators view concerns about using IT in criminal justice as misplaced. When they gather data or use IT in surveillance, police agencies may simply be trying to do their job more effectively and not attempting to create a "Big Brother" society. While the media and some civil liberties

Immigration

The Department of Homeland Security has implemented the United States Visitor and Immigrant Status Indicator Technology (US-Visit). US-Visit was developed to provide more security to the nation's airports while keeping transportation into and out of the country open. This is accomplished by using biometric scans to determine the identity of all travelers from foreign countries who attempt to enter the United States.

Almost all foreign citizens, regardless of country of origin, who wish to travel into the United States must comply with US-Visit requirements. The process of registering for travel into the United States under the new US-Visit starts far from U.S. soil. An individual who wishes to travel to the United States must first visit the U.S. consular office in their country and apply for a visa. When they apply for the visa they will have their biometrics collected in two separate ways. First, photographs will be taken of every applicant and those photographs will be entered into the US-Visit database along with digital finger scans. The digital finger scans will be taken of both the right and left index fingers of the applicant. This information will be loaded into a database and then checked to see if they match any criminals or suspected terrorists already in the system. Once applicants pass the database check they can be issued a visa to travel to the United States. Upon arrival at a U.S. port of entry, the traveler will be required to scan their left and right index fingers to determine if the individual at the point of entry is the same as the person who applied for the visa. Entry procedures were started in 115 airports at the beginning of 2004 and today all airports that receive international flights have US-Visit capabilities. Currently, there are 12 airports within the United States that are taking part in the US-Visit exit procedures, as well as two seaports. The exit procedure requires each traveler to scan their fingers before leaving the country to determine the identity of the individual leaving the country.

Homeland Security believes that implementing these new security features will result in fewer criminals or terrorists entering the country, and also reduce the amount of identity theft and fraud that may occur upon entry or exit. However, there are critics who say that the data available to U.S. Customs and Immigration provide too much personal information about travelers and U.S. citizens. Despite privacy concerns, the Department of Homeland Security is set on using the US-Visit program in conjunction with other government programs to increase the security of the United States.

CRITICAL THINKING

Are you afraid that futuristic security methods such as biometric technology will lead to the loss of personal privacy and the erosion of civil liberties? Would you want to be monitored by a computer recognition system as you travel and/or go about your daily activities?

Sources: United States Visitor and Immigrant Status Indicator Technology, Electronic Privacy Information Center, www.epic.org/privacy/us-visit/ (accessed April 27, 2007); US-Visit. Travel and Transportation, U.S. Department of Homeland Security, www.dhs.gov/dhspublic/interapp/content_multi_image/content_multi_image_0006.xml (accessed April 27, 2007).

advocates warn about the loss of privacy, the average citizen has much more to worry about from identity thieves—whose phishing expeditions compromise their financial and personal well-being and security—than from the police.[97]

2. *It really does work.* Modern IT may not be foolproof, but it increases safety. Intrusions into personal space may be warranted if lives are saved. Security cameras, for example, have proliferated in England and are now a vital tool in the government's war on terrorism. While they did not prevent the bombing of the London subway system that killed 56 Londoners in 2005, the images they produced encouraged thousands of tips and led to the arrest of other terrorists in the group, including one who had fled to Italy. While civil liberties groups fear that the success of the surveillance may lead to expanded coverage, that risk is offset by the fact that those bombers will not be able to strike again.[98]

3. *What's the big deal?* While IT makes surveillance and data storage more efficient, it does not gather information that human investigators did not collect in the past. It just does it more efficiently. The new technology is not invading homes but gathering information from public spaces, albeit in the real or electronic world. It is illogical to say that IT should not be used to collect data that any police officer or private citizen is free to observe and record.

4. *IT in criminal justice can be controlled.* There is no question that abuses may occur if law enforcement agents were given free rein to use IT for surveillance and control. However, strict national standards on the use of IT can keep it within acceptable boundaries. A number of national groups, including the American Bar Association (ABA), have already created model rules for IT. The ABA suggests that electronic surveillance must consider the following in order that it not invade people's privacy:

   a. The nature of the place, activity, condition, or location to be surveilled

   b. The care that has been taken to enhance the privacy of such place, activity, condition, or location

c. The lawfulness of the vantage point, including whether either the surveillance or installation of surveillance equipment requires a physical intrusion

d. The availability and sophistication of the surveillance technology

e. The extent to which the surveillance technology enhances the law enforcement officer's natural senses

f. The extent to which the surveillance of subjects is minimized in time and space

g. The extent to which the surveillance of nonsubjects is likewise minimized

h. Whether the surveillance is covert or overt.[99]

As the use of IT in criminal justice proliferates, whether to track and apprehend terrorists, cyber criminals, or common-law felons, its intrusion into the lives of the average citizen will also continue to grow. While civil libertarians warn of its overreach, the dangers present in contemporary society may override considerations of liberty and privacy

THINKING LIKE A CRIMINOLOGIST

The president's national security advisor approaches you with a problem. It seems that a tracking device has been developed that can be implanted under the skin, allowing people to be constantly monitored. Implanted at birth, the data surveillance device could potentially cover *everyone*, with a record of every transaction and activity they engage in entered into powerful computers where search engines would keep them under constant surveillance. The surveillance device would enable the government to keep tabs on their whereabouts as well as monitoring their biological activities such as brain waves, heart rate, and so on. The benefits are immense. Once a person becomes a suspect in a crime or is believed to be part of a terrorist cell, they can be easily monitored from a distance without danger to any government agent. They cannot hide or escape detection. Physical readings could be made to determine if they are under stress, using banned substances, and so on.

Writing Exercise Write a paper expressing your opinion on this device. Is it worthwhile considering the threats faced by America from terrorists and criminals or does it violate personal privacy and freedom?

Doing Research on the Web Before you begin writing your paper, go to the American Civil Liberties Union website. They say: "The United States is at risk of turning into a full-fledged surveillance society. The tremendous explosion in surveillance-enabling technologies, combined with the ongoing weakening in legal restraints that protect our privacy mean that we are drifting toward a surveillance society. The good news is that it can be stopped. Unfortunately, right now the big picture is grim."

You may also want to look at the website of the Center for Democracy and Technology (CDT)—a nonprofit public policy organization dedicated to promoting the democratic potential of today's open, decentralized global Internet. Their mission is to conceptualize, develop, and implement public policies to preserve and enhance free expression, privacy, open access, and other democratic values in the new and increasingly integrated communications medium.

Both websites can be accessed via **www.thomsonedu.com/criminaljustice/siegel**.

SUMMARY

- Cyber crime is a new breed of offenses that involves the theft and/or destruction of information, resources, or funds utilizing computers, computer networks, and the Internet.

- Cyber crime presents a challenge for the justice system because it is rapidly evolving, it is difficult to detect through traditional law enforcement channels, and its control demands that agents of the justice system develop technical skills that match those of the perpetrators.

- Cyber crime has grown because information technology (IT) has become part

When Michigan police, armed with a search warrant, came to the home of Booker T. Hudson, Jr., they knocked on the door, shouted "police," waited less than five seconds, *and broke into the apartment. They found crack cocaine in Hudson's pockets and a gun wedged in a chair nearby. Hudson was later convicted on drug charges despite the fact that state law required that police announce their presence during raids and give occupants a chance to come to the door—the so-called "knock and announce" rule. After his conviction, Hudson appealed his case all the way to the Supreme Court, arguing that his rights had been violated by this "no knock" search.[1]*

Should the police be forced to knock, announce their presence, wait for a few minutes, and give a wanted criminal such as Hudson the opportunity to arm himself and shoot first? On the other hand, should police officers have the right to burst into someone's home even if their purpose is to serve a search warrant? Doesn't such an unexpected entrance violate a person's right to privacy and dignity? And should the evidence seized in such a raid, in this case crack cocaine, be excluded from trial simply because the police violated a rule governing proper procedure? What is fair? What is just?

As every fan of the long-running series *Law and Order* knows, "In the criminal justice system, the people are represented by two separate, yet equally important, groups: the police, who investigate crime, and the district attorneys who prosecute the offenders." It is these two agencies of criminal justice—law enforcement and the courts—that are assigned the critical role of investigating crime, apprehending and arresting criminal suspects, charging them with an offense, and adjudicating their case. Given the delicate task of balancing the needs of the victim, the protection of society, and the civil rights of the accused, these agencies of justice must operate within the boundaries of the rule of law and be mindful of the legal restrictions placed on their behavior. The ruling in the Hudson case reflects this dynamic. The United States Supreme Court ruled that the search was constitutional and allowed Hudson's conviction to stand. The majority concluded that whether the premature entry had occurred or not, the police would have executed the warrant they had obtained, and would have discovered the gun and drugs inside the house. Therefore the discovery of the contraband was inevitable and should be allowed. The Court seemed to fear that if the "knock and announce" rule was inflexible, patently guilty defendants might go free because otherwise valid evidence would have to be thrown out of court. The "social cost" of freeing a dangerous drug dealer was too high, in their opinion, when compared to the loss of Hudson's privacy. Here we can see how the judicial branch must balance the greater needs of society with the more narrow rights of a criminal defendant. Their interpretation of such abstract legal concepts as "privacy" and "inevitable discovery," shape the scope of police behavior. Before *Hudson*, police executing a search warrant had to worry that evidence might be excluded if they did not first knock on the door, announce themselves, and wait a reasonable time for a response before forcing their way in. Now they can act first and ask later. The judiciary supported law enforcement's need to obtain valid evidence in as safe a manner as possible.

In this chapter we will review each of these institutions and evaluate their structure, goals, and process. We begin with a discussion of the police role as a crime fighting agency.

THE POLICE AND SOCIETY

The police and other law enforcement agents (such as federal agents and state investigators) are the gatekeepers of the criminal justice process. They initiate contact with law violators and decide whether to formally arrest them and start their journey through the criminal justice system, settle the issue in an informal way (by issuing a warning), or simply take no action at all.

Police officers' responsibilities are immense; they may suddenly be faced with an angry mob, an armed felon, or a suicidal teenager and be forced to make split-second decisions on what action to take. At the same time, they must be sensitive to the needs of citizens who are often of diverse racial and ethnic backgrounds. When police are present and visible, it creates a sense of security in a neighborhood and improves residents' opinions of the police.[2]

In carrying out these critical tasks, local police and law enforcement agents are given a great deal of discretion in their decision making. Some critics believe that they use this freedom in a biased fashion. Because of the repeated allegation that police officers harass minority citizens and use their arrest powers in a biased manner, the term *racial profiling* has become part of the vernacular. In response, police departments have undertaken efforts to train police in human relations and create more sensitivity toward the community. Though police agencies tend to be traditional organizations that are resistant to change, a great deal of progress has been made in improving community relations.[3] Programs have been created to improve relations between police and community as well as to help police officers on the beat be more sensitive to the needs of the public and cope more effectively with the stress of their jobs. Police officers have also become better educated and now routinely attend college. After graduation they seem willing to stay on the job and contribute their academic experiences to improve police performance and enhance police–community relationships.[4]

LAW ENFORCEMENT AGENCIES TODAY

Law enforcement duties are distributed across local, county, state, and federal jurisdictions. There are now approximately 800,000 full-time law enforcement officers in the United States, employed in almost 18,000 different agencies. Police and law enforcement agencies can be found at several levels of government.

Federal Law Enforcement

The federal government maintains about 50 organizations that are involved in law enforcement. Some of the most important of these are discussed here.

The Federal Bureau of Investigation In 1870 the U.S. Department of Justice became involved in actual policing when the attorney general hired investigators to enforce the Mann Act (which prohibited prostitution across state lines). In 1908 this group of investigators was formally made a distinct branch of the government, the Bureau of Investigation; in the 1930s the agency was reorganized into the Federal Bureau of Investigation (FBI) under the direction of J. Edgar Hoover.

Today's FBI is not a police agency but an investigative agency, with jurisdiction over all matters in which the United States is, or may be, an interested party. It limits its jurisdiction to federal laws, including all federal statutes not specifically assigned to other agencies. These include statutes dealing with

EXHIBIT 17.1

Top Priorities of the FBI

1. Protect the United States from terrorist attack.

2. Protect the United States against foreign intelligence operations and espionage.

3. Protect the United States against cyber-based attacks and high-technology crimes.

4. Combat public corruption at all levels.

5. Protect civil rights.

6. Combat transnational and national criminal organizations and enterprises.

7. Combat major white-collar crime.

8. Combat significant violent crime.

9. Support federal, state, county, municipal, and international partners.

10. Upgrade technology to successfully perform the FBI's mission.

Source: Federal Bureau of Investigation, www.fbi.gov/quickfacts.htm (accessed March 25, 2007).

espionage, sabotage, treason, civil rights violations, the murder and assault of federal officers, mail fraud, robbery and burglary of federally insured banks, kidnapping, and interstate transportation of stolen vehicles and property.

In addition to enforcing these laws, the FBI offers important services to local law enforcement agencies, including use of its vast fingerprint file and a sophisticated crime laboratory that aids local police in testing and identifying evidence, such as hair, fiber, blood, tire tracks, and drugs. The FBI's National Crime Information Center is a computerized network linked to local police departments by terminals. Through it, information on stolen vehicles, wanted persons, stolen guns, and so on is made readily available to local law enforcement agencies. As Exhibit 17.1 shows, in the post-9/11 world, the FBI has shifted its priority to counterintelligence, counterterrorism, and cyber terrorism.

In addition to the FBI, the following agencies are part of federal law enforcement:

▮ *Drug Enforcement Administration (DEA).* Investigates illegal drug use and carries out independent surveillance and enforcement activities to control the importation of narcotics.

▮ *U.S. Marshals.* Court officers who help implement federal court rulings, transport prisoners, and enforce court orders.

▮ *Bureau of Alcohol, Tobacco, Firearms, and Explosives (ATF).* Has jurisdiction over the sales and distribution of firearms, explosives, alcohol, and tobacco products.

▮ *Internal Revenue Service (IRS).* Established in 1862, the IRS enforces violations of income, excise, stamp, and other tax laws. Its intelligence division actively pursues gamblers, narcotics dealers, and other violators who do not report their illegal financial gains as taxable income.

County Law Enforcement

The county police department is an independent agency whose senior officer, the sheriff, is usually elected. The county sheriff's role has evolved from that of the early English shire reeve, whose main duty was to assist royal judges in trying prisoners and enforcing the law outside cities. From the time of U.S. westward expansion until municipal departments were developed, the sheriff often was the sole legal authority in vast territories.

Today, sheriff's offices contain about 330,000 full-time employees, including about 175,000 sworn personnel. Employment has risen an average of 4 percent per year since 1990.[5] Nearly all sheriffs' offices provide basic law enforcement services such as routine patrol, responding to citizen calls for service, and investigating crimes. It is also common for the sheriff's department to be keepers of the county jail, court attendants, and executors of criminal and civil processes. Typically, the sheriff's law enforcement functions today are carried out only in unincorporated areas within a county or in response to city departments' requests for aid in such matters as patrol or investigation.

State Police

The Texas Rangers, organized in 1835, are considered by some the first state police force. However, the Rangers were more a quasimilitary force that supported the Texas state militia than a law enforcement body. The first true state police forces emerged at the turn of the twentieth century, with Connecticut (1903) and Pennsylvania (1905) leading the way.

The impetus for creating state police agencies can be traced both to the low regard of the public for the crime-fighting ability of local police agencies and to the increasingly greater mobility of law violators. Using automobiles, thieves could strike at will and be out of the jurisdiction of local police before an investigation could be mounted. Therefore, it became necessary to have a law enforcement agency with statewide jurisdiction. Also, state police gave governors a powerful enforcement arm that was under their personal control and not that of city politicians.

Today there are about 60,000 full-time state police officers and 30,000 other full-time employees in 49 departments (Hawaii has no state police). The major role of state police is controlling traffic on the highway system, tracing stolen automobiles, and aiding in disturbances and crowd control.

In states with large, powerful county sheriff's departments, the state police function is usually restricted to highway patrol. In others, where the county sheriff's law enforcement role is limited, state police usually maintain a more active investigative and enforcement role and aid city and town police departments in criminal investigation.

Metropolitan Police

Metropolitan police agencies make up the vast majority of the law enforcement community's members. Today, there are more than 13,000 local police departments nationwide with an estimated 565,000 full-time employees, including about 450,000 sworn personnel.[6] About 50 departments employ 1,000 or more officers, and these agencies account for about a third of all local police officers; in contrast; nearly 800 departments employ just one officer.

Most larger urban departments are independent agencies operating without specific administrative control from any higher governmental authority. They are organized at the executive level of government. It is therefore common for the city mayor (or the equivalent) to control the hiring and firing of the police chief and, consequently, determine departmental policies. Traditionally, municipal departments were organized in a militaristic way, often using military terms to designate seniority (sergeant, lieutenant, captain). This organization is now changing as police departments become more decentralized.

Local police perform multiple roles, including but not limited to investigating crimes, identifying suspects, and making arrests. While most people are familiar with these law enforcement goals of police, there are actually many tasks performed by patrol officers:

- Enhance public safety by maintaining a visible police presence
- Maintain public order (i.e., peacekeeping) within the patrol area
- First response to fires and other emergencies
- Educate children about crime, drug abuse, safety, and so on
- Aid individuals and care for those who cannot help themselves
- Facilitate the movement of traffic and people
- Promote public safety and crime prevention[7]

The organization of a typical metropolitan police department is illustrated in Figure 17.1. This complex structure is

Figure 17.1 Organization of a Typical Metropolitan Police Department

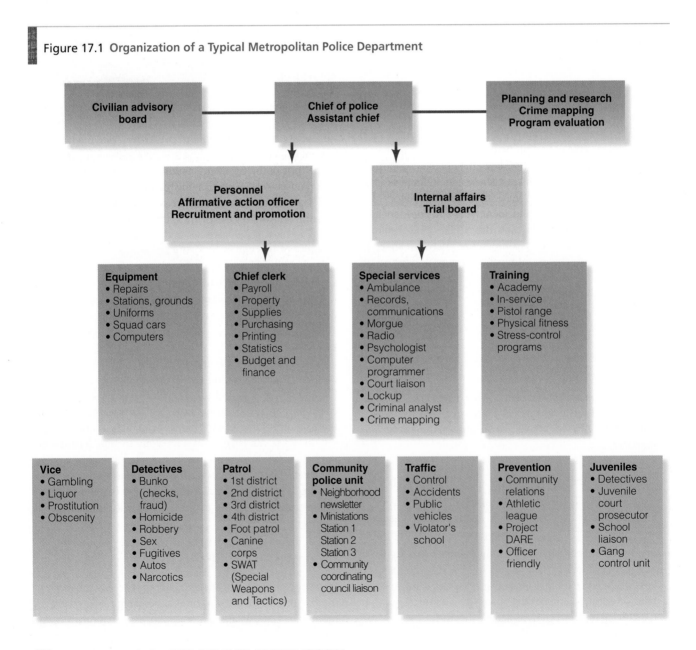

EXHIBIT 17.2

The Core Functions of Police

Law Enforcement Functions

▐ Identifying criminal suspects

▐ Investigating crimes

▐ Apprehending offenders and participating in their trials

▐ Deterring crime through patrol

Order Maintenance Functions

▐ Resolving conflict and keeping the peace

▐ Maintaining a sense of community security

▐ Keeping vehicular and pedestrian movement efficient

▐ Promoting civil order

Service Functions

▐ Aiding individuals in danger or in need of assistance

▐ Providing emergency medical services

▐ Public education and outreach

▐ Maintaining and administering police services

▐ Recruiting and training new police officers

a function of the multiplicity of roles with which the police are entrusted; these roles fall into three main categories (Exhibit 17.2).

PREVENTING AND DETERRING CRIME

One of the primary goals of police work is to deter criminal behavior. The visible presence of patrol cars on the street and the rapid deployment of police officers to the scene of a crime are viewed as an effective method of crime control. Unfortunately, research efforts designed to measure the effectiveness of patrol have not supported its deterrence capability. The most widely heralded attempt at measuring patrol effectiveness was undertaken during the early 1970s in Kansas City, Missouri, where researchers divided 15 separate police districts into three groups: one group retained normal patrol; the second (proactive) set of districts were supplied with two to three times the normal amount of patrol forces; and the third (reactive) group had its preventive patrol eliminated, with police officers responding only when summoned by citizens to the scene of a particular crime.[8] The Kansas City study found that these variations in patrol had little effect on the crime patterns in the 15 districts. The presence or absence of patrol officers did not seem to affect residential or business burglaries, motor vehicle thefts, larceny involving auto accessories, robberies, vandalism, or other criminal behavior, nor did it influence citizens' attitudes toward the police, their satisfaction with police, or their fear of future criminal behavior.

As a result of the Kansas City study, a number of innovative techniques have been developed to improve the effectiveness of the police as a crime deterring force.

Proactive Patrol

Although the mere presence of police may not be sufficient to deter crime, the manner in which they approach their task may make a difference. Improving response time and increasing the number of patrol cars that respond per crime may be one way of increasing police efficiency.[9] Jurisdictions that encourage patrol officers to stop motor vehicles to issue citations and to aggressively arrest and detain suspicious persons also experience lower crime rates than jurisdictions that do not follow such proactive policies.[10] Departments that more actively enforce minor regulations, such as disorderly conduct and traffic laws, are also more likely to experience lower felony rates.[11]

Pinpointing why proactive policing works so effectively is difficult. It may have a deterrent effect: aggressive policing increases community perception that police arrest many criminals and that most violators get caught; criminals are scared to commit crimes in a town that has such an active police force. Proactive policing may also help control crime because it results in conviction of more criminals. Because aggressive police arrest more suspects, there are fewer left on the street to commit crime; fewer criminals produce lower crime rates.

Aggressive police patrol efforts have been a critical success. The downturn in the New York City violent crime rate over the past decade has been attributed to aggressive police work aimed at lifestyle crimes: vandalism, panhandling, and graffiti.[12] Some commentators fear that aggressive policing will result in antagonism between proactive cops and the general public, especially if the police target racial minorities. However, recent research indicates that precinct level efforts to ensure that officers are respectful of citizens helped lower the number of complaints and improved community relations.[13]

Targeting Crimes

Evidence also shows that targeting specific crimes can be successful. *Directed patrol* involves assigning officers to a particular area to proactively investigate suspicious activities and to enforce existing gun, drug, traffic, and related laws.[14] Officers assigned to directed patrol areas are freed from having to respond to calls for service. The most common approach in a directed patrol effort is to make frequent traffic stops targeting drivers who seem suspicious or fit the profile of drug traffickers. The strategy generally includes increasing the number of police officers in a given location and the number of contacts with citizens.

Some efforts have targeted specific crimes such as gun possession or drug trafficking. The well-known Kansas City Gun Experiment was directed at restricting the carrying of guns in high-risk places at high-risk times. The program employed gun patrol officers who seized illegal weapons, made thousands of car and pedestrian checks and traffic stops, and over 600 arrests. As a result of this targeted effort, drive-by shootings dropped significantly, as did homicides. These improvements occurred without any displacement to other areas of the city.

Why did this program work (even though the actual number of guns seized was minimal)? It is possible that the

Two Los Angeles police officers question a suspected drug dealer and a woman in the Wilshire neighborhood of Los Angeles, California, after finding a small quantity of speed (methedrine) and a smoking pipe in their van. The area is known for its violent gangs and a flourishing drug trade. LAPD officers at the scene became interested after seeing the suspect run away from his van, abandoning the female passenger. The police assumed the male was making a purchase in a nearby house and had hidden the drugs. The woman was out on parole and faced a possible parole violation for the drug possession and being out after curfew. Active police patrol may have contributed to a falling crime rate in Los Angeles. Another reason: Sky-high real estate prices have driven criminals to outlying counties where real estate prices are more affordable.

over time; thus, studies using data collected annually may miss this immediate deterrent effect.

Adding Patrol Officers

One reason why patrol activity may be less effective than desired is the lack of adequate resources. Does adding more police help bring down the crime rate? At one time critics questioned whether adding police was effective because reviews of the existing research found that the actual number of law enforcement officers in a jurisdiction seemed to have little effect on area crimes.[19] However, a number of more recent studies have found that police presence may actually reduce crime levels and that adding police may bring crime levels down.[20] Evidence shows that cities with larger police departments that have more officers per capita than the norm also experience lower levels of violent crimes.[21] During the past decade larger cities have expanded their police forces and crime rates plummeted—a trend that indicates that adding police may in fact reduce crime rates.

Why does adding police reduce crime rates? The obvious reason is that an expanded police presence deters would-be criminals. There may also be residual effects. Increasing police resources may improve the overall effectiveness of the justice system. When resources are lacking, many cases are dropped before they ever get to trial because it becomes difficult to gather sufficient evidence to ensure a conviction; prosecutors are likely to drop these cases.[22] Adding police resources improves the quality of police work with the spillover effect of increasing the effectiveness of the entire justice process.

weapons were taken from high-rate offenders who were among the most likely perpetrators of gun-related crimes; their "lost opportunity" to commit violent crimes may have resulted in an overall crime and violence rate decrease. It is also possible that the gun sweeps caused some of the most violent criminals to be taken off the streets. And as word of the patrol got out, there may have been a general deterrent effect: people contemplating violent crime may have been convinced that apprehension risks were unacceptably high.[15]

Making Arrests

Can formal police action, such as an arrest, reduce crime? While the evidence is mixed, some research studies do show that contact with the police may cause some offenders to forgo repeat criminal behavior. Many first offenders will forgo criminal activity after undergoing arrest.[16] An arrest for drunk driving reduces the likelihood of further driving while intoxicated. An arrest apparently increases people's belief that they will be rearrested if they drink and drive and heightens their perception of the unpleasantness associated with an arrest.[17] Consequently, as the number of arrests per capita increases, crime rates go down.

Why do arrests inhibit crime? It is possible that news of increased and aggressive police arrest activity is rapidly diffused through the population and has an immediate impact on crime rates.[18] It is also likely that this impact on crime rates may erode

Using Technology

Police have made a concerted effort to deter crime with the aid of technology. CompStat, begun in New York City in 1994 as a means of directing police efforts in a more productive fashion, is one of the most famous police technology efforts.[23] CompStat is a computer-based system that gives local precinct commanders information about where and when crime is occurring in their jurisdiction. Commanders are provided with detailed data and electronic pin maps that show how crime is clustering geographically in the precinct and how patrol officers are being deployed. A key element of CompStat are weekly Crime Control Strategy Meetings during which the crime data are disseminated and the department's executives and commanders frankly

unanimous verdict is required when a six-person jury is used. When a twelve-person jury is used, the Supreme Court has maintained that the Sixth Amendment does not require a unanimous verdict, except in first-degree murder cases. In *Apodica v. Oregon*, the Court found constitutional an Oregon statute that required a finding of guilt by ten out of twelve jurors in cases of assault with a deadly weapon, burglary, and larceny.[162] However, it should be noted that the majority of states and the federal courts still require a unanimous verdict.

Right to be Free from Double Jeopardy

The Fifth Amendment provides that no person shall "be subject for the same offense to be twice put in jeopardy of life or limb." This means that a defendant cannot be prosecuted by a jurisdiction more than once for a single offense. For example, if a defendant is tried and found not guilty of murder in Texas, he cannot be tried again for the same murder in Texas. The right to be protected from double jeopardy was made applicable to the states through the Fourteenth Amendment in the case of *Benton v. Maryland*.[163] However, a person tried in federal court can be tried in state court, and vice versa.[164] And in 1985 the Court ruled in *Heath v. Alabama* that if a single act violates the laws of two states, the offender may be punished for each offense under the dual sovereignty doctrine: legal jurisdictions have the right to enforce their own laws, and a single act can violate the laws of two separate jurisdictions.[165]

Right to Legal Counsel

Regardless of the legal rights citizens command at trial, without legal counsel to aid them, they would be rendered defenseless before the law. Consequently, the Sixth Amendment provides the right to be represented by an attorney in criminal trials. However, the vast majority of criminal defendants are indigents who cannot afford private legal services. In a series of cases beginning in the 1930s, the U.S. Supreme Court established the defendant's right to be represented by an attorney and, in the event he or she cannot pay for representation, to have the state provide free legal services. First, in *Powell v. Alabama*, the Court held that an attorney was essential in capital cases where the defendant's life was at stake.[166] Then, in the critically important case of *Gideon v. Wainwright*, the Court granted the absolute right to counsel in all felony cases.[167] Finally, in *Argersinger v. Hamlin*, the defendant's right to counsel in misdemeanor cases was established.[168]

What about a case in which incarceration is not on the table but could be an issue later on? In *Alabama v. Shelton* (2002), the Court ruled that a defendant must be represented by counsel if he or she receives a probation sentence in which a prison or jail term is suspended but can later be imposed if the rules of probation are violated. In other words, if the sentence contains even a threat of future incarceration, the defendant must be afforded the right to counsel at trial.[169]

The Right to Be Competent at Trial

In order to stand trial, a criminal defendant must be considered mentally competent to understand the nature and extent of the legal proceedings. If a defendant is considered mentally incompetent, the trial must be postponed until treatment renders the defendant capable of participating in his or her own defense. Can state authorities force a mentally unfit defendant to be treated so that the person can be tried? In *Riggins v. Nevada*, the Supreme Court ruled that forced treatment does not violate a defendant's due process rights if it was (a) medically appropriate and (b) considering less intrusive alternatives, essential for the defendant's own safety or the safety of others.[170]

Right to Confront Witnesses

The accused has the right to confront witnesses to challenge their assertions and perceptions: Did they really hear what they thought they did? Or see what they think they saw? Are they biased? Honest? Trustworthy?

An important confrontation issue is the ability to shield child witnesses from the trauma of a court appearance. In *Maryland v. Craig* the Supreme Court ruled that child witnesses could testify via closed-circuit television as long as safeguards were set up to protect the defendant's rights.[171] Protections included the defendant being able to view the witness and being in communication with the witness's attorney at all times.

The Right to Press Coverage

There have been a number of specific points of contention between the press who want to report on a case and the judiciary who are concerned that publicity will taint the trial process. The clash can begin even before a trial takes place if a judge attempts to stifle press coverage or prohibit newspapers from printing articles about the case. In the most critical free press–fair trial case, *Richmond Newspapers Inc. v. Commonwealth of Virginia* (1980), the U.S. Supreme Court interpreted the First Amendment to mean that members of the press (and the public) have a right to attend trials.[172]

In the future the question of access of the press to nontrial judicial and administrative hearings may become significant. Should the press have the right to attend and report on deportation hearings involving illegal immigrants or quasimilitary hearings involving suspected terrorists? Procedures at these new and different types of hearings must still be mapped out.[173]

Televising Criminal Trials

Today, many state courts permit televised coverage of trials, often at the judge's discretion; the use of television cameras, video recorders, and still photography is banned in the federal court system.[174] Televising criminal proceedings could have significant advantages. Judges would be better prepared; the public would be informed about important legal issues; and the proceedings would serve an educational function, offsetting the simplistic views offered by television programs and feature films. On the other hand, televising trials can have some drawbacks. Broadcasting can feed the media frenzy that has turned some high profile cases into a three-ring circus. Lawyers might be encouraged to show off for the camera rather than prepare a sound legal defense—as may witnesses and possibly the judge and defendant as well. Security may become an issue. Witnesses are already reluctant to testify in high profile cases against organized crime and drug cartels. How will they react if forced to testify while their face is broadcast around the world? The same will apply to jurors fearful of retaliation. Under these circumstances, trial judges may be inclined to ban cameras from the very cases that the public is most interested in viewing.[175]

What the Future Holds

Not only is technology influencing law enforcement, it is also being applied in the courts in such areas as videotaped testimonies, new court-reporting devices, information systems, and data processing systems to handle such functions as court docketing and jury management.[176]

Contemporary relational databases now provide the flexibility to handle complex case management. To help programmers define the multiplicity of relationships that occur in a court setting, the National Center for State Courts in Williamsburg, Virginia, has developed a methodology for structuring a case management system that tracks a person to the case or cases in which he is a defendant, the scheduling of the cases to avoid any conflicts, and, of increasing importance, the fines that have been levied and the accounts to which the money goes.[177]

Court jurisdictions are also cooperating with police departments in the installation of communications gear that allows defendants to be arraigned via closed-circuit television while they are in police custody. Closed-circuit television has been used for judicial conferences and scheduling meetings. Courts are using voice-activated cameras to record all testimony during trials; these are the sole means of keeping trial records. Many high-tech courtrooms are now equipped for real-time transcription and translation, audio–video preservation of the court record, remote witness participation, computer graphics displays, television monitors for jurors, and computers for counsel and judge.[178]

Technology may not only improve case processing and ease court congestion, it may also help make the adjudicatory process more fair and unblemished. New scientific processes, such as the use of the DNA, will enhance the accuracy of the trial process. In an important 2006 case, *House v. Bell*, the U.S. Supreme Court expanded the ability of death row inmates to challenge their convictions in federal court based on DNA evidence produced long after their trials. *House* is the first case in which the Court considered the new evidentiary technology of DNA evidence when reexamining a death sentence. In its five to three decision, the Court held that new evidence, including DNA test results, raised sufficient doubt to merit a new hearing in federal court for Tennessee inmate Paul House, who had been on death row for more than 20 years for the rape and murder of his neighbor. The Court recognized that because DNA tests—not available at the time of conviction—pointed the finger at the victim's husband, House was entitled to a new trial. In his opinion, Justice Kennedy wrote "all the evidence, old and new, incriminating and exculpatory" must be taken into account . . . the court's function is not to make an independent factual determination about what likely occurred, but rather to assess the likely impact of the evidence on reasonable jurors."[179]

THINKING LIKE A CRIMINOLOGIST

A federal appellate judge asks your opinion about a tricky case. It seems that at 3 A.M. the local police were called about a loud party. When they arrived, they heard shouting inside, proceeded down the driveway, and saw two juveniles drinking beer in the backyard. Entering the yard, they saw through a screen door and windows an altercation in the kitchen between four adults and a juvenile, who punched one of the adults, causing him to spit blood in a sink. A police officer opened the screen door and announced his presence. Without a search warrant, the officer entered the kitchen and again cried out, whereupon the altercation gradually subsided. The officers arrested the adults and charged them with contributing to the delinquency of a minor and related offenses. However, the trial court granted the defendants' motion to suppress all evidence obtained after the officers entered the home on the grounds that the warrantless entry violated the Fourth Amendment. According to state and federal law, one exigency obviating the need for a search warrant is the need to render emergency assistance to occupants of private property who are seriously injured or threatened with such injury. However, the trial judge concluded that the juvenile's punch was insufficient to trigger the "emergency aid doctrine" because it did not give rise to an objectively reasonable belief that an unconscious, semiconscious, or missing person feared injured or dead was in the home. Furthermore, the judge suggested the doctrine was inapplicable because the officers had not sought to assist the injured adult but had acted exclusively in a law enforcement capacity.

> *Writing Exercise* The appellate court judge has to decide on the legality of the arrest and seizure of evidence. What would you advise? Write a brief paper explaining your position.

> *Doing Research on the Web* Before writing your paper, go to www.thomsonedu.com/criminaljustice/siegel and read over the case of *Brigham City v. Stuart* (No. 05-502) and learn more about the purpose of a search warrant.

SUMMARY

- Police officers are the gatekeepers of the criminal justice process. They use their power of arrest to initiate the justice process.

- There are several major law enforcement agencies. On the federal level, the FBI is the premier law enforcement organization. Other agencies include the Drug Enforcement Administration, the U.S. Marshals, and the Bureau of Alcohol, Tobacco, Firearms, and Explosives.

- County-level law enforcement is provided by sheriffs' departments.

- Most states maintain state police agencies. However, most law enforcement activities are carried out by local police agencies.

- The police role is multilevel. Police officers fight crime, keep the peace, and provide community services.

- Patrol officers are charged with deterring and preventing crime as well as other duties such as providing medical care and directing traffic.

- Police agencies are attempting to improve patrol through aggressive techniques that focus on particular crimes, adding officers, and using technology.

- Some police agencies have shifted the role of police through application of community policing models.

- The second prominent police role is investigation.

- Detectives collect evidence to identify perpetrators.

- In recent years many police operations have been controlled by court decisions. Most important, the courts have set limits on the extent of police interrogations and search and seizure of evidence.

- The judicatory process provides a forum for deciding the outcome of a conflict between two or more parties. This process is played out in the nation's court system.

- State courts usually involve a multitiered system—lower trial courts, superior trial courts, appellate courts, and supreme court. The federal system is similar; it contains trial courts, appellate courts, and the U.S. Supreme Court, which is the final court of appeals for all state and federal cases.

- There are three main actors in the judicatory process: the prosecutor, the defense attorney, and the judge.

- The prosecutor brings charges against the offender and then represents the state in all criminal matters.

- The defense attorney represents the accused at all stages of the judicatory process. Some defendants can afford to hire private attorneys for their defense, but the majority are represented by defense counsel appointed and paid for by the state.

- The judge controls the trial, rules on issues of evidence, charges the jury, and in some cases chooses the type and length of sentence.

- The pretrial stage of the justice process involves such issues as bail and plea bargaining.

- Bail is a money bond the defendant puts up to secure freedom before trial. It is controversial because those who cannot make bail must spend their time in detention.

- Critics charge that bail discriminates against the poor, who can neither afford bond nor borrow it from bonding agents. Consequently, reform programs, such as release on recognizance, have been employed.

- Plea bargaining involves the prosecutor allowing defendants to plead guilty as charged in return for some consideration—for example, a reduced sentence or dropped charges. Plea bargaining has been criticized because it represents the unchecked use of discretion by prosecutors. Often serious criminals can receive light sentences by bargaining, and some people may be coerced into pleading guilty because they fear a harsh sentence if they go to trial. An effort has

- been made to control plea bargains, but they are still frequently used.

- The second stage of the judicatory process is the criminal trial. The trial has a number of distinct stages, including jury selection, opening statements, presentation of evidence by prosecution and defense, closing arguments, instructions to the jury, verdict, sentence, and appeal.

- The rule of law also affects criminal trials. The Supreme Court has required that trials be speedy, public, and fair and has ruled that people have a right to be free from double jeopardy and to be represented by competent counsel.

- The judicatory process provides a forum for deciding the outcome of a conflict between two or more parties. This process is played out in the nation's court system.

- State courts usually involve a multitiered system—lower trial courts, superior trial courts, appellate courts, and supreme court. The federal system is similar; it contains trial courts, appellate courts, and the U.S. Supreme Court, which is the final court of appeals for all state and federal cases.

- There are three main actors in the judicatory process: the prosecutor, the defense attorney, and the judge.

- The prosecutor brings charges against the offender and then represents the state in all criminal matters.

- The defense attorney represents the accused at all stages of the judicatory process. Some defendants can afford to hire private attorneys for their defense, but the majority are represented by defense counsel appointed and paid for by the state.

- The judge controls the trial, rules on issues of evidence, charges the jury, and in some cases chooses the type and length of sentence.

- The pretrial stage of the justice process involves such issues as bail and plea bargaining.

- Bail is a money bond the defendant puts up to secure freedom before trial. It is controversial because those who cannot make bail must spend their time in detention.

- Critics charge that bail discriminates against the poor, who can neither afford bond nor borrow it from bonding agents. Consequently, reform programs, such as release on recognizance, have been employed.

- Plea bargaining involves the prosecutor allowing defendants to plead guilty as charged in return for some consideration—for example, a reduced sentence or dropped charges. Plea bargaining has been criticized because it represents the unchecked use of discretion by prosecutors. Often serious criminals can receive light sentences by bargaining, and some people may be coerced into pleading guilty because they fear a harsh sentence if they go to trial. An effort has been made to control plea bargains, but they are still frequently used.

- The second stage of the judicatory process is the criminal trial. The trial has a number of distinct stages, including jury selection, opening statements, presentation of evidence by prosecution and defense, closing arguments, instructions to the jury, verdict, sentence, and appeal.

- The rule of law also affects criminal trials. The Supreme Court has required that trials be speedy, public, and fair and has ruled that people have a right to be free from double jeopardy and to be represented by competent counsel.

- **ThomsonNOW** Maximize your study time by using ThomsonNOW's diagnostic study plan to help you review this chapter. The Personalized Study plan will help you identify areas on which you should concentrate; provide interactive exercises to help you master the chapter concepts; and provide a post-test to confirm you are ready to move on to the next chapter.

KEY TERMS

Federal Bureau of Investigation (FBI) (486)
state police (487)
proactive policing (489)
deterrent effect (489)
mug shots (491)
modus operandi (MO) (491)
sting operations (491)
morals squad (491)
vice squad (491)
Miranda warning (494)
inevitable discovery rule (494)
public safety doctrine (494)
search warrant (495)
community-oriented policing (COP) (498)
reactive policing (498)
problem-oriented policing (499)
adjudication process (500)

U.S. district courts (500)
federal courts of appeal (500)
U.S. Supreme Court (500)
writ of certiorari (500)
precedent (500)
landmark decision (500)
judge (501)
prosecutor (501)
defense attorney (501)
nolle prosequi (503)
assigned counsel system (505)
public defender system (505)
contract attorney system (505)
Missouri Plan (506)
criminal charge (506)
indictment (506)
information (506)
complaint (506)
bail (506)
preventive detention (508)

avertable recidivists (508)
bail bonding agent (509)
surety bond (509)
release on recognizance (ROR) (510)
deposit bail system (510)
bail guidelines (511)
plea bargaining (511)
venire (513)
jury array (513)
voir dire (513)
removed for cause (513)
peremptory challenges (514)
direct examination (515)
redirect examination (515)
cross-examination (515)
directed verdict (515)
rebuttal evidence (515)
double jeopardy (517)
dual sovereignty doctrine (517)

CRITICAL THINKING QUESTIONS

1. Distinguish between the duties of the state police, sheriff's departments, and local police departments.

2. What do you think are the social trends that may influence policing during the coming decade?

3. Should male and female officers have exactly the same duties in a police department? If not, why not?

4. A police officer orders an unarmed person running away from a burglary to stop; the suspect keeps running and is shot and killed by the officer. Do you believe the officer committed a crime? Explain.

5. Would you like to live in a society that abolished police discretion and used a full enforcement policy? Why or why not?

6. Should obviously guilty people go free because police originally arrested them with less than probable cause? Should illegally seized evidence be excluded from trial, even though it is conclusive proof of a person's criminal acts?

7. Have the courts given criminals too many rights? Should courts be more concerned with the rights of the victims or the rights of offenders?

NOTES

1. *Hudson v. Michigan* No. 04-1360 (2006).
2. James Hawdon and John Ryan, "Police-Resident Interactions and Satisfaction with Police: An Empirical Test of Community Policing Assertions," *Criminal Justice Policy Review* 14 (2003): 55–74.
3. William Wells, Julie Horney, and Edward Maguire, "Patrol Officer Responses to Citizen Feedback: An Experimental Analysis," *Police Quarterly* 8 (2005): 171–205.
4. David Jones, Liz Jones, and Tim Prenzler, "Tertiary Education, Commitment, and Turnover in Police Work," *Police Practice and Research* 6 (2005): 49–63.
5. Matthew Hickman and Brian Reaves, *Local Police Departments, 2003* (Washington, DC: Bureau of Justice Statistics, 2006).
6. Ibid.
7. American Bar Association, *Standards Relating to Urban Police Function* (New York: Institute of Judicial Administration, 1974), standard 2.2.
8. George Kelling, Tony Pate, Duane Dieckman, and Charles Brown, *The Kansas City Preventive Patrol Experiment: A Summary Report* (Washington, DC: Police Foundation, 1974).
9. Richard Timothy Coupe and Laurence Blake, "The Effects of Patrol Workloads and Response Strength on Arrests at Burglary Emergencies," *Journal of Criminal Justice* 33 (2005): 239–255.
10. James Q. Wilson and Barbara Boland, "The Effect of Police on Crime," *Law and Society Review* 12 (1978): 367–384.
11. Robert Sampson, "Deterrent Effects of the Police on Crime: A Replication and Theoretical Extension," *Law and Society Review* 22 (1988): 163–191.
12. For a thorough review of this issue, see Andrew Karmen, *Why Is New York City's Murder Rate Dropping So Sharply?* (New York: John Jay College, 1996).
13. Robert Davis, Pedro Mateu-Gelabert, and Joel Miller, "Can Effective Policing Also Be Respectful? Two Examples in the South Bronx," *Police Quarterly* 8 (2005): 229–247.
14. Edmund McGarrell, Steven Chermak, and Alexander Weiss, *Reducing Gun Violence: Evaluation of the Indianapolis Police Department's Directed Patrol* (Washington, DC: National Institute of Justice, 2002).
15. Lawrence Sherman, James Shaw, and Dennis Rogan, *The Kansas City Gun Experiment* (Washington, DC: National Institute of Justice, 1994).
16. Mitchell Chamlin, "Crime and Arrests: An Autoregressive Integrated Moving Average (ARIMA) Approach," *Journal of Quantitative Criminology* 4 (1988): 247–255.
17. Perry Shapiro and Harold Votey, "Deterrence and Subjective Probabilities of Arrest: Modeling Individual Decisions to Drink and Drive in Sweden," *Law and Society Review* 18 (1984): 111–149.
18. Stewart D'Alessio and Lisa Stolzenberg, "Crime, Arrests, and Pretrial Jail Incarceration: An Examination of the Deterrence Thesis," *Criminology* 36 (1998): 735–761.
19. Thomas Marvell and Carlisle Moody, "Specification Problems, Police Levels, and Crime Rates," *Criminology* 34 (1996): 609–646; Colin Loftin and David McDowall, "The Police, Crime, and Economic Theory: An Assessment," *American Sociological Review* 47 (1982): 393–401.
20. Tomislav V. Kovandzic and John J. Sloan, "Police Levels and Crime Rates Revisited: A County-Level Analysis from Florida (1980–1998)," *Journal of Criminal Justice* 30 (2002): 65–76; Steven Levitt, "Using Electoral Cycles in Police Hiring to Estimate the Effect of Police on Crime," *American Economic Review* 87 (1997): 270–291.
21. David Jacobs and Katherine Woods, "Interracial Conflict and Interracial Homicide: Do Political and Economic Rivalries Explain White Killings of Blacks or Black Killings of Whites?" *American Journal of Sociology* 105 (1999): 157–190.
22. Joan Petersilia, Allan Abrahamse, and James Q. Wilson, "A Summary of Rand's Research on Police Performance, Community Characteristics, and Case Attrition," *Journal of Police Science and Administration* 17 (1990): 219–229.
23. James Willis, Stephen Mastrofski, and David Weisburd, "Making Sense of COMPSTAT: A Theory-Based Analysis of Organizational Change in Three Police Departments," *Law & Society Review* 41 (2007): 147–188.
24. See generally Peter Greenwood and Joan Petersilia, *The Criminal Investigation Process*, vol. 1: *Summary and Policy Implications* (Santa Monica, CA: Rand Corporation, 1975); P. Greenwood, J. Chaiken, J. Petersilia, and L. Prusoff, *The Criminal Investigation Process*, vol. 3: *Observations and Analysis* (Santa Monica, CA: Rand Corporation, 1975).
25. Janice Puckett and Richard Lundman, "Factors Affecting Homicide Clearances: Multivariate Analysis of a More Complete Conceptual Framework," *Journal of Research in Crime and Delinquency* 40 (2003): 171–194.
26. C. Cotter and J. Burrows, *Property Crime Program, a Special Report: Overview of the STING Program and Project Summaries* (Washington, DC: Criminal Conspiracies Division, Office of Criminal Justice Programs, Law Enforcement Assistance Administration, U.S. Department of Justice, 1981).
27. Robert Langworthy, "Do Stings Control Crime? An Evaluation of a Police Fencing Operation," *Justice Quarterly* 6 (1989): 27–45
28. Robert Jackall, *Street Stories: The World of Police Detectives* (Cambridge, MA: Harvard University Press, 2005).
29. Ibid., p. 343
30. Greenwood and Petersilia, *The Criminal Investigation Process.*
31. Mark T. Willman and John R. Snortum, "Detective Work: The Criminal Investigation Process in a Medium-Size Police Department," *Criminal Justice Review* 9 (1984): 33–39.
32. John Eck, *Solving Crimes: The Investigation of Burglary and Robbery* (Washington, DC: Police Executive Research Forum, 1984).
33. See, for example, Susan Martin, "Policing Career Criminals: An Examination of an Innovative Crime Control Program," *Journal of Criminal Law and Criminology* 77 (1986): 1,159–1,182.
34. Charles L. Regini, "The Cold Case Concept," *FBI Law Enforcement Bulletin* 66 (1997): 1.
35. 500 U.S. 44, 111 S.Ct. 1661, 114 L.Ed.2d 49 (1991).
36. *Miranda v. Arizona*, 384 U.S. 436 (1966).
37. *Harris v. New York*, 401 U.S. 222 (1971).
38. *Michigan v. Tucker*, 417 U.S. 433 (1974).
39. *Moran v. Burbine*, 106 S.Ct. 1135 (1986); *Michigan v. Mosley*, 423 U.S. 96 (1975); *Fare v. Michael C.*, 442 U.S. 23 (1979).
40. *Nix v. Williams*, 104 S.Ct. 2501 (1984).
41. *New York v. Quarles*, 104 S.Ct. 2626 (1984).
42. *Oregon v. Elstad*, 105 S.Ct. 1285 (1985).
43. *Missouri v. Seibert*, No. 02-1371 (2004).
44. *Colorado v. Spring*, 107 S.Ct. 851 (1987).
45. *Colorado v. Connelly*, 107 S.Ct. 515 (1986).
46. *Moran v. Burbine*, 106 S.Ct. 1135 (1986).
47. *Colorado v. Connelly*, 107 S.Ct. 515 (1986).
48. *Minnick v. Miss.*, 498 U.S. 46; 111 S.Ct. 486; 112 L.Ed. 2d. 489 (1990).
49. *Arizona v. Fulminante*, 499 U.S. 279, 111 S.Ct. 1246; 113 L.Ed. 2d. 302 (1991).
50. *Davis v. United States*, 114 S.Ct. 2350 (1994).
51. *Chavez v. Martinez*, No. 01-1444. Decided May 27, 2003.
52. *United States v. Patane*, No. 02-1183 (2004).
53. *Dickerson v. United States*, 530 U.S. 428 (2000).
54. Victoria Time and Brian Payne, "Police Chiefs' Perceptions about *Miranda*: An Analysis of Survey Data," *Journal of Criminal Justice* 30 (2002): 77–86.

55. Richard A. Leo and Richard J. Ofshe, "The Consequences of False Confessions: Deprivations of Liberty and Miscarriages of Justice in the Age of Psychological Interrogation," *Journal of Criminal Law and Criminology* 88 (1998): 429–496.

56. *Terry v. Ohio*, 392 U.S. 1 (1968).

57. *Chimel v. California*, 395 U.S. 752 (1969).

58. *Carroll v. United States*, 267 U.S. 132 (1925).

59. *United States v. Ross*, 102 S.Ct. 2147 (1982).

60. *Whren et al. v. U.S.*, No. 95-5841 (1996).

61. (Drivers) *Pennsylvania v. Mimms*, 434 U.S. 106, 1977; and (passengers) *Maryland v. Wilson*, 117 U.S. 882 (1997).

62. Federal Bureau of Investigation, *Law Enforcement Officers Killed and Assaulted, 2003* (Washington, DC: Federal Bureau of Investigation, 2004).

63. *Bumper v. North Carolina*, 391 U.S. 543 (1960).

64. *Ohio v. Robinette*, 117 S. Ct. 417 (1996).

65. Brian Sutherland, "Whether Consent to Search Was Given Voluntarily: A Statistical Analysis of Factors that Predict the Suppression Rulings of the Federal District Courts," *New York University Law Review* 81 (2006): 2,192–2,233.

66. *United States v. Matlock*, 415 U.S. 164 (1974).

67. *Georgia v. Randolph*, No. 04-1067 (2006).

68. Limitations on the plain view doctrine have been defined in *Arizona v. Hicks*, 107 S.Ct. 1149 (1987); the recording of serial numbers from stereo components in a suspect's apartment could not be justified as being in plain view.

69. *Katz v. United States*, 389 U.S. 347 (1967).

70. *Kirk v. Louisiana*, No. 01-8419, U.S. Supreme Court, *per curiam* opinion, decided June 24, 2002.

71. Jon Gould and Stephen Mastrofski, "Suspect Searches: Assessing Police Behavior under the U.S. Constitution," *Criminology and Public Policy* 3 (2004): 315–362.

72. J. Q. Wilson, *Varieties of Police Behavior: The Management of Law and Order in Eight Communities* (Cambridge, MA: Harvard University Press, 1968).

73. Richard Sykes and Edward Brent, *Policing: A Social Behaviorist Perspective* (New Brunswick, NJ: Rutgers University Press, 1983).

74. Matthew Durose, and Patrick Langan, *Contacts Between Police and the Public Findings from the 2005 National Survey* (Washington, DC: Bureau of Justice Statistics, 2007).

75. Egon Bittner, *The Functions of Police in Modern Society* (Cambridge, MA: Delgeschlager, Gunn, and Hain, 1980), pp. 63–72.

76. James Q. Wilson and George Kelling, "Broken Windows: The Police and Neighborhood Safety," *Atlantic Monthly* (March 1982): 29–38.

77. Wilson and Kelling, "Broken Windows," p. 37.

78. John Worrall and Jihong Zhao, "The Role of the COPS Office in Community Policing," *Policing: An International Journal of Police Strategies and Management* 26 (2003): 64–87.

79. Jihong Zhao, Nicholas Lovrich, and Quint Thurman, "The Status of Community Policing American Cities," *Policing* 22 (1999): 74–92.

80. Albert Cardarelli, Jack McDevitt, and Katrina Baum, "The Rhetoric and Reality of Community Policing in Small and Medium–Sized Cities and Towns," *Policing* 21 (1998): 397–415.

81. Police Foundation, *The Effects of Police Fear Reduction Strategies: A Summary of Findings from Houston and Newark* (Washington, DC: Police Foundation, 1986).

82. Donald Green, Dara Strolovitch, and Janelle Wong, "Defended Neighborhoods, Integration, and Racially Motivated Crime," *American Journal of Sociology* 104 (1998): 372–403.

83. Lee Brown, "Neighborhood-Oriented Policing," *American Journal of Police* 9 (1990): 197–207.

84. Herman Goldstein, *Problem-Oriented Policing* (New York: McGraw-Hill, 1990).

85. Sherry Plaster Carter, Stanley Carter, and Andrew Dannenberg, "Zoning Out Crime and Improving Community Health in Sarasota, Florida: 'Crime Prevention Through Environmental Design,'" *American Journal of Public Health* 93 (2003): 1,442–1,445.

86. Tucson Police Department, Gang Tactical Detail. http://tpdinternet.tucsonaz.gov/Organization/divisions/sid.html#Gang_Tactical (accessed March 27, 2007).

87. Anthony Braga, David Kennedy, Elin Waring, and Anne Morrison Piehl, "Problem-Oriented Policing, Deterrence, and Youth Violence: An Evaluation of Boston's Operation Ceasefire," *Journal of Research in Crime and Delinquency* 38 (2001): 195–225.

88. Bill Goodwin, "Burglars Captured by Police Data Mining Kit," *Computer Weekly*, 8 August 2002, p. 3.

89. Raymond E. Foster, "Crime Scene Investigation," *Government Technology* (March 2005), www.govtech.net/magazine/story.php?id=93225&issue=3:2005 (accessed April 27, 2007).

90. Stephen Savage, John Grieve, and Sam Poyser, "Putting Wrongs to Right: Campaigns Against Miscarriages of Justice," *Criminology and Criminal Justice: An International Journal* 7 (2007): 83–105.

91. Matthew Durose and Patrick Langan, *State Court Sentencing of Convicted Felons, 2002* (Washington, DC: Bureau of Justice Statistics, 2004).

92. Steven Perry, *Prosecutors in State Courts, 2005* (Washington: DC: Bureau of Justice Statistics, 2006).

93. Ibid.

94. Jessie Larson, "Unequal Justice: The Supreme Court's Failure to Curtail Selective Prosecution for the Death Penalty," *Journal of Criminal Law and Criminology* 93 (2003): 1,009–1,031.

95. John Worrall, Jay Ross, and Eric McCord, "Modeling Prosecutors' Charging Decisions in Domestic Violence Cases," *Crime and Delinquency* 52 (2006): 472–503.

96. Teah Lupton, "Prosecutorial Discretion," *Georgetown Law Journal* 90 (2002): 1,279–1,295.

97. Rodney Kingsworth, John Lopez, Jennifer Wentworth, and Debra Cummings, "Adult Sexual Assault: The Role of Racial/Ethnic Composition in Prosecution and Sentencing," *Journal of Criminal Justice* 26 (1998): 359–372.

98. Myrna Dawson and Ronit Dinovitzer, "Victim Cooperation and the Prosecution of Domestic Violence in a Specialized Court," *Justice Quarterly* 18 (2001): 593–622.

99. Frank W. Miller, *Prosecution: The Decision to Charge a Suspect with a Crime* (Boston: Little, Brown, 1970).

100. Wayne LaFave, "The Prosecutor's Discretion in the United States," *American Journal of Comparative Law* 18 (1970): 532–548.

101. Carol DeFrances, Steven K. Smith, and Louise van der Does, *Prosecutors in State Courts, 1994* (Washington, DC: Bureau of Justice Statistics, 1996).

102. Cassia Spohn, Dawn Beichner, and Erika Davis-Frenzel, "Prosecutorial Justifications for Sexual Assault Case Rejection: Guarding the 'Gateway to Justice,'" *Social Problems* 48 (2001): 206–235.

103. Robert Davis, Barbara Smith, and Bruce Taylor, "Increasing the Proportion of Domestic Violence Arrests that Are Prosecuted: A Natural Experiment in Milwaukee," *Criminology and Public Policy* 2 (2003): 263–282.

104. Charles Breitel, "Controls in Criminal Law Enforcement," *University of Chicago Law Review* 27 (1960): 427–435.

105. See generally "A Symposium on Prosecutorial Discretion," *American Criminal Law Review* (1976): 379–399.

106. George Cole, "The Decision to Prosecute," *Law and Society Review* 4 (1970): 331–343.

107. Talia Roitberg Harmon and William Lofquist, "Too Late for Luck: A Comparison of Post-Furman Exonerations and Executions of the Innocent," *Crime and Delinquency* 51 (2005): 498–520.

108. *Gideon v. Wainwright*, 372 U.S. 335 (1963); *Argersinger v. Hamlin*, 407 U.S. 25 (1972).

109. Steven K. Smith and Carol J. DeFrances, *Indigent Defense* (Washington, DC: Bureau of Justice Statistics, 1996).

110. Carol J. DeFrances, *State-Funded Indigent Defense Services, 1999* (Washington, DC: Bureau of Justice Statistics, 2001).

111. Ibid.

112. See American Bar Association, *Special Committee on Evaluation of Ethical Standards, Code of Professional Responsibility* (Chicago: American Bar Association 1968), p. 81.

113. *Nix v. Whiteside*, 106 S.Ct. 988 (1986).

114. William Lineberry, ed., *Justice in America: Law, Order and the Courts* (New York: H. W. Wilson, 1972).

115. David Klein and Robert Hume, "Fear of Reversal as an Explanation of Lower Court Compliance," *Law and Society Review* 37 (2003): 579–607.

116. Roy Schotland, "2002 Judicial Elections," *Spectrum: The Journal of State Government* 76 (2003): 18–20.

117. *Examining the Work of State Courts, 1996.*

118. *Examining the Work of State Courts, 2000.*

119. Ric Simmons, "Re-Examining the Grand Jury: Is There Room for Democracy in the Criminal Justice System?" *Boston University Law Review* 82 (2002): 1–76.

120. M. Ozanne, R. Wilson, and D. Gedney, Jr., "Toward a Theory of Bail Risk," *Criminology* 18 (1980): 149.

121. Data in this section come from Thomas Cohen and Brian Reaves, *Felony Defendants in Large Urban Counties, 2002* (Washington, DC: Bureau of Justice Statistics, 2006).

122. Christopher Stephens, "'Bail' Section of the Criminal Procedure Project," *Georgetown Law Journal* 90 (2002): 1,395–1,416.

123. Caleb Foote, "A Study of the Administration of Bail in New York," *University of Pennsylvania Law Review* 106 (1960): 693–730; William Rhodes, *Pretrial Release and Misconduct* (Washington, DC: Bureau of Justice Statistics, 1985).

124. Cohen and Reaves, *Felony Defendants in Large Urban Counties, 2002.*

125. Goldkamp, *Two Classes of Accused.*

126. Vera Institute of Justice, *Programs in Criminal Justice* (New York: Vera Institute, 1972).

127. Reaves and Perez, *Pretrial Release of Felony Defendants, 1992*, p. 5.

128. Malcolm Feeley, *Court Reform on Trial* (New York: Basic Books, 1983); John Goldkamp, "Judicial Reform of Bail Practices: The Philadelphia Experiment," *Court Management Journal* (1983): 16–20.

129. John Goldkamp and Michael Gottfredson, *Judicial Decision Guidelines for Bail: The Philadelphia Experiment* (Washington, DC: National Institute of Justice, 1983).

130. Joseph Sanborn, "Philosophical, Legal, and Systemic Aspects of Juvenile Court Plea Bargaining," *Crime and Delinquency* 39 (1993): 509–527.

131. Carla Gaskins, *Felony Case Processing in State Courts, 1986* (Washington, DC: Bureau of Justice Statistics, 1990), p. 1. See also Donald Newman, "Making a Deal," in *Legal Process and Corrections*, eds. N.

Johnston and L. Savitz (New York: Wiley, 1982), p. 93.

132. Mike McConville and Chester Mirsky, *Jury Trials and Plea Bargaining: A True History* (Oxford, England: Hart Publishing, 2005).

133. George Fisher, "Plea Bargaining's Triumph," *Yale Law Journal* 109 (2000): 857–1,058.

134. Newman, "Making a Deal," pp. 96–97.

135. These sentiments are similar to those expressed by Abraham Blumberg in "The Practice of Law as a Confidence Game: Organizational Co-optation of a Profession," *Law and Society Review* 1 (1967): 15–39.

136. Again, these thoughts are similar to Blumberg's views as expressed in "The Practice of Law as a Confidence Game."

137. Shaila Dewan, "Prosecutors Say Cuts Force Plea Bargains," *New York Times*, 10 March 2003, p. B3.

138. Stephanos Bibas, "Plea Bargaining Outside the Shadow of Trial," *Harvard Law Review* 117 (2004): 2,464–2,547.

139. National Advisory Commission on Criminal Justice Standards and Goals, *Courts* (Washington, DC: U.S. Government Printing Office, 1976).

140. William Stuntz, "Plea Bargaining and Criminal Law's Disappearing Shadow," *Harvard Law Review* 117 (2004): 2,548–2,569.

141. Richard Kuh, "Plea Copping," *Bar Bulletin* 24 (1966–1967): 160.

142. Alan Alschuler, "The Defense Counsel's Role in Plea Bargaining," *Yale Law Journal* 84 (1975): 1,179.

143. See generally Milton Heumann, "A Note on Plea Bargaining and Case Pressure," *Law and Society Review* 9 (1975): 515.

144. John Kramer and Jeffrey Ulmer, "Downward Departures for Serious Violent Offenders: Local Court 'Corrections' to Pennsylvania's Sentencing Guidelines," *Criminology* 40 (2002): 897–933.

145. National Institute of Law Enforcement and Criminal Justice, *Plea Bargaining in the United States* (Washington, DC: Georgetown University, 1978), p. 8.

146. Michael Rubenstein, Stevens Clarke, and Teresa White, *Alaska Bans Plea Bargaining* (Washington, DC: U.S. Department of Justice, 1980).

147. Newman, "Making a Deal," p. 102.

148. National Advisory Commission on Criminal Justice Standards and Goals, *Courts*, p. 66.

149. See, for example, "Limiting the Peremptory Challenge: Representation of Groups on Petit Juries," *Yale Law Journal* 86 (1977): 1,715.

150. *Batson v. Kentucky*, 476 U.S. 79 (1986).

151. *Ham v. South Carolina*, 409 U.S. 524, 93 S.Ct. 848, 35 L.Ed.2d 46 (1973).

152. *Turner v. Murray*, 106 S.Ct. 1683 (1986).

153. *Taylor v. Louisiana*, 419 U.S. 522, 42 L.Ed.2d 690, 95 S.Ct. 692 (1975).

154. *In Ristaino v. Ross* (424 U.S. 589 [1976]), the Court said questioning the jury on racial issues was not automatic in all interracial crimes.

155. Edna Erez, "Victim Participation in Sentencing: Rhetoric and Reality," *Journal of Criminal Justice* 18 (1990): 19–31.

156. *Strunk v. United States*, 412 U.S. 434 (1973).

157. *Barker v. Wingo*, 404 U.S. 307 (1971).

158. *Duncan v. Louisiana*, 391 U.S. 145 (1968).

159. *Baldwin v. New York*, 399 U.S. 66 (1970).

160. *Blanton v. City of North Las Vegas*, 489 U.S. 538, 109 S.Ct. 1289, 103 L.Ed.2d 550 (1989).

161. *Williams v. Florida*, 399 U.S. 78 (1970).

162. *Apodica v. Oregon*, 406 U.S. 404 (1972).

163. *Benton v. Maryland*, 395 U.S. 784 (1969).

164. *United States v. Lanza*, 260 U.S. 377 (1922); *Bartkus v. Illinois*, 359 U.S. 121 (1959); *Abbate v. U.S.*, 359 U.S. 187 (1959).

165. *Heath v. Alabama*, 106 S.Ct. 433 (1985).

166. *Powell v. Alabama*, 287 U.S. 45 (1932).

167. *Gideon v. Wainwright*, 372 U.S. 335 (1963).

168. *Argersinger v. Hamlin*, 407 U.S. 25 (1972).

169. *Alabama v. Shelton*, 122 U.S. 1764 (2002).

170. *Riggins v. Nevada*, 504 U.S. 127 (1992).

171. *Maryland v. Craig*, 110 S.Ct. 3157, 111 L.Ed.2d 666 (1990).

172. 448 U.S. 555, 100 S.Ct. 2814, 65 L.Ed.2d 1 (1980).

173. Dale Edwards, "If It Walks, Talks and Squawks Like a Trial, Should It Be Covered Like One? The Right of the Press to Cover INS Deportation Hearings," *Communication Law and Policy* 10 (2005): 217–239.

174. T. Dyk and B. Donald, "Cameras in the Supreme Court," *American Bar Association Journal* 75 (1989): 34.

175. James Morton, "Court TV—The Cameras Are Switched On Again," *Journal of Criminal Law* 68 (2004): 451–453.

176. The following sections rely heavily on Elizabeth Wiggins, "The Courtroom of the Future Is Here: Introduction to Emerging Technologies in the Legal System," *Law and Policy* 28 (2006): 182–191; "Criminal Court Records Go Online," *Quill* 90 (2002): 39; Donald C. Dilworth, "New Court Technology Will Affect How Attorneys Present Trials," *Trial* 33 (1997): 100–114.

177. Wisconsin Circuit Court Access (WCCA), Access to the Public Records of the Consolidated Court Automation Programs (CCAP), http://wcca.wicourts.gov (accessed March 29, 2007).

178. Harris County Criminal Justice Center, http://aceav.com/cases/index.php?case_id=29 (accessed March 12, 2007).

179. *House v. Bell*, No. 04-8990, 547 U.S. ___ (2006).

18

Punishment and Correction

CHAPTER OUTLINE

A Brief History of Punishment
Reforming Correctional Punishment
The Rise of the Prison
Competing Correctional Models

The Goals of Criminal Punishment
Imposing Punishment
Sentencing Structures

Race, Culture, Gender, and Criminology:
Does Race Matter?

The Death Penalty
The Death Penalty Debate

Comparative Criminology: International
Use of the Death Penalty

Legal Issues

Correcting Criminal Offenders
Contemporary Corrections

Probation
Probation Services
Probation Rules and Revocation
Success of Probation

Intermediate Sanctions
Fines
Forfeiture
Restitution
Split Sentencing and Shock Probation
Intensive Probation Supervision
Home Confinement/Electronic Monitoring
Residential Community Corrections
Boot Camps/Shock Incarceration
Can Alternatives Work?

Jails
Jail Populations

Prisons
Types of Prisons

Prison Inmates: Male
Living in Prison
Prison Inmates: Female
Correctional Treatment
Prison Violence
Corrections and the Rule of Law
Cruel and Unusual Punishment

The Criminological Enterprise: The Problems of Reentry

Parole
The Parolee in the Community
How Effective Is Parole?

CHAPTER OBJECTIVES

1. Be familiar with the early history of punishment

2. Describe the development of the prison as a means of punishment

3. Describe the nature of probation and its various services

4. Discuss the effectiveness of probation and the concept of revocation

5. Be familiar with the various forms of alternative sanctions

6. Know the purpose served by the jail, its problems, and what is being done to improve jail conditions

7. Describe different types of correctional facilities and their level of security

8. Understand the experience of living in prison

9. Discuss correctional treatment and the nature of prison violence

10. Show how the problems of parolees and inmate reentry have influenced the correctional system

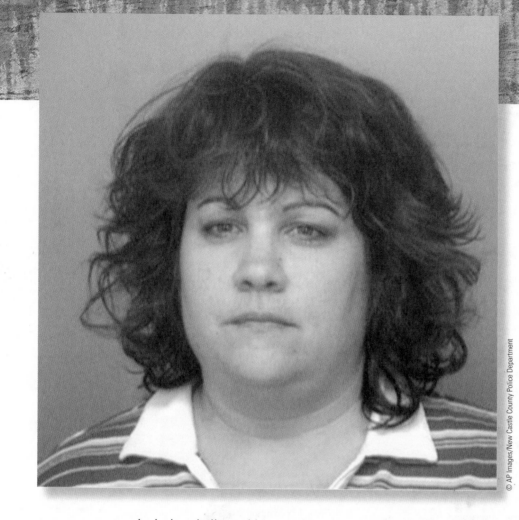

© AP Images/New Castle County Police Department

On March 18, 2007, Rachel Holt, 35, a sixth-grade science teacher, pleaded guilty to having sex with one of her 13-year-old students. During the sentencing hearing, prosecutors demanded that Holt be given the maximum sentence of 25 years, one for each of the times she had sex with the boy during an intense weeklong affair. She also gave the boy alcohol and allowed him to drive her car. In contrast, Holt's attorney reviewed 40 similar cases and found the average punishment was 18 months behind bars. Holt herself apologized "to everyone who suffered" as a result of her actions, including the victim and his family. "I hope you can forgive me," she said. "I know what I did was wrong." Speaking for the family, the boy's uncle claimed, "He had his innocence taken away through betrayal." After considering all arguments and statements, Superior Court Judge Calvin L. Scott sentenced Holt to 10 years in prison.[1]

Did Rachel Holt deserve a 10-year prison sentence or is her lawyer correct when he claims that she was punished excessively for her misdeeds? Should the sentence have been more in line with what other teachers received for similar crimes, or is each case unique? And was Holt's punishment overly severe considering the sentences routinely handed out for violent crimes? Table 18.1 contains data collected over a 12-year period of conviction offense and subsequent punishment in the nation's 75 largest counties. As the data show, almost 20 percent of convicted felons are given nonincarceration sentences such as probation. About 17 percent of rapists, 11 percent of robbers, and even 2 percent of murderers never set foot behind bars.[2] As Figure 18.1 indicates, the median sentence for a violent felony is five years in prison, half of the ten years received by Rachel Holt.

As the Holt case illustrates, formulating fair and effective punishments is a very difficult task. How can the proper sentence be formulated? Is it fair to punish one person more severely than another? And if so, what factors shape the contours of justice? What does society gain from keeping someone like Rachel Holt in prison for 10 years? Would five years be sufficient? What about three? Would we better off supervising her in the community with the condition that she stay away from young boys and devote her life to helping others?

In this chapter we will review the way we punish criminals. We begin by looking at the nature and purpose of sentencing criminals, review how sentences are distributed and then review contemporary forms of correction and supervision of those convicted of criminal offenses.

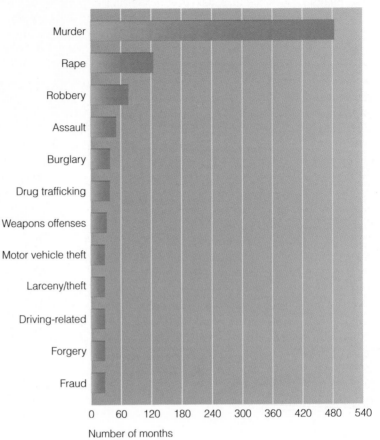

Figure 18.1 Median Sentence Received for Felony Convictions by Offense

Source: Thomas Cohen and Brian Reaves, *Felony Defendants in Large Urban Counties, 2002* (Washington, DC: Bureau of Justice Statistics, 2006), www.ojp.usdoj.gov/bjs/pub/pdf/fdluc02.pdf (accessed August 1, 2007).

Table 18.1 Most Severe Sentence Received by Most Serious Conviction Offense

Most Serious Conviction Charge	% Prison	% Jail	% Probation
All violent felonies	50	31	19
Murder	96	2	2
Rape	62	21	17
Robbery	69	20	11
Assault	38	38	23
Other violent crime	35	41	24

Note: From the 75 largest counties, 1990–2002.
Source: Brian Reaves, *Violent Felons in Large Urban Counties* (Washington, DC: Bureau of Justice Statistics, 2006), www.ojp.usdoj.gov/bjs/pub/pdf/vfluc.pdf (accessed August 1, 2007).

A BRIEF HISTORY OF PUNISHMENT

When a person is convicted of a criminal offense, society exercises the right to punish or correct his or her behavior. Equating crime and punishment is certainly not a new practice.[3] Criminal offenders have been punished by governmental authorities throughout recorded history. Over the centuries, there has been significant debate as to why people should be punished and what type of punishment is most appropriate to correct, treat, or deter criminal offenders. The style and purpose of criminal corrections have gone through many stages and have featured a variety of penal sanctions.[4]

From ancient times up until the fifteenth century, punishment for crime and misbehavior was immediate and severe, consisting of banishment, mutilation, branding, flogging, and death. Punishments became unmatched in their cruelty, featuring a gruesome variety of physical tortures. Punishment was also made into a public spectacle, presumably so the sadistic sanctions would act as a deterrent. But the variety and imagination of the tortures inflicted on even minor criminals before their death suggest that sadism and spectacle were more important than any presumed deterrent effect.

The discovery of the New World changed the nature of punishment. Rather than kill criminals, it became economically and politically more attractive to transport them to overseas colonies. They supplied labor, cost little, and were profitable for the government because manufacturers and plantation owners paid for convicts' services and transporting offenders served as a means of creating a native-speaking population abroad. The Old Bailey Court in London supplied at least 10,000 convicts between 1717 and 1775 to the Americas, helping secure the continent for Great Britain.[5] Convicts would serve a period as workers and then become free again.

Transportation to the colonies waned as a method of punishment with the increase in colonial population, further development of the land, and increasing importation of African slaves in the eighteenth century. The American Revolution ended transportation of felons to North America; the remaining areas used were Australia, New Zealand, and African colonies. Nonetheless, hanging and physical punishments were the norm and people went to their death after convictions of theft and were whipped for speaking out against the government. In 1795, English law included more than 200 felonies that were punishable by execution, including not only murder and rape, but also burglary, robbery, animal theft, the concealment of bankruptcy, and the malicious maiming of cattle.[6]

Reforming Correctional Punishment

Punishing people by incarcerating them in prisons and/or jails can actually be traced to a liberal reform effort instigated by William Penn (1644–1718), the founder of the state of Pennsylvania.[7] At the end of the seventeenth century, Penn revised Pennsylvania's criminal code to forbid torture and the capricious use of mutilation, physical punishment, and death, which heretofore had been the norm. These devices were replaced by the penalties of incarceration at hard labor, moderate flogging, fines, and forfeiture of property. All lands and goods belonging to felons were used to make restitution to the victims of crimes, with restitution limited to twice the value of the damages. Felons who owned no property were required by law to labor in the prison workhouse until the victim was compensated. Punishment was relatively mild for the times: burglary was punishable by three months' imprisonment and restitution to the victim; arson was punished by a year at hard labor and corporal punishment.

Though Penn's original reforms were later rescinded and English law re-adopted, the seeds had been planted for penal reform. In 1790, the Walnut Street Jail was built in Philadelphia as a "liberal reform" dedicated to replacing physical punishments. At this institution, most prisoners were placed in solitary cells, where they remained in isolation and did not have the right to work.[8] Overcrowding undermined the goal

of solitary confinement of serious offenders, and soon more than one inmate was placed in each cell. Despite these difficulties, similar institutions were erected in New York (Newgate in 1791), New Jersey (Trenton in 1798), and Massachusetts (Castle Island in 1785). By the turn of the nineteenth century, incarceration began to replace physical punishment as the preferred method of criminal sanction and has remained so ever since.

The Rise of the Prison

In 1816 New York built a new prison at Auburn, hoping to alleviate some of the overcrowding at Newgate. The Auburn prison design became known as the tier system because cells were built vertically on five floors of the structure. It was sometimes also referred to as the congregate system because most prisoners ate and worked in groups. In 1819 construction was started on a wing of solitary cells to house unruly prisoners. Three classes of prisoners were then created: one group remained continually in solitary confinement as a result of breaches of prison discipline; the second group was allowed labor as an occasional form of recreation; and the third and largest class worked and ate together during the days and went into seclusion only at night.

The philosophy of the Auburn system was crime prevention through fear of punishment and silent confinement. The worst felons were cut off from all contact with other prisoners, and although they were treated and fed relatively well, they had no hope of pardon to relieve their isolation. For a time, some of the worst convicts were forced to remain totally alone and silent during the entire day; this practice caused many prisoners to have mental breakdowns, resulting in suicides and self-mutilations. This practice was abolished in 1823.[9]

Competing Correctional Models

In 1818 Pennsylvania took the radical step of establishing a prison that placed each inmate in a single cell with no work to do. Classifications were abolished because each cell was intended as a miniature prison that would prevent the inmates from contaminating one another.

The new Pennsylvania prison, called the Western Penitentiary, had an unusual architectural design. It was built in a semicircle, with the cells positioned along its circumference. Built back-to-back, some cells faced the boundary wall while others faced the internal area of the circle. Its inmates were kept in solitary confinement almost constantly, being allowed about an hour a day for exercise. In 1820, a second, similar penitentiary using the isolate system was built in Philadelphia and called the Eastern Penitentiary.

The supporters of the Pennsylvania system believed that the penitentiary was truly a place to do penance. By advocating totally removing the sinner from society and allowing the prisoner a period of isolation in which to ponder alone upon the evils of crime, the supporters of the Pennsylvania system reflected the influence of religious philosophy on corrections. In fact, its advocates believed that solitary confinement (with in-cell labor as a recreation) would eventually make working so attractive that upon release the inmate would be well suited to resume a productive existence in society. The Pennsylvania system eliminated the need for large numbers of guards or disciplinary measures. Isolated from one another, inmates could not plan escapes or collectively break rules. When discipline was a problem, whips and iron gags were used (iron gags were jammed in inmates' mouths so they could not speak, causing great discomfort).

The congregate system eventually prevailed, however, and spread throughout the United States; many of its features are still used today. Its innovations included congregate working conditions, the use of solitary confinement to punish unruly inmates, military regimentation, and discipline. In Auburn-like institutions, prisoners were marched from place to place; their time was regulated by bells telling them to sleep, wake up, and work. The system was so like the military that many of its early administrators were recruited from the armed services.

Although the prison was viewed as an improvement over capital and corporal punishment, it quickly became the scene of depressed conditions; inmates were treated harshly and routinely whipped and tortured. As historian Samuel Walker notes,

> Prison brutality flourished. It was ironic that the prison had been devised as a more humane alternative to corporal and capital punishment. Instead, it simply moved corporal punishment indoors where, hidden from public view, it became even more savage.[10]

Yet in the midst of such savagery some inmates were able to adjust to institutional living and even improve their lives through prison-administered literacy programs.[11] Prison conditions began to slowly improve when state and federal court rulings gave inmates rights to freedom of religion and speech, medical care, due process, and proper living conditions. In the 1970s, when violence within the correctional system became a national scandal and major riots occurred at New York's Attica Prison and the New Mexico State Penitentiary, prison administrators responded with efforts to improve conditions and provide innovative programs that give inmates a voice in running the institution.

THE GOALS OF CRIMINAL PUNISHMENT

Why do we punish? What are the goals of criminal sentencing today? The sentencing decision is a key element of the adjudicatory process and its outcome may be influenced by a variety of goals and objectives. A number of factors have been found to influence sentencing outcomes, including general deterrence, specific deterrence, incapacitation, equity, diversion, rehabilitation, desert/retribution, and restoration (see Exhibit 18.1). In the case of Rachel Holt, the sentencing judge may have based his decision on (a) his belief that she *deserved* 10 years in prison for taking advantage of a minor, (b) his desire to *deter* other

teachers who might be pondering a similar act, (c) his belief that Holt needed to be *incapacitated* in order to protect other kids, or (d) all of the above.

Imposing Punishment

Sentencing is one of the most crucial functions of judges. Sentencing authority may also be exercised by the jury, an administrative body, a judge, or it may be mandated by statute.

In most felony cases, except where the law dictates mandatory prison terms, sentencing is usually based on a variety of information available to the judge. Some jurisdictions allow victims to make impact statements that are considered at sentencing hearings, although these often have little influence on sentencing outcomes.[12] Most judges consider a presentence investigation report by the probation department. This report, which is a social and personal history as well as an evaluation of the defendant, is used by the judge in making a sentencing decision.[13] Some judges heavily weigh the presentence investigation report; others may dismiss it completely or rely on only certain portions.

When an accused is convicted of two or more charges, he or she must be sentenced on each charge. A concurrent sentence means that both sentences are served at the same time, and the term of imprisonment is completed after the longest term has been served. A defendant may be sentenced to 3 years imprisonment on a charge of assault and 10 years for burglary, the sentences to be served concurrently. After the offender serves 10 years in prison, the sentences would be completed. Conversely, a consecutive sentence means that upon completion of one sentence, the other term of incarceration begins. A defendant sentenced to 3 years imprisonment on a charge of assault and 10 years for burglary, the sentences to be served consecutively, would serve a total of 13 years. In most instances sentences are given concurrently.

Sentencing Structures

When a convicted offender is sentenced to prison, the statutes of the jurisdiction in which the crime was committed determine the penalties that may be imposed by the court. Over the years, a variety of sentencing structures have been used, including determinate sentences, indeterminate sentences, and mandatory sentences.

The Indeterminate Sentence The indeterminate sentence is used in a majority of states. Created in the nineteenth century by penal reformers, its purpose is to encourage inmates to engage in treatment programs by promising them early release if they can convince correctional authorities that they have been rehabilitated while in prison. Under this scheme, those convicted of criminal offenses are given a short minimum sentence that must be served and a lengthy maximum sentence that is the outer boundary of the time that can possibly be served. For example, the legislature might set a sentence of a minimum of 1 year and a maximum of 20 years for burglary.

EXHIBIT 18.1

The Goals of Sentencing

1. *Deterrence*. By punishing the known offender for their misdeeds, society hopes to convince would-be offenders that the pains of punishment outweigh the potential benefits of criminal behavior. The validity of deterrence rests on the premise that punishing one offender will convince other potential criminals to abstain from crime. According to deterrence theory, people are not punished for what they have done but for the effect their punishment will have on the future behavior of others.

2. *Specific deterrence*. Experiencing harsh criminal punishments should convince convicted offenders that crime does not pay and recidivism is not in their best interests. The suffering caused by punishment should inhibit future law violations.

3. *Incapacitation*. By incapacitating a convicted offender in a secure facility, such as a prison or jail, the state seeks to reduce or eliminate his or her opportunity to commit future crimes. In some instances, incapacitation involves supervising an offender while the person remains in the community. It is hoped that close monitoring will restrict opportunities to commit future crime without the necessity of secure lockup. Incapacitation involves anticipating behavior patterns: offenders are confined not for what they have done but for what it is feared they might do in the future.

4. *Rehabilitation*. Correctional rehabilitation is aimed at reducing future criminality by treating and eliminating the underlying causes of crime. Offenders are believed to have one or more emotional or behavioral deficits that cause them to violate the law. Criminal behavior would cease if this problem could be successfully treated. Rehabilitation efforts focus on emotional stress, vocational training, education, or substance abuse. Rehabilitation also involves predicting future behavior: unless the offenders receive treatment, they will commit future crimes; treatment reduces the likelihood of their reoffending.

5. *Diversion*. In some instances, the court process is aimed at sparing nondangerous offenders from the stigma and labeling of a criminal conviction and involvement with the justice process. Instead of being convicted and sentenced to traditional forms of correction, such as a stay in a county jail, the judge may allow them to be diverted into a community correctional program for treatment.

6. *Desert/retribution*. Because criminals benefit from their misdeeds, they deserve to be punished for their criminal acts. Furthermore, if the state did not punish people for their misconduct (retribution), victims would be encouraged to seek personal vengeance for their loss (revenge), creating a chaotic society. In a just society, criminals are punished in a manner proportionate to the severity of their crimes. According to this view, it is only fair that criminals who have committed the most serious crime, murder, receive the most severe penalty, death.

7. *Equity/restitution*. Because criminals gain from their misdeeds, it seems both fair and just to demand that they reimburse society for its loss caused by their crimes. The equity goal of punishment means that convicted criminals must pay back their victims for their loss, the justice system for the costs of processing their case, and society for any disruption they may have caused. In a so-called victimless crime, such as drug trafficking, the social costs might include the expense of drug enforcement efforts, drug treatment centers, and care for infants born to drug-addicted mothers. In predatory crimes, the costs might include the services of emergency room doctors, lost workdays and productivity, and treatment for long-term psychological problems.

8. *Restoration*. Defendants may be asked to confront their behavior, the damage they caused the victim, and the shame they brought to their family, friends, and community. The goal is to restore them to good standing in society.

The actual length of time served is controlled by the corrections agency. Inmates can be paroled after serving the minimum sentence if they are considered rehabilitated and ready to live in the community. In addition, the minimum (or maximum) time served may be reduced if, while in prison, the convicted criminal earns "time off for good behavior" for participating in rehabilitation programs and behaving well. Inmates today serve less than half of their original sentences.

Most jurisdictions that use indeterminate sentences specify minimum and maximum terms but allow judges discretion to fix the actual sentence within those limits. If burglary is punishable by a sentence of 2 to 20 years, the judge could decide to give one offender 5 to 10 and another 2 to 5 years because they cooperated with the prosecution. The sentence must be no less than the minimum and no more than the maximum range of years set by the legislature.

The underlying purpose of indeterminate sentencing is to individualize each sentence in the interests of rehabilitating the offender. This type of sentencing allows for flexibility not only in the type of sentence imposed but also in the length of time served.

The Determinate Sentence Determinate sentences, which gave the convicted criminal a set number of years to be served in prison, were actually the first kind used in the United States but were eventually replaced by indeterminate sentencing models early in the twentieth century. However, the unbridled discretion given judges bothered critics who feared that it might be used in an unfair manner.

In 1969 Kenneth Culp Davis published *Discretionary Justice*, which was followed in 1972 by Judge Marvin Frankel's landmark study *Criminal Sentences—Law Without Order*.[14] These works exposed the disparity in the justice process and called for reform. Frankel stated, "The almost wholly unchecked and sweeping powers we give to judges in the fashioning of sentences are terrifying and intolerable for a society that professes devotion to the rule of law."[15]

In response to these concerns, a number of jurisdictions replaced indeterminate sentences and discretionary parole with a system of determinate sentencing that featured a single term of years without discretionary parole. Earned "good time" or time off for good behavior could still reduce the actual time served behind bars, in some cases, by up to one-half. These

Sentences can be either concurrent or consecutive and the difference can be dramatic. Former state House Speaker Jim Black (center) reacts as he is ordered to pay a $1 million fine on a state political corruption charge during his sentencing on July 31, 2007, in Raleigh, North Carolina. Wake County Superior Court Judge Donald Stephens also sentenced Black to serve up to ten months in prison, with the term to run concurrently with a federal 5-year sentence Black received earlier in the year.

modern versions of determinate sentencing reflect an orientation toward desert, deterrence, and equality at the expense of treatment and rehabilitation. Most jurisdictions have attempted to structure determinate sentences by suggesting appropriate prison terms for particular crimes.[16]

Structured Sentencing To ensure that the new determinate sentences would be applied in a fair manner, those jurisdictions that embraced determinate sentencing also developed guidelines to control and structure the sentencing process and make it more rational. **Sentencing guidelines** are usually based on the seriousness of a crime and the background of an offender: the more serious the crime and the more extensive the offender's criminal background, the longer the prison term recommended by the guidelines. Guidelines might require that all people convicted of robbery who had no prior offense record and who did not use excessive force or violence be given an average of a 5-year sentence; those who used force and had a prior record will have 3 years added on their sentence. In making their sentencing decisions, judges refer to the guideline manual and calculate the proper sentence based on the facts of the case and the characteristics of the defendant. Guidelines eliminate discretionary parole but also allow inmates to reduce their sentence by acquiring time off for good behavior. By eliminating judicial discretion, they are designed to reduce racial and gender disparity.[17]

The Nature of Guidelines Guidelines were created by appointed sentencing commissions whose members attempted to formulate what an "ideal" sentence would be for a particular crime and offender. In some instances their decisions were based on empirical analysis of existing sentencing practices while in other instances sentences were based on the beliefs of the commissioners. Regardless of the formulation there is a great deal of variation within guidelines. Some coexist with parole release and some do not. Some deal with all crimes and others only with felonies. Some set narrow sentencing ranges, and some set broad ones. Some address sentences of all types, and some address only state prison sentences.[18] North Carolina, Pennsylvania, and Ohio employ what is known as a "comprehensive structured sentencing system," which sets sentencing standards for felonies and misdemeanors, and for prison, jail, intermediate, and community punishments. They also include mechanisms for tying sentencing policy to correctional capacity and for distributing state funds to stimulate and support local corrections programs.[19]

There are a number of ways to formulate guidelines. One method is to create a grid with prior record and current offense as the two coordinates and set out specific punishments. Table 18.2 shows Minnesota's guidelines. Note that as prior record and offense severity increase, so does recommended sentence length. After a certain point, probation is no longer an option, and the defendant is expected to do prison time. A burglar with no prior convictions can expect to receive probation or an 18-month sentence for a house break-in; an experienced burglar with six or more prior convictions can get 54 months for the same crime. While following the guidelines is expected, they are recommendations based on typical circumstances. For a case that is not typical, the judge can depart from the recommended sentence. If the court does depart, the judge must state the reasons for departure and either the prosecution or the defense may appeal the pronounced sentence.

Legal Challenges The greatest challenge to the use of guidelines has been legal. In two recent decisions, *Blakely v. Washington* (2004) and *United States v. Booker* (2005), the Supreme Court found that the sentencing guidelines used both in Washington State and by the federal government were in violation of a defendant's Sixth Amendment rights.

Table 18.2 Sentencing Guidelines Grid (Presumptive Sentence Lengths in Months)

Severity Level of Conviction Offense		Criminal History Score						
		0	1	2	3	4	5	6 or more
Murder, 2nd-degree (intentional murder; drive-by shootings)	XI	306 *261–367*	326 *278–391*	346 *295–415*	366 *312–439*	386 *329–463*	406 *346–480[2]*	426 *263–480[2]*
Murder, 3rd-degree murder, 2nd-degree (unintentional murder)	X	150 *128–180*	165 *141–198*	180 *153–216*	195 *166–234*	210 *179–252*	225 *192–270*	240 *204–288*
Assault, 1st-degree controlled substance crime, 1st degree	IX	86 *74–103*	98 *84–117*	110 *94–132*	122 *104–146*	134 *114–160*	146 *125–175*	158 *135–189*
Aggravated robbery, 1st-degree controlled substance crime, 2nd degree	VIII	48 *41–57*	58 *50–69*	68 *58–81*	78 *67–93*	88 *75–105*	98 *84–117*	108 *92–129*
Felony DWI	VII	36	42	48	54 *46–64*	60 *51–72*	66 *57–79*	72 *62–86*
Assault, 2nd-degree felony in possession of a firearm	VI	21	27	33	39 *34–46*	45 *39–54*	51 *44–61*	57 *49–68*
Residential burglary Simple robbery	V	18	23	28	33 *29–39*	38 *33–45*	43 *37–51*	48 *41–57*
Nonresidential burglary	IV	12[1]	15	18	21	24 *21–28*	27 *23–32*	30 *26–36*
Theft crimes (over $2,500)	III	12[1]	13	15	17	19 *17–22*	21 *18–25*	23 *20–27*
Theft crimes ($2,500 or less) Check forgery ($200–$2,500)	II	12[1]	12[1]	13	15	17	19	21 *18–25*
Sale of simulated controlled substance	I	12[1]	12[1]	12[1]	13	15	17	19 *17–22*

Italicized numbers within the grid denote the range within which a judge may sentence without the sentence being deemed a departure. Offenders with nonimprisonment felony sentences are subject to jail time according to law.

☐ Presumptive commitment to state imprisonment. First-degree murder is excluded from the guidelines by law and continues to have a mandatory life sentence. See section II.E. Mandatory Sentences for policy regarding those sentences controlled by law.

☐ Presumptive stayed sentence; at the discretion of the judge, up to a year in jail and/or other nonjail sanctions can be imposed as conditions of probation. However, certain offenses in this section of the grid always carry a presumptive commitment to state prison. See sections II.C. Presumptive Sentence and II.E. Mandatory Sentences.

[1] One year and one day.

[2] M.S. § 244.09 requires the Sentencing Guidelines to provide a range of 15 percent downward and 20 percent upward from the presumptive sentence. However, because the statutory maximum sentence for these offenses is no more than 40 years, the range is capped at that number.

Source: Minnesota Sentencing Guideline Commission. August 1, 2006, www.msgc.state.mn.us/Guidelines/guide06. DOC (accessed July 31, 2007).

In these rulings, the court held that judges cannot impose sentences beyond the statutory maximum unless the facts supporting such an increase are found by a jury beyond a reasonable doubt.[20] In essence, the rulings made guidelines advisory rather than mandatory.

These cases did not in essence outlaw guidelines, but ruled that there must be changes in the way they are administered. State and federal courts are now addressing these issues and creating mechanisms for the proper administration of the guidelines, especially if the case involves sentencing enhancement. This work is ongoing. A recent (2006) report by the Federal Sentencing Commission found that even though federal courts interpreted the *Booker* decision in different ways, the majority of federal cases continue to be sentenced within the range of existing sentencing guidelines (about 86 percent). This conformance rate remained stable throughout the year that followed *Booker*. So even though the guidelines are now advisory rather than mandatory they still have a great deal of impact on sentencing decisions.[21]

Mandatory Sentences Another effort to limit judicial discretion has been the development of mandatory (minimum) sentences that require the incarceration of all offenders convicted of specific crimes. Some states, for example, exclude offenders convicted of certain offenses, such as drug trafficking or handgun crimes, from even the possibility of being placed on probation; some exclude recidivists; and others bar certain offenders from being considered for parole.

Mandatory sentencing generally limits the judge's discretionary power to impose any disposition but that authorized by the legislature. Mandatory sentencing legislation may supplement an indeterminate sentencing structure or be a feature of structured sentencing. For example, in Massachusetts, which uses indeterminate sentencing, conviction for possessing an unregistered handgun brings with it a mandatory prison term of at least 1 year.[22]

Truth in Sentencing First enacted in 1984, truth-in-sentencing laws require offenders to serve a substantial portion of their prison sentences behind bars.[23] Parole eligibility and good-time credits are restricted or eliminated. The truth-in-sentencing movement has been a response to prison crowding that in some instances has forced the early release of inmates from overcrowded institutions. The Violent Offender Incarceration and Truth-in-Sentencing Incentive Grant Program in the 1994 Crime Act offered the states funds to support the costs of longer sentences.[24] To qualify for federal funds, states must require those convicted of violent felony crimes to serve not less than 85 percent of their prison sentences. More than 25 states and the District of Columbia have met the federal Truth-in-Sentencing Incentive Grant Program eligibility criteria.[25] It is ironic that the United States is embracing these extremely punitive sentencing policies at the same time many other Western nations are moving in the opposite direction by employing more humane, moderate criminal punishments such as fines and community sentencing orders.[26]

Three Strikes Law Three strikes (and you're out) laws provide lengthy terms for any person convicted of three felony offenses, even if the third crime is relatively trivial. California's three strikes law is aimed at getting habitual criminals off the street. Anyone convicted of a third felony must do a minimum term of 25 years to life; the third felony does not have to be serious or violent. The federal Crime Act of 1994 also adopted a three strikes provision, requiring a mandatory life sentence for any offender convicted of three felony offenses; 26 states have so far followed suit and passed some form of the three strikes law.

Although welcomed by conservatives looking for a remedy for violent crime, the three strikes policy is controversial because a person convicted of a minor felony can receive a life sentence. Research shows that habitual offender sentencing laws have little effect on crime rates.[27]

Because of its use with petty offenders, there are ongoing legal challenges to the use of three strikes laws, and their future is still uncertain. However, on March 6, 2003, the U.S. Supreme Court in *Lockyer v. Andrade* upheld the three strikes sentence of Leandro Andrade, a man sentenced to prison in California for 50 years for stealing $153 worth of videotapes. It also upheld the conviction of Gary Ewing, who appealed a prior 25-year sentence for stealing a set of golf clubs. In both cases the Court ruled that the challenged sentences were not so grossly disproportionate as to violate the Eighth Amendment's prohibition against cruel and unusual punishment.[28] These cases solidified the legality of three strikes laws.

How People Are Sentenced The most recent data available show the following trends in sentencing:

▌ About 70 percent of all felons convicted in state courts are sentenced to a period of confinement—about 40 percent to state prisons and 30 percent to local jails. Jail sentences are for short-term confinement (usually for a year or less) in a county or city facility, while prison sentences are for long-term confinement (usually for over a year) in a state facility.[29]

▌ About 30 percent of convicted felons were sentenced to straight probation with no jail or prison time to serve. The ratio of confinement to community sentences has remained stable for the past 20 years (see Table 18.3).

▌ Felons sentenced to a state prison average about 4.5 years but were likely to serve only half of that sentence—or just 2.25 years—before release.

▌ The average sentence to local jail was 7 months. The average probation sentence was about 3 years.

▌ Besides being sentenced to incarceration or probation, more than one-third of convicted felons also were ordered to pay a fine, pay victim restitution, receive treatment, perform community service, or comply with some other additional penalty. A fine was imposed on at least 25 percent of convicted felons.

likely to result in a death sentence than homicides with female offenders or male victims.[43] Though African Americans make up less than 15 percent of the population, they account for about half of all death row inmates (Figure 18.4).

▎ Homicides involving strangers are more likely to result in a death sentence than homicides involving nonstrangers and acquaintances. Prosecutors are more likely to recommend the death sentence for people who kill white victims than they are in any other racial combination of victim and criminal, for example, whites who kill blacks.[44]

▎ Capital punishment may escalate the seriousness of criminal acts. Some critics fear that the introduction of capital punishment encourages criminals to escalate their violent behavior, consequently putting police officers at risk. A suspect who kills someone during a botched robbery may be inclined to "fire away" upon encountering police rather than surrender peacefully; the killer faces the death penalty already, what does he have to lose? Geoffrey Rapp studied the effect of capital punishment on the killings of police and found that, all other things being equal, the greater the number of new inmates on death row, the greater the number of police officers killed by citizens.[45] Rapp concludes that the death penalty seems to create an extremely dangerous environment for law enforcement officers because it (a) does not deter criminals and (b) may lull officers into a false sense of security because they believe that the death penalty will deter violence directed against them and may cause them to let their guard down.

▎ The death penalty is brutal and demeaning. Even if the general public voices approval of the death penalty, abolitionists argue that "social vengeance by death is a primitive way of revenge which stands in the way of moral progress."[46] And while early religious leaders accepted the death penalty, others such as the Catholic Church condemn the practice.[47] In *The Contradictions of American Capital Punishment*, Franklin Zimring links America's obsession with the death penalty, unique among westernized nations, with its vigilante tradition, in which people on the frontier took justice into their own hands, assuming that their targets were always guilty as charged.[48] The death penalty was widely practiced against slaves, and at one time mass executions were a brutal and common practice to stifle any thought of escapes or revolt.[49]

▎ Critics also question whether the general public gives blanket approval to the application of capital punishment. European Americans support capital punishment more than African Americans regardless of income or status.[50]

▎ While the Bible and religious leaders of bygone days may have supported the death penalty, religious people today, especially those who have a personal relationship with a loving God, tend to oppose the use of capital punishment.[51]

▎ Support for capital punishment among whites is skewed by racial attitudes; those holding racist attitudes are much more likely to support the death penalty.[52]

▎ People who generally support the death penalty may not want to see it used with juveniles, the mentally challenged, or the mentally ill.[53] Research suggests that most people may accept capital punishment in principle but also believe it should be used only rarely.[54] Surveys show that the general public is usually willing to forgo use of the death penalty when given choices of other penalties, such as life in prison without parole and compensation to the victim's family.[55] In a 2002 case, Kelly v. South Carolina, the Supreme Court ruled that jurors must be apprised of state laws that prohibit people convicted of first-degree murder from being eligible for parole.[56] Abolitionists believe that jurors who understand that dangerous criminals will never be released from prison may be less willing to recommend the death penalty.

▎ Opponents also object to the finality of the death penalty. It of course precludes any possibility of rehabilitation. Studies indicate that death row inmates released because of legal changes rarely recidivate and present little threat to the community.[57] It is also quite possible for an innocent person to be convicted of crime; once the person is executed, the mistake can never be rectified.[58] Many people convicted of murder are

Figure 18.4 Prisoners on Death Row by Race

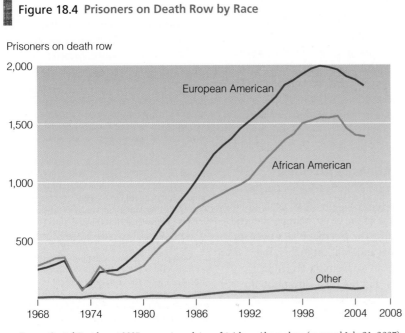

Prisoners on death row

European American

African American

Other

Source: *Capital Punishment 2005*, www.ojp.usdoj.gov/bjs/glance/drrace.htm (accessed July 31, 2007).

INTERNATIONAL USE OF THE DEATH PENALTY

The United States is not alone in using the death penalty though the trend has been to abolish its usage. According to the latest data from watchdog group Amnesty International, over half the countries in the world have now abolished the death penalty in law or practice. Amnesty International's latest information shows that:

- 89 countries and territories have abolished the death penalty for all crimes.

- 10 countries have abolished the death penalty for all but exceptional crimes such as wartime crimes.

- 29 countries can be considered abolitionist in practice: they retain the death penalty in law but have not carried out any executions for the past 10 years or more and are believed to have a policy or established practice of not carrying out executions, making a total of 128 countries which have abolished the death penalty in law or practice.

- 68 other countries and territories retain and use the death penalty, but the number of countries that actually execute prisoners in any one year is much smaller.

Progress Toward Worldwide Abolition

More than 40 countries have abolished the death penalty for all crimes since 1990. They include countries in Africa (recent examples include Liberia and Côte d'Ivoire), the Americas (Canada, Paraguay, and Mexico), Asia and the Pacific (Bhutan and Samoa), and Europe and Central Asia (Armenia, Bosnia-Herzegovina, Cyprus, Serbia and Montenegro, Turkey, and Turkmenistan).

Restating the Death Penalty

Once abolished, the death penalty is seldom reintroduced. Since 1985, more than 50 countries have abolished the death penalty in law or, having previously abolished it for ordinary crimes, have gone on to abolish it for all crimes. During the same period only four abolitionist countries reintroduced the death penalty. One of them—Nepal—has since abolished the death penalty again; one, the Philippines, resumed executions but later stopped. There have been no executions in the other two (Gambia and Papua New Guinea).

Death Sentences and Executions

During 2005, at least 2,148 people were executed in 22 countries and at least 5,186 people were sentenced to death in 53 countries. These are only minimum figures; the true figures were certainly higher. In 2005, 94 percent of all known executions took place in China, Iran, Saudi Arabia, and the United States.

Based on public reports available, Amnesty International estimated that at least 1,770 people were executed in China during the year, although the true figures were believed to be much higher. A Chinese legal expert was recently quoted as stating the figure for executions is approximately 8,000 based on information from local officials and judges, but official national statistics on the application of the death penalty remained classified as a state secret.

Iran executed at least 94 people, and Saudi Arabia at least 86. There were about 60 executions in the United States.

Executions of Juveniles

International human rights treaties prohibit anyone under 18 years old at the time of the crime being sentenced to death. The International Covenant on Civil and Political Rights, the American Convention on Human Rights, and the UN Convention on the Rights of the Child all have provisions to this effect. More than 100 countries have laws specifically excluding the execution of juvenile offenders or may be presumed to exclude such executions by being parties to one or another of the above treaties. A small number of countries, however, continue to execute juvenile offenders. Seven countries since 1990 are known to have executed prisoners who were under 18 years old at the time of the crime: Iran, Nigeria, Pakistan, the Congos, Saudi Arabia, the United States, and Yemen. Since 1994 there have been 20 executions of juvenile offenders, including 13 in the United States (before the practice was prohibited).

CRITICAL THINKING

1. The movement toward abolition in the United States is encouraged by the fact that so many nations have abandoned the death penalty. Should we model our own system of punishments after other nations or is our crime problem so unique that it requires the use of capital punishment?

2. Do you believe that someone who joins a terrorist group and trains to kill Americans deserves the death penalty even if they have never actually killed anyone?

Sources: Amnesty International's most recent data on the death penalty can be accessed at http://web.amnesty.org/pages/deathpenalty-index-eng (accessed July 17, 2007); "Nigeria: Stoning Sentence Stands," *New York Times*, 9 October 2002, Late Edition A6; Death Penalty News, "Saudi Arabia Executes Man for Sorcery," Amnesty International, March 2000; "USA Set to Break a Global Consensus—Execution of Child Offender Due," Amnesty International News Release, October 22, 2001; "China 'Striking Harder' than Ever Before," Amnesty International News Release, June 7, 2001; Associated Press, "Saudi Brothers Beheaded for Raping," *New York Times*, 20 July 2001, p. 3; Larry Rohter, "In Caribbean, Support Growing for Death Penalty," *New York Times*, 4 October 1998; Associated Press, "Chechen Pair Executed in Public," *Boston Globe*, 19 September 1997, p. 9; Reuters, "Saudi Beheadings over 100 for 1997," *Boston Globe*, 28 September 1997, p. A29.

later released because of mistaken identity or perjured testimony. For example, Rolando Cruz and Alejandro Hernandez, wrongfully convicted of murder, were released in 1995 after spending more than a decade on death row in the Illinois prison system; three former prosecutors and four deputy sheriffs who worked on the case were later charged with fabricating evidence against the pair.[59]

▌ "It is better that a thousand guilty go free than one innocent man be executed" is a statement abolitionists often make. This point has been convincingly made by Michael Radelet and Hugo Bedeau, who claim that there have been about 350 wrongful convictions this century, of which 23 led to executions. They estimate that about three death sentences are returned every two years in cases where the defendants have been falsely accused. More than half the errors stem from perjured testimony, false identification, coerced confessions, and suppression of evidence. In addition to the 23 who were executed, 128 of the falsely convicted served more than 6 years in prison, 39 served more than 16 years, and 8 died while serving their sentences.[60] Even though the system attempts to be especially cautious in capital cases, it is evident that unacceptable mistakes can occur.

▌ The death penalty is capricious; receiving death is similar to losing a lottery.[61] Of the 10,000 people who are convicted of murder each year, more receive probation as a sole sentence than get the death penalty. Is it fair to release one person who has taken a life into the community and execute another?

▌ Abolitionists claim that capital punishment has never been proven to be a deterrent, any more than has life in prison. In fact, capital punishment may encourage murder because it sets an example of violence and brutality.[62]

▌ Abolitionists also point out that nations such as Denmark and Sweden have long abandoned the death penalty and that 40 percent of the countries with a death penalty have active abolitionist movements.[63] See the Comparative Criminology feature "International Use of the Death Penalty" for more on this topic.

Legal Issues

The Supreme Court has upheld the legality of the death penalty as long as aggravating (such as extreme cruelty or killing for profit) or mitigating (such as the defendant's age and mental state) circumstances are taken into account.[64] However, the Court has placed limitations on the use of capital punishment:

1. The crimes for which the death penalty can be employed have been limited to intentional or felony murder. It is not permissible to punish rapists with death.[65]

2. People who are mentally ill may not be executed.[66] In a 2002 case, *Atkins v. Virginia*, the Court ruled that execution of mentally retarded criminals is "cruel and unusual punishment" prohibited by the Eighth Amendment.[67]

3. In *Roper v. Simmons* (2005), the Court set a limit of 18 years as the age of defendants who could be sentenced to death.[68] The Court said that executing young teens violates "the evolving standards of decency that mark the progress of a maturing society," and that American society regards juveniles as less responsible than adult criminals.

CORRECTING CRIMINAL OFFENDERS

Today there are more than 1,600 adult correctional facilities in the United States. These include prisons, prison hospitals, prison farms, and boot camps; centers for reception, classification, or alcohol and drug treatment; and community-based facilities such as halfway houses, group homes, and work-release centers. The overwhelming majority of these facilities are state-run institutions.[69] This vast correctional system provides many services in programs differentiated by level of security and intrusiveness. The least secure and intrusive programs involve community supervision by probation officers. Some offenders who need more secure treatment or control are placed under house arrest or held in community correctional centers. Those who require the most secure settings are placed in an incarceration facility. Felons are usually incarcerated in a state or federal prison; misdemeanants are housed in county jails or reformatories. As Figure 18.5 shows there are now more than 7 million people in some form of correctional supervision and the numbers have been increasing despite a decade long decline in the crime rate.

The entire correctional system has been a source of great controversy. Conservatives charge that the justice system is often too liberal and that serious offenders are all too often granted probation. Getting tough, they suggest, is the only way to keep crime rates down. They point out the fact that as the prison population has increased during the past decade, the crime rate has fallen. In contrast, liberals view prisons as warehouses that, far from helping rehabilitate inmates, are places of violence and degradation. Rather than deter people from future criminality, a prison stay actually reinforces or encourages their criminal offending.[70] And though it might surprise some "get tough" politicians, the general public may not be ready to embrace a prison-building boom at the expense of rehabilitation efforts.[71]

Contemporary Corrections

Correctional treatment can be divided today into community-based programs and secure confinement. Community-based corrections include probation, which involves supervision under the control of the sentencing court, and an array of intermediate sanctions, which provide greater supervision and treatment than traditional probation but are less intrusive than incarceration.

Figure 18.5 Adult Correctional Populations

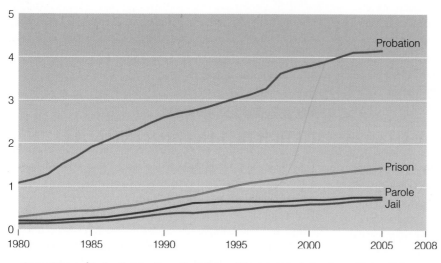

Millions

Probation

Prison

Parole

Jail

Source: Bureau of Justice Statistics Correctional Surveys (The Annual Probation Survey, National Prisoner Statistics, Survey of Jails, and The Annual Parole Survey) as presented in *Correctional Populations in the United States, Annual, Prisoners in 2005,* and *Probation and Parole in the United States, 2005,* www.ojp.usdoj.gov/bjs/glance/corr2.htm (accessed July 31, 2007).

Treatment in the community is viewed as a viable alternative to traditional correctional practices.[72] First, it is significantly less expensive to supervise inmates in the community than to house them in secure institutional facilities. Second, community-based corrections are necessary if the prison system is not to be overwhelmed by an influx of offenders. Third, community-based treatment is designed so that first-time or nonserious offenders can avoid the stigma and pain of imprisonment and be rehabilitated in the community.

In secure confinement, the jail houses misdemeanants (and some felons) serving their sentences, as well as felons and misdemeanants awaiting trial who have not been released on bail. State and federal prisons incarcerate felons for extended periods. Parole and aftercare agencies supervise prisoners who have been given early release from their sentences. Although parolees are actually in the community, parole is usually considered both organizationally and philosophically part of the secure correctional system. These institutions are discussed in the next sections.

PROBATION

Probation usually involves the suspension of the offender's sentence in return for the promise of good behavior in the community under the supervision of a probation department. In some cases the offender is first sentenced to a prison term, and then the sentence is suspended and the defendant placed on probation. In others, the imposition of a prison sentence is delayed or suspended while the offender is put on probation. Probation is not limited to minor or petty criminals; about one-third of people convicted of felony offenses receive a sentence of probation only with no prison or jail time.

As practiced in all 50 states and by the federal government, probation involves a contract between the court and the offender in which the latter is required to obey a set of rules or conditions required by the court. If the rules are violated, and especially if the probationer commits another criminal offense, probation may be revoked; this means that the contract is terminated, and the original sentence is enforced. If an offender on probation commits a second offense that is more severe than the first, he or she may be indicted, tried, and sentenced on that second offense.

Probation may also be revoked simply because its rules and conditions have not been met, even if the offender has not committed another crime. In a series of cases, most importantly *Gagnon v. Scarpelli,*[73] the Supreme Court ruled that before probation can be revoked, the offender must (1) be given a hearing before the sentencing court and (2) be provided with counsel if there is a substantial reason for him or her to require legal assistance.

Today, about 2,000 agencies nationwide monitor more than 4 million adults under federal, state, or local jurisdiction.[74] The adult probation population has grown rapidly during the past 25 years, increasing by 1 million since 1995 and 3 million since 1980, when 1.1 million people were on probation. Probation has become the sentence of choice for most offenders; about one-half of all offenders on probation have been convicted of a felony.

Probation Services

This vast array of offenders are treated, supervised, classified, and controlled by the nation's probation agencies and their probation officers. The services probation agencies provide can be divided into three broad categories.

Investigation After a person is convicted of a crime, the probation department investigates the case to determine if the defendant is a suitable candidate for probation or whether he or she needs to be placed in more secure confinement such as jail or prison. The investigation may involve interviews with friends and relatives, background checks, and so on. Based on this presentence investigation, the department makes a sentencing recommendation to the judge that typically controls the defendant's eligibility for community release.

Treatment If the offender is granted probation, the department will typically evaluate the case, assess the client's personality, and create an appropriate treatment program. This process, referred to as offender classification, is used to guide treatment and supervision practice.[75]

As part of the treatment function, probation officers help their clients cope with the personal problems that have put them at risk for criminal activity. Clients may be required to attend community mental health, substance abuse, and family counseling clinics. Probation officers can mandate that clients join support groups, report for polygraph testing and urinalysis, and complete homework assignments.[76]

Although placement in community-based treatment programs is the norm, it is not unknown for probation officers to provide direct treatment to offenders who have substance abuse problems in communities that lack adequate, effective community-based programs.[77] Probation officers also conduct special programs for clients, such as teaching childrearing skills to parents of juvenile offenders in their caseloads.[78]

Supervision Probation departments are charged with monitoring offenders while they are in the community. The level of supervision, depending on the probationer's risk potential and treatment needs, might range from daily checks to a yearly phone call. In some instances, probation officers may be asked to carry guns, especially when they are required to supervise felony clients and visit them in their neighborhoods and homes.[79]

To increase the effectiveness and lower recidivism risk, some communities are now experimenting with innovative supervision programs. In Maryland's HotSpot probation program, police officers, probation agents, neighbors, and social service professionals collaborate to form community probation supervision teams. Using a team approach, the program provides increased monitoring of offenders through home visits, drug testing, and regular meetings. Supervisors also work with the offenders to ease reentry through offender creation of work crews that aid in community cleanups, work on vacant houses, and participate in other projects.[80]

Probation Rules and Revocation

Each offender granted probation is given a set of rules to guide his or her behavior. Most jurisdictions have a standard set of rules that must be followed by probationers. These generally include:

- Maintaining steady employment
- Making restitution for loss or damage
- Cooperating with the probation officer
- Obeying all laws
- Meeting family responsibilities

Sometimes an individual probationer is given specific rules that relate to his or her particular circumstances, such as the requirement to enroll in an anger management or drug treatment program, to make a personal apology to the victim, or to have no contact with the ex-spouse.[81]

If rules are violated, a person's probation may be revoked by the court, and the probationer either begins serving the suspended sentence or, if he or she has not yet been sentenced, receives a prison sentence from the court. Revocation for violation of probation rules is called a technical violation; probation also can be revoked if the offender commits another offense.

Success of Probation

Probation is the most commonly used alternative sentence for a number of reasons: it is humane, it helps offenders maintain community and family ties, and it is cost effective. Incarcerating an inmate costs over $20,000 per year, while probation costs far less.[82]

Although unquestionably inexpensive, is probation successful? If most probation orders fail, the costs of repeated criminality would certainly outweigh the cost savings of a probation sentence. Overall, most probation orders do seem successful. National data indicate that about 60 percent of probationers successfully complete their probationary sentence while about 40 percent are rearrested, violate probation rules, or abscond.[83] Most revocations occur for technical violations that occur during the first three months of the probation sentence.[84]

© AP Images/Kevork Djansezian

Probation rules must be obeyed. Those who violate rules can have their probation revoked. In 2007, celebrity Paris Hilton made headlines when she was forced to serve a more than three-week sentence for violating probation in an alcohol-related reckless driving case.

How do serious offenders fare on probation? In an often-cited 1985 study, Joan Petersilia and her colleagues at the Rand Corporation followed the careers of 1,672 California men granted probation for felony offenses.[85] They found that 1,087 (65 percent) were rearrested, 853 (51 percent) were convicted, and 568 (34 percent) were incarcerated. The researchers uncovered the disturbing fact that 75 percent of the new arrests were for serious crimes, including larceny, burglary, and robbery; 18 percent of the probationers were convicted of serious violent crimes. They also found that about 25 percent of felons granted probation had personal and legal characteristics indistinguishable from people put in prison for the same original charges. The Petersilia research was an early indication that felons often qualified for and later failed on probation.

While the failure rate found by Petersilia seems disturbingly high, even the most serious criminals who receive probation are less likely to recidivate than those who are sent to prison for committing similar crimes.[86] In addition, studies of federal probationers indicate that the high recidivism rates found by Petersilia might be limited to the population she surveyed and that in some probation populations a 30 percent violation rate is more accurate.[87]

And there are some studies that have found a lower recidivism rate among particular classes of probationers (such as young, non–drug-using property offenders), indicating that probation may be a relatively effective correctional alternative for subgroups of offenders.[88] Those probationers who have a stake in conformity, such as a good job and economic resources, are the ones most likely to succeed on probation; a strong stake in society may be a more powerful determinant of probation success than participation in treatment programs.[89]

Because it costs far less to maintain an offender in the community than in prison, and because prison overcrowding continues, there is constant economic pressure to grant probation to serious felony offenders. Even if probation is no more successful than prison, it costs less and is therefore extremely attractive to policymakers.

INTERMEDIATE SANCTIONS

At a time when overcrowding has produced a crisis in the nation's prison system, alternative sanctions are viewed as a new form of corrections that falls somewhere between probation and incarceration.[90] Alternative sanctions include fines, forfeiture, home confinement, electronic monitoring, intensive probation supervision, restitution, community corrections, and boot camps.

The development of these intermediate sanctions can be tied to a number of different sources. Primary is the need to develop alternatives to prisons, which have proved both ineffective and injurious. Research indicates that about half of all prison inmates are likely to be rearrested and returned to prison, many soon after their release from an institution.[91]

High revocation rates indicate that probation alone may not be an effective solution to the prison crowding problem. Therefore, a sanction that falls somewhere between prison and probation might be a more effective alternative to traditional forms of correction.

Intermediate sanctions also meet the need to develop punishments that are fair, equitable, and proportional. It seems unfair to treat both a rapist and a shoplifter with the same method of correction, considering the differences in their criminal acts. Intermediate sanctions can provide the successive steps for a meaningful "ladder" of scaled punishments outside prison (Figure 18.6), thereby restoring fairness and equity to nonincarceration sentences.[92] A forger may be ordered to make restitution to the victim; an abusive husband may be ordered to reside in a community correctional center; a rapist would be sent to state prison. This feature of intermediate sanctions allows judges to fit the punishment to the crime without resorting to a prison sentence. Intermediate sanctions can be designed to be punitive by increasing punishments for people whose serious or repeat crimes make straight probation sentences inappropriate yet for whom prison sentences would be unduly harsh and dysfunctional.[93] The punitive nature of intermediate sanctions is not lost on offenders; some of whom prefer prison to the new, tougher forms of probation.[94]

The most likely candidates are convicted criminals who would normally be sent to prison but either have a low risk of recidivating or pose little threat to society (such as nonviolent property offenders). Used in this sense, intermediate sanctions are a viable solution to the critical problem of prison overcrowding.

The following sections more thoroughly discuss the forms of intermediate sanctions in use.

Fines

Fines are monetary payments imposed on an offender as an intermediate punishment for criminal acts. They are a direct offshoot of the early common-law practice requiring compensation to the victim and the state for criminal acts. Although fines are most commonly used in misdemeanors, they are also frequently employed in felonies where the offender benefited financially. Fines may be used as a sole sanction or combined with other punishment, such as probation or confinement. Quite commonly judges levy other monetary sanctions along with fines—such as court costs, public defender fees, probation and treatment fees, and victim restitution—to increase the force of the financial punishment.[95]

Some jurisdictions are experimenting with day fines, a concept originated in Europe that gears fines to an offender's net daily income in an effort to make them more equitable. In contrast to the traditional fixed-sum fining system, in which the fine amount is governed principally by the nature of the crime, the day-fine approach tailors the fine amount to the defendant's ability to pay. Thus, for a given crime, the day fine is larger for a high-income offender than for an irregularly employed or low-paid offender. The impact of the fine on each should be approximately equal. Under the traditional approach, a given fine

Figure 18.6 The Punishment Ladder

- Death penalty
- Prison
- Shock probation
- Residential community center
- Electronic monitoring
- House arrest
- Intensive probation
- Restitution
- Probation
- Forfeiture
- Fines
- Pretrial release
- Restorative justice

amount could be relatively severe for a low-income offender but trivial for a person of substantial means.[96]

Although it is far from certain that fines are an effective sanction, either alone or in combination with other penalties, they remain one of the most commonly used criminal penalties. Research sponsored by the federal government found that lower court judges impose fines alone or in tandem with other penalties in 86 percent of their cases, whereas superior court judges impose fines in 42 percent of their cases.[97]

Forfeiture

Another financially based alternative sanction is criminal (*in personam*) and civil (*in rem*) forfeiture. Both involve the seizure of goods and instrumentalities related to the commission or outcome of a criminal act. For example, federal law provides that after arresting drug traffickers, the government may seize the boat they used to import the narcotics, the car they used to carry them overland, the warehouse in which they were stored, and the home paid for with drug money; upon conviction, the drug dealers permanently lose ownership of these instrumentalities of crime.

The use of forfeiture was introduced in American law with the passage of the Racketeer Influenced and Corrupt Organizations (RICO) and the Continuing Criminal Enterprises acts, both of which allow the seizure of any property derived from illegal enterprises or conspiracies.

Restitution

Another popular intermediate sanction is restitution, used in about one-third of felony probation cases, which can take the form of requiring convicted defendants to either repay the victims of crime (monetary restitution) or serve the community to compensate for their criminal acts (community service restitution).[98]

Restitution programs offer convicted offenders a chance to avoid jail or prison sentences or lengthy probation. Restitution may also be used as a diversionary device that allows some offenders to avoid a criminal record altogether. In this instance, a judge continues the case "without a finding" while the defendant completes the restitution order; after the probation department determines that restitution has been made, the case is dismissed.[99]

Because restitution appears to benefit the crime victim, the offender, the criminal justice system, and society as a whole, national interest in the concept has been tremendous. Restitution is inexpensive, avoids stigma, and helps compensate crime victims. Offenders doing community service have worked in schools, hospitals, and nursing homes. Helping them avoid jail can save the public thousands of dollars that would have maintained them in secure institutions, free needed resources, and give the community the feeling that equity has been returned to the justice system. Most offenders successfully complete their restitution orders and consequently have equal or lower recidivism rates when compared to control groups of various kinds.[100]

Split Sentencing and Shock Probation

Split sentencing and shock probation are alternative sanctions that allow judges to grant offenders community release only after they have sampled prison life. These sanctions are based on the premise that if offenders are given a taste of incarceration sufficient to "shock" them into law-abiding behavior, they will be reluctant to violate the rules of probation or commit other criminal acts.

In a number of states and in the federal criminal code, a jail term can actually be a condition of probation; this is known as split sentencing. Under current federal practices, about 25 percent of all convicted federal offenders receive some form of split sentence, including prison and/or jail as a condition of probation.

Another approach, known as shock probation, involves resentencing an offender after a short prison stay. The shock comes because the offender originally receives a long maximum sentence but is then eligible for release to community supervision at the discretion of the judge (usually within 90 days of incarceration). Used in a number of states, shock probation has been praised as a program that limits prison time and allows offenders to be quickly integrated into the community, a mechanism that can maintain family ties, and a way of reducing prison populations and the costs of corrections.[101]

Intensive Probation Supervision

Intensive probation supervision (IPS) has been implemented in some form in most states, involving small caseloads of 15 to 40 clients who are kept under close watch by probation officers. The primary goals of IPS include:

▌ *Diversion.* Without intensive supervision, clients would normally have been sent to already overcrowded prisons or jails.

▌ *Control.* High-risk offenders can stay in the community under much closer security than traditional probation efforts can provide.

▌ *Reintegration.* Offenders can maintain community ties and be reoriented toward a more productive life while avoiding the pain of imprisonment.

Who is eligible for IPS? Most programs have admissions criteria based on the nature of the offense and the offender's criminal background. Some programs exclude violent offenders; others will not consider substance abusers. In contrast, some jurisdictions do not exclude offenders based on their prior criminal history. About 60 percent of IPS programs exclude offenders who have already violated probation orders or otherwise failed on probation.

Despite its promise, the failure rate in IPS caseloads is quite high, approaching 50 percent.[102] Younger offenders who commit petty crimes are the most likely to fail on IPS; ironically, people with these characteristics are the most likely to be included in IPS programs.[103] It is possible that closer supervision "produces" failures because supervisors are better able to detect technical and legal violations. Continuous drug testing alone should produce a higher failure rate among IPS clients than traditional probationers.

Home Confinement/ Electronic Monitoring

A number of states, including Florida, Oklahoma, Oregon, Kentucky, and California, have developed home confinement (HC) programs (also called house arrest or home detention) as an intermediate sanction. The HC concept requires convicted offenders to spend extended periods in their own homes as an alternative to incarceration. For example, an individual convicted of drunk driving might be sentenced to spend the period between 6 P.M. Friday and 8 A.M. Monday and every weekday after 5:30 P.M. in his or her home for the next six months. Current estimates indicate that as many as 10,000 people are placed under HC yearly.[104]

For house arrest to work, sentencing authorities must be assured that arrestees are actually at home during their assigned times. Random calls and visits are one way to check on compliance with house arrest orders. However, a more advanced method of control has been the introduction of electronic monitoring (EM) devices to manage offender obedience to home confinement orders.

Growth in the number of electronically monitored offenders has been explosive. Up to 1 million people may eventually be monitored electronically in the United States.[105] EM is being hailed as one of the most important developments in correctional policy.[106] It has the benefits of relatively low cost and high security while at the same time helping offenders avoid imprisonment in overcrowded, dangerous state facilities. Electronic monitoring is capital-intensive rather than labor-intensive. Because offenders are monitored by computers, an initial investment in hardware rules out the need for hiring many more supervisory officers to handle large numbers of clients. It can also be used at many stages of the justice process, including at the front end as a condition of pretrial release and at the back end as part of parole.

Residential Community Corrections

A more secure intermediate sanction is a sentence to a residential community corrections (RCC) program. These programs feature freestanding nonsecure buildings that are not part of a prison or jail and that house pretrial and adjudicated adults. The residents regularly depart to work, to attend school, and/or to participate in community corrections activities and programs.[107] Today the community correctional facility provides intermediate sanctions as well as a prerelease center for those about to be paroled from prison. RCC has been used as a direct sentencing option for judges who believe particular offenders need a correctional alternative halfway between traditional probation and a stay in prison.

Placement in an RCC center can be used as a condition of probation for offenders who need a nonsecure community facility that provides a more structured treatment environment than traditional probation.

Boot Camps/Shock Incarceration

Another intermediate sanction gaining popularity around the United States is boot camps or shock incarceration (SI). These programs typically include youthful, first-time offenders and feature military discipline and physical training. The concept is that short periods (90 to 180 days) of high-intensity exercise and work will shock young criminals into going straight. Tough physical training is designed to promote responsibility and improve decision-making skills, build self-confidence, and teach socialization skills. Inmates are treated with rough intensity by drill masters, who may call them names and punish the entire group for the failure of one of its members.

Is shock incarceration a correctional panacea or another fad doomed to failure? The results so far have not been encouraging. The costs of boot camps are no lower than those of traditional prisons, but because sentences are shorter, boot camps provide long-term savings. Some programs suffer high failure-to-complete rates, which makes program evaluations difficult (even if "graduates" are successful, it is possible that success is achieved because troublesome cases drop out and are placed in the general inmate population). What evaluations exist indicate that the recidivism rates of inmates who attend boot camps are in some cases no lower than those released from traditional prisons.[108] Because of these sketchy results, the future of the boot camp approach is clouded. Recently, the federal government announced the termination of its boot camp program.[109]

Even though these results are disappointing, it is possible that boot camps can be effective with some offenders by using a combination of treatment modalities. Older residents with ties to the community seem to do much better than younger, more impulsive clients who maintain deviant friends.[110] There is also evidence that how the boot camp experience is managed may shape its effect. A recent study of boot camp graduates shows that recidivism rates are significantly lowered if they are placed in residential aftercare program upon their release.[111]

Can Alternatives Work?

There is little evidence that alternative sanctions can prevent crime, reduce recidivism, or work much better than traditional probation or prison. Those who favor this approach argue that even without conclusive evidence that alternative sanctions are better than prison, they are certainly cheaper. Yet this rationale is valid only if the client population served would have been placed in more restrictive, costly secure confinement absent the opportunity for alternative sentencing. If, as some critics contend, placement is restricted to people who would have ordinarily been granted straight probation, then alternative sanctions are actually a more expensive method to achieve about the same result.

JAILS

The jail is a secure institution used to (a) detain offenders before trial if they cannot afford or are not eligible for bail and (b) house misdemeanants sentenced to terms of one year or less, as well as some nonserious felons. The jail is a multipurpose correctional institution whose other main functions are set out in Exhibit 18.2.

The jail originated in Europe in the sixteenth century and was used to house those awaiting trial and punishment. Jails were not used to house sentenced criminals because at that time punishment was achieved by fine, exile, corporal punishment, or death. Throughout their history, jails have been considered hellholes of pestilence and cruelty. In early English history, they housed offenders awaiting trial, as well as vagabonds, debtors, the mentally ill, and assorted others.[112] The early colonists adopted the European custom of detaining prisoners in jail. As noted previously, William Penn instituted the first jails to house convicted offenders while they worked off their sentences. The Walnut Street Jail, built in 1790, is considered the first modern jail.

Jail Populations

There has been a national effort to remove as many people from local jails as possible through bail reform measures and pretrial

---

EXHIBIT 18.2

Jail Functions and Services

Jails are locally operated correctional facilities that:

- Confine persons before or after adjudication. Inmates sentenced to jail usually have a sentence of one year or less.
- Receive individuals pending arraignment and hold them awaiting trial, conviction, or sentencing.
- Readmit probation, parole, and bail-bond violators and absconders.
- Temporarily detain juveniles pending transfer to juvenile authorities.
- Hold mentally ill persons pending their movement to appropriate mental health facilities.
- Hold individuals for the military, for protective custody for contempt, and for the courts as witnesses.
- Release convicted inmates to the community upon completion of sentence.
- Transfer inmates to federal, state, or other authorities.
- House inmates for federal, state, or other authorities because of crowding of their facilities.
- Sometimes operate community-based programs as alternatives to incarceration.

Source: Paige Harrison and Allen Beck, *Prison and Jail Inmates at Midyear 2005* (Washington, DC: Bureau of Justice Statistics, 2006), www.ojp.usdoj.gov/bjs/pub/ascii/pjim05.txt (accessed July 18, 2007).

diversion. Nonetheless, jail populations have been steadily increasing, due in part to the increased use of mandatory jail sentences for such common crimes as drunk driving and the use of local jails to house inmates for whom there is no room in state prisons. Today there are close to 800,000 people in jail on a daily basis, including almost 7,000 juveniles, despite a 20-year campaign by the federal government to remove minors from adult institutions.[113]

As might be expected, jail inmates tend to be troubled people, many of whom were sexually abused as children (about half the female inmates) and grew up in a single-parent household. A significant portion have alcohol and substance abuse problems and are repeat offenders. As Figure 18.7 shows, a disproportionate number of the minority population are jail inmates, a finding that reflects the social and economic disparities in our nation. African Americans are nearly five times more likely than whites, nearly three times more likely than Hispanics, and over nine times more likely than persons of other races to have been in jail.

PRISONS

State and federal governments maintain closed correctional facilities to house convicted felons. Usually called **prisons** or **penitentiaries**, these institutions have become familiar to most people as harsh, frightening places filled with dangerous men and women. San Quentin (California), Attica (New York), Joliet (Illinois), and Marion (Illinois) are but a few of the large state and federal prisons made well known by films, books, and other media.

Though the crime rate has fallen sharply for the past decade, the prison population has continued to rise. One reason is that there has been a recent trend for defendants convicted of a felony to be sent to prison (instead of jail or probation), a finding that may reflect a more conservative view of crime control. Similarly, increases in the prison population may also be linked to changing sentencing policies that force inmates to spend more time behind bars before they are released. And as more inmates are released on parole, the increasing number of returning parole violators has also helped fuel the growth in the prison inmate population.

As Figure 18.8 shows, the rapid increase in the prison population has finally begun to stabilize, though the number still trends upwards.

Types of Prisons

Prisons are usually categorized according to their level of security and inmate populations as maximum-, medium-, and minimum-security institutions. Large maximum-security prisons are surrounded by high walls, have elaborate security measures and armed guards, and house inmates classified as potentially dangerous. High security and stone walls give the inmates the sense that the facility is impregnable and reassure citizens that convicts will be completely incapacitated. During the day, the inmates engage in closely controlled activities: meals, workshops, education, and so on. Rule violators may be confined to their cells; working and other shared recreational activities are viewed as privileges.

Medium-security prisons have similar protective measures but usually contain less violent inmates. Consequently, they are more likely to offer a variety of treatment and educational programs to their residents. They may be similar in appearance to the maximum-security prison; however, security and atmosphere are neither so tense nor so vigilant. Medium-security prisons are also surrounded by walls, but there may be fewer guard towers or other security precautions. Visitor privileges may be more extensive, and personal contact may be allowed; in a maximum-security prison, visitors may be separated from inmates by Plexiglas or other barriers (to prohibit the passing of contraband). Although most prisoners are housed in cells, individual honor rooms in medium-security prisons are used to reward those who make exemplary rehabilitation efforts. Finally, medium-security prisons promote greater treatment efforts, and the relaxed atmosphere allows freedom of movement for rehabilitation workers and other therapeutic personnel.

Minimum-security prisons operate without armed guards or walls;

Figure 18.7 Jail Incarceration Rates by Race and Ethnicity

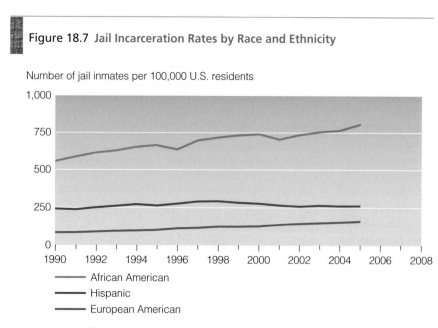

Number of jail inmates per 100,000 U.S. residents

— African American
— Hispanic
— European American

Source: Bureau of Justice Statistics Correctional Surveys (the National Probation Data Survey, National Prisoner Statistics, Survey of Jails, Census of Jail Inmates, and the National Parole Data Survey) as presented in *Correctional Populations in the United States, 1997,* and *Prison and Jail Inmates at Midyear, 2005,* www.ojp.usdoj.gov/bjs/glance/jailrair.htm (accessed July 31, 2007).

Figure 18.8 Prison Incarceration Rate

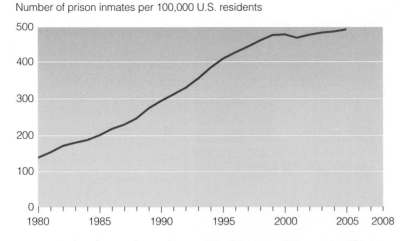

Number of prison inmates per 100,000 U.S. residents

Source: *Correctional Populations in the United States, 1997* and *Prisoners in 2005,* www.ojp.usdoj.gov/bjs/glance/incrt.htm (accessed July 31, 2007).

usually they are constructed in compounds surrounded by chain-link fences. Minimum-security prisons house the most trustworthy and least violent offenders; white-collar criminals may be their most common occupants. Inmates may be transferred to these nonrestrictive institutions as a reward for good behavior prior to their release. A great deal of personal freedom is allowed inmates. Instead of being marched to activities by guards, they are summoned by bells or loudspeaker announcements and assemble on their own. Work furloughs and educational releases are encouraged, and vocational training is of the highest level. Minimum-security prisons have been scoffed at for being too much like country clubs; some federal facilities catering to white-collar criminals even have tennis courts and pools. Yet they remain prisons, and the isolation and loneliness of prison life deeply affects the inmates at these facilities. And, of course, if an inmate cannot adjust to the relaxed security or attempts escape, he or she will be transferred to a higher-security institution.

Super Maximum Prisons More than 30 states now operate supermax prisons or units (also known as ultra-max prisons).[114] These high-security institutions can be independent correctional centers or locked wings of existing prisons operating under such names as the "secure housing unit" or "maximum control unit." The 484-bed federal facility in Florence, Colorado, is the model for the supermax prison. It has the most sophisticated security measures in the United States, including 168 video cameras and 1,400 electronically controlled gates. Inside the cells all furniture is unmovable; the desk, bed, and TV stand are made of cement. All potential weapons—including soap dishes, toilet seats, and toilet handles—have been removed. The cement walls are 5,000-pound quality, and steel bars are placed so they crisscross every 8 inches inside the walls. Cells are angled so that inmates can see neither each other nor the outside scenery. This cuts down on communications

and denies inmates a sense of location, in order to prevent escapes.

Getting out of the prison seems impossible. There are six guard towers at different heights to prevent air attacks. To get out, the inmates would have to pass through seven 3-inch-thick steel doors, each of which can be opened only after the previous one has closed. If a guard tower is ever seized, all controls are switched to the next station. If the whole prison is seized, it can be controlled from the outside. It appears that the only way out is via good works and behavior, through which an inmate can earn transfer to another prison within three years.

Some recent research by Daniel Mears and his colleagues finds that supermax prisons produce a mixed bag of results. Mears and Jamie Watson conducted surveys of correctional officials and found that supermax prisons may actually enhance the quality of life of inmates and consequently improve their mental health. Supermax prisons increase privacy, reduce danger, and even provide creature comforts such as TV sets that are unavailable in general population prisons. Staff report less stress and fear because they have to contend with fewer disruptive inmates.

On the other hand, Mears and Watson found that supermax prisons also bring some unintended negative consequences. Staff may have too much control over inmates, a condition that damages staff–inmate relationships. Long hours of isolation may be associated with mental illness and psychological disturbances. Supermax inmates seem to have a more difficult time readjusting upon release. A stay in a supermax prison inhibits reintegration into other prisons, communities, and families. In another study, Mears and Jennifer Castro surveyed wardens and found that although they seem to favor supermax prisons, they also express concern that the general public believes that supermax institutions are inhumane, that they drain limited funds away from state budgets, and that they produce increases in litigation and court interventions as well as increased recidivism and reentry failure among released inmates.

According to Mears and his associates, for supermax prisons to be effective they must achieve a number of hard-to-reach goals: identifying the most disruptive inmates, placing enough of them in supermax confinement, and reducing their misbehavior upon return to the general population. As well, other inmates must take their place as being disruptive, and so on. Failure to meet these requirements, Mears and company believe, undermines the overall effectiveness of the supermax concept.[115]

Private Prisons On January 6, 1986, the U.S. Corrections Corporation opened the first privately run state prison in Marion, Kentucky—a 300-bed minimum-security facility for

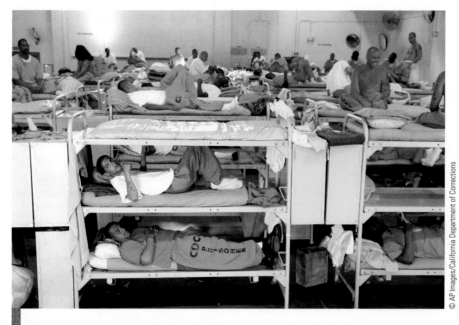

The number of inmates has skyrocketed. Here, inmates sit in their triple bunks in the California State Prison, Los Angeles. On July 23, 2007, two judges ordered creation of a special panel to examine ways to relieve California's overcrowded prisons, a move that could lead to the capping of the inmate population or the early release of some prisoners. Despite a rash of prison construction, overcrowding remains a national problem.

different from a private hospital or college, both of which offer services also provided by the state? The issues that determine the future of private corrections may be efficiency and cost effectiveness, not fairness and morality. Privately run correctional institutions have been found to provide better services at lower cost than public facilities.[120] They may experience some of the same problems as state-run institutions, but there is little conclusive evidence that they cannot operate as or even more efficiently than traditional institutions.[121]

In the abstract, a private correctional enterprise may be an attractive alternative to a costly correctional system, but these legal, administrative, and cost issues need to be resolved before private prisons can become widespread.[122] A balance must be reached between the need for a private business to make a profit and the integrity of a prison administration that must be concerned with such complex issues as security, rehabilitation, and dealing with highly dangerous people in a closed environment.[123]

Prison Inmates: Male

As expected, prisoners reflect the same qualities that are found in samples of arrestees. Inmates of state prisons are predominantly poor, young adult males with less than a high school education. However, although inmates tend to be young, longer sentences have dictated an aging inmate population; there is a growing pool of inmates aged 35 plus. Prison inmates who are aged 50 and beyond will make up 33 percent of the total prison population by the year 2010, placing pressure on prison administrators to devise ways of keeping aged inmates in the prison workforce, helping them maintain family ties, and assuring them access to medical and mental health specialists.[124]

Prison is not a new experience for many inmates: over 60 percent have been incarcerated before. About 80 percent of all inmates have had prior sentences to either probation or incarceration; about 5 percent have had 100 or more prior convictions! This criminal record is not surprising considering that most prison inmates have had extremely troubled backgrounds. Many grew up in single-parent households; many had parents who abused drugs or alcohol; the great majority have been substance abusers themselves.[125] Considering this background, it should come as no surprise that more inmates die from HIV-related disease than from prison violence.[126]

Inmates are educational and vocational underachievers. Only one-third have graduated from high school, and about

inmates who are within 3 years of parole.[116] By 2000, 264 privately operated facilities were under contract with state or federal authorities to house prisoners.[117] Today, privately run prisons hold many thousands of inmates. Corrections Corporation of America has approximately 71,000 beds in 63 facilities under contract for management in 19 states and Washington, D.C. The majority of these prisons are located in the South and Southwest, including 15 in Texas alone. About 62,000 inmates are currently under the company's supervision. Its main rival, Geo, currently operates 62 correctional and residential treatment facilities with capacity of about 51,000 beds in the United States, Australia, South Africa, Canada, and Britain. The third largest company, Cornell, has contracts to operate 82 facilities in 18 states and the District of Columbia with a service capacity of 19,500.[118]

Private facilities span the full range of correctional institutions. In addition to running stand-alone institutions, some correctional institutions outsource services such as medical care or food supply to private for-profit companies. Although privately run institutions have been around for a few years, their increased use may present a number of problems. Will private providers be able to effectively evaluate programs, knowing that a negative evaluation might cause them to lose their contracts? Will they skimp on services and programs to reduce costs? Might they not skim off the easy cases and leave the hard-core inmates for state care? And will the need to keep business booming require widening the net to fill empty cells? Some private service providers have been sued because their services were inadequate, causing harm to inmates.[119]

The notion of running prisons for profit may be unpalatable to large segments of the population. However, is this much

one-half are employed full-time before their incarceration; about half earned under $10,000 per year. Less than 20 percent are married, far below the standard rate for adult Americans.

The profile of the prison inmate supports the reality of a problem behavior syndrome. From birth, the path that led the inmate to prison was littered with insurmountable family, economic, and social problems.

Living in Prison

Inmates quickly learn what the term "total institution" really means.[127] When they arrive at the prison, they are stripped, searched, shorn, and assigned living quarters. Before they get there, though, their first experience occurs in a classification or reception center, where they are given a series of psychological and other tests and are evaluated on the basis of their personality, background, offense history, and treatment needs. Based on the classification they are given, they will be assigned to a permanent facility. Hard-core, repeat, and violent offenders will go to the maximum-security unit; offenders with learning disabilities may be assigned to an institution that specializes in educational services; mentally disordered offenders will be held in a facility that can provide psychiatric care; and so on. Some states have instituted rigorous classification instruments designed to maximize the effectiveness of placements, thereby cutting down on the cost of incarceration. If classification can be conducted in an efficient and effective manner, nondangerous offenders would not needlessly be kept in expensive high-security facilities.[128]

Inmates in large, inaccessible prisons find themselves physically cut off from families, friends, and former associates. Those who are fathers may become depressed because they are anxious about their kids.[129] Their families and friends may find it difficult to travel great distances to visit them; mail is censored and sometimes destroyed. The prison regulates dress, work, sleep, and eating habits.[130]

Inmates find themselves in a totally new world with its own logic, behavior, rules, and language. They must learn to live with the stress of prison life. The major losses are goods and services, liberty, heterosexual relationships, autonomy, and security.[131] Prisoners find they have no privacy; even when locked in their own cells, they are surrounded and observed by others.

Inmates must adjust to the incentives prison administrators have created to promote security and control behavior.[132] One type of incentive involves the level of comfort provided the inmate. Those obeying rules are given choice work assignments, privileges, and educational opportunities. Those who flout prison rules may be segregated, locked in their cells, or put in solitary confinement (the hole).

Administrators can also control the amount of time spent in prison. Furloughs can be dispensed to allow prisoners the opportunity to work or visit outside prison walls. Good-time credit can be extended to lessen sentences. Parole decisions can be influenced by reports on inmates' behavior. Inmates who maintain their innocence may find that their denial is communicated to paroling authorities, thereby putting their release date in jeopardy. This is especially vexing for those inmates who are actually innocent and who actively refuse to accept their institutional label of convicted criminal.[133]

The inmate must learn to deal with sexual exploitation and violence in the prison. One position says that this phenomenon is a function of racial conflict; another holds that inmates who become victims are physically weaker and less likely to form cohesive defensive groups.[134] In one study, criminologist Daniel Lockwood found that inmate aggressors come from a street culture that stresses violence and continue to behave violently while in prison.[135] Young males may be raped and kept as sexual slaves by older, more aggressive inmates. When these "slave holders" are released, they often sell their "prison wives" to other inmates.[136]

To avoid victimization, inmates must learn to adopt a lifestyle that shields them from victimization.[137] They must discover areas of safety and danger, whom to trust and whom to avoid. Some learn how to fight back to prove they are not people who can be exploited. People who viewed violence as an acceptable method of settling disputes before entering prison are the ones most likely to use violence while they are inmates.[138] Whereas some kill their attackers and get even longer sentences, others join cliques and gangs that provide protection and the ability to acquire power within the institution. Gangs are powerful in the larger prison systems, especially in California. Some inmates seek transfers to a different cell block or prison, ask for protective custody, or simply remain in their cells all the time.

Part of inmates' early adjustment involves becoming familiar with and perhaps participating in the hidden, black market economy of the prison—the hustle. Hustling provides inmates with a source of steady income and the satisfaction of believing they are beating the system.[139] Hustling involves the sale of such illegal commodities as drugs (uppers, downers, pot), alcohol, weapons, and illegally obtained food and supplies. When prison officials crack down on hustled goods, it merely drives the price up—giving hustlers a greater incentive to promote their black market activities.[140]

Inmates must also learn to deal with daily racial conflict. Prisoners tend to segregate themselves and, if peace is to reign in the institution, stay out of one another's way. Often racial groupings are quite exact; for example, Latinos may separate themselves according to their national origin (Mexicans, Puerto Ricans, Colombians, and so on). In large California prisons, segregation and power struggles create even narrower divisions. For example, Latino gangs are now organized by area of origin: northern California (Norteños), southern California (Sureños), and Mexican-born (Border Brothers).[141] Prisons represent one area in which minorities often hold power; as sociologist James B. Jacobs observed, "Prison may be the one institution in American society that blacks control."[142]

Prisoners must learn to deal with their frustrations over getting a "rotten deal." They may find that some other inmates received far lower sentences for similar crimes. They may be turned down for parole and then observe that others with similar records are granted early release. There is some evidence that perceived discrimination in the distribution of rewards and treatment may contribute to dissatisfaction, maladjustment, and prison violence.[143]

Finally, as the inmates' sentences wind down and their parole dates near, they must learn to cope with the anxiety of being released into the outside world. During this period, inmates may question their ability to make it in an environment in which they have failed before. Have their families stood by them? Are they outcasts? Facing release, these inmates often experience low self-esteem, become depressed, and suffer anxiety.[144]

Of course, not all inmates learn to cope. Some repeatedly violate institutional rules. One reason is that in the United States and abroad many inmates suffer from serious psychological and emotional problems. A review of inmate mental health in 12 countries, including the United States, found that many inmates suffered from psychotic illnesses, including 10 percent with major depression, and 65 percent had a personality disorder. Prisoners were several times more likely to have psychosis and major depression and about 10 times more likely to have antisocial personality disorder than the general population.[145]

As the prison population expands, the violence and danger of the streets will be imported into the prison culture. A recent (2006) report of the Commission on Safety and Abuse in America's Prisons funded by New York's Vera Institute of Justice found that violence, medical problems and segregation of inmates still plagues the nation's prisons (see Exhibit 18.3).[146]

Prison Inmates: Female

Women make up between 5 and 6 percent of the adult prison population. While their numbers are much smaller, the percentage of women in prison is increasing at a faster pace, a phenomenon that reflects the increasing presence of women in the crime rate. Female inmates are usually housed in minimum-security institutions more likely to resemble college dormitories than high-security male prisons. Women in prison tend to be of three basic types, described by Esther Heffernan: "the square," who is basically a noncriminal but who, in a fit of rage, may have shot or stabbed a husband or boyfriend; "the life," who is a repeat offender (shoplifter, prostitute, drug user, or pusher); and "the cool," who is part of the sophisticated criminal underworld. The square usually espouses conventional values and wants to follow the rules; the life rejects prison authority and is a rebel; the cool is aloof, manipulates the environment, and does not participate in prison life.[147]

Like men, female inmates must adjust to the prison experience. Female inmates generally first go through a period in which they deny the reality of their situation. Then comes a period of anger over the circumstances that led to their incarceration; during this phase, they begin to accept the circumstances of their imprisonment. A third stage finds female inmates greatly depressed because they can no longer deny that they are in prison to stay. Many female inmates eventually find reason to hope that their lives will improve.[148]

Daily life in the women's prison community is also somewhat different from that in male institutions. For one thing, women usually do not present the immediate physical danger to staff and fellow inmates that many male prisoners do. For another, the rigid, antiauthority inmate social code

EXHIBIT 18.3

Report of the Commission on Safety and Abuse in America's Prisons

Violence There is disturbing evidence of individual assaults and patterns of violence in some U.S. prisons and jails. Corrections officers told the Commission about a near-constant fear of being assaulted. Former prisoners recounted gang violence, rape, beatings by officers, and in one large jail, a pattern of illegal and humiliating strip-searches. Former Florida Warden Ron McAndrew described small groups of officers operating as "goon squads" to abuse prisoners and intimidate other staff. Inmate-on-inmate violence is common even if the prison death rate has been in sharp decline.

Medical Problems High rates of disease and illness among prisoners, coupled with inadequate funding for correctional health care, endanger prisoners, staff, and the public. Much of the public dismisses jails and prisons as sealed institutions, where what happens inside remains inside. In the context of disease and illness, which travel naturally from one environment to another, that view is clearly wrong. Left untreated, staph infections and diseases such as tuberculosis, hepatitis C, and HIV directly affect our families, neighborhoods, and communities. As a result of poverty, substance abuse, and years of poor health care, prisoners as a group are much less healthy than average Americans. Every year, more than 1.5 million people are released from jail and prison carrying a life-threatening contagious disease. At least 350,000 prisoners have a serious mental illness.

Segregation Separating dangerous or vulnerable individuals from the general prison population is now commonplace. In some systems, prisoners who should be housed at safe distances from particular individuals or groups of prisoners end up locked in their cells 23 hours a day, every day, with little opportunity to be productive and prepare for release. People who pose no real threat to anyone and also those who are mentally ill are placed for months or years in high-security units and supermax prisons. In some places, the environment is so severe that people end up completely isolated, confined in constantly bright or constantly dim spaces without any meaningful human contact—torturous conditions that are proven to cause mental deterioration. Prisoners often are released directly from solitary confinement and other high-security units to the streets, despite the clear dangers of doing so.

Source: John Gibbons and Nicholas de Belleville Katzenbach, *Confronting Confinement: A Report of the Commission on Safety and Abuse in America's Prisons* (New York: Vera Institute of Justice, 2006).

found in many male institutions does not exist in female prisons. Recent research conducted in the California prison system finds that few female inmates experience the violent atmosphere common in male institutions, nor do they suffer the racial and ethnic conflict and divisiveness.[149] Female inmates seem to receive more social support from both internal sources (inmate peers and correctional staff) and external sources (families and peers), a factor that may help lessen the pains of prison life, help them adjust, and improve the social climate within female institutions.[150]

Confinement for women, however, may produce severe anxiety and anger because they are separated from families and loved ones and unable to function in normal female roles. Low self-esteem is a major problem among female inmates.[151] Unlike men, who direct their anger outward, female prisoners may revert to more self-destructive acts to cope with their problems. Female inmates are perhaps more likely than males to mutilate their own bodies and attempt suicide. It is not surprising, considering these circumstances, that female inmates are more likely to be treated with mood-altering drugs and placed in psychiatric care, whereas male inmates' adjustment difficulties are viewed as disciplinary problems.[152]

One common form of adaptation to prison employed by women is the surrogate family. This group contains masculine and feminine figures acting as fathers and mothers; some even act as children and take on the role of either brother or sister. Formalized marriages and divorces may be conducted. Sometimes multiple roles are held by one inmate, so that a "sister" in one family may "marry" and become the "wife" in another.[153]

Helping the Female Inmate The special needs of female inmates must be addressed by correctional authorities. Health care is an issue. Many institutions have inadequate facilities to care for women who are pregnant when they enter prison or become pregnant during their prison stay.[154] There is a growing problem of HIV-related illnesses as the ongoing war on drugs increases the number of substance-abusing female inmates who are at risk for AIDS.[155]

Helping women to adjust after they leave the institution is another goal. Surveys indicate that the prison experience does little to prepare women to reenter the workforce after their sentences have been completed. Gender stereotypes still shape vocational opportunities.[156] Female inmates are still being trained for "women's roles," such as childrearing, and are not given the programming to make successful adjustments in the community.[157]

Female offenders are more likely than males to be convicted of a nonviolent crime and incarcerated for a low-level involvement in drug offenses, such as driving a boyfriend to make a drug deal. The female offender may end up serving a longer sentence than the boyfriend simply because they are less likely to work out a plea arrangement.[158] It is not surprising that many women display psychological problems, including serious psychopathology.[159] The picture that emerges of the female inmate is troubling. After a lifetime of emotional turmoil, physical and sexual abuse, and drug use, it seems improbable that overcrowded, underfunded correctional institutions can forge a dramatic turnaround in the behavior of at-risk female inmates. Many have lost custody of their children, a trauma that is more likely to afflict those who are already substance abusers and suffer from depression.[160] While some who receive emotional support can be helped to adjust and reenter society, it should come as no surprise that many female inmates feel strain and conflict, psychological conditions related to violent episodes.[161]

Correctional Treatment

Correctional treatment has been an integral part of prison life since warden Z. R. Brockway introduced it as part of the daily regimen at the Elmira Reformatory in the nineteenth century. Today more than 90 percent of all prison inmates participate in some form of program or activity after admission.[162] A recent survey of correctional treatment found that substance abuse education and awareness is the most common form of treatment provided, being offered in 74 percent of prisons, 61 percent of jails, and 53 percent of community correctional agencies; remedial education is the most frequently available correctional program in prisons (89 percent) and jails (60 percent).[163]

There are many approaches to treatment. Some, based on a medical model, rely heavily on counseling and clinical therapy. Others attempt to prepare inmates for reintegration into the community; they rely on work release, vocational training, and educational opportunities. Still others stress self-help through 12-step or Alcoholics Anonymous programs. Some programs have a religious theme and involve Bible clubs and other pious activities.[164] Under the Bush administration, faith-based rehabilitation efforts have flourished, and some have shown to be positive influences on inmate behavior.[165]

Although it is beyond the scope of this book to describe the vast number of correctional treatment programs, a few important types are listed in Exhibit 18.4.

Does Correctional Treatment Work? Despite the variety and number of treatment programs in operation, some question their effectiveness. In an often-cited study from 35 years ago, Robert Martinson and his associates found that, with few exceptions, rehabilitative efforts seemed to have no appreciable effect on recidivism.[166]

Martinson's work was followed by efforts that found, embarrassingly, that some high-risk offenders were more likely to commit crimes after they had been placed in treatment programs than before the onset of rehabilitation efforts.[167] Even California's highly touted community treatment program, which matched youthful offenders and counselors on the basis of their psychological profiles, was found by Paul Lerman to exert negligible influence on its clients.[168]

These less-than-enthusiastic reviews of correctional rehabilitation helped develop a more conservative view of corrections, which means that prisons are viewed as places of incapacitation and confinement; their purpose is punishment, not treatment.[169] Current social policy stresses eliminating the nonserious offender from the correctional system while increasing the sentences of serious, violent offenders. The development of lengthy mandatory and determinate sentences to punish serious offenders and the simultaneous evolution of alternative sanctions to limit the nonserious offender's interface with the system are manifestations of this view.

Some criminologists continue to challenge the "nothing works" philosophy.[170] Recent analysis of education, vocation, and work programs indicate that they may be able to lower recidivism rates and increase postrelease employment.[171] Inmates who have completed higher levels of education find it easier to gain employment upon release and consequently are less likely to recidivate over long periods.[172]

EXHIBIT 18.4

Correctional Treatment Program Types

Therapy and Counseling

The most traditional type of treatment in prison involves psychological counseling and therapy. Counseling programs exist in almost every major institution. Some stress individual treatment with psychotherapy or other techniques. However, because of lack of resources, it is more common for group methods to be used. Some groups are led by trained social workers, counselors, or therapists; others rely on lay personnel as leaders.

Therapeutic Communities

Because drug abuse is so prevalent among inmates, some institutions have been organized into therapeutic communities (TCs) in order to best serve their clientele. The TC approach to substance abuse uses a psychosocial, experiential learning process that relies on positive peer pressure within a highly structured social environment. The community itself, including staff and program participants, becomes the primary method of change. They work together as members of a "family" in order to create a culture where community members confront one another's negative behavior and attitudes and establish an open, trusting, and safe environment; TC relies then on mutual self-help. The TC approach encourages personal disclosure rather than the isolation of the general prison culture.

Educational Programs

Almost all correctional institutions provide some type of educational experience. Some prisons allow inmates to obtain a high school diploma through equivalency exams or general educational development (GED) certificates. Some prisons provide college courses, usually staffed by teachers who work at nearby institutions. These services are extremely important because about two-thirds of all state prison inmates did not receive a high school diploma. Recent federal surveys indicate that about one-quarter of state prison inmates were able to complete the GED while serving time in a correctional facility; more than half take education courses while confined.

Vocational Programs

Most prisons operate numerous vocational training programs designed to help inmates develop skills for securing employment on their release. In the past, the traditional prison industries of laundry and license plate manufacture failed to provide these skills. Today programs stress such marketable skills as dental laboratory work, computer programming, auto repair, and radio and television work.

Private Industry

A new version of vocational rehabilitation is the development of private industry in prison. This can take many different forms, including private citizens sitting on prison industry boards, private vendors marketing goods from prison industry, inmates manufacturing and marketing their own goods, private management of state-owned prison industry, franchising within the prison system in which manufactured goods are marketed under license from a private firm, and privately owned industries on prison grounds employing inmate labor.

Self-Help Groups

Recognizing that the probability of failure on the outside is acute, inmates have attempted to organize self-help groups to provide the psychological tools needed to prevent recidivism. Some are chapters of common national organizations such as Alcoholics Anonymous. Membership in these programs is designed to improve inmates' self-esteem and help them cope with common problems such as alcoholism, narcotics abuse, or depression.

In general, treatment seems to be most effective if it is matched with the needs of inmates.[173] Programs that teach interpersonal skills, utilize individual counseling, and make use of behavioral modification techniques to improve cognitive reasoning and develop social skills have produced positive results both in the community and within correctional institutions.[174] Among the characteristics associated with the most successful programs are these:

- Services are intensive, lasting only a few months.
- Programs are cognitive, aimed at helping inmates learn new skills in order to better cope with personality problems such as impulsivity.
- Program goals are reinforced firmly and fairly, using positive rewards rather than negative punishment.
- Therapists relate to clients sensitively and positively. Therapists are trained and supervised appropriately.
- Clients are insulated from disruptive interpersonal networks and placed in environments where prosocial activities predominate.[175]

So although the concept of correctional treatment is often questioned, many criminologists still believe that it is possible to help some inmates within prison walls.

Prison Violence

On August 9, 1973, Stephen Donaldson, a Quaker peace activist, was arrested for trespassing after participating in a pray-in at the White House. Sent to a Washington, D.C., jail for two nights, Donaldson was gang raped approximately 60 times by numerous inmates. Donaldson later became president of Stop Prisoner Rape, a nonprofit organization that advocates for the protection of inmates from sexual assault and offers support to victims. On July 18, 1996, at the age of 49, Donaldson passed away from infections complicated by AIDS.[176]

Conflict, violence, and brutality are sad but ever-present facts of institutional life. Violence can involve individual conflict: inmate versus inmate, inmate versus staff, staff versus inmate. One common threat is sexual assault. Research has shown that prison rapes usually involve a victim who is viewed as weak and submissive and a group of aggressive rapists who can dominate the victim through their collective strength. Sexual harassment leads to fights, social isolation, fear, anxiety, and crisis. Nonsexual assaults may stem from an aggressor's desire to shake down the victim for money and personal favors, may be motivated by racial conflict, or may simply be used to establish power within the institution. Surveys indicate that at least 20 percent of all inmates are raped during the course of their prison stay.[177] The problem is so severe that Congress enacted the Prison Rape Reduction Act of 2003, which established three programs in the Department of Justice:

1. A program dedicated to collecting national prison rape statistics, data, and conducting research

2. A program dedicated to the dissemination of information and procedures for combating prison rape

3. A grant program to assist in funding state programs[178]

What are the causes of prison violence? There is no single explanation for either collective or individual violence, but theories abound. One position holds that inmates are often violence-prone individuals who have always used force to get their own way. In the crowded, dehumanizing world of the prison, it is not surprising that they resort to force to dominate others.[179]

A second view is that prisons convert people to violence by their inhumane conditions, including overcrowding, depersonalization, and threats of rape. Even in the most humane prisons, life is a constant put-down, and prison conditions threaten the inmates' sense of self-worth; violence is a consequence of these conditions.[180]

Still another view is that prison violence stems from mismanagement, lack of strong security, and inadequate control by prison officials.[181] This view has contributed to the escalated use of solitary confinement in recent years as a means of control. Also contributing to prison violence is the changing prison population. Younger, more violent inmates, who often have been members of teenage gangs, now dominate prison life. The old code of "do your own time" and "be a right guy" may be giving way to a prison culture dominated by gangs, whose very nature breeds violence.

Corrections and the Rule of Law

For many years, the nation's courts did not interfere in prison operations, maintaining what is called the hands-off doctrine (see Chapter 16). The judiciary's reluctance to interfere in prison matters was based on the belief that it lacked technical competence in prison administration, society's general apathy toward prisons, and the belief that prisoners' complaints involved privileges rather than rights.[182] The hands-off doctrine was lifted in the 1960s. General concern with civil and human rights, increasing militancy in the prison population, and the reformist nature of the Warren Court created a climate conducive to change.

For many years the Supreme Court upheld inmates' rights, granting them access to the courts to seek legal redress for improper or damaging prison conditions. Recently claims that prisoner-inspired lawsuits were clogging the courts swayed a more conservative Court to limit the methods by which inmates can seek release or redress, for example, by discouraging inmates from filing "frivolous" lawsuits.[183] Then in 1996 Congress enacted the Prison Litigation Reform Act (PLRA), which makes it harder for prisoners to file lawsuits in federal court. The PLRA mandates that before an inmate can file a lawsuit, the inmate must try to resolve the complaint through the prison's grievance procedure, which usually requires filing a written description of the complaint or grievance with a prison official.[184]

Nonetheless, some of the gains won by inmates continue in force, including the following:

▌ *Freedom of speech and press.* The courts have ruled that inmates retain freedom of speech and press unless correctional authorities can show that it interferes with or threatens institutional freedom. In *Procunier v. Martinez,* a court ruled that an inmate's mail could be censored only if there existed substantial belief that its contents would threaten security. However, in *Saxbe v. Washington Post,* the right of an inmate to grant press interviews was limited; the Supreme Court argued that such interviews would enhance the reputations of particular inmates and jeopardize authorities' desire to treat everyone equally.[185]

▌ *Medical rights.* After many years of indifference, inmates have been given the right to secure proper medical attention. To gain their medical rights, prisoners have generally resorted to class action suits to ask courts to require adequate medical care.[186] In 1976, after reviewing the legal principles established over the preceding 20 years, the Supreme Court in *Estelle v. Gamble* clearly stated the inmate's right to medical care. The court said:[187]

> *Deliberate indifference to serious medical needs of prisoners constitutes the "unnecessary and wanton infliction of pain,"* . . . *proscribed by the Eighth Amendment. This is true whether the indifference is manifested by prison doctors in their response to the prisoner's needs or by prison guards in intentionally denying or delaying access to medical care or intentionally interfering with the treatment once prescribed.*[188]

▌ Lower courts will decide, case by case, whether "deliberate indifference" has actually occurred.

Cruel and Unusual Punishment

Prisoners have long suffered severe physical punishment in prison, ranging from whipping to extended periods of solitary confinement. The courts have held that such treatment is unconstitutional when it

▌ Degrades the dignity of human beings.[189]

▌ Is more severe than the offense for which it has been given.[190]

▌ Shocks the general conscience and is fundamentally unfair.[191]

The courts have also ruled on the necessity of maintaining the general prison system in a humane manner. For example, in 1970, the entire prison system in Arkansas was declared unconstitutional because its practices of overt physical punishment were ruled to violate the Eighth Amendment.[192]

In *Rhodes v. Chapman,* the Supreme Court upheld the practice of double-bunking two or more inmates in a small cell (50 square feet).[193] "Conditions of confinement," the Court argued, "must not involve the wanton and unnecessary infliction of pain nor may they be grossly disproportionate to the severity of the crime warranting imprisonment," but "conditions that cannot be said to be cruel and unusual under contemporary standards are not unconstitutional. To the extent that such conditions are restrictive and even harsh, they are part of the penalty that criminal offenders pay for their offenses against society."[194]

In a recent case, *Hope v. Pelzer,* the Supreme Court ruled that correctional officials who knowingly violate the Eighth

THE PROBLEMS OF REENTRY

Because of America's two-decade-long imprisonment boom, more than 500,000 inmates are now being released back into the community each year. As criminologist Joan Petersilia warns, there are a number of unfortunate consequences to this release back into the community because many of those being released have not received adequate treatment and are unprepared for life in conventional society. The risks they present to the community include increases in child abuse, family violence, the spread of infectious diseases, homelessness, and community disorganization. Many have no way to cope and wind up in homeless shelters. A recent (2006) study of shelters in New York City found that 23 percent of the occupants had been released from New York prisons and jails in the past two years.

The increased reentry risks can be tied to legal changes in how people are released from prison. In the past, offenders were granted early release only if a parole board believed they were rehabilitated and had ties to the community—such as a family or a job. Inmates were encouraged to enter treatment programs to earn parole. Changes in sentencing law have resulted in the growth of mandatory release and limits on discretionary parole. People now serve a fixed sentence, and the discretion of parole boards has been blunted. Inmates may be discouraged from seeking involvement in rehabilitation programs (they do not influence the chance of parole), and the lack of incentive means that fewer inmates leaving prison have participated in programs to address work, education, and substance use deficiencies. Nor does the situation improve upon release. Many inmates are not assigned to supervision caseloads once back in the community. About 200,000 released inmates go unsupervised each year, three-quarters of whom have been released after completing their maximum sentence and are therefore not obligated to be supervised.

Petersilia argues that most leave prison with no savings, no immediate entitlement to unemployment benefits, and few employment prospects. Upon release, some find that they are no longer welcome in subsidized public housing complexes due to the U.S. Department of Housing and Urban Development's "one strike and you're out" policy, where all members of the household are evicted if one member is involved in crime. A year after release, as many as 60 percent of former inmates are not employed in the regular labor market, and there is increasing reluctance among employers to hire ex-offenders. Ex-offenders are commonly barred from working in the fields in which most jobs are being created, such as child care, education, security, nursing, and home health care. More jobs are also now unionized, and many unions exclude ex-offenders.

Being barred from work opportunities produces chronic unemployment, a status closely related to drug and alcohol abuse. Losing a job can lead to substance abuse, which in turn is related to child and family violence. Mothers released from prison have difficulty finding services such as housing, employment, and child care, and this causes stress for them and their children. Children of incarcerated and released parents may suffer confusion, sadness, and social stigma, and these feelings often result in difficulties in school, low self-esteem, aggressive behavior, and general emotional dysfunction. If the parents are negative role models, children fail to develop positive attitudes about work and responsibility. Children of incarcerated parents are five times more likely to serve time in prison than are children whose parents are not incarcerated.

Prisoners have significantly more physical and mental health problems than the general population. More than

---

Amendment rights of inmates can be held liable for damages.[195] Hope, an Alabama prison inmate, was twice handcuffed to a hitching post for disruptive conduct. He was handcuffed above shoulder height, and when he tried moving his arms to improve circulation, the handcuffs cut into his wrists, causing pain and discomfort. Hope filed a suit against three guards, charging them with violating his civil rights. The Supreme Court ruled that Hope's treatment amounted to "unnecessary and wanton" inflictions of pain, constituting cruel and unusual punishment forbidden by the Eighth Amendment. The Court reasoned that any reasonable security or safety concerns had long since ended by the time Hope was handcuffed to the hitching post, because he had already been subdued, handcuffed, placed in leg irons, and transported back to prison. The *Hope* case shows that correctional officials can be sued if their behavior violates an inmate's constitutional rights and that officials or any reasonable person should have surmised that the behavior was in violation of accepted practices.

PAROLE

Parole is the planned release and community supervision of incarcerated offenders before the expiration of their prison sentences. It is usually considered a way of completing

three-fourths of the inmates leaving prison report a history of drug and/or alcohol abuse in the next year. Inmates with mental illness (about 16 percent of all inmates) are also increasingly being imprisoned—and then released. Even when public mental health services are available, many mentally ill individuals fail to use them because they fear institutionalization, deny they are mentally ill, or distrust the mental health system. The situation will become more serious as more and more parolees are released back into the disorganized communities whose deteriorated conditions may have motivated their original crimes.

Fear of a prison stay has less of an effect on behavior than ever before. As the prison population grows, the negative impact of incarceration may be lessening. In neighborhoods where "doing time" is more the rule than the exception, it becomes less of a stigma and more of a badge of acceptance. However, it also becomes a way of life from which some ex-convicts do rebound. Teens may encounter older men who have gone to prison and have returned to begin their lives again. With the proper skills and survival techniques, prison is considered "manageable." Although a prison stay is still unpleasant, it has lost its aura of shame and fear. By becoming commonplace and mundane, the "myth" of the prison experience has been exposed and its deterrent power reduced.

The Effect on Communities

Parole expert Richard Seiter notes that when there were only a few hundred thousand prisoners, and a few thousand releasees per year, the issues surrounding the release of offenders did not overly challenge communities. Families could house ex-inmates, job-search organizations could find them jobs, and community social service agencies could respond to their individual needs for mental health or substance abuse treatment. Today, the sheer number of reentering inmates has taxed the communities to which they are returning. Charis Kubrin and Eric Stewart have found that communities that already face the greatest social and economic disadvantages are ones that produce the highest recidivism rates. Obviously, the influx of returning inmates can magnify their problems.

Research shows that high rates of prison admissions produce high crime rates. Clearly, the national policy of relying on prison as a deterrent to crime may produce results that policy makers had not expected or wanted.

CRITICAL THINKING

1. All too often, government leaders jump on the incarceration bandwagon as a panacea for the nation's crime problem. Is it a "quick fix" whose long-term consequences may be devastating for the nation's cities, or are these problems counterbalanced by the crime-reducing effect of putting large numbers of high-rate offenders behind bars?

2. If you agree that incarceration undermines neighborhoods, can you think of some other, indirect ways that high incarceration rates help increase crime rates?

Sources: Stephen Metraux and Dennis Culhane, "Recent Incarceration History Among a Sheltered Homeless Population," *Crime and Delinquency* 52 (2006): 504–517; Charis Kubrin and Eric Stewart, "Predicting Who Reoffends: The Neglected Role of Neighborhood Context in Recidivism Studies," *Criminology* 44 (2006): 165–197; Joan Petersilia, *When Prisoners Come Home: Parole and Prisoner Reentry* (New York: Oxford University Press, 2003); Joan Petersilia, "Hard Time Ex-Offenders Returning Home After Prison," *Corrections Today* 67 (2005): 66–72; Joan Petersilia, "When Prisoners Return to Communities: Political, Economic, and Social Consequences," *Federal Probation* 65 (2001): 3–9; Richard Seiter, "Prisoner Reentry and the Role of Parole Officers," *Federal Probation* 66 (2002).

a prison sentence in the community and is not the same as a pardon; the paroled offender can be legally recalled to serve the remainder of his or her sentence in an institution if parole authorities deem the offender's adjustment inadequate or if the offender commits another crime while on parole.

The decision to parole is determined by statutory requirement and usually involves the completion of a minimum sentence. Parole is granted by a state (or federal) parole board: a body of men and women who review cases and determine whether an offender has been rehabilitated sufficiently to deal with the outside world. The board also dictates the specific parole rules a parolee must obey.

Some states with determinate sentencing statutes do not use parole boards but release inmates at the conclusion of their maximum terms less accumulated good time. This form of mandatory parole release has been increasing rapidly as states adopt various forms of determinate sentencing. State inmates released from prison as a result of a parole board decision dropped from 50 percent of all adults entering parole in 1995 to about 30 percent today.[196]

In states where discretionary parole is used, the decision is made at a parole grant hearing. There the full board or a subcommittee reviews information, may meet with the offender, and then decides whether the parole applicant has a reasonable chance of succeeding outside prison. Candidates

Fewer than half of all parolees succeed in the community and most eventually return to prison. Here, Detroit police officer Tracey Burgess (left) looks through a screen door as her partner Michael Jordan talks on the radio during a search for a parole violator in River Rouge, Michigan. "What does it take to keep these people locked up?" asked Burgess, frustrated because too often parole violators are back on a street just days after being arrested. State corrections officials are hoping to alleviate some of that frustration and prevent parolees from returning to prison, with a new policy that could mean 30 days in jail for those who violate parole rules.

In some jurisdictions, parolees in need of closer surveillance are placed on intensive supervision parole (ISP). These programs use limited caseload sizes, treatment facilities, the matching of parolee and supervisor by personality, and shock parole (which involves immediate short-term incarceration for parole violators to impress them with the seriousness of a violation). ISP clients are required to attend more office and home visits than routine parolees. ISP may also require frequent drug testing, a term in a community correctional center, and electronic monitoring in the home. More than 17,000 parolees are under intensive supervision, 1,400 of whom are monitored electronically by computer.

Evaluations of ISP programs have produced mixed results. Some show that they may actually produce a higher violation rate than traditional parole supervision because limiting caseload size allows parole officers to supervise their clients more closely and spot infractions more easily.[199] Some recent research shows that under some conditions a properly run ISP program can significantly reduce recidivism upon release. The key factors may be parole officer orientation (a balance between social service and law enforcement seems to work best) and a supportive organizational environment in which the program is being run.[200]

for parole may be chosen by statutory eligibility on the basis of time served in relation to their sentences. In most jurisdictions, good time reduces the minimum sentence and therefore hastens eligibility for parole. In making its decision, the board considers the inmate's offense, time served, evidence of adjustment, and opportunities on the outside.

To help these parole decision makers, parole prediction tables have been developed.[197] These tables correlate personal information on inmates who were released in the past with their rates of rearrest. The best-known predictive device is the Salient Factor Score Index. The salient factor score includes age, type of offense, prior parole revocations, history of heroin use, and employment background.[198]

The Parolee in the Community

Once community release has begun, the offender is supervised by a trained staff of parole officers who help the offender adjust to the community and search for employment as they monitor behavior and activities to ensure that the offender conforms to the conditions of parole.

Parolees are subject to strict standardized or personalized rules that guide their behavior and limit their activities. If at any time these rules are violated, the offender can be returned to the institution to serve the remainder of the sentence; this is known as a technical parole violation. Inmates released in determinate sentencing states can have part or all of their good time revoked if they violate the conditions of their release.

How Effective Is Parole?

Conservative thinkers criticize parole because it allows possibly dangerous offenders into the community before the completion of their sentences. Parole decision making relies on human judgment, so it is quite possible that dangerous offenders, who should actually have remained inside a secure facility, are released into society while others who would probably make a good adjustment to the community are denied release.

The evaluation of parole effectiveness has produced some disturbing results. Despite all efforts to treat, correct, and rehabilitate incarcerated offenders, the fact remains that a majority return to prison shortly after their release. Federal surveys indicate that about two-thirds of all released inmates are rearrested within three years of leaving prison for a felony or serious misdemeanor.[201] About half are reconvicted for a new crime. Within three years, about half were back in prison, serving time for a new prison sentence or for a technical violation of their release, such as failing a drug test, missing an appointment with their parole officer, or being arrested for a new crime.

What factors predict parole failure? Prisons may do little to help inmates adjust on the outside. As correctional expert Stephen Duguid maintains, by their very nature, prisons seek to impose and maintain order and conformity rather than to help inmates develop skills such as independence and critical thinking, factors that may be essential once the inmate is forced to cope outside the prison's walls.[202]

Inmates themselves may have a long history of criminal behavior, an antisocial personality, a record of substance abuse, and childhood experiences with family dysfunction— factors that are correlated with postrelease recidivism.[203] Many releasees have suffered from a lifetime of substance abuse or dependence disorder.[204] A history of physical and sexual abuse has also been linked to recidivism.[205] More than 10 percent exhibit both mental illness and substance abuse. Parolees who have had a good employment record in the past and who maintain jobs after their release are the most likely to avoid recidivating.[206]

The specter of recidivism is especially frustrating to the American public: it is so difficult to apprehend and successfully prosecute criminal offenders that it seems foolish to grant them early release so they can prey on more victims. As corrections expert Joan Petersilia puts it:

> Persons released from prison face a multitude of difficulties. They remain largely uneducated, unskilled, and usually without solid family support systems—to which are added the burdens of a prison record. Not surprisingly, most parolees fail, and rather quickly—rearrests are most common in the first six months after release.[207]

The Criminological Enterprise feature "The Problems of Reentry" on pages 554–555 discusses Petersilia's research and the work of others on the problems of parole failure.

In sum, many parolees are returned to prison for technical violations. It is therefore likely that one of the reasons for prison overcrowding is the large number of technical parole violators who are returned within three years of their release. If overcrowding is to be successfully dealt with, a more realistic parole violation policy may have to be developed in areas where the correctional system is under stress.

THINKING LIKE A CRIMINOLOGIST

The director of the American Civil Liberties Union has contacted you, asking for your professional opinion. She has read a paper by criminologists William Bowers and Glenn Pierce, who argue that far from being a deterrent, capital punishment actually produces more violence than it prevents; they label this the brutalization effect. Executions, they say, actually increase murder rates because they raise the general violence level in society and because violence-prone people identify with the executioner, not with the target of the death penalty. Consequently, when violence-prone people are confronted or their authority is challenged, they execute their challengers in the same manner that the state executes people who violate its rules.

Writing Exercise Assuming that Bowers and Pierce are correct, the ACLU director asks, does this mean that the death penalty violates the general public's civil rights? She asks whether it might be possible to turn public opinion against the death penalty on the basis that it actually does more harm than good, thereby endangering their lives. Write a brief response to the director answering these concerns.

Doing Research on the Web Before you write your response, visit sites that advocate for and against the death penalty. Abolitionist sites and pro–death penalty arguments can be found via www.thomsonedu.com/criminaljustice/siegel.

SUMMARY

- After a conviction, sentencing occurs. Each state, as well as the federal government, has its own types of sentences and punishments.

- Today's correctional institutions can trace their development from European origins.

- Early punishments were physical and brutal.

- The mercantile system and the development of overseas colonies created the need for labor, so slavery and forced labor began to replace physical punishment.

- Punishment methods developed in Europe were modified and improved by American colonists, most notably William Penn.

- Later, as needs grew, the newly formed states created their own large facilities. Discipline was harsh within them, and most enforced a code of total and absolute silence.

- New York developed the system of congregate working conditions during the day and isolation at night at Auburn Prison. Pennsylvania adopted an isolate system that required inmates be locked into their cells for the duration of their sentence.

- Fines, suspended sentences, community supervision, and prison are the most common forms of punishment. Prison sentences are divided into determinate and indeterminate types.

- There are also mandatory sentences that must be served upon conviction and carry no hope of probation.

- Efforts to control sentencing disparity include the use of sentencing guidelines, as well as determinate and mandatory sentences.

- Corrections involve the punishment, treatment, and incapacitation of convicted criminal offenders.

- Probation is the community supervision of convicted offenders by order of the court. It is a sentence reserved for defendants whom the magistrate views as having potential for rehabilitation without needing to serve prison or jail terms.

- Probation is practiced in every state and by the federal government and includes both adult and juvenile offenders. In the decision to grant probation, most judges are influenced by their personal views and the presentence reports of the probation staff.

- Once on probation, the offender must follow a set of rules or conditions, the violation of which may lead to revocation of probation and reinstatement of a prison sentence. These rules vary from state to state but usually involve such demands as refraining from using alcohol or drugs, obeying curfews, and terminating past criminal associations.

- In recent years, the U.S. Supreme Court has granted probationers greater due process rights; today, when the state wishes to revoke probation, it must conduct a full hearing on the matter and provide the probationer with an attorney when that assistance is warranted.

- To supplement probation, intermediate sanctions have been developed. Widely used intermediate sanctions include fines and forfeiture, intensive probation supervision, electronic monitoring, and community-based correctional facilities.

- Alternative sentencing options may allow residents to be eligible for work and educational release during the day while attending group sessions at night. Although these options are less costly and can free up prison space for more violent offenders, their effectiveness has not been adequately tested.

- Jails are used for misdemeanants and minor felons. Because conditions are so poor in jails, they have become a major trouble spot for the criminal justice system. New generation jails have improved security and reduced violence.

- Federal and state prisons—classified as minimum, medium, and maximum security—house most of the nation's incarcerated felons. Their poor track record has spurred the development of other correctional models, specifically boot camps, halfway houses, and community correctional centers.

- One newer development is privately run correctional institutions operated by private companies, which receive a fee for their services.

- The prison population has skyrocketed in the past few years, but recent data indicate that the boom may be leveling off.

- On entering prison, offenders must make tremendous adjustments to survive. Inmates learn to obey the inmate social code, which dictates proper behavior and attitudes. If inmates break the code, they may be unfavorably labeled. Prison violence is very common.

- Inmates are eligible for a large number of treatment devices designed to help them readjust to the community once they are released. Some programs include individualized and group psychological counseling, therapeutic communities, and vocational training with work furloughs.

- The courts have recognized that inmates have rights—which include access to the courts and legal counsel, the exercise of religion, the rights to correspondence and visitation, and the right to adequate medical treatment.

- Most inmates are paroled before the completion of their maximum term. Parole can be revoked if the offender violates the rules of parole or commits a new crime.

- Ex-inmates have a tough time adjusting on the outside, and the recidivism rate is disturbingly high.

- **ThomsonNOW** Maximize your study time by using ThomsonNOW's diagnostic study plan to help you review this chapter. The Personalized Study plan will help you identify areas on which you should concentrate; provide interactive exercises to help you master the chapter concepts; and provide a post-test to confirm you are ready to move on to the next chapter.

KEY TERMS

Walnut Street Jail (527)
Auburn system (527)
congregate system (528)
mandatory prison terms (528)
impact statements (528)
concurrent sentence (528)
consecutive sentence (528)
indeterminate sentence (528)
determinate sentence (529)
sentencing guidelines (530)
truth-in-sentencing laws (532)
sentencing disparity (533)

brutalization effect (536)
intermediate sanctions (542)
forfeiture (543)
monetary restitution (543)
community service
    restitution (543)
split sentencing (543)
shock probation (543)
intensive probation
    supervision (IPS) (544)
home confinement (HC) (544)
electronic monitoring (EM) (544)

residential community
    corrections (RCC) (544)
boot camps (544)
shock incarceration (544)
jail (545)
prison (546)
penitentiary (546)
supermax prison (546)
surrogate family (550)
parole (554)
parole grant hearing (555)
intensive supervision parole (556)

CRITICAL THINKING QUESTIONS

1. Do you approve of mandatory sentencing laws? Should every convicted felon be given the option of community treatment?

2. What rights should a probationer have before his community sentence is revoked? Is probation a privilege or a right? And if a privilege, would you recommend that it be revoked for the slightest rule violation?

3. Should a convicted criminal make restitution to a wealthy victim who does not really need the money? When is restitution inappropriate?

4. Should offenders be fined based on the severity of what they did or according to their ability to pay? Is it fair to gear fines to wages? Should some offenders be punished more severely because they are financially successful?

5. Do house arrest and electronic monitoring involve a violation of personal freedom? Does wearing an ankle bracelet smack of Big Brother? Would you want the government monitoring your daily activities? Could this practice be expanded, for example, to monitor the whereabouts of AIDS patients or political protestors?

6. Should private companies be allowed to run correctional institutions? What are the drawbacks to having a private company take on a sensitive and sometimes dangerous function such as administering prisons and jails?

NOTES

1. Sean O'Sullivan, "Teacher Gets 10 Years in Sex Case," *The News Journal*, 17 March 2007.
2. Brian Reaves, *Violent Felons in Large Urban Counties* (Washington, DC: Bureau of Justice Statistics, 2006), www.ojp.usdoj.gov/bjs/pub/pdf/vfluc.pdf (accessed April 27, 2007).
3. Graeme Newman, *The Punishment Response* (Philadelphia: Lippincott, 1978), p. 13.
4. Among the most helpful sources for this section are Jean Kellaway, *The History of Torture and Execution: From Early Civilization through Medieval Times to the Present* (Guilford, CT: Lyons Press, 2002); Lawrence Meir Friedman, *Crime and Punishment in American History* (New York: Basic Books, 1994 reprint ed.); Samuel Walker, *Popular Justice* (New York: Oxford University Press, 1980); Newman, *The Punishment Response*.

5. G. Ives, *A History of Penal Methods* (Montclair, NJ: Patterson-Smith, 1970).
6. J. J. Tobias, *Crime and Police in England, 1700–1900* (New York: Gill and Macmillan, 1979), p. 140.
7. Walker, *Popular Justice*, p. 34.
8. Orlando Lewis, *The Development of American Prisons and Prison Customs*, reprint ed. (Kila, MT: Kessinger Publishing, 2005), p. 17.
9. Gustave de Beaumont and Alexis de Tocqueville, *On the Penitentiary System in the United States* (Philadelphia: Carey, Lea & Blanchard, 1833), p. 49.
10. Walker, *Popular Justice*, p. 70.
11. Larry Goldsmith, "History from the Inside Out: Prison Life in Nineteenth-Century Massachusetts," *Journal of Social History* 31 (1997): 109–136.
12. Edna Erez and Pamela Tontodonato, "The Effect of Victim Participation in Sentencing

on Sentencing Outcome," *Criminology* 28 (1990): 451–474.
13. Kriss Drass and J. William Spencer, "Accounting for Presentencing Recommendations: Typologies and Probation Officers' Theory of Office," *Social Problems* 34 (1987): 277–293.
14. Kenneth Culp Davis, *Discretionary Justice: A Preliminary Inquiry* (Baton Rouge: Louisiana State University Press, 1969).
15. See Marvin Frankel, *Criminal Sentences—Law Without Order* (New York: Hill and Wang, 1972), p. 5.
16. Thomas Marvell and Carlisle Moody, "Determinate Sentencing and Abolishing Parole: The Long-Term Impacts on Prisons and Crime," *Criminology* 34 (1996): 105–128.
17. Jo Dixon, "The Organizational Context of Criminal Sentencing," *American Journal of Sociology* 100 (1995): 1,157–1,198.

18. Michael Tonry, *The Fragmentation of Sentencing and Corrections in America* (Washington, DC: National Institute of Justice, 1999).

19. Ibid., p. 11.

20. *Blakely v. Washington*, 124 S.Ct. 2531 (2004); *United States v. Booker*, No. 04-104 (2005).

21. United States Sentencing Commission, "Final Report on the Impact of *United States v. Booker* on Federal Sentencing," March 2006, www.ussc.gov/booker_report/ Booker_Report.pdf (accessed April 27, 2007).

22. Michael Tonry, *Sentencing Reform Impacts* (Washington, DC: U.S. Government Printing Office, 1987), pp. 26–27.

23. This section is based on Paula M. Ditton and Doris James Wilson, *Truth in Sentencing in State Prisons* (Washington, DC: Bureau of Justice Statistics, 1999).

24. Pub.L. No. 103-322, 108 Stat. 1796 (1994).

25. Ditton and Wilson, *Truth in Sentencing in State Prisons*.

26. Michael Tonry, "Parochialism in U.S. Sentencing Policy," *Crime and Delinquency* 45 (1999): 48–65.

27. Tomislav Kovandzic, "The Impact of Florida's Habitual Offender Law on Crime," *Criminology* 39 (2001): 179–204.

28. *Lockyer v. Andrade*, 538 U.S. 63 (2003) 270 F.3d 743; *Ewing v. California*, 538 U.S. 11 (2003).

29. Bureau of Justice Statistics, "Criminal Sentencing Statistics, 2007," www.ojp.usdoj. gov/bjs/sent.htm (accessed April 27, 2007).

30. Brent Smith and Kelly Damphouse, "Terrorism, Politics, and Punishment: A Test of Structural-Contextual Theory and the 'Liberation Hypothesis,'" *Criminology* 36 (1998): 67–92.

31. For a general review of this issue, see Florence Ferguson, "Sentencing Guidelines: Are (Black) Offenders Given Just Treatment?" paper presented at the annual meeting of the American Society of Criminology, Montreal, November 1987.

32. Alfred Blumstein, "On the Racial Disproportionality of the United States Prison Population," *Journal of Criminal Law and Criminology* 73 (1982): 1,259–1,281; Darnell Hawkins, "Race, Crime Type, and Imprisonment," *Justice Quarterly* 3 (1986): 251–269; Martha Myers, "Offended Parties and Official Reactions: Victims and the Sentencing of Criminal Defendants," *Sociological Quarterly* 20 (1979): 529–540.

33. Raymond Paternoster, "Race of the Victim and Location of the Crime: The Decision to Seek the Death Penalty in South Carolina," *Journal of Criminal Law and Criminology* 74 (1983): 754–785.

34. For more on this issue, read Hugo Adam Bedau and Paul Cassell, *Debating the Death Penalty: Should America Have Capital Punishment? The Experts on Both Sides Make Their Best Case* (London, Oxford University Press, 2003).

35. Dennis Wiechman, Jerry Kendall, and Ronald Bae, "International Use of the Death Penalty," *International Journal of Comparative and Applied Criminal Justice* 14 (1990): 239–259.

36. Marilyn Peterson Amour and Mark Umbreit, "Exploring 'Closure' and the Ultimate Penal Sanction for Survivors of Homicide Victims," *Federal Sentencing Reporter* 19 (2006): 105–112.

37. Lisa Stolzenberg and Stewart D'Alessio, "Capital Punishment, Execution Publicity, and Murder in Houston, Texas," *Journal of Criminal Law and Criminology* 94 (2004): 351–380.

38. Steven Messner and Kenneth Tardiff, "Economic Inequality and Level of Homicide: An Analysis of Urban Neighborhoods," *Criminology* 24 (1986): 297–317.

39. William Bowers and Glenn Pierce, "Deterrence or Brutalization: What Is the Effect of Executions?" *Crime and Delinquency* 26 (1980): 453–484.

40. John Cochran, Mitchell Chamlin, and Mark Seth, "Deterrence or Brutalization? An Impact Assessment of Oklahoma's Return to Capital Punishment," *Criminology* 32 (1994): 107–134.

41. William Bailey, "Deterrence, Brutalization, and the Death Penalty: Another Examination of Oklahoma's Return to Capital Punishment," *Justice Quarterly* 36 (1998): 711–734.

42. Marian Borg, "The Southern Subculture of Punitiveness? Regional Variation in Support for Capital Punishment," *Journal of Research in Crime and Delinquency* 34 (1997): 24–45.

43. Marian Williams and Jefferson Holcomb, "Racial Disparity and Death Sentences in Ohio," *Journal of Criminal Justice* 29 (2001): 207–218.

44. Jon Sorenson and Donald Wallace, "Prosecutorial Discretion in Seeking Death: An Analysis of Racial Disparity in the Pretrial Stages of Case Processing in a Midwestern County," *Justice Quarterly* 16 (1999): 559–578.

45. Geoffrey Rapp, "The Economics of Shootouts: Does the Passage of Capital Punishment Laws Protect or Endanger Police Officers?" *Albany Law Review* 65 (2002): 1,051–1,084.

46. See, for example, Ernest Van Den Haag, *Punishing Criminals: Concerning a Very Old and Painful Question* (New York: Basic Books, 1975), pp. 209–211; Walter Berns, "Defending the Death Penalty," *Crime and Delinquency* 26 (1980): 503–511.

47. Thoroddur Bjarnason and Michael Welch, "Father Knows Best: Parishes, Priests, and American Catholic Parishioners' Attitudes Toward Capital Punishment," *Journal for the Scientific Study of Religion* 43 (2004): 103–118.

48. Franklin Zimring, *The Contradictions of American Capital Punishment* (London: Oxford University Press, 2003).

49. Vance McLaughlin and Paul Blackman, "Mass Legal Executions in Georgia," *Georgia Historical Quarterly* 88 (2004): 66–84.

50. James Unnever and Francis Cullen, "Reassessing the Racial Divide in Support for Capital Punishment: The Continuing Significance of Race," *Journal of Research in Crime and Delinquency* 44 (2007): 124–158.

51. James Unnever, Francis Cullen, and John Bartkowski, "Images of God and Public Support for Capital Punishment: Does a Close Relationship with a Loving God Matter?" *Criminology* 44 (2006): 835–866.

52. James Unnever and Francis Cullen, "The Racial Divide in Support for the Death Penalty: Does White Racism Matter?" *Social Forces* 85 (2007): 1,281–1,301.

53. Denise Paquette Boots, Kathleen Heide, and John Cochran, "Death Penalty Support for Special Offender Populations of Legally Convicted Murderers: Juveniles, the Mentally Retarded, and the Mentally Incompetent," *Behavioral Sciences and the Law* 22 (2004): 223–238.

54. Norman Finkel and Stefanie Smith, "Principals and Accessories in Capital Felony-Murder: The Proportionality Principle Reigns Supreme," *Law and Society Review* 27 (1993): 129–146.

55. Marla Sandys and Edmund McGarrell, "Attitudes Toward Capital Punishment: Preference for the Penalty or Mere Acceptance?" *Journal of Research in Crime and Delinquency* 32 (1995): 191–213.

56. *Kelly v. South Carolina*, 534 U.S. 246 (2002).

57. James Marquart and Jonathan Sorensen, "Institutional and Postrelease Behavior of Furman-Commuted Inmates in Texas," *Justice Quarterly* 26 (1988): 677–693.

58. Kilman Shin, *Death Penalty and Crime* (Fairfax, VA: George Mason University, 1978), p. 1.

59. "Illinois Ex-Prosecutors Charged with Framing Murder Defendants," *Criminal Justice Newsletter* 28 (2 January 1997): 3.

60. Michael Radelet and Hugo Bedeau, "Miscarriages of Justice in Potentially Capital Cases," *Stanford Law Review* 40 (1987): 121–181. For an opposing view, see Stephen Markman and Paul Cassell, "Protecting the Innocent: A Response to the Bedeau-Radelet Study," *Stanford Law Review* 41 (1988): 121–170; for their response, see Hugo Adam Bedeau and Michael Radelet, "The Myth of Infallibility: A Reply to Markman and Cassell," *Stanford Law Review* 42 (1988): 161–170.

61. Richard Berk, Robert Weiss, and Jack Boger, "Chance and the Death Penalty," *Law and Society Review* 27 (1993): 89–108. For an opposing view, see Raymond Paternoster, "Assessing Capriciousness in Capital Cases," *Law and Society Review* 27 (1993): 111–122.

62. William Bowers and Glenn Pierce, "Deterrence or Brutalization: What Is the Effect of Executions?" *Crime and Delinquency* 26 (1980): 453–484.

secondary prevention programs Treatment programs aimed at helping offenders after they have been identified.

second-degree murder A homicide with malice but not premeditation or deliberation, as when a desire to inflict serious bodily harm and a wanton disregard for life result in the victim's death.

selective incapacitation The policy of creating enhanced prison sentences for the relatively small group of dangerous chronic offenders.

self-control A strong moral sense that renders a person incapable of hurting others or violating social norms.

self-control theory According to Gottfredson and Hirschi, the view that the cause of delinquent behavior is an impulsive personality. Kids who are impulsive may find that their bond to society is weak.

self-report survey A research approach that requires subjects to reveal their own participation in delinquent or criminal acts.

semiotics The use of language elements as signs or symbols beyond their literal meaning.

sentencing circle A peacemaking technique in which offenders, victims, and other community members are brought together in an effort to formulate a sanction that addresses the needs of all.

sentencing disparity People convicted of similar criminal acts may receive widely different sentences.

sentencing guidelines Guidelines to control and structure the sentencing process and make it more rational; the more serious the crime and the more extensive the offender's criminal background, the longer the prison term recommended by the guidelines.

serial murder The killing of a large number of people over time by an offender who seeks to escape detection.

serial rape Multiple rapes committed by one person over time.

sexual abuse Exploitation of a child through rape, incest, or molestation by a parent or other adult.

sexual predator law Law that allows authorities to keep some criminals convicted of sexually violent crimes in custody even after their sentences are served.

shame The feeling we get when we don't meet the standards we have set for ourselves or that significant others have set for us.

sheriff The chief law enforcement officer in a county.

Sherman Antitrust Act Law that subjects to criminal or civil sanctions any person "who shall make any contract or engage in any combination or conspiracy" in restraint of interstate commerce.

shield laws Laws designed to protect rape victims by prohibiting the defense attorney from inquiring about their previous sexual relationships.

shire Counties in England and much of Europe in the eleventh century.

shock incarceration A short prison sentence served in boot camp–type facilities.

shock probation A sentence in which offenders serve a short prison term to impress them with the pains of imprisonment before they begin probation.

shoplifting The taking of goods from retail stores.

siblicide Sibling homicide. The median age of sibling homicide offenders is 23, and the median age of their victims is 25. The vast majority of sibling homicide offenders are males (87 percent), and they are most likely to kill their brothers. When lethal violence by brothers against their sisters occurs, it is more likely in juvenile sibling relationships rather than adult sibling relationships (31 percent versus 14 percent). Sisters killing their brothers or sisters are relatively rare events.

siege mentality Residents who become so suspicious of authority that they consider the outside world to be the enemy out to destroy the neighborhood.

situational crime prevention A method of crime prevention that stresses tactics and strategies to eliminate or reduce particular crimes in narrow settings, such as reducing burglaries in a housing project by increasing lighting and installing security alarms.

situational inducement Short-term influence on a person's behavior, such as financial problems or peer pressure, that increases risk taking.

skeezers Prostitutes who trade sex for drugs, usually crack.

skilled thieves Thieves who typically work in the larger cities, such as London and Paris. This group includes pickpockets, forgers, and counterfeiters, who operated freely.

skip tracer An individual hired by the bonding agent to track down a fugitive in order to recover the lost bond. These modern bounty hunters receive a share of the recovery, and unlike police, bounty hunters can enter a suspect's home without a warrant in most states; also called a recovery agent.

smugglers Thieves who move freely in sparsely populated areas and transport goods, such as spirits, gems, gold, and spices, without bothering to pay tax or duty.

snitches Amateur shoplifters who do not self-identify as thieves but who systematically steal merchandise for personal use.

social altruism Voluntary mutual support systems, such as neighborhood associations and self-help groups, that reinforce moral and social obligations.

social bond Ties a person has to the institutions and processes of society. According to Hirschi, elements of the social bond include commitment, attachment, involvement, and belief.

social capital Positive relations with individuals and institutions that are life sustaining.

social code The unwritten prison guidelines that express the values, attitudes, and types of behavior older inmates demand of younger inmates. Passed on from one generation of inmates to another, the inmate social code represents the values of interpersonal relations within the prison.

social conflict theory The view that crime is a function of class conflict and power relations. Laws are created and enforced by those in power to protect their own interests.

social control function The ability of society and its institutions to control, manage, restrain, or direct human behavior.

social control theory The view that people commit crime when the forces that bind them to society are weakened or broken.

social development model (SDM) A developmental theory that attributes criminal behavior patterns to childhood socialization and pro- or antisocial attachments over the life course.

social disorganization theory Branch of social structure theory that focuses on the breakdown of institutions such as the family, school, and employment in inner-city neighborhoods.

social ecologists Criminologists who study the ecological conditions that support criminality.

social ecology Environmental forces that have a direct influence on human behavior.

social harm A view that behaviors harmful to other people and society in general must be controlled. These acts are usually outlawed, but some acts that cause enormous amounts of social harm are perfectly legal, such as the consumption of tobacco and alcohol.

socialization Process of human development and enculturation. Socialization is influenced by key social processes and institutions.

socialization view One view is that people learn criminal attitudes from older, more experienced law violators. Another view is that crime occurs when children develop an inadequate self-image, which renders them incapable of controlling their own misbehavior. Both of these views link criminality to the failure of socialization, the interactions people have with the various individuals, organizations, institutions, and processes of society that help them mature and develop.

social learning theory The view that human behavior is modeled through observation of human social interactions, either directly from observing those who are close and from intimate contact, or indirectly through the media. Interactions that are rewarded are copied, while those that are punished are avoided.

social process theory The view that criminality is a function of people's interactions with various organizations, institutions, and processes in society.

social psychology The study of human interactions and relationships, emphasizing such issues as group dynamics and socialization.

social reaction theory The view that people become criminals when significant members of society label them as such and they accept those labels as a personal identity. Also known as labeling theory.

social reality of crime The view that the main purpose of criminology is to promote a peaceful, just society.

social structure theory The view that disadvantaged economic class position is a primary cause of crime.

sodomy Illegal sexual intercourse. Sodomy has no single definition, and acts included within its scope are usually defined by state statute.

somatotype A system developed for categorizing people on the basis of their body build.

specific deterrence A crime control policy suggesting that punishment be severe enough to convince convicted offenders never to repeat their criminal activity.

spam An unsolicited advertisement or promotional material, typically in the form of an unwanted e-mail message. While e-mail is the most common form of spam, it can also be sent via instant messaging, Usenet newsgroup, and mobile phone messaging, among other media.

split sentencing A jail term is part of the sentence and is a condition of probation.

stalking A pattern of behavior directed at a specific person that includes repeated physical or visual proximity, unwanted communications, and/or threats sufficient to cause fear in a reasonable person.

stalking statutes Laws that prohibit "the willful, malicious, and repeated following and harassing of another person."

state account system Prisoners produce goods in prison for state use.

state police A law enforcement agency with statewide jurisdiction; the major role of state police is controlling traffic on the highway system, tracing stolen automobiles, and aiding in disturbances and crowd control.

state political crime Political crime that arises from the efforts of the state to either maintain governmental power or to uphold the race, class, and gender advantages of those who support the government. It is possible to divide state political crimes into five varieties: (1) political corruption, (2) illegal domestic surveillance, (3) human rights violations, (4) state violence such as torture, illegal imprisonment, police violence and use of deadly force, and (5) state-corporate crime committed by individuals who abuse their state authority or who fail to exercise it when working with people and organizations in the private sector.

state-sponsored terror Terrorism that occurs when a repressive government regime forces its citizens into obedience, oppresses minorities, and stifles political dissent.

status frustration A form of culture conflict experienced by lower-class youths because social conditions prevent them from achieving success as defined by the larger society.

statutory crimes Crimes defined by legislative bodies in response to changing social conditions, public opinion, and custom.

statutory rape Sexual relations between an underage individual and an adult; though not coerced, an underage partner is considered incapable of giving informed consent.

stigma An enduring label that taints a person's identity and changes him or her in the eyes of others.

stigmatize To apply negative labeling with enduring effects on a person's self-image and social interactions.

sting An undercover police operation in which police pose as criminals to trap law violators.

sting or swindle A white-collar crime in which people use their institutional or business position to trick others out of their money.

strain The emotional turmoil and conflict caused when people believe they cannot achieve their desires and goals through legitimate means. Members of the lower class might feel strain because they are denied access to adequate educational opportunities and social support.

strain theorists Criminologists who view crime as a direct result of lower-class frustration and anger.

strain theory Branch of social structure theory that sees crime as a function of the conflict between people's goals and the means available to obtain them.

stratified society Grouping according to social strata or levels. American society is considered stratified on the basis of economic class and wealth.

street crime Common theft-related offenses such as larcenies and burglaries, embezzlement, and theft by false pretenses.

street efficacy A concept in which more cohesive communities with high levels of social control and social integration foster the ability for kids to use their wits to avoid violent confrontations and to feel safe in their own neighborhood. Adolescents with high levels of street efficacy are less likely to resort to violence themselves or to associate with delinquent peers.

strict liability crimes Illegal acts whose elements do not contain the need for intent, or *mens rea*; they are usually acts that endanger the public welfare, such as illegal dumping of toxic wastes.

structural theory The view that criminal law and the criminal justice system are means of defending and preserving the capitalist system.

subculture A group that is loosely part of the dominant culture but maintains a unique set of values, beliefs, and traditions.

subculture of violence Norms and customs that, in contrast to society's dominant value system, legitimize and expect the use of violence to resolve social conflicts.

submission Passive obedience to the demands of others, such as submitting to physical or sexual abuse without response.

substantive criminal law A body of specific rules that declare what conduct is criminal and prescribe the punishment to be imposed for such conduct.

subterranean values Morally tinged influences that have become entrenched in the culture but are publicly condemned. They exist side by side with conventional values and while condemned in public may be admired or practiced in private.

sufferance The aggrieved party does nothing to rectify a conflict situation; over time, the unresolved conflict may be compounded by other events that cause an eventual eruption.

suitable target According to routine activities theory, a target for crime that is relatively valuable, easily transportable, and not capably guarded.

superego Incorporation within the personality of the moral standards and values of parents, community, and significant others.

supermax prison An enhanced high-security facility that houses the most dangerous felons in almost total isolation. Also called ultra-max prison.

surety bond The 10 percent the defendant pays to the bonding agent, which serves as the bonding agent's commission.

surplus value The Marxist view that the laboring classes produce wealth that far exceeds their wages and goes to the capitalist class as profits.

surrogate family A common form of adaptation to prison employed by women, this group contains masculine and feminine figures acting as fathers and mothers; some even act as children and take on the role of either brother or sister. Formalized marriages and divorces may be conducted. Sometimes multiple roles are held by one inmate, so that a "sister" in one family may "marry" and become the "wife" in another.

symbolic interaction theory The sociological view that people communicate through symbols. People interpret symbolic communication and incorporate it within their personality. A person's view of reality, then, depends on his or her interpretation of symbolic gestures.

synthesis A merger of two opposing ideas.

systematic forgers Professionals who make a living by passing bad checks.

systematic review A research technique that involves collecting the findings from previously conducted studies, appraising and synthesizing the evidence, and using the collective evidence to address a particular scientific question.

target-hardening strategies Making one's home or business crime proof through the use of locks, bars, alarms, and other devices.

target-removal strategies Displaying dummy or disabled goods as a means of preventing shoplifting.

technical violation Revocation of parole because conditions set by correctional authorities have been violated.

temperance movement An effort to prohibit the sale of liquor in the United States that resulted in the passage of the Eighteenth Amendment to the Constitution in 1919, which prohibited the sale of alcoholic beverages.

terror cells Divisions of terrorist group affiliates, each of which may be functionally independent so that each member has little knowledge of other cells, their members,

locations, and so on. The number of cells and their composition depend on the size of the terrorist group. Local or national groups will have fewer cells than international terrorist groups that may operate in several countries, such as the al-Qaeda group.

terrorism The illegal use of force against innocent people to achieve a political objective.

terrorist group Any group practicing, or that has significant subgroups that practice, international terrorism.

tertiary prevention programs Crime control and prevention programs that may be a requirement of a probation order, part of a diversionary sentence, or aftercare at the end of a prison sentence.

testosterone The principal male steroid hormone. Testosterone levels decline during the life cycle and may explain why violence rates diminish over time.

thanatos According to Freud, the instinctual drive toward aggression and violence.

theory of anomie A modified version of the concept of anomie developed by Merton to fit social, economic, and cultural conditions found in modern U.S. society. He found that two elements of culture interact to produce potentially anomic conditions: culturally defined goals and socially approved means for obtaining them.

therapeutic communities (TCs) A treatment approach using a psychosocial, experiential learning process that relies on positive peer pressure within a highly structured social environment.

thesis In the philosophy of Hegel, an original idea or thought.

three strikes Policies whereby people convicted of three felony offenses receive a mandatory life sentence.

thrill-seeking hate crimes Acts by hate-mongers who join forces to have fun by bashing minorities or destroying property; inflicting pain on others gives them a sadistic thrill.

ticking bomb scenario A scenario that some experts argue in which torture can perhaps be justified if the government discovers that a captured terrorist knows the whereabouts of a dangerous explosive device that is set to go off and kill thousands of innocent people.

tithing During the Middle Ages, groups of about ten families who were responsible for maintaining order among themselves and dealing with disturbances, fires, wild animals, and so on.

torture An act that causes severe pain or suffering, whether physical or mental, that

is intentionally inflicted on a person for such purposes as obtaining a confession, punishing them for a crime they may have committed, or intimidating or coercing them into a desired action.

trait theory The view that criminality is a product of abnormal biological and/or psychological traits.

transitional neighborhood An area undergoing a shift in population and structure, usually from middle-class residential to lower-class mixed use.

treason An act of disloyalty to one's nation or state.

Trojan horse A computer program that looks like a benign application but contains illicit codes that can damage the system operations. Though Trojan horses do not replicate themselves like viruses, they can be just as destructive.

truly disadvantaged Wilson's term for the lowest level of the underclass; urban, inner-city, socially isolated people who occupy the bottom rung of the social ladder and are the victims of discrimination.

truth-in-sentencing laws Laws that require offenders to serve a substantial portion of their prison sentence behind bars.

turning points According to Laub and Sampson, the life events that alter the development of a criminal career.

tying arrangement A corporation requires customers of one of its services to use other services it offers.

underclass The lowest social stratum in any country, whose members lack the education and skills needed to function successfully in modern society.

Uniform Crime Report (UCR) Large database, compiled by the Federal Bureau of Investigation, of crimes reported and arrests made each year throughout the United States.

USA Patriot Act (USAPA) Legislation giving U.S. law enforcement agencies a freer hand to investigate and apprehend suspected terrorists.

U.S. district courts Trial courts that have jurisdiction over cases involving violations of federal law, such as interstate transportation of stolen vehicles and racketeering.

U.S. marshals Court officers who help implement federal court rulings, transport prisoners, and enforce court orders.

U.S. Supreme Court The court of last resort for all cases tried in the various federal and state courts.

utilitarianism The view that people's behavior is motivated by the pursuit of pleasure and the avoidance of pain.

venire The group called for jury duty from which jury panels are selected.

viatical investments The selling of a death benefit policy, at less than face value, by a terminally ill person to a third party.

vice squad Police officers assigned to enforce morally tinged laws, such as those governing prostitution, gambling, and pornography.

victim compensation The victim ordinarily receives compensation from the state to pay for damages associated with the crime. Rarely are two compensation schemes alike, however, and many state programs suffer from lack of both adequate funding and proper organization within the criminal justice system. Compensation may be made for medical bills, loss of wages, loss of future earnings, and counseling. In the case of death, the victim's survivors can receive burial expenses and aid for loss of support.

victimization (by the justice system) While the crime is still fresh in their minds, victims may find that the police interrogation following the crime is handled callously, with innuendos or insinuations that they were somehow at fault. Victims have difficulty learning what is going on in the case; property is often kept for a long time as evidence and may never be returned. Some rape victims report that the treatment they receive from legal, medical, and mental health services is so destructive that they cannot help but feel "re-raped."

victimization survey A statistical survey (such as the NCVS) that measures the amount, nature, and patterns of victimization in the population.

victimless crimes Crimes that violate the moral order but in which there is no actual victim or target. In these crimes, which include drug abuse and sex offenses, it is society as a whole and not an individual who is considered the victim.

victimologist A person who studies the victim's role in criminal transactions.

victim precipitation theory The idea that the victim's behavior was the spark that ignited the subsequent offense, as when the victim abused the offender verbally or physically.

victim-witness assistance programs Government programs that help crime victims and witnesses; may include compensation, court services, and/or crisis intervention.

vigilantes Individuals who go on moral crusades without any authorization from legal authorities. The assumption is that it is okay to take matters into your own hands if the cause is right and the target is immoral.

violentization process According to Lonnie Athens, the process by which abused children are turned into aggressive adults. This process takes violent youths full circle from being the victims of aggression to its initiators; they are now the same person they grew up despising, ready to begin the process with their own children.

virility mystique The belief that males must separate their sexual feelings from needs for love, respect, and affection.

voir dire The process in which a potential jury panel is questioned by the prosecution and the defense to select jurors who are unbiased and objective.

voluntary manslaughter A homicide committed in the heat of passion or during a sudden quarrel; although intent may be present, malice is not.

Walnut Street Jail At this institution, most prisoners were placed in solitary cells, where they remained in isolation and did not have the right to work.

warez A term computer hackers and software pirates use to describe a game or application that is made available for use on the Internet in violation of its copyright protection.

watch system In medieval England, men organized in church parishes to guard against disturbances and breaches of the peace at night; they were under the direction of the local constable.

website defacement A type of cyber vandalism that occurs when a computer hacker intrudes on another person's website by inserting or substituting codes that expose visitors to the site to misleading or provocative information. Defacement can range from installing humorous graffiti to sabotaging or corrupting the site.

Wechsler Adult Intelligence Scale One of the standard IQ tests.

Wernicke-Korsakoff disease A deadly neurological disorder.

white-collar crime Illegal acts that capitalize on a person's status in the marketplace. White-collar crimes can involve theft, embezzlement, fraud, market manipulation, restraint of trade, and false advertising.

Wickersham Commission Created in 1931 by President Herbert Hoover to investigate the state of the nation's police forces, a commission that found police training to be inadequate and the average officer incapable of effectively carrying out his duties.

workplace violence Irate employees or former employees attack coworkers or sabotage machinery and production lines; now considered the third leading cause of occupational injury or death.

writ of certiorari An order of a superior court requesting that the record of an inferior court (or administrative body) be brought forward for review or inspection.

zealot The original Zealots were Hebrew warrior groups active during the Roman occupation of Palestine during the first century BCE. Today the term commonly refers to a fanatical or over-idealistic follower of a political or religious cause.

CASE INDEX

Abbate v. U.S.
   359 U.S. 187 (1959), 523 n.164
Alabama v. Shelton
   122 U.S. 1764 (2002), 517
Alberts v. California
   354 U.S. 476 (1957), 415
Apodica v. Oregon
   406 U.S. 404 (1972), 517
Argersinger v. Hamlin
   407 U.S. 25 (1972), 517, 522 n.108
Arizona v. Fulminante
   499 U.S. 279, 111 S.Ct. 1246; 113
   L.Ed.2d 302 (1991), 521 n.49
Arizona v. Hicks
   107 S.Ct. 1149 (1987), 522 n.68
Atkins v. Virginia
   No. 00-8452 (2002), 539
Atwater v. Lago Vista
   532 U.S. 318 (2001), 493
Baldwin v. New York
   399 U.S. 66 (1970), 516
Barker v. Wingo
   404 U.S. 307 (1971), 516
Bartkus v. Illinois
   359 U.S. 121 (1959), 523 n.164
Batson v. Kentucky
   476 U.S. 79 (1986), 514
Benton v. Maryland
   395 U.S. 784 (1969), 517
Blakely v. Washington
   124 S.Ct. 2531 (2004), 530, 532
Blanton v. City of North Las Vegas
   489 U.S. 538, 109 S.Ct. 1289, 103
   L.Ed.2d 550 (1989), 516
Brigham City v. Stuart
   No. 05-502, 518
Bumper v. North Carolina
   391 U.S. 543 (1960), 522 n.63
Carpenter v. United States
   484 U.S. 19 (1987), 397 n.35
Carroll v. United States
   267 U.S. 132 (1925), 522 n.58
Chavez v. Martinez
   No. 01-1444 (May 27, 2003), 521 n.51
Chimel v. California
   395 U.S. 752 (1969), 522 n.57
Coker v. Georgia
   430 U.S. 349, 97 S.Ct. 1197, 51
   L.Ed.2d 393 (1977), 560 n.65
Colorado v. Connelly
   107 S.Ct. 515 (1986), 521 nn.45, 47
Colorado v. Spring
   107 S.Ct. 851 (1987), 521 n.44
Davis v. United States
   114 S.Ct. 2350 (1994), 521 n.50
Dickerson v. United States
   530 U.S. 428 (2000), 495

Duncan v. Louisiana
   391 U.S. 145 (1968), 516, 523 n.158
Estelle v. Gamble
   429 U.S. 97 (1976), 553
Ewing v. California
   538 U.S. 11 (2003), 559 n.28
Fare v. Michael C.
   442 U.S. 23 (1979), 521 n.39
Ford v. Wainwright
   477 U.S. 399 (1986), 560 n.66
Furman v. Georgia
   408 U.S. 238, 92 S.Ct. 2726, 33
   L.Ed.2d 346 (1972), 563 n.189
Gagnon v. Scarpelli
   411 U.S. 778, 93 S.Ct. 1756, 36
   L.Ed.2d 656 (1973), 540
Georgia v. Randolph
   No. 04-1067 (2006), 496
Gideon v. Wainwright
   372 U.S. 335 (1963), 517, 522 n.108
Gregg v. Georgia
   428 U.S. 153, 96 S.Ct. 2909, 49
   L.Ed.2d 859 (1976), 560 n.64
Ham v. South Carolina
   409 U.S. 524, 93 S.Ct. 848, 35
   L.Ed.2d 46 (1973), 514
Harris v. New York
   401 U.S. 222 (1971), 521 n.37
Heath v. Alabama
   106 S.Ct. 433 (1985), 517
*Hillary Goodridge et al. v. Department of
   Public and Another*
   SJC -08860, November 18, 2003, 433
   n.28
Hope v. Pelzer
   No. 01-309, June 27, 2002, 553
House v. Bell
   No. 04-8990, 547 U.S. (2006), 518
Hudson v. Michigan
   No. 04-1360 (2006), 485, 486
*Illinois Ex Rel. Madigan v. Telemarketing
   Associates*
   No. 01-1806 (2003), 384
In re Gault
   87 U.S. 1, 87 S.Ct. 1428, 18 L.Ed.2d
   527 (1967), 472
Katz v. United States
   389 U.S. 347 (1967), 522 n.69
Kelly v. South Carolina
   No. 00-9280 (2002), 537
Kirk v. Louisiana
   No. 01-8419 (June 24, 2002), 496
Lawrence v. Texas
   No. 02-102 (June 26, 2003), 22, 405
Lee v. Tahash
   352 F.2d 970 (3th Cir., 1965), 563
   n.191

Lewis v. Casey
   93.1511 (1996), 563 n.183
Lockyer v. Andrade
   538 U.S. 63 (2003) 270 F.3d 743,
   532
Maryland v. Craig
   110 S.Ct. 3157, 111 L.Ed.2d 666
   (1990), 517
Maryland v. Wilson
   117 U.S. 882 (1997), 522 n.61
Memoirs v. Massachusetts
   383 U.S. 413 (1966), 415
MGM Studios, Inc. v. Grokster
   125 S.Ct. 2764 (2005), 442–443
Michigan v. Lucas
   90-194 (1991), 295
Michigan v. Mosley
   423 U.S. 96 (1975), 521 n.39
Michigan v. Tucker
   417 U.S. 433 (1974), 521 n.38
Miller v. California
   413 U.S. 15 (1973), 415
Minnick v. Miss.
   498 U.S. 46; 111 S.Ct. 486; 112
   L.Ed.2d 489 (1990), 521 n.48
Miranda v. Arizona
   384 U.S. 436 (1966), 494, 495
Missouri v. Seibert
   No. 02–1371 (2004), 521 n.43
Moran v. Burbine
   106 S.Ct. 1135 (1986), 521 nn.39, 46
New Jersey v. Timmendequas
   161 N.J. 515, 356-44 (1999), 82
Newman v. Alabama
   349 F.Supp. 278 (M.D.Ala., 1974),
   563 n.186
New York v. Quarles
   104 S.Ct. 2626 (1984), 521 n.41
Nix v. Whiteside
   106 S.Ct. 988 (1986), 505
Nix v. Williams
   104 S.Ct. 2501 (1984), 521 n.40
Northern Pacific Railways v. United States
   356 U.S. 1 (1958), 398 n.73
Ohio v. Robinette
   117 S.Ct. 417 (1996), 522 n.64
Oregon v. Elstad
   105 S.Ct. 1285 (1985), 521 n.42
Payne v. Tennessee
   111 S.Ct. 2597, 115 L.Ed.2d 720
   (1991), 87 n.116
Pennsylvania v. Mimms
   434 U.S. 106 (1977), 522 n.61
Pope v. Illinois
   481 U.S. 497 (1987), 415, 416
Powell v. Alabama
   287 U.S. 45 (1932), 517

Procunier v. Martinez
    416 U.S. 396 (1974), 553
Rhodes v. Chapman
    452 U.S. 337 (1981), 553
Richmond Newspapers Inc. v. Commonwealth
    of Virginia
    448 U.S. 555, 100 S.Ct. 2814, 65
    L.Ed.2d 1 (1980), 517
Riggins v. Nevada
    504 U.S. 127 (1992), 517
Ristaino v. Ross
    424 U.S. 589 (1976), 523 n.154
Riverside County v. McLaughlin
    384 U.S. 436 (1966), 493
Roe v. Wade
    314 F.Supp. 1217 (1973), 410 U.S.
    113, 40
Roper v. Simmons
    No. 03-0633 (2005), 539
Roth v. United States
    354 U.S. 476 (1957), 415
Saxbe v. Washington Post
    41 L.Ed.2d 514 (1974), 553

Strunk v. United States
    412 U.S. 434 (1973), 523 n.156
Taylor v. Louisiana
    419 U.S. 522, 42 L.Ed.2d 690, 95
    S.Ct. 692 (1975), 514
Terry v. Ohio
    392 U.S. 1 (1968), 522 n.56
Trop v. Dulles
    356 U.S. 86, 78 S.Ct. 590 (1958),
    563 n.189
Turner v. Murray
    106 S.Ct. 1683 (1986), 514
United States v. Bishop
    412 U.S. 346 (1973), 398 n.65
United States v. Booker
    No. 04-104 (2005), 530, 532
United States v. Holy Land Foundation for Re-
    lief and Development Criminal Action
    No. 3:04-CR-240-G, 462 n.68
United States v. Lanza
    260 U.S. 377 (1922), 523 n.164
United States v. Matlock
    415 U.S. 164 (1974), 495–496

United States v. Miller
    307 U.S. 174 (1939), 48
United States v. Patane
    No. 02-1183 (2004), 521 n.52
United States v. Ross
    102 S.Ct. 2147 (1982), 522 n.59
United States v. 12200-ft Reels of Super
    8mm Film
    413 U.S. 123 (1973), 432 n.10
Virginia v. Black
    No. 01-1107 (2003), 308
Weems v. United States
    217 U.S. 349, 30 S.Ct. 544, 54 L.Ed.
    793 (1910), 563 n.190
Whitner v. State
    Supreme Court of South Carolina, Opin-
    ion Number 24468, July 15, 1996, 297
Whren et al. v. U.S.
    No. 95-5841 (1996), 522 n.60
Williams v. Florida
    399 U.S. 78 (1970), 516–517
Young v. American Mini Theaters
    427 U.S. 50 (1976), 415

Aaronson, Robert, 312 n.6
Abbey, Antonia, 312 n.21
Abbott, Robert, 224 n.43; 225 n.53;
  282 n.145
Ablow, Jennifer, 156 n.146
Abrahamse, Allan, 521 n.22
Abram, Karen, 27 n.41
Abramoff, Jack, 377; 377
Abu-Jamal, Mumia, 238; 238
Acierno, Ron, 85 n.27
Ackerman, Jeff, 62 n.107
Adams, Anthony, 313 n.51
Adams, Kenneth, 116 n.96
Adams, Mike, 227 nn.147, 161
Adams-Curtis, Leah, 314 n.89
Adamson, Gary, 84 n.18
Aday, David, 282 n.119
Addington, Lynn, 60 n.16
Addison, Laura, 561 n.124
Addison, Tamara, 414; 434 nn.94, 98
Adler, Alfred, 138
Adler, Freda, 62 n.102
Adler, Howard, 398 n.108
Adler, Nancy, 193 n.92
Ageton, Suzanne, 61 n.70; 227 n.160
Aggleton, John, 156 n.126
Agnew, Robert, 61 n.79; 62 n.87; 178–181;
  185; 190; 194 nn.137, 148, 152, 154,
  156, 162, 165, 171, 174, 219; 220;
  223 n.12; 224 nn.18, 42; 225 n.97;
  226 nn.126, 142; 262; 278; 281 n.95
Agopian, Michael, 561 n.102
Agozino, Biko, 250 nn.15, 22
Ahmed, Eliza, 252 nn.116–117
Ahrens, Courtney, 66–67; 84 n.11
Ahsan, Habibul, 153 n.25
Aichorn, August, 138; 157 n.185
Aiken, Leona, 223 n.6
Aind, R. W., 155 n.89
Ainsworth-Darnell, James, 191 n.9
Ajzen, Icek, 435 n.162
Akagi, H., 153 n.24
Akers, Ronald, 54; 62 n.109; 115 n.29;
  206–207; 225 nn.80–81, 83–84, 86,
  88, 90; 226 n.123; 281 n.107
Akutagawa, Donald, 316 n.177
Alarid, Leanne Fiftal, 62 n.97; 98; 116 n.62
Albert, Alexa, 413; 434 n.92
Albrecht, Steve, 309; 317 n.256
Alexander, Deanna, 251 n.40
Alison, Laurence, 315 n.169; 369 n.102
Allen, Chris, 312 n.15
Allen, Mark, 483 n.24
Allen, Terry, 227 n.167
Allison, Graham, 337; 343 n.62
Allison, Julie, 314 nn.94, 97, 100
Almovist, Frederik, 223 n.9

Alongo, Nicholas, 280 n.35
Alpert, Geoffrey, 119 n.185
Alschuler, Alan, 523 n.142
Altschuler, Andrea, 193 n.92
Altschuler, David, 252–253 n.132; 483 n.39
Alvi, Shahid, 314 nn.107, 114
Amarasiriwardena, Chitra J., 154 n.77
Amato, Paul, 224 n.17
Amendolla, Jean, 85 n.33
Ames, Aldrich Hazen, 323; 325; 325
Ames, Rosario, 325; 325
Amir, Menachem, 73; 85 n.57
Amos, H. E., 154 n.62
Amour, Marilyn Peterson, 560 n.36
Anderson, Bobbi Jo, 226 n.116
Anderson, Craig, 41; 43; 61 n.55; 144
Anderson, Curt, 407
Anderson, Elijah, 170–171; 185;
  192 nn.55, 76
Anderson, Jerry, 84 n.9
Anderson, Karen, 277
Anderson, Kevin B., 252 n.108
Anderson, Linda, 118 n.151
Anderson, Mark, 315 n.166
Anderson, Patrick, 561 n.123
Andrade, Leandro, 532
Andreason, P. J., 155 n.91
Andres, Greg, 394
Andrews, D. A., 157 n.186; 159 n.251; 281
  n.65; 483 n.28; 562–563 n.173
Andrews, Howard, 158 n.204
Andrews, Sara K., 434 n.86
Angell, Jeannette, 115 n.25
Anglin, M. Douglas, 436 nn.192, 185
Angold, Adrian, 158 n.203
Anselin, Luc, 312 n.16; 313 n.47
Anslinger, Harry, 404
Anthony, J. C., 192 n.61
Apospori, Eleni, 119 n.185
Appelbaum, Mark, 153 n.33
Applegate, Brandon, 118 n.171; 483 n.30
Arafat, Yassir, 333
Arcand, Philip, 356
Aristotle, 359
Armstrong, James, 397 n.32
Arndt, Craig, 462 n.97
Arneklev, Bruce J., 118 n.153; 275; 281
  n.102; 282 n.130
Arnold, Sandy, 158 n.202
Arnold, Suzanne, 153 n.22
Arnulf, Isabelle, 153 nn.20, 25
Arrigo, Jean Maria, 342 n.22
Arrillaga, Pauline, 315 n.141, 145
Arrington, Michael, 460–461 n.10
Arseneault, Louise, 156 n.146
Arter, Michael, 60 n.30
Arum, Richard, 63 n.136; 281 n.66

Arvanites, Thomas, 40; 43; 251 n.56
Asigian, Nancy, 72; 85 n.51
Astone, Nan Marie, 224 n.14
Athens, Lonnie, 288; 313 n.40
Atherton, Janet Bond, 348
Atkins, Daryl, 150
Atwater, Gail, 493
Augustine, St., 406
Auletta, Ken, 118 n.158
Austin, James, 115 n.14; 483 n.34
Austin, Roy, 63 n.139; 483 n.24
Avakame, Edem, 85 n.59
Avants, Ernest, 492
Avary, D'Aunn Wester, 115 n.43, 47; 116
  n.57; 363–364; 368 n.24; 369 n.90
Avery, Ginny, 369 n.101
Ayres, Ian, 117 n.105; 369 n.62
Azrael, Deborah, 43; 50

Babcock, Charles R., 397 n.40
Babcock, Ginna, 436 n.200
Bachman, Esther, 498
Bachman, Jerald, 60 nn.21–22; 62 n.111;
  435 nn.132, 157
Badger, Kelly, 314 n.80
Bae, Ronald, 560 n.35
Baek, Jong-Ho, 562 n.128
Baer, D., 435 n.156
Baer, Judith, 159 n.242
Baertlein, Lisa, 315 n.135
Bagli, Charles V., 397 n.38
Baier, Colin, 225 n.58
Bailey, Barbara, 339
Bailey, Carol, 227 n.170
Bailey, R., 563 n.179
Bailey, Susan, 428
Bailey, William, 560 n.41
Baker, Al, 343 n.66
Baker, Debra, 461 n.41
Baker, Stephen, 461 n.15
Balboni, Jennifer, 317 n.247
Bales, William, 227 n.177; 535
Balfour, Gillian, 251 n.80
Bali, J. P., 153 n.29
Ball, Robert A., 225 n.96
Ballard, Danny, 159 n.244, 249, 279
Baller, Robert, 313 n.47
Ballezza, Richard A., 399 n.127
Ballou, Brian R., 227 n.172
Balter, Mitchell, 280 n.34
Ban, Rachel, 156 n.149
Bandura, Albert, 141; 146; 158 n.222
Banville, Richard, 375–376
Bao, Wan-Ning, 194 n.163
Barak, Gregg, 250 nn.20, 23
Barbaree, Howard, 434 n.102
Barber, Nigel, 312 n.13

Bardo, Robert John, 22
Bardsley, Marilyn, 482–483 n.10
Barkan, Steven, 192 n.89
Barkley, Russell, 155 n.106
Barlow, David, 250–251 n.35
Barnes, Grace, 435 n.143
Baron, R. A., 61 n.54
Baron, Stephen W., 194 n.149; 225 n.55
Barr, Kellie, 435 n.143
Barr, Robert, 117 n.106
Barrett, David, 433 n.63; 434 n.73
Barrios, Lisa, 315 n.166
Barrueco, Sandra, 280 n.35
Bartko, J., 155 n.116
Bartkowski, John, 560 n.51
Bartos, Omar, 399 n.128
Bartusch, Dawn Jeglum, 280 n.37
Basciano, Vincent "Vinnie Gorgeous," 394
Basile, Kathleen, 309–310; 317 n.262
Baskin, Deborah, 562 n.152
Baskin-Sommers, Arielle, 14–15; 27 n.38
Bass, Patricia, 119 n.194
Bateman, Alicia, 316 n.180
Bateman, Richard W., 563 nn.199, 206
Bates, John, 193 n.96; 224 n.15; 280 n.45
Bates, William, 435 n.127
Batiuk, Mary Ellen, 562 n.172
Battin, Sara, 224 n.43; 225 n.53
Bauer, John, 316 n.217
Baum, K., 85 n.42
Baum, Katrina, 522 n.80
Baumann, Barbara, 224 n.26
Baumeister, Roy, 314 n.113
Baumer, Eric, 97; 115 n.41; 193 n.99; 313
    n.52; 316 n.218
Baumhover, Lorin, 117 nn.113, 116
Bayer, Ronald, 115 n.10
Bayley, David, 117 n.122
Bazemore, Gordon, 246; 252 nn.129–130
Beach, Laura, 368 n.1
Bean, Lydia, 43
Bearn, Jenny, 437 n.219
Beasley, Shanna, 315 n.147
Beattie, Irenee, 281 n.66
Beaumont, Gustave de, 559 n.9
Beaver, Kevin, 224 n.50; 281 n.99
Beccaria, Cesare, 6; 25; 92; 93; 107;
    113–114
Beck, Allen, 118 n.175; 545; 561 n.91; 561
    n.113; 562 n.162
Beck, Robert, 445
Becker, Howard, 18; 27 n.47; 215; 227
    n.151; 433 n.19
Becker, Jill, 154 n.44
Bedeau, Hugo Adam, 539; 560 nn.34, 60
Bedford, Olwen, 434 n.77
Beech, Anthony, 159 n.247
Behr, Peter, 379
Beichner, Dawn, 314 nn.90, 122; 522 n.102
Beittel, Marc, 109
Belanger, Albert, 434 n.96
Belanger, Erin, 255
Belcher, Anthony, 246
Belfrage, Henrik, 139; 158 n.206
Bell, Paul, 61 n.56
Bell, Rachael, 482–483 n.10

Bellair, Paul, 86 n.81; 99; 116 n.71; 191
    n.22; 192 n.86; 193 nn.100, 104
Bellinger, David, 154 nn.69, 77
Belliston, Lara, 281 n.105
Bellucci, Patricia, 312 n.24
Belluck, Pam, 397 n.28; 398 n.79
Beloof, Douglas E., 87 n.118
Bench, Lawrence, 227 n.167
Benda, Brent, 282 nn.114, 117
Benedict, W. Reed, 561 n.88
Benjamin, David, 461 n.59
Bennett, Brian, 461 n.53
Bennett, Katherine, 483 n.33
Bennett, Neil, 153 n.2
Bennett, Susan, 307; 317 n.233
Benson, Michael, 281 n.106; 398 nn.94,
    103
Bentham, Jeremy, 5; 92; 93; 115 n.6
Berg, Ellen, 433 n.62
Bergaström, Sandra, 434 n.71
Bergen, Raquel Kennedy, 313 n.71
Berk, Richard, 109–110; 119 n.182; 436
    n.208; 560 n.61; 562 n.128
Berkowitz, David ("Son of Sam"), 139; 300
Berliner, Howard, 437 n.220
Bernard, Thomas, 61 n.45; 194 n.175
Bernasco, Wim, 116 n.70; 369 nn.78, 82
Bernburg, Jön Gunnar, 194 n.144; 218;
    227 nn.162, 168, 186
Berner, Wolfgang, 155 n.83; 159 n.259
Berns, Walter, 560 n.46
Bernstein, Elizabeth, 433 n.45
Berroya, A., 153 n.24
Best, Connie, 86 n.100
Best, David, 436 n.186
Beswick, Tracy, 437 n.219
Beucke, Dan, 461 n.30
Beutel, Ann, 62 n.97
Beverlin, Matt, 109
Beyers, Jennifer, 158 n.197; 193 n.96;
    224 n.15; 279 n.7
Bhaskar, Roy, 251 n.44
Bhattacharya, Rina, 343 n.43
Bianchi, Herbert, 483 n.35
Bibas, Stephanos, 523 n.138
Bibel, Daniel, 62 n.106; 157 n.175
Bieneck, Steffen, 313 n.69
Bier, I., 127
Biesecker, Gretchen, 154 n.73
Bihrle, Susan, 155 n.81
Bijleveld, Catrien, 159 n.255
Bilefsky, Dan, 290
Billy the Kid, 466
Bimbi, David S., 436 n.179
Binder, Arnold, 483 n.34
Binder, David, 399 n.126
Bingenheimer, Jeffrey B., 313 n.45
Bin Laden, Osama, 319; 322; 334; 336
Binsfield, Peter, 5
Birkbeck, Chrisophter, 116 n.81
Birmaher, Boris, 157 n.190
Birnbaum, Jean, 292; 314 nn.83, 115
Birt, Angela, 314 n.112
Bistolaki, E., 156 n.119
Bittner, Egon, 522 n.75

Bjarnason, Thoroddur, 560 n.47
Bjerk, David, 191 n.23
Bjerregaard, Beth, 60 n.25; 313 n.56
Black, Donald, 193 n.95
Black, Jim, 530
Blackman, Vance, 560 n.49
Blackstone, E., 369 n.75
Blackwell, Brenda Sims, 118 n.154; 242;
    252 nn.93–94, 101
Blair, James, 157 n.156; 159 n.257
Blair, Tony, 448
Blake, Laurence, 86 n.89; 369 n.77; 521 n.9
Blalock, Hubert, Jr., 63 n.122
Blankenship, Michael, 225 n.99; 398 n.86;
    483 n.30
Blann, Angela, 25
Blanton, Thomas, Jr., 492
Blanton, Zachariah, 145
Blau, Judith, 61 n.76; 193 n.129
Blau, Peter, 61 n.76; 193 n.129
Blickle, Gerhard, 159 n.258
Block, Alan, 399 nn.118–119
Block, Carolyn Rebecca, 304; 436 n.173
Block, Richard, 61 n.76; 193 n.131
Blount, William, 313 n.33
Blumberg, Abraham, 523 nn.135–136
Blumberg, Mark, 435 nn.136, 140
Blumer, Herbert, 27 n.46; 214; 227 n.144
Blumstein, Alfred, 41; 43; 60 n.35; 119
    n.193; 559 n.32
Blunt, Anthony, 323
Boatwright, Jeffrey, 477
Bobadilla, Leonardo, 156 n.153
Bodine, George, 60 n.18
Boehnke, Klaus, 194 n.145
Boer, Douglas, 314 n.112
Boesky, Ivan, 386
Bogaerts, Jef, 224 n.29
Boger, Jack, 560 n.61
Bohm, Robert, 234; 250 n.27
Bohman, Michael, 157 n.166
Boivin, Michel, 156 n.154
Boland, Barbara, 483 n.11; 521 n.10
Bolen, Rebecca M., 314 n.109
Bonacci, Angelica, 314 n.113
Bonczar, Thomas, 560 n.74; 561 n.83
Bond, Dale, 282 n.147
Bonett, Douglas, 155 n.79
Bonger, Willem, 232; 233
Bonnie, Richard, 151
Bonta, James, 157 n.186; 158 n.213; 483
    n.28; 562–563 n.173; 563 n.203
Bontrager, Stephanie, 227 n.177; 535
Bookless, Clara, 158 n.217
Booth, Alan, 62 n.96; 154 nn.42, 46
Boots, Denise Paquette, 560 n.53
Borg, Marian, 560 n.42
Boruch, Victor, 27 n.56
Borum, Randy, 158 n.221; 315 n.167; 321;
    342 n.5
Bosket, Willie, 55
Bothwell, Robert, 315 n.123
Botsis, A., 156 n.119
Bottcher, Jean, 53; 62 n.98
Bouchard, Thomas, 157 n.157
Boulerice, Bernard, 155 n.80

Bourgois, Philippe, 94; 115 *n*.21
Bowden, Blake Sperry, 85 *n*.40
Bowers, William, 557; 560 *nn*.39, 62
Bowling, Benjamin, 280 *n*.56
Box, Steven, 62 *n*.105; 250 *n*.34
Boyd, Carol, 435 *n*.158
Boyer, Richard, 368 *n*.38
Bradley, Stacey, *414*
Brady, James, 48
Braga, Anthony A., 50; 117 *nn*.131, 134; 297; 315 *n*.149; 522 *n*.87
Bragason, Ólafur Örn, 149
Braithwaite, John, 61 *n*.71; 193 *n*.127; 244–245; 250 *n*.21; 252 *nn*.113, 116, 118, 131; 316 *n*.212; 397 *n*.27; 398 *nn*.100, 103
Braithwaite, Valerie, 252 *n*.116
Brame, Robert, 227 *nn*.184, 189; 279 *n*.17; 280 *nn*.45, 55, 61; 281 *n*.110; 282 *n*.128
Branch, Kathryn, 304
Branscomb, Anne, 461 *n*.32
Bratingham, Patricia, 116 *nn*.85, 97
Bratingham, Paul, 116 *nn*.85, 97
Breaux, Marie-Anne, 315 *n*.123
Brecher, Edward, 433 *n*.20; 435 *n*.125
Breitel, Charles, 504; 522 *n*.104
Breivik, Gunnar, 368 *n*.37
Brems, Christiane, 34; 60 *n*.20
Brenda, Brent B., 561 *n*.110
Brennan, Patricia, 155 *n*.84; 156 *n*.124; 157 *n*.178; 158 *n*.208; 312–313 *n*.27
Brennan, Pauline, 535
Brennan, Robert T., 313 *n*.45
Brent, Edward, 522 *n*.73
Brents, Barbara G., 434 *n*.78
Breslin, Beau, 252 *n*.127
Breverlin, Matt, 108
Brewer, Robert, 312 *n*.19
Brewer, Victoria, 61 *n*.64; 119 *n*.192; 279 *n*.26; 562 *n*.155
Brewster, Mary, 310; 317 *n*.266
Brezina, Timothy, 154 *n*.45; 185; 194 *nn*.162, 164–165, 171; 224 *n*.42; 280 *n*.48
Briar, Scott, 226 *nn*.103, 106
Brick, Michael, 43
Briere, John, 314 *n*.117; 433 *n*.34
Briken, Peer, 129; 155 *n*.83; 159 *n*.259
Briscoe, Suzanne, 118 *n*.141
Brison, Susan, 68; 85 *n*.32
Britain, R. P., 155 *n*.90
Britt, Chester, 437 *n*.215
Britt, David, 251 *n*.47
Britton, Lee, 63 *n*.149; 119 *n*.196
Brockway, Z. R., 551
Broidy, Lisa, 62 *n*.100; 158 *n*.198; 194 *nn*.170, 173–174; 280 *n*.45
Bronte-Tinkew, Jacinta, 224 *n*.30
Bronwfield, David, 191 *n*.25
Brook, Judith, 43; 144
Brooke, James, 317 *n*.225
Brooks, Judith, 279 *n*.27; 435 *n*.152
Brooks-Gunn, Jeanne, 191 *nn*.11–13
Browdy, Jennifer, 316 *n*.181
Brown, Alan, 154 *n*.75

Brown, Alyson, 433 *n*.63; 434 *n*.73
Brown, Charles, 117 *n*.125; 521 *n*.8
Brown, Christopher M., 398 *n*.107
Brown, Garrett, 250 *n*.26
Brown, Jerry, 476
Brown, Jocelyn, 433 *n*.64; 434 *n*.74
Brown, Lee, 522 *n*.83
Brown, Roy, III, 315 *n*.123
Brown, Sandra, 225 *n*.66
Brown, Shayna, 483 *n*.30
Brown, Thomas, 155 *n*.101
Browne, Angela, 315 *nn*.152, 154
Browne, C., 158 *n*.207
Browne, Derek, 158 *n*.217
Browne, Kevin D., 563 *n*.205
Brownfield, David, 61 *n*.72; 86 *n*.66; 225 *n*.89; 226 *n*.137; 281 *n*.102; 282 *n*.116
Browning, Christopher, 195 *n*.178
Brownmiller, Susan, 313 *n*.72
Brownstein, Henry, 312 *n*.17
Bryan, Nicole, 436 *n*.209
Bryant, Susan Leslie, 85 *n*.21
Buchanan, Christy Miller, 154 *n*.44
Buchsbaum, Monte, 155 *nn*.92, 98
Buchting, Francisco, 156 *n*.149
Buck, Andrew, 87 *n*.124; 115 *n*.48
Buck, Janeen, 562 *n*.164
Buck, Philip, 312 *n*.21
Buddie, Amy, 314 *n*.95
Budtz-Jorgensen, E., 153 *n*.20
Bufacchi, Vittorio, 342 *n*.22
Buffett, Jimmy, 378
Buffett, Warren, 177
Buitelaar, Jan, 154 *n*.48
Bukovec, Paul, 313 *n*.71
Bukowski, William, 224 *n*.49; 313 *n*.60
Bullogh, V., 433 *n*.36
Burger, Timothy, 461 *n*.53
Burgess, Ernest W., 9; 27 *n*.24; 162; 168
Burgess, Guy, 323
Burgess, P., 158 *n*.207
Burgess, Robert, 206; 225 *n*.81
Burgess, Tracey, 556
Burke, Jeffrey, 157 *n*.190
Burkett, Steven, 118 *n*.147
Burnett, Ros, 560 *n*.70
Burns, Barbara, 158 *n*.221
Burns, Ronald, 317 *n*.261; 398 *nn*.93, 98
Burr, Aaron, 322–323
Burrell, Amy, 86 *n*.84; 115 *n*.18
Burrows, J., 521 *n*.26
Bursik, Robert, 117 *n*.118; 118 *nn*.145, 152–154; 191 *nn*.35, 40; 192 *nn*.82, 88; 193 *nn*.105, 114, 124; 281 *n*.102; 282 *n*.130
Burt, Callie Harbin, 282 *n*.124
Burton, Thomas, 397 *n*.49
Burton, Velmer, 61 *nn*.69, 74; 62 *n*.97; 116 *n*.62; 194 *n*.159; 225 *n*.60; 226 *n*.134
Bush, George H. W., 425
Bush, George W., 337; 338; 412; 448; 551
Bushman, Brad, 41; 43; 61 *n*.55; 144; 314 *n*.113
Bushway, Shawn, 227 *n*.189; 280 *n*.63; 483 *n*.31; 534; 535

Buswell, Brenda, 62 *n*.97
Butterfield, Ethan, 446
Butterfield, Fox, 55; 63 *n*.121; 313 *n*.57
Bynum, Timothy, 191 *n*.24; 192 *n*.57
Byrne, Donn, 157 *n*.184
Byrne, James, 191 *n*.38; 193 *n*.98; 561 *nn*.90, 107
Byrne, John A., 379; 398 *n*.87

Cadoret, R. J., 157 *n*.164
Caesar, Julius, 329
Caeti, Tory, 116 *n*.95; 117 *n*.132
Cain, C., 157 *n*.164
Cairncross, John, 323
Calavita, Kitty, 397 *n*.5
Calden, Paul, 308
Calder, James, 316 *n*.217
Caldwell, Roslyn, 223 *n*.7
Calnon, Jennifer, 62 *n*.116
Calvan, Bobby Caina, 119 *n*.186
Cameron, Mary Owen, 354; 368 *n*.34
Campbell, Alec, 436 *n*.208
Campbell, Anne, 62 *nn*.97, 106; 157 *n*.175; 281 *n*.101
Campbell, Doris, 304
Campbell, Jacquelyn, 304
Campbell, Kathryn, 562 *n*.133
Campbell, Neve, 309
Campbell, Rebecca, 84 *n*.10; 87 *n*.111
Campbell, Rosie, 433 *n*.50
Campbell, Suzanne, 43; 117 *n*.126
Campbell, Thomas, 287
Campo-Flores, Arian, 191 *n*.1
Cancino, Jeffrey Michael, 192 *n*.90; 193 *n*.93
Canela-Cacho, Jose, 119 *n*.193
Cantor, David, 87 *n*.124
Cao, Liqun, 313 *n*.51
Capachin, Jeanne, 462 *n*.74
Capaldi, Deborah, 224 *n*.48; 279 *n*.20; 312 *n*.27
Capell, Kerry, 462 *n*.95
Capone, Al, 390
Capowich, George E., 193 *n*.106; 194 *nn*.109, 160
Carbonell, Joyce, 159 *n*.256
Cardarelli, Albert, 522 *n*.80
Carey, Gregory, 156 *n*.129; 157 *n*.159
Caringella-MacDonald, Susan, 252 *n*.88
Carlen, Pat, 251 *n*.73
Carlson, Allan Eric, 447
Carlson, Bonnie, 560 *n*.77
Carlson, Eric, 560 *n*.71
Carlson, Robert, 436 *n*.180
Carmichael, Stephanie, 117 *n*.121
Carmichael-Jones, Clive, 441
Carney, Cormac J., 271
Carr, Jackson, 72
Carr, Joetta, 434 *n*.101
Carrano, Jennifer, 224 *n*.30
Carrero Blanco, Luis, 333
Carrington, Frank, 81; 87 *n*.137
Carrington, Tim, 398 *n*.74
Carroll, Douglas, 159 *n*.277
Carrozza, Mark, 226 *nn*.120, 131
Carter, Chris, 561 *n*.125; 563 *n*.204
Carter, David, 428

Carter, Ricki, 277
Carter, Sherry Plaster, 434 n.83; 522 n.85
Carter, Stanley, 434 n.83; 522 n.85
Cartier, Jerome, 436 n.190
Cartwright, Desmond, 225 n.96
Casintahan, D., 153 n.24
Caspi, Avshalom, 61 n.78; 117 n.120; 136; 156 nn.146, 151; 157 nn.179, 188; 159 n.263; 279 n.9, 19, 26; 280 nn.44, 51; 282 n.142
Cassell, Paul, 119 n.197; 483 n.13; 560 nn.34, 60
Castellano, Thomas, 562 n.144
Castro, Jennifer, 561 n.115
Catalano, Richard, 224 n.43; 225 n.53; 262; 282 n.145; 435–436 n.166; 436 n.184
Catalano, Shannan, 60 nn.6, 32; 61 n.47; 68; 69; 70; 71; 84 n.3; 85 n.41; 314 n.79
Cauce, Mari, 86 n.64
Cauchon, Dennis, 561 n.114
Cauffman, Elizabeth, 62 n.100; 158 nn.198, 233; 282 n.136
Causey, Richard, 378
Cecchi, Matthew, 98
Cecil, Joe, 27 n.56
Cederblad, Marianne, 159 n.280
Cernkovich, Stephen, 60 n.24; 178; 194 n.143; 226 n.132; 279 n.12; 281 n.79; 282 n.144
Chachere, J. Gregory, 144
Chafetz, Janet Saltzman, 251 n.76
Chaiken, J., 521 n.24
Chaiken, Marcia, 436 n.170
Chakrabarti, Nandini, 127
Chakravarti, Shamit, 343 n.43
Chalk, Peter, 343 n.39
Chambliss, William, 233; 250 n.16; 368 n.13; 399 n.118
Chamlin, Mitchell, 117 n.118; 274; 282 n.132; 521 n.16; 560 n.40
Chaplin, Terry, 369 n.100
Chapman, Jane Roberts, 251 n.81
Chappell, Duncan, 60 n.7
Chard-Wierschem, Deborah, 61 n.82
Charlebois, P., 63 n.153
Chase, Peter, 339
Chaseling, Janet, 369 n.95
Chayet, Ellen, 118 n.177
Chen, C.-Y., 192 n.61
Chen, Henian, 433 n.64; 434 n.74
Chen, Jieming, 225 n.70
Chen, Jieru, 317 n.262
Chen, Xiaojin, 435 n.159
Chen, Yi Fu, 194 n.153
Cheng, Zhongqi, 153 n.25
Cheng Chui Ping, 23
Cherbonneau, Michael, 368 n.48
Chermak, Steven, 63 n.126; 521 n.14
Cherry, Bobby Frank, 492
Chesney-Lind, Meda, 251 nn.73, 75; 252 n.88
Chien-Peng, Chung, 343 n.38
Chilcoat, Howard, 280 n.35
Chilton, Roland, 227 n.156

Chin, Ko-lin, 13
Chiricos, Ted, 40; 43; 117 n.118; 118 nn.151, 159; 171; 192 nn.69, 72; 227 n.177; 251 n.54; 534; 535
Cho, Adrian, 397 n.52
Cho, Seung-Hui, 48; 75; 99; 121–122; 121
Choudhury, Muhtashem, 397 n.31
Christakis, Dmitri, 144
Christakos, Antigone, 436 n.173
Christenson, Cornelia, 314 n.111
Christenson, R. L., 224 n.38
Christian, George M., 339
Christiansen, A., 435 n.160
Christodoulou, G., 156 n.119
Chronis, Andrea, 224 n.26
Chung, He Len, 280 n.33
Chung, Ick-Joong, 280 n.46
Cicchetti, Dante, 224 n.33
Cirillo, Kathleen, 159 nn.244, 249, 279
Clark, John, 60 n.28
Clark-Daniels, Carolyn, 117 nn.113, 116
Clarke, Gregory n., 157 n.193
Clarke, Ronald, 86 n.94; 87 n.122; 100–101; 102; 115 nn.16, 22; 116 nn.89, 91; 117 nn.101–102, 107, 109; 368 n.61; 369 n.93
Clarke, Stevens, 523 n.146
Clarkson, Lana, 506
Clason, Dennis L., 225 n.87
Classen, Gabriele, 194 n.145
Clayton, Richard, 315 n.165; 428
Clear, Todd, 315 n.131
Cleckley, Hervey, 148; 149
Cleland, Charles, 563 n.174
Clements, Benedict, 343 n.43
Clinard, Marshall, 397 nn.17, 46
Clines, Francis X., 316 n.187
Clingempeel, Glenn, 280 n.40
Clinton, Bill, 503
Clinton, Monique, 312 n.21
Clooney, George, 346
Cloward, Richard, 186–187; 188; 190; 195 n.196
Coatsworth, J. Douglas, 85 n.40
Cochran, John, 116 n.82; 226 n.123; 281 n.102; 304; 560 nn.40, 53
Cochran, Johnny, 505
Cogan, Jeanine, 317 n.238
Cohen, A., 563 n.179
Cohen, Albert, 182–184; 186; 188; 190; 194 n.136; 195 nn.187, 192
Cohen, Jacqueline, 11; 27 n.33; 60 n.35; 86 n.68; 105; 116 n.52; 117 n.130; 119 n.193
Cohen, Lawrence, 74; 75; 86 nn.82, 96; 157 n.167
Cohen, Mark A., 84 n.7; 398–399 n.112
Cohen, Morris, 402–403; 432 n.6
Cohen, Patricia, 43; 144; 279 n.27; 433 n.64; 434 n.74
Cohen, Robert, 225 n.56; 313 n.59
Cohen, Thomas, 509; 510; 511; 512; 523 nn.121, 124; 526; 533
Cohen-Bendahan, Celina, 154 n.48
Cohen-Kettenis, Peggy, 154 n.48
Cohn, Bob, 434 n.113

Cohn, Ellen, 46; 61 nn.53, 56, 59
Cohn, Steven, 192 n.89
Cole, Christopher, 398 n.78
Cole, George, 522 n.106; 561 nn.95, 97
Coley, Rebekah Levine, 193 n.103
Coll, Xavier, 279 n.18
Colletti, Patrick, 155 n.81
Collin, Barry C., 461 n.54
Collins, James, 312 n.20
Collins, Mark, 280 n.64
Collins, Thelma, 492
Colony, Catherine, 312 n.3
Colvin, Mark, 268
Colwell, Brian, 159 nn.244, 249, 279
Comer, James, 63 n.120
Comiskey, Most Rev. Brendan, 405
Comte, Auguste, 6
Conger, Rand, 227 n.163; 281 n.77; 282 n.126; 313 nn.32, 41
Conklin, John, 305
Conley, Dalton, 153 n.2
Conly, Catherine, 483 n.11
Conwell, Chic, 349; 368 n.16
Cook, Kimberly, 115 n.15
Cook, Philip, 48–49; 50; 115 n.16; 297; 315 n.149
Cook, William, 238
Cooke, Alistair, 353
Cooley, Charles Horton, 17; 214; 227 n.144
Coomer, Brandi Wilson, 60 n.34
Coontz, Phyllis, 154 n.51
Cooper, Cary, 61 n.58; 154 n.49
Cooper, Chris, 323
Cooper, Kylie, 398 n.70
Copes, Heith, 225 n.72; 368 nn.48, 51
Copper, Janet R., 317 n.253
Coppola, Michael, 391
Corill, Dean, 300
Cornish, Derek, 100–101; 115 nn.16, 22; 116 n.91
Corrado, J., 435 n.156
Correa, Vanessa, 562 n.164
Cortese, Samuele, 153 nn.20, 25
Costa, Francis, 279 n.18
Costanzo, Michael, 115 n.50
Costello, Jane, 158 n.203
Cota-Robles, Sonia, 224 n.28
Coto, Danica, 561 n.119
Cotter, C., 521 n.26
Couey, John Evander, 407; 407
Coupe, Richard Timothy, 86 n.89; 521 n.9
Coupe, Timothy, 369 n.77
Court, John, 434 n.105
Courtney, Robert R., 375; 385–386; 385
Courtwright, David, 289–290; 313 n.66; 437 n.228
Couzens, Michael, 60 n.10
Covington, Jeanette, 192 nn.68, 83; 193 n.131
Cowan, Alison Leigh, 368 n.1
Cox, Archibald, 503
Cox, Louis, 27 n.55; 93; 115 n.9; 119 n.184; 562 n.167
Cragin, Kim, 343 n.39
Craig-Moreland, Delores, 561 n.124

Crane, Jonathan, 191 n.28
Craven, Wes, 309
Crawford, Charles, 251 n.54; 534; 535
Crawford, Krysten, 379
Creamer, Vicki, 225 n.66
Crenshaw, Martha, 343 n.51
Cressey, Donald, 4; 16; 27 nn.3, 42; 203–205; 225 n.64; 386; 398 n.82; 399 n.121
Cretacci, Michael, 226 n.125
Crews, F. T., 153 n.23
Croisdale, Tim, 63 n.149; 119 n.196
Cromwell, Paul, 115 nn.43, 47; 116 n.57; 354; 363–364; 368 nn.24, 36; 369 n.90
Cronan, John P., 563 n.176
Crosby, L., 280 n.42
Crosby, Rick, 279 n.22
Crosnoe, Robert, 226 n.111
Crossette, Barbara, 433 nn.16, 18
Crouch, Ben, 119 n.192; 561 n.94; 562 n.155
Crowder, Martin J., 127
Crowe, R. R., 157 n.164
Crowther, Betty, 435 n.127
Cruise, Keith, 312 n.8
Cruz, M. C. Vince, 153 n.24
Cruz, Rolando, 537
Culhane, Dennis, 555
Cullen, Charles, 299
Cullen, Francis, 60 n.19; 61 nn.69, 74; 62 n.97; 85 n.62; 86 n.69; 116 n.62; 158 n.204; 185; 194 nn.159, 162, 165; 223 n.12; 224 nn.18, 24; 225 n.60; 226 nn.114, 119, 120, 131, 134; 227 n.145; 253 n.135; 274; 282 nn.132–133; 314 nn.88, 96; 317 n.263; 398 n.94; 483 nn.28, 30; 560 nn.50–52; 562–563 n.170, 173
Cullen, Keven, 433 n.32
Cummings, Andrea, 116 n.78; 314 n.86
Cummings, Debra, 522 n.97
Cuniff, Mark, 561 n.102
Cunningham, Randy "Duke," 377
Cunningham-Niederer, Michele, 399 n.116
Cupach, William, 310; 317 nn.264, 267
Currie, Elliott, 480; 483 n.40
Curry, G. David, 192 nn.52, 73
Curry, Mary Ann, 304
Cuvelier, Steven, 116 n.62
Czaja, Ronald, 60 n.27

Dadds, Mark, 369 n.102
Dafeamekpor, Denise Spriggs, 314 n.120
Dahlberg, Linda, 13; 316 n.191
Dahrendorf, Ralf, 232; 233
Daigle, Leah, 280 n.53; 282 n.133; 314 nn.88, 96
D'Alessio, Stewart, 63 n.123; 108; 109; 521 n.18, 536
Daley, Suzanne, 434 n.90
Dal Forno, Gloria, 282 n.122
D'Allessio, Stewart, 560 n.37
Dalton, Katharina, 128; 154 n.57
Daly, Kathleen, 251 nn.73, 75, 79; 252 nn.88, 109; 386; 398 n.80

Daly, Martin, 62 n.88; 85 n.60; 135; 157 nn.168–171; 192 n.65; 193 n.128; 282 n.121; 316 n.199
Daly, Sara A., 343 n.39
Damphouse, Kelly, 559 n.30
Danesh, John, 562 n.145
Daniels, R. Steven, 117 nn.113, 116
Dann, Robert, 108; 109
Dannefer, Dale, 62 n.110
Dannenberg, Andrew, 434 n.83; 522 n.85
Dantzler, Joyce, 314 n.120
Darrow, William, 433 n.66
Darwin, Charles, 6
Davey, Monica, 397 n.41
David, David, 437 n.219
Davidson, Laura, 61 n.73
Davies, Garth, 191 n.29
Davies, Mark, 225 n.75; 226 n.133; 435 n.154
Davies, Priscilla, 159 n.272
Davies, Susan, 279 n.22
Davies-Netley, Sally, 85 n.21
Daviglus, M., 127
Davis, Derek, 562 n.165
Davis, Gray, 476
Davis, Joanne, 435 n.146
Davis, Kenneth Culp, 529; 559 n.14
Davis, Robert, 60 n.12; 85 nn.31, 45; 86 n.104; 87 nn.117, 123; 436 n.210; 437 n.212; 483 n.37; 521 n.13; 522 n.103
Davis, Roy, 314 n.103
Davis-Frenzel, Erika, 314 nn.90, 122; 522 n.102
Davison, Elizabeth, 116 n.69
Davoli, Charles, 561 n.123
Dawkins, Marvin, 436 n.181
Dawson, Myrna, 503–504; 522 n.98
Day, H. D., 159 n.272
Day, Jennifer Cheeseman, 163
Dean, Charles, 119 n.183; 279 n.17; 280 n.55
Deane, Glenn, 60 n.5; 312 n.16; 313 n.47
DeBartolo, Eddie, Jr., 376
DeBaryshe, Barbara, 279 n.14
DeBeir, Georges, 448
Deboutte, Dirk, 224 n.29
Decker, Michele, 433 n.47
Decker, Scott, 116 n.75; 226 n.135; 306; 315 n.157; 317 n.224; 361; 369 nn.80, 85; 435 n.137
DeCoster, Stacy, 158 n.216; 170; 191 n.39; 194 n.157
Dedjinou, Adrienne, 398 n.70
Dee, Henry, 492
Defina, Robert, 40; 43
DeFrances, Carol J., 505; 522 nn.101, 109–110
DeFronzo, James, 61 n.81; 193 n.116; 195 n.209
DeGostin, Lucille, 563 n.197
De Gruchy, John W., 247
DeHart, Erica, 67–68; 85 n.29
Dejong, Christina, 118 nn.172, 176, 178; 227 n.155
DeJong, M. J., 155 n.116
DeKeseredy, Walter, 251 nn.71–72; 252 n.87; 314 nn.107, 114

DeLamatre, Mary, 86 n.68
DeLay, Tom, 377; 377
De Li, Spencer, 119 n.181; 225 n.58; 280 n.62; 281 n.73
DeLisi, Matt, 225 n.72
DeLone, Gregory, 462 n.81
DeLone, Miriam, 63 n.125; 218; 227 n.179
Del Regato, Guillermo, 477
Deluca, Stefanie, 192 n.80
Demaray, Michelle Kilpatrick, 315 n.163
Dempsey, Jared, 85 n.35
Demuth, Stephen, 63 n.127; 251 n.51; 534; 535
DeNavas-Walt, Carmen, 191 nn.6, 17
DeNevi, Don, 368 n.7
Dengate, Sue, 153 n.21
Denney, Robert, 313 n.61
Denno, Deborah, 129; 154 n.72; 155 nn.80, 85; 157 nn.176–177
Denov, Myriam, 562 n.133
Dentler, Robert, 61 n.66
Deptula, Daneen, 225 n.56; 313 n.59
DeRios, M. D., 435 n.155
Dershowitz, Alan, 327
Derzon, James, 279 n.21
Desai, Manisha, 154 n.75
Deschenes, Elizabeth Piper, 62 n.104; 282 n.127
De Silva, W. P., 433 n.33
Deutsch, Joseph, 115 n.51
Devine, Francis Edward, 115 n.2
Devine, Shannon, 433 n.46
Devlin, Sir Patrick, 403; 432 n.7
DeVoe, Jill, 85 n.42; 315 n.161
Dewan, Shaila, 523 n.137
Dezhbakhsh, Hashem, 109
Dhami, Mandeep, 386; 398 n.85
Diaz, Ornelio, 477
DiClemente, Ralph, 279 n.22
Dieckman, Duane, 117 n.125; 521 n.8
Dietz, Park, 140
Dietz, Robert D., 195 n.178
Dietz, Tracy, 85 n.46
DiGiuseppe, David, 144
DiLalla, David, 156 n.129
Di Luigi, Massimo, 282 n.122
Dilulio, John, 561 n.116
Dilworth, Donald C., 523 n.176
DiMaio, Vincent, 516
Dinitz, Simon, 226 n.108
Dinovitzer, Ronit, 503–504; 522 n.98
Dionne, Ginette, 156 n.154
Dirie, Waris, 402
Dishion, Thomas, 224 n.48
Dishman, Chris, 335; 343 n.50
Ditton, Paula M., 559 nn.23, 25
Dixon, Jo, 559 n.17
Dobash, R. Emerson, 316 nn.208, 211
Dobash, Russell, 316 nn.208, 211
Dobrin, Adam, 86 nn.68, 70; 192 n.52; 282 n.133
Dodge, Kenneth, 156 n.151; 158 n.230; 193 n.96; 224 n.15; 280 n.45
Dohrenwend, Bruce, 227 n.145
Dominici, Cinzia, 282 n.122
Dominick, Joseph, 461 n.39

Donald, B., 523 *n*.174
Donaldson, Stephen, 552
Dong, Jie, 445
Donker, Andrea, 280 *n*.54
Donnelly, Patrick, 86 *n*.97
Donnerstein, Edward, 314 *n*.116; 434 *nn*.101, 103
Donohue, John J., III, 40–41; 43; 109
Donovan, John, 279 *n*.18; 435 *n*.159
Doob, Anthony, 118 *n*.140
Dorahy, Martin, 84 *n*.18
Doran, Michael Scott, 334; 343 *n*.44
Doraz, Walter, 153 *n*.31
Dornfeld, Maude, 279 *n*.28
Doughterty, Carter, 397 *n*.47
Downey, Douglas, 191 *n*.9
Downey, Robert, Jr., 98
Downs, William, 85 *n*.21; 227 *n*.165
Doyle, Daniel, 313 *n*.49
Drago, Harry Sinclair, 368 *n*.7
Drake, Francis, 330
Drake, J. J. P., 154 *n*.62
Drass, Kriss, 193 *n*.131; 315 *n*.151; 559 *n*.13
Dressler, Joshua, 22
Drew, Christopher, 316 *n*.187
Driver, Edwin, 157 *n*.182
Drugge, Jeff, 314 *n*.112
Duffee, David, 560 *n*.77
Dugan, Laura, 100; 116 *n*.80; 561 *n*.89
Dugdale, Richard, 122; 153 *n*.5
Duguid, Stephen, 556; 563 *n*.202
Duhart, Detis, 317 *n*.257
Dunaway, R. Gregory, 61 *nn*.69, 74; 62 *n*.97; 225 *n*.60; 226 *n*.134; 281 *n*.104
Duncan, David, 378
Duncan, Greg J., 191 *nn*.11–13; 192 *n*.80
Dunford, Franklyn, 119 *n*.183
D'Unger, Amy, 63 *n*.156; 280 *n*.47
Dunlop, Eloise, 281 *n*.78
Dunn, Linda Wade, 359
Dunn, Patricia, *51*
Durkheim, Émile, 8; 10; 25; 27 *nn*.18–19; 175–176; 181
Durose, Matthew, 436 *n*.207; 522 *nn*.74, 91
Durrant, Lynne, 282 *n*.147
Duwe, Grant, 301; 316 *n*.184
Dwiggins, Donna, 62 *n*.97
Dworkin, Andrea, 402; 432 *n*.4; 434 *n*.88
Dwyer, Jim, 483 *n*.26
Dyk, T., 523 *n*.174
Dyson, Laronistine, 84 *n*.9

Earls, Felton, 63 *n*.154; 193 *nn*.94, 118; 289; 313 *nn*.44–45
Earnest, Terri, 192 *n*.56
Earp, Wyatt, 466
Eaves, Lindon, 156 *n*.149
Ebbers, Bernie, 379
Eccles, Jacquelynne, 154 *n*.44
Eck, John, 117 *nn*.98–99; 521 *n*.32
Eckholm, Erik, 191 *n*.21
Edelhertz, Herbert, 398 *n*.84
Edens, John, 561 *n*.125; 563 *n*.204
Edwards, Charles Marcus, 492
Edwards, Dale, 523 *n*.173
Edwards, Edwin, 376
Edwards, Jessica, 411; 433 *n*.60

Egelko, Bob, 315 *n*.140
Eggleston, Carolyn, 62 *n*.97
Egley, Arlen, Jr., 191 *n*.2
Eichenwald, Kurt, 379; 398 *n*.60
Einarsson, Emil, 149
Einstein, Stanley, 399 *n*.122
Eisen, Seth, 156 *n*.149
Eitle, David, 63 *n*.123
Eitzen, Stanley, 398 *n*.96
Elder, Glen, 226 *n*.124; 281 *n*.77; 282 *n*.126
Eley, Thalia, 157 *n*.161
El Hawaa, Iyad Abu, 381
Elifson, Kirk, 437 *n*.217
Elis, Lori, 275
Elizabeth I, Queen, 330
Elkind, Peter, 379
Ellingworth, Dan, 85 *n*.48
Elliott, Amanda, 193 *nn*.115, 120
Elliott, Delbert, 61 *nn*.70–71; 62 *n*.110; 116 *n*.93; 119 *n*.183; 192 *n*.54; 193 *nn*.115, 120; 227 *n*.160; 282 *n*.118
Elliott, F. A., 155 *n*.110
Ellis, Cynthia, 78
Ellis, Lee, 153 *nn*.9, 12, 14, 16; 154 *nn*.50–51; 155–156 *nn*.118, 120, 123; 157 *n*.172; 281 *nn*.82, 97; 314 *n*.105
El-Magd, Nadia Abou, 342 *n*.20
Elonheimo, Henrik, 223 *n*.9
Elstein, Sharon, 314 *n*.103
Emerson, Robert M., 317 *n*.260
Endresen, Inger, 225 *n*.82
Engel, Robin Shepard, 62 *n*.116; 158 *n*.212
Engels, Friedrich, 27 *n*.26; 230; 232; 250 *nn*.8, 12
Engels, Rutger, 158 *n*.229
Engen, Rodney, 227 *n*.177; 535
Ennett, Susan, 63 *n*.135
Enrich, David, 433 *n*.48
Epstein, Gil, 115 *n*.51
Epstein, Joel, 398 *n*.91
Epstein, Kitty Kelley, 250 *n*.24
Erez, Edna, 87 *n*.117; 523 *n*.155; 559 *n*.12
Erickson, Kai, 215; 227 *n*.149
Erickson, Maynard, 118 *n*.151
Erickson, Rosemary, 27 *n*.35
Ericsson, Kjersti, 252 *n*.89
Erikson, Erik, 138
Erkanli, Alaattin, 158 *n*.203
Ernst, Frederick, 312 *n*.5
Eron, L., 159 *n*.240
Erwin, Brigette, 85 *n*.37
Esagian, Gkaro, 312 *n*.5
Esbensen, Finn-Aage, 62 *n*.104; 192 *n*.79; 195 *n*.203; 282 *n*.127
Eskridge, Chris, 560 *n*.71
Esmail, Aneez, 316 *n*.172
Espelage, Dorothy, 62 *n*.100; 158 *n*.198
Espinoza, Edward, 95
Estabrook, Arthur, 122; 153 *n*.5
Estes, Richard J., 412; 433 *n*.31; 434 *n*.76
Estrich, Susan, 85 *n*.58; 315 *n*.129
Ethridge, Philip, 561 *n*.121
Evano, Ronald and Mary, 31
Evans, Davis, 285–286; *285*
Evans, Gary, 191 *n*.15
Evans, Jeff, 154 *n*.71

Evans, Michelle, 194 *nn*.155, 161
Evans, Rhonda, 398 *n*.83
Evans, T. David, 61 *nn*.69, 74; 62 *n*.97; 194 *n*.159; 225 *n*.60; 226 *n*.134
Eve, Raymond, 62 *n*.103
Eves, Anita, 127
Ewing, Charles Patrick, 313 *n*.35; 317 *n*.230
Ewing, Gary, 532
Eysenck, Hans, 10; 27 *n*.27; 147; 159 *nn*.253–254, 256
Eysenck, M. W., 159 *nn*.254, 256
Ezell, Michael, 63 *n*.156

Facciaabrutto, Anthony J., 395
Factor-Litvak, Pamela, 153 *n*.25; 154 *n*.75
Fader, James, 63 *n*.147
Fagan, Abigail, 156 *n*.143
Fagan, Jeffrey A., 119 *n*.183; 185; 191 *nn*.29, 37; 195 *n*.186
Fairweather, David, 314 *n*.112
Falck, Russel, 436 *n*.180
Falshaw, Louise, 563 *n*.205
Falwell, Jerry, 404
Famularo, Richard, 158 *n*.199
Fantaye, Dawit Kiros, 369 *n*.73
Farabee, David, 436 *n*.190
Farahan, Victoria, 375
Faraone, Stephen, 155 *n*.100; 156 *n*.149
Fargeon, Samantha, 155 *n*.108
Farley, Reynolds, 63 *n*.140
Farnworth, Margaret, 61 *n*.66; 262
Farr, Kathryn Ann, 437 *n*.230
Farrall, Stephen, 280 *nn*.41, 56
Farrell, Graham, 85 *nn*.49, 52; 364; 369 *n*.94
Farrell, Michael, 224 *n*.16; 435 *n*.143
Farrington, David P., 13; 38; 60 *nn*.31, 36, 41; 63 *n*.145; 86 *nn*.68, 88; 103; 117 *n*.110; 133; 156 *nn*.133, 135–136, 140–142; 199; 224 *nn*.20–23; 268; 279 *nn*.16, 26; 280 *n*.36; 313 *nn*.42, 62; 368 *n*.33
Farroque, Rokeya, 312 *n*.5
Fass, Simon, 368 *n*.22
Fassbender, Pantaleon, 159 *n*.258
Fastow, Andrew, 96; 378–379
Faulkner, Daniel, 238
Faupel, Charles, 436 *nn*.176–178, 192
Fazel, Seena, 312 *n*.23; 562 *n*.145
Feder, Lynette, 561 *n*.89
Feeley, Malcolm, 523 *n*.128
Fein, Robert, 315 *n*.167
Feinberg, Joel, 432 *n*.8
Feinberg, Seth, 195 *n*.178
Feingold, Alan, 282 *n*.112
Fejes-Mendoza, Kathy, 62 *n*.97
Fell, James, 117 *n*.135
Felson, Marcus, 74; 75; 76; 86 *nn*.82, 96; 101; 116–117 *nn*.90, 98
Felson, Richard B., 60 *n*.5; 86 *n*.92; 99; 116 *nn*.64–65, 76; 195 *n*.185; 224 *n*.51; 306; 313 *n*.52; 314 *n*.119; 315 *n*.155; 316 *n*.218
Fendrich, Michael, 60 *n*.26; 433 *n*.59; 435 *n*.165
Fenton, Terence, 158 *n*.199
Ferguson, Florence, 559 *n*.31
Ferguson, H. Bruce, 153 *n*.32

Fergusson, David, 43; 279 *n*.29; 280 *n*.45
Ferracuti, Franco, 11; 27 *n*.31; 313 *n*.48
Ferrell, Jeff, 116 *n*.83
Ferri, Enrico, 153 *n*.4
Ferris, Kerry O., 317 *n*.260
Feucht, Thomas, 315 *n*.166
Fidler, Larry P., *506*
Fiedler, Mora, 192 *n*.58
Fields, Monique, 561 *n*.84
Fienberg, Stephen, 154 *n*.73
Figert, Anne E., 154 *n*.56
Figlio, Robert M., 56; 57; 63 *nn*.141, 143, 150; 279 *n*.4
Figuerdo, Aurelio Jose, 157 *n*.173
Finckenauer, James O., 13; 27 *n*.57; 393
Finkel, Norman, 560 *n*.54
Finkelhor, David, 67; 72; 84 *n*.15; 85 *n*.51; 302; 314 *n*.99; 316 *nn*.197, 201, 203–204; 433 *n*.65; 434 *n*.75
Finn, Kristin, 435 *n*.134
Finn, Peter, 86 *n*.106; 87 *n*.135
Finnerty, Collin, 285–286; *285*
Fireman, Gary, 85 *n*.35
Firestone, David, 397 *n*.18
Fischer, Mariellen, 155 *n*.106
Fishbein, Diana, 128; 154 *nn*.35, 60; 155 *n*.86
Fisher, Bonnie, 85 *n*.62; 86 *nn*.69, 71; 281 *n*.94; 310; 314 *nn*.88, 96; 317 *n*.263
Fisher, Gene, 43
Fisher, George, 523 *n*.133
Flaccus, Gillian, 271
Flaherty, Austin, 87 *n*.119
Flaherty, Sara, 87 *n*.119
Flaming, Karl, 192 *n*.58
Flannery, Daniel, 62 *nn*.97, 103; 281 *n*.83
Flay, Brian, 116 *n*.61; 435 *n*.151
Fletcher, Beverly, 562 *n*.151
Fletcher, Kenneth, 155 *n*.106
Flewelling, Robert, 60 *n*.29; 63 *n*.135; 428
Flitter, Jill Klotz, 85 *n*.23; 434 *n*.68
Flynn, Kevin, 316 *n*.190
Flynn, Stephen, 343 *n*.66
Flynt, Larry, 301
Fogel, C. A., 155 *n*.79
Fogel, David, 483 *n*.20
Foglia, Wanda, 118 *nn*.144, 159–160
Fong, Grace, 155 *n*.93
Foote, Caleb, 509; 523 *n*.123
Forbes, Gordon, 314 *n*.89
Forde, David, 281 *n*.91
Formby, William, 117 *nn*.113, 116
Formoso, Diana, 223 *n*.6
Forney, Matthew, 461 *n*.53
Forrest, Walter, 282 *n*.125
Forster, Bruce, 149
Forsythe, Lubica, 369 *n*.89
Foster, Hilliard, 158 *n*.212
Foster, Holly, 252 *n*.92; 279 *n*.13
Foster, Jodie, 143; 294
Foster, Raymond E., 522 *n*.89
Fowler, Tom, 156 *n*.126
Fox, Ben, 116 *n*.63
Fox, James Alan, 44; 300; 301; 315 *n*.146; 316 *nn*.173, 179, 182–183; 317 *nn*.250, 255; 414; 434 *n*.104

Fox, Kirstan, 63 *n*.124
Francis, Janice, 368 *n*.22
Francis, Myrna, *306*
Frank, Blanche, 436 *n*.195
Frank, Nancy, 397 *n*.7; 398 *n*.67
Frank, Steven, 462 *n*.91
Frankel, Marvin, 529; 559 *n*.15
Franklin, J. M., 159 *n*.272
Franklin, John Paul, 301
Franklin, Megan, *46*
Franklin, Richard H., 561 *n*.114
Franks, John, 432 *n*.12
Fraser, Jennifer, 369 *n*.102
Frauenheim, Ed, 460 *n*.3
Frazee, Sharon Glave, 116 *n*.69
Freedman, Jonathan, 144
Freeman-Gallant, Adrienne, 156 *n*.137
Freemon, Melinda, 60 *n*.20
Freud, Sigmund, 7; 137–138; 146; 151; 286; 312 *n*.11
Frey, William, 63 *n*.140
Fricker-Elhai, Adrienne, 435 *n*.146
Friday, Paul, 224 *n*.44
Fridman, Daniel, 86 *n*.98
Fried, Gabriela, 343 *n*.45
Friedlander, Robert, 342 *n*.27; 343 *n*.31
Friedman, Andrea, 404; 433 *n*.25
Friedman, Lawrence Meir, 559 *n*.4
Friedrichs, David, 236; 251 *n*.37; 397 *n*.4
Friedrichs, Jessica, 236; 251 *n*.37
Friendman, Richard, 158 *n*.205
Friesthler, Bridget, 192 *n*.78
Fritsch, Eric, 116 *n*.95; 117 *n*.132
Fromm-Auch, Delee, 159 *n*.272
Frone, Michael, 314 *n*.78
Frye, Victoria, 304
Fuchs, Siegmund Fred, 313 *n*.70
Fuentes, Angel Ilarraza, 317 *n*.261
Fuentes, Thomas V., 399 *n*.120
Fukurai, Hiroshi, 227 *n*.170
Fulton, Betsy, 253 *n*.135
Fyfe, James, 43; 117 *n*.126

Gabrielli, William, 157 *n*.166
Gacy, Wayne, 300
Gadd, David, 280 *n*.41
Gaffney, Michael, 192 *n*.90
Gagnon, C., 63 *n*.153
Gagnon, John, 314 *n*.111
Gainey, Randy, 193 *n*.104; 227 *n*.177; 535
Gajewski, Francis, 117 *nn*.131, 134
Gale, Nathan, 115 *n*.50
Gall, Franz Joseph, 7
Gallagher, Catherine, 562 *n*.171
Galvin, Jim, 227 *n*.156
Galway, Roberta, 356
Gamble, Wendy, 224 *n*.28
Gans, Dian, 154 *n*.34
Gant, Charles, 155 *n*.107
Garcia, Luis, 193 *n*.98; 317 *n*.247
Gardner, Carol Brooks, 317 *n*.260
Garland, David, 483 *nn*.14, 16
Garner, Connie Chenoweth, 226 *nn*.114, 119
Garner, Joel H., 119 *n*.183
Garnier, Helen, 226 *n*.117
Garofalo, James, 86 *n*.75; 87 *n*.134; 317 *nn*.227, 238

Garofalo, Raffaele, 122; 153 *n*.3
Garrett, Carol, 483 *n*.28
Gartin, Patrick, 119 *n*.184
Gartner, Rosemary, 85 *n*.61; 109; 562 *n*.149
Gary, Faye, 304
Gasca, Johnny Ray, 91–92; *91*
Gaskins, Carla, 523 *n*.131
Gates, Bill, 177
Gaylor, Rita, 157–158 *n*.197
Gebhard, Paul, 314 *n*.111
Geis, Gilbert, 60 *n*.7; 368 *n*.15; 397 *n*.16; 483 *n*.34
Geller, Susan Rose, 282 *n*.146
Gelles, Richard, 303–304; 316 *nn*.198, 202, 213
Gendreau, Paul, 483 *n*.28; 562–563 *n*.173; 563 *nn*.175, 200
George, David, 155 *n*.93
Georges-Abeyie, Daniel, 63 *n*.117; 342 *n*.28
Gerber, Jurg, 436 *n*.200
Gerdes, D., 154 *n*.42
Gere, Richard, 410
Gersheli, Eduard, 371
Gerstein, Dean, 279 *n*.27
Gertz, Marc, 46; 50; 61 *n*.62; 116 *n*.67; 118 *n*.168; 192 *nn*.69, 72; 473
Gesch, C. Bernard, 126; 127
Ghosh, Palash, 561 *n*.118
Giallombardo, Rose, 562 *n*.153
Giancola, Peter, 435 *n*.144
Gibbons, Donald, 159 *n*.251; 368 *n*.48
Gibbons, John, 550; 562 *n*.146
Gibbs, Jack, 118 *n*.151; 227 *n*.187; 251 *n*.59; 342 *n*.26
Gibbs, John, 62 *n*.97; 115 *n*.45; 116 *n*.72
Gibbs, Natalie, 116 *n*.78; 314 *n*.86
Gibson, Chris, 192 *n*.90; 280 *n*.53
Gibson, Evelyn, 305
Giever, Dennis, 281 *n*.98
Gifford, Robert, 369 *n*.91
Gilbert, Karen, 562 *n*.170
Gilchrist, Lewayne, 280 *n*.46
Gillis, A. R., 252 *n*.91
Gillis, Roy, 317 *n*.238
Gillman, Matthew W., 154 *n*.77
Ginzberg, Eli, 437 *n*.220
Giordano, Peggy, 60 *n*.24; 194 *n*.143; 225 *n*.65; 226 *n*.132; 279 *n*.12; 281 *n*.79; 282 *nn*.120, 144; 368 *n*.47
Giordano, Philip, 405
Giroux, Bruce, 279 *n*.31
Gjeruldsen, Susanne Rogne, 312 *n*.23
Glass, Nancy, 304
Glaze, Lauren E., 560 *n*.74; 561 *n*.83; 563 *n*.196
Gleason, Sandra, 562 *nn*.139–140
Glick, Barry, 60 *n*.9
Glueck, Eleanor, 10; 27 *n*.29; 146–147; 159 *n*.252; 223 *n*.5; 256; 263; 265–266; 278 *n*.2
Glueck, Sheldon, 10; 27 *n*.29; 146–147; 159 *n*.252; 223 *n*.5; 256; 263; 265–266; 278 *n*.2
Goddard, Henry H., 122; 147; 153 *n*.5
Godfrey, Barry, 396 *n*.2
Godney, D., Jr., 523 *n*.120
Goetz, Barry, 437 *n*.226

Goffin, Claire, 563 n.175
Goffman, E., 562 n.130
Gohm, Carol, 314 n.93
Gold, Martin, 62 n.103
Goldberg, Jack, 156 n.149
Goldkamp, John, 43; 117 n.126; 437
    n.215; 523 nn.125, 128–129
Goldman, David, 155 n.117
Goldman, M. S., 435 n.160
Goldsmith, Larry, 559 n.11
Goldstein, Herman, 499; 522 n.84
Goldstein, Michael, 434 n.100
Goldstein, Paul, 312 nn.17, 24; 433 nn.56–
    57, 59; 435 n.165
Golub, Andrew, 436 nn.167–168
Gonzales, Martha Denise, 381
Gonzales, Nancy, 223 n.6
Gooch, Erik, 316 n.175
Gooch, Teresa, 60 n.42
Goodman, Robert, 157 n.192
Goodman, Sam, 349–351
Goodsell, Mill, 498
Goodstein, Laurie, 227 n.152
Goodwill, Alasdair, 315 n.169
Goodwin, Bill, 522 n.88
Goodwin, D. W., 435 n.149
Gootman, Elissa, 316 n.185
Gordon, Kristina Coop, 85 n.25
Gordon, Leslie, 281 n.77; 313 n.32
Gordon, Rachel, 313 n.62
Gordon, Robert, 225 n.96
Gorge, Mathieu, 461 n.57
Goring, Charles, 136–137; 157 n.181
Gorr, Wilpen, 27 n.33; 117 n.130
Gossop, Michael, 436 n.186; 437 n.219
Gottfredson, Denise, 86 nn.65, 85; 193
    nn.102, 125
Gottfredson, Gary, 86 n.65; 193 nn.102,
    125
Gottfredson, Michael, 51; 60 n.17; 61 n.83;
    62 n.86; 211; 269–274; 278; 281
    nn.87–88, 92, 96, 108; 282 n.115;
    387; 398 nn.88–89; 437 n.215; 523
    n.129
Gottfredson, Stephen, 115 n.49
Gottman, John Mordechai, 304
Gottschalk, Earl, 397 n.23
Gould, Arthur, 434 n.89
Gould, Jon, 497; 522 n.71
Gould, Leroy, 54; 62 n.109
Gould, Stephen Jay, 153 n.6
Gove, Walter, 116 n.82; 154 n.41; 156
    n.121
Gowdy, Voncile, 561 n.96
Goyer, P. F., 155 n.91
Grandison, Terry, 84 n.9
Grandjean, P., 153 n.20
Grann, Martin, 312 n.23
Grasmick, Harold, 117 n.118; 118 nn.145,
    152–154; 192 n.82; 193 nn.105, 114,
    124; 281 n.102; 282 nn.113, 123, 130
Gray, Gregory, 153 n.32
Gray, Louis n., 93; 115 n.17; 159 n.237
Gray, M. Kevin, 561 n.84
Gray, Tara, 535
Gray-Ray, Phyllis, 227 nn.147, 161

Graziano, Heidi, 562 n.128
Graziano, Joseph, 153 n.25; 154 n.75
Green, Donald, 118 n.151; 522 n.82
Green, Lorraine, 102; 117 nn.103–104
Green, Rebecca, 461 nn.33–34; 462 n.83
Green, Stuart P., 388; 398 n.97
Green, William, 313 nn.67, 73
Greenbaum, Paul, 561 n.125; 563 n.204
Greenbaum, Robert, 312 n.2
Greenberg, David, 119 n.187; 251 n.57
Greenberg, Stephanie, 192 n.59
Greene, Michael, 313 n.46
Greenemeir, Larry, 460 n.7
Greenfeld, Lawrence, 85 n.53; 118 n.174
Greenhouse, Joel, 154 n.73
Greening, Leilani, 159 n.245
Greenwell, Lisa, 562 n.160
Greenwood, Peter, 437 n.218; 521 nn.24, 30
Gregg, Heather S., 343 n.39
Gregory, Alice, 157 n.161
Gregory, Carol, 62 n.108
Grella, Christine, 562 n.160
Grierson, Jeffrey, 433 n.40
Grieve, John, 522 n.90
Griffiths, Curt Taylor, 252 n.129
Grigoryan, Konstantin, 371
Grigoryan, Mayya Leonidovna, 371
Griswold, David, 226 nn.113, 137
Groff, Elizabeth, 369 n.76
Gross, Alan, 314 n.93
Gross, Harriet, 149
Gross, Kate, 461 n.43
Gross, Samuel, 15; 27 n.39
Groth, A. Nicholas, 292; 294; 314 nn.83,
    115
Grove, H., 398 n.55
Groves, W. Byron, 27 nn.26, 44–45; 193
    nn.102, 125; 234; 250 nn.5, 8, 29
Grow, Brian, 461 n.15
Grubstein, Lori, 63 n.147
Gruenewald, Paul, 192 n.78
Grus, Catherine, 84 n.16
Gu, Joann, 317 n.247
Gudjonsson, Gisli, 149
Guess, Teresa, 251 n.55
Guijarro, Margarita, 279 n.25
Gulderyan, Haroutyun, 371
Gulley, Bill, 156 n.144
Gumz, Edward, 253 n.136
Gundry, Gwen, 156 n.142
Gupta, Humka, 433 n.47; 461 n.58
Gupta, Sanjeev, 343 n.43; 450
Gusfield, Joseph, 403; 432 n.11; 435 n.129
Gutierrez, Francisco, 436 n.204
Gutner, Cassidy, 86 n.101
Guttfredson, Michael, 115 n.24
Gwlasda, Victoria, 85 n.33

Haack, D., 154 n.42
Haapanen, Rudy, 63 n.149; 119 n.196; 281
    n.110
Haas, Ain, 194 n.163
Habermann, Niels, 155 n.83; 159 n.259
Haden, Sara Chiara, 84 n.13
Hagan, John, 27 n.2; 191 n.19; 241–242;
    251 n.43; 252 nn.90–92; 279 n.13

Hagelstam, Camilla, 159 n.273
Hagn, John, 194 n.145
Haikkanen, Helina, 369 n.102
Hakim, Simon, 87 n.124; 115 n.48; 369
    n.86
Häkkänen, Helinä, 159 n.273
Halbfinger, David M., 397 n.44
Hale, Benjamin, 462 n.94
Hale, Chris, 62 n.105
Hale, Matthew, 293
Halkitis, Perry n., 436 n.179
Hall, Andy, 507
Hall, Jerome, 369 n.71
Hall, Joseph S., 398 n.69
Hallam, J., 434 n.103
Halleck, Seymour, 157 n.189
Haller, Mark, 397 n.6
Hallet, Amanda, 279 n.25
Halperin, William, 115 n.50
Halpern, Carolyn, 411; 433 n.60
Halvorsen, Jessica, 314 n.80
Hamilton, Alexander, 322
Hamilton, Catherine, 563 n.205
Hamilton, Thomas, 286
Hamlin, John, 225 n.100
Hammett, Theodore, 398 n.91
Hammock, Georgina, 86 n.86
Hammond, Rodney, 315 n.166
Hammond, Sean M., 127
Hammurabi, 18
Hampson, Sarah E., 127
Hampton, Tracy, 435 n.148
Hanlon, Thomas, 563 nn.199, 206
Hannon, Lance, 61 n.81
Hansell, Saul, 461 nn.14, 29
Hansell, Stephen, 436 n.184
Hansen, Ellen Beate, 368 n.37
Hanson, Karl, 158 n.213; 561 n.81; 563
    n.203
Hanson, Roger, 561 nn.95, 97
Hanssen, Robert, 323
Hansson, Kjell, 159 n.280
Harden, Philip, 155 n.80; 156 n.138
Hardin, John Wesley, 466
Harding, Alan, 27 n.5
Harding, Karen, 155 n.107
Hardt, Robert, 60 n.18
Hare, Robert, 149
Harer, Miles, 44–45; 61 nn.49–50
Harlow, Caroline Wolf, 87 n.127
Harmon, Talia Roitberg, 505; 522
    n.107
Harr, Robin, 562 n.157
Harries, Keith, 191 n.42; 316 n.189
Harrington, Kathy, 279 n.22
Harris, Angela P., 252 n.85
Harris, Anthony, 42; 43; 297
Harris, Eric, 121
Harris, Grant, 149
Harris, Mark, 193 nn.107, 126
Harris, Nathan, 252 n.116
Harris, Patricia, 368 n.61; 560 n.75
Harris, Philip, 63 n.147
Harrison, Lana, 562 n.163
Harrison, Paige, 545; 561 nn.113, 117
Harry, Joseph, 118 n.159; 195 n.195

Hart, Ariel, 60 *n*.11
Hart, Elizabeth, 155 *n*.105
Hart, H. L. A., 403; 432 *n*.9
Hartjen, Clayton, 225 *n*.74
Hartman, Jennifer, 117 *n*.128
Hartnagel, Timothy, 226 *n*.138
Hartstone, Eliot, 191 *n*.37
Hartwig, Holly, 280 *n*.43
Hasday, Jill Elaine, 314 *n*.102
Hathaway, Jeanne, 316 *n*.215
Hathaway, R. Starke, 159 *nn*.260–261
Hausbeck, Kathryn, 434 *n*.78
Hawdon, James, 521 *n*.2
Hawke, W., 153 *n*.30
Hawkins, Darnell, 313 *n*.47; 535; 559 *n*.32
Hawkins, Gordon, 46; 61 *n*.60
Hawkins, J. David, 224 *n*.43; 225 *n*.53;
    262; 280 *nn*.36, 39, 46; 282 *n*.145;
    435–436 *n*.166; 436 *n*.184
Hawkins, John, 330
Hawkins, Yusuf, 307
Hawton, Keith, 279 *n*.18
Hay, Carter, 194 *nn*.155, 161; 224 *n*.27;
    252 *n*.120; 282 *nn*.125, 127; 473
Hay, Dale, 62 *n*.97; 159 *n*.241; 312 *n*.26
Hayes, Frank, 462 *n*.64
Hayes, Roxanne, *110*
Haynie, Dana, 86 *n*.67; 156 *n*.145; 192
    n.52; 224 *n*.51; 225 *n*.65; 282 *n*.120
Hazelbaker, Kim, 368 *n*.50; 369 *n*.63
Hazlewood, Robert, 116 *n*.78; 314 *n*.86
He, J., 153 *n*.23
Heald, F. P., 155 *n*.95
Heath, Linda, 144
Hecker, Jeffrey, 159 *n*.239
Heffernan, Esther, 550; 562 *n*.147
Hefler, Gerd, 194 *n*.145
Heflinger, Craig Anne, 224 *nn*.42, 47
Heide, Kathleen, 300; 313 *n*.33; 316 *n*.174;
    560 *n*.53
Heimer, Karen, 116 *n*.81; 158 *n*.216; 191
    n.39; 227 *n*.169
Heitgerd, Janet, 192 *n*.88
Helenius, Hans, 223 *n*.9
Hellström, Tomas, 461 *n*.56
Hemenway, David, 43; 50
Hemmens, Craig, 483 *n*.33; 562 *n*.126
Henderson, Russell A., 307; 308
Hendriks, Jan, 159 *n*.255
Henggeler, Scott, 158 *nn*.227, 229; 280
    n.40
Henley, Wayen, Jr., 300
Hennard, George, 301
Hennessy, James, 155 *nn*.82, 91
Henry II, King of England, 19
Henson, Trudy Knicely, 368 *n*.47
Hentig, Hans von, 15; 27 *n*.40; 85 *n*.55
Hepburn, John, 368 *n*.11
Hepburn, Lisa, 50
Herek, Gregory, 317 *n*.238
Herenkhol, Todd, 312 *n*.25
Hernandez, Alejandro, 537
Hernandez, Daphne, 193 *n*.103
Hernandez, Jeanne, 316 *n*.202
Hernandez, Michael "Shorty," 477
Herrenkohi, Todd, 280 *nn*.36, 39

Herrnstein, Richard, 24; 27 *n*.55; 62 *n*.90;
    118 *n*.170; 148; 159 *nn*.270, 274; 195
    n.206; 281 *n*.84
Herve, Huues, 314 *n*.112
Hessing, Dick, 281 *n*.105
Hetu, Celine, 368 *n*.38
Heumann, Milton, 523 *n*.143
Hibbeln, J. R., 127
Hickey, Eric, 116 *n*.77
Hickey, J., 158 *n*.226
Hickman, Matthew J., 482 *n*.6; 521 *n*.5
Hickman-Barlow, Melissa, 250–251 *n*.35
Hidaym, Virginia, 158 *n*.221
Hilbert, Richard, 194 *n*.134
Hill, Andreas, 155 *n*.83; 159 *n*.259
Hill, D., 154 *n*.36
Hill, Karl G., 224 *n*.43; 225 *n*.53; 280 *n*.46
Hillbrand, Marc, 158 *n*.212
Hilton, Paris, 98; *541*
Hinckley, John, 48; 143
Hindelang, Michael, 27 *n*.54; 60 *n*.35; 61
    n.71; 62 *n*.103; 147–148; 159 *nn*.261,
    265; 214; 225 *n*.97; 226 *n*.136; 368
    n.39
Hinduja, Sameer, 449; 461 *nn*.46–47
Hinshaw, Stephen, 131; 155 *n*.108
Hintikka, Jukka, 127
Hippchen, Leonard, 153 *nn*.17–18
Hirky, A. Elizabeth, 435 *n*.153
Hirsch, David, 43
Hirschel, J. David, 119 *n*.183
Hirschfield, Paul, 141; 158 *n*.220
Hirschi, Travis, 27 *n*.54; 51; 60 *nn*.17, 35;
    61 *nn*.71, 83; 62 *n*.86; 115 *n*.24;
    147–148; 159 *n*.265; 201; 210–214;
    222; 225 *nn*.57, 80; 226 *n*.109;
    269–274; 278; 281 *nn*.87–88, 92, 96,
    108; 282 *n*.115; 387; 398 *nn*.88–89
Hitchcock, Alfred, 122
Hitler, Adolf, 301; 330
Ho, Ching-hua, 157 *n*.196
Hochstetler, Andy, 86 *n*.91; 225 *n*.72
Hodge, Carole, 227 *n*.146
Hodgins, Sheilagh, 158 *n*.208
Hoffer, A., 153 *n*.31
Hoffman, John, 194 *n*.152; 279 *n*.27
Hoffman, Peter, 563 *nn*.197–198
Hoffmann, John, 194 *n*.172
Hogan, Michael, 191 *n*.44; 192 *n*.69
Hoge, Robert, 281 *n*.65; 483 *n*.28;
    562–563 *n*.173
Hogg, J., 159 *n*.275
Hoheimer, Francis, 361; 369 *n*.79
Holcomb, Jefferson E., 63 *n*.127; 535; 560
    n.43
Hollander, Yona, 461 *n*.40
Holleran, David, 118 *n*.179; 295; 315
    n.128; 561 *n*.86
Hollywood, Jesse James, 213; *213*
Holmes, Malcolm, 226 *n*.116
Holmes, Neville, 462 *n*.93
Holmes, Oliver Wendell, 19; 27 *n*.49
Holmes, Ronald, 315 *n*.170; 316 *n*.178
Holmes, Stephen, 315 *n*.170; 316 *n*.178
Holsinger, Alexander, 117 *n*.128; 224 *n*.33
Holsinger, Kristi, 224 *n*.33

Holt, Rachel, 525–526; 525; 528
Holtzworth-Munroe, Amy, 312 *n*.8
Homant, Robert, 368 *n*.41; 561 *n*.100
Homel, Ross, 116 *n*.91; 369 *n*.95
Homes, Malcolm, 251 *n*.50
Hommer, Daniel, 155 *n*.93
Hong, Rachelle, 87 *n*.116
Hook, Edward, III, 279 *n*.22
Hooker, "Fighting Joe," 410
Hoover, Herbert, 466
Hoover, J. Edgar, 486
Hope, Tim, 85 *n*.48
Hope, Trina, 212; 226 *n*.122
Horney, Julie, 60 *n*.30; 154 *n*.59; 282
    n.121; 313 *n*.52; 314 *n*.120; 521 *n*.3
Horowitz, Ruth, 421; 435 *n*.163
Horwood, L. John, 43; 279 *n*.29; 280 *n*.45
Hoskin, Anthony, 60 *n*.5
Hotaling, Gerald, 433 *n*.65; 434 *n*.75
Hough, Richard, 85 *n*.21
House, James, 281 *nn*.70, 74
House, Paul, 518
Howard, C. Vyvyan, 153 *n*.28
Howard, Gregory, 116 *n*.74; 279 *n*.25
Howell, Harold, 375–376
Howell, James, 63 *n*.152; 116 *n*.74; 313
    n.58
Hoyt, Dan, 86 *n*.64; 314 *n*.92; 435 *n*.159
Hoza, Betsy, 224 *n*.49; 313 *n*.60
Hsieh, Chin-Chi, 61 *n*.77
Hu, Howard, 154 *n*.77
Huang, Bu, 312 *n*.25; 435–436 *n*.166; 436
    n.184
Hubbell, Amy, 435 *n*.158
Huberty, James, 301
Hudson, Booker T., 485; 486
Huebner, Beth, 191 *n*.24; 192 *n*.57
Huesman, L., 159 *n*.240
Huff-Corzine, Lin, 561 *n*.88
Hughes, Donna, 409
Hughes, Lorine, 462 *n*.81
Hughes, Timothy, 563 *n*.201
Huh, David, 200
Huie, S. A., 193 *n*.130
Huizinga, David, 61 *n*.71; 62 *n*.110; 86
    n.72; 117 *n*.119; 119 *n*.183; 192 *n*.79;
    193 *nn*.115, 120; 195 *n*.203
Hulsman, L., 483 *n*.35
Hume, Robert, 506; 523 *n*.115
Hummer, R. A., 193 *n*.130
Humphries, Drew, 252 *n*.88
Hunt, Eric, *125*
Hunt, Geoffrey, 526 *n*.141
Hunter, John, 227 *n*.146
Hurlburt, Michael, 85 *n*.21
Hurley, Jimmy, 84 *n*.13
Hurley, Robert S., 159 *nn*.244, 249, 279
Husted, David, 279 *n*.23
Hutchings, Barry, 135; 157 *nn*.165–166
Hutchison, Ira, 119 *n*.183
Hwang, Shu-ling, 434 *n*.77
Hyde, Janet Shibley, 62 *n*.97

Iacono, William, 156 *n*.153
Ialongo, Nicholas, 280 *n*.35
Immarigeon, Russ, 252 *n*.109

Inciardi, James, 368 *n.*12; 421; 423; 433 *n.*52; 435 *nn.*122, 126, 128, 163; 436 *nn.*169, 185; 437 *n.*229
Inglis, Ruth, 316 *n.*200
Innes, Christopher, 85 *n.*53
Iovanni, Leeann, 62 *n.*108; 218; 227 *n.*190
Ireland, Jane, 461 *n.*44
Ireland, Timothy, 85 *n.*36; 313 *n.*37
Iribarren, Carlos, 126; 127
Irwin, John, 115 *n.*14
Ives, G., 559 *n.*5

Jackall, Robert, 521 *n.*28
Jackson, Jennifer, 314 *n.*80
Jackson, Kenneth, 227 *n.*155
Jackson, Kristina, 435 *n.*150
Jackson, Linda, 227 *n.*146
Jackson, Lori, 312 *n.*6
Jackson, Patrick, 60 *n.*8
Jackson, Rebecca, 562 *n.*159
Jacob, Ayad, 436 *n.*173
Jacob, Da'Mon, 78
Jacobs, Bruce, 96; 97; 115 *nn.*33, 37–38; 368 *n.*59
Jacobs, David, 63 *n.*133; 251 *nn.*39, 47; 521 *n.*21
Jacobs, D. R., Jr., 127
Jacobs, George, 6
Jacobs, James B., 526 *n.*142; 549
Jacobs, K. J., 154 *n.*65
Jacobson, Heather, 461 *nn.*33–34; 462 *n.*83
Jacobson, Neil, 304
Jacoby, Kristen, 27 *n.*39
Jaffe, Pater, 87 *n.*114
Jaffe, Richard S., 29
Jaffee, Sara, 134; 156 *nn.*146, 151, 155
James, Susan, 435 *n.*141
James, William, 142
Janes, Nicole, 398 *n.*78
Jang, Kerry, 156 *n.*127
Jang, Sung Joon, 225 *nn.*58–59
Janis, Irving, 224 *n.*40
Jansen, Robert, 116 *n.*68; 305
Janus, Mark-David, 433 *n.*49
Jarjoura, G. Roger, 194 *n.*151; 224 *n.*38
Jaworski, Leon, 503
Jeanmard, Matthew, 315 *n.*123
Jeffery, C. Ray, 100; 116 *n.*87
Jenkins, Patricia, 226 *nn.*120–121
Jenkins, Philip, 413; 434 *n.*97
Jensen, Eric, 436 *n.*200
Jensen, Gary, 62 *n.*103; 86 *n.*66; 225 *n.*89; 226 *n.*137; 252 *nn.*96–97
Jensen, Vickie, 313 *n.*51
Jerskey, Beth, 156 *n.*149
Jesilow, Paul, 252 *n.*128
Jessor, Richard, 61 *n.*78; 279 *nn.*18–19, 24
Jesus, 244
Jeter, Lynne W., 379
Jiang, Shanhe, 562 *n.*150
Joe, Karen Ann, 96; 115 *n.*31
Johansson, Peter, 149
John Paul II, Pope, 405
Johnson, Bruce D., 281 *n.*78; 436 *nn.*167–168, 170
Johnson, Byron, 225 *nn.*58–59

Johnson, Carrie, 379
Johnson, Christine, 282 *n.*126
Johnson, David, 397 *n.*31
Johnson, Dawn, 85 *n.*25
Johnson, Holly, 157 *n.*170
Johnson, Janice, 435 *n.*141
Johnson, Jeffery G., 144
Johnson, Jeffrey, 41; 43; 433 *n.*64; 434 *n.*74
Johnson, Lee Michael, 227 *n.*163
Johnson, Lyndon B., 188; 467
Johnson, Margaret, 462 *n.*93
Johnson, Mark, 60 *n.*20
Johnson, Robert, 227 *n.*170, 180; 279 *n.*27
Johnson, Wendell, 85 *n.*33
Johnson, W. Wesley, 250–251 *n.*35
Johnston, David Cay, 398 *n.*66
Johnston, Eric, 560 *n.*70
Johnston, Lloyd, 60 *nn.*21–22; 62 *n.*111; 435 *n.*132
Johnstone, J., 195 *n.*195
Jolin, Annette, 433 *n.*38
Jolliffe, Darrick, 279 *n.*16
Jon, Nina, 252 *n.*89
Jones, David, 521 *n.*4
Jones, Donald, 135; 157 *nn.*162–163
Jones, Guitana, 405
Jones, Heather, 224 *n.*26
Jones, Lisa, 316 *nn.*197, 203–204
Jones, Liz, 521 *n.*4
Jones, Mark, 560 *n.*75
Jones, Marshall, 135; 157 *nn.*162–163
Jones, Peter, 63 *n.*147; 437 *n.*215; 561 *n.*102
Jones, Philip B. C., 25
Jones, Shayne, 192 *n.*60
Jonsson, Patrik, 87 *n.*133
Jonzon, Eva, 316 *n.*205
Jordan, Carol, 317 *n.*268
Jordan, Lamar, 85 *n.*44
Jordan, Michael, 556
Jorgensen, Jenel S., 157 *n.*193
Jorgensen, P. J., 153 *n.*20
Jose-Kampfner, Christina, 562 *n.*148
Joyce, James, 413
Joyner, James, 434 *n.*87
Juan Carlos, King, 333
Judah, Richard, 155 *n.*107
Junger, Marianne, 226 *n.*128; 279 *n.*25; 281 *n.*105
Junger-Tas, Josine, 226 *n.*128
Jussim, Lee, 224 *n.*34

Kadleck, Colleen, 117 *n.*100
Kageyama, Yuri, 313 *n.*74
Kahan, Susan, 561 *n.*85
Kahler, Christopher, 85 *n.*25
Kahn, Arnold, 314 *n.*80
Kaine, Timothy, 48
Kakoulidis, Christos, 312 *n.*5
Kalb, Larry, 86 *n.*72; 279 *n.*16
Kaloupek, Danny, 85 *n.*37
Kaltiala-Heino, Rittakerttu, 157 *n.*194
Kandel, Denise, 225 *n.*75; 226 *n.*133; 435 *n.*154
Kandel, Elizabeth, 154–155 *n.*79
Kane, John, 462 *nn.*67, 69
Kane, Robert, 193 *n.*112; 313 *n.*54

Kanka, Megan, 22; 81; 82
Kanka, Richard and Maureen, 82
Kant, Immanuel, 353
Kanth, Sarita, 13
Kaplan, David, 433 *n.*17
Kaplan, Howard, 210; 227 *nn.*170–71, 180
Kaplan, Steven, 374; 374
Karasik, Theodore W., 343 *n.*39
Karberg, Jennifer, 560 *n.*69; 561 *n.*117
Karmen, Andrew, 87 *n.*115; 315 *n.*133; 521 *n.*12
Karp, David R., 252 *n.*127
Kasen, Stephanie, 43; 144
Kasza, Kristen, 153 *n.*19
Kates, Don, 116 *n.*54
Katz, Jack, 132; 156 *n.*122
Katz, Janet, 144
Katzenbach, Nicholas de B., 550; 562 *n.*146
Kauffman, K., 158 *n.*226
Kaufman, Jeanne, 84 *n.*19
Kaufman, Joanne, 63 *n.*131; 313 *n.*42; 315 *n.*166
Kavilanz, Parija B., 250 *n.*1
Kawai, Eriko, 313 *n.*62
Kay, Barbara, 226 *n.*108
Kaysen, Debra, 62 *n.*101
Kazemian, Lila, 60 *n.*31; 63 *n.*148
Keeler, Gordon, 158 *n.*203
Keels, Micere, 192 *n.*80
Keenan, Kate, 224 *n.*45; 279 *n.*31
Keeney, Belea, 300; 316 *n.*174
Keire, Mara, 434 *n.*80
Keith, Bruce, 224 *n.*17
Kellam, Sheppard, 280 *n.*35
Kellar, Mark, 562 *n.*138
Kellaway, Jean, 559 *n.*4
Kellett, Sue, 149
Kelley, Thomas, 368 *n.*41
Kelling, George, 117 *n.*125; 498; 521 *n.*8; 522 *nn.*76–77
Kellogg, Michael, 330; 343 *n.*32
Kelly, Kathryn, 157 *n.*184
Kelly, Linda, 561 *n.*107
Kelly, Thomas, 561 *n.*100
Kempe, C. Henry, 316 *n.*194
Kempe, Ruth S., 316 *n.*194
Kempf, Kimberly, 226 *n.*130
Kempf-Leonard, Kimberly, 57; 63 *nn.*151–152; 118 *n.*173
Kempinen, Cynthia, 561 *n.*111
Kendall, Jerry, 560 *n.*35
Kendziora, Kimberly, 316 *n.*214
Kennedy, Anthony M., 518
Kennedy, Daniel, 368 *n.*41; 561 *n.*100
Kennedy, David, 50; 522 *n.*87
Kennedy, John F., 188
Kennedy, Leslie, 87 *n.*121; 281 *n.*91
Kennedy, Sean, 432 *n.*1
Kenney, T. J., 155 *n.*95
Kerbs, Jodi, 157–158 *n.*197
Kercher, Kyle, 62 *n.*85
Kerich, Michael, 155 *n.*93
Kerner, Hans-Jürgen, 224 *n.*44
Kerns, Suzanne, 280 *n.*39
Kerr, Margaret, 149
Kershaw, Sarah, 316 *n.*185

Kershner, J., 153 n.30
Kessler, Daniel, 106; 117 n.139
Kethineni, Sesha, 226 n.134
Keys, David, 251 n.55
Khan, A. Q., 337
Kidd, Sean, 435 n.147
Kiehl, Kent, 149
Kiley, Marion, 433 n.52
Killen, Edgar Ray, 492
Killias, Martin, 42–43; 43
Killip, Steve, 87 n.114
Kilpatrick, Dean, 84 n.14; 85 n.27; 86 n.100; 312 n.20
Kim, D., 153 n.23
Kim, Julia Yun Soo, 60 n.26
Kim, KiDeuk, 118 n.167
Kim, Sang-Weon, 193 n.132
Kim, Yeora, 461 n.39
Kimble, Charles, 86 n.97
King, Harry, 348; 368 n.13
King, John, 317 n.252
King, Kate, 119 n.194
Kingery, Paul M., 159 nn.244, 249, 279
Kingree, J. B., 157 n.196
Kingsbury, Kathleen, 192 n.53
Kingsworth, Rodney, 315 n.127; 522 n.97
Kinkade, Patrick, 317 n.261
Kinlock, Timothy, 280 n.34
Kinney, Linda, 314 n.120
Kinscherff, Robert, 158 n.199
Kinsey, Karyl, 118 nn.145, 153
Kinsey, Richard, 251 n.70
Kinsie, Paul, 433 nn.51, 55
Kipp, Heidi, 224 n.26
Kiritsy, Mary, 153 n.33
Kivivuori, Janne, 27 n.32; 60 n.3; 85 n.28; 157 n.194
Kjelsberg, Ellen, 157 n.191
Klackenberg-Larsson, Ingrid, 159 n.272
Klaus, Patsy, 305; 368 nn.58, 60
Klebold, Dylan, 121
Kleck, Gary, 40; 43; 46; 49; 50; 61 n.62; 80; 87 nn.128–131; 116 nn.54, 67; 118 n.168; 251 n.54; 534; 535
Klein, David, 506; 523 n.115
Klein, Uwe, 159 n.258
Kleinknecht, William, 399 n.122
Kleinman, Ken P., 154 n.77
Kletschka, H. K., 155 n.112
Kline, Jennie, 153 n.25
Kling, Kristen, 62 n.97
Klinger, David, 118 n.164; 193 n.110; 496; 497
Klockars, Carl, 251 n.62; 349; 368 n.21; 436 nn.176, 178, 192
Kluger, Jeffrey, 343 n.49
Knight, Raymond, 314 n.84
Knigt, Zelda, 316 n.176
Knoller, Marjorie, 296
Knowles, Gordon, 96; 115 n.36
Kobrin, Solomon, 188; 192 n.84; 195 n.210
Kocieniewski, David, 397 n.44
Koenen, Karestan, 156 n.149
Kohlberg, Lawrence, 142; 158 nn.225–226
Kohn, Robert, 85 n.25
Kolbo, Jerome, 85 n.40

Konofal, Eric, 153 nn.20, 25
Koons, Barbara, 191 n.43
Koons-Witt, Barbara, 535
Koops, Willem, 159 n.238
Kopie, Kathy, 316 n.204
Kornhauser, Ruth, 191 n.27; 195 n.204
Koroloff, Nancy, 157–158 n.197
Kort-Butler, Lisa, 194 n.157
Koss, Mary, 414; 434 nn.94, 98
Kosterman, Rick, 280 nn.36, 39; 282 n.145; 435–436 n.166; 436 n.184
Kovandzic, Tomislav V., 49; 50; 117 n.124; 315 n.160; 521 n.20; 559 n.27
Koziol-McLain, Jane, 304
Kozlowski, L. Dennis, 378
Krafft-Ebing, Richard von, 406
Krah, Barbara, 313 n.69
Krahn, Harvey, 226 n.138
Kramer, John, 523 n.144
Kramer, Lisa, 433 n.62
Kramer, Ronald, 397 n.12; 398 n.105
Kreager, Derek, 117 n.119
Kreps, Janet, 315 n.144
Kreuger, A., 154 n.68
Krisberg, Barry, 483 n.34
Kristol, Irving, 403; 433 n.14
Krivo, Lauren, 61 n.75; 191 n.16; 193 nn.107, 109, 126
Krohn, Marvin, 61 nn.78, 82; 62 n.109; 116 nn.73–74; 156 n.137; 218; 224 nn.39, 48; 225 nn.77, 84, 86; 226 n.139; 227 nn.162, 168, 186; 262; 279 nn.6, 19, 24; 314 n.119; 435 n.142; 436 n.196
Krueger, P. M., 193 n.130
Krueger, Robert, 157 n.188; 159 n.263
Krug, Etienne, 13; 316 n.191
Kruger, Natalie, 201
Kruttschnitt, Candace, 63 n.119; 144; 279 n.28; 280 n.64; 281 n.67; 562 n.149
Krynicki, V. E., 155 n.113
Krystal, John, 158 n.212
Ku, Simon, 86 n.90
Kubik, Elizabeth, 159 n.239
Kubrin, Charis, 191 n.46; 192 n.49; 289; 313 n.53; 555
Kuczera, Leszek, 360
Kuh, Richard, 523 n.141
Kully, Christine, 314 n.80
Kumar, Virendra, 13
Kumpulkinen, Kirsti, 223 n.9
Kunarac, Dragoljub, 291
Kurki, Leena, 247
Kurlychek, Megan, 227 n.189; 561 n.111
Kurtz, Ellen, 191 n.43
Kurtz, Steven, 433 n.52
Kurz, Gwen, 57; 63 n.146
Kutchinsky, Berl, 434 n.99

Lab, Steven, 562 n.169; 563 n.173
Labouvie, Erich, 62 n.92
Lacasse, Lori, 155 nn.81, 92, 98
Lacerte-Lamontagne, Celine, 368 n.38
Lacey, Marc, 314 n.76
Ladd, Heather, 562 n.128

LaFave, Wayne, 315 nn.137–138; 368 nn.25, 43; 369 nn.65, 72, 74; 504; 522 n.100
Lafree, Gary, 63 n.136; 100; 116 nn.80–81; 118 n.142; 193 n.131; 313 n.65; 315 n.130
LaGrange, Randy, 226 n.141
LaGrange, Teresa, 86 n.83; 195 n.177; 226 nn.118, 129
Lahey, Benjamin, 224 n.26; 313 n.62
Laidler, Karen Joe, 13
Laird, Robert, 280 n.45
Lalumiere, Martin, 149
Lambert, Paul, 562 n.159
Lambert, Sharon, 280 n.35
Lamontagne, Yves, 368 n.38
Land, Kenneth, 86 nn.80, 96; 87 n.120; 192 n.62; 280 n.47
Landau, Simha, 86 n.98
Landwehr, Patricia, 315 n.123
Lane, Jodi, 192 n.71
Langan, Patrick A., 13; 436 n.207; 522 nn.74, 91; 561 n.102; 563 n.201
Langley, Kate, 156 n.126
Langworthy, Robert, 521 n.27
Lanier, C. S., 562 n.129
Lansky, Meyer, 390
Lanza-Kaduce, Lonn, 62 n.109; 118 n.159; 225 n.84
Laplante, David, 156 n.154
LaPrairie, Carol, 252 n.125
Laqueur, Walter, 343 n.30
Lardiere, John "Johnny Coca Cola," 391
Larivee, S., 63 n.153
Larkin, Nancy, 119 n.187
La Rooy, David, 434 n.71
LaRosa, John, 62 nn.89, 91
Larson, David, 225 n.58
Larson, Jessie, 522 n.94
Larson, Reed, 86 nn.74, 76
Lascala, Elizabeth, 192 n.78
Lasley, James, 226 n.140
Latessa, Edward, 561 n.122
Lattimore, Pamela, 312 n.25
Lau, Karen, 153 n.28
Laub, John, 27 n.30; 43; 63 n.155; 153 n.8; 156 nn.132, 139; 199; 227 nn.184–185; 256; 262–267; 278; 278–279 nn.3, 15; 280 nn.57–58; 281 n.68
Laucht, M., 154 n.42
Laughon, Kathryn, 304
Lauritsen, Janet, 85 n.47; 115 n.41; 313 n.52
Lavater, J. K., 7
LaVigne, Nancy, 116 n.94; 369 n.76
Law, Cardinal Bernard, 405
Law, Fergus, 279 n.18
Law, Moira, 158 n.213; 563 n.203
Lawrence, D. H., 413
Lawrence, Frederick M., 308; 317 n.242
Lay, Kenneth, 96; 378–379
Lazoritz, Martin, 279 n.23
Lea, John, 239–240; 251 nn.66, 70
Leaf, Philip, 280 n.35
LeBeau, James, 314 n.87
Lebed, Jonathan, 443

Lebel, Thomas, 227 n.191
LeBlanc, Marc, 63 nn.148, 153; 226 n.115; 256; 279 n.5; 280 n.36; 281 n.102
Lecendreux, Michel, 153 nn.20, 25
Lechter, Jonathan, 399 n.114
Leclerc, Benoit, 116 n.79
Lee, Beverly, 86 n.106
Lee, Cheryl Hill, 191 nn.6, 17
Lee, Daniel, 192 n.52
Lee, Felicia, 317 n.241
Lee, Gang, 225 n.88
Lee, L. V., 153 n.24
Lee, Matthew, 43; 67–68; 85 n.29; 192 n.56; 312 n.14
Lefforge, Noelle, 223 n.7
Legault, Richard, 50
Legon, Jeordan, 461 n.12
Leiber, Michael, 63 n.124; 251 n.36; 252 n.99
Leisring, Penny, 313 n.39
Lemert, Edwin M., 217; 222; 227 n.175; 355; 368 nn.19, 41; 483 n.32
Lemmon, John, 313 n.29
Lemos, Robert, 461 n.35
Lencz, Todd, 155 n.81
Lengua, Liliana, 280 nn.36, 39
Lenza, Michael, 251 n.55
Leo, Richard A., 522 n.55
Leonard, Kenneth, 304
Leonard, Kimberly Kempf, 226 n.135
Leonardsen, Dag, 13
Lerman, Paul, 552; 562 n.168
Leschied, Alan, 281 n.65
Leukefeld, Carl, 428
Levander, M. T., 158 n.218
Levenson, Michael, 227 n.172
Levin, Brian, 317 n.240
Levin, David J., 563 n.201
Levin, Jack, 300; 301; 307; 316 nn.173, 179, 182–183; 317 nn.232–234, 250, 255; 414; 434 n.104
Levine, David M., 461 n.20
Levine, Murray, 252 n.97
Levitt, Steven D., 40–41; 43; 44; 61 n.48; 106; 107; 110; 117 nn.105, 124, 139; 118 n.162; 119 n.189; 274; 282 n.137; 369 n.62; 521 n.20
Levrant, Sharon, 253 n.135
Levy, Clifford, 398 n.58
Levy, Diane, 153 n.25
Lewicka, S., 154 n.42
Lewis, Dorothy Otnow, 286; 288; 312 nn.6–7; 313 nn.34, 36
Lewis, James Paul, 271
Lewis, John, 60 n.30
Lewis, Orlando, 559 n.8
Lewis, Oscar, 163; 191 n.7
Lewis, S. A., 155 n.90
Li, Fuzhong, 224 n.48
Li, Spencer, 118 n.168
Libby, Therese J., 20
Liddick, Don, 399 n.122
Liddle, Peter F., 149
Lieberman, Joseph, 405
Lillard, Lee, 281 n.70
Lin, Kuei-Hsiu, 313 n.32

Lind, Bronwyn, 86 n.90
Lindblad, Frank, 316 n.205
Linder, Douglas, 342 n.7
Lindgren, Scott, 153 n.33
Lindh, John Walker, 322; 322; 323
Lindner, Charles, 561 n.106
Lineberry, William, 523 n.114
Link, Bruce, 158 n.204; 227 n.145
Linnoila, Markku, 155 nn.116–117
Linster, Richard, 312 n.25
Linz, Daniel, 314 n.116; 434 n.101
Lipsey, Mark, 279 n.21; 483 n.29; 563 n.174
Liptak, Adam, 87 n.132
Lipton, Douglas, 159 n.246; 483 n.15; 562 n.166; 563 n.174
Liska, Allen, 86 n.81; 192 n.86; 193 n.104; 226 n.143
Litan, Avivah, 462 n.76
Littlejohn, Darryl, 65
Litton, Roger, 369 n.92
Liu, Jianhong, 127; 193 n.104
Liu, Xiaoru, 227 n.159
Liu, Xinhua, 153 n.25
Liu, Zhiqiang, 109
Livaditis, Miltos, 312 n.5
Livesley, W. John, 156 n.127
Livingston, Jennifer, 314 nn.78, 80, 82
Lizotte, Alan, 61 nn.78, 82; 87 n.125; 116 nn.73–74; 156 n.137; 224 n.39; 251 n.51; 262; 279 nn.6, 19, 24; 313 nn.56, 59; 435 n.142; 436 n.196
Lo, Celia, 437 n.223
Lochman, J. E., 159 n.243
Locke, John, 353
Locker, John, 396 n.2
Lockwood, Daniel, 549; 562 nn.134–135
Loeber, Rolf, 62 n.97; 63 n.153; 86 nn.68, 72; 153 n.19; 157 n.190; 158 nn.197, 220; 159 n.241; 224 nn.35, 45; 256; 258–260; 279 nn.5, 7, 16, 26, 28, 31; 280 n.36, 45, 51–52; 312 n.26; 313 nn.42, 62; 436 n.193
Lofland, John, 227 n.173
Lofquist, William, 505; 522 n.107
Loftin, Colin, 521 n.19
Loftus, Margaret, 368 n.30
Logan, Charles, 561 n.120; 562 n.169
Logan, T. K., 317 n.268; 428
Lögdberg, B., 158 n.218
Logie, Robert, 369 n.80
Logio, Kim, 84 n.17
Lohan, Lindsay, 98
Lohr, David, 482–483 n.10
Lolacono, Nancy J., 153 n.25
Lombroso, Cesare, 7–8; 25; 27 n.12; 52–53; 62 n.93; 122; 151
Lonczk, Heather, 282 n.145
Loney, Bryan, 156 n.153
Longmore, Monica, 225 n.65; 282 n.120
Longshore, Douglas, 282 n.127; 420; 435 n.138
Loomis, Dana, 317 n.259
Lopez, John, 522 n.97
Lorenz, Konrad, 287; 290; 312 n.12
Lotke, Eric, 191 n.20; 483 n.23

Lott, John, Jr., 50
Love, Craig T., 159 n.268
Lovrich, Nicholas, 192 n.90; 522 n.79
Lowenstein, George, 118 n.157
Lozano, Rafael, 13; 316 n.191
Lu, Chunmeng, 86 n.69
Luciano, Lucky, 390
Lucken, Karol, 560 n.76
Luckenbill, David, 298–299; 313 n.49; 315 n.158
Ludwig, Jens, 48–49; 50; 297; 315 n.149
Lueck, Monika, 312 n.10
Lueck, Thomas J., 434 n.115
Lui, Kung-Jong, 87 n.126
Lunde, Donald, 315 n.135
Lundman, Richard, 117 n.127; 521 n.25
Lunsford, Jessica, 406; 407
Luntz, Sarah, 434 n.72
Luo, Michael, 398 n.58
Lupton, Teah, 522 n.96
Luque, Luis, 315 n.123
Lurigio, Arthur, 84 n.4; 85 n.31; 87 n.123; 436 n.210; 437 n.212; 561 n.90
Lussier, Patrick, 280 n.36
Luukkaala, Tiina, 157 n.194
Lyght, C. E., 155 n.114
Lykken, David, 27 n.10; 118 n.156; 149
Lynam, Donald, 154 n.79; 157 n.179; 158 n.234; 159 nn.255, 267; 279 n.26; 280 nn.37, 45, 51; 281–282 n.111; 428
Lynch, James, 84 n.12; 87 n.124; 119 n.195
Lynch, Kathleen Bodisch, 282 n.146
Lynch, Michael, 27 nn.26, 44–45; 154 n.70; 234; 250 nn.5–6, 8, 10, 13, 29, 33; 251 n.36; 388; 397 n.7; 398 nn.67, 98
Lyons, Charles R., 58
Lyons, Michael, 156 n.149
Lyttle, Robert, 446

Maakestad, William, 398 n.94
MacCoun, Robert, 436 n.175
MacDonald, John, 265; 281 n.75; 282 n.133
MacDonald, Julia, 369 n.91
Mace, David E., 157 n.193
Machalek, Richard, 157 n.167
Machon, Ricardo, 155 n.79
MacIntosh, Randall, 315 n.127
Mack, Kristin, 252 n.99
Mackenzie, Doris Layton, 119 n.181; 281 n.73; 562 n.171
Mackesy-Amiti, Mary Ellen, 435 n.165
Maclean, Donald, 323
Macmillan, Ross, 66; 84 n.8; 281 n.67
Maercker, Andreas, 85 n.38; 87 n.112
Maguin, Eugene, 224 n.35
Maguire, Edward, 521 n.3
Maguire, Kathleen, 195 n.208
Mahanna, Paul, 483 n.11
Maher, Dennis, 295
Maher, Lisa, 433 n.53
Maheshwari, Ayonija, 433 n.47
Mahoney, Barry, 561 nn.95, 97
Maier, Jeanette, 406
Maier, Timothy W., 368 n.31
Maier-Katkin, Daniel, 194 n.175

Makepeace, James, 316 *n*.214
Malamuth, Neil, 314 *n*.117; 414; 434
   nn.94, 98
Malecki, Christine Kerres, 315 *n*.163
Malin, Tom, 401–402
Malisova, L., 154 *n*.42
Malvo, John Lee, 301
Man, Christopher D., 563 *n*.176
Mancini, Christina, 473
Mandela, Nelson, 247
Manganello, Jennifer, 304
Manning, Wendy, 225 *n*.65; 282 *n*.120
Mantell, Michael, 309; 317 *n*.256
Manzano, Thaddeus, *34*
Maples, Michelle, 227 *n*.191
Maras, A., 154 *n*.42
Marchak, Patricia, 336–337
Marchbanks, Polly, 87 *n*.126
Marenin, Otwin, 274; 282 *n*.129
Marescialli, Mauro, 13
Maric, Alexandra, 434 *n*.102
Marimuthu, Jaisankar, 439
Marini, Margaret Mooney, 62 *n*.97
Marino, Raymond, *360*
Markianos, M., 156 *n*.119
Markman, Stephen, 119 *n*.197; 560 *n*.60
Markovitz, J. H., 127
Markowitz, Benjamin, 213
Markowitz, Fred, 193 *n*.104; 195 *n*.185
Markowitz, Nick, 213
Marneros, Andreas, 158 *n*.209
Marquart, James, 116 *n*.62; 119 *n*.192;
   279 *n*.26; 560 *n*.57; 561 *n*.121; 562
   nn.126, 155
Marschak, Patricia, 343 *n*.60
Marshall, D. D., 159 *n*.272
Marshall, Ineke Haen, 226 *n*.128; 282
   n.121
Marshall, John, 323
Marshall, Paul, 154 *n*.64
Marshall, Stephen, 317 *n*.259
Martens, Frederick, 399 *n*.116
Martin, Adrian, *201*
Martin, Catherine, 428
Martin, Neilson, 156 *n*.153
Martin, Robert, 49–50
Martin, Susan, 436 *n*.194; 521 *n*.33
Martines, Laura, 316 *n*.209
Martinez, Amos, 225 *n*.101
Martinez, Ramiro, Jr., 40; 43; 312 *n*.14
Martinson, Robert, 93; 115 *n*.8; 483 *n*.15;
   552; 562 *n*.166
Maruna, Shadd, 158–159 *n*.235; 227
   n.191; 560 *n*.70
Marvell, Thomas, 50; 117 *nn*.123–124,
   138; 119 *n*.189; 521 *n*.19; 559 *n*.16
Marx, Karl, 9; 10; 25; 27 *n*.26; 230–232;
   250 *nn*.8–9, 11
Marziano, Vincent, 159 *n*.247
Maschi, Tina, 158 *n*.220; 159 *n*.242
Mason, W. Alex, 280 *nn*.36, 39
Massey, James, 225 *n*.86; 226 *n*.139
Massino, Joseph, 394
Masters, Kimberly, 562 *n*.154
Masterson, Bat, 466
Mastrofski, Stephen, 497; 521 *n*.23; 522 *n*.71

Mastromarino, Michael, 353; *353*
Mateu-Gelabert, Pedro, 521 *n*.13
Mathers, Richard, 226 *nn*.114, 119
Matheson, Daniel, 27 *n*.39
Matsueda, Ross, 104; 116 *n*.81; 117 *n*.119;
   227 *nn*.158, 169
Matteson, T. H., *6*
Matthews, Steven "Cutthroat," *476*
Matusko, Jacqueline, 312 *n*.22
Matza, David, 207–209; 222; 225 *nn*.91–94
Maudsley, Henry, 7
Mauer, Marc, 119 *n*.190
Maughan, Barbara, 279 *n*.31
Mawson, A. R., 154 *n*.65
Maxwell, Christopher, 119 *n*.183; 279–280
   n.32; 434 *n*.67; 436 *n*.194
Maxwell, Sheila Royo, 279–280 *n*.32; 434
   n.67; 561 *n*.84
May, David, 74; 86 *n*.73
Mazerolle, Lorraine Green, 117 *nn*.100,
   131, 134
Mazerolle, Paul, 158 *n*.198; 194 *nn*.152,
   158–160; 279 *nn*.11, 17; 280 *n*.55;
   281 *n*.110
Mazzetti, Mark, 343 *n*.43
McAndrew, Ron, 550
McAuslan, Pam, 312 *n*.21
McBride, Duane, 437 *n*.229
McCaffrey, Shannon, 223 *n*.3
McCaghy, Charles, 27 *n*.43; 368 *n*.47; 369
   n.68; 397 *n*.53; 433 *nn*.39, 42; 435
   n.130
McCall, Andrew, 368 *n*.2
McCall, Patricia, 63 *n*.132; 192 *n*.87; 280
   n.47
McCarthy, Bill, 85 *n*.61; 118 *n*.163; 225
   n.67; 252 *n*.92
McCarty, Carolyn, 144
McCauley, Elizabeth, 280 *nn*.36, 39
McCleary, Richard, 118 *n*.142
McClelland, Gary, 27 *n*.41
McClintock, F. H., 305
McCluskey, John, 191 *n*.24
McConnell, Mike, 337
McConville, Mike, 523 *n*.132
McCord, Eric, 522 *n*.95
McCord, Joan, 279 *n*.10
McCorkle, Richard, 483 *n*.27
McCue, Colleen, 60 *n*.42
McCurdy, Sheryl, 433 *n*.61
McDaniel, Charles, 562 *n*.165
McDevitt, Jack, 307; 308; 317 *nn*.232–233,
   247; 522 *n*.80
McDonel, E. C., 159 *n*.246
McDowall, David, 61 *n*.82; 84 *n*.12; 86
   n.77; 435 *n*.142; 521 *n*.19
McEntire, Ranee, 192 *n*.72
McFall, R., 159 *n*.246
McFarland, Christine, 154 *n*.73
McFarlane, Alexander, 158 *n*.217
McFarlane, Judith, 304
McFeely, Richard, 399 *n*.132
McGahey, Richard, 192 *n*.52
McGarrell, Edmund, 521 *n*.14; 560 *n*.55
McGee, Rob, 157 *n*.188
McGloin, Jean Marie, 158 *n*.232

McGlothlin, W., 436 *n*.185
McGriff, Bill, 561 *n*.120
McGue, Matt, 156 *n*.153
McGuffin, Peter, 156 *n*.153
McGuire, Stryker, 312 *n*.4
Mchugh, Suzanne, 156 *n*.145
McKay, Henry D., 168–170; 190; 191
   nn.30, 32
McKenzie, Roderic, 27 *n*.24
McKibben, André, 116 *n*.79
McKinney, Aaron J., 307; 308
McKinney, Joseph R., 437 *n*.216
McLanahan, Sara, 224 *n*.14
McLaughlin, Vance, 560 *n*.49
McLean, Bethany, 379
McLean, W. Graham, 153 *n*.28
McLeod, Jane, 279 *n*.28
McLeod, Maureen, 87 *n*.134
McMackin, Robert, 85 *n*.37
McMillan, Richard, 43; 86 *n*.95; 192 *n*.50
McMorris, Barbara J., 281 *n*.67
McMurray, Scott, 397 *n*.33
McNamara, Grace, 435 *n*.153
McNeill, Richard, 193 *nn*.102, 125
McNulty, Thomas, 191 *n*.22; 193 *n*.119
McPhee, Mike, 317 *n*.231
McVeigh, Gloria, 127
McVeigh, Timothy, 21
Mdzinarishvili, A., 153 *n*.23
Mead, George Herbert, 17; 214; 226–227
   n.144
Meadows, Susannah, 312 *n*.1
Mears, Daniel, 62 *n*.99; 225 *n*.78; 473;
   547; 561 *n*.115
Measelle, Jeffrey, 156 *n*.146
Medina-Ariza, Juanjo, 85 *n*.45
Medlicott, Sandra, 275
Mednick, Sarnoff A., 127; 135; 153 *n*.17;
   154 *n*.55; 155 *nn*.79, 84; 156
   nn.124–125, 131; 157 *nn*.165–166,
   178; 158 *n*.208; 312–313 *n*.27
Meehan, Albert, 239; 251 *n*.49
Meeker, James, 192 *n*.71
Meesters, Cor, 155 *n*.104; 282 *n*.131
Megargee, Edward, 159 *n*.262
Meier, Robert, 50; 61 *n*.68; 86 *n*.93; 191
   n.26; 223 *n*.4
Meili, Trisha, *79*
Mellingen, Kjetil, 127
Meloy, Reid, 316 *n*.175; 317 *n*.265
Meltzer, Howard, 157 *n*.192
Menard, Scott, 192 *n*.54; 282 *n*.118
Mendenhall, Ruby, 192 *n*.80
Mendes, Silvia, 117 *n*.112
Mendrek, Adrianna, 149
Mercy, James, 13; 49; 87 *n*.126; 315 *n*.153;
   316 *n*.191
Merkens, Hans, 194 *n*.145
Mero, Richard, 281 *n*.70
Merton, Robert, 176–177; 190; 194
   n.133
Meseck-Bushey, Sylvia, 156 *nn*.128, 144
Mesquita, Ethan Bueno de, 343 *n*.58
Messer, Julie, 157 *n*.192
Messerschmidt, James, 241; 251 *nn*.78, 84
Messerschmidt, Pamela, 312 *n*.20

Messner, Steven, 43; 60 n.5; 61 n.80; 75; 86 n.95; 116 nn.65, 76; 144; 177–178; 190; 191 n.3; 192 nn.50–51; 193 n.99; 194 nn.138–139, 141, 168; 224 n.41; 312 n.16; 313 nn.47, 55; 316 n.218; 560 n.38

Metraux, Stephen, 555

Metz, Tim, 398 n.81

Meyer, Joanne, 156 n.149

Meyer, Jon'a, 535

Michalowski, Michael, 398 n.105

Michalowski, Raymond, 27 n.44; 397 n.12

Michelson, n., 155 n.79

Miech, Richard, 61 n.78; 279 n.19

Miethe, Terance, 86 nn.77, 80, 93; 251 n.52; 315 n.151

Milan, Stephanie, 279 n.8

Miles, William, 60 n.25

Mileusnic, Darinka, 27 n.41

Milich, Rich, 428

Milken, Michael, 386

Miller, Alan, 194 n.152

Miller, Amanda, 315 n.161

Miller, Amy, 562 n.149

Miller, Bobbi Viegas, 86 nn.74, 76

Miller, Brenda, 85 n.21

Miller, Darcy, 62 n.97

Miller, Frank W., 504; 522 n.99

Miller, Henry, 413

Miller, Jack, 48

Miller, Jerome, 55; 63 n.128

Miller, Jerry, 478

Miller, Jody, 96; 115 n.37; 306; 317 n.222

Miller, Joel, 521 n.13

Miller, John, 409

Miller, Joshua, 158 n.234; 159 n.255

Miller, Kirk, 60 n.27

Miller, Lawrence, 343 nn.40, 47

Miller, L. E., 156 n.130

Miller, Lisa, 193 n.123

Miller, Matthew, 41; 43; 50

Miller, Michael, 398 n.81

Miller, Susan, 62 n.108

Miller, Ted R., 84 n.7

Miller, Thomas, 312 n.24

Miller, Todd, 116 n.61; 279 n.25; 435 n.151

Miller, Walter, 182; 183; 188; 195 n.183; 225 n.61

Mills, Michael, 397 n.13

Milman, Harold, 153 n.22

Milner, Trudie, 118 n.150

Mincy, Ronald, 191 n.21

Miner, Michael, 85 n.23; 434 n.68

Minniti, Maria, 399 n.122

Minor, Kevin, 561 n.87

Minor, M. William, 118 n.159; 225 n.96

Mio, J. S., 435 n.155

Mirowsky, John, 62 n.97; 192 n.75

Mirsky, Chester, 523 n.132

Mischel, Walter, 159 n.250

Misson, Sebastian, 433 n.40

Mitchell, Nick, 227 n.191

Mitchell, Ojmarrh, 535

Moch, Annie, 191 n.15

Modzeleski, Wliam, 315 nn.166–167

Moffitt, Terrie, 61 n.78; 63 n.154; 117 n.120; 154 nn.78–79; 155 n.103; 156 nn.146, 151; 157 nn.156, 179; 159 nn.257, 263, 267; 261; 273; 279 nn.9, 19, 26; 280 nn.37, 44, 45, 49–51; 281–282 nn.109, 111, 142

Moilanen, Irma, 223 n.9

Moke, Paul, 562 n.172

Mokherjee, Jessica, 194 n.147

Mokhiber, Russell, 399 n.113

Momenan, Reza, 155 n.93

Monachesi, Elio, 159 nn.260–261

Monaghan, Rachel, 461 n.44

Monahan, John, 158 n.211

Money, J., 154 n.54

Monroe, Laura, 314 n.120

Monroe, Lawrence, 61 n.66

Monroe, R. R., 155 n.96

Monson, Candice, 86 n.101

Montada, Leo, 85 n.38

Montgomery, Nicholas, 27 n.39

Montgomery, Paul, 153 n.26

Monzon, Cinnamon, 477

Monzon, Karls, 477

Moody, Carlisle, 117 nn.123–124, 138; 119 n.189; 521 n.19; 559 n.16

Moon, Dreama, 562 n.151

Moon, Melissa, 483 n.30

Moore, Charles, 251 n.52; 492

Moore, Elizabeth, 281 n.106; 397 n.13

Moore, Kristin, 224 n.30; 226 n.127

Moore, Mark, 374; 397 n.17; 436 n.206

Moore, Melaine, 224 n.38

Moore, Thomas, 492

Moore, Todd M., 85 n.25

Morales, Tomas, 526 n.141

Moran, Jonathan, 343 n.54

Moran, Kenneth, 561 n.106

Morash, Merry, 191 n.37; 562 n.157

More, Thomas, 353

Morenoff, Jeffrey D., 189; 191 n.45; 193 nn.94, 118

Morgan, Lynn, 434 n.95

Morgan, Patricia, 96; 115 n.31

Morgan, Stephen J., 343 n.51

Moriarty, Laura, 561 n.123

Morris, George, 399 n.114

Morris, Gregory, 281 n.104

Morris, Jodi Eileen, 193 n.103

Morris, Miranda, 62 n.101

Morrissey, Carlo, 85 n.37

Morse, Barbara, 116 n.93

Morse, Edward, 279 n.26

Morselli, Carlo, 115 n.27; 225 n.67

Morton, James, 434 n.91; 523 n.175

Moses, 18

Mouren, Marie Christine, 153 nn.20, 25

Mousain-Bosc, M., 153 n.29

Moy, Ernest, 312 n.6

Mrug, Sylvie, 224 n.49; 313 n.60

Mucci, Lorelei, 316 n.215

Mufti, Lisa, 194 n.142

Mugford, Jane, 252 nn.119, 121

Mugford, Stephen, 252 nn.119, 121

Muhammad, John Allen, 301

Mullen, Joan, 561 n.116

Mullen, P., 158 n.207

Mullings, Janet, 119 n.192; 562 n.155

Mullins, Christopher, 362

Mulvey, Edward, 60 n.30; 62 nn.89, 91

Muncer, Steven, 62 n.106; 157 n.175

Murakami, Haruki, 343 nn.46, 59

Murata, K., 153 n.20

Muraven, Mark, 282 n.139

Muris, Peter, 155 n.104; 282 n.131

Murphy, Fred, 60 n.18

Murray, Charles, 24; 27 n.55; 93; 115 n.9; 119 n.184; 148; 159 n.274; 562 n.167

Murray, Ellen, 226 n.108

Murray, Joseph, 224 n.23

Mustaine, Elizabeth Ehrhardt, 116 n.53; 436 n.174

Mustard, David, 50

Muth, Stephen, 433 n.66

Myers, Jane, 280 n.43

Myers, Martha, 559 n.32

Myers, Wade, 316 n.175

Myrdal, Gunnar, 163; 191 n.8

Myrvang, Bjøn, 312 n.23

Nachshon, Israel, 153 n.15; 157 n.177

Nadelmann, Ethan, 429–430; 437 n.227

Nagin, Daniel, 117 nn.111, 114, 117, 137; 118 nn.151, 157; 259; 280 nn.38, 45–47, 59; 281 n.103

Nagin, David, 483 n.18

Nahimana family, 129

Najman, Jake, 156 n.143

Nalla, Mahesh, 251 n.36

Nanjundappa, G., 435 n.155

Nansel, Tonja, 315 n.162

Napoleon, 328

Napoleoni, Loretta, 462 n.70

Nardelli, Robert, 229; 229

Nas, Coralijn, 159 n.238

Nasheri, Hedieh, 342 n.13

Nasr, Osama Hassan Mustafa, 326

Nasrallah, Hassan, 329

Nation, Carrie, 418

Nation, Maury, 224 nn.42, 47

Navarro, Mireya, 433 n.58

Neal, David, 60 n.20

Neapolitan, Jerome, 62 n.114; 289; 313 n.63

Nee, C., 369 n.91

Needleman, Herbert, 129; 154 n.73

Neeley, Connie L., 561 n.124

Neff, Sabrina, 562 n.165

Negroponte, John, 337

Neisser, Ulric, 154 n.74

Nelken, David, 396–397 n.3

Neller, Daniel, 313 n.61

Ness, Eliot, 418

Ness, Roberta, 154 n.73

Neufeld, Peter, 483 n.26

Neuman, Craig, 562 n.159

Newman, Donald, 483 n.12; 523 nn.131, 134, 147

Newman, Elana, 85 n.37

Newman, Graeme, 304; 559 nn.3–4

Newman, Oscar, 100; 116 n.86

Newton, Huey, 331

Ney, Bob, 377

Neziroglu, F., 154 n.38
Ngo, Jennifer, 409
Nicelli, Joseph, 353
Nicewander, W. Alan, 267; 281 n.81
Nickles, Laura, 483 n.37
Nielsen, Amie, 43
Nielsen, Arnie, 312 n.14
Niemelä, Solja, 223 n.9
Nieuwbeerta, Paul, 85 n.47; 86 n.87; 116
    n.70; 369 n.82
Nieves, Evelyn, 315 n.139
Nifong, Mike, 285
Nilsson, L. L., 158 n.218
Nisbet, Robert, 27 n.15
Nixon, K., 153 n.23
Nobiling, Tracy, 63 n.125; 251 n.53; 535
Nocek, Janet, 339
Noel, Robert, 296
Noonan, M., 85 n.42
Novak, Kenneth, 117 n.128
Novak, Scott, 428
Nurco, David n., 280 n.34; 563 nn.199, 206
Nuutila, Art-Matti, 223 n.9
Nye, F. Ivan, 50; 61 nn.65–66

Oakes, Jeannie, 224 n.36
O'Brien, Kevin A., 343 n.39
O'Brien, Mary, 433 n.40
O'Brien, Robert, 60 n.13
O'Callaghan, Mark, 159 n.277
Odgren, John, 216–217
Odiah, Chuk, 312 n.9
O'Donovan, Michael, 156 n.126
O'Faolain, Julia, 316 n.209
Ofshe, Richard J., 522 n.55
Ogle, Robbin, 194 n.175
Ogloff, James, 149
O'Grady, Kevin, 563 nn.199, 206
O'Hara, Terence, 397 n.51
O'Hear, Michael M., 78; 86 n.105
Ohlin, Lloyd, 60 n.36; 186–187; 188; 190;
    195 n.196
Oken, Emily, 154 n.77
O'Leary, Cecilia, 250 n.25
O'Leary, K. Daniel, 85 n.26
O'Leary, Susan, 316 n.214
Oliveira, Andrew, 398 n.78
Olligschlaeger, Andreas, 27 n.33
Olsen, Virgil, 61 n.66
Olson, James, 115 nn.43, 47; 116 n.57;
    363–364; 368 n.24; 369 n.90
Olson, Lynn, 85 n.33
Olsson, Martin, 159 n.280
Olweus, Dan, 225 n.82; 461 n.45
O'Malley, Patrick, 60 nn.21–22; 62 n.111;
    435 n.132
O'Neil, John, 397 n.41
Opjordsmoen, Stein, 312 n.23
Opler, Mark, 154 n.75
Orbuch, Terri, 281 nn.70, 74
Orlebeke, Jacob, 154 n.48
Ormrod, Richard, 84 n.15
Ornstein, Miriam, 60 n.29
Orobio de Castro, Bram, 159 n.238
Orth, Ulrich, 85 n.38; 87 n.112
Ortiz, Madeline, 561 n.125; 563 n.204

Osborn, Denise, 85 n.48
Osgood, D. Wayne, 60 n.22; 62 n.96; 134;
    154 nn.42, 46; 156 n.150; 267; 279
    n.20; 281 n.81; 282 n.121
Osman, Suzanne, 314 n.106
Ostresh, Erik, 226 n.116
Ostrow, Miriam, 437 n.220
Ostrowsky, Michael, 194 n.168
O'Sullivan, Sean, 559 n.1
Otis, Melanie, 317 n.226
Ott, John, 154 n.68
Ouellet, Lawrence, 433 n.59
Ouimet, Marc, 281 n.102
Ouimette, Paige Crosby, 157 n.187
Ousey, Graham, 282 nn.119, 141
Ovanessian, Rafi, 15
Overpeck, Mary, 315 n.162
Owen, David, 342 n.11
Owen, Michael, 156 n.126
Owens, Elizabeth, 155 n.108
Ozanne, M., 523 n.120
Özbay, Özden, 226 n.113
Özcan, Yusuf Ziya, 226 n.113

Packer, Herbert L., 478; 482 n.9; 483 n.22
Pagulayan, O., 153 n.24
Pahlavi, Shah Mohammad Reza, 329
Paige, Karen, 154 n.61
Palacio, Manuel, 477
Palermo, Mark, 282 n.122
Palfrey, Deborah Jeane, 406
Pallone, Nathaniel, 155 nn.82, 91
Palloni, Alberto, 27 n.2
Palmer, S., 158 n.207
Pan, En-Ling, 224 n.16
Paparozzi, Mario, 563 n.200
Papillo, Angela Romano, 226 n.127
Paradis, Emily, 85 n.24
Parisi, Nicolette, 562 nn.132, 143
Park, Robert Ezra, 9; 27 nn.20, 24; 162; 168
Parker, Jocelyn, 343 n.34
Parker, Karen, 63 nn.123, 132; 192
    nn.47–48, 87; 265; 281 n.75
Parker, Robert Nash, 61 n.63; 312 n.3
Parra, Gilbert, 435 n.150
Parsons, Deborah, 252 n.128
Parsons, Jeffrey T., 436 n.179
Parvez, Faruque, 153 n.25
Paschall, Mallie, 60 n.29; 63 n.135
Pasqualetti, Patrizio, 282 n.122
Passas, Nikos, 396–397 n.3; 397 nn.20–21
Pastore, Ann, 195 n.208
Patchin, Justin, 191 n.24; 449; 461
    nn.46–47
Pate, Tony, 117 n.125; 521 n.8
Patel, Vipul, 433 n.47
Paternoster, Raymond, 107; 117 n.120; 118
    nn.151, 157, 159, 165, 167, 178; 194
    n.152; 218; 227 n.190; 251 n.73; 279
    n.17; 280 nn.55, 59, 61; 282 n.128;
    560 nn.33, 61
Patil, Sujata, 27 n.39
Pattavina, April, 193 n.98
Patterson, Gerald R., 279 nn.14, 20; 280
    n.42; 312 n.27
Patterson, Orlando, 436 n.201

Pattison, Philippa, 159 n.247
Paulozzi, Len, 315 n.166
Payne, Brian, 117 n.138; 521 n.54
Payne, Gary, 194 n.159; 226 n.134
Payne, Monique, 191 n.19
Pazniokas, Mark, 433 n.29
Peacock, Mark, 561 n.110
Pearson, Frank, 563 n.174
Pearson-Nelson, Benjamin, 312 n.16
Pease, Ken, 85 n.52; 117 n.106; 364;
    369 n.94
Pease, Susan, 159 n.268
Peete, Thomas, 118 n.150
Pelham, Molina, Jr., 155 n.104
Pelham, William, Jr., 224 n.26
Pender, Kathleen, 250 n.4
Penn, William, 527; 545
Penrod, Steven, 314 n.116; 434 n.101
Pepinsky, Harold, 243
Perdoni, Matthew, 562 n.163
Perea, Ignacio, 296
Perez, Cynthia, 61 n.78; 279 nn.6, 19, 24;
    436 n.196
Perez, Jacob, 523 n.127
Perez-Melara, Carlos Enrique, 449
Pérez-Peña, Richard, 397 n.26
Perkins, Elizabeth, 369 n.93
Perry, Rick, 242
Perry, Steven, 522 n.92
Perusse, Daniel, 156 n.154
Petchesky, Rosalind, 251 n.46
Peter, K., 85 n.42
Peter, Katharin, 315 n.161
Peters, Roger, 561 n.125; 563 n.204
Petersilia, Joan, 227 n.157; 521 nn.22, 24,
    30; 541–542; 554; 555; 557; 561
    nn.82, 85, 90, 101, 104–105; 563
    nn.199, 207
Peterson, David, 226 n.126
Peterson, Joyce, 561 n.85
Peterson, Ruth, 61 n.75; 191 n.16; 193
    nn.107, 109, 126
Petraitis, John, 116 n.61; 435 n.151
Petras, Hanno, 280 n.35
Petras, Tricia, 312 n.2
Petrocelli, Matthew, 251 n.63
Petrosino, Anthony, 27 n.57; 252 n.115;
    483 n.25
Petrosino, Carolyn, 252 n.115; 483 n.25
Pettit, Gregory, 193 n.96; 224 n.15; 280
    n.45
Pezzin, Liliana, 115 n.28
Philaretou, Andreas, 460 n.9
Philby, Kim, 323
Philip, Michael, 63 n.118
Phillips, Coretta, 85 n.52; 364; 369 n.94
Phillips, David, 141; 158 n.223
Phillips, Julie A., 63 n.138; 191 n.22
Phillips, Monte, 155 n.93
Phillips, Scott, 312 n.22
Phillips, Susan, 158 n.203
Phillips, Tim, 192 n.63
Phillips-Plummer, Lynanne, 433 n.66
Pi, Yijun, 194 n.163
Piaget, Jean, 142; 158 n.224
Pickering, Lloyd, 281 n.105

Pickett, Kate, 153 n.19; 194 n.147
Piehl, Anne Morrison, 522 n.87; 534; 535
Pierce, Glenn, 557; 560 nn.39, 62
Pietz, Christina, 313 n.61
Piha, Jorma, 223 n.9
Pihl, Robert, 155 n.80; 156 n.138
Piliavin, Irving, 210; 226 nn.103, 106
Pilla, Ramani, 315 n.162
Pinderhughes, Ellen, 279 n.8
Pinel, Philippe, 7; 137
Piquero, Alex, 86 n.67; 100; 107; 116 n.80;
    117 n.121; 118 nn.161, 178; 119
    n.180; 148; 154 n.45; 158 nn.198,
    233; 159 n.269; 194 nn.158–160; 251
    n.63; 252 n.101; 265; 279 n.17; 280
    nn.33, 48, 53, 55; 281–282 nn.75–76,
    90, 110–111, 133, 136
Piquero, Nicole Leeper, 194 n.176; 225
    n.99; 280 n.53; 398 n.86; 561 n.80
Pitt, Brad, 346
Pittman, David, 435 n.123
Pitts, Marian, 433 n.40
Planty, Mike, 315 n.161
Platt, Anthony, 191 n.31; 251 n.65
Platt, Jerome J., 435 n.145; 437 n.222
Platt, Tony, 250 n.25
Pliska, Lawrence, 360
Ploeger, Matthew, 62 n.99; 225 nn.69, 78
Plomin, Robert, 157 nn.156, 161; 159
    n.257
Podolsky, E., 154 n.37
Pogarsky, Greg, 84 n.12; 117 nn.111, 114,
    117, 137; 118 nn.143, 167; 119
    n.180; 281 n.103; 282 n.139
Pogrebin, Mark, 225 n.101
Polge, A., 153 n.29
Polk, Kenneth, 195 n.207
Pollack, Otto, 62 n.94
Pollitt, Mark, 449; 461 n.55
Pomeroy, Wardell, 314 n.111
Ponder, Michael, 239; 251 n.49
Pontell, Henry, 397 n.5; 462 n.77
Poole, Eric, 225 nn.97, 101
Popkin, Susan, 85 n.33
Porche, Dianne, 398 n.83
Port, Otis, 462 n.95
Porter, David, 462 n.78
Porter, Father James, 405
Porter, Rebecca, 399 n.136
Porter, Stephen, 314 n.112
Porterfield, A. L., 60 n.18
Posner, Daniel, 399 n.114
Post, Jerrold M., 336; 343 nn.53, 56
Potter, Lloyd, 315 n.166
Potterat, John, 433 n.66
Potterton, Dave, 462 n.74
Pottieger, Anne, 421; 435 n.163
Poussin, Nicolas, 291; 291
Powell, Andrea, 191 n.42
Powell, Michael, 353
Powers, Edward, 102; 117 n.108
Powers, Ronald, 317 n.228
Poyser, Sam, 522 n.90
Pradai-Prat, D., 153 n.29
Pranis, Kay, 252 n.124
Prasad, Monica, 407; 433 n.41

Pratt, Travis, 158 n.232; 483 n.21; 535
Prendergast, Michael, 436 n.190
Prenzler, Tim, 521 n.4
Presser, Lois, 253 n.133; 483 n.38
Preston, Julia, 184
Pribesh, Shana, 192 n.75
Price, Jamie, 192 n.52
Price, Virginia, 433 n.49
Pridemore, William, 193 n.132
Prinz, Ronald, 153 n.27; 280 n.39
Priyadarsini, S., 225 n.74
Proctor, Bernadette D., 191 nn.6, 17
Proffitt, Fiona, 343 n.36
Proietti, Luca, 282 n.122
Proulx, Jean, 116 n.79; 280 n.36
Pruitt, B. E., 159 nn.244, 249, 279
Pruitt, Matthew, 192 n.47
Prusoff, L., 521 n.24
Przybylski, Roger, 436 n.173
Puckett, Janice, 117 n.127; 521 n.25
Pugh, Meredith D., 60 n.24; 61 n.77; 226
    n.132
Pullmann, Michael, 157–158 n.197
Puzzanchera, Charles M., 473

Qin, Ping, 156 n.152
Quetelet, L. A. J., 8; 10; 27 n.16
Quigley, Brian, 304
Quinet, Kenna Davis, 85 n.47; 316 n.173,
    182
Quinney, Richard, 243; 249; 250 n.17; 251
    n.41; 252 nn.107–108; 397 nn.17, 27
Quinney, Robert, 233
Quinsey, Vernon, 369 n.100
Quiñones, Alan, 184
Quisenberry, Neil, 192 n.60

Raab, Selwyn, 399 n.134
Raaijmakers, Quinten, 158 n.229
Rabasa, Angel, 343 nn.39, 41, 68
Rada, Richard, 314 n.111
Radelet, Michael, 537; 539; 560 n.60
Rader, Dennis, 299; 469
Radosevich, Marcia, 62 n.109; 225 n.84
Radosh, Polly, 562 n.158
Raffalovich, Lawrence, 43; 86 n.95; 192 n.50
Rafter, Nicole Hahn, 25; 27 nn.8–9, 13, 28
Raghavan, Chitra, 435 n.141
Raine, Adrian, 126; 127; 129; 132; 153
    n.18; 155 nn.81, 84, 92, 94, 98; 156
    nn.124–125; 157 n.178; 158 n.231;
    280 n.51; 312–313 n.27
Rainone, Gregory, 436 n.195
Rainville, Gerard, 561 n.98
Raitt, F. E., 154 n.58
Raj, Anita, 316 n.215; 433 n.47
Raja, Sheela, 84 n.10
Raley, R. Kelly, 63 n.137
Ramanathan, Chockalingam, 439
Ramanathan, Thirugnanam, 439
Ramirez, G. B., 153 n.24
Ramsey, Elizabeth, 279 n.14
Ramsey, Susan, 85 n.25
Rand, Michael, 315 n.161; 368 n.57
Randall, Susan, 313 n.68
Randolph, Scott, 496

Range, Lillian, 85 n.21
Rankin, Bruce, 193 nn.115, 120
Rankin, Joseph, 60 n.33; 223 n.13
Rapin, J., 153 n.29
Rapp, Geoffrey, 109; 537; 560 n.45
Rashbaum, William K., 343 n.66
Ratcliffe, Jerry, 61 n.43
Rathouz, Paul, 224 n.26
Rathus, Spencer, 60 n.28; 159 n.261; 225
    n.98; 433 n.37
Raudenbush, Stephen W., 189; 191 n.45;
    193 n.91
Rawlings, Robert, 155 n.93
Ray, Melvin, 227 nn.147, 161, 165
Reagan, Ronald, 48; 78; 93; 143; 477
Reaves, Brian, 482 nn.6, 8; 509; 510; 511;
    512; 521 n.5; 523 nn.121, 124, 127;
    526; 533; 559 n.2
Reaves, Brian A., 561 n.98
Rebellon, Cesar, 194 n.150; 223 n.11; 226
    n.139; 435 n.165
Reboussin, Roland, 116 n.78; 314 n.86
Reckless, Walter, 109; 210; 226
    nn.107–108
Reddy, Marisa, 315 n.167
Reed, M. D., 226 n.143
Rees, Sian, 437 n.219
Regini, Charles L., 521 n.34
Regnerus, Mark, 226 n.124
Regoeczi, Wendy, 315 n.151
Regoli, Robert, 225 n.97
Reidel, Marc, 315 n.150
Reilly, Michael, 248
Reiman, Jeffery, 250 n.30
Reisig, Michael, 192 n.77; 193 n.93
Reiss, Albert, 144; 154 n.48; 155 n.115;
    159 n.278; 210; 226 n.105; 312 n.18;
    398 n.99
Reitzel, Deborah, 87 n.114
Rekart, Michael, 434 n.69
Remy, Nicholas, 5
Ren, Xin, 224 n.44
Rengert, George, 84 n.6; 87 n.124; 107;
    115 nn.19, 42, 48; 116 n.84; 118
    n.161; 436 n.202
Reno brothers, 347
Resick, Patricia, 62 n.101; 86 n.101
Resig, Michael, 274; 282 n.129
Resnick, Heidi, 85 n.27; 312 n.20
Resnick, Patricia, 86 n.99
Restifo, Nicholas, 312 n.6
Reuter, Peter, 436 n.175
Reynolds, B. J., 155 n.95
Reynolds, Margan, 113
Reynolds, Matthew, 314 n.120
Reynolds, Morgan, 115 n.16
Rheingold, Alyssa, 85 n.27
Rhodes, William, 523 n.123
Rhoter, Larry, 538
Rice, Frances, 156 n.126
Rice, Harvey, 381
Rice, Marnie, 149
Rice, Stephen, 63 n.123
Richard, Chris, 460 n.8
Richards, Maryse, 86 nn.74, 76
Richards, Stephen, 562 n.127

Richardson, Alexandra, 153 *n*.26
Richardson, Deborah, 86 *n*.86
Richardson, Samuel, 291
Rich-Edwards, Janet W., 154 *n*.77
Richie, Nicole, *508*
Richmond, F. Lynn, 195 *n*.207
Ridde, James, 281 *n*.80
Ridder, Elizabeth, 43; 279 *n*.29
Riddle, David, 153 *n*.27
Rideau, Wilbert, 562 *n*.136
Rideout, Greta, 293
Rideout, John, 293
Rideout, Victoria, 144
Ridgway, Ric, 407
Riegel, Stephanie, 526 *n*.141
Riess, Julie, 154 *n*.73
Rigas, John, 389
Rigas, Timothy, 389
Rijsdijk, Fruhling, 156 *n*.146
Rimpelä, Matti, 157 *n*.194
Ringo, Johnny, 466
Ringwalt, Chris, 428
Risser, Jan, 433 *n*.61
Ritakallio, Minna, 157 *n*.194
Ritz, Christina E., 191 *n*.2
Riveland, Chase, 561 *n*.114
Rivera, A. Francisco, 153 *n*.24
Rivera, Craig, 227 *nn*.162,
Rizvi, Shireen, 62 *n*.101; 86 *n*.101
Roache, Declan, 246
Roberts, Aki, 313 *n*.65
Roberts, Albert, 87 *n*.107
Roberts, Jennifer, 60 *n*.30
Roberts, Julia, 410
Roberts, Mary K., 226 *nn*.113, 137
Roberts, Miguel, 314 *n*.93
Roberts, Ron, 434 *n*.71
Roberts, Sam, 191 *n*.4
Roberts, Staci, 74; 86 *n*.73
Robertson, Alison, 369 *n*.101
Robertson, Craig, 227 *nn*.147, 161
Robespierre, Maximilien, 330
Robin, D. R., 155 *n*.95
Robin, Gerald, 315 *n*.125
Robins, Lee, 63 *n*.154
Robinson, Beatrice, 85 *n*.23; 434 *n*.68
Robinson, Matthew, 115 *n*.46; 369 *n*.81
Robles, Albert, 95; *95*
Roby, Charles, 336
Roche, Declan, 253 *n*.134
Roche, M., 153 *n*.29
Rockefeller, John D., 382
Rodeheaver, Daniel, 118 *n*.166
Rodgers, Joseph, 157 *n*.159
Rodriguez, Diego, 184
Rodriguez, Jose, *67*
Roehl, Jan, 117 *n*.100
Roehling, P. V., 435 *n*.160
Rogan, Dennis, 226 *n*.104; 227 *n*.166; 521 *n*.15
Rogers, Joseph, 156 *nn*.128, 144
Rogers, Michael, 369 *n*.106
Rogers, R. G., 193 *n*.130
Rogers, Richard, 312 *n*.8; 562 *n*.159
Rogosch, Fred, 224 *n*.33
Rogovin, Charles, 398 *n*.84

Rohde, David, 343 *n*.43; 434 *n*.116
Rohde, Paul, 157 *n*.193
Roman, Caterina, 562 *n*.164
Romero-Daza, Nancy, 434 *n*.70
Rooney, James P., 277
Rose, Vicki McNickle, 313 *n*.68
Rosenau, William, 343 *n*.39
Rosenbaum, Alan, 313 *n*.39
Rosenbaum, Dennis, 85 *n*.33; 87 *n*.123; 428; 436 *n*.210; 437 *n*.212
Rosenbaum, James, 192 *n*.80
Rosenbaum, Jill Leslie, 226 *n*.140
Rosenfeld, Richard, 43; 60 *n*.35; 75; 86 *n*.95; 115 *n*.41; 116 *nn*.65, 76; 144; 177–178; 190; 191 *n*.3; 193 *nn*.99, 131; 194 *nn*.138–139, 141; 435 *n*.137
Rosenmerkel, Sean, 398 *n*.111
Rosenthal, Lawrence, 192 *n*.74
Roshier, Bob, 115 *n*.5
Rosner, Richard, 158 *n*.201
Ross, Catherine E., 62 *n*.97; 192 *n*.75
Ross, Edward Alsworth, 372; 382; 397 *n*.8
Ross, H. Laurence, 118 *n*.142
Ross, Jay, 522 *n*.95
Ross, Jeffrey Ian, 342 *nn*.1, 16, 19; 562 *n*.127
Ross, Michael, 433 *n*.61
Rossi, Peter, 99; 116 *n*.66; 436 *n*.208
Roth, Gerhard, 312 *n*.10
Roth, Jeffrey, 117 *n*.138; 144; 154 *n*.48; 155 *n*.115; 159 *n*.278; 312 *n*.18
Roth, Loren, 153 *n*.17
Rothenberg, Richard, 433 *n*.66
Rotton, James, 46; 61 *n*.59
Rountree, Pamela Wilcox, 85 *n*.30; 86 *n*.80; 87 *n*.120; 192 *n*.62; 562 *n*.172
Rowe, Alan, 117 *n*.115
Rowe, David, 62 *nn*.97, 103; 134; 155 *n*.87; 156 *nn*.128, 141, 144, 147, 150; 157 *nn*.158–159, 173; 267; 281 *nn*.81, 83
Rowe, Richard, 157 *n*.192
Ruben, Alan, 153 *n*.21
Rubenstein, Michael, 523 *n*.146
Rubin, Paul H., 109
Rubin, Robert, 154 *n*.53
Ruby, Charles, 343 *n*.55
Ruchkin, Vladislav, 224 *n*.29
Rucker, Lila, 562 *n*.157
Ruddy, Sally, 315 *n*.161
Rudolph, Eric, 29–30; 29; 60 *nn*.1–2
Rudolph, Jennifer, 194 *n*.143; 279 *n*.12
Ruggiero, Kenneth, 312 *n*.20
Ruibal, Sal, 312 *n*.1
Ruppert, Carol, 225 *n*.98
Ruschena, D., 158 *n*.207
Rush, Benjamin, 7; 137
Rushton, Phillipe, 62 *n*.114
Russell, Diana, 294; 303; 314 *nn*.98, 108–109, 116; 316 *n*.201
Rustigan, Michael, 237; 251 *n*.45
Rutter, Michael, 156 *n*.151; 280 *n*.44
Ryales, Robert, *34*
Ryan, George, 315 *n*.166; 377
Ryan, James, 561 *n*.103
Ryan, John, 521 *n*.2
Ryan, Kimberly, 86 *n*.64
Ryan, Patrick, 312 *n*.17

Sabathia, Jessica, 441
Sabol, William, 119 *n*.195
Sachs, Carolyn, 304
Sack, Kevin, 397 *n*.37
Sagi, Philip, 315 *n*.159
Said, Carolyn, 250 *n*.4
Sakheim, George, 369 *n*.99
Salekin, Randall, 312 *n*.8
Salfati, Gabrielle, 316 *n*.180
Salty, Robert, 477
Saltzman, Linda, 118 *n*.159; 315 *n*.153; 317 *n*.262
Samaha, Joel, 22
Samaha, Reema, 75
Samakouri, Maria, 312 *n*.5
Sambucioni, Augusto, 282 *n*.122
Sami, Nilofar, 155 *n*.108
Sample, Barry, 63 *n*.118
Sampson, Gary L., 277
Sampson, Robert J., 27 *n*.30; 40; 43; 61 *n*.76; 63 *nn*.117, 155; 116 *n*.52; 153 *n*.8; 156 *nn*.132, 139; 189; 191 *nn*.36, 38, 45; 193 *nn*.91, 94, 102, 113, 115, 118, 120, 125, 131; 199; 227 *nn*.184–185; 256; 262–267; 278–279 *nn*.3, 15; 280 *nn*.57–58; 281 *n*.68; 313 *n*.50; 521 *n*.11
Samuelson, Leslie, 226 *n*.138
Sanborn, Joseph, 523 *n*.130
Sanders, Teela, 410; 433 *nn*.50, 54
Sandys, Marla, 560 *n*.55
Saner, Hilary, 436 *n*.175
Sanfiel, Michael, 477
Sansone, Lori, 85 *n*.21
Sansone, Randy, 85 *n*.21
Santiago, Edwin, 184
Santtila, Pekka, 369 *n*.102
Sao, Khon, *186*
Sarat, Austin, 342 *n*.8
Sarbin, T. R., 156 *n*.130
Sargent, W., 154 *n*.36
Sarkar, n. n., 84 *n*.20
Sarkar, Rina, 84 *n*.20
Saul, Stephanie, 250 *n*.3
Saunders, Benjamin, 84 *n*.14; 86 *n*.100; 312 *n*.20
Savage, Stephen, 522 *n*.90
Savitz, Leonard, 60 *n*.14
Savolainen, Jukka, 194 *n*.146; 223 *n*.10
Scanlon, Barbara, 433 *n*.49
Scarborough, Kathryn, 144
Scarpa, Angela, 84 *n*.13
Scarpitti, Frank, 226 *n*.108
The Scary Guy, *214*
Schaefer, Catherine, 154 *n*.75
Schaefer, Diane, 252 *n*.126
Schaeffer, Cindy, 280 *n*.35
Schaeffer, Rebecca, 22
Schafer, Joseph, 192 *n*.57
Schafer, Stephen, 15; 27 *n*.40; 60 *n*.7; 342 *n*.4
Schaffner, Laurie, 560 *n*.78
Scharf, P., 158 *n*.226
Schauer, Cathrin, 409
Schauss, Alexander G., 153 *n*.31; 154 *n*.67

Scheck, Barry, 483 *n*.26; *536*
Scheinberger-Olwig, Renate, 313 *n*.69
Schenck, Christopher, 398 *n*.78
Scheurman, Leo, 192 *n*.84
Schiff, Mara, 252 *n*.130
Schlaupitz, Sheila, 252 *n*.93
Schlegel, Alexander, 159 *n*.258
Schlegel, Kip, 397 *n*.11; 398 *n*.104
Schlesinger, Traci, 63 *n*.124
Schmeidler, James, 436 *n*.195
Schmid, A. P., 328
Schmidt, Janell, 226 *n*.104; 227 *n*.166
Schmidt, Melinda G., 282 *n*.146
Schmidt, M. H., 154 *n*.42
Schmidt, Randall, 87 *n*.108
Schmutte, Pamela, 159 *n*.263
Schnurer, Eric B., 58
Schoenthaler, Stephen, 126; 127; 153 *n*.31
Schollenberger, Janet, 304
Schotland, Roy, 523 *n*.116
Schrader, Geoff, 158 *n*.217
Schrag, Clarence, 61 *n*.44; 195 *n*.191
Schram, Pamela, 562 *n*.156
Schreck, Christopher, 86 *n*.71; 281 *n*.94
Schreiner, P. J., 127
Schroeder, Ryan, 266; 281 *n*.79
Schuck, Amie, 191 *n*.44
Schumacher, Joseph, 560 *n*.63
Schumacher, Michael, 57; 63 *n*.146
Schur, Edwin, 227 *n*.150; 432 *n*.3
Schutt, Russell, 62 *n*.110
Schwab-Stone, Mary, 224 *n*.29
Schwartz, Jennifer, 62 *n*.107
Schwartz, Martin, 251 *nn*.71–72; 252 *n*.87;
        314 *nn*.107, 114; 315 *n*.131
Schwartz, Miguel, 316 *n*.214
Schwarzenegger, Arnold, *476*
Schweitzer, Louis, 510
Schwendinger, Herman, 60 *n*.40; 251
        nn.74, 78
Schwendinger, Julia, 60 *n*.40; 251 *nn*.74, 78
Scott, Austin, 315 *nn*.137–138; 368 *nn*.25,
        43; 369 *nn*.65, 72, 74
Scott, Calvin L., 525
Scott, Peter, 27 *n*.11
Scourfield, Jane, 156 *n*.153
Scudder, Robert, 313 *n*.33
Scuro, Pedro, 13
Seale, Bobby, 331
Seale, Clyde, 492
Seale, James Ford, 492; *492*
Sealock, Miriam, 62 *n*.113; 194 *n*.176
Sechrest, Dale, 561 *n*.108
Segal, David, 353
Segal, Nancy, 156 *n*.147
Seguin, Jean, 155 *n*.80
Seidman, David, 60 *n*.10
Seidman, Robert, 233; 250 *n*.16
Seiter, Richard, 555; 560 *n*.71
Seligmann, Reade, 285–286; *285*
Sellers, Christine, 225 *n*.87; 252 *n*.93; 304
Sellers, Courtenay, 158 *n*.219
Selley, John R., 157 *n*.193
Sellin, Thorsten, 56; 57; 63 *nn*.141–142;
        182; 195 *n*.179; 279 *n*.4
Semple, W. E., 155 *n*.91

Sennott, Charles M., 433 *n*.32
Sepper, Elizabeth, 342 *n*.23
Serra, Susan, 312 *n*.6
Seth, Mark, 560 *n*.40
Seto, Michael, 414; 434 *n*.102
Sevander, S., 158 *n*.218
Sever, Brion, 118 *n*.168
Sewell, Kenneth, 312 *n*.8
Shachmurove, Yochanan, 369 *n*.86
Shackelford, Todd, 315 *n*.147
Shah, Saleem, 153 *n*.17
Shahar, Yael, 461 *n*.62
Shakespeare, William, 291
Shalhoub-Kevorkian, Nadera, 290
Shane, Jon, 158 *n*.219
Shannon, Elaine, 461 *n*.53
Shannon, Lyle, 63 *n*.144
Shapira, Nathan, 279 *n*.23
Shapiro, Perry, 119 *n*.184; 521 *n*.17
Sharkey, Patrick, 193 *n*.121
Sharon, Ariel, 448
Sharpe, Kimberly, 158 *n*.212
Sharps, Phyllis, 304
Shaughnessy, Rita, 155 *n*.109
Shaver, Lynda Dixon, 562 *n*.151
Shaw, Clifford R., 168–170; 188; 190; 191
        nn.30, 32
Shaw, Daniel, 224 *n*.19
Shaw, James, 521 *n*.15
Shea, William, 447
Shedd, Carla, 191 *n*.19
Sheldon, William, 122; 153 *n*.7
Shelley, Louise I., 393
Shelly, Peggy, 115 *n*.45; 116 *n*.72
Shelton, Kelly, 280 *n*.64
Shepard, Matthew, 306–307; 308
Shepherd, Joanna M., 109
Sheppard, David, 313 *n*.59
Sher, Kenneth, 435 *n*.150
Sherman, Lawrence, 60 *n*.9; 105; 109–110;
        117 *n*.129; 119 *n*.182; 226 *n*.104; 227
        n.166; 521 *n*.15
Sherman, William, 353
Shevlin, Mark, 67; 84 *n*.18
Shields, Ian, 225 *n*.96
Shifley, Rick, 252 *n*.123
Shin, Hee-Choon, 279 *n*.27
Shin, Kilman, 560 *n*.58
Shinnar, Reuel, 119 *n*.188
Shinnar, Shlomo, 119 *n*.188
Shipley, Bernard, 118 *n*.175
Shipman, Harold Frederick, 300
Shirley, Mary, 60 *n*.18
Shmueli, Dikla, 282 *n*.139
Short, James, 50; 61 *nn*.65–66; 205; 225
        nn.71, 96
Shotland, R. Lance, 314 *n*.91
Shover, Neal, 115 *n*.30; 363; 368 *n*.8; 369
        n.88
Showers, Carolin, 62 *n*.97
Shrout, Patrick, 227 *n*.145
Sidwell, Clare, 436 *n*.186
Siedfer, Jill Jordan, 368 *n*.40
Siegel, Jane, 85 *n*.22; 316 *n*.206
Siegel, Larry, 60 *nn*.7, 28; 159 *n*.261; 225
        n.98; 514; 561 *n*.99

Sieler, DeDe, 158 *n*.197
Sigel, S., 154 *n*.68
Sigurdsson, Jon Fridrik, 149
Silbereisen, Ranier, 279 *n*.30
Silberman, Charles, 563 *n*.180
Silberman, Matthew, 118 *n*.151
Silke, Andrew, 343 *n*.52
Sillanmäki, Lauri, 223 *n*.9
Silva, Phil, 61 *n*.78; 63 *n*.154; 154 *n*.79; 155
        n.103; 157 *nn*.179, 188; 159 *n*.263;
        279 *nn*.9, 19; 280 *nn*.37, 44; 282 *n*.142
Silver, Clayton, 223 *n*.7
Silver, Eric, 158 *nn*.212, 214–215; 193
        n.123
Silverman, Ira, 313 *n*.33
Silverman, Jay, 316 *n*.215; 433 *n*.47
Silverman, Jenna, 223 *n*.7
Silverman, Robert, 195 *n*.177; 226 *nn*.118,
        129
Simeon, Jovan, 153 *n*.32
Simeon, Quentin, *261*
Simister, John, 61 *n*.58; 154 *n*.49
Simmons, Ric, 523 *n*.119
Simon, David, 398 *n*.96
Simon, Leonard, 60 *n*.23
Simon, Leonore M. J., 155 *nn*.100, 102;
        280 *n*.60
Simon, Patricia, 279 *n*.26
Simon, Rita James, 27 *n*.35; 62 *n*.102
Simon, Thomas, 315 *n*.166
Simons, Leslie, 282 *n*.124
Simons, Marlise, 314 *n*.75
Simons, Ronald, 227 *n*.163; 265; 273–274;
        281 *n*.77; 282 *nn*.124–125; 313 *n*.32,
        41
Simonsen, C., 153 *n*.31
Simos, Alexander, 312 *n*.6
Simpson, John, 252 *n*.91
Simpson, M. K., 159 *n*.275
Simpson, Murray, 159 *n*.275
Simpson, O. J., 474; 505
Simpson, Sally, 62 *n*.113; 194 *n*.169; 562
        n.161
Sims, Barbara, 87 *n*.113; 250 *nn*.19, 32;
        560 *nn*.70, 75
Sims, Crissy, 561 *n*.87
Singer, Jane, 369 *n*.97
Singer, Merrill, 434 *n*.70
Singer, Simon, 144; 252 *n*.97
Singh, Piyusha, 117 *n*.130
Singhvi, Nikhil S., 398 *n*.107
Singleton, Lawrence, *110*
Sinha, V. K., 127
Sitren, Alicia, 118 *n*.171
Skilling, Jeffrey, *96*; 378–379
Skinner, William, 225 *n*.86
Skogan, Wesley, 192 *nn*.64, 66, 81; 193
        n.101
Skoler, Daniel, 398 *n*.90
Skondras, M., 156 *n*.119
Slade, Eric, 224 *n*.33; 313 *n*.30
Slaughter, Ellen, 191 *n*.37
Slavkovich, Vesna, 153 *n*.25
Sloan, John J., 86 *n*.69; 117 *n*.124; 315
        n.160; 521 *n*.20
Sloat, Alison, 158 *n*.202

Slocum, Lee Ann, 194 *n*.169; 562 *n*.161

Smailes, Elizabeth, 43; 144; 433 *n*.64; 434 *n*.74

Small, Albion W., 8–9

Smallish, Lori, 155 *n*.106

Smart, Carol, 62 *n*.105

Smeenk, Wilma, 280 *n*.54

Smiley, Edward Forbes, III, 345–346

Smiljanich, Kathy, 433 *n*.34

Smith, Andra, 149

Smith, Anthony, 433 *n*.40

Smith, Barbara, 87 *n*.117; 483 *n*.37; 522 *n*.103

Smith, Brent, 559 *n*.30

Smith, Carolyn, 156 *nn*.135, 137, 140; 224 *nn*.22, 32, 39; 279 *n*.25; 313 *n*.37; 435 *n*.142

Smith, Daniel, 84 *n*.14; 435 *n*.146

Smith, David S., 368 *n*.1, 447

Smith, Donald, 369 *n*.93

Smith, Douglas, 50; 61 *nn*.67, 73; 119 *n*.184; 194 *n*.169; 226 *n*.104; 227 *n*.166, 184; 251 *n*.73; 562 *n*.161

Smith, G. T., 435 *n*.160

Smith, Judith, 191 *n*.13

Smith, M. Dwayne, 61 *n*.64

Smith, Michael, 117 *n*.133; 251 *n*.63

Smith, Oklahoma, 361

Smith, Philip, 192 *n*.63

Smith, Stefanie, 560 *n*.54

Smith, Steven K., 522 *nn*.101, 109

Smith, Timothy, 279 *n*.25

Smith, William, 116 *n*.69

Smolej, Mirka, 27 *n*.32; 60 *n*.3; 85 *n*.28

Smons, Ronald, 194 *n*.153

Snedker, Karen, 85 *n*.34

Snell, Tracy, 119 *n*.198

Snook, Brent, 369 *n*.83

Snortum, John R., 118 *n*.149; 521 *n*.31

Snyder, Scott, 144

Snyder, Thomas, 85 *n*.42; 315 *n*.161

Socrates, 8

Soderstrom, Irina, 562 *n*.144

Solomon, Brett Johnson, 224 *n*.46

Solon, 406

Somers, Leigh Edward, 369 *n*.105

Somkin, Carol, 193 *n*.92

Sommers, Ira, 14–15; 27 *n*.38; 562 *n*.152

Sones, Ronald, 483 *n*.11

Sorensen, Jonathan, 560 *n*.57

Sorenson, Ann Marie, 281 *n*.102; 282 *n*.116

Sorenson, Jon, 109; 398 *n*.55; 560 *n*.44

Sorenson, T., 398 *n*.55

Sorrells, James, 158 *n*.200

Soulé, David, 86 *n*.85

Sourander, Andre, 223 *n*.9

Spaccarelli, Steve, 85 *n*.40

Sparks, Richard, 250 *n*.18; 251 *n*.61

Speck, Richard, 132–133

Speckart, George, 436 *n*.192

Spector, Phil, *506*; *516*

Spelman, William, 117 *nn*.131, 134; 191 *n*.41

Spencer, J. William, 559 *n*.13

Spergel, Irving, 192 *nn*.52, 73

Spitzberg, Brian, 310; 317 *nn*.264, 267

Spohn, Cassia, 63 *n*.125; 118 *n*.179; 218; 227 *n*.179; 295; 314 *nn*.90, 121–122; 315 *n*.128; 522 *n*.102; 561 *n*.86

Spracklen, Kathleen, 224 *n*.48

Springett, Gwynneth, 158 *n*.202

Spunt, Barry, 312 *n*.24

Spurzheim, Johann K., 7

Squires, Gregory, 191 *n*.46

Stack, Steven, 109

Stafford, Mark C., 93; 115 *n*.17; 159 *n*.237

Stahelski, Anthony, 343 *n*.57

Stalin, Joseph, 239; 337

Stanley, Jay, 462 *n*.92

Stark, Benjamin, 446

Stark, Rodney, 86 *n*.78; 193 *n*.111; 201; 225 *n*.57

Starles, R. M., 155 *n*.95

Starr, Kenneth, 503

Stattin, Hakan, 159 *n*.272

Steele, Bruce, 432 *n*.1

Steele, Tracey, 108; 109

Steen, Sara, 227 *n*.177; 535

Steffensmeier, Darrell, 44–45; 54; 61 *nn*.49–50; 62 *nn*.84–85, 95, 105, 107; 192 *n*.52; 251 *n*.51; 349–351; 368 *n*.21; 534; 535

Steffensmeier, Renee Hoffman, 62 *n*.105

Stegink, Lewis, 153 *n*.33

Stein, Judith, 226 *n*.117

Stein, Nancy, 252 *n*.86

Steinberg, Laurence, 158 *n*.233; 282 *n*.136

Steiner, Hans, 158 *n*.198

Steinhardt, Barry, 462 *n*.92

Stephan, James, 119 *n*.198; 560 *n*.69; 561 *n*.117

Stephens, Christopher, 523 *n*.122

Stephens, Donald, *530*

Stephens, Gene, 13; 252 *n*.122

Sterk, Claire, 437 *n*.217

Sterk-Elifson, Claire, 38; 60 *n*.37; 421; 435 *n*.161

Stermac, Lana, 85 *n*.24

Stern, Howard, 404; 433 *n*.24

Stetler, Linda, 375

Stetson, Barbara, 225 *n*.66

Steury, Ellen Hochstedler, 158 *n*.204

Stevens, Douglas Richard, 3–4

Stevens, Ed, 117 *n*.138

Stevens, Tomika, 312 *n*.20

Stevenson, Richard, 369 *n*.89

Stewart, Claire, 159 *n*.236

Stewart, Eric, 86 *n*.71; 194 *n*.153; 281 *nn*.77, 94; 313 *n*.41; 437 *n*.217; 555

Stewart, Martha, 386; 388; 388

Stewart, Potter, 413

St. Gerard, Vanessa, 561 *n*.109

St. Guillen, Imette, 65–66; 65

Stice, Eric, 200

Stigler, George J., 115 *n*.4

Stoddart, Clare, 153 *n*.32

Stolzenberg, Lisa, 63 *n*.123; 108; 109; 521 *n*.18; 560 *n*.37, 536

Stone, Emily, 60 *n*.42

Stone, Laurence, 316 *n*.210

Stone, Sharon, 213

Stone-Meierhoefer, Barbara, 563 *n*.198

Storr, C. L., 192 *n*.61

Stout, Ronnie, 312 *n*.5

Stouthamer-Loeber, Magda, 86 *n*.68; 159 *nn*.263, 267; 224 *n*.45; 279 *nn*.16, 18, 26, 28, 31; 280 *n*.51; 313 *n*.42, 62

Strang, John, 437 *n*.219

Stratton, Howard, 282 *n*.148

Straus, Murray, 224 *n*.31; 288; 303–304; 313 *nn*.31, 38; 316 *nn*.207, 213

Streifel, Cathy, 62 *n*.84

Stretesky, Paul, 154 *n*.70; 191 *n*.44; 398 *n*.98

Streuning, Elmer, 227 *n*.145

Strodtbeck, Fred, 225 *n*.96

Strolovitch, Dara, 522 *n*.82

Strom, Kevin J., 317 *n*.237

Strueber, Daniel, 312 *n*.10

Stuart, Gregory, 85 *n*.25; 312 *n*.8

Stults, Briam, 63 *n*.123

Stumbo, Phyllis, 153 *n*.33

Stuntz, William, 523 *n*.140

Su, S. Susan, 194 *n*.172; 279 *n*.27

Sudermann, Marlies, 87 *n*.114

Sullivan, Christopher, 158 *n*.219; 224 *n*.25

Sullivan, Dennis, 243; 252 *nn*.103–106

Sun, Ivan, 193 *n*.104

Surratt, Hilary, 410; 433 *n*.52

Susser, Ezra S., 154 *n*.75

Sutherland, Brian, 522 *n*.65

Sutherland, Edwin H., 4; 9; 10; 14; 16; 27 *nn*.3, 42; 147; 159 *n*.264; 203–205; 210; 225 *nn*.62–64; 348–349; 368 *nn*.14, 16; 372; 382; 397 *nn*.9–10; 398 *n*.68

Swaggi, Vincent, 349

Swahn, Monica, 312 *n*.19; 317 *n*.262

Swango, Michael, 300

Swanson, Christopher B., 224 *n*.37

Swartz, Bruce, 462 *n*.88

Swartz, Marc, 378

Swartz, Marvin, 158 *n*.221

Sweeten, Gary, 227 *n*.164; 266

Sykes, Gresham, 207–209; 222; 225 *nn*.91, 93–94; 251 *n*.38; 562 *n*.131

Sykes, Richard, 522 *n*.73

Symons, Donald, 314 *n*.104

Ta, Mydue, 317 *n*.259

Tabias, J. J., 559 *n*.6

Tait, David, 314 *nn*.107, 114

Tajima, Emiko, 312 *n*.25

Takagi, Paul, 251 *n*.46

Talbert, Regina, 246

Tamminen, Tuulk, 223 *n*.9

Tannenbaum, Frank, 217; 227 *n*.174

Tanskanen, Antti, 127

Tarde, Gabriel, 137; 157 *n*.183

Tardiff, Kenneth, 192 *n*.51; 313 *n*.55; 560 *n*.38

Tark, Jongyeon, 49; 80; 87 *n*.131

Tatchell, Renny, 282 *n*.147

Tatchell, Thomas, 282 *n*.147

Taub, Richard P., 166

Taxman, Faye, 562 *n*.163

Taylor, Alan, 156 *nn*.146, 151

Taylor, Bruce, 60 n.12; 85 n.31; 522 n.103
Taylor, Dawn, 158 n.202
Taylor, Ian, 233; 240; 250 n.14; 251 n.68
Taylor, Jeanette, 156 n.153
Taylor, John, 369 n.101
Taylor, Mark Lewis, 244; 252 n.111; 369 n.91
Taylor, Natalie, 397 n.15
Taylor, Ralph, 115 n.49; 191 n.43; 192 nn.68, 83; 193 nn.97, 131
Taylor, Robert, 116 n.95; 117 n.132
Taylor, Terrance, 224 n.44
Taylor, Wendy, 116 nn.85, 97
Teplin, Linda, 27 n.41
Terrill, William, 192 n.77
Tesoriero, James, 116 n.73
Testa, Maria, 314 nn.78, 80, 82, 95
Tewksbury, Richard, 116 n.53; 436 n.174
Thapar, Anita, 156 n.126
Thatcher, Robert, 155 n.86
Thaxton, Sherod, 194 n.156
Theall, Katherine, 437 n.217
Theerathorn, Pochara, 116 n.88
Thomas, Chandra, 223 n.2
Thomas, Evan, 312 n.1
Thomas, Melvin, 63 n.134
Thomas, Stephen, 43
Thomas, Suzie Dod, 252 n.86
Thomas, W. I., 9; 17
Thomas Aquinas, St., 406
Thomlinson, R. Paul, 313 n.61
Thompson, Carol, 398 n.93
Thompson, Kevin, 252 nn.97–98; 282 n.140
Thompson, Marti, 157 n.196
Thompson, Melissa, 95; 115 nn.20, 26
Thompson, Wright, 223 n.1
Thornberry, Terence, 60 n.25; 61 nn.66, 82; 63 n.150; 116 n.73; 156 n.137; 224 nn.32, 38–39, 48; 225 n.77; 262; 279 n.25; 313 n.37; 435 n.142
Thornburgh, Nathan, 461 n.53
Thorne, Ian, 369 n.101
Thorton, Marlene, 561 nn.95, 97
Thrasher, Frederick, 27 n.22
Thurman, Quint, 354; 368 n.36; 522 n.79
Tibbetts, Stephen, 225 n.99; 280 n.53; 281 n.90; 398 n.86
Tice, Peter, 279 n.28
Tifft, Larry, 60 n.28; 243; 252 nn.103–104, 106; 483 n.36
Time, Victoria, 521 n.54
Timmendequas, Jesse, 82; 82
Timpson, Sandra, 433 n.61
Tippetts, Scott, 117 n.135
Tita, George, 86 n.68; 312 n.2
Titchener, Edward, 142
Titterington, Victoria, 85 n.43; 251 n.83
Tittle, Charles, 50; 61 nn.67–68; 117 n.115; 118 n.146; 191 n.26; 195 n.205; 218; 223 n.4; 227 nn.183, 188; 268; 281 n.102; 282 nn.113, 123, 130
Tjaden, Patricia, 317 n.260
Tmberlake, Justin, 213
Tobias, Aurelio, 279 n.18
Tobias, J. J., 368 n.4

Tobin, Kimberly, 116 n.74
Tobin, Michael, 154 n.73
Tobler, Nancy, 282 n.148
Toby, Jackson, 251 n.60
Toch, Hans, 563 n.181
Tocqueville, Alexis de, 559 n.9
Tolmunen, Tommi, 127
Tomas, Joseph, 279 n.18
Tomaskovic-Devey, Donald, 60 n.27
Tomasovic, Elizabeth, 312 n.22
Tonn, Jessica, 461 n.48
Tonry, Michael, 13; 115 n.13; 559 nn.18, 22, 26; 561 nn.92–93
Tontodonato, Pamela, 87 n.117; 559 n.12
Toombs, Nancy J., 561 n.110
Toomey, Rosemary, 156 n.149
Topalli, Volkan, 207; 368 n.59
Tosouni, Anastasia, 462 n.77
Townsley, Michael, 369 n.95
Towns-Miranda, Luz, 369 n.99
Tracy, Paul, 57; 62 n.112; 63 nn.143, 151, 152; 118 n.173
Trapani, Catherine, 62 n.97
Traub, Leah Goldman, 158 n.220
Travis, Lawrence, 561 n.122
Trebach, Arnold, 435 n.121
Tremblay, Pierre, 115 n.27; 225 n.67
Tremblay, Richard, 63 n.153; 155 n.80; 156 n.154; 259; 280 nn.38, 45; 281 n.102
Trendle, Giles, 460 n.4
Treno, Andrew, 192 n.78
Treynker, Aleksandr, 371
Trickett, Alan, 85 n.48
Triplett, Ruth, 193 n.104; 227 n.181
Tristan, Jennifer, 200
Trumbetta, Susan, 116 n.78; 314 n.86
Trump, Donald, 177
Tseng, Li-Jung, 435 n.152
Tsuang, Ming, 156 n.149
Tuch, Steven, 63 n.130; 239; 251 n.48
Tully, Lucy, 156 n.151
Tunnell, Kenneth, 97; 116 n.55; 205; 225 n.76; 422; 436 n.171
Turic, Darko, 156 n.126
Turner, Charles, 279 n.25
Turner, Heather, 84 n.15
Turner, Michael, 85 n.62; 117 n.128; 314 n.96; 317 n.263
Turner, Scott, 369 n.104
Turner, Susan, 561 n.85; 563 n.199
Turpin-Petrosino, Carolyn, 27 n.57
Tyler, Kimberly, 314 n.92; 435 n.159
Tzavaras, Nikos, 312 n.5

Uggen, Christopher, 95; 115 nn.20, 26; 252 nn.95, 100; 280 n.64; 281 n.69
Ullman, Sarah, 314 n.85
Ullrich, Simone, 158 n.209
Ulman, Arina, 303; 316 n.207
Ulmer, Jeffrey, 350–351; 523 n.144
Ulrich, Yvonne, 304
Umbreit, Mark, 560 n.36
Umhau, John, 155 n.93
Unfold, Douglas, 369 n.100
Unnever, James, 223 n.12; 224 n.18; 560 nn.50–52

Vaccaro, Donato, 435 n.153
Vaillant, George, 267
Valier, Claire, 191 n.34
Van Den Bergle, Pierre, 153 n.10
Van den Bree, Marianne, 156 nn.126, 153
Van Den Haag, Ernest, 118 n.155; 560 n.46
Van der Does, Louise, 522 n.101
Van der Laan, Peter, 280 n.54
Vander Ven, Thomas, 226 nn.120, 131
VanDeusen, Karen, 434 n.101
Vandewater, Elizabeth, 144
Van de Weyer, Courtney, 127
Van Dijk, Mirjam, 314 n.113
Van Geen, Alexander, 153 n.25
Van Goozen, Stephanie, 154 n.48
Van Gundy, Karen, 226 n.139; 435 n.165
Van Hoof, Anne, 158 n.229
Van Kammen, Welmoet, 224 n.45; 279 n.31
Van Koppen, Peter J., 116 n.68; 305; 317 n.221
Van Loh, Timothy, 281 n.105
Van Voorhis, Patricia, 226 nn.114, 119; 253 n.133; 483 n.38
Van Wormer, Katherine, 312 n.9
Vanzile-Tamsen, Carol, 314 nn.78, 80, 82
Varano, Sean, 191 n.24
Vardi, Nathan, 461 n.52
Vargas, Elizabeth, 308
Vashista, Anish, 397 n.31
Vatis, Michael A., 460 n.2
Vazsonyi, Alexander, 62 nn.97, 103; 157 n.173; 272; 281 nn.83, 105
Veach-White, Ernie, 157–158 n.197
Vega, Hector, 184
Velez, Maria, 191 n.16; 193 nn.108–109
Venables, Peter, 127; 156 n.125; 158 n.231
Veneziano, Carol, 158 n.228
Veneziano, Louis, 158 n.228
Venkatesh, Sudhir Alladi, 107; 118 n.162; 274; 282 n.137
Verhulst, Frank, 280 n.54
Verlur, D. E., 435 n.155
Vermeiren, Robert, 158 n.210; 224 n.29; 280 n.55
Vernon, Philip, 156 n.127
Verona, Edelyn, 159 n.256
Veronen, Lois, 86 n.100
Veysey, Bonita, 61 n.80; 158 n.219
Vicomandi, David, 282 n.122
Victor, Timothy, 27 n.56
Victorino, Sharon, 255
Victorino, Troy, 255; 255
Viding, Essi, 134; 157 n.156; 159 n.257
Vieraitis, Lynne, 50; 315 n.160
Vigdor, E. R., 49
Viinamäki, Heimo, 127
Villaume, Alfred, 252 n.112
Villemez, Wayne, 50; 61 n.67
Vincent, Mary, *110*
Virkkunen, Matti, 154 n.39; 155 nn.79, 116–117
Viscusi, W. Kip, 462 n.96
Visher, Christy, 227 n.153; 312 n.25
Vitaro, Frank, 280 n.45
Vito, Gennaro, 561 n.122
Vitter, David, 406

Voas, Robert, 117 *n*.135
Volavka, Jan, 153 *n*.17; 154 *n*.55; 155 *n*.90;
  156 *n*.131
Vold, George, 232; 233; 392; 399 *n*.129
Von, Judith, 86 *n*.100
Von Hirsch, Andrew, 112; 119 *n*.199
Von Zielbauer, Paul, 560 *n*.79
Voronin, Yuri A., 393
Voss, Harwin, 54; 62 *n*.109
Vossekuil, Bryan, 315 *n*.167
Votey, Harold, 119 *n*.184; 521 *n*.17
Vowell, Paul, 225 *n*.70
Vuchinich, S., 280 *n*.42
Vungkhanching, Martha, 435 *n*.150

Wadsworth, Tim, 192 *n*.49
Wagner, Charles, 369 *n*.99
Wagner, Richard, 158 *n*.202
Wagner, Ryan, 158 *n*.221
Waite, Linda, 281 *n*.70
Waite, Phillip, 282 *n*.147
Wakschlag, Lauren, 153 *n*.19
Waldo, Gordon, 117 *n*.118; 118 *nn*.151,
  159
Waldorf, Dan, 526 *n*.141
Walker, Alice, 403
Walker, Jesse, 563 *n*.177
Walker, Richard, 461 *n*.20
Walker, Robert, 317 *n*.268
Walker, Samuel, 218; 227 *n*.179; 482 *nn*.2–
  3; 528; 559 *nn*.4, 6, 10
Walker, Stephanie, *479*
Wall, April, 462 *nn*.67, 69
Wallace, C., 158 *n*.207
Wallace, Donald, 560 *n*.44
Wallace, John, 435 *n*.157
Wallace, Rodrick, 191 *n*.28
Wallace-Carpretta, Suzanne, 561 *n*.81
Wallerstedt, John, 119 *n*.191
Walsh, Anthony, 153 *nn*.13–14; 154 *nn*.43,
  47; 194 *n*.167; 281 *n*.97; 314 *n*.105
Walsh, Marilyn, 368 *nn*.6, 20–21, 23
Walters, Glenn, 157 *nn*.160, 180
Walton, Paul, 233; 250 *n*.14
Walz, Liz, 252 *n*.102
Wang, Eugene, 85 *n*.35
Wang, Fahui, 40; 43
Wang, Hsiao-Ming, 562 *n*.138
Wang, Jichuan, 436 *n*.180
Wang, Morgan, 61 *n*.55
Wanson, Jeffrey, 158 *n*.221
Ward, David, 93; 115 *n*.17; 118 *n*.147;
  144; 159 *n*.237; 282 *n*.113
Ward, Tony, 159 *nn*.236, 247
Waring, Elin, 117 *nn*.131, 134; 118 *n*.177;
  398 *n*.110; 522 *n*.87
Warner, Barbara, 60 *n*.34; 191 *n*.10; 313
  n.43
Warner, Lynn, 483 *n*.11
Warr, Mark, 62 *n*.99; 205; 224 *n*.52; 225
  nn.54, 73, 78; 265; 281 *n*.71; 314 *n*.81
Warren, Earl, 474; 500
Warren, Janet, 116 *n*.78; 292; 314 *n*.86
Wartella, Ellen, 144
Wasilchick, John, 115 *nn*.19, 42
Wasserman, Gail, 153 *n*.25

Watson, Jamie, 547; 561 *n*.115
Watt, Toni Terling, 212; 226 *n*.122
Watzke, Stefan, 158 *n*.209
Wayner, Peter, 368 *n*.44
Weatherburn, Don, 86 *n*.90; 280 *n*.64; 369
  n.89
Weatherston, David, 343 *n*.54
Weaver, Bob, 462 *n*.90
Webb, Barry, 116 *n*.92
Webb, Nancy, 369 *n*.99
Weber, Egen, 27 *n*.6
Webster, Cheryl Marie, 118 *n*.140
Webster, Daniel, 304
Webster, Pamela, 281 *nn*.70, 74
Wechsberg, Wendee, 411; 433 *n*.60
Weekes-Shackelford, Viviana, 315 *n*.147
Weeks, Margaret, 434 *n*.70
Wei, Evelyn, 279 *n*.18; 436 *n*.193
Weihe, P., 153 *n*.20
Weinberg, Heather, 158 *n*.202
Weiner, Neil Alan, 412; 433 *n*.31; 434 *n*.76
Weingart, Saul, 437 *n*.211
Weinmann, Gabriel, 462 *n*.66
Weis, Joseph, 60 *n*.35; 61 *n*.71; 62 *n*.105;
  159 *n*.261
Weis, Robert, 239
Weisburd, David, 117 *nn*.102–103, 131,
  134; 118 *n*.177; 397 *n*.11; 398 *n*.110;
  521 *n*.23
Weiser, Benjamin, 369 *n*.67
Weiser, Carl, 317 *n*.249
Weisheit, Ralph, 61 *n*.52; 434 *n*.117
Weisman, Jonathan, 397 *n*.40
Weiss, Alexander, 63 *n*.126; 521 *n*.14
Weiss, P., 369 *n*.64
Weiss, Robert, 251 *n*.58; 560 *n*.61
Weist, Mark, 314 *n*.120
Weitekamp, Elmar, 224 *n*.44
Weitzer, Ronald, 63 *n*.130; 239; 251 *n*.48;
  289; 313 *n*.53; 434 *n*.82
Welch, Michael, 118 *n*.150; 436 *n*.209; 560
  n.47
Wells, James, 561 *n*.87
Wells, L. Edward, 60 *n*.33; 61 *n*.52; 223
  n.13
Wells, Nancy, 191 *n*.15
Wells, William, 521 *n*.3
Wellsmith, Melanie, 86 *n*.84; 115 *n*.18
Welsh, Brandon, 38; 60 *n*.41; 86 *n*.88; 103;
  117 *n*.110
Welte, John W., 86 *n*.63; 435 *n*.143; 436
  n.172
Wentworth, Jennifer, 315 *n*.127; 522 *n*.97
West, Donald J., 63 *n*.145; 133; 156
  nn.133–134, 142; 224 *n*.20
West, Valerie, 251 *n*.57
Westcott, Kathryn, 153 *n*.1
Western, Bruce, 227 *n*.177; 534; 535
Weston, Eugene, 139
Whaley, Rachel Bridges, 314 *n*.110
Whatley, Mark, 314 *n*.122
Wheeler, Stanton, 398 *n*.110
Whine, Michael, 461 *n*.61
Whipple, Diane, 296
Whitbeck, Les, 314 *n*.92; 435 *n*.159
White, Ben, 492

White, Garland, 116 *n*.58; 144
White, Helene Raskin, 158 *n*.220; 226
  n.141; 279 *n*.28; 435–436 *n*.166; 436
  nn.184, 193–194
White, Helene White, 194 *n*.152
White, Jennifer, 63 *n*.154
White, Michael, 42; 43; 117 *n*.126
White, Rob, 250 *n*.31
White, Teresa, 523 *n*.146
White, Thomas, 157 *n*.180
Whitehall, George, 225 *n*.96
Whitehead, John, 562 *n*.169; 563 *n*.173
Whiteman, Martin, 279 *n*.27
Whitman, Charels, 301
Whitman, Terry, 316 *n*.177
Whitney, Stephen, 312 *n*.25
Whittinger, Naureen, 156 *n*.126
Whitworth, Keith, 398 *n*.93
Whyte, Carrie, 369 *n*.102
Whyte, Laurence, 369 *n*.102
Whyte, William F., 38; 60 *n*.39
Wiatrowski, Michael, 226 *nn*.113, 137
Widom, Cathy Spatz, 84 *n*.19; 85
  nn.36# 39
Wiebe, Richard, 282 *n*.135
Wiechman, Dennis, 560 *n*.35
Wieczorek, William F., 86 *n*.63; 436 *n*.172
Wiederman, Michael, 85 *n*.21
Wiersema, Brian, 84 *n*.7
Wiesel, Elie, *125*
Wiesner, Margit, 279 *n*.30
Wiggins, Elizabeth, 523 *n*.176
Wikberg, Ron, 562 *n*.136
Wikstrom, Per-Olof, 280 *n*.52
Wilcox, Norma, 108; 109
Wilcox, Pamela, 74; 86 *n*.73; 192 *n*.60; 282
  n.141; 315 *n*.165
Wild, Jack, 346; 348
Wilder, Esther, 212; 226 *n*.122
Wilhelm, C., 154 *n*.42
Wilkinson, Deanna, 428
Wilkinson, Paul, 342 *n*.25
Wilkinson, Richard, 194 *n*.147
Wilks, Judith, 483 *n*.15; 562 *n*.166
Will, Richard, 561 *nn*.92–93
Williams, Dominic P., 153 *n*.28
Williams, James, 118 *n*.166
Williams, Kirk, 315 *nn*.152, 154
Williams, Linda, 85 *n*.22; 290; 316
  n.206; 409
Williams, Marian, 560 *n*.43
Williams, Marian R., 63 *n*.127; 535
Williams, Mark, 158 *n*.231; 433 *n*.61
Williams, Stanley "Tookie," 272
Williams, Stephanie Hall, 224 *n*.26
Williams, Wendol, 155 *n*.93
Williard, Jennifer, 432 *n*.5
Willingham, David, *46*
Willis, Bruce, 213
Willis, James, 521 *n*.23
Willman, Mark T., 521 *n*.31
Wills, Thomas Ashby, 435 *n*.153
Wilmoth, Charles, 156 *n*.121
Wilson, B., 436 *n*.185
Wilson, Brandon, 98–99; *99*
Wilson, Clyde, 462 *n*.71

Wilson, David, 483 n.29; 562 n.171; 563 n.174
Wilson, Dennis, 14; 27 n.36
Wilson, Doris James, 559 nn.23, 25; 563 n.201
Wilson, Edmund O., 123; 151; 153 n.11
Wilson, Genarlow, 197–198
Wilson, James Q., 60 n.36; 62 n.90; 93; 115 n.11; 116 n.82; 118 nn.169–170; 125; 154 n.40; 159 n.270; 195 n.206; 281 n.84; 497; 498; 521 nn.10, 22; 522 nn.72, 76–77
Wilson, Janet, 102; 117 n.108
Wilson, Margaret, 561 n.112
Wilson, Margo, 62 n.88; 85 n.60; 135; 157 nn.168–171; 192 n.65; 193 n.128; 282 n.121; 316 n.199
Wilson, Pete, 476
Wilson, R., 523 n.120
Wilson, William Julius, 74; 86 n.81; 165–166; 193 nn.115, 120; 313 n.50
Wilt, Susan, 304
Winfree, L. Thomas, Jr., 225 n.87; 562 n.150
Wingood, Gina, 279 n.22
Winick, Charles, 433 nn.51, 55
Winslett, Andrea, 314 n.93
Wirth, Louis, 9; 27 n.23; 162
Wish, Eric, 226 n.102
Wislar, Joseph S., 60 n.26
Wissow, Lawrence, 224 n.33; 313 n.30
Witner, Helen, 60 n.18
Wittebrood, Karin, 85 n.47; 86 n.87
Wittekind, Janice Clifford, 281 n.105
Wittrock, Stacy, 191 n.39
Wohlfarth, Harry, 154 n.68
Wolf, Jim, 461 n.21
Wolf, Mark L., 277
Wolfendale, Jessica, 342 n.21
Wolfers, Justin, 109
Wolff, Ashley, 562 n.164
Wolff, Russell, 436 n.209
Wolfgang, Marvin, 11; 14; 27 nn.7, 31, 37; 56; 57; 63 nn.141–143, 150; 85 n.56; 256; 279 n.4; 313 n.48
Wolfner, Glenn, 316 nn.198, 202
Wolraich, Mark, 153 n.33
Wong, Frank, 144

Wong, Janelle, 522 n.82
Wong, Stephen, 149
Woo, Hyung-jim, 461 n.39
Wood, Peter, 116 n.82; 281 nn.102, 104
Wood, Wendy, 144
Wooden, Wayne, 365; 369 n.103
Woods, Katherine, 63 n.133; 521 n.21
Wooldredge, John, 227 n.178; 562 nn.137, 154
Woolford, Andrew, 250 n.7
Wooton, Barbara, 156 n.132
Wormith, J. Stephen, 159 n.251
Worrall, John, 193 n.117; 368 n.28; 369 n.84; 522 nn.78, 95
Woyke, Elizabeth, 461 n.30
Wozniak, John, 253 n.135
Wright, Bradley Entner, 61 n.78; 117 n.120; 225 n.58; 276; 279 nn.9, 19; 282 n.142
Wright, Cynthia Pfaff, 60 n.27
Wright, James, 85 n.46; 99; 116 n.66
Wright, John Paul, 60 n.19; 185; 194 nn.162, 165; 224 nn.24, 50; 226 nn.120, 131; 274; 281 n.99; 282 n.132; 483 n.30
Wright, Joy, 158 n.202
Wright, Richard, 115 n.41; 306; 317 n.224; 361; 362; 368 n.59; 369 nn.80, 85
Wright, Robert O., 154 n.77
Wrightsman, Lawrence, 314 nn.94, 97, 100
Wrinkle, Robert, 109
Wu, Chyi-in, 313 n.32
Wu, Lawrence, 194 n.166
Wunderlich, Ray, 154 n.63
Wundt, Wilhelm, 142
Wung, Phen, 279 n.31
Wuornos, Aileen, 300

Xie, Min, 84 n.12
Xu, Xiao, 304

Yager, Tom, 461 n.51
Yamamoto, T., 155 n.89
Yang, Catherine, 462 n.95
Yang, Yaling, 155 n.81
Yaryura-Tobias, J. A., 154 n.38
Yates, Andrea, 140; 140
Yeager, Peter, 397 n.46

Yee, Dorline, 563 n.174
Yeudall, Lorne, 155 nn.88, 96, 110; 159 n.272
Yeung, W. Jean, 191 n.13
Yili, Xu, 192 n.58
Yllo, K., 314 n.99
Yodanis, Carrie, 251 n.82
Young, Amy, 435 n.158
Young, Jock, 233; 239–240; 250 n.14; 251 nn.66, 70
Young, Lawrence, 159 n.261
Yunker, James, 109

Zaff, Jonathan, 226 n.127
Zahman, Marvin, 514
Zahn, Margaret, 315 nn.150, 159
Zakaria, Fareed, 436 n.203
Zalman, Marvin, 483 n.26
Zaslow, Jeffrey, 369 n.96
Zatz, Marjorie, 227 n.154
Zawacki, Tina, 312 n.21
Zawitz, Marianne, 315 n.146; 437 n.213
Zayed, Z. A., 155 n.90
Zeckhauser, Richard J., 462 n.96
Zeedyk, M. S., 154 n.58
Zehr, Howard, 243–244; 252 n.110
Zernike, Kate, 428
Zhang, Lening, 86 n.63; 227 n.182; 436 n.172
Zhang, Quanwu, 224 nn.41, 45
Zhang, Yan, 436 n.194
Zhao, Jihong, 192 n.90; 522 nn.78–79
Zhe, Zhu, 13
Zheng, Wei, 154 n.75
Zheng, Yan, 153 n.25
Zhong, Hua, 62 n.107
Ziebell, John, 175
Ziff, John, 342 n.8
Zimmerman, Frederick, 144
Zimmerman, Rick, 428
Zimmermann, Grégoire, 157 n.195
Zimring, Franklin, 46; 61 n.60; 118 n.140; 437 n.218; 537; 560 n.48
Zinger, Ivan, 483 n.28; 562–563 n.173
Zlotnick, Caron, 85 n.25
Zorbaugh, Harvey, 9; 27 n.21
Zwi, Anthony, 13; 316 n.191

SUBJECT INDEX

ABA (American Bar Association), 293, 457–458, 505

Abortion, 29, 40–41, 331

Abu Ghraib prison (Iraq), 326

Abuse. *See* Child abuse; Child sexual abuse; Domestic violence; Sexual abuse

The Accused, 294

ACLU (American Civil Liberties Union), 93, 326, *339*, 454, 455

Acquaintance rape, 292–293

Acquaintance robbery, 305–306

Active precipitation, 73

Actual authority, 383

Actus reus, 21, 22

Adaptation, modes of, 176, *177*

ADC (Aid to Dependent Children), 188

ADHD (attention deficit hyperactive disorder), 124, 127, 130–131, *131*

Adjudication process, 500. *See also* Courts

Adolescent-limited offenders, 261, 273

Adolescents. *See also* Gangs; Juvenile justice system; Schools
  adolescent-limited offenders, 261, 273
  attitudes of, toward juvenile court, 107
  automobiles and, 76
  as chronic offenders, 56–57
  cognitive deficits of delinquent youth, 145
  crime rates and patterns involving, 40, 51–52, 111
  desistance of, 265–267
  drunk-driving by, 105
  friendships of delinquents, 213
  Gluecks' research on, 10
  guns and, 41, 74, 289, 423, 499
  labeling of, and criminal behavior, 218
  latent delinquency and, 138
  media violence and, 41, 143–144
  mood disorders and, 139–140
  parental deviance and delinquency of, 133, 199–200
  parental efficacy and, 199–200, 273–274
  posttraumatic stress disorder (PTSD) and, 67
  property crimes by, 44, 45, 51–52
  school shootings and, 48, 75, 99, 121–122, 286, 287, 299
  self-reporting on criminal activity by, 44–45, 52
  sexual behavior of, 197–198
  social bond theory and, 212–213
  street efficacy and, 173–174
  substance abuse by, 418–423
  victimization of, 67, 69, 69–70, 71, 73–74
  violent crime by, 44, 45, 51–52, 66, *145*

Adoption, 375

Adoption studies, 135

Afghanistan, 322, 334, 425–426

Africa
  criminal enterprises in, 392
  death penalty in, 538, 539
  diet and crime research, 126
  genital mutilation of females in, 403
  rape in, 291
  state sponsored terrorism in, 334
  substance abuse in, 416
  violence in, 289

African Americans. *See also* Race and ethnicity
  arrests of, 54–55, 478
  bail for, 55
  Black Panther Party and, 238, 331–332
  burglary rates and, 360
  community deterioration and, 170
  contextual discrimination by judges against, 218
  crime rates and, 170
  death penalty for, 536, 537
  DWB (Driving While Black) and, *54*, 55
  economic and social disparity for, 55–56
  families of, 56, 198–199
  hate crimes against, *306*, 307
  high school graduation rates of, 200
  jury service by, 514
  marriage of, and age-graded theory, 265
  murders of, 297, 301, 492
  police contacts with, 498
  population statistics on, 54
  poverty of, 164–166, *164*, 170
  in prisons and jails, 55, 164, 478, 536, 537, 549
  property crime by, 54
  racial profiling of, 54–55, 216, 238–239, 486
  self-reporting by, 35, 54
  sentencing of, 55, 534
  unemployment and underemployment of, 164, 165
  victimization of, 72, 297, 306, 360
  violent crime by, 54, 55, 297, 302
  voting privileges for, 55
  whites' fear of, 171

Aftermath: Violence and the Remodeling of a Self (Brison), 68

Age. *See also* Adolescents; Children; Developmental theories; Elderly persons
  aging out of crime, 52
  crime patterns and trends regarding, 40, 51–52

early-onset criminals, 56–57, 259–261
  poverty and, 163–164
  victimization and, 69–70, 71

Age-graded theory
  cumulative disadvantage and, 263–264
  definition of, 262–263
  future research on, 265–266
  marriage factor and, 264–265
  principles of, 263–264
  public policy implications of, 267
  social capital and, 264
  summary of, 275
  testing, 264

Aggravated assault. *See* Assault and battery

Aggravated rape, 294. *See also* Rape

Aggression. *See also* Violence and violent crime
  behavior modeling and, 141
  family influences on, 141
  gender and, 53
  hormonal influences on, 126–127
  media violence and, 143–144
  punishment linked with, 288

Aging out of crime, 52. *See also* Desistance

AIDS
  medication for, 375
  murder conviction for person with, 296
  prisoners and, 111, 548, 551
  prostitutes and, 411–412
  siege mentality and, 171
  substance abuse and, 420, 423, 430

Aid to Dependent Children (ADC), 188

Airplane hijackers, 100

Airport security, 456

Alcohol abuse. *See also* Drunk-driving
  by adolescents, 418–420
  ban on sales of, 102, 418
  biochemical influences on, 124
  chronic offenders and, 57
  crime and, 423
  differential reinforcement theory and, 206–207
  domestic violence and, 304
  pregnancy and, 297, 430
  Prohibition of, 418, 430
  robbery and, 305
  self-report surveys on, 43–44
  statistics on, 418–420
  summary of, 417
  trends in, 43–44
  victimization and, 73

Alcoholics Anonymous, 551

Alexithymia, 139

ALF (Animal Liberation Front), 332, 333

Alienation. *See* Anomie

Alienation view of terrorists, 336
Alien conspiracy theory, 391
Al Jazeera website, 448
Allergies, 128
All God's Children: The Bosket Family and the American Tradition of Violence (Butterfield), 55
Al-Qaeda, 322, 333–334, 340
Amateur receivers, 351
Amerada Hess oil company, 379
American Bar Association (ABA), 293, 457–458, 505
American Bar Foundation, 466–467
American Civil Liberties Union (ACLU), 93, 326, 339, 454, 455
American Convention on Human Rights, 538
American Dream, 177–178
American Indians. *See* Native Americans
American Psychiatric Association, 151
American Psychological Association, 148
American Taliban, 322, 322
Amnesty International, 242, 320, 334, 403
Amphetamines, 417, 425. *See also* Drugs
Anal stage, 138
Androgens, 53, 125–128
Anesthetics, 417
Anger rape, 292
Angola, 289
Animal Liberation Front (ALF), 332, 333, 335
Annie E. Casey Foundation, 164
Anomie
    American Dream and, 177–178
    definition of, 8, 175
    evaluation of Merton's anomie theory, 176–177
    impact of, 177–178
    institutional anomie theory, 177–178, 181
    mechanical solidarity and, 175
    Merton's theory of, 176–177, 181
    organic solidarity and, 175
    social adaptations and, 176
ANS (autonomic nervous system) dysfunction, 149
Anti-Drug Abuse Act (1986, 1988), 425
Antipsychotic drugs, 132. *See also* Mental illness/mental disorders
Anti-Saloon League, 418
Antisocial behavior
    antisocial personality, 147, 148–149
    arousal theory and, 132
    diet and, 125
    differential association theory of, 205
    integrated cognitive antisocial potential (ICAP) theory of, 268, 275
    peer relations and, 201
    personality and, 146–149
    psychodynamic theory of, 138–139
    of siblings, 133
    of victims, 68
Antisocial personality, 147, 148–149
Antithesis, 232
Apparent authority, 383

Appeal, 471
Arbitrage, 386
Argentina, 126, 333
Armenia, 538
Army of God, 29
Arousal theory, 132
Arraignment, 471, 471, 518
Arrests
    of African Americans, 54–55, 478
    cleared crime due to, 31, 32
    definition of, 469
    for domestic violence, 109–110
    drug–crime connection and, 424
    drug-related arrests, 416
    inhibition of crime by, 49
    in justice process, 469
    probable cause for, 469
    process of, 492–493
    for traffic violations, 493
Arson
    by adolescents, 45, 52
    arson for profit, 365
    arson fraud, 365
    common-law description of, 20
    costs to victims of, 66
    flashover and, 365
    juvenile fire starter, 365
    motivation for, 365
    as Part I crime, 30, 31
    professional arson, 365
    statistics on, 33, 364
    underreporting of, 33
Arson for profit, 365
Arson fraud, 365
ART Act (Artists' Rights and Theft Prevention Act), 453
Asia. *See* specific countries
Asian Americans. *See also* Race and ethnicity
    high school graduation rates of, 200
    poverty of, 164
    single-parent families and, 198–199
Asphyxiophilia, 406
Assault and battery. *See also* Child abuse; Domestic violence; Rape
    by adolescents, 44, 45, 52
    age of victims of, 71
    aggravated assault, 30
    common-law description of, 20
    definition of, 301
    firearms used in, 46
    in home, 302–304
    nature and extent of, 301–302
    as Part I crime, 30, 31
    percentage of cleared cases involving, 32
    plea bargaining for charge of, 512
    pretrial detention for charge of, 509
    road rage, 301
    sentences for, 113, 526, 531
    statistics on, 301–302
    in workplace, 309
Assigned counsel system, 505
Atavistic anomalies, 7–8
ATF (Bureau of Alcohol, Tobacco, Firearms, and Explosives), 487

Atlanta bombing during Olympics (1997), 29
ATMs (automatic teller machines), 441
Attachment, 211, 212, 213–214
Attempted crime, 20
Attention deficit hyperactive disorder (ADHD), 124, 127, 130–131, *131*
Attorneys. *See* Defense attorneys; Prosecutors; Right to legal counsel
Auburn system, 527
Aum Shinrikyo, 334–335
Australia
    crime trends in, 13
    diet and crime research, 126
    domestic violence in, 302
    drunk-driving penalties in, 106
    prostitution in, 412
    restorative justice in, 247
    substance abuse in, 416
Authority conflict pathway, 259, *260*
Autoerotic asphyxia, 406
Automatic teller machines (ATMs), 441
Automobiles. *See also* Automobile theft; Drunk-driving
    adolescents and, 76
    DWB (Driving While Black) and, *54*, 55
    joyriding and, 356
    LoJack auto protection system for, 102, 358
    plea bargaining for driving-related charges, 512
    police search of, 495
    pretrial detention for driving-related charges, 509
    road rage, 301
    sentences for driving-related convictions, 526
Automobile theft
    by adolescents, 45
    car cloning, 465
    carjacking, 305, 358
    categories of, 356–357
    combating, 358
    international trends in, 13
    models of cars most frequently stolen, 357
    as Part I crime, 30, 31
    percentage of cleared cases involving, 32
    plea bargaining for charge of, 512
    pretrial detention for charge of, 508
    sentences for, 526
    situational prevention of, 101, 102
    statistics on, 356
    stealing car parts, 357–358
Autonomic nervous system (ANS) dysfunction, 149
Avertable recidivists, 508, 510
Azerbaijan, 320

Bad checks, 355
Bail, 55, 471, 507, 507–511
Bail bonding agents, 509
Bail guidelines, 511
Balanced and restorative justice (BARJ), 246
Balkan criminal organizations, 392

Bank fraud, 382, 383
Bank of Credit and Commerce International (BCCI), 374–375, 385
Barbiturates, 417, 425. *See also* Drugs
Bar girls (B-girls), 410
BARJ (balanced and restorative justice), 246
Basque Fatherland and Liberty (ETA), 332–333
Battery, 20, 301. *See also* Assault and battery
Bayship Management Inc. (BSM), 376
BCCI (Bank of Credit and Commerce International), 374–375, 385
BEAM (brain electrical activity mapping), 130
Behaviorism, 137, 141–142, 146, 150
Behavior modeling, 141
Beliefs. *See also* Morality
    General Theory of Crime (GTC) and, 273
    institutional belief and socialization, 201–202
    social bond theory and, 211, 212
The Bell Curve (Herrnstein and Murray), 24, 148
The Best Little Whorehouse in Texas, 410–411
Beyond Probation (Murray and Cox), 93
Beyond Tolerance: Child Pornography on the Internet (Jenkins), 413
B-girls (bar girls), 410
Bhutan, 539
Bias crimes. *See* Hate crimes
Bill of Rights, 474–475
Biochemical conditions and crime
    allergies, 128
    chemical and mineral influences, 124–125
    diet, 125, 126–127
    environmental contaminants, 128
    glucose metabolism/hypoglycemia, 125
    hormonal influences, 125–128
    lead levels, 128–129, *129*
    premenstrual syndrome (PMS), 128
    summary of, 137
Biological determinism, 8
Biologically oriented therapy, 150
Biological positivism, 7–8, 11
Biometric technology, 456–457, 478
Biophobia, 123
Biosocial theory, 8
Biosocial trait theories
    arousal theory, 132
    biochemical conditions and crime, 124–129, 137
    evaluation of, 136
    evolutionary theory, 135–136, 137
    genetics and crime, 132–135, 137
    neurophysiological conditions and crime, 129–132, 137
    summary of, 137
Bipolar disorder, 138
Black Panther Party, 238, 331–332
Blended families, 303
Body snatchers case, 353

Boggs Act (1951), 425
Bombings, 29–30, 319–320, 331, 332, 333. *See also* Terrorism
Boosters, 98, 354
Boot camps, 544–545
Borat, 17
Border Patrol, 338
Bosnia-Herzegovina, 538
Bosnian war, 291
Boston Community Disorder Unit, 307, 308, 310
Bourgeoisie, 9, 230–231
Box Man: A Professional Thief's Journal (King), 348
Brady Handgun Violence Prevention Act, 48–49
Brain. *See also* Head injuries; Neurophysiology
    brain scanning techniques, 129–130
    cerebral allergies, 128
    chemistry of, 131–132
    hormones and, 128
    impairment in executive brain function, 129
    minimal brain dysfunction (MBD), 130
    neocortex of, 128
    phrenologists on, 7
    psychopaths and brain abnormality, 149
    tumors, lesions, injury, and disease of, 131
Brain electrical activity mapping (BEAM), 130
Brain surgery, 150
Brazil, 12, 334, 412–413
Breach, 323
Bribery, 376–379
The Bridge overthe Racial Divide: Rising Inequality and Coalition Politics (Wilson), 165–166
Britain. *See* Great Britain
Brothel (Albert), 413
Brothels, 410–411, 412, 413. *See also* Prostitution
Brutalization effect, 536, 557
BSA (Business Software Alliance), 451
BSM (Bayship Management Inc.), 376
Buddhism, *186*
Bullying
    of children, 448
    cyber bullying, 448–449
Bureau of Alcohol, Tobacco, Firearms, and Explosives (ATF), 487
Bureau of Justice Statistics, 30, 36, 113
Burglars on the Job (Wright and Decker), 361
Burglary. *See also* Robbery; Theft
    careers in, 363–364
    commercial burglary, 361–363
    common-law description of, 20, 360
    definition of, 360
    good burglars, 363
    greed and, 107
    history of, 360
    international trends in, 12, 13
    nature and extent of, 360

as Part I crime, 30, 31
    percentage of cleared cases involving, 32
    planning of, 361
    plea bargaining for charge of, 512
    pretrial detention charge of, 508, 509
    rational choice theory and, 98
    repeat burglary, 364
    sentences for, 526, 531
    statistics on, 360
    targets of burglars, 97
Burkino Faso, 403
Burma, 335, 425
Businesses. *See also* Corporate crime; Shoplifting; White-collar crime
    burglary of, 361–363
    executive pay packages and, 229–230
    Home Depot Company, 229
    influence peddling in, 377–379
    workplace violence in, 308–309
Business Software Alliance (BSA), 451

California
    Anti-Terrorism Information Center (CATIC), 338
    gangs in, 162
    organized crime in, 391
    Proposition 8 in, 106
    rape law in, 295
    three strikes law, 110, 352
California Personality Inventory (CPI), 147
Call girls, 411. *See also* Prostitution
Call houses, 411. *See also* Prostitution
Cambodia, 12, 425
Cambridge Five, 323
Cambridge Study in Delinquent Development (CSDD), 133, 199
Canada
    capital punishment abolished in, 539
    crime trends in, 12, 13
    diet and crime research, 126
    domestic violence in, 302
    Doorsteps Neighbourhood Program in, 101
    Internet child pornography in, 454–455
    IQ–crime relationships research, 148
    marital rape law in, 293
    social bond theory, 212–213
    substance abuse in, 416
Cannabis, 417
Capable guardians, 74, 75
Capitalism. *See* Businesses; Corporate crime
Capitalism, Patriarchy, and Crime (Messerschmidt), 241
Capitalist bourgeoisie, 230–231
Capital punishment
    ACLU on, 93
    comparative research on, 108
    debate on, 535–537, *536*, 539
    deterrent effect of, 106, 108–109, 112
    DNA evidence for death row inmates, 518
    exoneration of death row inmates, 15
    false convictions and, 537, 539
    immediate impact of, for deterrence, 108
    international use of, 538, 539
    for juveniles, 538, 539

legal issues on, 539
opposition to, 242
sentence of, for murder, 55, 255, 277
statistics on, 533, 538
time-series studies on, 108–109
Car cloning, 465. *See also* Automobile theft
Carding (phishing), 443–444, 451–452
Career criminals. *See also* Chronic offenders
burglars, 363–364
cultural deviance theory and, 183
definition of, 56
professional thieves, 348–351
strain and, 180
Carjacking, 305, 358. *See also* Automobile theft
Cars. *See* Automobiles
Cartographic school of criminology, 8
CASA (National Center on Addiction and Substance Abuse), 419–420, 429
Castle doctrine, 80
CATIC (California Anti-Terrorism Information Center), 338
Causes of Delinquency (Hirschi), 210–214
CCTV (closed-circuit television), 103
CD (conduct disorder), 131, 139
CDC (Centers for Disease Control), 128–129
Celebrities and criminal justice system, 474, *508, 541*
Center for Democracy and Technology, 458
Centers for Disease Control (CDC), 128–129
Central African Republic, 403
Central America. *See* Latin America
Central Intelligence Agency. *See* CIA (Central Intelligence Agency)
Cerebral allergies, 128
CERT Coordination Center, 445
CFAA (Computer Fraud and Abuse Act), 442
The Challenge of Crime in a Free Society, 467
Change
in communities, 172
cultural change and crime trends, 42–43
General Theory of Crime (GTC) and, 273
in life influences, 257–258
Check fraud, 355
Chemical influences on crime. *See* Biochemical conditions and crime
Chemical restraints, 132, 150
Chemical straitjackets, 132, 150
Chevron oil company, 379
Chicago
Crime Commission, 467
crime prevention (Chicago Area Project), 188
Project on Human Development in Chicago Neighborhoods, 165–166, 289, 290
Shaw and McKay's concentric zones theory based on, 168–170
Chicago School, 8–9, 162
Child abuse. *See also* Child sexual abuse
causes of, 302–303
definition of, 302

delinquency and other problems due to, 200
distorted thinking patterns of abusers, 145–146
drug use later in life and, 34
international trends in, 13
posttraumatic stress disorder and, 67
statistics on, 302, 405
violence–abuse association, 288
Child Online Protection Act (1998), 442, 453
Child pornography, 413–414, *414*, 454–455. *See also* Child sexual abuse; Pornography
Child Pornography Prevention Act (1996), 453
Children. *See also* Child abuse; Child pornography; Child sexual abuse; Juvenile justice system; Life course theory; Schools
bullying of, 448
conduct disorder (CD) and, 131, 139
disruptive and antisocial children, 57
and early onset of criminal behaviors, 56–57, 259–261
exposure of, to violence, 288–289
as fire starter, 365
health problems of, 164
murders of, 72, 82, 98–99, 297
neglect of, 302
parental deviance and delinquency, 133, 199–200
parental efficacy and, 199–200, 273–274
poverty of, 163–164, *164*
in single-parent families, 198–199
street efficacy and, 173–174
television violence and, 143–144
victimization of, 67
Children's Internet Protection Act (2000), 442
Child sexual abuse, 67, 82, 145–146, 200, 303, 405–412. *See also* Sexual abuse
Child Sexual Abuse Prevention Act, 412
Chile, 329
China
crime trends in, 12, 13
criminal gangs from, 392
death penalty and executions in, 538
honor killing in, 290
labeling effects and, 218
opium in, 430
revolution in, 329
terrorism in, 333
in World Trade Organization, 234
Chiseling, 375–376
Chivalry hypothesis, 53
Choice theories. *See* Classical criminology; Rational choice theory
Chronic offenders. *See also* Career criminals
adolescents as, 56–57
antisocial personality and, 149
causes of chronicity, 56–58
characteristics predicting, 57
continuity of crime and, 57
definition of, 56

early onset and, 56–57
patterns in, 56–58
persistence and, 57, 261, 273
personality traits of, 147
recidivism and, 111, 477, 508, 556–557
three strikes policy and, 58, 110, 234, 352, 532
Chronic victimization, 72
Churches. *See* Religion
CIA (Central Intelligence Agency)
Ames's espionage and, 325
citizens' mistrust of, 171
Lindh's treason, 322
terrorism fight by, 338
torture used by, 326
Circuit travelers, 411. *See also* Prostitution
CITA (Crime Identification Technology Act), 455
Civil liberties. *See also* ACLU (American Civil Liberties Union)
biometric identification systems and, 478
death penalty and, 93
information technology in criminal justice and, 455–458
sex offender registration and, 478
USA Patriot Act and, 340
Class. *See* Social class
Classical criminology, 5–6, 11, 92–93
Clean Air Act, 388, 389
Clean Water Act, 388
Cleared crime, 31, 32
Client fraud, 380–382
Climate and crime, 45
Cliques, 216. *See also* Gangs
Closure, 355
Club drugs, 13, 417, 423
Cocaine, 38, 95, 392, 416, 417, 423. *See also* Crack cocaine; Drugs
Cocaine Anonymous, 427, 430
Code of Hammurabi, 18
Code of the street, 185
Cognitive differences, gender and, 53
Cognitive theory
definition of, 137
history of, 142
information processing, 142, 145–146
moral and intellectual development theory, 142
shaping perceptions, 145–146
summary of, 146, 150
Cognitive therapies, 146, 150
Cohort research, 37, 56–57, 256
Collective efficacy
definition of, 172
effect of, 173–174
forms of, 172–173
informal social control, 172–173
institutional social control, 173
public social control, 173
street efficacy and, 173–174
College boy, 186
Colombia
crime trends in, 12
drug cartels in, 335, 375, 426
terrorism in, 334, 335

Columbia/HCA Healthcare Corporation, 381
Columbia University, 144, 429
Columbine High School shootings, 121
Commerce Clause, 387
Commercial burglary, 361–363. *See also* Burglary
Commission on Safety and Abuse in America's Prisons, 549, 550
Commitment and social bond theory, 211, 212
Commitment to conformity, 210
Common law, 19, 20, 290, 301, 352, 360. *See also* Laws
Communications Decency Act (1996), 442, 453
Communist Manifesto (Marx), 9, 230
Communities and neighborhoods
    change and change cycles in, 172
    collective efficacy and, 172–174
    concentric zones of, 169, *169*
    crime control by, 80–81
    decent values in, 185
    deterioration of, and social ecology school, 170
    drug use prevention and control in, 426–427
    fear in, 171
    gentrification and, 172
    informal social control in, 173
    institutional social control of, 173
    minority group poverty and, 165–166
    parolees in, 555–556
    permeable neighborhoods, 98
    preemptive deterrence by, 240
    prevention/control of crime by community organizations, 80–81, 173, 426–427
    public social control in, 173
    restorative justice and, 245
    social control and, 167–168
    social disorganization theory and, 167–174
    sources of strain in, 180
    street values in, 185, 209
    transitional neighborhoods, 168–169
Community-based corrections, 539
Community-oriented policing (COP), 498–499, *498*
Community service restitution, 543
Comparative criminology. *See also* specific countries
    capital punishment, 108, 538, 539
    crime trends, 12–13
    diet and crime, 126–127
    IQ–crime relationships, 148
    labeling effects, 218
    marital rape, 293
    national values and, 289–290
    restorative justice, 247
    self-control, 274
    sex trade, 408–410
    situational crime prevention, 103
    social bond theory, 212–213
    substance use, 416
    women's status, 241

Complaint (pretrial procedure), 507
Compliance strategies, 388–389
Comprehensive Crime Control Act (1984), 78
Comprehensive Drug Abuse Prevention and Control Act (1970), 425
CompStat, 490–491
Computer crime. *See* Cyber crime; Internet
Computer fraud, 441
Computer Fraud and Abuse Act (CFAA), 442
Computer security breaches, 451
Computer Security Institute (CSI), 451, 452
Computer virus, 446–447
Computer worms, 446–447
Concentric zones of neighborhoods, 169, *169*
Concurrent sentence, 528
The Condition of the Working Class in England in 1844 (Engels), 232
Conduct disorder (CD), 131, 139
Conduct norms, 182
Confessions of a Dying Thief (Steffensmeier and Ulmer), 350–351
Confidence games, 359
Conflict gangs, 187. *See also* Gangs
Conflict view, 9, 11, 17, 18
Conformity, 176
Congos, 538
Congregate system, 528
Conscience, 138
Consecutive sentence, 528
Consensus view, 16, 18
Consent, and rape cases, 295
Consent search, 495
Conspiracy, 20
Constant latent traits, 257
Constitutional amendments. *See* specific amendments, such as First Amendment
Constructive possession, 352
Contagion effect, 135
Containment theory, 210
Contextual discrimination, 218
Continuity of crime, 57
Contract attorney system, 505
The Contradictions of American Capital Punishment (Zimring), 537
Control. *See* Social control; Social control theory
Control balance theory, 268, 275
Controlled Substances Act (1984), 425
Controlling crime. *See* Prevention/control
Convention on Cyber Crime, 453–454, 455
COP (Community-oriented policing), 498–499, *498*
Coping with strain, 180
Copyright Act, 453
Copyright infringement, 442–443, 451, 453
Corner boy, 184
Corporate crime. *See also* White-collar crime

deceptive pricing, 384
    definition of, 372, 382–383
    Enron case, *96*, 378–379, 387
    false claims advertising, 384
    fraud by Facciabrutto Holdings, Inc., 385
    illegal restraint of trade, 384
    Ponzi scheme, 271
    price fixing, 384
    Tyco case, 378
    worker safety/environmental crimes, 384–385, 387, 388, 389, 390
    WorldCom case, 379
Corporate espionage, 323–324
Corrections. *See also* Jails; Prisons
    community-based corrections, 539
    elements of, 469
    intermediate sanctions, 542–545
    parole, 469, 537, 554–557
    probation, 469, 532, 540–542
    rule of law and, 533
    secure confinement, 539–540
    statistics on, 539, 540
    and steps in justice process, 470, 471
    summary of, 468
    treatment programs and, 551–552
Cosa Nostra, 391
Costs
    of criminal justice system, 66, 467, 468
    of cyber crime, 451–452
    of domestic violence, 106
    of drug control, 429
    of incarceration, 111
    of juvenile justice system, 66
    of situational crime prevention, 102–104
    of substance abuse, 66
Côte d'Ivoire, 539
Counseling. *See* Treatment programs
Counterfeit Access Device and Computer Fraud and Abuse Law (1984), 452
County law enforcement, 487
Courtroom work group, 474
Courts. *See also* Judges; Jury; Supreme Court
    arraignment and, 471, *471*, 518
    contextual discrimination against African Americans in, 218
    defense attorneys in, 501–502, 504–505
    federal courts, 500, 502, 506
    judges in, 501, 505–506
    jury selection and, 513–514
    law of criminal procedure and, 474
    procedural laws for, 474–476
    prosecutors in, 501–504
    racial profiling and, 238–239
    restorative justice and, 245–246
    state courts, 500, 501, 506
    statistics on, 467, 500, 506
    steps in jury trial, 514–516
    and steps in justice process, 469–471
    structure of, 500–501
    summary of, 468
    technology used by, *471*, 518
    trials and rule of law, 516–518
Covert pathway, 259
CPI (California Personality Inventory), 147

Crack cocaine, 41, 96–97, 411, 416, 417, 423, 430, 485. See also Cocaine; Drugs
Crackdowns, 105
Credit card fraud, 451
Credit card theft, 355–356
Crime. See also headings beginning with Crime and Criminal; specific types of crimes; and names of criminals in Name Index
    cleared crime, 31, 32
    conflict view of, 9, 11, 17, 18
    consensus view of, 16, 18
    criminality distinguished from, 94
    criminologists' views of, 16–18
    definitions of, 18, 234–235
    expressive crimes, 47
    instrumental crimes, 47
    interactionist view of, 17–18
    legal definition of, 21
    offender-specific crime, 94
    offense-specific crime, 94
    Part I and Part II crimes, 30, 31, 39
    as rational, 98–100
    social harm and, 16
    as social phenomenon, 4
Crime Act (1994), 532
Crime and Everyday Life (Felson), 76
Crime and Human Nature (Wilson and Herrnstein), 269
Crime and Personality (Eysenck), 10
Crime and Punishment in America (Currie), 480
Crime and the American Dream (Messner and Rosenfeld), 177–178
Crime Commission (1967), 467
Crime control. See Prevention/control
Crime control model, 476–478, *476*, 480
Crime discouragers, 101
Crime Identification Technology Act (CITA), 455
Crime in Context: A Critical Criminology of Market Societies (Taylor), 240
Crime in the Making (Sampson and Laub), 262–263
Crime mapping, 39
Crime prevention. See Prevention/control
Crime Prevention through Environmental Design (Jeffery), 100
Crime rates. See Crime statistics; Trends in crime
Crime statistics. See also National Crime Victimization Survey (NCVS); Patterns in crime; Uniform Crime Reports (UCR); and specific crimes
    cohort research for, 37
    crime mapping and, 39
    criminologists' use of, 11
    data mining and, 39
    evaluation of primary sources of data, 36
    experimental research and, 37–38
    international crime trends, 12–13
    meta-analysis and systematic review, 38–39
    observational and interview research and, 38

    primary sources of, 30–33
    Quetelet's use of, in nineteenth century, 8
    secondary sources of, 37–39
    self-report surveys, 34–35, 36, 37
    summary on data collection methods, 37
    variations in, 270–271
Crime trends. See Trends in crime
Crime typology, 14. See also specific types of crime
Crime Victims' Rights Act (2004), 78
Criminal anthropology, 8
Criminal charge, 507
Criminal gangs. See Gangs
Criminality. See also headings beginning with Crime and Criminal; and names of criminals in Name Index
    crime distinguished from, 94
    definition of, 94
    disruption promoting, 257
    exploitation and, 241
    intelligence and, 147–148, *150*
    rational choice theory on, 94–97
Criminal justice. See also Criminal justice system; Juvenile justice system
    concepts of, 476–480
    crime control model, 476–478, *476*, 480
    crime rates and, 42
    criminology distinguished from, 4, 5
    definition of, 5
    due process model, 478, 480
    information technology in, 455–458
    justice model, 478, 480
    nonintervention model, 479–480
    rehabilitation model, 478–479, 480
    restorative justice model, 480
    rule of law and, 474–476
Criminal justice system. See also Corrections; Courts; Juvenile justice system; Police
    abuse of victims by, 66–67
    adjudication process and, 500
    celebrity cases in, 474, *508*, *541*
    components of, 468
    cost of, 66, 467, 468
    criminal justice funnel, 474, 475
    definition of, 467
    discretion in, 474, 500
    hands-off doctrine for, 474
    history of, 466–467
    juvenile justice system compared with, 472–473
    overview of, 467–469
    procedural laws for, 474–476
    process of justice, 469–475
    rule of law and, 474–476
    statistics on, 467
Criminal law. See Laws
Criminals. See also specific types of crimes; and specific criminals in Name Index
    career criminals, 56, 180, 183, 363–364
    early-onset criminals, 56–57, 259–261
    offender-specific crime and, 94
    professional criminals, 348–351
    reasoning criminal, 94
    relationship between victims and, 72, 297–299

Criminal Sciences—Law Without Order (Frankel), 529
Criminal terrorism, 335
Criminal trials. See Trials
Criminological enterprise, 11, 14–15, 16
Criminologists. See also Criminology
    choice of topics and subjects for study by, 24
    criminal behavior systems and crime typologies and, 14–15, 16
    criminal statistics and research methodology of, 11
    criminological enterprise and, 11, 14–16
    critical criminologists, 230
    definition of, 11
    ethics for, 23–24
    funds for research by, 24
    penology and social control and, 15, 16
    sociology of law and, 14, 16
    theory construction and testing by, 14, 16
    training of, 4, 11
    victimology and victimologists, 15, 16, 66
    views of crime and, 16–18
Criminology. See also Criminologists
    Chicago School and, 8–9
    classical criminology, 5–6, 11, 92–93
    conflict and crime, 9, 11
    contemporary criminology, 10–11
    criminal justice distinguished from, 4, 5
    criminal law and, 18–23
    criminological enterprise and, 11, 14–16
    definition of, 4–5
    developmental criminology, 10, 11
    deviance and, 4–5
    ethics and, 23–24
    history of, 5–10
    as multidisciplinary science, 4
    positivism and, 6–11, 93
    social–psychological views of, 9
    summary of perspectives in, 11
    views of crime and, 16–18
Crisis intervention, 79
Critical criminologists, 230
Critical criminology
    on cause of crime, 235–236
    contemporary critical criminology, 234
    creation of, 232–233
    critical feminist theory, 240–243
    definition of, 230
    definition of crime and, 234–235
    emerging forms of, 239–243
    evaluation of, 239
    globalization and, 236, *236*
    instrumental theory and, 236–237
    left realism, 239–240, 243
    marginalization and, 235
    Marxism and, 230–232
    peacemaking criminology, 242–243
    public policy and, 243–248
    research on, 237–239
    restorative justice and, *242*, 243–248
    structural theory and, 237
    surplus value and, 235, *235*

Critical feminist theory. *See also* Feminism
  on crime and patriarchy, 241
  definition of, 240
  on exploitation and criminality, 241
  on patriarchy, 240–241
  power-control theory and, 241–242, 243
  summary of, 243
Cross-cultural differences. *See* Comparative
  criminology
Cross-examination, 515
Cross-sectional survey, 34
Cruel and unusual punishment, 553
Crusted over, 289
CSDD (Cambridge Study in Delinquent
  Development), 133, 199
CSI (Computer Security Institute), 451, 452
Cuba, 326, 329
Cult terrorism, 334–335
Cultural change and crime trends, 42–43
Cultural deviance critique, 205–206
Cultural deviance theory
  conduct norms and, 182
  cultural transmission and, 167
  culture conflict and, 182
  definition of, 167
  delinquent subcultures theory, 182–186,
    188
  differential opportunity theory, 186–187,
    188
  elements of, 183
  focal concerns of lower class, 182, 183,
    188
  middle-class measuring rods and,
    183–184
  status frustration and, 183
  subcultures and, 167, 181–182, 183
  summary of, 188
Cultural retaliatory homicide, 289
Cultural transmission, 167
Cultural view of white-collar crime, 387
Culture conflict, 182, 203–204
Culture Conflict and Crime (Sellin), 182
Culture of poverty, 163
Cultures. *See* Comparative criminology;
  Subcultures
Cumulative disadvantage, 263–264
Curfew laws, 101, 105
Custodial interrogation, 494–495
Cyber bullying, 448–449
Cyber crimes. *See also* Internet
  computer fraud, 441
  computer security breaches, 451
  computer worms and viruses, 446–447
  control of, 452–455
  copyright infringement, 442–443, 451
  cyber bullying, 448–449
  cyber spying, 449
  cyber stalking, 448
  cyber terrorism, 440, 449–451
  cyber theft, 440–445
  cyber vandalism, 440, 446–449, 452
  definition of, 440
  denial-of-service attack, 442
  distribution of illegal sexual material,
    441–442

enforcement agencies for, 454–455
  etailing fraud, 445
  extent and costs of, 451–452
  identity theft, 443–445, 451–452
  international treaties on, 453–454, *454*
  Internet securities fraud, 443
  laws on, 452–453
  local enforcement efforts on, 454–455
  logic bombs, 446–447
  pirating of software and films, 451, 453
  spam, 447
  Trojan horses, 446–447
  Website defacement, 447–448
Cyber spying, 449
Cyber stalking, 448
Cyber terrorism, 440, 449–451, *450*
Cyber theft
  computer fraud, 441
  copyright infringement, 442–443, 451
  definition of, 440
  denial-of-service attack, 442
  distribution of illegal sexual material,
    441–442
  identity theft, 443–445, 451–452
  Internet securities fraud, 443
  phishing, 443–444, 451–452
  pirating of software and films, 451, 453
  vishing, 444–445
Cyber vandalism
  bomb threats, 446
  cost and extent of, 452
  cyber bullying, 448–449
  cyber spying, 449
  cyber stalking, 448
  definition of, 440
  logic bombs, 446–447
  spam, 447
  Trojan horses, 446–447
  viruses and worms, 446–447
  Website defacement, 447–448
Cycle of violence, 68
Cyprus, 538

DaimlerChrysler, 379
D.A.R.E. (Drug Abuse Resistance
  Education), 428
Data mining, 39, 499
Date rape and physical abuse, 74, 145,
  293, 304. *See also* Rape
Day of week and crime, 45
DBD (Disruptive behavior disorder), 139
DEA (Drug Enforcement Administration),
  487
Deadly force by crime victims, 80
Death penalty. *See* Capital punishment
Deceptive pricing, 384
Defective intelligence, 137
Defense attorneys
  assigned counsel system and, 505
  contract attorney system and, 505
  courtroom work group and, 474
  ethical code of, 505
  jury selection and, 513–514
  public defender and, 505
  right to counsel and, 474, 505, 517

role conflicts of, 505
  role of, 501–502, 504–505
  during trials, 515
Defense of Marriage Act (1996), 404–405
Defenses
  insanity defense, 151
  justification defense, 22
  lack of mental capacity defense, 22
  types of, 21–22
Defensible space, 100
Defensive hate crimes, 307
Deliberation, 296
Delinquency. *See* Adolescents; Juvenile
  justice system
Delinquency and Opportunity (Cloward and
  Ohlin), 186–187
Delinquency in a Birth Cohort (Wolfgang,
  Figlio, and Sellin), 56
Delinquent boy, 186
Delinquent Boys (Cohen), 182–184, 186
Delinquent subcultures theory, 182–186, 188
Demystify, 237
Denial, as neutralization technique,
  207–208
Denial-of-service attack, 442
Denmark
  adoption study, 135
  crime trends in, 13
  death penalty abolished in, 539
  IQ–crime relationships, 148
  mental illness and crime in, 139
  neurophysiological conditions and
    crime, 129
Department of Homeland Security (DHS),
  338, 457
Departments of U.S. government. *See*
  specific departments, such as Justice
  Department
Deposit bail system, 510
Desistance
  age of onset/continuity of crime and,
    259–260
  aging out of crime, 52
  definition of, 256
  of delinquents, 265–267
  gender and, 260
  marriage factor and, 264–265
Determinate sentence, 529–530
Deterrence. *See also* General deterrence
  capital punishment as, 535–536, 539
  general deterrence, 104–107, 112
  marginal deterrence, 92
  police responsibility for, 489–491
  preemptive deterrence, 240
  as sentencing goal, 529
  specific deterrence, 108–110, 112
  for white-collar crime, 389–390
Deterrence theory, 10, 104–107
Deterrent effect, 489
Developmental theories
  age-graded theory, 262–267, 275
  control balance theory, 268, 275
  definition of, 256
  differential coercion theory, 268, 275
  evaluation of, 275–276

foundations of, 256–257
general theory of crime and delinquency (GTCD), 262, 275
integrated cognitive antisocial potential (ICAP) theory, 268, 275
interactional theory, 262, 275
latent trait theories, 256, 257, 267–275
life course theory, 256, 257–267
public policy implications of, 276
social development model (SDM), 262
summary of, 10, 11, 275
Deviance
criminology and, 4–5
cultural deviance theory, 167, 181–188
definition of, 5
joining deviant cliques, 216
labeling theory and, 214–218
parental deviance, 133, 199–200
primary deviance, 217
retrospective reading of, 216–217
secondary deviance, 217
Deviant place theory, 74, 75, 77
DHHS. See Health and Human Services Department (DHHS)
DHS (Homeland Security Department), 338, 457
Dialectic method, 232
Diet
antisocial behavior and, 125
crime and, 125, 126–127
Differential association theory
analysis of, 205–206
cultural deviance critique of, 205–206
definition of, 203
principles of, 203–205
summary of, 221
testing, 205
Differential coercion theory, 268, 275
Differential enforcement, 215–216
Differential opportunity theory, 186–187, 188
Differential reinforcement, 206
Differential reinforcement theory, 206–207, 221
Diffusion of benefits, 102
Digital Millennium Copyright Act (DMCA), 442
Direct conditioning, 206
Directed verdict, 515
Direct examination, 515
Director of National Intelligence (DNI), 337, 340
Discouragement, 102
Discretion, 474, 500, 503–505, 533
Discrimination. See Contextual discrimination; Racial profiling; Racism
Disinhibition, 143
Disorders, 139. See also Mental illness/mental disorders
Disorganization. See Social disorganization theory
Displacement, 102
Disposition, 471
Disputatiousness, 289
Disruptive behavior disorder (DBD), 139

Diversion programs, 219, 529
The Division of Labor in Society (Durkheim), 8
Divorce, 198–199
Djibouti, 403
DMCA (Digital Millennium Copyright Act), 442
DNA evidence, 15, 295, 478, 518
DNI (Director of National Intelligence), 337, 340
Doing Justice (Van Hirsch), 112
Domestic violence. See also Child abuse
arrests for, 109–110
history of, 303
Minneapolis domestic violence study, 109–110
murder of violent spouse by victim, 298
nature and extent of, 303–304
posttraumatic stress disorder (PTSD) and, 67
predictive factors for, 304
social cost of, for spouse abusers, 106
statistics on, 302, 303–304
Dopamine, 131
Double jeopardy, 471, 517
Dramatization of evil, 217
Drift, 207
Driving. See Automobiles; Drunk-driving
Driving While Black (DWB), 54, 55
Drug Abuse Control Act (1965), 425
Drug Enforcement Administration (DEA), 487
Drug Policy Alliance, 429–431, 481
Drugs. See also specific drugs
adolescents' use of, 418–422
AIDS and, 420, 423, 430
arrests related to, 416
causes of drug abuse, 420–421
child abuse and later drug use, 34
chronic offenders and, 57
community strategies for control of, 426–427
control of drug use, 425–429, 481
cost of addiction to, 66
cost of drug control, 429
crime and, 41, 423–424
D.A.R.E. (Drug Abuse Resistance Education), 428
differential reinforcement theory and, 206–207
drug dealers and, 96–97, 98, 184, 205, 422, 490
drug-testing programs, 427, 544
female drug abusers and drug dealers, 38, 96, 98
gangs and, 41
gateway model of, 421
as high-risk lifestyle for victimization, 73
interdiction strategies for control of, 426
law enforcement strategies for control of, 426
laws on, 404, 424–425
legalization of, 429–430
list of commonly used drugs, 417
prostitutes' abuse of, 411

psychological characteristics of drug users, 420
punishment strategies for drug use, 426
rational choice theory and, 98
robbery and, 305
and routine activities theory of victimization, 77
self-report surveys on, 35, 36, 43–44, 423
situational crime prevention for, 102
source control of, 425–426
stabilized junkies and, 423
statistics on, 418–420
street junkies and, 422–423
street price of, 426
subcultural view of, 420
treatment programs for drug users, 427–429, 427
trends in, 43–44
types of drug users, 421–423
violent crime and, 14–15, 287
women's use of, 423, 430
Drug-testing programs, 427, 544
Drug trade
control of, 481
drug dealers and, 96–97, 98, 184, 205, 422, 423, 490
international drug cartels and drug trafficking, 335, 375, 392, 425, 426
plea bargaining for charge of drug trafficking, 512
pretrial detention for drug trafficking charge, 509
sentences for drug trafficking, 526, 531
women as drug dealers, 96, 98
Drunk-driving. See also Alcohol abuse
by adolescents, 105
banning alcohol sales and, 102
deaths from, 105, 430
minimum legal drinking age (MLDA) and, 105
Dual sovereignty doctrine, 517
Due process model, 478, 480
Due process rights, 22, 478, 517
DUI. See Drunk-driving
Duke rape case, 285–286
Dunblane, Scotland, school shootings, 286, 287
Durham-Humphrey Act (1951), 425
DWB (Driving While Black), 54, 55

Early onset, 56–57, 259–261
Earth Liberation Front (ELF), 332, 332
Eastern Europe. See also specific countries
capital punishment abolished in, 538
crime trends in, 13
organized crime in, 392
EC (electronic monitoring), 544
Ecological view, 9, 11
Ecology of crime. See also Social ecology
day, season, and climate, 45, 46
regional differences, 46, 47, 273
temperature, 45–46
Economic crime, 346. See also Arson; Automobile theft; Burglary; Larceny; Property crimes; Theft; White-collar crime

614 SUBJECT INDEX

Economic Espionage Act (EEA), 324
Economics. *See also* Property crimes; Social
    class
    crime trends and, 40, 42–43
    globalization and, 236, *236*, 324
    race and economic disparity, 55–56
    victims' economic loss, 66
Eco-terrorism, 332, *332*, 333
Ectomorphs, 122
Edgework, 100
Edna McConnell Clark Foundation, 24
Education. *See also* Schools
    Head Start Program, 188, 219
    high school dropouts, 164, 200–201
    of prisoners, 551
    problems with, and criminality, 200–201
    on victimization, 79
EEA (Economic Espionage Act), 324
EEG (electroencephalograph), 129–130
Egalitarian families, 242
Ego, 137–138
Ego ideal, 138
Egypt
    al-Qaeda and, 340
    ban on genital mutilation in, 403
    honor murders in, 302
Eighteenth Amendment, 418
Eighth Amendment, 92, 532, 553
Elder abuse, 70
Eldercide, 297
Elderly persons
    crime rate of, 52
    eldercide, 297
    fraud against, 70, 395
    murder of, 297
    population statistics on, 52, 70
    victimization of, 70, 71
Election fraud, 321–322
Electra complex, 138
Electroencephalograph (EEG), 129–130
Electronic Communications Privacy Act,
    453
Electronic monitoring (EC), 544
ELF (Earth Liberation Front), 332, *332*
Eliminating crime. *See* Prevention/control
El Salvador, 161–162
Embezzlement, 359–360, 380, 386
EMCDDA (European Monitoring Centre for
    Drugs and Drug Addiction), 481
Employment and employees
    actual authority to employee, 383
    African Americans and, 164
    blue-collar pilferage and, 380
    chronic unemployment and social
        ecology theory, 170–171
    crime trends and, 40
    drug-testing programs and, 427
    employee fraud, 380
    Internet abuse by employees, 452
    vocational rehabilitation for drug
        abusers, 429
    worker safety and, 384–385
    workplace violence and, 308–309
Endomorphs, 122
England. *See* Great Britain

The English Convict (Goring), 136–137
Enron case, *96*, 378–379, 387
Enterprise crime, 372. *See also* Corporate
        crime; Cyber crime; Organized crime;
        White-collar crime
Enterprise theory of investigation (ETI), 394
Environmental crimes, 384–385, 387, 388,
        389, 390. *See also* Pollution
Environmental factors
    aggression, 141
    environmental contaminants, 128
    lead levels, 128–129, *129*
    lighting, 128
Environmental Protection Agency (EPA),
        385, 387
Equipotentiality, 123
Equity, as sentencing goal, 529
Eros, 138, 286
Escort services, 411. *See also* Prostitution
Espionage
    cyber espionage, 449
    definition of, 323
    Economic Espionage Act (EEA), 324
    foreign industrial espionage, 323–324
    industrial espionage, 323
ETA (Basque Fatherland and Liberty),
        332–333
Etailing fraud, 445
Ethics. *See also* Morality
    conflict of interests and, 24
    criminology and, 23–24
    of defense attorneys, 505
    research decisions and, 24
Ethnicity. *See* African Americans; Asian
        Americans; Latinos; Native Americans;
        Race and ethnicity
ETI (enterprise theory of investigation),
        394
Europe. *See* specific countries
European Monitoring Centre for Drugs and
        Drug Addiction (EMCDDA), 481
*European Sourcebook of Crime and Criminal
        Justice Statistics*, 12
Evil, dramatization of, 217
Evolutionary theory
    definition of, 135
    gender and, 136
    of rape, 293
    summary of, 137
    violence and, 135, 286–287
Evolving latent traits, 257
Exclusionary rule, 476
*The Executed God: The Way of the Cross in
        Lockdown America* (Taylor), 244
Exhibitionism, 406
Experimental research, 37–38. *See also*
        Research
Exploitation, 241, 376
Expressive crimes, 47
Expressive violence, 286
Extinction, 102
Extroversion–introversion, 147

Facciabrutto Holdings, Inc., 385
Failure to act, 21

False claims advertising, 384
False pretenses, 31, 70, 271, 358–359, 371
Familicide, 301
Family. *See also* Domestic violence; Siblings
    ADHD children and, 130
    African American families, 56
    aggression in, 141
    antisocial personality and, 148–149
    blended families, 303
    chronic offenders and, 57
    decent values and, 185
    divorce and, 198–199
    egalitarian families, 242
    Gluecks' research on, 10
    informal social control of, 172
    parental deviance and, 133, 199–200
    parental efficacy and, 199–200, 273–274
    paternalistic families, 242
    sibling similarities and criminal tenden-
        cies, 133
    single-parent families, 198–199
    socialization and, 198–200
    surrogate family in prisons, 550
    twin behavior, 133–135
Family Entertainment and Copyright Act
        (2005), 453
Fast Track program, 276
FBI (Federal Bureau of Investigation)
    on assault, 301
    on confidence games, 359
    crime data from, 30–33
    cyber crime and, 439, 454
    on cyber terrorism, 449
    eco-terrorism targeted by, 332
    on embezzlement, 360
    enterprise theory of investigation (ETI)
        and, 394
    espionage by Hanssen in, 323
    on hate crimes, 307
    investigation of city corruption by, 405
    jurisdiction and priorities of, 486–487
    on larceny, 352
    National Crime Information Center of, 499
    organized crime and, 394
    on robbery, 304
    surveillance of Ames by, 325
    terrorism and, 337–338
    Uniform Crime Report (UCR) from,
        30–33
    white-collar crime and, 376, 387
    on workplace violence, 308–309
FCC (Federal Communication
        Commission), 404
FCPA (Foreign Corrupt Practices Act),
        378–379
FDA (Food and Drug Administration), 353
Fear
    community fear, 171
    of crime, 67–68, 171–172
    gangs and, 171
    mistrust and, 171–172
    psychopaths and low fear quotient, 149
    race-based fear, 171–172
    siege mentality and, 171–172
    victims' fear, 68

Federal Bail Reform Act (1984), 510
Federal Bureau of Investigation. *See* FBI
    (Federal Bureau of Investigation)
Federal Bureau of Narcotics, 404
Federal Communication Commission
    (FCC), 404
Federal courts, 500, 502, 506. *See also*
    Courts; Supreme Court
Federal courts of appeals, 500
Federal law enforcement, 486–487. *See also*
    specific government agencies
Federal Sentencing Commission, 532
Federal Trade Commission (FTC), 454
Felony murder, 296. *See also* Murder
The Female Offender (Lombroso), 52–53
Feminism. *See also* Gender; Women
    critical criminology and, 233
    critical feminist theory, 240–243
    on exploitation and criminality, 241
    liberal feminist theory, 53–54
    on patriarchy, 240–241
    power-control theory and, 241–242, 243
    on prostitution, 413
    on rape, 293
Fences
    associational fences, 351
    burglars and, 363
    definition of, 346
    occasional fences, 351–352
    professional fence, 349–350
Feticide, 296–297
Fifth Amendment, 494
File sharing, 442–443
Filicide, 297
Films. *See also* Media; and specific films
    piracy of, and Internet, 453
    violence in, 122
Fines, 532, 543
Finland, 13, 126
Firearms. *See also* Gun control
    adolescents and, 41, 74, 289, 423, 499
    crime trends and, 41
    as deterrent to crime and violence, 46,
        49, 80
    domestic violence and, 304
    gangs and, 289
    legislation on, 48–49
    national values and, 289
    patterns in use of, 46
    plea bargaining for charge of weapons
        offenses, 512
    police involvement in control of,
        489–490
    pretrial detention for charge of weapons
        offenses, 509
    pros and cons of gun control, 48–49
    right-to-carry concealed handguns, 49
    school shootings, 48, 75, 99, 121–122,
        286, 287, 299
    for self-protection, 49, 80
    sentences for weapons offenses, 526
    use of, in violent crime, 46
    victimization of people carrying, 74
FireSafe Families, 365
Fire-setting. *See* Arson

First Amendment
    hate crimes and, 308
    obscenity and, 454
    pornography and, 415, 442, 454
    press coverage of trials and, 517
    USA Patriot Act and, 340
First-degree murder, 296
FISA (Foreign Intelligence Surveillance
    Act), 339
Fixated, 138
Flash houses, 346
Flashover, 365
Focal concern theory (Miller), 182, 183, 188
Food and Drug Administration (FDA), 353
Forcible rape. *See* Rape
Ford Foundation, 510
Foreign Corrupt Practices Act (FCPA),
    378–379
Foreign countries. *See* Comparative
    criminology; and specific countries
Foreign industrial espionage, 323–324
Foreign Intelligence Surveillance Act
    (FISA), 339
Foreign Travel or Transportation in Aid of
    Racketeering Enterprises Act (Travel
    Act), 392
Forfeiture, 543
Forgery
    plea bargaining for charge of, 512
    pretrial detention for charge of, 509
    sentences for, 526
Fourteenth Amendment, 474–475, 516,
    517
France
    bribery in, 377
    crime trends in, 13
    Declaration of the Rights and Man, 92
    Reign of Terror in, 330
    revolution in, 92, 329, 330
    terrorism in, 332–333
Fraud
    arson fraud, 365
    bank fraud, 382, 383
    check fraud, 355
    client fraud, 380–382
    computer fraud, 441
    credit card fraud, 451
    definition of, 358–359
    elderly as victims of, 70, 395
    election fraud, 321–322
    employee fraud, 380
    etailing fraud, 445
    health care fraud, 380–382
    hedge fund fraud, 383
    insurance company fraud, 31
    Internet securities fraud, 443
    management fraud, 378–380
    Medicaid fraud, 380
    Medicare fraud, 371
    National Association of Fraud
        Investigation, 374
    plea bargaining for charge of, 512
    Ponzi scheme, 271
    pretrial detention for charge of, 509
    sentences for, 526

Freebase, 417
French Revolution, 92, 329, 330
Friendships. *See* Peer relations
Frotteurism, 406
FTC (Federal Trade Commission), 454

GABA, 131
Gambia, 538
Gambling, 442, 491
Gang rape, 292
Gangs
    adolescent self–reporting on, 45, 52
    in California, 162
    chronic offenders and, 57
    conflict gangs, 187
    crime trends and, 41
    criminal gangs, 187
    cultural deviance theory and, *182*
    differential opportunity and, 187
    drugs and, 41, 426
    drug-trafficking gangs, 41
    in El Salvador, 161–162
    fear and, 171
    firearms and, 289
    hand signs of, *38*
    information resources on, 222
    lower-class culture and, 182, 183
    in New York, *34*
    police and, 499
    in prisons, 549
    recruitment into, 173, 174
    retreatist gangs, 187
    strain theory and, 175
    in Texas, *38*
    types of, 187
Gateway model, 421
Gay men. *See* Homosexuality
Gender. *See also* Feminism; Women
    burglary and, 361, 362
    chivalry hypothesis, 53
    cognitive differences and, 53
    crime patterns/crime rate and, 52–54,
        125–128, 136
    critical feminist theory on, 240–243
    desistance and, 260–261
    deviant peers and, 205
    evolutionary theory and, 136
    feminist views of, 53–54
    General Theory of Crime (GTC)
        and, 273
    hormonal influences on crime rate,
        125–128
    male socialization and rape, 293
    masculinity hypothesis, 53
    self-control and crime and, 273
    socialization and development and, 53
    stalking and, 309–310
    victimization and, 69, 70
    virility mystique and, 293
General deterrence
    analysis of, 106–107
    capital punishment as, 106, 108–109,
        112
    certainty of punishment as, 104
    crackdowns as, 105

definition of, 104
increasing police activity as, 105
informal sanctions as, 106
perception of punishment as, 104–105
severity of punishment as, 105–106
shame and humiliation as, 106
summary of, 112
General strain theory (GST)
coping with strain, 180
criminal careers and, 180
definition of, 178
evaluation of, 181
multiple sources of strain, 178–179
negative affective states and, 178–180
sources of strain, 179–180
summary of, 181
General theory of crime and delinquency
(GTCD), 262, 275
A General Theory of Crime (Gottfredson and
Hirschi), 269–274
General Theory of Crime (GTC)
analysis of, 272–274
impulsivity and, 270, 272–273, 274
self-control and, 269–274
summary of, 275
support for, 272
Genetics
adoption studies, 135
crime and, 132–135, 137
evaluation of genetic research, 134–135
Eysenck on, 10
Lombroso on, 7
mental illness and, 132
parental deviance and criminal
tendencies, 133
personality and, 132, 147
sibling similarities, 133
substance abuse and, 421
twin studies, 133–135
Genital mutilation, 403
Genocide rape, 291
Germany
bribery in, 377–378
crime trends in, 13
Holocaust in, 330, 336–337
Marshall Plan for, 340
motor vehicle theft in, 101
sex tourism in, 408
terrorism in, 330
Ghana, 403
The Ghetto (Wirth), 9
Globalization, 236, 236, 324
Glucose metabolism, 125
Godfather films, 390
The Gold Coast and the Slum (Zorbaugh), 9
Good burglars, 363
Government. See also specific agencies
conservative agenda of, 93, 234
cost of drug control, 429
as funding source for criminology
research, 24
illegal activities by local officials, 95
influence peddling in, 377
minority group poverty and, 165–166
response of, to terrorism, 337–340

response of, to victimization, 78–80
welfare programs and, 173, 188
Grand jury, 470
Grand larceny, 352
Great Britain
arson in, 364–365
burglary in, 12, 13, 98
common law in, 19
crime trends in, 12, 13
diet and crime research in, 126
drug-crime connection in, 423, 424
identity theft in, 452
London Metropolitan Police in, 466
motor vehicle theft in, 101
Old Bailey Court in London, 527
prostitution in, 413
shoplifting in, 354
situational crime prevention in, 103
substance abuse in, 416, 423, 424
thieves in, 346
treason in, 323
working class in, 232
Greed, 107, 385–386
GST. See General strain theory (GST)
GTC. See General Theory of Crime (GTC)
GTCD. See General theory of crime and
delinquency (GTCD)
Guantanamo base, 326
Guardianship, 74, 75
Guatemala, 334
Guerillas, 328
Guilt
actus reus and, 21, 22
criminals' expression of, 207
failure to act and, 21
mens rea and, 21, 22
proof of, historically, 18–19
in rape case, 294–295
Guilty by Reason of Insanity (Lewis), 286
Guilty pleas. See Plea bargaining
Guinea, 403
Gun control, 48–49. See also Firearms
Gun Control Act (1968), 48

Haldol, 132
Hallucinogens, 417
Handguns. See Firearms; Gun control
Hands-off doctrine, 474
Harrison Narcotics Act (1914), 424
Harvard University, 10, 256, 304
Hate crimes
control of, 308
factors producing, 307
legal controls of, 308
mission hate crimes, 307
nature and extent of, 307–308
reactive (defensive) hate crimes, 307
retaliatory hate crimes, 307
roots of hate, 307
statistics on, 307
thrill-seeking hate crimes, 307
victims of, 306–307, 306
Hate Crimes (McDevitt and Levin), 307
HC (home confinement), 544
Head injuries, 131. See also Brain

Head Start Program, 188, 219
Health and Human Services Department
(DHHS), 219, 302, 380, 419
Health care
fraud in, 380–382
homicide rate and medical technology,
42
in prisons, 553
Health care fraud, 380–382
Health Insurance Portability and Account-
ability Act (HIPAA), 381–382
Hedge fund fraud, 383
Heels, 354
Heredity. See Genetics
Heroin, 66, 95, 335, 392, 416, 417, 423.
See also Drugs
Hezbollah, 333
High-risk lifestyle for victimization, 73
Highway Loss Data Insurance (HLDI), 357,
358
Hijackers. See Airplane hijackers
HIPAA (Health Insurance Portability and
Accountability Act), 381–382
Hispanics. See Latinos
History
of burglary, 360
of cognitive theory, 142
of crime trends, 39
of criminal justice system, 466–467
of criminal law, 18–19
of criminology, 5–10, 52–53
of drug use, 416
of embezzlement, 359–360
of female criminals, 52–53
of juvenile justice system, 472
of moral crusades and crusaders, 404
of prostitution, 406, 410, 412
of psychological trait theories, 136–137
of punishment, 5, 18–19, 92–93,
526–528, 545
of rape, 291, 291
of revolutionaries, 329
of spousal abuse, 303
of terrorism, 329–330
of theft, 346–348
of trait theory, 122–123
of treason, 322–323
HIV. See AIDS
HLDI (Highway Loss Data Insurance), 357,
358
Holland, 412, 413
Home confinement (HC), 544
Home Depot Company, 229
Homeland Security Department (DHS),
338, 457
Homicide. See Murder
Homicide (Daly and Wilson), 135
Homosexuality
gay political candidate as former
prostitute, 401–402
hate crimes against gay men, 306–307
marriage and, 404–405
sodomy laws and, 22, 405
Honduras, 334
Hong Kong, 13

Honor killing, 182, 290, 302
Hormones
    brain and, 128
    influence of, on crime, 125–128
    premenstrual syndrome (PMS) and, 128
    sex hormones, 53, 125–128
Hot pursuit/exigency, 496
Hot spots for crime, 74–75
Humanistic psychology, 142
Human nature and crime, 269
Human rights violations, 326
Human Rights Watch, 327
Humiliation as deterrence for crime, 106
Hung jury, 471
Hyperactivity. See ADHD (attention deficit
    hyperactive disorder)
Hypoglycemia, 125
Hypotheses, 7, 14. See also Scientific
    method

I Am the Central Park Jogger (Meili), 79
ICAP (integrated cognitive antisocial
    potential) theory, 268, 275
ICVS (International Crime Victims
    Survey), 12
Id, 137, 138
Identity crisis, 138
Identity theft, 443–445, 451–452
Identity Theft and Assumption Deterrence
    Act (1998), 444, 453
Ideological view of terrorists, 336
Illegal domestic surveillance, 325
Immigration
    crime trends and, 40
    protest on immigration reform, 236
    smuggling of illegal immigrants, 23
    US-Visit technology and, 457
Immorality. See also Morality; Public order
        crimes
    social harm and, 403–404
Impact statements, 80, 528
Imprisonment. See Prisons
Impulsivity, 270, 272–273, 274. See also
    Self-control
Incapacitation, 110–111, 112, 529. See also
    Prisons
Incarceration. See also Jails; Prisons
    costs of, 111
    deterrent effect of, 106, 108–111
    shock incarceration, 544–545
Incivilities, 171
Income statistics, 162. See also Poverty;
    Wealth
Index crimes. See Part I crimes
India
    diet and crime research in, 126
    honor killing in, 290
    Thugee cult and Kali in, 329–330
Indians. See Native Americans
Indictment, 507
Indigent defendants. See Right to counsel
Individual strain, 175
Industrial espionage, 323
Inevitable discovery rule, 494
Infanticide, 297

Inferiority complex, 138
Influence peddling, 376–379
Informal sanctions, 106
Informal social control, 172–173
Information (pretrial procedure), 507
Information processing, 142, 145–146
Information technology (IT), 440, 455–458
Inheritance school, 122
Innovation, 176
Insanity defense, 151
Institute for Child and Family, 203
Institute for Social Research (ISR), 34–35,
    418
Institutional anomie theory, 177–178, 181
Institutional involvement and belief,
    201–202
Institutional racism, 55, 478. See also
    Racism
Institutional social control, 173
Instrumental crimes, 47
Instrumental theory, 236–237
Instrumental violence, 286
Insurance company fraud, 31
Insurgents, 328–329
Integrated cognitive antisocial potential
    (ICAP) theory, 268, 275
Integrated theories, 262
Intellectual and moral development theory,
    142
Intellectual property (IP) crime, 451, 452
Intelligence
    crime and, 147–149
    criminality and, 147–148, 150
    defective intelligence, 137
    of psychopaths, 148
    testing of, 148–149
Intensive probation supervision (IPS), 544
Intensive supervision parole (ISP), 556
Interactional theory, 262, 275
Interactionist view, 17–18
Interagency Telemarketing and Internet
        Fraud Working Group, 454
Intermediate sanctions
    boot camps, 544–545
    community service restitution, 543
    definition of, 542
    effectiveness of, 545
    electronic monitoring (EC), 544
    fines, 543
    forfeiture, 543
    home confinement (HC), 544
    intensive probation supervision (IPS), 544
    monetary restitution, 543
    punishment ladder and, 542
    residential community corrections
        (RCC), 544
    shock incarceration, 544–545
    shock probation, 543–544
    split sentencing, 543
Internal Revenue Service (IRS), 382, 387,
    487
International Covenant on Civil and
        Political Rights, 538
International Crime Victims Survey
        (ICVS), 12

International trends in criminology. See
        Comparative criminology
Internet. See also Cyber crime
    child pornography on, 413–414, 414,
        454–455
    cyber bullying, 448–449
    cyber spying, 449
    cyber stalking, 448
    employee abuse of, 452
    etailing fraud, 445
    gambling on, 442
    pirating of software and films, 451, 453
    pornography on, 413–414, 414,
        441–442
    Website defacement, 447–448
Internet False Identification Prevention Act
    (2000), 453
Internet Fraud Complaint Center, 454
INTERPOL, 12
Interrogation by police, 469, 494–495. See
        also Investigation of crime
Interview research, 38
Introversion–extroversion, 147
Investigation of crime
    consent search during, 495
    custodial interrogation, 494–495
    effectiveness of, 491–492
    hot pursuit/exigency during, 496
    inevitable discovery rule, 494
    interrogation of suspects during, 469,
        494–495
    "knock and announce" rule during, 485
    legal controls over, 493–494
    Miranda warning and, 494–495
    modus operandi (MO) of criminals
        and, 491
    mug shots and, 491
    by police, 469, 491–497
    by prosecutor, 503
    public safety doctrine and, 494
    search and seizure during, 485, 495–496
    second party consent during, 495–496
    sting operations and, 491
    threshold inquiry (stop-and-frisk)
        during, 495
Involuntary manslaughter, 296. See also
        Manslaughter
Involvement, and social bond theory,
    211–212
IPS (intensive probation supervision), 544
IQ. See Intelligence
Iran, 329, 430, 538
Iraq, 326, 334
Ireland, 247, 248, 330
IRS (Internal Revenue Service), 382, 387,
    487
Islam. See Muslims
ISP (intensive supervision parole), 556
Israel, 293, 333
ISR (Institute for Social Research), 34–35
IT (information technology), 440, 455–458
Italy
    bribery in, 377
    crime trends in, 13
    terrorism in, 330

Jails. *See also* Prisons
  characteristics of inmates of, 545, 546
  definition of, 545
  as element of correctional system, 469
  functions and services of, 545
  history of, 545
  sentences to, 526, 532, 533
  statistics on, 545
Jamaica, 425
Japan
  crime trends in, 12, 289
  labeling effects, 218
  Marshall Plan for, 340
  terrorism in, 334
Jemaah Islamiyah, 330
Jobs. *See* Employment and employees
Joyriding, 356
Judges. *See also* Courts; Supreme Court
  contextual discrimination against African Americans and, 218
  judicial overload and, 506
  role of, 501, 505–506
  selection of, 506
  sentencing by, 528–533
Judiciary system. *See* Courts; Judges
Jury. *See also* Trials
  African Americans on, 514
  hung jury, 471
  impartial juries, 514
  instructions to, during trial, 515
  jury array and, 513
  peremptory challenges and, 514
  removal for cause and, 513
  right to jury trial, 516–517
  selection of, 513–514
  voir dire and, 513
Jury array, 513
Just desert, 112
Justice. *See also* Criminal justice; Criminal justice system
  concepts of, 476–480
  crime control model, 476–478, 476
  criminal justice funnel, 474, 475
  definition of, 4
  due process model, 478, 480
  justice model, 478, 480
  nonintervention model, 479–480
  rehabilitation model, 478–479, 480
  restorative justice model, 480
  steps in process of, 469–475
Justice Department. *See also* FBI (Federal Bureau of Investigation)
  Anti-Trust Division of, 389, 390
  Criminal Division of, 439
  cyber crime and, 439
  funding of research by, 24
  on influence peddling in business, 377–378
  National Institute of Justice and, 24
  prevention of prison rapes and, 552
  on restorative justice, 248
  Violent Criminal Apprehension Program (VICAP) of, 300
  white-collar crime and, 387

Justice model, 478, 480
Justice system. *See* Criminal justice system
Justification defense, 22
Juvenile delinquency. *See* Adolescents; Juvenile justice system
Juvenile justice system. *See also* Adolescents; Criminal justice system
  adolescents' view of, 107
  adult justice system compared with, 472–473
  cost of, 66
  history of, 472
  statistics on, 467
  Supreme Court cases on, 472

Kaiser Foundation media violence study, 143
Kansas City Gun Experiment, 489–490
Kansas City study of police department, 105, 489
Kidnapping, 213, 477
Kids Count project, 164
KKK (Ku Klux Klan), 307, 308, 331, 492
Knapp Commission, 377
Korea, 13, 302
Ku Klux Klan (KKK), 307, 308, 331, 492

Labeling theory
  consequences of labeling, 216–217
  contextual discrimination and, 218
  definition of, 202
  differential enforcement and, 215–216
  diversion programs and, 219
  dramatization of evil and, 217
  effects of labeling, 218
  evaluation of, 218
  interpretation of crime and, 215
  joining deviant cliques and, 216
  positive versus negative labels, 214–215
  primary and secondary deviance and, 217
  process of labeling, 215
  public policy and, 219
  racial profiling and, 216
  reflected appraisals and, 216
  research on, 217–218
  retrospective reading of deviance, 216–217
  stigma and, 216
  summary of, 221
  symbolic interaction theory and, 214
Lack of mental capacity defense, 22
Landmark decisions, 500
Laos, 335
Larceny. *See also* Automobile theft; Fraud; Shoplifting; Theft
  bad checks, 355
  common-law description of, 20, 352
  definition of, 352
  grand larceny, 352
  as Part I crime, 30, 31
  percentage of cleared cases involving, 32
  petit (petty) larceny, 352
  plea bargaining for charge of, 512
  pretrial detention for charge of, 509
  sentences for, 526

statistics on, 352
types of, 352–353
Latency, 138
Latent delinquency, 138
Latent traits
  constant latent traits, 257
  definition of, 267
  evolving latent traits, 257
Latent trait theories
  constant latent traits, 257
  control balance theory, 268
  crime and human nature, 269
  definition of, 256
  definition of latent trait, 267–268
  differential coercion theory, 268
  evolving latent traits, 257
  General Theory of Crime (GTC), 269–275
  integrated cognitive antisocial potential (ICAP) theory, 268, 275
  summary of, 275
Latin America. *See also* specific countries
  drug cartels in, 335, 375, 425, 426
  honor killing in, 290
  terrorism in, 333, 334, 335
Latinos. *See also* Race and ethnicity
  bail for, 55
  burglary rates and, 360
  fear of crime and, 171
  high school graduation rates of, 200
  marriage of, as age-graded theory, 265
  police contacts with, 498
  poverty of, 164
  in prisons and jails, 546, 549
  single-parent families and, 198–199
Law, Order and Power (Chambliss and Seidman), 233
Law and Order, 486
Law enforcement. *See also* Arrests; Police; Sheriffs
  county law enforcement, 487
  drug control and, 426
  federal law enforcement, 486–487
  fence's relationship with, 350
  labeling theory and differential enforcement, 215–216
  metropolitan police, 487–489
  pornography and, 415
  racial profiling and, 54–55, 216, 238–239, 486
  reporting practices by, and UCR, 32–33
  society and, 486
  state police, 487
  statistics on, 467
  terrorism fight by, 337–339
  white-collar crime and, 387–390
Law Enforcement Assistance Administration (LEAA), 467
Law of criminal procedure, 474
Laws
  actus reus and, 21, 22
  on bail, 510
  on child sexual abuse, 412
  common law, 19, 20, 290, 301, 352, 360
  conflict view of crime and, 17, 18

on copyright, 442, 453
on crime control, 467
Crime Identification Technology Act (CITA), 455
criminal defenses and, 21–22
curfew laws, 101, 105
on cyber crime, 452–453
on deadly force by crime victims, 80
in definition of criminology, 4
on drugs, 404, 424–425
elements of criminal law, 21–22
environmental protection laws, 388, 389
evolution of criminal law, 22–23
failure to act and, 21
on firearms, 48–49
goals of criminal law, 19
health care fraud and, 381–382
history of criminal law, 18–19
on identity theft, 444
on industrial espionage, 324
legal definition of crime, 21
Megan's Law, 82
mens rea and, 21, 22
merchant privilege laws, 354
morality and, 402–405
on organized crime, 392, 394
perceptions of, as influence on motives and drives, 203–204
on pornography, 415–416, 442
on prisons, 552
on prohibition of alcohol, 418
on prostitution, 412, 413
public opinion and, 19
on rape, 294–296, 552
registration laws for sex offenders, 22, 81, 82, 244
Sherman Antitrust Act, 384, 389
shield laws, 295
sociology of law, 14, 16
sodomy laws, 22, 405
stalking statutes, 22
statutory crimes, 19
strict liability and, 21
substantive criminal law, 16
three strikes law, 58, 110, 234, 352, 532
truth-in-sentencing laws, 532
USA Patriot Act, 234, 339–340, 339, 453
on victims' rights, 78–79, 81
Welfare Reform Act (1996), 188
on white-collar crime, 384, 388, 389
LEAA (Law Enforcement Assistance Administration), 467
Lead levels, 128, 128–129, 129
Learning. See Social learning theory
Lebanon, 333
Left realism, 239–240, 243
Left-wing political groups, 331–332
Legislation. See Laws
Liberal feminist theory, 53–54
Liberia, 539
Life course persisters, 261, 273
Life course theory
  adolescent-limited offenders, 261, 273
  age of onset/continuity of crime, 259–261

changing life influences and, 257–258
continuity and desistance and, 259–260
criminal life course theories, 261–267
definition of, 256
disruption promoting criminality, 257
gender and desistance, 260–261
general theory of crime and delinquency (GTCD), 262, 275
as integrated theories, 262
interactional theory, 262, 275
life course persisters, 261, 273
pathways to crime, 258–259, 260
problem behavior syndrome (BPS), 258
social development model (SDM), 262
summary of, 275
Lifestyle theory, 73–74, 77
Lighting, 128
The Limits of the Criminal Sanction (Packer), 478
Lineup, 469
Live from Death Row (Mumia), 238
Logic bombs, 446–447
LoJack auto protection system, 102, 358
London. See Great Britain
Lower classes. See also Poverty; Underclass
  child poverty and, 163–164
  code of the streets and, 185
  crime patterns and, 46–47, 50–51
  focal concerns of, 182, 183, 188
  media influence on, 163
  middle-class measuring rods and, 183–184
  minority group poverty and, 164
  poverty and, 164–165
  theory of delinquent subcultures and, 182–186
  truly disadvantaged and, 165–166
  underclass and, 163
LSD, 425, 426. See also Drugs
Lumpen proletariat, 231

Macedonia, 330
Madam (brothel), 410
Mafia, 391, 394. See also Organized crime
Mala in se, 19
Mala prohibitum, 19
Malaysia, 439
Malware, 447
Management fraud, 378–380
Mandatory prison terms, 528, 532
Mann Act, 412, 486
Manslaughter
  common-law description of, 20
  definition of, 296
  involuntary manslaughter, 296
  negligent manslaughter, 296
  nonnegligent manslaughter, 296
  as Part I crime, 30, 31
  voluntary manslaughter, 20
MAO (monoamine oxidase), 131, 132
Marathon oil company, 379
Marginal deterrence, 92
Marginalization, 235
Marijuana, 404, 417, 423, 424, 430. See also Drugs
Marijuana Tax Act (1938), 404, 424

Marital exemption, 293
Marital rape, 293
Mark (confidence games), 359
Marriage. See also Domestic violence
  age-graded theory and, 264–265
  Defense of Marriage Act (1996), 404–405
  divorce and, 198–199
  murder of spouse, 297–298, 302
  rape in, 293
  same-sex marriage, 404–405
  victimization and marital status, 70, 72
Marxism
  capitalist bourgeoisie, 230–231
  crime as seen by, 232
  dialectic method of, 232
  lumpen proletariat, 231
  productive forces and productive relations, 230–232
Masculinities and Crime (Messerschmidt), 241
Masculinity hypothesis, 53
Massachusetts Brady-Fox Law, 49
Massage parlors, 411
Mass murder, 300–301
Master traits. See Latent trait theories
Mauritania, 126
MBD (minimal brain dysfunction), 130
Mechanical solidarity, 175
Media. See also Television
  coverage of trials by, 517
  crime coverage by, 11
  on criminals, 93
  violence in, 41, 122, 143–144
Medicaid fraud, 380
Medical care. See Health care
Medical technology, 42. See also Technology
Medicare fraud, 371
Megan's Law, 82
Mens rea, 21, 22
Mental illness/mental disorders
  alexithymia, 139
  antipsychotic drugs for, 132
  antisocial personality, 147, 147–148
  bipolar disorder, 138
  conduct disorder (CD), 131, 139
  crime and, 139–141
  death penalty and, 539
  disruptive behavior disorder (DBD), 139
  genetics and, 132
  insanity defense, 151
  Miranda warning and, 494
  mood disorders, 139
  narcissistic personality disorder, 294
  oppositional defiant disorder (ODD), 139
  paranoid schizophrenia, 139
  of prisoners, 549, 555
  psychodynamic theory of, 139–141
  psychosis, 139
  of rapists, 294
  right to be competent at trial and, 517
  schizophrenia, 121, 139, 141, 494
  of school shooters, 121
  of terrorists, 336
  of women, 139, 140

Mental retardation. *See* Intelligence
Merchant privilege laws, 354
Mesomorphs, 122
Meta-analysis, 38–39
Methadone, 428–429
Methamphetamine, 14–15, 416. *See also* Drugs
Metropolitan police, 487–489. *See also* Police
Mexico, 539
Michigan State University, 222
Middle-class measuring rods, 183–184
Middle East
    domestic violence in, 302
    drug cartels in, 425
    genital mutilation of females in, 403
    honor killing in, 290, 302
    organized crime in, 392
    Palestinian Liberation Organization
        (PLO) in, 333
    terrorism in, 330, 333
Military. *See also* War
    domestic violence and, 304
    rape by, 291
Minimal brain dysfunction (MBD), 130
Minimum legal drinking age (MLDA), 105
Minneapolis domestic violence study, 109–110
Minnesota Multiphasic Personality Inventory (MMPI), 147
Minnesota Study of Twins Reared Apart, 134
Minnesota Twin Family Study, 134
Minorities. *See* African Americans; Asian Americans; Latinos; Native Americans; Race and ethnicity
Minors. *See* Children
Miranda warning, 494–495
Mission hate crimes, 307
Missouri Plan, 506
MLDA (minimum legal drinking age), 105
MMPI (Minnesota Multiphasic Personality Inventory), 147
Modus operandi (MO), 491
Monetary restitution, 543
Monitoring the Future (MTF) study, 34–35, 36, 44, 45, 418–419
Monoamine oxidase (MAO), 131, 132
Montenegro, 538
Mood disorders, 139
Moral crusaders, 404–405
Moral development, 142
Moral entrepreneurs, 18, 215
Morality. *See also* Beliefs; Ethics; Public order crimes; Values
    criminal law and, 19
    debates on, 402–403
    General Theory of Crime (GTC) and, 273
    law and, 402–405
    moral crusades and, 404–405
    moral entrepreneurs, 215
    social harm of immoral acts, 403–404
The Moral Sense (Wilson), 125
Morals squads, 291
Mosaic Code, 18
Motivated offenders, 74, 75

Motor vehicle theft. *See* Automobile theft
Mousetrapping, 442
Movies. *See* Films
MPQ (Multidimensional Personality Questionnaire), 147
MTF (Monitoring the Future) study, 34–35, 36, 44, 45, 418–419
Mug shots, 491
Multidimensional Personality Questionnaire (MPQ), 147
Multidisciplinary science, 4
Murder. *See also* Capital punishment; Violence and violent crime
    of children, 72, 82, 98–99, 297
    common-law description of, 20
    costs to victims of, 66
    cultural retaliatory homicide, 289
    definition of, 296
    degrees of, 296–297
    deliberation and, 296
    eldercide, 297
    familicide, 301
    felony murder, 296
    feticide, 296–297
    filicide, 297
    firearms used in, 46
    first-degree murder, 296
    honor killings, 182, 290, 302
    infanticide, 297
    international trends in, 12
    manslaughter distinguished from, 296
    mass murder, 300–301
    nature and extent of, 297
    as Part I crime, 30, 31
    percentage of cleared cases involving, 32
    personal relations between victim and murderer, 298–299
    plea bargaining for charge of, 512
    premeditation and, 296
    pretrial detention for charge of, 508, 509
    rational choice theory and, 98–99
    repeat convictions for, 112
    school shootings, 48, 75, 99, 121–122, 286, 287, 299
    second-degree murder, 296
    sentences for, 113, 500, 526, 531, 536
    serial killers, 67–68, 139, 299–300, 414
    siblicide, 72
    by spouse, 297–298, 302
    spree killers, 301
    statistics on, 297, 539
    by strangers, 299
    U.S. trends in, 39, 42, 44
    victim–murderer relationship, 297–300
    victims of, 65–66, 72, 78, 82, 98–99, 99, 255, 277, 297, 301, 407, 492
    by women, 140
    in workplace, 309
Muslims, 333–334, 403, 412
Myanmar (formerly Burma), 335, 425

Naive check forgers, 355
Narcissistic personality disorder, 294
Narcotics, 417, 424, 430. *See also* Heroin
Narcotics Anonymous, 427, 430

Narcotics Control Act (1956), 425
National Association of Fraud Investigation, 374
National Center for Policy Analysis, 106, 277
National Center for State Courts (NCSC), 501, 518
National Center for Victims of Crime, 68
National Center on Addiction and Substance Abuse (CASA), 419–420, 429
National Center on Elder Abuse, 70
National Child Abuse and Neglect Data System (NCANDS), 302
National College of Juvenile Justice, 506
National Commission on Terrorist Attacks Upon the nited States, 337
National Conference of State Court Judges, 506
National Counterintelligence Center, 323
National Counterterrorism Center (NCTC), 337–338, 340
National Crime Information Center, 499
National Crime Victimization Survey (NCVS)
    on assault, 302
    on burglary, 360
    definition of, 36
    evaluation of, 36, 37
    on firearm use, 46
    on rape, 292, 294
    statistics on victimization, 66, 68
    trends in, 43, 44
    validity of, 36
National Deviancy Conference (NDC), 232–233
National Health Care Anti-Fraud Association (NHCAA), 380
National Household Survey on Drug Abuse (NHSDA), 419
National Incident-Based Reporting System (NIBRS), 33, 36
National Information Infrastructure Protection Act (NIIPA), 452–453
National Institute of Justice, 24
National Institute of Mental Health, 24
National Insurance Crime Bureau (NICB), 357
Nationalist terrorism, 332–333
National Mental Health Association (NMHA), 146
National Organization for Victim Assistance, 81
National Science Foundation, 24
National Sex Offender Public Registry, 81
National Stolen Property Act, 453
National Surveys on Drug Use and Health (NSDUH), 419, 423, 424
National Whistleblower Center, 385
National White-Collar Crime Center, 373, 454
National Youth Gang Center, 222
Native Americans, 199, 200
Naxalone, 429
Nazism, 330, 336–337
NCANDS (National Child Abuse and Neglect Data System), 302

NCSC (National Center for State Courts), 501, 518
NCTC (National Counterterrorism Center), 337–338, 340
NCVS. *See* National Crime Victimization Survey (NCVS)
Negative affective states, 178–180
Negative reinforcement, 206
Neglect, 302
Negligent manslaughter, 296
Neighborhood hustler, 351
Neighborhoods. *See* Communities and neighborhoods
Neocortex, 128
Nepal, 538
Networks of terror groups, 335
Neuroallergies, 128
Neurophysiology
 antisocial personality and, 149
 attention deficit hyperactive disorder (ADHD), 124, 127, 130–131, *131*
 brain chemistry, 131–132
 brain tumors, lesions, injury, and disease, 131
 crime and, 129–132, 137
 definition of, 129
 measuring neurological impairment, 129–130
 minimal brain dysfunction (MBD), 130
 summary of, 137
Neuroticism, 147
Neurotransmitters, 131–132
Neutralization theory
 definition of, 207
 shoplifting and, 354
 summary on, 221
 techniques of neutralization, 207–209
 testing, 208
 white-collar crime and, 386
The New Criminology (Taylor, Walton, and Young), 233
New York City Counterterrorism Bureau, 338–339
New York Crime Victim Board, 81
New York Electronic Crimes Task Force (NYECTF), 454
New Zealand, 276, 293
NHCAA (National Health Care Anti-Fraud Association), 380
NHSDA (National Household Survey on Drug Abuse), 419
NIBRS (National Incident-Based Reporting System), 33, 36
Nicaragua, 329
NICB (National Insurance Crime Bureau), 357
Nigeria, 538
NIIPA (National Information Infrastructure Protection Act), 452–453
9/11 attacks, 319–320, 334, 404
9/11 Commission, 337
NMHA (National Mental Health Association), 146
Nolle prosequi, 503
Nonintervention model, 479–480
Nonnegligent manslaughter, 296

Norepinephrine, 131
Northwestern University/University of Chicago Joint Center for Poverty Research, 164
Norway, 13
NSDUH (National Surveys on Drug Use and Health), 419, 423, 424
Nuclear Terrorism (Allison), 337
Nuclear weapons, 337
Nutrition. *See* Diet
NYECTF (New York Electronic Crimes Task Force), 454

Obscenity, 404, 413, 415. *See also* Pornography
Observational research, 38
Obsessive-compulsive disorder, 67
Occasional fences, 351–352
Occasional thieves, 348
Occupational Safety and Health Administration (OSHA), 384–385
Oceanis Eleven/Twelve/Thirteen, 346
ODD (oppositional defiant disorder), 139
Oedipus complex, 138
Offender-specific crime, 94
Offense-specific crime, 94
Office for Victims of Crime (OVC), 81
Office on National Drug Control Policy (ONDCP), 5, 426
Oil companies, 375, 379
Old Bailey Court, London, 527
Olympics (1997) bombing, 29
Omnibus Victim and Witness Protection Act, 78
On Aggression (Lorenz), 287
"On Crimes and Punishment" (Beccaria), 6
ONDCP (Office on National Drug Control Policy), 5, 426
Operation Backfire, 332
Operation Bullpen, 374
Operation Ceasefire, 499
Operation Weed and Seed, 188–189
Opium, 416, 430
Oppositional defiant disorder (ODD), 139
Oral stage, 138
Organic solidarity, 175
Organizational crime, 382. *See also* Corporate crime
Organized crime
 activities of, 390–391
 alien conspiracy theory and, 391
 characteristics of, 390
 concept of, 391
 contemporary organized crime groups, 391–392
 control of, 392, 394
 Cosa Nostra, 391
 definition of, 372, 390
 future of, 394
 Mafia, 391, 394
 Russian organized crime, 392, 393
Organized Crime Control Act (1970), 392, 394
OSHA (Occupational Safety and Health Administration), 384–385

OVC (Office for Victims of Crime), 81
Overt pathway, 259

Pakistan, 340, 538
Palestinian Liberation Organization (PLO), 333
Palestinian women, domestic violence against, 302
Papua New Guinea, 538
Paraguay, 539
Paranoid schizophrenia, 139. *See also* Schizophrenia
Paraphilias, 405–406, 407
Parental abuse, 303
Parents. *See* Family
Parole
 definition of, 554
 effectiveness of, 556–557
 as element of correctional system, 469
 intensive supervision parole (ISP), 556
 parolees in community, 555–556, *556*
 parole grant hearing, 555
 problems of reentry and, 554–555
 prohibition of, for murder convictions, 537
 statistics on, 554
Parole grant hearing, 555
Particular deterrence. *See* Specific deterrence
Part I crimes, 30, 31, 39, 54. *See also* Violence and violent crime
Part II crimes, 31, 54
Passive precipitation, 73
Paternalistic families, 242
Patriarchal system, 240–241
Patriot Act, 234, 339–340, *339*, 453
Patterns in crime. *See also* Crime statistics; National Crime Victimization Survey (NCVS); Uniform Crime Reports (UCR)
 age and, 51–52
 aging out of crime, 52
 chronic offenders/criminal careers, 56–58
 ecology of crime, 45–46, *47*
 firearms, 46
 gender and, 52–54, 125–128, 136
 race and, 54–56
 regional differences, 46, *47*
 social class and socioeconomic conditions and, 46–47, 50–51
Patterns in Criminal Homicide (Wolfgang), 14
Payola, 377
PBS (problem behavior syndrome), 258, 421
PCP, 426
Peacemaking, 242–243
Pedophilia, 22, 406. *See also* Sexual abuse
Peer relations
 differential association theory and, 205
 friendships of delinquents, 213
 General Theory of Crime (GTC) and, 273
 social bond theory and, 213
 socialization and, 201, *201*
 subculture of violence and, 289

Penitentiaries, 546. *See also* Prisons
Pennsylvania prison system, 527–528
Penology, 15. *See also* Prisons
Peremptory challenges, 514
Permeable neighborhoods, 98
Persistence, 57, 261, 273
Personality
  antisocial behavior and, 146–149
  antisocial personality, 147, 147–148
  California Personality Inventory (CPI), 147
  of chronic offenders, 147
  crime and, 146–147, 150
  definition of, 146
  extroversion–introversion, 147
  genetics and, 132, 147
  Minnesota Multiphasic Personality Inventory (MMPI), 147
  Multidimensional Personality Questionnaire (MPQ), 147
  psychopathic personality, 147
  research on, 147
  sociopathic personality, 147
  stability–instability, 147
Peru, 334
Petit (petty) larceny, 352. *See also* Larceny
PET (positron emission tomography), 130
Phallic stage, 138
Pharmacist, chiseling by, 375, 385, *385*
Philadelphia cohort research, 256
Philippines, 289, 538
Phishing, 443–444, 451–452
Photo studios, prostitutes in, 411
Phrenologists, 7
Physiognomists, 7
Pickpockets, 349
Pigeon drop, 359
Pilferage, 380
Pinkerton Detective Agency, 347
Pirating of software and films, 451, 453
Pittsburgh Youth Study, 73–74
Playboy, 413
Plea bargaining, 471, 503, 511–513
Pleasure principle, 137
PLRA (Prison Litigation Reform Act), 553
PMS (premenstrual syndrome), 128
Poachers, 346
Police. *See also* Arrests; Investigation of crime; Law enforcement
  addition of parole officers, 490
  booking of suspect by, 469
  changing role of, 497–498
  community-oriented policing (COP), 498–499, *498*
  contacts between civilians and, 497–498
  crackdowns by, 105
  drug control and, 426
  functions of, 489
  increasing police activity as deterrence, 105
  interrogation of suspects by, 469
  investigation of crime by, 469, 491–497
  Kansas City study of, 105, 489
  metropolitan police, 487–489

  morals (vice) squads of, 291
  organization of metropolitan police department, 488
  prevention and deterrence of crime by, 489–491
  proactive policing, 489
  problem-oriented policing (POP), 499
  prosecutor's cooperation with, 503
  public social control of, in neighborhoods, 173
  racial profiling by, 54–55, 216, 238–239, 486
  reactive policing, 498
  responsibilities of, 486
  restorative justice and, 245
  shootings by, 496–497
  society and, 486
  state police, 487
  statistics on, 487–488
  and steps in justice process, 469, 470
  sting operations by, 491
  summary of, 468
  targeting crimes and, 489–490
  tasks of patrol officers, 488
  technology used by, 490–491, 499
Police Executive Research Forum, 491
Policy making. *See* Public policy
Political corruption, 325
Political crime. *See also* Terrorism
  definition of, 320
  election fraud, 321–322
  espionage, 323–324
  goals of, 320–321
  human rights violations, 326
  illegal domestic surveillance, 325
  nature of, 320
  political corruption, 325
  stages in becoming political criminal, 321
  state-corporate crime, 326
  state political crime, 324–326
  state violence, 326
  torture, 326, 327
  treason, 322–323, *322*
  types of, 321–326
Political solutions to terrorism, 340
Political terrorists, 331–332
Pollution. *See also* Environmental crimes
  environmental contaminants, 128
  lead levels, 128–129, *129*
Ponzi scheme, 271
POP (problem-oriented policing), 499
Population statistics, in eighteenth century, 8
Population (survey), 34
Pornography. *See also* Obscenity
  child pornography, 413–414, *414*, 454–455
  control of, 415–416
  history of, 413
  Internet distribution of, 441–442
  laws on, 415–416, 442
  violence caused by, 414
Portugal, 13
Positivism, 6–11, 93

Positron emission tomography (PET), 130
Posttraumatic stress disorder (PTSD), 67, 77, 303
Poverty. *See also* Lower classes; Underclass; Welfare
  age and, 163
  child poverty, 163–164, *164*
  code of the streets and, 185
  community deterioration and, 170
  crime patterns and, 47, 51
  cultural deviance theory and, 182
  culture of poverty, 163
  minority group poverty, 164–166, *164*, 170
  statistics on, 162, 163
  strain theory and, 175
  truly disadvantaged and, 165–166
  victimization and, 70
  welfare programs and, 173, 188
Power-control theory, 241–242, 243
Power rape, 292
Precedent, 500
Preliminary hearing, 470–471, 503
Premeditation, 296
Premenstrual syndrome (PMS), 128
Presentencing investigation, 471
President's Commission on Law Enforcement and the Administration of Justice, 467
Pretrial detention, 508–509
Pretrial procedures. *See* Bail; Plea bargaining
Pretty Woman, 410
Prevention/control
  of automobile theft, 358
  Chicago Area Project, 188
  community organizations for, 80–81, 173, 426–427
  of cyber crime, 452–455
  developmental theories and, 276
  Fast Track Program, 276
  general deterrence and, 104–107, 112
  of hate crimes, 307
  incapacitation and, 110–111, 112
  Operation Weed and Seed and, 188–189
  of organized crime, 392, 394
  police responsibility for, 489–491
  of pornography, 415–416
  preemptive deterrence and, 240
  primary prevention programs, 149–150
  of prostitution, 412
  rational choice theory and, 100–112
  secondary prevention programs, 150
  of serial killers, 300
  of shoplifting, 354–355
  situational crime prevention and, 100–104, 112
  SMART program, 276
  specific deterrence and, 108–110, 112
  of substance abuse, 276, 425–429, 481
  tertiary prevention programs, 150
  War on Poverty and, 188
  white-collar crime, 388–389
  workplace violence, 309

Preventive detention, 508–509
Price fixing, 384
Primary deviance, 217
Primary prevention programs, 149–150
Princeton University Survey Research
    Center, 36
Principles of Criminology (Sutherland), 203
Prison Litigation Reform Act (PLRA), 553
Prison Rape Reduction Act (2003), 552
Prisons. *See also* Incarceration; Jails
    African Americans in, 55, 164, 478, 536,
        537, 549
    congregate system of, 528
    costs of, 111
    cruel and unusual punishment and, 553
    definition of, 546
    deterrent effect of, 106, 108–111
    drug offenders in, 416, 424, 555
    as element of correctional system, 469
    female inmate characteristics, 550
    health care in, 553
    history of, 527–528
    living in prison, 548–549
    male inmate characteristics, 548
    maximum-security prisons, 546
    medium-security prisons, 546
    minimum-security prisons, 546
    private prisons, 548
    rape in, 549, 552
    rehabilitation of prisoners, 477,
        478–479, 479
    sentences for violent crimes, 113
    social class of prisoners, 47
    statistics on, 110, 547
    super maximum prisons, 546–548
    types of, 546–548
    violence in, 528, 552–553
Privacy. *See* Civil liberties
Private property. *See* Property crimes
Proactive policing, 489
Probable cause, 469
Probable cause hearing, 470–471
Probation
    as element of correctional system, 469
    intensive probation supervision (IPS),
        544
    investigation and, 540
    revocation of, 540, 541
    rules of, 541
    service categories for, 540–541
    shock probation, 543–544
    statistics on, 540
    success of, 541–542
    supervision and, 541
    treatment and, 540–541
    trends in, 532
Problem behavior syndrome (PBS), 258, 421
Problem-oriented policing (POP), 499
Productive forces, 230–232
Productive relations, 230–232
Professional arson, 365. *See also* Arson
The Professional Thief (Sutherland), 349
Professional thieves, 348–351. *See also*
    Career criminals; Theft
Prohibition of alcohol, 418, 430

Project on Human Development in Chicago
    Neighborhoods, 165–166, 289, 290
Proletariat, 9, 231
Prolixin, 132
Property crimes. *See also* Arson; Automo-
    bile theft; Burglary; Larceny; Theft
    by adolescents, 44, 45, 51–52
    by African Americans, 54
    regional differences in, 47
    trends in, 42–43, 44, 69
    victimization rates for, 69
*Prosecution: The Decision to Charge a Subject
    with a Crime* (Miller), 504
Prosecutorial discretion, 103–104
Prosecutors
    charges determined by, 503
    complaint/charging by, 469
    courtroom work group and, 474
    investigation of law violations by, 503
    jury selection and, 513–514
    plea bargaining and, 471, 503, 511–513
    preliminary hearings and, 470–471, 503
    prosecutorial discretion and, 503–504
    role of, 501, 505–506
    sentencing and, 503
    special investigations by, 503
    during trials, 515
    types of, 502–503
Prostitution
    becoming a prostitute, 411–412
    brothel prostitutes, 410–411, 413
    child sexual abuse and, 411, 412
    control of, 412
    definition of, 406–407
    economic opportunity and, 95
    feminist views on, 413
    gay political candidate as former
        prostitute, 401–402
    history of, 406, 410, 412
    international sex trade, 408–410, 412
    legalization of, 412–413
    police vice squad and, 491
    statistics on, 407–409
    types of, 410–411
Protect Act (2003), 412
Psychodynamic theory
    of antisocial behavior, 138–139
    definition of, 137
    elements of, 137–138
    mental illness, 139–141
    mood disorders, 139
    psychosexual stages of human
        development, 138
    summary of, 146, 150
Psychological trait theories
    behavioral theory, 141–142, 146, 150
    cognitive theory, 142, 145–146, 146,
        150
    history of, 136–137
    intelligence and crime, 147–149, 150,
        150
    personality and crime, 146–147, 150
    psychodynamic theory, 137–141, 146, 150
    summary of, 150
Psychological view

of criminology, 9
    of substance abuse, 420
    of terrorism, 336
Psychopathic personality, 7, 147, 148–149.
    See also Antisocial personality; Mental
    illness/mental disorders
Psychosexual stages of human develop-
    ment, 138
Psychosis, 139. *See also* Mental illness/
    mental disorders
Psychosurgery, 150
PTSD (posttraumatic stress disorder), 67,
    77, 303
Public defender, 505
Public order crimes. *See also* Alcohol abuse;
    Drugs; Substance abuse
    definition of, 402
    law and morality, 402–405
    paraphilias, 405–406, 407
    pornography, 413–416
    prostitution, 406–413
Public policy
    age-graded theory and, 267
    crime trends and, 42
    critical criminology and, 243–248
    developmental theories and, 276
    just desert and, 112
    rational choice theory and, 111–112
    social structure theories and, 188–189
    trait theory and, 149–150
Public safety doctrine, 494
Public social control, 173
Puerto Rico, 425
*Punishing Hate: Bias Crimes under American
    Law* (Lawrence), 308
Punishment. *See also* Capital punishment;
    Corrections; General deterrence; Jails;
    Prisons; Sentencing; Specific deterrence
    aggression linked with, 288
    capitalism's impact on, 239
    certainty of, and deterrence, 104
    criminal law and, 19
    cruel and unusual punishment, 553
    of drug use, 426
    goals of criminal punishment, 528–533
    of hate crimes, 308
    history of, 5, 18–19, 92–93, 526–528
    objectives of, in classical theory of
        crime, 92
    perception of, and deterrence, 104–105
    punishment ladder, 542
    racial profiling in, 238–239
    severity of, and deterrence, 105–106
Punishment ladder, 542
Pure Food and Drug Act, 424

Quasi-experimental research design, 37–38
Quorum Health Group, 381

Race and ethnicity. *See also* African Ameri-
    cans; Asian Americans; Latinos; Native
    Americans
    code of the street and, 185
    contextual discrimination and, 218
    crime patterns and, 54–56

death penalty and, 536, 537
discrimination based on, 55–56,
165–166, 218, 478, 533–535
family dissolution and, 56
fear of crime and, 171–172
General Theory of Crime (GTC) and,
273
hate crimes against, 307
institutional racism and, 55
jail inmates, 545, 546
marriage and age-graded theory, 265
murders of African Americans, 297, 301,
492
poverty and, 164–166
in prison, 549
racial profiling and, 54–55, 216,
238–239, 486
self-control and crime and, 273
sentencing and, 533–535
single-parent families and, 198–199
strain theory and, 174–175
victimization and, 69, 72
Racial profiling, 54–55, 216, 238–239, 486
Racial threat hypothesis, 172
Racism. *See also* Race and ethnicity; Racial
profiling
contextual discrimination and, 218
crime patterns and, 55
institutional racism, 55, 478
in sentencing, 533–535
subtle nature of, 165–166
Racketeer Influenced and Corrupt Organization Act (RICO), 394
Radical feminism. *See* Critical feminist
theory
Rand Corporation, 491, 541
Rape. *See also* Sex offenders
abuse of victims of, by criminal justice
system, 66
accusations of, against Duke lacrosse
team members, 285–286
acquaintance rape, 292–293
age of victims of, 71
aggravated rape, 294
anger rape, 292
of Bosnian and Kosovar women, 291
causes of, 293–294
common-law description of, 20, 290
consent and, 295
costs to victims of, 66
date rape, 74, 145, 293
definitions of, 290–291
evolutionary and biological factors on,
294
firearms used in, 46
gang rape, 292
genocide rape, 291
history of, 291, *291*
international trends in, 12–13
law on, 294–296
male socialization and, 293
marital rape, 293
military and, 291
as Part I crime, 30, 31

percentage of cleared cases involving, 32
plea bargaining for charge of, 512
pornography and, 414
posttraumatic stress disorder (PTSD)
and, 68
power rape, 292
pretrial detention for charge of, 508, 509
in prisons, 549, 552
proof of, 294–295
psychological abnormality of rapists, 294
rational choice theory of, 99–100
relationship of victim and rapist in, 72
sadistic rape, 292
sentences for, 113, 526
serial rapes, 292
sexual motivation for, 294
shield laws and, 295
social learning perspective on, 294
speak-out rally for survivors of, 67
statistics on, 36, 292, 302
statutory rape, 292–293
types of rape and rapists, 292–293
virility mystique and, 293
in workplace, 309
Rational choice theory
airplane hijackers and, 100
choice of time and place of crime, 97
choice of type of crime, 97
classical theory of crime, 92–93
concepts of, 10, 11, 94–97
controlling/eliminating crime and,
100–112
development of, 92–93
drug use and, 98
economic opportunity and crime,
94–95, *96*
general deterrence and, 104–107, 112
incapacitation and, 110–111, 112
just desert and, 112
knowledge of criminal techniques and,
96–97
learning and experience in criminal
decision making, 96
murder and, 99
offense- and offender-specific crimes
and, 94
public policy implications of, 111–112
robbery and, 99
sex offenders and, 99–100
situational crime prevention and,
100–104, 112
specific deterrence and, 108–110, 112
structuring crime and, 97
structuring criminality and, 94–97
of substance abuse, 421
substance abuse and, 421
targets of crime and, 97
theft and, 98
violent crime and, 98–100
white-collar crime and, 385–386
Rationalization of white-collar crime, 386
Rational robbery, 306
RCC (residential community corrections),
544
Reaction formation, 186

Reactive (defensive) hate crimes, 307
Reactive policing, 498
Reality principle, 138
Reasoning criminal, 94
Rebellion, 176
Rebuttal evidence, 515
Recidivism, 111, 477, 508, 556–557. *See
also* Chronic offenders
Reciprocal altruism, 123
Redirect examination, 515
Registration laws for sex offenders, 22, 81,
82, 244
Rehabilitation model, 478–479, 480, 529.
See also Treatment programs
Reign of Terror, 330
Reigns of Terror (Marchak), 336–337
Reinforcement
differential reinforcement, 206
differential reinforcement theory,
206–207, 221
negative reinforcement, 206
Reintegrative shaming, 244–245
Relationships. *See also* Family; Marriage;
Peer relations
murderous relations, 297–299
rapist–victim relationship, 72
stalker–victim relationship, 310
victim–criminal relationship, 72,
297–299
Relative deprivation, 174–175, 181
Release on recognizance (ROR), 510
Religion
Buddhism, *186*
clergy sex scandal, 405
death penalty and, 535, 537
institutional social control by churches,
173
and prohibition of alcohol, 416, 418
socialization and, 201–202
substance abuse and, 416
swindling of religious people, 375
terrorism and, 329–330
Remarriage. *See* Blended families
Removed for cause, 513
Repeat burglary, 364
Repeat offenders. *See* Chronic offenders
Reporting. *See* Uniform Crime Reports
(UCR)
Research. *See also* Self-report surveys
adoption studies, 135
cohort research, 37, 56–57, 256
ethics and, 24
experimental research, 37–38
funds for, 24
interview research, 38
meta-analysis, 38–39
observational research, 38
quasi-experimental design, 37–38
retrospective cohort study, 37
scientific method, 4, 6–7, 11, 14
systematic review, 38–39
time-series studies, 108–109
twin studies, 133–135
Residential community corrections (RCC),
544

Resource Conservation and Recovery Act, 388

Respect game, 185

Restitution
community service restitution, 543
monetary restitution, 543
as sentencing goal, 529

Restitution agreements, 79, 219

Restoration, as sentencing goal, 529

Restorative justice
balanced and restorative justice (BARJ), 246
challenge of, 246, 248
as criminal justice model, 480
definition of, 243–244
information resources on, 248
in international community, 247, 248
process of, 245–246
protest against death penalty, *242*
reintegrative shaming and, 244–245
restoration programs and, 245–246, *246*
sentencing circle and, 245
in workplace, 309

Restorative Justice (Sullivan and Tifft), 243

Restorative justice model, 480

Restraint of trade, 384

Retaliatory hate crimes, 307

Retreatism, 176

Retreatist gangs, 187

Retribution, as sentencing goal, 529

Retributive terrorism, 333–334

Retrospective cohort study, 37

Retrospective reading, 216–217

Revenge, 19

Revolutionaries, 329

Revolutionary terrorists, 330

Revolutionary War, 330

RICO (Racketeer Influenced and Corrupt Organization Act), 394

Right to be competent at trial, 517

Right to counsel, 474, 505

Right to jury trial, 516–517

Right to legal counsel, 474, 505, 517

Right to speedy trial, 514, 516

Right-wing political groups, 331

Risk factor, 15

Risperdal, 132

Ritualism, 176

Road rage, 301

Robbery. *See also* Burglary; Theft
acquaintance robbery, 305–306
by adolescents, 44, 45, 52
age of victims of, 71
Brinks robbery at Miami International Airport, 477
common-law description of, 20, 304
definition of, 304
firearms used in, 46
international trends in, 13
as Part I crime, 30, 31
percentage of cleared cases involving, 32
plea bargaining for charge of, 512
pretrial detention for charge of, 508, 509
rational choice theory and, 99
rational robbery, 306

relationship of victim and criminal in, 72
sentences for, 113, 526, 531
statistics on, 304
train robbery, 347, *347*
types of robbery and robbers, 305
U.S. trends in, 42
in workplace, 309

Rochester Youth Development Study (RYDS), 73–74, 133

Role exit behavior, 242

ROR (release on recognizance), 510

Routine activities theory, 74–77

Rule of law
corrections and, 533
criminal justice system and, 474–476
sentencing and, 529
trials and, 516–518

Runaways, 67, 73

Russia/Soviet Union
chechen terrorists in, 333
organized crime and, 392, 393
prostitution in, 409
revolution in, 329, 330
secret service of, 323, 325
spies for, 323, 325
Stalin's gulags and purges in, 239, 337

RYDS (Rochester Youth Development Study), 73–74, 133

Sadistic rape, 292

Sadomasochism, 406

Safecracking, 347–348

Safe Streets and Crime Control Act (1968), 467

SAMHSA (Substance Abuse and Mental Health Services Administration), 419, 429

Samoa, 539

Sampling, 34

Sarbanes-Oxley (SOX) law, 389

Saudi Arabia
al-Qaeda and, 340
crime trends in, 13
death penalty and executions in, 538

Scared Straight program, 24

Schering-Plough Corporation, 379

Schizophrenia, 121, 139, 141, 494

Schools. *See also* Education
chronic offenders and, 57
D.A.R.E. (Drug Abuse Resistance Education) in, 428
drug-testing programs at, 427
high school dropouts, 164, 200–201
institutional social control by, 173
problems with, and criminality, 200–201
restorative justice and, 245
speaker at, *214*
victimization at, 69
violence in, 48, 75, 99, 121–122, 286, 287, 299

School shootings, 48, 75, 99, 121–122, 286, *287*, 299

Scientific method, 4, 6–7, 11, 14

Scotland
marital rape law in, 293
school shootings in, 286, *287*

Scream movies, 309

SDM (social development model), 262

SDS (Students for a Democratic Society), 332

Search and Destroy (Miller), 55

Search warrant, 495

Season of year and crime, 45, *46*

SEC (Securities and Exchange Commission), 376–379, 386, 387, 388, 439, 454

Second Amendment, 48

Secondary deviance, 217

Secondary prevention programs, 150

Second-degree murder, 296

Second party consent, 495–496

Secret Service, 338, 387, 454

Securities Act (1933), 443

Securities and Exchange Commission (SEC), 376–379, 386, 387, 389, 439, 454

Securities chiseling, 375–376

Securities fraud, 443

Self-concept and crime, 210

Self-control
General Theory of Crime (GTC) and, 269–274
impulsivity versus, 270, 272–273, 274

Self-control theory
definition of, 271–272
white-collar crime and, 387

Self-protection
firearms for, 80
victimization and, 80–81

Self-report surveys. *See also* Research; Surveys
by African Americans, 54
on class–crime relationship, 50
conducting, 34
definition of, 34
on drug use, 35, 36, 43–44, 423
evaluation of, 36, 37
Monitoring the Future (MTF) study, 34–35, 44, 45, 418–419
patterns in, 34–35
sample questions, 35
trends in, 43–44
validity of, 35

Senegal, 403

Sentencing. *See also* Jails; Prisons; Punishment
concurrent sentence, 528
consecutive sentence, 528
determinate sentence, 529–530
goals of, 529
guidelines for, 530–532
indeterminate sentence, 528–529
by judges, 528–533
mandatory prison terms and, 528, 532
by prior record, 533
prosecutor's role in, 503
racial discrimination in, 55, 238–239, 533–535
sentencing circle and, 245
sentencing disparity, 533–535
split sentencing, 543

structured sentencing, 530
structures for, 528–533
of teacher for sex offense, 525–526
three strikes policy for, 58, 110, 234,
    352, 532
trends in, 532–533
during trial, 516, *530*
truth-in-sentencing laws, 532
victim impact statements and, 80, 528
for violence crime, 113, 500, 526, 536
Sentencing circle, 245
Sentencing Commission, U.S., 389
Sentencing disparity, 533–535
September 11 attacks, 319–320, 333, 404
Serbia and Serbian army, 291, 538
Serial killers. *See also* Murder
    control of, 300
    definition of, 299
    fear of, 67–68
    female serial killers, 300
    motivations of, 300
    pornography and, 414
    schizophrenia and, 139
    types of, 299–300
Serial rapes, 292
Serotonin, 131
Sex hormones, 53, 125–128
Sex offenders. *See also* Rape; Sexual abuse
    clergy sex scandal, 405
    distorted thinking patterns of, 145–146
    hormonal treatment of, 128
    pedophiles, 22
    psychosurgery for, 150
    rational choice theory and, 99–100
    registration laws on, 22, 81, 82, 244,
        478
    teacher as, 525–526
Sex tourism, 408–409, 412
Sex trade, international, 408–410
Sexual abuse. *See also* Child abuse; Sex
    offenders; Victims and victimization
    child sexual abuse, 67, 82, 145–146,
        200, 303, 405–412
    clergy sex scandal, 405
    definition of, 303
    distorted thinking patterns of abusers,
        145–146
    international trends in, 13
    posttraumatic stress disorder (PTSD)
        and, 67, 303
    prostitutes and child sexual abuse, 411,
        412
    rational choice theory, 99–100
    statistics on, 302, 303, 405
    by teacher, 525–526
    victims' problems due to, 67, 200, 303
Sexual assault. *See* Rape
Sexual motivation for rape, 294
Shame
    as deterrence for crime, 106
    reintegrative shaming, 244–245
Sheriffs, 487. *See also* Law enforcement;
    Police
Sherman Antitrust Act, 384, 389
Shield laws, 295

Shock incarceration, 544–545
Shock probation, 543–544
Shoplifting
    by adolescents, 44, 45, 52
    definition of, 353
    photograph of, *259*
    prevention/control of, 354–355
    profile of shoplifter, 354
    statistics on, 354
Siblicide, 72
Siblings
    antisocial behavior of, 133
    murder of, 72
Siege mentality, 171–172
Siemens, 378
Situational crime prevention
    CCTV (closed-circuit television) for, 103
    costs and benefits of, 102–104
    crime discouragers and, 101
    defensible space and, 100
    definition of, 100
    diffusion of benefits and, 102
    discouragement and, 102
    displacement and, 102
    encouragement and, 103
    extinction and, 102
    in Great Britain and U.S., 103
    increase of efforts for, 101
    increase of risk for, 101–102
    increase of shame and reducing
        provocation for, 102
    reducing rewards for, 101
    removing excuses for, 102
    summary of, 112
    targeting specific crimes for, 100–101
Situational Crime Prevention (Clarke), 100
Situational inducements, 348
Sixth Amendment, 505, 514, 530
Skeezers, 411. *See also* Prostitution
Skilled thieves, 346
Skull shapes, 7, *7*
SMART program, 276
Smugglers, 346
Smuggling of illegal immigrants, 23
Snitches, 354
Social bond theory
    definition of, 211
    elements of social bond, 211–212
    opposing views on, 213–214
    summary of, 221
    supporting research for, 212–213
    testing, 212
Social capital, 264
Social class. *See also* Lower classes; Poverty;
    Underclass; Wealth
    class–crime controversy, 50–51
    crime and, 162–166
    crime patterns and, 46–47, 50–51
    middle-class measuring rods, 183–184
    self-reports on class–crime relationship, 50
    strain theory and, 174–175
    stratified society and, 162
    victimization and, 70
Social conflict. *See* Conflict view; Critical
    criminology

Social control
    as goal of criminal law, 19
    informal social control, 172–173
    institutional social control, 173
    neighborhoods and, 167–168
    power-control theory, 241–242, 243
    public social control, 173
Social control theory
    commitment to conformity and, 210
    containment theory and, 210
    definition of, 202
    Hirschi's social bond theory, 211–214, 221
    public policy and, 219
    self-concept and crime, 210
Social development model (SDM), 262
Social disorganization theory
    collective efficacy and, 172–174
    concentric zones of neighborhoods, 169,
        169
    definition of, 166–167
    foundations of, 168
    Shaw and McKay's concentric zones
        theory, 168–170, 174
    social ecology theory, 170–174
    summary of, 168, 174
    transitional neighborhoods and,
        168–169
Social ecologists, 170
Social ecology. *See also* Ecology of crime
    chronic unemployment and, 170–171
    community deterioration and, 170
    community fear and, 171
    definition of, 9
    summary of, 174
    of victimization, 69
Social facts, 14
Social harm, 16
Socialization. *See also* Social learning theory
    antisocial personality and, 148–149
    crime and, 9, 11, 198–203
    cultural deviance theory and, 182
    definition of, 9, 198
    educational experience and, 200–201
    effects of, on crime, 202–203
    family deviance and, 199–200
    family relations and, 198–199
    gender and, 53
    institutional involvement and belief,
        201–202
    male socialization and rape, 293
    peer relations and, 201, *201*
    terrorists' motivation and, 336
    violence and, 287–288
Social learning theory
    behaviorism and, 141–142
    definition of, 202
    differential association theory, 203–206,
        221
    differential reinforcement theory,
        206–207, 221
    of domestic violence, 304
    evaluation of, 208, 210
    neutralization theory, 207–209, 221
    of rape, 294
    of substance abuse, 421

Social order, and criminal law, 19
Social positivism, 8, 11
Social process theories
    definition of, 198
    differential association theory, 203–206, 221
    differential reinforcement theory, 206–207, 221
    evaluation of, 218–219, 221
    Hirschi's social bond theory, 211–214, 221
    neutralization theory, 207–209, 221
    public policy implications of, 219
    social control theory, 202, 210–214
    socialization and crime, 198–203
    social learning theory, 202–210
    social reaction theory (labeling theory), 202, 214–218
    storylines and, 220
    summary of, 221
Social psychology, 9
Social reaction theory
    consequences of labeling, 216–217
    contextual discrimination and, 218
    definition of, 202
    differential enforcement and, 215–216
    diversion programs and, 219
    dramatization of evil and, 217
    effects of labeling, 218
    evaluation of, 218
    interpretation of crime and, 215
    joining deviant cliques and, 216
    positive versus negative labels, 214–215
    primary and secondary deviance and, 217
    process of labeling, 215
    public policy and, 219
    racial profiling and, 216
    reflected appraisals and, 216
    research on, 217–218
    retrospective reading of deviance, 216–217
    stigma and, 216
    summary of, 221
    symbolic interaction theory and, 214
The Social Reality of Crime (Quinney), 233
Social structure theories
    cultural deviance theory, 167, 181–187, 188
    definition of, 166
    evaluation of, 187–188
    public policy implications of, 188–189
    social disorganization theory, 166–174
    socioeconomic structure and crime, 162–166
    strain theory, 167, 168, 174–181
Sociobiology, 123
Sociobiology (Wilson), 123
Socioeconomic conditions, 46–47, 50–51. See also Economics; Poverty; Wealth
Sociology of law, 14, 16
Sociopathic personality, 147. See also Antisocial personality
Sodomy laws, 22, 405
Solicitation, 20
Somatype, 122
The Sopranos, 394
South Africa

drug trafficking and, 392
restorative justice in, 247
substance abuse in, 416
South America. See Latin America
Soviet Union. See Russia/Soviet Union
SOX (Sarbanes-Oxley) law, 389
Spain
    crime trends in, 13
    terrorism in, 330, 332–333
Spam, 447
Specific deterrence, 108–110, 112, 529
Split sentencing, 543
Spoofing (phishing), 443–444, 451–452
Spousal abuse. See Domestic violence
Spree killers, 301
Spying, 323–324
SQUID (superconducting quantum interference device), 130
Sri Lanka, 289
Stability–instability, 147
Stabilized junkies, 423
Stalking
    cyber stalking, 448
    definition of, 309
    laws on, 22
    mental illness of stalker, 121
    statistics on, 309–310
    victims of, 309–310
State-corporate crime, 326
State courts, 500, 501, 506
State Department, 328
State police, 487
State political crime, 324–326
State sponsored terrorism, 334, 336–337
State violence, 326
Statistics. See Crime statistics; National Crime Victimization Survey (NCVS); Patterns in crime; Uniform Crime Reports (UCR); and specific crimes
Status frustration, 183
Statutory crimes, 19
Statutory rape, 292–293
Stelazine, 132
Steroids, 417
Stigma, 216. See also Social reaction theory
Stigmatize, 18
Sting operations (police), 491
Stings (white-collar crime), 374–375
St. Kitts, 425
Storylines, 220
Strain. See also Stress
    community sources of, 180
    coping with, 180
    criminal careers and, 180
    definition of, 167
    individual strain, 175
    multiple sources of, 178–179
    social sources of, 180
    sources of, 179–180
    structural strain, 175
Strain theory
    American Dream and, 177–178
    anomie and, 175–178, 181
    definition of, 167
    general strain theory (GST), 178–181
    institutional anomie theory, 177–178, 181

Merton's theory of anomie, 176–177, 181
    relative deprivation and, 174–175, 181
    summary of, 181
Stratified society, 162
Street Corner Society (Whyte), 38
Street crime, 346
Street efficacy, 173–174
Street Gang Resource Center, 222
Street junkies, 422–423
Street values, 185, 209
Streetwalkers, 410. See also Prostitution
Stress. See also Strain
    of adolescent victims, 67
    spousal abuse and, 67
    of victims, 67
Strict liability, 21
Structural strain, 175
Structural theory, 237
Structured sentencing, 530
Students for a Democratic Society (SDS), 332
Subculture of violence, 289–290
Subcultures
    code of the streets and, 185
    college boy, 186
    corner boy, 184
    cultural deviance theory and, 167, 181–182, 183
    delinquent boy, 186
    delinquent subcultures theory, 182–186, 188
    formation of deviant subcultures, 184–186
    substance abuse and, 420
    of violence, 289–290
Substance abuse. See also Alcohol abuse; Drugs
    by adolescents, 418–420
    AIDS and, 420, 423, 430
    causes of, 420–421
    chronic offenders and, 57
    drug-related arrests, 416
    genetic factors in, 421
    as high-risk lifestyle for victimization, 73
    history of, 416
    as illegal versus deviant, 4–5
    international examples of, 416
    prevention programs for, 276
    problem behavior syndrome (PBS) and, 421
    psychological view of, 420
    rational choice theory and, 421
    robbery and, 305
    social learning and, 421
    statistics on, 418–420
    subcultural view of, 420
    violence and, 287
Substance Abuse and Mental Health Services Administration (SAMHSA), 419, 429
Substantive criminal law, 16
Subterranean values, 207
Sudan, 291, 334
Sufferance, 309
Suitable targets, 74, 75
Superconducting quantum interference device (SQUID), 130
Superego, 138